SOCIAL STRATIFICATION

*Oxford in India Readings
in Sociology and Social Anthropology*

**GENERAL EDITOR
T. N. MADAN**

SOCIAL STRATIFICATION

Edited by

DIPANKAR GUPTA

OXFORD
UNIVERSITY PRESS

OXFORD
UNIVERSITY PRESS

Oxford University Press is a department of the University of Oxford.
It furthers the University's objective of excellence in research, scholarship,
and education by publishing worldwide. Oxford is a registered trademark of
Oxford University Press in the UK and in certain other countries

Published in India by
Oxford University Press
22 Workspace 2nd Floor 1/22 Asaf Ali Road New Delhi 110002 India

First edition published in 1991
Oxford India Paperbacks 1992
44th impression 2023

ISBN-13: 978-0-19-563088-6
ISBN-10: 0-19-563088-2

Printed in India by Manipal Technologies Limited, Manipal

To Dipayan
amor fati, have a great time young friend!

OTHER BOOKS IN THE SERIES

Preface

The most appealing aspect of all utopias is that in these enchanted places everyone is equal. There is no difference of class, rank, or prestige. This however does not mean that utopias are boring places to be in, for equality in this case certainly does not imply dull uniformity. All worthwhile utopias have energetically supported the right and freedom to be different but have refused to rank these differences either politically, economically or culturally. Even in Marx's utopia, the communist society, where there would be no state, no classes, and no class struggles, there would nevertheless continue to be writers, poets, musicians, fisherfolk—and of course, men and women.

What then separates our real lived-in world from the 'best of all possible worlds' is our understanding of social stratification. In utopia, social stratification would only take into account differences, but in our world differences often imply ranking, inequality and hierarchy. By social stratification we mean not just the differences that separate fellow human beings in society, whether on the grounds of culture, economy or biology, but we also include within it's scope hierarchical rankings which ordain positions of superiority and inferiority within the society.

This added dimension, viz., that of hierarchy, has become so dominant in our thinking that we often go to the other extreme in believing that stratification has to do with inequality and hierarchy alone. Therefore both the utopians and the conventional this-worldly savants of social stratification are extremists in their own ways.

Through this volume I would really like to argue out an alternative position which at first sight might sound like a compromise between the two extremes, but is in fact not quite so. In my view studies on social stratification can enrich our social existence if we realize how often what are merely different are not seen as being just different but somehow as also unequal. On the other hand to deny the reality of inequality would be futile. All human societies from the dawn of written history have been organized around the principles of hierarchy and ranking. But at the same time history has presided over great changes, some cataclysmic, resulting in the constant reordering of hierarchies. New ranks, orders and hierarchies have emerged not because human beings at certain points in history inexplicably become rebellious, but rather because all hierarchies and principles of inequality strive to impose a ranked order over human differences but succeed only temporarily in doing so. To say this is not to deny the existence of inequality, but it certainly helps one to intellectually humble existing hierarchies. In doing so, we certainly won't succeed in establishing an utopia but might make this world a slightly more congenial place to live in.

What I am thinking of now more than anything else is of the blood that has been spilt down the ages under the mistaken assumption that one community was not only different from another but was somehow superior to it. Great wars and petty jealousies have been occasioned by this universal and popular tendency to believe that where there is difference there must necessarily be a hierarchy.

That such instances should continue unabated even today should sober many of us who take pride in the so-called scientific temper of our age. Sociologists and anthropologists can contribute somewhat in bringing about a better understanding by asking and searching for the bases of such prejudicial constructions of hierarchy. Many social scientists have been remiss on this count and this can best be illustrated with the help of mainstream scholarship on caste as a system of social stratification. Instead of seeing the Brahmins version of Hindu society as one which is as capricious as the various non-Brahmin versions, specialists on the caste system have generally tended to elevate the Brahminical view above all else.

Yet, if the caste system admits different castes within its fold, then should it not also be part of our task to demonstrate that any one kind of hierarchy, even the Brahminical one, is perhaps a deliberate construction, and not one which naturally predominates, for it is constructed over a field where differences (in this case, caste differences) are significant? In such a situation there may be different deliberated hierarchies, all equally valid, though each is contextualized by different socio-economic co-ordinates. To stress, in otherwords, that differences can be celebrated in their own right, and that they need not always be ironed out in a single hierarchy, is admittedly to partake of a bit of utopia, but very intentionally, and with calculated reason.

In a book of readings of this kind one must necessarily abide by the extant literature on the subject and therefore no message can be bluntly

put across. Additionally, a worthwhile reader should represent a wide
cross section of respectable positions on the subject. A lot still depends
on how the Readings are read. I would like to believe that the selection
and arrangement of the essays are such that they excite independent
theoretical assessments on the subject of social stratification as a
whole. Perhaps at the end of the book the reader will feel that the
essays in this volume, not individually, but collectively, have added to
his/her understanding of social stratification. The legitimacy of this
volume will reside whenever such a sentiment rises.

The task of selecting papers for volumes of this kind can be difficult
if there is either too much or too little on the subject. Here, it is a case
of too much. The constraint of space has led to the exclusion of many
excellent papers. It was indeed very difficult excising those pieces
away as I have personally gained so much from them. There is
practically no straight paper on the history of caste or class in this
volume, though many essays allude to them. This is a gap that I miss
most, but to include such papers would add to the size of the volume
and commit it to a length which most readers would find taxing on their
purses and patience. Moreover, the state of the art in sociological and
anthropological studies on social stratification, by the large, begins
from this side of history. Therefore, the most effective intervention
that this book can make is if it is able to churn familiar waters and
dredge unsuspected insights from within, while at the same time
remaining well within the bounds of professional competence.

This Reader is divided into the following four sections: (I) Caste,
(II) Caste Profiles, (III) Class, and (IV) Caste, Class and Conflict. All
the papers have to do with India, though there are three papers in the
Appendices which are purely theoretical. No book on social
stratification in India can ignore the subject of caste or class, but we
have included the section on caste profiles and on caste, class and
conflict, to demonstrate how significant the understanding of
differences can be in the study of social stratification. This is done
pointedly with the section on caste profiles because in the study of the
caste system the overwhelming tendency is to see it only in terms of an
hierarchical ordering.

Not that hierarchy is unimportant—far from it. But an exclusive
obsession with hierarchy undermines the existence of differences and
leads one to conclude, rather unreflexively, that one hierarchy is
somehow intrinsically more durable or more viable, than the others.

The last part of the book devoted to caste, class and conflict, gives expression to the interaction between hierarchy and differences; it brings out, through the essays in that section, how often social tensions and conflicts emerge from disputes over hierarchy. The potentialities for such conflict situations always exist but need propitious socio-economic conditions for bringing them out in the open.

It has not been possible to reproduce entire articles here, mainly due to constraints of space. I have therefore used three dots to indicate missing words and four dots to indicate missing lines. Four dots on a separate line have been used to indicate missing paragraphs and pages. Compiling this book took several months of work. In the course of these months I must confess I learnt a lot from the readings I had to go through in order to make, edit and adapt the selections. I hope that the students of sociology and anthropology, their teachers, and my colleagues will consider, in balance, that my time was well spent.

Dipankar Gupta

Acknowledgements

This book took a long time to prepare and my indebtedness to others
kept growing all the while. My wife, Harmala, helped me with proof-
reading and indexing. Oxford University Press, demonstrated great
patience and provided editorial help with the several, often barely
legible, drafts of this book. Krityanand Bhagat helped me immensely
in chasing references in libraries and in relieving me of some of the
drudgery that goes with the production of a volume such as this.
Gaurang Sahay and Abul Hayat never turned down any of my requests
for help. I am indebted to Patricia Uberoi, Baburao Baviskar and
Ramchandra Guha for their support and encouragement especially
during those early uncertain weeks when the book needed direction.
My statement on hierarchy and difference in the study of social
stratification would have remained a shame-faced, unexpressed idea
had not Yogendra Singh and Jit Uberoi given it the nod. T.N. Madan as
General Editor of the series was always extremely co-operative and
academically stimulating: he certainly did more than his share to make
this volume stand. I should at least take the responsibility for all the
shortcomings of the book.

Contents

APPENDICES

APPENDICES

Hierarchy and Difference:
An Introduction

DIPANKAR GUPTA

The Idea of Stratification and the Caste System

Social stratification has a special place in the study of Indian society. India has long been reckoned as the most stratified of all known societies in human history. The caste system with its myriad forms of superordination and subordination, its many customs and taboos, is perhaps most responsible for conferring on India this dubious honour. But this is not all. Economically too India is highly stratified. Miserable slums border expensive residential areas in city after city in India. The indescribable poverty of the very poor has even led to a review of the limits of physical endurance at pitifully low nutritional levels. This vast polarity notwithstanding, India is also a significant economic power with a sizeable bureaucracy and technically trained personnel. Add to this the diversity of linguistic groups that make up our Indian nation state and the fact of India being the most stratified society becomes near incontrovertible.

India is also a very self-conscious society. There are endless debates in India on what should be the path of development, and what internal arrangements of power and wealth, of cultural status and economic wherewithal, are best suited to propel the country into the modern, industrial epoch. As a people Indians have been deeply involved in moral and ethical questions regarding the caste system, cultural diversity and economic inequality—all central issues of social stratification. This is reflected in our Constitution which makes any discrimination

based on caste, language, religion or creed illegal. Clearly the founders of independent India had pondered deeply over the cardinal features of social stratification in our society.

Very often when we talk of social stratification in India we concentrate almost exclusively on the caste system. The uniqueness of this
outstanding institution has captivated sociologists · and anthropologists
for generations. It would be hard to think of a sociologist working on
India who has not written or commented extensively on it. Quite naturally, with all this literature, some of exceptional quality, discussions
on the caste system tend to subsume the entire field of social stratification.

The Visibility Postulate

But social stratification includes a lot more. The fact that the caste
system is seen as an example *par excellence* of social stratification,
gives an indication of the specificity of the term and the range it can
include. The caste system, as it is understood widely, separates and
hierarchizes Hindus. However, it is not sufficient if this separation and
hierarchization are wholly internalized or intellectualized. It is only
when hierarchy and differences are externalized and socially demonstrated that we can truly talk about social stratification. Rituals, dress,
tonsorial styles, marriage practices, and a host of other such phenomena
help in socially separating one caste from another. It is these phenomena too that are appropriately valorized for the purposes of hierarchical ranking. It is for this reason that when we talk of social stratification
we not only mean differentiation but differentiation that is made
socially visible. It is not just stratification but social stratification. In
other words there is a general acknowledgement within society of the
social markers that separate the population, and an awareness also of
the crucial criterion (sometimes a set of criteria) on which such
forms of differentiation are based (see Béteille 1977: 4, 9, 40-1).
Social stratification then deals with the ways in which the human population is socially differentiated, i.e. differentiated publicly and demonstrably. The criterion for differentiation may be one but the social display of differentiation usually includes a host of factors. The principal
criterion on which the caste system is based is the principle of *natural
superiority*. Natural superiority in this case is not physical prowess or
intelligence, though these often work their way in, but the endowment
of bodily purity. It is a known fact that there is no unambiguous physical criterion by which individuals can be differentiated on the basis of

the extent of purity of their bodies. This is why it is essential that social practices, occupations, life styles, rituals and taboos demonstratively differentiate one caste from another for all to see.

Even in cases where there are clear biological differences such as sex or race, these differences are not retained in their natural form when we include them under the rubric of social stratification. Social stratification is not satisfied with biological differences *per se*. These biological differences must be socially amplified with respect to dress, or food, or occupation, or residence, or mobility, or a combination of all these and more. Differences in race or sex become important for social stratification because of the modalities by which the social lives of people belonging to different sexes or races are socially separated and distinguished. Those biological differences that are not thus amplified upon become socially irrelevant and do not factor in the reckoning of any system of social stratification.

That human kind everywhere demonstrates actively this propensity to differentiate may seem a rather trivial and pointless failing (and some orders or differentiations are arguably pointless), yet a closer look will tell us that social stratification manifests itself in almost every aspect of social life—even in the most intimate ones. The family, the school, the office, the neighbourhood, all are marked deeply by internal divisions of authority, wealth, or status; or language, culture and customs. As a matter of fact, one might even say that order and coherence in a society, or in any of its aspects thereof, eventually rest on its system of social stratification (ibid.: 17).

Naturally a lot depends on what aspect of social life we are interested in for our analytical pursuits. Need one be reminded that social reality is diverse and no one factor can serve as a durable key to its many secrets? Social stratification too is just one aspect of this multifaceted social reality, but it is a factor that weighs rather heavily in politics, in economics, and in moral considerations of right and wrong. Politicians from the earliest of times have sought to transform or better existing systems of unequal power distribution; economists—even before university economists arrived—talked at length about the rich and the poor; and of course, there have been renowned thinkers, philosophers and men of religion, who have pondered over the questions of inequality and social differences in order to ferret out their inner essence. It is for this reason that a confrontation with the issues of social stratification at the intellectual level is inescapable. Quite appropriately some of the greatest sociologists have in the last century contributed significantly to our understanding of social stratification (see Appendices).

Need for Conceptual Clarity

One must not forget that it is not at all the case that a society should exhibit only one form of social stratification. In India, for instance, the extant forms of social stratification are many. There is of course the caste system, but even this 'extreme form of social stratification' (Dumont 1988:3) coexists with occupational stratification, linguistic stratification, sexual stratification and religious stratification (to name a few). It is important for sociologists to remember that each of these forms of stratification have their own axial principles. It would do us no good if we were to be careless on this score. Any carelessness or untidiness in this matter would lead to quite basic conceptual difficulties. For instance, the oft asked query of whether caste is giving way to class, is an outcome of conceptual fogginess. There is no reason to believe that if there is caste there cannot be class, nor is it the case that as one grows the other must wane. We should not forsake an elementary methodological tenet namely that a *concept should be independently defined.* Caste and class after all do not constitute a continuum.

The important point to bear in mind is that the various forms of social stratification are analytically separate and separable. Empirically we often find one form of stratification overlaid by another. Gender stratification may correspond with economic stratification, class and caste may demonstrate significant statistical correlation, or linguistic/regional groups may show a great degree of co-variation with occupational stratification. This should not tempt us to conflate or submerge one category of stratification with another. The co-variation between two or more forms of stratification asks for a higher order of explanation, and not the abandonment of one for the other, e.g. caste for class, or class for caste.

The lines of social stratification in India are so deep and variegated that their uniqueness often overwhelms the scholar. The temptation to abandon 'theory' (or general laws?) when it comes to social stratification in India is strong, but stronger still is the temptation to construct an 'Indian theory' of the social phenomenon. This Indian theory of social stratification, it is believed, would be faithful to the idiosyncracies of the Indian situation and would fully flesh out the wholesomeness of caste, linguistic and religious diversity in this country. Much as this 'territorial orientation' (Singh 1985 : 53) is attractive it has not yet yielded anything which has risen above the capriciousness of the author. There is good reason for this too. The advantage of theory is not only that it attempts to explain and frame observations, but it also performs the vital function of helping us communicate our varied experiences. We must move from the particular to the general if we are to share our experiences meaningfully. What is more, we get a deeper insight into our own experiences as a result of such theoretical communication. Only a fool-hardy mountaineer would attempt to scale the Everest without learning from the experiences of other mountaineers who may have scaled other mountains. Theories presume concepts, and concepts by their very nature allow us to group and categorize manifold experiences. All theories, Indian and non-Indian, must utilize concepts, and all concepts ought to satisfy certain basic logical principles if they are to be of any theoretical use. The difficulty, it seems to me, is that one is not always very careful about what the principal concepts of the various theories of social stratification imply. This is probably why there is some discomfort in certain quarters with respect to the application of general theories of social stratification to the Indian condition.

It is for this reason that it was felt that it would be best to devote the following pages to a clarification of the concepts of `hierarchy' and difference' as they are central to all theories of social stratification (see Appendices, I, II, III, IV and Madan 1980). In addition, 'hierarchy' and 'difference' inform other commonly used concepts like caste, class and status, as we shall soon see. Once we realize the importance of the basic principles that govern these terms our usage of them will be more sophisticated, and our understanding of terms like caste, status, class, prestige, will become more amenable to rigorous theoretical treatment. No claim is being made at this point of the relative merits and demerits of the various general theories of social stratification, such as those of Marx, Weber, functionalism, or culturology. What we wish to underline is that a clarity of the key concepts, namely, hierarchy and difference, will help us in our individual theoretical drives.

Hierarchy and Differences : The Key Concepts

Before we settle down to a close scrutiny of the logical properties of the concepts of *hierarchy* and *difference*, we should spend a little while in carefully going over the more general term *stratification* itself, and what it implies.

Stratification spontaneously signifies a multi-layered phenomenon, much like the earth's crust (Béteille 1977: 129). The point to remember in this connection is that the geological metaphor can be misleading in

the case of social stratification in so much as it might figuratively persuade one to believe that stratification always implies layers that are
vertically or hierarchically arranged. For a true understanding of stratification we should be able to conceptually isolate it from hierarchy, as
the latter is but one of the manifestations of the former.

The various layers that stratification spontaneously signifies do not
imply unconditional differentiation. The differentiation is always on
the basis of a criterion, or a set of criteria. Stratification therefore implies a common axis (or axes) that straddles the differences. Quite unlike geology again, social stratification does not manifest itself readily
or 'naturally' to the naked eye. A deliberate act is required on the part
of the observer or analyst to unite certain kinds of differences in order
to construct a particular system of stratification. In discussing any system of social stratification we acknowledge an overarching commonality (or similarity) which like a thread links the manifest differences together. Social stratification is not like distinguishing between cabbages
and kings: it does not group disparate entities without a clearly stated
criterion or a declared set of criteria.

Commonality then exists as a pre-condition for all systems of stratification. If only differentiation were to be emphasized then how would
systems of stratification emerge? How also could one justify the inclusion of certain elements and not of others. Cabbages, kings, ships and
sealing wax do not after all make for any system. But when the population is stratified, say on the criterion of income, then we have an uniform criterion which can bring together sweepers, managers, white collar workers, and agricultural labourers into a single system of stratification where monetary income is the regnant principle. Likewise when we
construct a social stratification of language groups the unifying basis is
language and it does not matter if the language speaker is a sweeper or a
college professor. Finally these sweepers, managers, white collar workers, and professors can also constitute a system of stratification based on
the criterion of occupation. We are not really interested if these managers, sweepers, etc. are short or tall, married or unmarried. The only factor that interests us is that they all perform a manifest occupation. In
each case then there is a presumption of a commona'ity that systema-
tizes the differentiation of the various strata and binds the universe of
a particular form of stratification.

(a) *Hierarchy* implies the regular ordering of a phenomenon on a
continuous scale 'such that the elements of the whole are ranked in relation to the whole' (Dumont 1988: 66). Height, weight, income and even
power (once it has been quantified) can be arranged in a hierarchy. Tall

and short people can be arranged in a hierarchy of height. You cannot position short or understand shortness unless you have a hierarchical scale that tells you what is tall and tallness. Hierarchy is but one form of social stratification and it certainly does not constitute the essence of social stratification. Indeed this is just the mistake that the famous sociologist Pitrim Sorokin made when he wrote :

Social stratification means the differentiation of a given population into *hierarchically* super-posed classes. It is manifested in the existence of upper and lower layers (the geological metaphor, D.G.). Its basis and very essence consists in an unequal distribution of rights and privileges ... social power and influences among the members of a society (Sorokin 1961: 570; emphasis added).

Quite obviously for Sorokin, inequality and hierarchy were the stuff of social stratification. The geological model of layers too is quite evident. The various layers are always arranged vertically. If, for instance, we were to be discussing the stratification of power then those at the top have more power than those below them and so on till we come to the last layer that has the least power. The same can be said about wealth and examples proliferate.

But not all systems of stratification are hierarchical. Some are, but many are not. In the latter case 'difference' is valorized, and notions of hierarchy may or may not surface.

(b) *Differences* rather than hierarchy are dominant in some stratificatory systems. In other words, the constitutive elements of these differences are such that any attempt to see them hierarchically would do offence to the logical property of these very elements. The layers in this case are not arranged vertically or hierarchically, but horizontally or even separately. Such an arrangement can be easily illustrated in the case of language, religion or nationalities. It would be futile, and indeed capricious, if an attempt was made to hierarchize languages or religions or nationalities. In these cases it does not matter at all if the schematic representation of stratification places the different strata contiguously or separately, as long as they are horizontally positioned. India again is an appropriate place to demonstrate this variety of social stratification. The various languages that are spoken in India speak eloquently of an horizontal system of social stratification where differences are paramount. Secular India again provides an example of religious stratification where religions are not hierarchized or unequally privileged in law, but have the freedom to exist separately in full knowledge of their intrinsic differences.

A system of *social stratification* then implies differentiation among one or more features in such a fashion that they can be grouped along a common axis. But as stratification speaks not only of differentiation but differentiation grouped along such axes, the factor that is common indicates the nature of stratification. If it is language then we are delineating a stratification of language; if it is income, then we are hierarchizing a stratification of income; if it is religion then we are stratifying the different religions.

Hierarchy is only one kind of stratification where the strata are arranged vertically. This is appropriate only when this vertical arrangement is along a variable that can be measured on a continuous scale, as in the case of numbers. One cannot measure the proletariat, or the capitalist, but one can measure income. Likewise one cannot measure languages but one can measure the prestige accorded to a certain language in a certain region. It is possible then to have a hierarchy of income or of prestige, such that in one case different income earners and, in another, different language groups, can be placed along a continuous hierarchical scale. The crucial fact in all this is that the differences in prestige or in income should be either quantitative, or quantifiable (in terms of more or less of a certain property).

Difference is salient when social stratification is understood in a 'qualitative' sense. According to this scheme, there are incommensurable entities or units, that constitute different systems of stratification. In place of a continuous scale one encounters instead discrete categories. Thus in a stratification of classes, for example, different occupations may be listed without any scalar or hierarchical ranking; likewise in the stratification of religious groups one might mention the various religious denominations without imposing on them the uniformity of a scale based either on prestige, or on wealth, or on rationality. Once this is clear then there is little reason to believe with Sorokin that social stratification principally concerns itself with inequality and hierarchy.

To sum up then, social stratification is the ordering of social differences with the help of a set of criteria or just a single criterion (which is generally the case) which ties the differentiated strata into a *system*. Secondly, systems of social stratification just do not exist. They emerge only after a deliberate act on the part of the observer or analyst to opt for that common criterion or criteria. Thirdly, because these systems of social stratification are pivoted on mental constructions there is often a good deal of heart burning, house burning, and even wife burning on this account. Different people have different reckonings of stratification, and when these systems do not match there is friction, often fire.

Differences and Inequality

We have already said that social stratification implies differentiation, but does this also mean that the strata thus differentiated are also unequal? It is important to reiterate that there can be separate classes of stratification, or strata, without there necessarily being any inequality (whether of wealth, power or prestige) between them. To bear this in mind is to guard against an oft adopted assumption that inequality pervades all forms of social differentiation. This then quite unthinkingly leads one to hierarchize systems of social stratification which are essentially horizontal. Unexamined prejudices thus find their way into academic exercises.

A social differentiation that separates without implying inequality is not always easy to appreciate. This is why an awareness of one's prejudices as well as those of others is so essential to the study of social stratification. Humankind, unfortunately, has not yet developed to a stage where we can all indulge in and celebrate our differences. Differences in language, religion, race or sex are differences that in themselves do not contain the property of inequality. This may however not be the popular understanding of these differences.

In the eyes of most people religions, languages, sexes, nationalities are all hierarchized—though it would be difficult to get an unambiguous statement of the criteria on the basis of which these hierarchies are constructed. In fact, a worthwhile question for a sociologist is to ask: Why is it that people tend to hierarchize horizontal differentiations whose logical property is equality?

Caste and class both bring to our minds inequality and hierarchy. And yet only certain operationalizations of these terms justify the implication of inequality. One can in fact talk of the various castes, both rural and urban, without directly implying inequality of caste, wealth or status. As a matter of fact, A.M. Shah in a recent study on the Vanias and Rajputs of Gujarat has treated each caste as a separate entity without making any statement on the nature of hierarchy that might pertain between them (Shah 1988: 3-29). Indeed on many occasions attempts to hierarchize different castes are fraught with ambiguous and contradictory postulates. Where can one place the Jat farmer of west UP? If one adopts the *varna* system then he would be placed quite low in the hierarchy, perhaps even deserving the contempt that the Manusmriti accords to the Sudra. But try calling any of these proud and prosperous Jats Sudras to their face, and immediately another hierarchy will become readily visible. The proud Jat bows to no one, not even to the Brahmin (see Pettigrew pp. 163-75 in this volume). As a matter of fact the Brahmin is a butt of ridicule in all of Jat land, especially in Punjab and west UP. And his is not the only caste which is made fun of. Jat opprobrium falls abundantly on other castes as well: the unctuous and oily merchants, the lowly Chamars, Nais, and Valmikis—in fact on everyone who is not a Jat.

Likewise one need not imply at all that the white collar worker is inferior to the capitalist entrepreneur, unless we are talking of power within the organization or work place, or wealth and material possessions. But once we move away from these attributes and go on to detail and discuss the differences in life styles, aesthetic tastes, world views etc., between the white collar worker and the capitalist entrepreneur we quickly realize that it would be futile, indeed tendentious, if any attempt were made to hierarchize these differential traits. A little careful reflection therefore will tell us that certain kinds of strata which we quite uncritically assume to be concepts denoting a hierarchical system of stratification may not be just that alone. Such concepts as the white collar or even middle class may have a life quite distinct from their popular placement in a hierarchical scale.

It is therefore of the utmost importance to situate concepts in their appropriate contexts. There are at least two common terms used in the sociology of social stratification which sometimes emphasize hierarchy and sometimes difference. These two concepts are class and caste. It would be useful to spend some time in working out the varying dimensions of hierarchy and difference in the application of these terms. This we believe will give us useful insights into the variety of ways in which caste and class manifest themselves.

Hierarchy and Difference in Caste

Caste has resisted definition quite successfully precisely because its two dimensions, namely, hierarchy and difference, deflect any single unifying definitional probe. After a long deliberation Leach (1960: 2-3) settled more or less for J.H. Hutton's descriptive statement of the caste system where endogamy, pollution, occupational differentiation and hierarchy, with the Brahmins at the top, are the important diacritical features of the phenomenon. Bouglé too essentially described the caste system though he believed he was defining it. Yet Bouglé perhaps more than any one else clearly emphasized the two aspects of *hierarchy* and *difference* in it. According to him hierarchy, repulsion and hereditary specialization are the three important characteristics of the caste system (Bouglé 1971: 9). Today we know that both in traditional India, as well as in modern India (of course) castes cannot be linked to occupations except in exceptional cases. To be fair Bouglé noticed this fact too (ibid.: 18-19). But the reason we commend Bouglé is because he gave hierarchy and repulsion equal importance in his description of the caste system.

According to Bouglé the spirit of the caste system is determined in an important way by the mutual repulsion that exists between castes. In other words Bouglé is here emphasizing the differences that exist between different castes. Repulsion, Bouglé argued, manifested itself in endogamy, commensal restriction, and even contact (ibid.: 9). For this reason different castes stayed as discrete entities, 'atomized', 'opposed', and even 'isolated'. The methodologically relevant point is that Bouglé did not see any problem in the coexistence of hierarchy with repulsion. The logic of the situation should have however led him to allow for differences in hierarchies as well, but he stops well short of that and provides for only one hierarchy (presumably the Brahmin variety); and this is where he is logically at fault.

In most popular renditions of the caste system, hierarchy alone is emphasized and that too from the Brahmin point of view. The *Purusasukta* legend whereby the Brahmins are said to have come from the head of the primeval being and the Sudras from the feet is too well known to bear repetition here. But what is generally not equally well known is that there are as many such legends, or origin tales, as there are castes. These origin tales, or *jati puranas*, justify different hierarchies and the Brahmin is not always at the top. As a matter of fact, there are castes that find even the Brahmin defiling (Dumont 1988: 59). The presence of such multiple hierarchies is in consonance with the reality that there are also varying models of emulation which castes employ for purposes of upward mobility. The Brahmin model is one such model but there are other non-Brahmin models, such as those of the Kshatriya, Rajput, Maratha, and even the Vania, and they are all equally persuasive to their adherents. It would be incorrect to consider these other non-Brahmin models to be less worthy of attention because each instance of model adoption implies the conscious and deliberate rejection of the other available models. The reason for this variation in templates of emulation lies in the notion of 'difference' and its obverse 'equality'. Nobody, no matter what their caste may be, would ever accept that they are made of impure substances, or that the substances in them are less pure than those of another. Caste legends of Doms, Chamars, Chasa Dhoba, Kahars, all proclaim exalted origins (see Risley 1891) which of course the Brahminical texts vehemently deny. Yet each of these tales captures independently the essence of 'difference' between castes and are therefore logically of equal status. Gerald Berreman writes of an incident that portrays this tension over hierarchy accurately. During the course of his fieldwork he once related to some of his low caste respondents the orthodox hierarchy according to which the Brahmin was unequivocally on top. After listening carefully to Berreman these low caste respondents laughed, and one of them said, 'You have been talking with Brahmins' (Berreman pp. 84-92 in this volume).

If this is the case then any attempt to study the caste system in terms of a single clearly ranked hierarchy would obviously run into great difficulties. If we look at castes closely then we find that each maintains its own traditions and customs zealously and clearly distinguishes itself from others in its universe. Often this has been understood as a kind of 'caste patriotism'.[1] But to make matters difficult, caste is not just a separation between different castes. Each case of separation and valorization of differences is accompanied by a unique hierarchical ordering of castes. It is another matter that there are disagreements over this hierarchy, and that not all hierarchies can be socially enforced on a single scale, yet castes as such are never quite rested even after they have repulsed one another. Differentiation involves a cathective judgement regarding the elements of bodily purity and impurity, and this quite spontaneously suggests different, yet specific attempts to construct hierarchical rankings of castes. It should however be underlined that such hierarchies are idiosyncratic and *equally* valid.

We are thus forced to disagree with Dumont in so much as he posits

---

[1] This caste patriotism differs from self-identification on racial grounds by the fact that as one goes down to the finer and lower order divisions within a caste till one finally comes to the level of the endogamous *jati*, one continually finds a proliferation of *differences* all the way. Thus the maintenance of the first order division such as of the Vania, or the Brahmin, hardly exhausts the plentitude of other distinguishing markers that exist at lower levels. Thus one cannot say that endogamous *jatis* are segmented groups of the first order caste rankings. These *jatis* are not simply smaller segments of the bigger whole (see Dumont 1988 : 42).

Race identity, on the other hand, moves in the opposite direction. The passion with which one identifies first order divisions like 'white' or 'black' is far greater than if the white and blacks were seen at lower and more disaggregated levels. The significance of being a white is far greater in South Africa than being a white of Dutch, German or English origin (for other views on this subject see Dumont 1988 : 247-66).

a single hierarchy for understanding and explaining the caste system. In this true hierarchy the Brahmins are unanimously at the top and the Untouchables without dissension are at the bottom. The hierarchy is therefore a ritual hierarchy (and that is why it is 'true', says Dumont) which is dependent upon a state of mind and is not influenced by secular forces of economics and politics (see Dumont 1988: 19, 34, 66; Madan, 1970: 1-13). In our opinion such unanimity over the Brahminic hierarchy does not really exist; and the reason for this lack of consensus is remarkably simple. As castes are different and separate it is but a logical corollary that they should also hierarchize differently and separately.[2]

Notwithstanding our disagreement with Dumont it is incontrovertible however that Dumont introduced, perhaps for the first time in sociology and social anthropology, a technical understanding of the concept of hierarchy. True hierarchies, Dumont clarifies, 'are ranked in relation to the whole' (Dumont 1988: 66), with the added proviso that 'that which encompasses is more important than that which is encompased' (Dumont 1988: 76). Thus it is clear that hierarchies suggest an overall unity such that the differentiated strata within the hierarchy are encompassed by the defining criterion of the system. This is why he advised, contra Bouglé, that to understand the caste system it was all important to grasp the principle of the *true hierarchy* and not wander among *differences* (Dumont 1988: xlviii, 43). It is perhaps because Dumont did not pay attention to the active principle of differences in the caste system that the Hindu caste order is presented as one without internal tension and dynamism, and the Hindu person as an archetypal representative of the species, *Homo Hierarchicus* (see also Desai 1988 : 49).

One might, at this stage, ask the question whether hierarchy comes before differences or differences before hierarchy (see Desai ibid.: 42)? There are good grounds to dodge the question but it would be more forthright to suggest that the existence of different hierarchies encourages one to take the position that differences dominate the articulation of a hierarchy in the caste system. Those hierarchies that are socially enforced on a general scale do not subsume the number

[2] Gerald Berreman's works are most instructive on this account. In recent times Berreman has time and again emphasized the fact that different castes have different evaluations of the caste hierarchy. It is unfortunate that Berreman's views are not as well known in India as Dumont's ideas are (see Berreman 1963 : 214-15, 222-3; 1979 : 77-80).

that exist in an intraverted form in the more closeted observances
and beliefs of the subjugated castes. The ideological motivation to Sanskritize does not appear only when the hitherto subordinated castes
have either money or power to fancifully conjure another hierarchy.
The other hierarchy is always there waiting for a propitious moment to
extravert itself generally over the entire society.

Hierarchy and Difference in Class

The importance of distinguishing between hierarchy and difference can
be exemplified with reference to the concept of class as well. Like caste,
the concept of class finds its way into a large number of theoretical formulations of social stratification. Not always is it made clear whether it
is being used in a hierarchical sense or in the sense of a horizontally
differentiated and separate stratum. Most often any mention of class
stratification presumes a hierarchical ordering though the concept is not
logically limited to such operationalizations alone.

Class refers to a system of stratification that is economic in character. We are all familiar with terms like upper class, middle class and
lower class; or, rich, middle and poor farmer. Sometimes these terms
can be increased depending upon how fine one would like the categories to be. Therefore, it is often the case that one separates the upper
middle class from the middle class or the lower middle class, and so
on. There is no analytical problem in adding to the numbers of strata
thus, because they are all being read off a hierarchical scale. Therefore
we can have a class category depending upon the criterion of land, or
one depending on the variable of money, or one on marketable yield, or
one on disposable income. The important thing is that all of these criteria are convertible directly into money and that is why in class stratifications money or wealth is always central.

In spite of the matter appearing so simple one must exercise a number of precautions when using these terms. First, it ought to be realized that the cut-off points on a hierarchical scale which signify strata
like upper class, upper middle class, middle class, lower middle class,
lower class, and so on are essentially arbitrary. At what point the lower
middle class becomes a lower class depends on considerations not
imminent in the hierarchy. That is why it is important to remember that
cut-off points on the hierarchy are justified on the basis of cohort factors which do not figure in the hierarchy itself, but are employed by
the analyst to justify the demarcations for the purposes of a specific
analysis (see also Singh 1977: 21-2). For each analysis therefore the

cohort factors justifying the demarcations in the hierarchy will differ. For this reason agrarian classifications which use such strata, as 0-5 acres, 6-10 acres, 11-15 acres, 16 acres and above, have to be revalidated with every fresh analysis. The problem in many cases is that these classifications are often seen as absolute in themselves, thus committing the analyst to elementary errors of reification. In one area a person with 5 acres may be an impoverished and marginal peasant, but elsewhere a farmer with 5 acres may be a prosperous member of the yeomanry.

This leads us to the second point of caution while employing strata that eponymously signify a hierarchical scale. The middle peasant, or the middle class, refers quite obviously to a stratum which is in the middle of the hierarchy of land and wealth respectively. But the manner in which these terms have been used and have gained salience urges us to a construct a much fuller picture than the flat one-dimensional one that is read off a hierarchical scale. The understanding of the term middle peasant has attained a certain analytical status because its first approximation as one belonging in the middle of the land hierarchy has been abundantly superimposed by a host of other characteristics which are well outside the scope of the criterion that defined the land hierarchy. Some of the factors that give the concept of the middle peasant its analytical leverage in contemporary literature are ideological innocence, thriftiness, the employment of family labour, negligible interactions with the market, production for consumption, and so forth. The middle class too is often conceptualized in a similar manner. The attribute of cultural pretension, or the propensity for urban occupations are not features of the income hierarchy on which the concept of the middle class may receive its initial validation. Income or land ownership then become only one of the many characteristics by which such classes are understood. But as many of their other features cannot be merged into a single hierarchy, these strata gain much of their salience from their other attributes, namely, those that signify 'difference'. Even when certain features can be hierarchized, such as the employment of family labour, in the case of the middle peasant, the change in quantity on the continuum is regarded as so significant that when the peasant employs hired labour in the main he undergoes a qualitative transformation. In keeping with this qualitative transformation other attributes peculiar to the rich peasantry, such as entrepreneurship, urban preferences, ideological aggression, and so on become critical cohort factors—some of these are not amenable to hierarchization, and those which are call out to other hierarchies based

on different criteria. One should then, with a little care, be able to distinguish between pure hierarchical strata, and those which are eponymously so but depend in addition on attributes of difference.

While we have so far discussed hierarchical strata based on a single
hierarchy, the same principal obtains even when a composite index
is made up of different variables which have been quantitatively opera-
tionalized. In other words the aim of fashioning such composite indices
is to arrive at one hierarchial measure. In the formulation of the indices
of Socio-Economic Status (SES), education, occupation, prestige, income were first hierarchized and then merged together. Thus though
each strata in the hierarchy have a variety of attributes they are visualized as being causally linked. For instance, Yogendra Singh and B.
Kuppuswamy write:

Education has been considered to be a deciding factor of one's occupation.
occupation an important intervening variable in the translation of educational
advantage into income advantage, and the income a positive factor in deciding one's social prestige which, in turn, influences the educational level
of the succeeding generation and possibly of the same also (quoted in Singh
1977: 21).

The differences are here *merged* and united reinforcing thus the
single criterion hierarchies. Qualitative differences between the
different variables that go into the making of SES, like composite indices, are deliberately sublated in order that these indices be quantifiable
and obey the principle of hierarchy.

Hierarchy and Differences in Order and Conflict

Rarely do social classes present themselves simply as clusters around a
continuous hierarchy. Life styles, beliefs, family size, etc., come in to
characterize, almost uniquely, strata which, in the first quick look, may
be considered to belong to the continuous hierarchy alone. Distinguishing between classes on the hierarchy from those that may only be reminiscent of it has other advantages too. It predisposes us, for instance, to
anticipate the different analytical consequences that follow when one
uses them especially with reference to conflict, continuity, order and
change. If hierarchy alone is emphasized then there is little scope for
allowing for change, conflict and dissension. In a hierarchy, as we
know with the help of Dumont, 'that which encompasses is more
important than that which is encompassed' (Dumont 1988: 76). Classes

understood simply in terms of their hierarchical placement cannot be utilized analytically for the study of change or class conflict. The principle of the true hierarchy, namely, that of encompassment undermines the potentialities of conflict if it does not negate them altogether. Hierarchy with its principle of encompassment signifies order and conformity. When one makes a hierarchy of wealth, or of power, or of prestige, then in each case continuity, conformity, order and objectifiable acquiescence to the hierarchy are valorized. Even multiple SES indices conform to this logical rule. While they help us make synchronic comparison, they are 'essentially static' (Singh 1988 : 23-4).

In order to understand the dimensions of conflict within the framework of social stratification it is essential to realize that conflict and tension can only be examined with the aid of concepts which do not owe complete allegiance to a hierarchical order but which have significant diacritical features of their own. While the manager, the superintendent, the white collar worker, and the dirty white collar worker, may be placed in a hierarchy within an organization, yet, if one is to understand organization tension and conflict then, these very classes must step out of their one dimensional profile in the hierarchy and assume a more qualitatively rounded presence. This is a logical requirement. As the hierarchy emphasizes unity and conformity, therefore any attempt to go beyond this level will necessitate an absorption of characteristics outside the criterion of the hierarchy or, in other words, attention must be paid to the multiple features that spell differences. With differences comes the notion of equality. Thus though the hierarchy may spell out unambiguously the inequality within the system we are still within an interiority whose sovereignty cannot be undermined without bringing in 'differences' from without. Thus though a manager remains a manager, a worker remains a worker, and a bobbin boy remains a bobbin boy, yet in an industrial dispute an alternative dimension comes into play. Now there is scope to, and room enough for, protest, agitation, or strike, for the hierarchically subordinated seek *equality* at other levels through the medium of differences. Political commitment, world views, aesthetic tastes and ethical values, are some of the differences that come into focus that separate the working class from the managers. For any agitation to take place in a hierarchically ordered organization it is an unconditional necessity that the dimension of 'differences' become salient.

In the case of castes, too, if there is a single true hierarchy (as Dumont posits) then that logically forecloses the possibility of conflict within the system. This is because the caste hierarchy, like all hierarchies, inheres in the relation between that which encompasses and that which is encompassed. Caste conflicts and caste mobility occur because there are full-fledged *differences* between castes. Because of these differences, as we said before, alternative hierarchies, which are logically of equal status, arise. And as Dumont said correctly in another context, conflict arises only among equals (Dumont 1972). But Dumont's context was restricted to the rivalry for supremacy in village factions and caste *panchayats*. Dumont allows for conflict in these limited areas such as the caste *panchayat* because the members of a caste *panchayat*, or of a dominant caste, belong to the same caste and hence are equals. This led to 'plurality' of power (Dumont 1988 : 164, 182-3). Once again, we believe, Dumont is logically correct but is empirically too restrictive. His mistake in this case is that he is restricting the play of equality far too strictly. Conflicts arise on a far more general scale in caste societies because of the existence of multiple caste hierarchies, which are all separate and 'equal' and support their positions through their own caste ideologies.

While such a position is initially perhaps a little difficult to accept with reference to caste and class, a fidelity to the logical requirements of the terms, hierarchy and difference, help us see the matter somewhat freed from our reigning prejudices. As we all, researchers and respondents alike, live in stratified societies, prejudices of one kind or the other are bound to exist even within the most self-conscious amongst us. This is why it is useful to look at the logical requirements of the key concepts of social stratification, namely those of hierarchy and difference, and then examine how these concepts imbrue the more empirically determined concepts like caste and class.

Conclusion : Hierarchy and Difference in Weber and Marx

Hierarchy and difference not only add to our understanding of concepts like caste and class but also help us to get a deeper reading of the various received theories of social stratification. Not always have the authors, or the exegetes of these theories, spelt out the logical implications of their concepts such that it would further our appreciation of the basic principles of social stratification.

Weber's formulation of the three axes of stratification, namely, class, status, and party, has many interesting possibilities from our point of view (see Appendix III).Of the three, 'status' received far greater attention, for Weber was always keen to delineate the alternative ways by which men gave meaning to their different life styles. But for Weber each of these axes revolved around a single variable. Class was determined by reward in the market place;[3] status centred around the concept of social prestige; and the crucial variable behind the party was power. As can easily be seen, rewards, prestige and power can be hierarchized and measured along univariate axes and this is probably why Weber despaired that all changes were only superficial. The only change that he foresaw with great trepidation and heightened distaste was the further consolidation of the principle of hierarchy in bureaucracies that dominated every aspect of society. For this reason he argued for the persistence of the democratic system for when it decides among various demagogues there is a fleeting moment during which bureaucracy is temporarily checked. Even such ephemeral correctives were welcomed by Weber as the scene was otherwise too bleak. The fact that Weber saw no alternatives to the present may explain why he should be the leading figure with a large number of generally conservative behaviourial scientists of today. This is no small irony for unlike many later Weberians the master himself never glorified the present but reviled instead the 'iron cage' in which modern European societies were trapped (see Weber 1948 : 120-5; see also Loewenstein 1966 : 24-5).

In Weber's understanding of status group there lies a great potentiality for emphasizing differences. But as we just mentioned, Weber himself chose to unite these divergences in the hierarchy of prestige. For this reason caste was seen by him as a case of closed status groups (Weber 1958 : 39) and differences within the caste system were thus unfortunately sublated. In his understanding of caste perhaps Weber was not to blame, for such has been the power of popular conception on caste, that even today hierarchy is often emphasized over all else in the understanding of this unique Indian system of stratification.

This is not to suggest that Weber saw no 'difference' at all. But in Weber's understanding of difference, such as in his typology of world religions, the different religions are portrayed as unique totalities quite independent of one another. For instance, the world affirming religions exist quite independently of the world abnegating religions. This is quite different from the manner in which different classes are dialectically related in Marx's works. Change impulses exist in Marx because, with the exception of Marx's distinction between literate and pre-literate societies, differences are integrally related and not uniquely isolated.

[3] Dumont rightly observes that for Weber 'all buyers and all sellers are as such identical' (Dumont 1988 : 105; see also Parkin 1982 : 93).

To refine then what has been said earlier, it is not just 'differences', but linked (or related) 'differences' that allow for an appreciation of the forces of social change and for a more dynamic frame of reference. Marx too accepted the primacy of hierarchy in the caste system, for which reason he was compelled to suspend the logic of historical materialism when it came to India. Marx has numerous passages to this effect where he talks of an unchanging India trapped timelessly by superstition and caste dogma till such time as it was shaken by British colonialism (see in particular Marx and Engels 1959: 15-18, 31, 34). This tradition in Marxist thinking still remains a vital strain with many (see for a good review treatment, Hindess and Hirst 1975).

Quite in contrast to his description of India, Marx saw great potentialities for change in all class societies.*The Manifesto of the Communist Party* quite clearly states on the first page that class societies are coterminous with literate societies where the first distinctions were made between manualand mental labour(Marx and Engels1969: 108-9). India then should have also been examined as a class society replete with the potentialities of historical materialism. Even so, Marx, persuaded by Orientalist literature, quite uncharacteristically chose to view pre-British India in the main as a society still outside the process of history.

To return to the *Manifesto of the Communist Party* we see two types of classes, and not just two classes, as it is popularly believed. The first type of classes are the so-called social classes, like freeman, journeyman, apprentice, and guildmaster. The second type of classes are the analytical classes, such as the bourgeois and the proletariat, whose dialectically contradictory relationship defines and constrains specific social epochs and also shapes social change. But the social classes of the first type are descriptive classes and historical change does not hinge on them. In the Middle Ages there existed 'subordinate gradations' (ibid.: 109) beginning at the top with the feudal lord, who was followed by vassals, guildmaster, journeyman, apprentices and serfs. But such 'gradations' (hierarchy?) were of little use to Marx in his formulation of the laws of motion in society. In order to get the laws of motion, the contradictions (differences in their extreme form) between the determinate classes in society (or classes of the second type) were of critical importance and as such had to be unearthed for each specific social formation. In feudal societies, Marx contended, the basic classes in contradiction were the classes of the feudal lord and serf; and in capitalist society the contradiction was between the bourgeois class and the proletariat (ibid.). All this was packed in the first two pages of the *Manifesto of the Communist Party.*

The fact that Marx spent very little time on hierarchical gradations led him to undermine the aspects of order, continuity and stability in class societies. But this again was a logical denoument for he understood classes in terms of contradictions, i.e. in terms of extreme mutual 'differences', such that the interest of the two determinate classes in opposition would always remain irreconcilable. There is just no question of the encompassing and the encompassed being applicable here. These irreconcilable differences can only be overcome by a qualitative transformation of society as a whole. Wesolowski is thus wide off the mark when he attributes to Marx a hierarchical understanding of these very basic classes. According to Wesolowski (1969 : 128),

The bourgeoisie enjoy a higher income, a higher level of education and higher prestige. The workers have a low income, a low level of income and low prestige. The petit-bourgeoisie have an intermediate income, enjoy medium prestige and their level of education is higher than that of the bourgeoisie.

To mistake Marx's clear postulation of class contradiction as a species of strata continuum again demonstrates that the sociologists of social stratification quite uncritically tend to assume that all forms of stratification must necessarily be hierarchical in character. This was the mistake that we mentioned elsewhere in this paper that Pitrim Sorokin committed and is repeated again as we just saw by Wesolowski (see also Fried 1967 : 52). Perhaps a conscious awareness of the logical properties of *hierarchy* and *difference* will pre-empt such errors in the future and allow for a more systematic exposition of the basic principles that underpin the sources of continuity and change in diverse systems of social stratification.

I
Caste

Some of the most outstanding works on social stratification in India have to do with the caste system. Both descriptively and conceptually scholarship on the caste system has contributed significantly to our general understanding of social stratification over and above enriching our comprehension of this peculiarly Indian system of stratification. In this section one can get only a glimpse of the richness and variety of the material on castes. While the first few papers clarify the descriptive field, the later papers, particularly beginning with Bouglé's essay, are more analytical in character. In the more analytical essays the focus is on conceptual issues like hierarchy, separation, holism, individualism and on the competing theoretical perspectives which unite the studies of the caste system with general theoretical problems in sociology and social anthropology.

M.N. Srinivas opens this secton by clarifying the difference between *varna* and *jati*. This distinction is extremely important to sort out the different levels at which *varna* and *jati* become salient. The pan-Indian four-tiered *varna* system of the Brahmin, Kshatriya, Vaishya and Sudra does not operate on the ground. Srinivas points out that the *varna* scheme is primarily a fiction for it does not in fact regulate the social order. What empirically constitute the caste system are the numerous *jatis* which are specific to a region. Marriage rules, commensal taboos, occupational rigidity and even village politics operate at the *jati* level.

With this as a backdrop we are better placed to appreciate some of the major contributions which have attempted to conceptualize and define the caste system. The effort in all these cases is to analytically distinguish it from other forms of stratification. There seems to be a broad consensus that the caste system is a typically Indian phenomenon and therefore it is essential to first describe it faithfully and then to theoretically account for its characteristics and consequenses. Ghurye's essay helps us to get a detailed description of the essential features of the caste system. This essay adequately sums up the aggregate characteristics of the caste system such as endogamy, occupational specialization and hierarchy with a wealth of illustrations. In Ghurye's opinion, as well as in M.N. Srinivas's, the relevant level at which the caste system should be analysed is that of the *jati*.

McKim Marriott's famous essay on 'Multiple Reference in Indian Caste Systems' delineates with enviable lucidity the different levels at which the various aspects of the caste system become salient. At the level of the village what is important is the interaction between *jatis*, because it is these groups or categories which predominate the consciousness of the local people. In a closed rural society one's *jati* position is known on a very intimate basis. Where family backgrounds and histories are common folk knowledge, local caste customs inhibit as well as condition one's style of life. There is not much scope for the parvenu, nor is there much point in trying to wear a *jati* persona that is not traditionally one's own.

It is a different story however, once we enter the urban setting. Here it is not the interactional network of the *jati* that is relevant but the attributes or life styles one displays. Outside the village one's acquaintance with one's neighbours or colleagues is not nearly as rich and informed as at the rural level. Family backgrounds cannot be readily authenticated, nor can there be any common tradition as to how certain *jatis* must conduct themselves. Indeed, in an urban setting *jatis* have little meaning as they are regionally specific, and people from different regions come together in the cities. It is for this reason that one's life styles become relatively free of both the past and caste and there is greater scope for social mobility. As a person's status is known primarily on the basis of what he or she can display, the interactional *jati* world of the village slides into the background. In urban India, consequently, the notion of the *varna* classification becomes salient. There are certain accepted pan-Indian stereotypical styles of life attributed to each *varna*. Marriott thus fleshes out in detail what Srinivas had earlier indicated in his distinction between *varna* and *jati*.

Pauline Kolenda's essay is a summary of McKim Marriott and Ronald Inden's work on the 'dividual-particle' theory of pollution. It explains from the emic point of view how the Hindus themselves expain the natural/physical basis of caste distinctions. According to this native Hindu theory, individuals belonging to a particular caste share identical particles. These particles are different from the particles that constitute other individuals in other castes. This is why it is necessary to maintain distance between castes, lest these particles co-mingle. Marriott and Inden believe that this dividual-particle theory held by the Hindus must be paid attention to if one is to understand the resilience of the caste system. It should be mentioned in this connection that the 'dividual-particle theory' justifies the notion of natural superiority which is central to the caste system. Unlike racial stratification where visible differences govern social interaction, the caste system has to rest eventually on the belief in natural differences. The 'dividual-particle' theory is appropriate for it upholds natural differences and at the same time does not demand that these differences be perceptible to the senses. It is worthwhile keeping this in mind while discussing purity and pollution in Dumont's pure hierarchy to which we shall come soon.

Bouglé's work on the caste system continues to provide inspiration today much as it did when it was first published in 1908. Bouglé's understanding of the caste system is extraordinarily rich considering that his information came from secondary sources. He was also one of the early scholars who tried to define the caste system. He felt that the manifold caste observances and practices could be reduced to three principal characteristics, namely, occupational specialization, hierarchy and repulsion.

In this connection there are two important points which should be noted. First, though Bouglé considered occupational specialization to be an important feature of the caste system, he also realized that even the Brahmin, when prodded by hunger, would take up the so- called low-caste jobs. This observation is significant for very often, even today, there is a marked tendency towards viewing the caste system as an inflexible phenomenon. Secondly, the fact that Bouglé laid emphasis on repulsion as a crucial characteristic of the caste system meant that he too understood castes as discrete entities, i.e. as units which were sufficiently distinct, separate and isolatable.

We can appreciate Louis Dumont's contribution to the subject in *Homo Hierarchicus* best if we begin where Dumont himself began, i.e. with Bouglé. Like Bouglé Dumont too is interested in understanding the principle behind the caste system. But whereas Bouglé underlined 'repulsion', Dumont emphasizes 'hierarchy'. For Dumont, hierarchy is the all embracing principle behind the caste system. The units of the caste system, which Bouglé saw as separable and distinct, are encompassed and ordered by the encompassing criterion of the caste hierarchy. According to Dumont, caste hierarchy is determined by the principle of purity and pollution and that is why, argues Dumont, it should be seen as a true religious hierarchy (See appendix IV).

Scholarship on the caste system took a definite turn after *Homo Hierarchicus*. To a large extent T.N. Madan's lucid and precise presentation of Dumont's major thesis, which has been acknowledged as such by Dumont himself, has made the book accessible to a wider audience. It is for this reason that Madan's essay has been included here. The debates are now more analytically centred on issues such as whether or not caste is a religious hierarchy, and if it is, then can it explain such social phenomena as change, dynamism, individualism and freedom, adequately? One of the earliest and most pointed criticisms of Dumont came from Gerald Berreman, author of *Hindus of the Himalayas*. Berreman found much to disagree with Dumont for his own field study indicated that the principle of the true hierarchy was not uniformly adhered to by all Hindus. His strongly argued (and worded) critique of Dumont is built around the position that Dumont is generalizing on the basis of the Brahminical version of the caste system.

Joan Mencher asks a related question when she urges us to take a look at the caste system from below. In this connection she highlights the elements of coercion and caste-economic oppression that actually dominate the day to day experience of people. The openings for peasant mobilization are examined not strictly with reference to economic factors, but in conjunction with caste identities, traditional problems of behaviour and modern political processes.

Berreman and Mencher both encourage a non-Brahminical view of caste, or to be more accurate, a view of caste that is not limited to the Brahmin's version. My piece, which is the concluding essay in this section, follows this line of thought and attempts to provide an alternative conspectus for understanding the caste system. Instead of hierarchy, I propose that castes should be seen as discrete units with their own ideological self-images and notions of hierarchy. In this case there is no one ideology and no one hierarchy but there are ideologies and hierarchies in conflict. This is because a hierarchy, in my view, emerges from self-valuation whereas in Dumont the all encompassing hierarchy gives meaning to, as well as positions, the different castes.

Clearly the issues are still highly contentious. It is impossible to capture the full flow of articles and contributions that have been generated by *Homo Hierarchichus*. Dumont's ideas are not entirely original, for many before him had said that the Hindu order is essentially a religious one and yet the presentation of his thesis became an important landmark in the study of the subject. Even though many may disagree with Dumont, it is Dumont more than any other person in recent times who has reinvigorated conceptual discussions on the caste system.

Varna and Caste

M. N. SRINIVAS

An attempt is made in this brief essay to consider the relation between caste as it is in fact, and as it is subsumed by the traditional
concept of *varna*. The consideration of this relationship is both important and overdue, as the concept of *varna* has deeply influenced the
interpretation of the 'ethnographic reality' of caste. *Varna* has been
the model to which the observed facts have been fitted, and this is true
not only of educated Indians, but also of sociologists to some extent.

The layman is unaware of the complexities of *varna*. To him it
means simply the division of Hindu society into four orders, viz.,
Brahmana (Brahmin, traditionally, priest and scholar), Kshatriya (ruler
and soldier), Vaishya (merchant) and Shudra (peasant, labourer and
servant). The first three castes are 'twice-born' as the men from them
are entitled to don the sacred thread at the Vedic rite of *upanayana*,
while the Shudras are not. The Untouchables are outside the *varna*
scheme.

The layman's view of *varna* is a comparatively late view, and
varna, which literally means colour, originally referred to the distinction between the Arya and Dasa. Ghurye writes,

... in the Rg-Veda the word '*varna*' is never applied to any one of these
classes [Brahamana, Kshatriya, etc]. It is only the Arya *varna* or the Aryan
people that is contrasted with the Dasa *varna*. The Satapatha Brahamana, on
the other hand, describes the four classes as the four *varnas*. '*Varna*' means
'colour', and it was in this sense that the word seems to have been employed in contrasting the Arya and the Dasa, referring to their fair and dark
colours respectively. The colour connotation of the word was so strong that
later on when the classes came to be regularly described as *varnas*, four different colours were supposed to be distinguished (Ghurye 1950 : 47).

From M. N. Srinivas, 'Varna and Caste', in *Caste in Modern India and Other Essays*,
Asia Publishing House, Bombay, 1962.

He states later that the Rg-Vedic distinction between Arya and Dasa gave place to the distinction between the Arya and the Shudra (ibid : 52). In the Rg-Veda, along with the distinction between Arya and Dasa, there is a division of society into three orders, viz., Brahma, Kshatriya and Vish.

The first two represented broadly the two professions of the poet-priest and the warrior-chief. The third division was apparently a group comprising all the common people. It is only in one of the later hymns, the celebrated Purushasukta, that a reference has been made to four orders of society as emanating from the sacrifice of the Primeval Being. The names of those four orders are given there as *Brahmana, Rajanya (Kshatriya), Vaishya* and *Shudra,* who are said to have come from the mouth, the arms, the thighs, and the feet of the Creator. The particular limbs associated with these divisions and the order in which they are mentioned probably indicate their status in the society of the time, though no such interpretation is directly given in the hymn (ibid : 45).

It is interesting to note that though three orders are mentioned in the Rg-Veda, there is no single term to describe them. A term which originally referred to the distinction in colour and appearance between the conquerors (Arya) and the conquered aborigines (Dasyu) was used later to refer to the hierarchical division of the society.

In the *varna* scheme of the Vedas there are only four orders, and the Untouchables have no place in it. But there are references in Vedic literature to groups such as the Ayogava, Chandala, Nishada and Paulkasa, who are outside the *varna* scheme, and who seem to be despised.

It is more reasonable to hold that both these groups, Chandala and Paulkasa, were sections of the aborigines that were, for some reason or another, particularly despised by the Aryans. The Nishadas, on the other hand, seem to have been a section liked by the Aryans, probably because they were amenable to their civilized notions. The Vedic expression *'pancajanah'* is explained by tradition, belonging to the latter part of the period, to mean the four *varnas* and Nishadas, a fact which shows that these people had, by this time, become quite acceptable to the Aryans (ibid : 54).

In brief, '. . . the three classes of the early portion of the Rg-Veda were later solidified into four groups, more or less compact, with three or four other groups separately mentioned' (ibid). And 'the ideas of untouchability were first given literary expression in connection with the Shudras and the sacrifice' (ibid : 52-8).

I shall now describe the features of the caste system *implicit* in the *varna* scheme and then try to see how they differ from, or conflict with, the system as it actually functions.

Firstly, according to the *varna* scheme there are only four castes excluding the Untouchables, and the number is the same in every part of India. But even during Vedic times there were occupational groups which were not subsumed by *varna* even though it is not known whether such groups were castes in the sense sociologists understand the term. Today, in any linguistic area there are to be found a number of castes. According to Ghurye, in each linguistic region, there are about 200 caste groups which are further sub-divided into about 3000 smaller units each of which is endogamous and constitutes the area of effective social life for the individual (ibid : 28). The *varna* scheme refers at best only to the broad categories of the society and not to its real and effective units. And even as referring only to the broad categories of the society it has serious shortcomings. It has already been seen that the Untouchables are outside the scheme, but as a matter of actual fact they are an integral part of the society. The fact that they are denied privileges which the higher castes enjoy does not mean that they are not an integral part of the society.

The category of Shudra subsumes in fact the vast majority of non-Brahminical castes which have little in common. It may at one end include a rich, powerful and highly Sanskritized group and at the other tribes whose assimilation into the Hindu fold is only marginal. The Shudra category spans such a wide structural and cultural gulf that its sociological utility is very limited.

It is well known that occasionally a Shudra caste after the acquisition of economic and political power, Sanskritized its customs and ways, and succeeded in laying claim to be Kshatriyas. The classic example of the Raj Gonds, originally a tribe, but who successfully claimed to be Kshatriyas after becoming rulers of a tract in Central India, shows up the *varna* classification. The term Kshatriya, for instance, does not refer to a closed ruling group which has always been there since the time of the Vedas. More often it refers to the position attained or claimed by a local group whose traditions and luck enabled it to seize politico-economic power. In fact, in peninsular India there are no genuine Kshatriyas and Vaishyas. In this area these two categories only refer to the local castes which have claimed to be Kshatriyas and Vaishyas by virtue of their occupation and martial tradition, and the claim is not seriously disputed by others. Claims to being Brahmins are much less common.

The *varna* model has produced a wrong and distorted image of caste. It is necessary for the sociologist to free himself from the hold of the *varna* model if he wishes to understand the caste system. It is hardly necessary to add that this is more difficult for Indian sociologists than it is for non-Indians.

The position which each caste occupies in the local hierarchy is frequently not clear. It is true, however, that in most areas of the country Brahmins are placed at the top and Untouchables at the bottom, and most people know who are the Brahmins, and who, the Untouchables. But in southern India the Lingayats claim equality with, if not superiority to the Brahmin, and orthodox Lingayats do not eat food cooked or handled by the Brahmins. The Lingayats have priests of their own caste who also minister to several other non-Brahmin castes. Such a challenge of the ritual superiority of the Brahmin is not unknown though not frequent. The claim of a particular caste to be Brahmin is, however, more often challenged. Food cooked or handled by Marka Brahmins of Mysore, for instance, is not eaten by most Hindus, not excluding Harijans.

One of the most striking features of the caste system as it actually exists is the lack of clarity in the hierarchy, especially in the middle regions. This is responsible for endless argumentation regarding mutual ritual rank: it is this ambiguity which makes it possible for a caste to rise in the hierarchy. Each caste tries to prove that it is equal to a 'superior' caste and superior to its 'equals'. And arguments are advanced to prove superiority. The vegetarian castes occupy the highest position in the hierarchy and approximation to vegetarianism is adduced as evidence of high status. The drinking of liquor, the eating of the domestic pig which is a scavenger, and of the sacred cow, all these tend to lower the ritual rank of a caste. Similarly, the practice of a degrading occupation such as butchery, or a defiling occupation such as cutting hair, or making leather sandals, tends to lower the ritual rank of a caste. There is a hierarchy in diet and occupation, though this varies somewhat from region to region. The castes from which a man accepts cooked food and drinking water are either equal or superior, while the castes from which he does not, are inferior. Similarly the practice of certain customs such as shaving the heads of widows, and the existence of divorce, are also criteria of hierarchical rank. Not infrequently, the member of a caste points to some customs of his caste as evidence of high rank, while others point to the existence of certain other customs as evidence of low rank. In cases such as that of the Smith (Achari) the disparity between the position claimed by the caste and that conceded by others is indeed great. The Smiths of South India seem to have tried to move high up in the caste system by a thorough Sanskritization of their rites and customs, and this, instead of gaining them what they wanted, has roused the disapproval, if not the hostility, of all the others. Today, very few castes including the Harijan, eat food cooked by Smiths. Until recently, Smiths were not entitled to perform a wedding inside the village, or wear red slippers and so on.[1] It is necessary to stress here that a vast number of small castes in a region do not occupy clear and permanent positions in the system. Nebulousness as to position is of the essence of the system in operation as distinct from the system in conception. The *varna* model has been the cause of misinterpretation of the realities of the caste system. A point that has emerged from recent field research is that the position of a caste in the hierarchy may vary from village to village. It is not only that hierarchy is nebulous here and there, and that castes are mobile over a period of time; but the hierarchy is also to some extent local. The *varna* scheme offers a perfect contrast to this picture.

The *varna* scheme is a 'hierarchy' in the literal sense of the term because ritual considerations form the basis of the differentiation. It is true that generally speaking the higher castes are also the better-off castes, and the lowest castes are also among the poorest, but a ranking of castes on principally economic or political considerations would produce a stratification somewhat different from that based on ritual considerations. The disparity between the ritual and economic or political position of a caste is often considerable. In the Mysore village, Rampura, for instance, the Brahmin priest is accorded every respect by the village headman who is a Peasant (Okkaliga) by caste. But the headman is the richest man in the village and in the area, the biggest land-owner and money-lender, the official headman of the village, and generally a very influential man, and one of the managers of the Rama temple at which the Brahmin is a priest. In secular matters the priest is dependent on the headman. In the summer of 1952, the priest's eldest son passed the lower secondary examination in the first class, and he went to the headman's house as soon as he heard the news. He was pleased, confused and even worried. He wanted his son to study further,

---

[1] As to why the Lingayats succeeded in obtaining a high position while the Smiths did not, is an extremely interesting problem for the historical sociologist. Both the castes seem to have employed 'shock tactics', but while in one case they came off in the other, they did not.

See William L. Rowe, 'The New Cauhans ...' , in this volume to get a better idea on this question. Editor.

which cost money, and also meant his going to Mysore which the priest considered a strange and distant city. (As a matter of actual fact, Mysore was only 22 miles from Rampura.) The priest discussed the matter with the headman, who treated his worries half-jokingly, and then went to the headman's mother, an old matriarch of seventy odd years. He sat a few feet away from her and talked to her, addressing her every few minutes as *avva* or mother. The Brahmin equivalent of *avva* would be *amma* or *tayi*, but it is interesting to note that the priest made use of a term of respect which every peasant used, exactly as a peasant would. He was treating her advice with respect though according to the *varna* scheme she was a member of the Shudra caste.

A member of a higher caste often goes to a rich and powerful member of a lower caste for help and advice. It is clear that in such cases the former is dependent upon the latter. When members of different castes come together, their mutual positions are determined by the context in which the contact takes place. Thus, for instance, in a ritual context, the priest would occupy the higher position while in a secular context, the headman would occupy the higher position. This way of formulating the situation is not very satisfactory as behind the particular contexts there lie the permanent positions. In the example given above, the headman and his mother knew they were dealing not with an ordinary peasant, but with a Brahmin and a priest at that. He normally occupied a position of respect; and as priest of the Rama temple he had a special claim on the headman's help and support. Helping him would result in the acquisition of *punya* or spiritual merit. Helping any poor man confers spiritual merit, but more merit would accrue when the poor man is also a Brahmin and a priest. The headman also needs the services of the priest, and when any important Brahmin friends visited Rampura, he asked the priest to provide food for them.

The *varna* scheme has certainly distorted the picture of caste but it has enabled ordinary men and women to grasp the caste system by providing them with a simple and clear scheme which is applicable to all parts of India. *Varna* has provided a common social language which holds good, or is thought to hold good, for India as a whole. A sense of familiarity even when it does not rest on facts, is conducive to unity.

It is interesting to note that the mobility of a caste is frequently stated in *varna* terms rather than in terms of the local caste situation. This is partly because each caste has a name and a body of customs and traditions which are peculiar to itself, in any local area, and no other caste would be able to take up its name. A few individuals or families may claim to belong to a locally higher caste, but not a whole caste. Even the former event would be difficult as the connections of these individuals or families would be known to all in that area. On the other hand, a local caste would not find it difficult to call itself Brahmin, Kshatriya or Vaishya. Even here there might be opposition, but the parvenus may distinguish themselves from the local Brahmin, Kshatriya or Vaishya by suitable prefixes. Thus the Bedas of Mysore would find it impossible to call themselves Okkaligas (Peasants) or Kurubas (Shepherds), but would not have difficulty in calling themselves Valmiki Brahmins. The Smiths of South India long ago, in pre-British times, changed their names to Vishvakarma Brahmins. In British India this tendency received special encouragement during the periodical census enumerations when the low castes changed their names in order to move up in hierarchy.

Features of the Caste System

G. S. GHURYE

A foreign visitor to India is struck by the phenomenon known as the caste system. He may not understand the full working of the system, but he is aware of the fact that Hindu society is divided into groups, known as castes with varying degrees of respectability and circles of social intercourse.... This is due not only to the fact that caste is the most general form of social organization in India but also because it presents such a marked contrast to the social grouping prevalent in Europe or America. Owing to these two features—ubiquity and strangeness—the institution has found many able scholars devoted to its study. With all the labours of these students, however, we do not possess a real general definition of caste. It appears to me that any attempt at definition is bound to fail because of the complexity of the phenomenon. On the other hand, much literature on the subject is marred by a lack of precision about the use of the term. Hence I propose to give a description of the factors underlying this system of castes.

The earliest account of this institution, given by a foreigner of the third century BC, mentions two of the features characterizing it before it was modified by close cultural contact with Western Europe during the last century.

It is not permitted to contract marriage with a person of another caste, nor to change from one profession or trade to another, nor for the same person to undertake more than one, except when he is of the caste of philosophers, when permission is given on account of his dignity.

Excerpted from G. S. Ghurye, 'Features of the Caste System', *Caste and Race in India*, Popular Prakashan, Bombay, 1969.

In this paper, I have quoted many authorities that are chronologically later by half a century or more than the period I have here in view. But other and older authorities are almost everywhere indicated. The reason is that the later authorities give more details and are easily accessible to most people.

Though this statement of Megasthenes brings two of the most salient features of the institution to the forefront, yet it fails to give a complete idea of the system.

The outstanding features of Hindu society when it was ruled by the social philosophy of caste, unaffected by the modern ideas of rights and duties, may be discerned to be six.

Segmental Division of Society

. . . . Castes were groups with a well developed life of their own, the membership whereof, unlike that of voluntary associations and of classes, was determined not by selection but by birth. The status of a person depended not on his wealth as in the classes of modern Europe, but on the traditional importance of the caste in which he had the luck of being born. . . . To restrict myself to the Marathi region, a person is born either a Brahmin, Prabhu, Maratha, Vani, Sonar, Sutar, Bhandari, Chambhar, or a Mahar, etc. If he chances to take a vocation which is not earmarked for a particular caste—say the military—he remains a casteman all the same. A Brahmin general and a Maratha general, though of equal status in the army, belong to two different status-groups in their private life and there cannot be any social intercourse between them on equal terms. But this is not the case in a class society where status is determined by vocation and consequent income. A class has no standing or occasional council, to regulate the conduct and guide the morals of its members, apart from the laws of the community as a whole. Members of one class follow different vocations, which, when organized, possess standing executive committees, which govern the members of their profession according to their rules. These rules generally exclude the legitimate province of the wider community, and refer only to professional·etiquette or economic gain! . . . . Most of the castes on the other hand, excepting the high ones like the Brahmin and the Rajput, have regular standing councils deciding on many more matters than those taken cognizance of by the committees of the trade unions, associations, or guilds, and thus encroaching on the province of the whole community. . . . The governing body of a caste is called the *panchayat*. Some of the offences dealt with by it are: (a) eating, drinking, or having similar dealings with a caste or sub-caste; with which such social intercourse is held to be forbidden; (b) keeping as concubine a woman of another caste; (c) seduction of or adultery with a married woman; (d) fornication; (e) refusal to fulfil a promise of marriage; (f) refusing to send a wife to her

husband when old enough; (g) refusing to maintain a wife; (h) non-
payment of debt; (i) petty assaults; (j) breaches of the customs of the
trade peculiar to the caste; (k) encroaching on another's clientele, and
raising or lowering prices; (l) killing a cow or any other forbidden
animal; (m) insulting a Brahmin and (n) defying the customs of the
caste regarding feasts, etc., during marriage and other ceremonies. It
will be seen from this list that some of the offences tried by the governing bodies of castes were such as are usually dealt with by the State
in its judicial capacity. Thus, a caste was a group with a separate arrangement for meting out justice to its members apart from that of the
community as a whole, within which the caste was included as only
one of the groups. Hence the members of a caste ceased to be members
of the community as a whole, as far as that part of their morals which is
regulated by law was concerned. This quasi-sovereignty of the caste
is particularly brought to notice by the fact that the caste council was
prepared to re-try criminal offences decided by the courts of law. This
means that in this caste-bound society the amount of community-feel-
ing must have been restricted, and that the citizens owed moral
allegiance to their caste first, rather than to the community as a whole.
By segmental division I wish to connote this aspect of the system. The
punishments that these councils awarded were: (1) out-casting, either
temporary or permanent; (2) fines; (3) feasts to be given to the castemen; (4) corporal punishment and (5) sometimes religious expiation. . .
This description of the activities of a caste-council will enable us to
appreciate the remark, 'The caste is its own ruler'. The diversity in
the administration of law necessarily led to differences in moral
standards of the various castes. There was thus created a cultural gulf
between the castes. I may note some of the items of cultural differences
among the castes to bring out clearly the implications of the segmentation. Many of the castes have their special deities. Among such
castes the following may be noted from southern India, Komati,
Kamsalai, Gamalla, Idiga, Mala and Madiga; from the Central Provinces, Ahir; from the Uttar Pradesh, Aheriya, Baheliya, Kharwar,
Korwa, Chero, Bhuiyar, Dom, Musahar, and Nai; and from Gujarat,
Vaishyas. About the differences in religious outlook of the Madras
castes it has been said :

Amongst the Brahmin community this one fact stands off clear and distinct,
that they do not indulge in the worship of Grama Devata, the village gods,
to which the aboriginal population almost exclusively bows down (*Madras
Census*, 1871: 137).

The customs about marriage and death vary widely among the different castes. Brahmins did not permit widow-marriage nor tolerate concubinage as a caste-practice. This could not be said of many lower castes. . . . These differences of morals and customs were so manifest that the early British Courts in India not merely asked the opinion of their pundits, but took the evidence of the heads of the castes concerned as to their actual usages. . . . Hence castes are small and complete social worlds in themselves, marked off definitely from one another, though subsisting within the larger society.

Hierarchy

In my discussion of the subject so far I have used the comparative degree with reference to the status of different castes, thus assuming beforehand one of the principal characteristics of the caste society, viz., the hierarchy of the groups. Everywhere in India there is a definite scheme of social precedence amongst the castes, with the Brahmin at the head of hierarchy. Only in southern India the artisan castes

have always maintained a struggle for a higher place in the social scale than that allowed to them by Brahmanical authority. . . . There is no doubt as to the fact that the members of this great caste (Kammalan) dispute the supremacy of the Brahmins, and that they hold themselves to be equal in rank with them (*Madras Census*, 1871 : 137).

John Fryer, who visited India in 1670, seems to refer to this attitude. In any one of the linguistic divisions of India there are as many as two hundred castes which can be grouped in classes whose gradation is largely acknowledged by all. But the order of social precedence amongst the individual castes of any class cannot be made definite, because not only is there no ungrudging acceptance of such rank but also the ideas of the people on this point are very nebulous and uncertain. The following observation vividly bring out this state of things.[1]

As the society now stands . . . the place due to each community is not easily distinguishable, nor is any common principle of precedence recognized by the people themselves by which to grade the castes. Excepting the Brahmin at one end and the admittedly degraded castes like the Holeyas at the other, the members of a large proportion of the intermediate castes think or profess to think that their caste is better than their neighbours' and should be ranked accordingly. . . .

[1] For more detailed treatment of this issue see Gerald Berreman, 'Brahmanical View of Caste', or Dipankar Gupta, 'Continuous Hierarchies and Discrete Castes', in this volume.

Restrictions on Feeding and Social Intercourse

There are minute rules as to what sort of food or drink can be accepted by a person and from what castes. But there is very great diversity in this matter. The practices in the matter of food and social intercourse divide India into two broad belts. In Hindustan proper, castes can be divided into five groups: first, the twice-born castes; second, those castes at whose hands the twice-born can take *pakka* food; third, those castes at whose hands the twice-born cannot accept any kind of food but may take water; fourth, castes that are not untouchable, yet are such that water from them cannot be used by the twice-born; last come all those castes whose touch defiles not only the twice-born but any orthodox Hindu. All food is divided into two classes, *kachcha* and *pakka*, the former being any food in the cooking of which water has been used, and the latter all food cooked in 'ghee' without the addition of water. 'As a rule a man will never eat *kachcha* food unless it is prepared by a fellow caste-man, which in actual practice means a member of his own endogamous group, whether it be caste or sub-caste, or else by his Brahmin Guru or spiritual guide. But in practice most castes seem to take no objection to *kachcha* food from a Brahmin'. A Brahmin can accept *kachcha* food at the hands of no other caste; some of them, like the Kanaujia Brahmins, are so punctilious about these restrictions that, as a proverb has it, three Kanaujias require no less than thirteen hearths. As for the *pakka* food, it may be taken by a Brahmin at the hands of some of the castes only. On the whole, however, as E.A. Blunt has made out, there is 'no relation between a caste's social position and the severity of its cooking taboo' (Blunt 1969 : 90-4); as many as thirty-six out of seventy-six castes of U.P. take *kachcha* cooked food from only their own members and none others.

The ideas about the power of certain castes to convey pollution by touch are not so highly developed in northern India as in the South. The idea that impurity can be transmitted by the mere shadow of an Untouchable or by his approaching within a certain distance does not seem to prevail in Hindustan. No Hindu of decent caste will touch a Chamar, or a Dom; and some of the very low castes themselves are quite strict about contact. . . .

In Bengal the castes are divided into two main groups: (1) the Brahmins, and (2) the Shudras. The second class is further divided into four sub-classes, indicating their status as regards food and water: (a) the Sat-Shudra group includes such castes as the Kayastha and Nabashakh, (b) then come the Jalacharaniya-Shudras, 'being those castes, not technically belonging to the Nabashakh group, from whom Brahmins and members of the higher castes can take water', (c) then follow the Jalabyabaharya-Shudras, castes from whose hands a Brahmin cannot take water, (d) last stand the Asprishya-Shudras castes whose touch is so impure as to pollute even the Ganges water, and hence their contact must be avoided. They are thus the Untouchables (Risley 1891, II: 270). In the matter of food western Bengal resembles Hindustan except in this that in Bengal there are some people who will not accept any *kachcha* food even from the hands of a Brahmin; *pakka* food can be ordinarily taken not only from one's own or any higher caste, but also from the confectioner class, the Myras and Halwais. As regards the position of the Untouchables the following observation will give a clear idea. 'Even wells are polluted if a low caste man draws water from them, but a great deal depends on the character of the vessel used and of the well from which water is drawn. A masonry well is not so easily defiled as one constructed with clay pipes, and if it exceeds three and a half cubits in width so that a cow may turn round in it, it can be used even by the lowest castes without defilement. . . .' (*U.P. Census,* 1911 : 329) Certain low castes are looked down upon as so unclean that they may not enter the courtyard of the great temples. These castes are compelled to live by themselves on the outskirts of villages.

In eastern and southern Bengal and in Gujarat and the whole of southern India there is no distinction of food as *kachcha* for the purposes of its acceptance or otherwise from anyone but a member of one's own caste. In Gujarat and southern India, generally speaking, a Brahmin never thinks of accepting water, much less any cooked food, from any caste but that of the Brahmins, and all the other castes or groups of castes more or less follow the principle of accepting no cooked food from any caste that stands lower than itself in the social scale. This rule does not apply with the same strictness to accepting water. Again as a rule, a lower caste has no scruples in accepting cooked food from any higher caste. Thus all the castes will take cooked food from the Brahmin.

The theory of pollution being communicated by some castes to members of the higher ones is also more developed in Gujarat. Theoretically, the touch of a member of any caste lower than one's own defiles a person of the higher caste; but in actual practice this rule is not strictly observed. In the Maratha country the shadow of an Untouchable is sufficient, if it falls on a member of a higher caste, to pollute him. In Madras, and especially in Malabar, this doctrine is still further elaborated, so that certain castes have always to keep a stated distance between themselves and the Brahmin and other higher castes so as not to defile the latter. Thus the Shanar, toddy-tapper of Tamilnad, contaminates a Brahmin if he approaches the latter within twenty-four paces. Among the people of Kerala, a Nayar may approach a Nambudiri Brahmin but must not touch him; while a Tiyan must keep himself at the distance of thirty-six steps from the Brahmin, and a Pulayan may not approach him within ninety-six paces.[2] A Tiyan must keep away from a Nayar at twelve paces, while some castes may approach the Tiyan, though they must not touch him. A Pulayan must not come near any of the Hindu castes. So rigid are the rules about defilement which is supposed to be carried with them by all except the Brahmins, that the latter will not perform even their ablutions within the precincts of a Shudra's habitation. Generally the washerman and the barber, who serve the general body of villagers, will not render their services to the unclean and Untouchable castes.

Civil and Religious Disabilities and Privileges of the Different Sections

Segregation of individual castes or of groups of castes in a village is the most obvious mark of civil privileges and disabilities, and it has prevailed in a more or less definite form all over India. Southern India as in the matter of ceremonial purity and untouchability stands out distinct in the rigidity of these rules. In nothern India generally, in the Maratha country and, as it appears, sometimes in the Telugu and Kanarese regions, it is only the impure castes that are segregated and made to live on the outskirts of villages. It does not seem that other groups of castes have distinct quarters of the town or village allotted to them excepting in parts of Gujarat. In the Tamil and Malayalam regions very frequently different quarters are occupied by separate castes or sometimes the village is divided into three parts : that occupied by the dominant caste in the village or by the Brahmins, that allotted to the Shudras, and the one reserved for the Panchamas or Untouchables. In a village of the Ramnad District, the main portion is occupied by the Nayakars, shepherds, artisans, washermen, and barbers, forming a group living in the north-east corner of the village while the Untouchables ply their trades in the north-west and the south-east corners. . . .

[2] For a slightly different scale of distances see Rao.(1957: 21).

In southern India certain parts of the town or village are inaccessible to certain castes. The agitation by the impure castes to gain free access to certain streets in Vaikam in Travancore brings into clear relief some of the disabilities of these castes. It is recorded that under the rule of the Marathas and the Peshwas, the Mahars and Mangs were not allowed within the gates of Poona after 3 p.m. and before 9 a.m. because before nine and after three their bodies cast too long a shadow, which falling on a member of the higher castes—especially a Brahmin —defiles him. However, in the Dravidian South,[3] the very land of the supreme dominance of the Brahmin, the Brahmin was restricted in his rights of access to any part of the village. It is well known that in a village which is a gift to the Brahmins, a Paraiyan is not allowed to enter the Brahmin quarter; but it is not known to many students that the Paraiyans will not permit a Brahmin to pass through their street; so much so that if one happens to enter their quarters they greet him with cow-dung water. . . . All over India the impure castes are debarred from drawing water from the village well, which is used by the members of other castes. In the Maratha country a Mahar—one of the Untouchables—might not spit on the road lest a pure caste Hindu should be polluted by touching it with his foot, but had to carry an earthen pot, hung from his neck, in which to spit. Further he had to drag a thorny branch with him to wipe out his footprints and to lie at a distance prostrate on the ground if a Brahmin passed by, so that his foul shadow might not defile the holy Brahmin. In the Punjab, where restrictions regarding pollution by proximity have been far less stringent than in other parts of India, a sweeper, while walking through the streets of the larger towns, was supposed to carry a broom in his hand or under his armpit as a mark of his being a scavenger and had to shout out to the people warning them of his polluting presence. . . . In Gujarat the depressed castes used to wear a horn as their distinguishing mark. From certain decisions noted by the Peshwas in their diaries one can form some idea about disabilities of some of the castes in the Maratha country. The rulers upheld the claim of the potters, opposed by the carpenters, that they could lead their bridal processions on horse-back, and that of the copper-smith, against the Lingayats, to go in procession through public streets.

In Dravidian India the disabilities of the lower castes went so far as to prescribe what sort of houses they should build and what material

[3] Specifically speaking, Tamilnadu

they might employ in the construction thereof. The Shanars and Izhavas, toddy-tappers of the eastern and the western coasts, were not allowed to build houses above one storey in height. In Malabar the house is called by different names according to the occupant's caste; and peoples of inferior castes dare not refer to their own homes in the presence of Nambudiri Brahmin in more flattering terms than as 'dung-heaps'.

The toddy-tappers of Malabar and the east coast, Izhavas and Shanars were not allowed to carry umbrellas, to wear shoes or golden ornaments, to milk cows or even to use the ordinary language of the country. In Malabar, Brahmins alone were permitted to sit on boards formed in the shape of a tortoise, and if a member of any other caste were to use such a seat he was liable to capital punishment. Members of all castes, except the Brahmins, were expressly forbidden to cover the upper part of their body above the waist. In the case of women also, until 1865 they were obliged by law to go with the upper part of their bodies quite bare, if they belonged to the Tiyan or other lower castes. Under the Peshwas a greater distinction was made in the punishment on account of the caste of the criminal than of the nature of the crime itself. Hard labour and death were punishments mostly visited on criminals of the lower castes.

In Tamilnad there has been for ages a faction among the non-Brahmin castes dividing most of them into two groups, the right-hand castes and the left-hand castes. The right-hand castes claim certain privileges which they strongly refuse to those of the left-hand, viz., riding on horse-back in processions, carrying standards with certain devices, and supporting their marriage booths on twelve pillars. They insist that the left-hand castes must not raise more than eleven pillars to the booth nor employ on their standards devices peculiar to the right-hand castes.

. . . .

Certain sacraments cannot be performed by any caste other than the Brahmins. The most sacred literature cannot be studied by the Shudras. No caste can employ any other priests than the Brahmins, with very few exceptions, in southern India. The artisans of Madras seem to employ their own priests; and the goldsmith caste of the Maratha region established their right of employing their caste-fellows as priests during the last part of the Peshwa rule. The innermost recesses of temples can only be approached by the Brahmins, clean Shudras and other high castes having to keep outside the sacred precincts. The impure castes,

and particularly the Untouchables, cannot enter even the outer portions of a temple but must keep to the courtyards. In south Malabar,
the high castes do not allow the Tiyans to cremate their dead.

A Brahmin never bows to anyone who is not a Brahmin, but requires
others to salute him; and when he is saluted by a member of a non-
Brahmin caste he only pronounces a benediction. Some of the lower
castes carry their reverence for the Brahmins, especially in northern
India, to such extremes that they will not cross the shadow of a Brahmin, and sometimes will not take their food without sipping water in
which the big toe of a Brahmin is dipped.

In the Maratha country, at the beginning of the seventeenth century, the great preacher Ramdas tried to inculcate in the minds of the
people the idea of unity based on the bond of common locality. During
the latest period of the Peshwa rule (latter half of the eighteenth century), however, this ideal dwindled into the orthodox one wherein
Brahmins figure prominently; the State having no higher function than
that of pampering them. Under the Hindu rulers the Brahmins must
have secured to themselves many pecuniary privileges, denied to others, on the strength of this orthodox theory of the proper function of the
State, and perhaps more because they happened to occupy the posts of
importance. Thus in the Maratha region during the period referred to
above, the Konkanasth Brahmin clerks obtained the privilege of their
goods being exempted from certain duties and their imported corn
being carried to them without any ferry-charges. Brahmin landholders of a part of the country had their lands assessed at distinctly
lower rates than those levied from other classes. Brahmins were exempted from capital punishment, and when confined in forts, they
were more liberally treated than the other classes.

. . . .

Lack of Unrestricted Choice of Occupation

Generally a caste or a group of allied castes considered some of the
callings as its hereditary occupation, to abandon which in pursuit of
another, though it might be more lucrative, was thought not to be right.
Thus a Brahmin thought that it was correct for him to be a priest,
while the Chamar regarded it as his duty to cure hides and prepare
shoes. This was only generally true, for there were groups of occupations like trading, agriculture, labouring in the field, and doing military service which were looked upon as anybody's, and most castes
were supposed to be eligible for any of them. Among the artisans

occupations, which were more or less of the same status, were open to the members of these castes without incidental degradation. No caste would allow its members to take to any calling which was either degrading, like toddy-tapping and brewing, or impure, like scavenging or curing hides. It was not only the moral restraint and the social check of one's caste-fellows that acted as a restraint on the choice of one's occupation, but also the restriction put by other castes, which did not allow members other than those of their own castes to follow their callings. Of such restrictive regulations there were in operation only those concerning the profession of priest, no one not born a Brahmin being allowed to be a priest. The effect of these rules was that the priestly profession was entirely monopolized by the Brahmins, leaving aside the ministrants of the aboriginal deities, while they were seen plying any trade or calling which suited their tastes and which was not polluting. The majority of the Konkanasth and Deshasth Brahmins of the Maratha country were devoted to secular pursuits filling offices of every kind, including the village accountantship. During the Maratha upheaval and after, the Brahmins entered the profession of arms in fairly large numbers. Before the Indian Mutiny the Kanaujia Brahmins used to enter the Bengal army as sepoys in large numbers. Some of the Rarhi Brahmins of Bengal accepted service under Mohammedan rulers. Some of the Brahmins of Rajasthan served their Marwadi masters. The majority of the Brahmins in the lower Karnatak, according to Buchanan, almost entirely filled the different offices in the collection of revenue and even acted as messengers. Of the Hindustani Brahmins of Central India [Madhya Pradesh] it is said that a considerable population of them are concerned in trade. The Havig Brahmins of the Tulu country did all kinds of agricultural labour except hold the plough. About the Kanaujia Brahmins of Uttar Pradesh it is asserted that they even till the soil with their own hands, while shop-keeping and hawking form the main source of livelihood for the Sanadhya Brahmins of that region. In Rajasthan the Brahmin is not only willing to do all the labour that his piece of land requires, but is also ready to sell his labour to other more fortunate occupants. Brahmins in Madras appear as civil, public, and military servants, traders, cultivators, industrialists, and even labourers. It seems that in the days of Akbar, too, the Brahmins were engaged in trade, cultivation, or any advantageous pursuit in general.

More castes than one are engaged in agriculture. Thus we have the Vellalas, the Pallis, the Agamudaiyans and the Malaiyalis in Madras. As regards the five artisan castes, grouped together as Panchakalsi, it is observed that it is not impossible for individuals to pass from one occupation to another without any alteration of social status or loss of right of intermarriage. Weaving is practised by many of the menial castes including even the impure castes of Mahars and Chamars. If one looks at the Census Reports, especially those for 1901, one finds groups, which are regarded as separate castes, following more calling than one. . . . In 1798 Colebrooke wrote :

Daily observation shows even Brahmins exercising the menial profession of a Shudra. We are aware that every caste forms itself into clubs or lodges, consisting of the several individuals of that caste residing within a small distance, and that these clubs or lodges govern themselves by particular rules or customs or by-laws. But though some restrictions and limitations, not founded on religious prejudices, are found among their by-laws, it may be received as a general maxim that the occupation appointed for each tribe is entitled to a preference. Every profession, with few exceptions is open to every description of person (*Ency. Brit.* V, 1798 : 465).

Restrictions on Marriage

Most of the groups, whose features I have attempted to characterize above, are further divided into a number of sub-groups every one of which forbids its members to marry persons from outside it. Each of these groups, popularly known as sub-castes, is thus endogamous. This principle of strict endogamy is such a dominant aspect of caste-society that an eminent sociologist is led to regard endogamy as 'the essence of the caste system'. There are, however, a few exceptions to this general rule of marrying within one's own group which are due to the practice of hypergamy. In some parts of Punjab, especially in the hills, a man of a higher caste can take to wife a girl from one of the lower castes, while, in Malabar, the younger sons of the Nambudiri and other Brahmins consort with the Kshatriya and Nayar women, among whom mother-right prevails. Excepting for these cases of inter-caste hypergamy each group has to contract matrimonial alliances within its own limits. Outside of this practice the only other authentic case where inter-caste marriage is allowed is that of some of the artisan castes of Malabar. Any man venturing to transgress this law will be put out of his own sub-caste and it is doubtful if he will be admitted into the folds of any other respectable caste. To illustrate from the Maratha region, a Konkanasth Brahmin must marry a girl born in a Konkanasth Brahmin family, while a Karhada Brahmin must similarly seek his partner from amongst the Karhada Brahmins, and so on, the principle being that marriage must be arranged within the group which is most effectively considered to be one's own. If this rule is violated expulsion from the membership of the group is generally the penalty which the offending parties have to suffer. In Gujarat the unit within which all matrimonial alliances must be contracted is very often still smaller than the so-called sub-caste of the Marathi region. Among the Banias, the trading caste, for example, there are not only the division of Shrimali, Porwal, Modh, etc., but there are further sub-divisions like Dasa Porwal and Visa Porwal. This is not all. The Dasa are still further required to contract their marriages either from amongst the Dasas of Surat or of Bombay according to whether they belong to Surat or Bombay. When the groups are so much subdivided the penalty for transgressing the rule of endogamy in reference to the smallest unit is not expulsion of the offending parties but the gratification by them of the offended group.

To regard endogamy as the chief characteristic of a caste is to treat all so-called sub-castes as the real castes. There are two reasons against this procedure of raising sub-castes to the position of castes, viz., it would be contrary to the native feeling on the subject, and would be highly inconvenient in practice, as it would create a bewildering multiplicity of castes. As for the second objection, we may safely pass it over, as it concerns only an administrative difficulty. As regards the Indian sentiment against making a sub-caste into a caste, it must be pointed out that, at best, this is the representation of only one side of the problem; for if, to confine myself to the Marathi country, a Saraswat Brahmin is known to the outsiders as a Saraswat, to a Saraswat he is better known either as a Shenvi or as a Sashtikar or Pednekar. Stated generally, though it is the caste that is recognized by the society at large it is the sub-caste that is regarded by the particular caste and the individual. It is mainly indifference towards others, so characteristic of the Indian system, that is responsible for this attitude. For a Brahmin most others are Shudras, irrespective of high or low status; and for two or three higher castes that are allied to the Brahmins in culture, the rest of the population, excepting the impure castes and some other specific groups, is Kulwadi or Shudra—a generic term for manual workers. The higher castes are grouped together as either Ashrafin in Bihar, Bhadralok in Bengal, or Pandhar-peshe in Maharashtra. Futher, if we are to take some kind of Indian sentiment as our guide in our analysis, then, ac ording to the orthodox theory on this matter, there are only two, or at the most three castes in the present age, and we shall have to divide the whole population of any major linguistic province into two castes, Brahmin and Shudra, or at the most three, where the existence of the Kshatriya is grudgingly granted. Evidently no scientific student of caste, not even Gait himself, has proposed to follow Indian opinion on this matter. There is ample reason why, to get a sociological correct idea of the institution we should recognize sub-castes as real castes.

....

To sum up, in each linguistic area there were about two hundred groups called castes with distinct names, birth in one of which, usually, determined the status in society of a given individual, which were divided into about two thousand smaller units—generally known as sub-castes fixing the limits of marriage and effective social life and making for specific cultural tradition. These major groups were held together by the possession, with few exceptions of a common priesthood. There was a sort of an overall counting which grouped all of them into five or six classes, overtly expressed or tacitly understood. Over a large part of the country they were welded together for civil life in the economy and civics of village communities. Common service to the civic life, prescriptive rights of monopolist service, and specific occasions for enjoying superiority for some of the castes, considered very low, made the village community more or less a harmonious civic unit. Complete acceptance of the system in its broad outlines by the groups making up that system and their social and economic interdependence in the village not only prevented the exclusivist organization of the groups from splitting up the system into independent units, but created a harmony in civic life. Of course, this harmony was not the harmony of parts that are equally valued, but of units which are rigorously subordinated to one another.

Multiple Reference
in Indian Caste Systems

McKIM MARRIOTT

Modern Urban Stratification

The modern Indian urban or metropolitan type of stratification . . . presents several special features. First, it is an open, unbounded system in which any person or group coming from outside may take a position. Damle (1968) tells us that new arrivals in the city, or newly formed urban groups, or even merely aspirant groups in rural areas may all include themselves conceptually within a metropolitan system of stratification. Urban stratification thus seems universalistic as well as infinitely expansible. 'Reference behaviour'—for example, the imitative identification of an individual or group with another to whose status it aspires—may occur in the Indian metropolitan type of stratification with pehaps no more frustration than would be met in the social class system of the urban West.

Second, high or low positions in the metropolitan type of system are measured largely according to the qualities (behaviour and attributes) exhibited currently by a given individual or group, set against the general urban scale of higher and lower qualities. Many Indian cities, like Bombay, seem to have been dominated culturally by a generically high-caste, middle-class style of life. The Pamckalsis mentioned by Damle provide an example of measurement by such a standard in the city of Bombay: by removing meat from their diet, altering their marriage rules, and raising their educational level, members of the

Excerpted from McKim Marriott, 'Multiple Reference in Indian Caste Systems', in J. Silverberg, ed., *Social Mobility and the Caste System in India: An Interdisciplinary Symposium*, Mouton, Hague, 1968.

Pamckalsi group persuaded the urban audience to accept them as having rank equivalent to that of the urban Brahmans. Currently demonstrable traits must be emphasized by most new participants in the urban type of stratification, for in a metropolitan society of many newcomers, the particular hereditary identities which have been established locally or regionally in earlier times are rarely meaningful. Castes whose very names imply clear positions of rank in their original localities cannot be placed precisely among the heterogeneous hundreds of castes assembled in the cities from far distant regions: each must be judged by its members' approximation to the more general urban class styles.

Third, in the urban type of stratification, the units to be ranked are increasingly regarded not as representatives of ritually corporate castes,[1] but rather as individuals or groups of individuals. The deference accorded to the individual B.R. Ambedkar for his educational and occupational achievements is not intended for the Mahar caste as a ritual corporation, even though the deference paid to Ambedkar personally may in urban eyes contribute to a raising of the average standing of Mahars taken as a collection of individuals which includes Ambedkar. A test of this individualism of the city actually occurred: Ambedkar's marriage with a lady of Brahman caste was not generally taken to prove that the corporate Mahar caste is superior to the corporate Brahman caste in question, as it would have been if we had been dealing here with a rural ranking of castes as such. Instead, the individualistic interpretation of this marriage proves the irrelevance of caste as corporation on the metropolitan scene. What Damle tells us of stratification in the new metropolis permits us in fact to do without that separate level of corporate analysis which is indispensable in dealing with all rural Hindu systems of stratification which are known to us.

Can this open, qualitative, and noncorporate metropolitan type of stratification characterize only the greatest Indian cities of recent decades, or can it characterize also the Indian cities of earlier centuries?

---

[1] The term 'corporate' refers to the element of identity in ritual rank which is shared by all members of a caste and which is implicit in each caste member's ritual transactions with members of other castes. The term as used here does not refer to the caste as a concrete group or set of persons. Stein argues that 'corporate mobility' is a modern phenomenon unknown to medieval South India, he refers to the effective political organization of an extensive concrete group or set of persons to achieve their common caste goals by adopting some explicit behavioural policy. The lack of evidence for such consciously organized group efforts in medieval South India does not, of course, deny the powerful if implicit assumption that the ritual rank of the whole corporate caste is affected and possibly altered by the ritual deference given and received by its members to and from members of other castes.

Knowledge of earlier Indian urban social systems is slight, yet fragmentary information and logic suggest that at least commercial cities may have exhibited similar tendencies for millennia. Anonymity, individual mobility, and the reduction of communal controls would at any time have tended to favour the metropolitan type of stratification.

Rural Stratification

All these typical features of urban stratification contrasts with the features of stratification in rural village communities. Rural systems of stratification are, in the first place, closed rather than open. They are composed of known and limited sets of castes, groups, and individuals which can admit and place newcomers only when the identities of the newcomers can be fully established and linked with units in the pre-existing local order. Here arise most acutely the difficulties of applying reference group theory, as Damle tells us, since subjective identification with and imitation of a group other than one's own, if it transgresses hereditarily established local identities, can never lead to actual absorption. Reference behaviour in villages would then generally be 'dysfunctional' for the behaving unit, in Merton's sense (Merton 1957).

A second contrasting feature of rural stratification as depicted in these papers and others is that the ranks of units tend to be assigned not by comparative ratings of the qualities, behaviour, or symbolic attributes of the units, but rather by the outcomes of mutual confrontations. Rural stratification has been called typically 'international' rather than 'attributional' (Marriott 1959: 92-107). Thus the Holeru Untouchables studied by Edward Harper could not raise their local caste standing merely by abandoning the dietary attribute of beef. Similarly, achieving a higher local rank through the merely symbolic aspects of their 'Cauhan' movement seems dubious to Noniyas themselves, according to William L. Rowe. Assertions have sometimes been made that a shift towards more 'Sanskritic' attributes has gained a higher local rank for rural groups, such as some of the Kodagus of rural Coorg, but such assertions are as yet unattested by local evidence. What does undeniably affect people's estimates of rank in rural systems of stratification is the giving and receiving of pollution, especially through food and services. Kodagus in Coorg villages occupy high positions as feeders and ritual masters of other castes and as sponsors of temple rituals in which other castes provide the lower services (Srinivas 1952 : 38-45, 185-99). The Noniya Cauhan myth also exemplifies this rural way of thought: the fall of the ancestral Rajputs is attributed to their acceptance of food from an Untouchable. In the same way, reformers of the Holeru correctly point out that the Holeru caste is locally low because some of its members directly subordinate the caste by accepting dead cattle and other pollutions from the houses of their indenture-holders. The adoption of a sacred thread, or a lofty name, or even a vegetarian diet by some members of the caste may not alter the kind of pollution received by other Holerus from members of higher castes. Such gestures thus may remain ineffective for altering the rank ascribed to the caste locally.

The third and perhaps most fundamental contrast between metropolitan and rural stratification is the obvious contrast between a type in which corporate ranking are of little or no importance on the one hand and a type in which corporate rankings are of the essence. By rural logic, what the single member of one caste does with the single member of another caste by way of giving or receiving pollution is sufficient to upgrade or degrade the whole or either of the two castes in relation to the other. The great concern for unanimous action on the part of rural leaders of such castes as the Holerus and Noniyas is a consequence of this rural structural assumption as to the corporate nature of caste rank. Without the feature of corporateness in rank, a 'caste' would be little different from any other collection of individuals sharing some element of identity such as a group having a distinctive ethnic or national background. A noncorporate group may often be regarded correctly as having the sum or average rank of its parts, that is, of its component individuals' ranks. Thus those leaders who attempt to raise the rank of an urban, noncorporate 'caste' group will typically concern themselves not with uniform action to avoid subordination in intercaste relations, but with helping the group's heroes, and with raising the average level of income and the qualitative style of life of the group's members. Their concern would be incorrect for the village but is correct for the metropolis. If urbanite-led movements for raising the ranks of certain caste groups have often been ineffective in rural areas, the reason for their failure may lie in their stress upon qualitative or attributional changes by individuals where only changes in corporate ritual interaction would be locally relevant.

Individual Prestige

To emphasize the importance of corporate caste considerations in rural stratification is not to deny the importance of a distinct phenomenon of individual prestige in rural as well as urban communities. Caste rank is an important component, but only one component of an individual's prestige in the rural type of stratification (Marriott 1052 : 869-74). Like individuals and groups in cities, individual members of ranked castes in villages may further gain or lose in rank according to their individual attributes and behaviour, but especially according to their wealth and power. Recognized rural indices of prestige include the elegance of ceremonial performances and the numbers of other persons who can be mustered to participate in them. Striving for individual prestige, and on the opposite side, declining in prestige through loss of wealth and power—these do not distinguish the urban from the rural type of stratification discussed above. Individual effort to rise above the standing of one's caste appears to be a common and persisting feature of Indian society, as important among the individualistic 'renouncers' of medieval Tirupati studied by Stein as among the ambitious twentieth-century villagers studied now by Rowe and Harper.

Individuals stand to gain in one component of their prestige if their castes can rise as corporations. But for far too long, observers of Hindu society have assumed that individual striving is always and wholly absorbed in group efforts toward caste mobility. Actually the ambitions of an individual villager or a rural family may conflict with the ambitions of the caste, as in the poignant Holeru example: if these low-caste rural labourers refuse to perform their traditional, caste-defiling services for Brahman landowners, they must give up their individually profitable and prestige-helping indentures. It was the initial income from his indenture which permitted an individual Holeru to gain prestige among his caste-fellows, perhaps among villagers generally, and now certainly a better average standing for members of his caste in the city-dominated larger society. If he keeps his indentured status, the individual Holeru may gain immediate economic power and long-term security, but be forced into caste-polluting services in relation to his Brahman master, thus retaining a lower caste rank locally.

On the other hand, the ambitions of individual Noniyas who had adequate means of livelihood independent of providing local services seem to have given added impetus to the corporate movement of the whole caste outward and upward. Where there are external sources of income, individuals need not suffer losses of prestige as the caste strives to climb out from under. A local source of increased income from land may do as well as external sources to promote agreement between individual and caste interests.

Zones of Reference

The two contrasting types of stratification systems—the closed, interactionally ranked corporate caste systems of rural communities on the one hand, and the open, attributional, noncorporate rankings of individuals and groups in cities on the other hand—are by no means sufficient to account for the many intermediate, overlapping, and apparently conflicting reference phenomena reported in the present and in previous studies. One insufficiency of these initial types is obvious where I argue above that reference behaviour cannot relevantly occur within a typical rural, local caste system. Apparently against my argument, the papers of Rowe and Harper, as well as many other cases, indicate that rural caste groups do in fact often identify themselves as belonging properly to higher and more attractive categories than those to which they are ordinarily assigned according to their local relations of pollution-giving and pollution-receiving.

The Noniyas provide one clear case in point and represent the policies of many other rural groups: by identifying themselves as belonging to a category called 'Cauhan' they claim not an existing local rank which is higher than that of their caste at present, but rather membership in a social category which is nonexistent as a caste group in hierarchies of the localities where Noniyas live. 'Cauhan' is the name of a clan (*kula*) of the mythical 'Fire race' (Agni Vamsa) of the Rajput cluster of castes, and the designation 'Rajput' is one taken regionally by the dominant Thakur caste groups to symbolize their pretended descent from members of the classical Kshatriya *varna*. The Noniyas' Claim to be Cauhans is thus a claim for high rank in a regional and in a grand civilizational scheme of categories. Their claim refers only indirectly and by roundabout implications to the local ladder of caste groups. The claim of rural Kodagus to be classical 'Ugras' is a similar case is point (Srinivas 1952 : 33-4).

If we are to think clearly now about the mobility of castes, we cannot neglect the consipicuous lesson of these cases: a local caste group may perceive itself as living and striving in at least three successively larger zones, each of which has its different ordering of categories.

These three zones are: (1) the zone of the village community and its directly connected part of the countryside, (2) the zone of the recognized cultural or linguistic region and (3) the zone of the whole civilization.

(1) In the village zone, the relevant categories are caste ranks. Caste ranks are established most directly by the local degrees of relative ritual

dominance exercised among the particular local groups which represent their castes as corporate bodies. The relative rank of a caste may vary somewhat from village to village, and instances of such variation may be known to residents of each village; nevertheless, the rank of a caste is conceived as being properly uniform, so that known variants tend to be argued out in each locality as cases are applied in a court to the interpretation of a general law.

(2) The zone of regional scope is likely to encompass whole endogamous castes. Regional conceptions of ranking usually include notions as to the relative standings of clusters of separate, but similarly named or occupied whole castes, often grouped further within larger categories of rank, such as the lord and servant categories of northern India, the water-bearing and nonwater-bearing categories of Bengal, the light people and dark people of Gujarat, etc.

(3) In the civilizational zone there are the familiar categories of universal scopesomewhat ambiguously ranked classical styles of life which necessarily have no exact reference to castes. These are the four varnas, Brahman, Kshatriya, Vaishya, and Sudra.

I call the ranking of these styles of life 'ambiguous' because they do not stand one above another representing different degrees of any unitary quality. The ideals of the Brahman and Kshatriya *varnas*, for example, are in several ways mutually divergent and incompatible. The commonly understood Brahman ideal stresses intellectual refinement, ascetic standards of consumption and nonviolence, while the Kshatriya ideal stresses, on the other hand, strength, readiness for violence, luxurious consumption, including meat-eating, etc. A caste cannot smoothly work its way upwards, becoming more Brahman-like by first becoming the perfect Kshatriya. It cannot evolve into a Kshatriya by first becoming a good Vaishya, for Vaishya and Kshatriya values are again opposed, the Vaishya ideal emphasizing conservation of wealth, purity in religion, a vegetarian diet, etc. Finally, the Vaishya and Kshatriya ideals together oppose the servile values of the Sudra. That small section of the Kodagus which chose to identify itself as 'Brahman' necessarily cut itself off from the majority of the same caste who chose as 'Udgras' to refer their behaviour to the Kshatriya scale. Patidars of central Gujarat have shifted as a whole from a Kshatriya claim to a Vaishya claim, and have had to alter their diet, 'downward', as it were, accordingly (Shah and Shroff 1959 : 62-3). The *varnas* thus appear to function as competing, dialectically related models, rather than as a single scale of precedence. When rural castes choose the same *varna* ideal, they may sometimes be ranged in degrees of rank according to their realization of that one ideal, but generally the civilizational *varna* scheme offers a variety of aristocratic postures which are parallel or roughly equal in value. Only in those rather anomalous situations where Brahmans became soldiers, landlords, or kings, or where warriors became philosophers or ascetics have inevitable compromises even suggested a unitary system of values.

To these three, approximately territorial zones—locality, region, and civilization—with their distinct categories of rank must be added still other, sometimes only partially enclosing hierarchies of categories, such as those based on religious affiliation (e.g., 'born' versus 'converted' Sikhs), or on sectarian values in diet and in other ritual conduct. Finally there is the newer national and cosmopolitan hierarchy of values implied by Damle's discussion and most evident in cities—education, individual achievement, independence, secular dominance. Based in the metropolitan areas, it is gaining increasing sway over the rural areas.

A given piece of behaviour by members of a local caste group in a village or town may allude to any of these several superimposed or cross-cutting zonal hierarchies of values, and may have different meanings in each of them. In the dramas of social mobility enacted upon the village stage, if the actors often seem to be talking past one another, it is no doubt, often because they are playing roles in different scripts. They aim their performances towards different, sometimes distant audiences of diverse tastes.

Before we can judge the effectiveness, or the 'functionality' and 'dysfunctionality' of a given piece of behaviour, we must specify for which of these several zonal or other audiences the action is intentionally performed. The Noniya Cauhan movement, like similar movements by Bhars, Chamars, Lohars, and *Ahirs*, in the same area (Cohn 1955 : 72-6), may be irrelevant to Senpur villager's conceptions of their own ritual ranking of castes, since the movement may effect no alteration in the local patterns regarding intercaste transfer of food and services. Or such movements, if strongly organized, may go so far as to take one or more castes out of the existing interactional hierarchy, and may ultimately threaten the continuance of the local system. On the other hand, the same movements may have both relevance and system-maintaining effects considered in relation to the sectarian, civilizational, or national moral systems to which they make symbolic reference. These movements may then be regarded as 'anticipatory' to the

socialization of certain caste members, if not in ways of behaviour
appropriate to traditional village society, then perhaps in ways useful
to those persons as groups or as individuals in the social life of the
cities to which so many rural people are now en route. What the ambitious castes lose at home through their new contempt for local custom they may ultimately gain in the books of the state and nation,
politically and economically as well as in the positive evaluation of
their style of life.

Considering the pains and inherent contradictions of referring one's
behaviour to nonlocal scales and models, we may reasonably ask why
such behaviour occurs, and why it occurs now at an apparently accel-
erating pace? Rowe and Harper both illuminate an essential dynamic:
the discrepancy between the low local ritual rank of a caste and its
higher economic or political standing either outside or inside the community. Wealthy Noniya highway contractors were the first to become
'Cauhans' while the Holerus wooed by the Congress Party were leaders
of the agitation for caste reform. The external stimuli in these cases are
like those noted by Bailey for the state monopoly-holding Boad Distillers or the politically patronized Pan Untouchables ('Boad Outcastes')
of Bisipara in Orissa (Bailey 1957 : 186-98, 211-27). In each case, dis-
crepancies between local and external rank in the initial situation
were evidently felt as more painful than the difficulties that would ensure from attempting mobility. If opportunities for greater achievement or influence by low-caste people outside the village increase,
then external reference behaviour must also tend to increase.

Inherently, of course, broader references to more famous models
have a grander sound. Inherently, too, the broader the scope of the reference, the less capable it may prove of precise application at local
levels. One may speculate that a part of the seeing flexibility and
changeability of caste participation in the rituals of the Tirupati temple
examined by Stein may be due to the disjunction between such vague
scriptural *varna* categories as 'twice-born' and 'Sudra' on the one hand
and the diversity of South Indian regional caste groups on the other.
Broader, more external reference also helps a rural caste group to escape denial of its claims locally. For this reason, if for no other, references to the civilization-wide *varna* categories would seem favoured
over claims of more local, regional, or sectarian scope. Certain small
kingdoms of Kerala, like the Kandyan kingdom in Ceylon, seem to
have had means for establishing ranks and adjudicating claims by
whole castes throughout a small region. But regular procedures for
legitimizing claims are typically lacking from the higher levels of

Hinduism. When the seventeenth-century Maratha ruler Sivaji wished to have himself (and thus his caste) recognized as 'Kshatriya', he sought this favour from a certain learned Maharashtrian priest, resident in Banaras. This priest had no formally superior jurisdiction, so that contention could be allayed ultimately only to the extent that Marathas as conquerors could command general deference. Claims referring to regional categories, such as the claims of Kunbis to be 'Marathas', or Marathas to be 'Rajputs', seem typically to occur and to succeed only when the aspirant group can support its claims by preponderant power in the relevant zone of reference.

The Noniyas of Senapur, when they first organized themselves for an advance in caste rank, in no way held preponderant power. Their external reference to the regional scale of Rajput clans through the verbal claim of 'Cauhan' descent might well have been passed over without local political testing, and without conflict between Noniyas and the local Dobhi Thakurs. But the Noniyas' visible gesture of donning the sacred thread which had been the local Thakurs' prerogative subjected them to immediate reprisals by the Thakurs, who evidently felt aped and insulted. (Only later, it seems, as the Thakurs themselves began to doubt the crucial value of their own civilizational 'twice-born' claim, and as Noniyas recruited greater political support for their movement, was thread-wearing by Noniyas and other low-caste groups finally tolerated by the Thakurs.) The externality of reference on the part of poor and politically weak rural low-caste groups thus may be dictated not only by a desire to move symbolically out of the confining village into larger, freer worlds, but also by a desire, while so doing, to avoid the immediate local application of negative sanctions.

Historically we can note that changes in the favoured scope of inter-caste reference behaviour have in these examples as elsewhere tended to accompany changes in the modes of communication. Claims of less extreme scope, often modified by sectarian membership, seem to have been common during the centuries preceding British domination, although the absolute number of such claims may have been fewer. As printing and increased education helped to disseminate knowledge of a simplified and redefined classical Indian culture more widely, references to the civilizational *varna* categories became more frequent. The recent developments of mass education, radio, and other media, and of a national search for international respect, have been accompanied by more frequent rural orientation towards occupational achievement and class values of metropolitan type. Since the new, national hierarchy built upon such values counts individuals and groups rather than corporate castes as its units, behaviour directed towards the imagined audience of the nation represents a diminution of interest in the localized mobility of castes as such.

The shift of symbolic reference towards wider zones, and the movement of all Indian stratification systems towards the metropolitan type are by no means complete, of course. Indeed, both movements are subject to reversals and counter-references, as even cosmopolitan urbanites look back to memories of clearer caste hierarchies in the villages of their origins.

Conclusion

The main import of these remarks is to stress the need for a number of new analytic notions in order to understand what any given effort at caste mobility is about. I think that we must at the outset be aware of the contrast between closed, interactional, rural systems of stratification on the one hand and open, attributional, urban systems on the other hand. Since orientations to the city or village are states of mind, rural or urban residents may refer their behaviour to either or both kinds of contrasting systems.

We need further distinguish the ranking and movement of castes as corporations concerned with ritual dominance and pollution from the ranking and movement of individuals or groups concerned with wealth, power, or prestige, for a given act may relate to either or both kinds of units in mutually affirming or mutually denying ways.

Finally, to understand the ranking and mobility of castes, we must determine the felt locus of each caste and specify to which of the several possibly relevant hierarchies and audiences—local, regional, sectarian, civilizational, or national—its behaviour is referred by itself and others. Only with these multiple worlds in our minds can we hope to comprehend that castes move not only among social positions, but also among realms of thought.

The Ideology of Purity

PAULINE KOLENDA

Biological Substantialism: The Dividual-Particle Theory of Pollution

... The issue of the natives' understandings, or cognitive view of their own societies was not ascendant in anthropology at the time Dumont, Stevenson, Srinivas and Harper were writing in the 1950s and 1960s. Most scholars did not address that issue. In the 1970s, however, the issue of 'emic' versus 'etic' conceptualizations was in the forefront of social-cultural anthropology.

The contrast between 'emic' and 'etic' has been borrowed from linguistics (Pike 1967 : 27-39). In linguistics the term 'phonemes' refers to the minimal sounds in a language recognized by the native speakers themselves. In contrast, 'phonetics' refers to the minimal sounds in the language recognized by trained linguistic anthropologists as they record the sounds in a general linguistic system of notation. These terms are now applied to other aspects of a culture besides language. An 'emic' analysis gives the insider's, the native's interpretation or 'model' of some cultural phenomena; an 'etic' analysis gives the outsider's, the anthropologist's interpretation or 'model'.

McKim Marriott, an anthropologist, and Ronald B. Inden, a historian well-versed in Bengali and Sanskrit, have tried to characterize the 'emic' view—the natives' 'model' of the Hindu caste system (1973, 1977). Their 'ethnosociology of the caste system' takes major account of what others, such as Stevenson, have considered as the 'Hindu pollution concept' but treats this concept as part of what Hindus believe about physics, biology, and sociology. Specifically, their view

Excerpted from Pauline Kolenda, 'The Ideology of Purity and Pollution', in *Caste in Contemporary India: Beyond Organic Solidarity*, Waveland Press, Prospect Heights, Illinois, 1985.

takes up the human bodily contribution to social processes. It can answer such questions as: What is it that actually defiles water for a higher-caste person when it comes from the hands of an Untouchable? What is it about the semen of a higher-caste man that does not pollute a lower-caste female sexual partner?

. . . .

Marriott and Inden draw their understanding not only from the ethnography of everyday avoidances and exchanges, but from Hindu writings, including the Vedas, which concern sacrificial worship, from Brahmans, Upanishads, classical books of moral and medical sciences, and from late medieval moral code books of certain castes in Bengal. They do not consider these texts to be ethnographic; that is, accurate descriptions of Hindus' actual behaviour in olden times. But they do not treat them merely as records of the 'ideal culture' either. These writings are sometimes seen by outsiders as 'prescriptive'—as giving principles for behaviour—but Marriott and Inden see in them more than that. They see them as records of the cognitive concepts, the ways of thinking of reflective, educated Hindus. Hindu native models today may be derived from such writings. By using such sources, Marriott and Inden claim to have found some ways in which Hindus themselves understand caste processes.

What they find is this: Unlike Westerners who think in terms of a duality of separable body and spirit, or body and mind, Hindus think monistically. Hindus believe that a person inherits a *unitary coded-substance*. The code 'programmed' into the person's substance or body relates to his or her *varna, jati,* sex, and personality.

With respect to *varnadharma*, the code for members of each of the four *varnas* (priests, warrior-rulers, herdsmen-agriculturalists, servants), Marriott and Inden explain the sacrificial superman found in the Rig Veda. He is a 'Code Man' from which the 'genera' (*varnas*) of human beings were derived. Each genus (*varna*) is believed to have received its particular code from a different part of the body of the 'Code Man'.

Similarly, one's *jatidharma*, the duty of one's *jati*, is encoded into one's bodily substance, as are the duties for one's sex and personality. Such a code does not determine exact behaviour, however, but represents 'internal formulae for uplifting conduct', prescriptions for what one knows one should do as *naturally* appropriate for one's own kind of person.

There are features of the coded-substances that explain the process of pollution. First of all, this coded-substance is made of coded-particles (in Sanskrit, *pindas* and other terms). These particles—bits of hair, sweat, saliva, etc.—may be shared or exchanged with others, and it is such particles that mix into food, water, and other things transferred in interpersonal transactions. Thus, one gives off coded-particles and gains coded-particles from others. One should try to gain suitable or better coded-particles (those coming from gods or higher castes), not worse coded-particles (those coming from lower castes or defiled persons) than one's own. One may get better particles through 'right eating, right marriage, and other right exchange and actions' (Marriott and Inden 1977: 233). One may rid oneself of inferior particles through disposal as in excretion, or other processes 'often aided by persons of suitably lower genera'. As understood by Hocart and Gould, lower caste persons absorb pollution, here specified as inferior coded-particles, from higher caste persons.

A second important feature of a coded-substance is that its parts or particles can be loosened to separate and combine with other kinds of coded-substances. Marriott and Inden explain:

Heat is catalytic in many of these internal processes and external exchanges: it creates an instability that facilitates either separation or combination among particles of different kinds of substance. Processes like digestion and sexual intercourse require heat to separate, to distill, and to mix different substances. You are always likely to become what you eat, and you may also be atomically involved in what you feed to others, but especially so if and when the food is hot. Hence cooking and the serving and eating of warm foods like boiled rice and ordinary fresh, unleavened bread are liminal processes in which bodily and nutritive substances must be very carefully managed (Marriott and Inden 1977 : 233).

This theory of coded-substances which are inherited, and which break up into coded-particles, especially through the catalyst of heat, to recombine with other kinds of particles, offers a theory of pollution contagion. Presumably some of the coded-particles of the lower caste person's coded-substance is actually transferred to the higher caste person, through food, water, touch, or contact with the lower caste person's bodily products. Such a theory may strike a Western reader as strange. It is a theory, however, which is to be found in revered writings of Hindus themselves, and thus represents the native point of view, according to Marriott and Inden.

Marriott and Inden say that the instability of the coded-substance of the person, its ready break-up into particles, shows that the Hindu view of the person is of one that is 'dividual', one which divides up into separable portions. Such a 'dividual' image contrasts with the Western image of the person as an 'individual', these authors say. They also assert that the monistic Hindu view which does not separate substance from code—i.e., body from morality—marks it as very different from Westerners' typically dualistic mode of thinking. Because of the instability of a person's coded-substance, the Hindu person must strive to maintain his appropriate coded-substance and possibly better it, not just avoid pollution. Marriott and Inden claim '. . .the players have at stake also the preservation and transformation of their own natures' (Marriott 1976 : 112).

The Essence and Reality
of the Caste System

C. BOUGLÉ

Definition of the Caste System

. . . If we consider the current usage of the word, caste seems first of all
to arouse the idea of hereditary specialization. The son of a blacksmith
will be a blacksmith just as the son of a warrior will be a warrior. In the
assigning of tasks no account is taken of expressed desires nor of
manifest aptitudes but only of filiation. Race and occupation are bound
together. No other than the son can continue the work of the father and
the son cannot choose any other occupation than that of his father.
Professions become the obligatory monopolies of families, to perform
them is not merely a right but a duty imposed by birth upon the childern.
Such a spirit must reign in a society before we can say that that society
is subject to the rule of caste.

But is this sufficient? It seems to us that in addition we must be able
to recognize the existence of different levels in that society, the existence, in other words, of a hierarchy. The word caste makes us think not
only of hereditarily appointed work but also of unequally divided rights.
Caste does not mean monopoly only but privilege as well. By the fact
of his birth one individual is bound to pay heavy taxes while another
escapes them. In the eyes of justice this man is 'worth' a hundred
pieces of gold and that one only fifty. The golden ring, the red robe
and yellow girdle which are the dress of one are strictly forbidden to

Excerpted from C. Bouglé, The Essence and Reality of the Caste System', in *Contributions to Indian Sociology*, No. 2, 1958.

another. Personal 'status' for life is determined by the rank of the group to which one belongs. We are bound to say then that inequality is also the product of the caste system.

But another element also appears to us to call for definition. When we say that the spirit of caste reigns in a society, we mean that the different groups of which that society is composed, repel each other rather than attract, that each retires within itself, isolates itself, makes every effort to prevent its members from contracting alliances or even from entering into relations with neighbouring groups. A man refuses to seek a wife outside his traditional circle, he will moreover refuse any food not prepared by his fellows and regard the mere contact of 'strangers' as impure and degrading. Such is the man who obeys the 'spirit of caste'. Horror of misalliance, fear of impure contacts and repulsion for all those who are unrelated, such are the characteristic signs of this spirit. It seems to us that it is, as it were, designed to atomize the societies into which it penetrates; it divides them not merely into superimposed levels but into a multitude of opposed fragments; it brings each of their elementary groups face to face, separated by a mutual repulsion.

The spirit of caste unites these three tendencies, repulsion, hierarchy and hereditary specialization, and all three must be borne in mind if one wishes to give a complete definition of the caste system. We shall say that a society is subject to this system if it is divided into a large number of mutually opposed groups which are hereditarily specialized and hierarchically arranged if, on principle, it tolerates neither the *parvenu*, nor miscegenation, nor a change of profession. . . . Only by keeping these three constituent elements of caste before our eyes can we see in which civilizations it has flourished and with what social forms it is associated. If in our search for a caste system in historical reality we are guided by this integral definition we can see at a glance that easy as it is to perceive the scattered elements of the system it is less easy to find it complete and perfect in its entirety. If there are few civilizations into which one or other of its characteristic tendencies has not penetrated, there are also few in which all three united are to be seen flourishing freely.

. . . .

The Caste System in India

Does this system encounter obstacles in India? Or on the contrary can we see the three essential tendencies freely at play there?

First of all we can nowhere find specialization pushed to such a degree as in India. Certainly the number of differentiated occupations is less than in our own contemporary society; but in order for a society to have ten thousand professions and to have seen them increase by more than four thousand in thirteen years that society must have a 'scientific' industry which alone is capable of multiplying and varying both the means and the needs of production. So far as India was left to itself it did not see such progress.

But while her methods of production remained relatively simple she still divided the various tasks as far as was possible among different groups. We have only to think of the number of sub-groups of which each major occupational group is composed in order to appreciate this. Thus we may distinguish six merchant castes, three of scribes, forty of peasants, twenty-four of journeymen, nine of shepherds and hunters, fourteen of fishermen and sailors, twelve of various kinds of artisans, carpenters, blacksmiths, goldsmiths and potters, thirteen of weavers, thirteen of distillers, eleven of house servants. No doubt these internal subdivisions do not all correspond to professional distinctions. But in many cases what distinguishes a caste from its fellows is that it abstains from certain procedures, does not use the same materials, does not manufacture the same products.

In Buddhist legends different castes are distinguished according to the instruments that they use or according to the fish that they catch. In the matter of clothing those who make turbans will have nothing to do with those who make sashes. Amongst leather workers one caste makes shoes, another repairs them and yet another fashions leather flasks. One may not see, we are told, the same man driving the plough as tends the beast. Among the Ghosi clans one looks after the cows and only sells milk; others buy milk and sell butter. The Kumhars of Orissa are divided into Uria Kumhars who work standing at large urns and Kattya Kumhars who sit down at a wheel to make little pots. The coolie who carries a load on his head will refuse to carry it on his shoulders; he who uses a pole will not use a knapsack. Each of the house-servant castes has its own work and each energetically refuses to do the work of others. From the top to the bottom of Hindu society the accumulation of function is forbidden in principle.

A change of function is no less forbidden. Work is divided once for all and each has his allotted task from his childhood. Heredity of occupation is the rule and has been since antiquity. . . . In the Jatakas which give us a glimpse of Hindu society in the sixth century the expression 'son of a caravan leader' signifies caravan leader; 'son of a blacksmith' signifies blacksmith, the families of potters and stone-masons are designated there, allusion is made to the streets and villages where certain hereditary specializations are localized. Each class in India has its particular occupation. Even the names of castes, of which the greater part are the names of professions also, sufficiently prove the antiquity of specialization in Hindu society.

No doubt there are many exceptions to the rule. It is not a question here of recent changes of profession which have inclined many of all castes to agriculture or to the administrative service: these result from the disturbance of Hindu tradition by English invasion. But at all times the Brahmans have kept all kinds of occupation open for themselves. So far from being confined to the study of sacred texts, we find some who are ploughmen, soldiers, tradesmen and cooks. To fill one's belly one must play many parts, said one of them to the Abbe Dubois (Dubois 1981 : 292).

Their superiority opens greater possibilities to them than the common run of mortality. This superiority implies purity and it is true that the concern to preserve purity excludes many kinds of activity. Does not the doctrine of *ahmisa*, which forbids the wounding of even the smallest living creature, forbid the priest to cut open the soil with a plough blade. But faced with material necessities such prohibitions must be softened. Indeed the theory itself plays a part in this: the Brahmanic codes recognized the right of the Brahman to practise different occupations in times of distress. If Manu formally forbids him to traffic in liquor, perfumes, meat and wool, he permits him to engage in military service, agriculture, the care of herds, and a certain number of commercial enterprises.

In their turn members of other castes, which these same codes tie to their traditional occupation, in fact, and following the Brahman's example, take certain liberties with the rule. We have just observed that the names of castes are commonly those of ancient occupations. But let us also add that it is relatively rare today to find a caste practising the occupation which its name designates. The Atishbaz are indeed, as their name indicates, artificers and the N'Albauds farriers. But it is not the case that all Chamars are tanners today; the Ahir shepherds, the Banjara porters, and Luniya salt-workers. The Baidya, according to their tradition, are a caste of doctors. But hardly a third of them practise medicine : many are teachers in schools, farmers, and stewards. . . .

In estimating the position of hereditary specialization in Hindu society we are bound to remember that this society is hierarchically organized. Nowhere may we observe distinctions more clearly cut, nowhere such extravagance of both respect and disdain.

Travellers have frequently painted the sad picture of Paria life. Thus the Abbe Dubois (1981) has written :

Hardly anywhere are they allowed to cultivate the soil for their own benefit, but are obliged to hire themselves out to the other castes. . . . Their masters may beat them at pleasure; the poor wretches having no right either to complain or to obtain redress . . . . What chiefly disgusts other natives is the revolting nature of (their) food, they contend for carrion with dogs.

On the Malabar coast they are not even allowed to build huts. If a Nayar meets them he may kill. On other hand, see the account of the guru's entry :

They ride on a richly caparisoned elephant or in a superb palanquin. Many have an escort of cavalry, and are surrounded by guards. . . . Bands of musicians playing all sorts of instruments precede them . . . along the route incense and other perfumes are burnt . . . new clothes are perpetually spread for him to pass over; triumphal arches . . . are erected.

A pinch of the cow-dung ash with which he marks his brow is an inestimable gift; his curse is petrifying, his blessing will save (ibid. 49, 55, 61, 128, 125-6).

Not all Brahmans lead this royal life but the greater part live at the expense of other castes. In principle the Brahman should live upon the alms of others, . . . for he is made to receive and not to give.

When one passes through a hamlet, one might believe that the Brahman caste is the most numerous for they remain indolently at home while others work. Another traveller tells us of the ferryman of Benares who is sufficiently honoured if a Brahman deigns to employ his boat. Another says, speaking of the Brahmans, that they walk with an air of self-satisfaction and conscious superiority which is inimitable. It is not surprising, as the Abbe Dubois tells us, that they are superbly egotistic (ibid.: 99), for are they not brought up to believe that all is owing to them and that they owe nothing? Their absolute superiority is as uncontested as the absolute inferiority of the Parias.

Between these two extremes the great multiple of castes are arranged in their different degrees, each one preoccupied to hold its rank and to preserve its prerogatives from usurpation.[1] In order to gauge rank, different considerations enter into account: purity of food, fidelity

---

[1] According to Dubois, questions of precedence sometimes gave rise to bloody battles

to the traditional occupation, and abstention from forbidden foods. Practically speaking the eminence or baseness of a caste is determined above all by the relations which it has with the Brahman caste. Will the Brahmans accept a gift of any sort whatever from a man of this caste? Will they without hesitation take a cup of water from his hand? Will they make difficulties? Will they refuse with horror? Here is the true criterion of the dignity of a caste : the measure of its relative nobility is the Brahman's esteem.

If we consult the sacred codes we find these broad social divisions expressed with the precision of mathematical relations. We discover that the number of ceremonies practised, the total amount of fines imposed, even the rate of interest paid, varies with the rank of castes and that in all circumstances the Brahman receives the maximum profit and suffers the minimum loss.

No doubt, as we shall see we cannot trust the codes in matters of detail. The actual distinctions are far from being as strict as the ideal ones. At many points the hierarchy is uncertain. The position of a caste varies in different regions[2] and questions of precedence give rise to frequent disputes. But these uncertainties leave the principle unquestioned ; the very disputes and the fights to which they lead, prove to what a point the members of Hindu society are imbued with the idea that they ought to be hierarchically organized.

All observers have been struck by the fact that these specialized elements of Hindu society are not only superimposed but also mutually opposed and that the force which animates the whole system of the Hindu world is a force of repulsion which keeps the various bodies separate and drives each one to retire within itself.

The disgust which Europeans inspire in Hindus has frequently been noted. A traveller recounts that a Brahman with whom he was

---

(Dubois 1981: 26). Since the recent census [1951] attention has been drawn to the fear of some castes, that they were not classed according to their rank. The Khattris convened a meeting of protest at Bareilly and sent a memorandum to the census authorities, in order to insist upon their right to be classed as Kshatriyas (*Census of India, 1901*, General Report by Risley and Gait, I, p. 539).

[2] When low castes improve their position they look for a genealogy which will exalt them: for their old name they invent a new etymology, or even try to change their name. But their rivals tolerate this rise with difficulty, whence the interminable disputes. Many examples could be given : the Khattris claim to be Kshatriyas and observe the rites laid down for martial castes, but others class them as Banias. The enriched Sunris have for long striven to be recognized as a pure caste. But only the degraded prophets of Hinduism flatter their ambition. Risley tells us that even those who work for the Sunris do not like to touch their food. A Chandala would lose caste if he touched the seat upon which a Sunri was seated (See Risley 1891, II p. 279).

acquainted used to visit him very early in the morning: the Brahman preferred to see him before taking his bath so that he might then cleanse himself of the impurities which he had incurred. A Hindu with self-respect would die of thirst rather than drink from the cup which had been used by a '*Mleccha*'. But what is noteworthy is that the Hindus appear to feel something of the same repugnance in regard to each other ; a proof that they are to a certain extent foreigners to each other. In Calcutta great difficulty was experienced over the establishment of a water system : how could people of different castes use the same tap ? The contact of the Paria inspires such horror that they are obliged, as their name implies, to carry warning bells which announce their presence. On the Malabar coast there are people who are forced to go almost naked for fear that others may be touched by the billowing of their clothes. The fear of an impure atmosphere is from all time, one of the dominating traits of the Hindu soul. The Jatakas are full of stories which bear witness to the disgust which has, in all ages, been inspired by contact with, or even sight of, the impure races. A Brahman discovers that he has been travelling with a Chandala : 'Damn you, Candala, raven of ill-omen; move out of the wind'. Two friends, the daughters of a Gahapati and a Purohit, are playing by the city gate. Two Chandala brothers come on the scene and the girls flee to wash their eyes.

Undoubtedly not all races provoke an equal disgust. Nevertheless in the eyes of an orthodox Hindu any caste, other than his own, is in a sense impure. This sentiment of latent repulsion manifests itself clearly in certain circumstances.

For example, someone may not fear the contact of the man of another caste but nevertheless refuse to eat with him. It is above all from food that contamination is feared. It can only be eaten amongst caste-fellows: it should not even be touched by a stranger,[3] whose glance is sometimes sufficient to pollute it. If a Paria so much as looks into a kitchen all the utensils should be broken. . . . Scruples of this kind are naturally more lively in the high castes. But from the top to the bottom of the social scale, one encounters the same concern. In time of famine the Santal allowed themselves to die of hunger rather than touch food prepared by Brahmans. He who eats food forbidden by his caste becomes an 'out-cast' an 'out-law'. . . .

---

[3] We have to distinguish amongst foods. The manner in which they are prepared makes them, if one may say so, more or less 'dangerous'. Brahmans will take food from certain castes which has been cooked with clarified butter (*pakki*) and not food cooked in other ways (*kachchi*).

There is however one sphere in which the protectionism of caste raises yet higher barriers : more than a matter of food, caste is a 'matter of marriage'. Marriage outside the caste is strictly forbidden : the caste is rigorously endogamous. We must add that this endogamy is coupled with an internal exogamy. While there is a wide circle within which a Hindu must find a wife there is a narrow circle within the first in which he may not marry. Many castes, in imitation of the Brahmans, divide themselves into *gotras*, the members of the same *gotra* may not inter-marry. Sometimes the prohibition applies to the eponymous group composed of the descendants of the same ancestor, sometimes to a territorial group composed of the inhabitants of the same locality. These rules of exogamy are complex and vary according to the caste. What we have to bear in mind for the present is the rigour of the general rule which isolates castes and tends to keep them eternally closed to one another.

No doubt there are many exceptions to this rule also. The notions brought into being by the existence of hierarchy sometimes triumph over the feelings of mutual repulsion which otherwise separate castes. Many families seek husbands for their daughters in higher castes; 'hypergamy' then overcomes endogamy. Certain Radhya of high rank are so sought after as grooms that they make marriage their profession: they keep registers in which they write the names of the women they have honoured by their union. Even in high castes derogation of the rule of endogamy is not rare. According to Carnegy, the Rajputs of Oudh used to take their wives from the aborigines without any degrada-tion of their descendants. In the same way it is habitual, according to Crooke, for Jats to seek out girls of low caste, pass them off as girls of their own blood, and marry them.

Even lacking such observations the analysis of (physical) anthro-pology could prove that, despite the most strict prohibitions there have been innumerable mixtures of all kinds. Nevertheless the fact remains that the only

pure marriage is that contracted between people of the same caste, that the public conscience, by the sanctions which it applies, manifests its concern to maintain this ideal and that, even more than a change of occupation, a mar-riage outside the caste carries with it a degradation of status; to such an extent is this separatist tendency inherent in Hindu society.

We could, moreover, measure the strength of this tendency by its re-sults. The multiplicity of the groups into which Hindu society is divided is the best proof of the existence of a reciprocal repulsion between its elements.

If we were to confine ourselves to her sacred books, India would not appear to be so divided. According to Manu, there are four castes and 'there are not five'. This tradition has, upto the present day, dominated both historians and travellers. But it is precisely the value of this tradition that the recent work of indologists invites us to suspect. Criticizing the Brahmanic theory of caste, Senart has pointed out its waverings and incertitudes : on more than one point it masks and falsifies the reality more than it records it. In the particular matter of the number of castes, the sacred codes, immediately after having affirmed that there are only four, implicitly recognize a considerable number. The 'theory of mixed castes' offers us, in fact, a certain number of degraded castes resulting from illicit unions between pure castes. But the theory is transparently a theory constructed after the event, to explain what could not be denied. It is an avowal of the multiplicity of castes whose names, professional or geographical, betray for the most part a very ancient origin. Furthermore if, to test the veracity of the Brahmanic codes we consult the Buddhist literature, we certainly find the theory of four castes mentioned, but rather as a system for discussion than as a picture of facts. Throughout the legends of the sixth century, Hindu society appears already divided into a multiplicity of sections, Sanskrit literature also shows the same multiplicity. . . .

Contemporary observations tend to show that the theory of four castes, the *caturvarnya* has never been more than an ideal, blending a simplified and as it were shortened picture of the reality with a reiteration of frequently violated prescriptions. It would be useless to look at the castes of the present as the descendants of the four traditional castes; the Brahmans who had the monopoly of prayer and sacrifice, the Kshatriyas, warriors born, the Vaishyas destined to commerce, the Shudras created for the service of others.

The Brahmans as we see them today correspond best to the type described in the codes but again we must mark the differences. Not only do Brahmans exercise many more professions than the Brahmanic law ordains but in addition, and most important of all, so far from constituting one caste only, as might be believed from the sacred books they are divided into a host of castes separating one from the other. As far as the other castes are concerned the gap is even more striking. There are the Rajputs who claim descent from the Kshatriyas, but first of all, apart from the fact that many of their pretensions are obviously untrue, they also form a mass of families rather than one caste. The occupations assigned by tradition for the Vaishya do not appear in fact to be reserved to one caste only, but are divided amongst very diverse castes. Finally it is a waste of labour to look for the caste which would correspond to the Shudras. This is why the census no longer uses these traditional names in order to distinguish the different categories of the population. One has only to look at present reality to realize that castes must be counted in their thousands. The Brahmanic theory tries in vain to conceal this essential multiplicity. The caste system has divided Hindu society into a considerable number of small opposed societies.

To sum up on these points : hereditary specialization, hierarchical organization, reciprocal repulsion : as far as any social form can realize itself in its purity, the caste system is realized in India. At the very least it penetrates Hindu society to a level unknown elsewhere. It plays some part in other civilizations but in India it has invaded the whole. It is in this sense that we may speak of the caste system as a phenomenon peculiar to India.

Dumont on the Nature of Caste in India

T.N. MADAN

Louis Dumont's credentials as an Indianist are of an exceptionally high order. He is a scholar of international renown who is equally at home in the domains of sociology, social anthropology, and Indology. The subjects on which he has written have an impressive range and include Hinduism, caste, kinship, kingship in ancient India, and social-political movements in modern India. His recent *magnum opus, Homo Hierarchicus,*[1] is an unusual work in its conception, design and execution. It is deserving of our most serious study.

The task that Dumont set himself is succinctly announced in the subtitle of the book: an inquiry into 'the caste system and its implications'.[2] The first question that will, therefore, occur to the reader is: How does Dumont define castes? Definitions, which should constitute

Adapted from T.N. Madan, 'On the Nature of Caste in India, A Review Symposia on Louis Dumont's *Homo Hierarchicus'* , *Contributions to Indian Sociology*, No. 5, 1971.

[1] *Homo Hierarchicus : Essai surele systemdes castes* (445 pages) was originally written in French and published by Gallimard of Paris in 1966. An English translation by Mark Sainsbury, under the title of *Homo Hierarchicus : The Caste System and its Implications* (xxii + 386 pages), was published in 1970 in the USA and in England by the University of Chicago Press and Weidenfeld and Nicolson respectively. It was published in India in 1971 by Vikas Publications of Delhi.

The first draft of the translation was revised by Dumont. We are therefore assured of its faithfulness to the original text. The English version differs from the original work only in as much as three of the four essays forming the Appendices of the latter have been omitted and a new Preface added. All these essays were originally published in *Contributions to Indian Sociology* (1957-66). The three omitted pieces have been published again in a collection of the author's essay called *Religion, Politics and History in India* (1970a).

[2] Dumont writes in the Preface to the English edition that its subtitle is what he had chosen for the original work, but it had been abandoned on the French publisher's insistence who found it 'too technical' (xi).

part of the conclusions of a scientific inquiry, by necessity have to be its starting point as well. This fact is often at the root of considerable confusion as all kinds of *a priori* assumptions creep into a chosen definition which influences the course of inquiry and almost predetermines its conclusions. One of the refrains of Dumont's book is that the Western scholars' definition of caste as a type of social stratification is sociocentric. They must therefore liberate themselves from their preconceived ideas (such as egalitarianism, individualism, the pre-eminence of politics and economics in society) by which they are trapped. Caste, which undoubtedly stands for 'inequality', in theory as well as in practice, should not be interpreted as a notion which is the opposite of 'equality', and therefore an anomaly or, worse, a perversion. The inequality of the caste system is a special type of inequality, and the sociologist's principal task is to lay bare its nature. Let us see how Dumont does this.

Dumont writes in the Preface to the French edition :

In a work of this nature, everything depends in the last analysis on the theoretical orientation. On this point it is not enough to say that I owe everything, or almost everything, to the French tradition of sociology. For not only has it nurtured me, my ambition is to extend it (xv-xvi).[3]

Suffice it to point out here that it is the intellectualist or idealist orientation in this tradition which is the dominant element in Dumont's conceptions of the office of sociology. Sociologists should concern themselves with forms or essences. They must penetrate the facade of observable behaviour to get at the 'ideas and values' which the people being studied assume, recognize and express themselves.

The ideas which they [the people] express are related to each other by more fundamental ideas *even though these are unexpressed*. Fundamental ideas literally 'go without saying', and have no need to be distinct, that is tradition. Only their corollaries are explicit. The caste system for example appears as a perfectly coherent theory once one adds the necessary but implicit links to the principles that the people themselves give (1970b : 7).

Dumont has consistently put forward this point of view for quite some time now; we find its most extended application in the present

---

[3] Page numbers in parenthesis, without reference to their source, throughout this review symposium refer to the English edition of *Homo Hierarchicus* (Dumont 1970b).

work. Needless to emphasize here, the search for latent, underlying structures, is a first principle of the methodology of structuralism.

The French (and German?) sociological tradition leads Dumont to stress the role of ideology in moulding human behaviour and, therefore, to seek to bring together sociology and Indology. Following Bouglé, one of the masters, he chooses the Hindu notion of the fundamental opposition between the pure and the impure as his starting point for an understanding of the caste system. Bouglé, at the beginning of the century, had defined the caste system as consisting of hierarchically arranged hereditary groups, separated from each other in certain respects (caste endogamy, restrictions on eating together and on physical contact), but interdependent in others (traditional division of labour). Dumont stresses the importance of recognizing these three features, or 'principles', as mutually entailed, resting on 'one fundamental conception', for the atomization into simple elements is the student's need and not a characteristic of the system itself. What we need in order to transcend the distinctions we make is 'a single true principle'. Such a principle, Dumont maintains, is the opposition of the pure and the impure.

This opposition underlies hierarchy, which is the superiority of the pure to the impure, underlies separation because the pure and the impure must be kept separate, and underlies the division of labour because pure and impure occupations must likewise be kept separate. *The whole is founded on the necessary and hierarchical coexistence of the two opposites.*[4]

Hierarchy, defined as the superiority of the pure over the impure, then, is the 'keystone' in Dumont's model of the caste system. It is of the greatest importance to realize at once that, as employed by him, the notion 'is quite independent of natural inequalities or the distribution of power'. It is

the principle by which the elements of a whole are ranked in relation to the whole, it being understood that in the majority of societies it is religion which provides the view of the whole and that the ranking will thus be religious in nature (66).

---

[4] Among Indian students of the caste system writing in English, Ketkar (1909) probably was the first to emphasize the notion of purity-pollution. He called it 'the chief principle on which the entire system depends ... the pivot on which the entire system turns' (121-2). He also distinguished caste gradation from socio-economic ranking. And his authority was Manu.

In other words, hierarchy is the relationship between 'that which encompasses and that which is encompassed' (xii). Such a perspective helps us to obtain a holistic view of the system and to overcome the dualism of opposition.

Dumont's starting point—his definition of caste—is clearly stated. The questions which arise next are : What does he do with it? Where does he proceed from it and how?

Dumont's concern in the present work is with 'the traditional social organization of India from the point of view of theoretical comparison' (xv). He sees his task as the construction of a model of the traditional caste system, of an ideal type. He is concerned only secondarily with ascertaining the 'fit' between it and contemporary social reality. His construction of the model does not proceed in the manner of the chronology-oriented historian, either. In fact, Dumont declares at the very outset that he has 'not set out to provide a *history* of the caste system' (xix) though he employs historical data in his analysis. His method is that of a theorist : he begins with a key idea and then proceeds deductively and dialectically, working out its implications step by step. He calls his work an 'experiment' (xiii) : if the reader remembers this, he will better appreciate what Dumont does in the book and the manner in which he does it. Dumont's regret seems to be that 'the work as a whole remains semi-deductive, which is hardly surprising in the present state of the social sciences' (xix).

An important problem that arises in the context of Dumont's method is his use of ethnographical materials. He does this in two distinct ways; one might say he employs it at two different levels. Having declared his foremost concern to be with ideology, i.e. with 'a system of ideas and values' (36), he hastens to caution that 'ideology is not everything' (37). Ideology will not *explain* everything, though it encompasses the whole of social reality; nor does observation of actual behaviour *reveal* everything. There remains a 'residue' (not necessarily of inferior ontological status) which is deduced from a 'confrontation of ideology with observation' (77). In the main text of the book ethnographical materials are employed in such a confrontation—but more about this in the next section.

At another level, Dumont uses ethnographical data to elucidate, elaborate or qualify various aspects of the main argument. They are presented in the form of notes which cover over 83 pages (set in thinner type than the main text). The bibliographical references cited in the notes come to about 400 items. They are in the nature of a supplementary work, as it were. It was this feature of the book which I had in mind when I described it above as being unusual in design.

I have so far made an attempt briefly to describe the scope of Dumont's work and the methodology employed by him. I will now give a chapter-wise synopsis of the contents of the book to show how he constructs his argument.

The introductory chapter, we are told, was written with the French reader in mind, to pinpoint for him why the understanding of caste should be of interest to him, given his devotion to the values of egalitarianism and individualism: 'the castes teach us a fundamental social principle, hierarchy' (2). And we can fully understand equality only after we have contrasted it with the opposite notion, which should be hierarchy and not inequality. Hierarchy is an indispensable element of social life anywhere, but it is in India, where it is explicitly affirmed that it is best studied.

Chapters 1, 2 and 3 deal with the concepts employed in the work and outline the ideology of caste. Dumont begins with a critique of the Western scholars' sociocentric conceptions of caste during the nineteenth and twentieth centuries, and also complains of the pernicious separation between the so-called textual and contextual studies. The notions of 'system' and 'structure' are then introduced :

the caste system is above all a system of ideas and values, a formal comprehensible, rational system, a system in the intellectual sense of the term. . . . Our first task is to grasp this intellectual system, this ideology (35).

Castes, we are further told, are mutually related through 'a system of oppositions, a structure' (39), i.e. in terms of the opposition between the pure and the impure. A discussion of purity-pollution follows.

Chapter 3 deals with hierarchy and the theory of *varna*. It is a most crucial discussion and focuses on the differentiation (disjunction) of status and power and the subordination of the king to the priest in Hindu society. Hierarchy is said to involve gradation, but is asserted to be distinct from both power and authority. It is 'religious ranking and classifies things and beings' according to their 'degree of dignity' (65).[5] It is an all-embracing, comprehensive concept. Hierarchy and the scheme of *varnas* are found to be in consonance with each other, as are *varna*

---

[5] It may be of some interest to recall that Durkheim associated hierarchy with sacredness and dignity. He wrote of . . . the hierarchy of things [wherein the sacred objects] are naturally considered superior in dignity and power to profane things (1964: 37).

and *jati*. In fact, hierarchy encompasses both the *varna* divisions and the caste system. What remains problematic, however, is the connexion of hierarchy with power, for

hierarchy cannot give a place to power as such, without contradicting its own principle. Therefore, it must give a place to power without saying so, and it is obliged to close its eyes to this point on pain of destroying itself (77).

At this point, Dumont undertakes a somewhat detailed examination of ethnographical evidence (Risley, Mayer and Marriott) to examine the interaction between purity and power in 'actual situations'. He concludes that though both 'interaction' and 'attributions' (as distinguished by Marriott) are present in such situations, the ideological orientation prevails.

Having introduced the ideology, Dumont proceeds to consider aspects of behaviour within and between castes in terms of it. Chapter 4 shows that the traditional division of labour (the *jajmani* system) is based on religious values rather than on economic logic. It does not, however, account for all economic transactions, and Dumont admits this. Chapter 5 considers the regulation of marriage (endogamy, iso gamy, hypergamy) in terms of the key concept of hierarchy. Chapter 6 carries the argument further to cover rules concerning contact, untouchability, food and vegetarianism. The opposition between the pure and the impure emerges clearly and convincingly in these three chapters.

Chapter 7 deals with power and territory and Chapter 8 with justice and authority. It is here that the confrontation of ideology with observed social reality is most prominent : 'in conformity with our method, we shall now begin to set out what is actually encountered in caste society while not figuring directly in the ideology' (152). We are now brought face to face with territory, power, village dominance, and ownership of wealth, and their mutual relationship. These are said to be questions of fact and not at all of theory. In fact, in terms of the theory, they enter 'surreptitiously' on the scene; power pretends to be the equal of status (153). Dominant castes, factions and economics also are discussed in this very framework. The final conclusion expectedly is:

just as religion in a way encompasses politics, so politics encompasses economics within itself. The difference is that the politico-economic domain is separated, named, in a subordinate position as against religion, whilst economics remains undifferentiated within politics (165).

The results of the 'experiment' are not yet complete, however. Chapter 8 passes on (from power) to authority. Ethnographical data on caste goverment from Uttar Pradesh are examined. Such matters as the source of authority, the village *panchayat*, the caste assembly, caste jurisdiction, and excommunication are discussed. Here also Dumont makes a major concession in favour of ethnographical evidence as against ideology. To understand the exercise of authority, the principle of hierarchy is held to be applicable but incomplete; it is 'completed by dominance' (183).

The problems discussed in Chapters 7 and 8 are described as difficult and controversial and are said to

hinge round a simple dilemma. Either power must be accommodated within the theory of caste, as here, or else the theory of caste must be brought under the notion of power and 'politico-economic' relations. . . . It is a matter of approach. . . . The fact remains that the empirical approach [which highlights politics and economics] is a misconstruction of Indian civilization: it amounts to assimilating *dharma* to *artha*. . . . (308).

The *Brahmin-Kshatriya* relationship too, is one of the most crucial structural elements in Dumont's model of the caste system. He defines caste in terms of it :

We shall say that there is caste only where this characteristic (the disjunction between *brahman* and *ksatra*, i.e., between status and power) is present, and we shall request that any society lacking this characteristic, even if it is made up of closed status groups, be classified under another label (214). . . .

The notion of disjunction between status and power—the subordination of the latter to the former—does indeed create difficulties. I do not see, however, how one can call such a distinction false (or true) at the level at which Dumont employs it. Moreover, he is aware of the difficulties and devises his methodology of confronting ideology with observation . . . to deal with it. The approach is ingenious but the results are not wholly satisfactory. Dumont criticizes Bailey's model in which there is 'a high degree of coincidence between politico-economic rank and the ritual ranking of caste' (Bailey 1957: 266). He points out that when Bailey finds this congruence disappear at the two extremes of the hierarchy, he explains it always as 'a peculiar rigidity in the system of caste' in the middle rungs of which 'ritual rank tends to follow . . . economic rank' (Bailey 1957 : 266-7). Dumont emphasizes the expression 'peculiar rigidity' and calls it delightful' (76)!

If Bailey fails to make full allowance for status, does Dumont fare much better with power? He writes : '. . . power, devalued to the advantage of status at the overall level, *surreptitiously makes itself the equal of status in the interstitial levels*'(153, emphasis supplied). This is very well put, but I find an uncomfortable similarity between Bailey's and Dumont's predicaments. The 'peculiar rigidity' of the two extremes of the hierarchy in Bailey's model is matched by the 'surreptitious' entry of power into the middle rungs of Dumont's model.

The main argument of Dumont's essay ends with Chapter 8. Chapter 9 deals with renunciation and sects—the opposites of the notions of 'collective man' and caste. An examination of these is a methodological necessity (device) for Dumont, for he seeks understanding of India (and of Western society) through a dialectical process, through the juxtaposition of logically opposite cultural types. He writes :

It may be doubted whether the caste system could have existed and endured independently of its contradictory, renunciation. The point is important for comparison with the West : we are not dealing with a solid opposition, as if in one case there was nothing but the individual, in the other nothing but collective man. For India has both distributed in a particular way(186).

This is a most important conclusion: the fundamental structural elements of these two (all?) societies are the same: highly significant differences between them arise out of the different patterns of relationship between the elements, however.

Chapter 10 takes up the problem of comparison : are there castes among non-Hindus and outside India (201)? Given Dumont's emphasis upon ideology and upon hierarchy, it is not surprising to read:

One is therefore led to see the caste system as an Indian institution having its full coherence and vitality in the Hindu environment, but continuing in existence, in more or less attenuated forms, in groups adhering to other religions (210).

Enlarging the scope of comparison, Dumont suggests that caste should be deemed to be present only where the disjunction between status and power is present and where castes exhaust the entire society (214-15).

In Chapter 11 (the last) comparison is continued, but in temporal, rather than spatial, terms. In other words, Dumont takes up the problem of change: 'What is the caste system becoming nowadays' (217)? The

tone of the whole discussion is set by his statement made at the very
outset that contemporary literature 'exaggerates' change. 'One thing is
certain : the society as an overall framework has not changed, *there
has been change in* the society and not *of* the society' (218). And again:

Given our way of thinking, we must face the fact that the anticipated links between technico-economic change and social change did not operate, and that
caste society managed to digest what was thought [by Marx, among others]
must make it burst asunder (218).

In Dumont's view, the only significant change that does seem to
have taken place is that the traditional interdependence of castes has
been replaced by 'a universe of impenetrable blocks, self-sufficient,
essentially identical and in competition with one another' (222).
Dumont calls this 'the substantialization of caste'. An inventory of
sources of change in the caste system lists juridical and political
changes, social-religious reform, Westernization, growth of modern
professions, urbanization, spatial mobility, and the growth of market
economy. But, despite all these factors making for change, the most
ubiquitous and general form that change has taken in contemporary
times is one of a 'mixture', or 'combination', of traditional and modern features (228-31).

Dumont concludes by asserting that hierarchy is 'a universal necessity' and that, if it is not formally recognized in a society, it may assert
itself in a pathological form (e.g., racism). It is, therefore, of the greatest importance for Western man to endeavour to study and understand a
social system in which hierarchy is recognized, and, in fact, accorded
the status of a first principle. That is why the book is offered to the
French public.

The Appendix contains Dumont's well-known essay, 'Caste, Racism, "Stratification" ' first published in 1960. It contains all the principal ideas elaborated in *Homo Hierarchicus* and should help the
reader to recapitulate the argument.

Homo Hierarchicus is a most impressive achievement and shall long
remain a basic work for the students of Indian societies. Dumont's view
of caste stands a long way off from that of Henry Summer Maine, one
of the founding fathers of comparative sociology, who writing about a
hundred years ago condemned it as 'the most disastrous and blighting
of all human institutions' (1917 : II). Not that Dumont is interested in
defending caste; he does regard it worthy of serious study, however, if
only to better understand that Western society itself which Maine and

his contemporaries regarded as the acme of human history.

To what extent Dumont is successful in the latter enterprise—i.e. in his effort to understand *Homo equalis* in terms of the opposite type of *Homo hierarchicus*—remains to be seen. It is even more difficult for an Indian to judge whether the Western reader—the Frenchman— to whom Dumont says the present work is addressed, is going to have a better appreciation of his own culture and society as a result of reading it. It may well be argued that the intellectualist vision is but a mirage for the empiricist—that those who unremittingly pursue political and economic *interests* are unlikely to find a sociology of *values* the most useful of analytical frameworks. Such speculation is not very relevant right now, however. *Homo Hierarchicus* is a work complete in itself and must be judged as such.

What distinguishes this work from the usual social anthropological discussions of caste is that it does not proceed from fieldwork to a model of how the system works. Instead it begins with a cardinal explanatory principle—hierarchy—and boldly sets out to build a model thereon, throughout maintaining the position that theory or ideology overrides and encompasses ethnography. A conscious and single-minded preoccupation with the ideology of complementarity and separation leads Dumont to ask fundamental questions about Hindu society and about the structuralist method. . . .

The chief virtue of Dumont's exercise lies exactly in that he holds up for public view, as it were, the potentialities and limitations of his view of caste and of his methodology. If his critics are able to highlight the limitations, they are enabled to do so better because of his intensive inquiry. To that extent even they are in his debt. As for himself, Dumont believes that his choice of hierarchy as the cardinal explanatory principle was 'a good one and enabled us to test the consistency of the system' (212).

The Brahmanical View of Caste

GERALD D. BERREMAN

Homo Hierarchicus is a scholarly book by a learned man. It contains much truth and insight about caste and society in India. More than that, it puts what its author has to say into the context of social theory, especially as it has developed in France. This is laudable, for most discussions of caste in India ignore their theoretical underpinnings and implications, leaving the reader to speculate about them himself if he is so inclined. But the truth we find here about caste is a very special version, derived from very particular, though carefully documented, sources. As such it is a truth I find to be so incomplete, selective and biased as to amount to a serious distortion of the nature of caste as it is experienced by those who live it, and it is well nigh irrelevant to an understanding of how the system works in India. . . .

The book is introduced with a brief statement anticipating its major contribution: 'The castes teach us a fundamental social principle, hierarchy'(2). Hierarchy is said to distinguish Indian society from 'modern' societies whose fundamental social principle is equality. The major theme of this review can be anticipated thus : any hierarchy, like any equalitarian system, is opposed by those who see its effect upon themselves as disadvantageous, no matter how loudly or piously it is advocated by those who benefit from it. Those low in an hierarchical system universally see it as disadvantageous to themselves and object either to the system or to the manner in which it is applied to themselves. Any social hierarchy, then, is perpetrated and perpetuated by elites and is struggled against as circumstances permit, by those they oppress. This is true in India and anywhere else. There are four specific facets of

From Gerald D. Berreman, 'The Brahamanical View of Caste', *Contributions to Indian Sociology* (n.s), No. 5, 16-25.

Dumont's argument with which I will take specific issue. Each reinforces the others, progressively refracting the data and interpretations into the peculiarly distorted image which the book presents.

(1) *The assumption that there is a clear and consistent, universal and fundamental disparity between what the author terms 'traditional' or 'simpler' societies (e.g., Indian), and 'modern' ones (e.g., French, British).* Dumont finds 'traditional' societies to be characterized by conceptions of the collective nature of man, by the primacy of social rather than individual goals, and thus by 'hierarchy' (by which he means ritual hierarchy, based on the purity/pollution opposition). 'Modern' societies are characterized contrastively by individualism and hence by egalitarianism (the antithesis of hierarchy). In his words : As opposed to modern society, traditional societies, which know nothing of equality and liberty as values, which know nothing, in short, of the individual, have basically a collective idea of man, and our (residual) apperception of man as a social being is the sole link which unites us to them, and is the only angle from which we can come to understand them(8).

And Dumont describes those who write of 'stratification' in the Indian caste system as ethno- or 'socio'-centric. He claims to derive his own view of caste from purely Indian sources, thereby discovering the truth which has escaped those less capable than he of transcending their modern, Western biases. The result of his insights, however, is an explanation of caste and culture in India, based on a series of oppositions or dualities (modern/traditional, hierarchy/equality, purity/pollution, status/power, etc.), which is remarkably consistent with the dialectical and structural viewpoints of his European, and especially French, intellectual forebearers. His analysis is at least as suspect of ethonocentrism as those of the stratification sociologists he criticizes, for it, as much as they, reflects alien, Western perspectives.

The Indian world of ritual hierarchy described by Dumont is as sterile and unreal as the world of stratification depicted by sociologists he vilifies. In each case the people who comprise the system are depicted as unfeeling, regimented automatons ruled by inexorable social forces, conforming unquestioningly and unerringly to universal values. Does Dumont really believe that individuals are as submerged by Indian society, as submissive to it, as conformist to its ideologies, as this book implies? If so, how can he reconcile this notion with first-hand experience in India where, as all empirical studies have demonstrated, people are as wilful, factionalized and individually variable as people anywhere else. Like people everywhere they are doubters and believers, conformists and non-conformists; they are defiant, compliant, selfish, magnanimous, independent, innovative, tradition-bound, fearful, courageous, optimistic, pessimistic; they hope, aspire, despair, subvert, connive, abide, enforce, manipulate and choose among alternatives as they cope with their society and its values. This is the way the people I have known in village and city have responded to the caste system. To assert that members of 'traditional' societies behave otherwise is a blanket denial of individuality and initiative which reflects a kind of ethnocentrism and condescension no less distorting in its effect than the 'socio-centrism' which Dumont deplores. Indians are not so simple, so consistent or slavish to custom or to one another as he implies. Surely among the conspicuous strengths of Indian society are its tolerance for deviance, for non-conformity and for diversity, and the many outlets it provides for their expression. Dumont's assertions are as inconceivable to me as the bland and erroneous claims made by other authors that Indians are not progressive or innovative, or are not motivated to achieve. Such characterizations are simply not true to the Indian experience, however much they may satisfy their authors' theories.

(2) *The notion that power and economic and political factors are distinct from and epiphenomenal to caste, and that ritual hierarchy is the central fact of caste, independent of power.* I would assert that the power-status opposition is a false dichotomy in the context of caste. The two are inseparable. Thus, for example, Dumont notes the status claims of upwardly mobile castes, but says, 'to make a claim is one thing, and for it to be accepted is another' (73). True enough. The history of myriad cases of this kind (and we may note that they are endemic to India's caste system—the Census of India did not generate them, though it did afford a new arena in which to fight them out) demonstrates that the *claim* is made by reference to behaviours and attributes Dumont would call hierarchical, but that the claim is *granted* or *denied* on the basis of power. Special circumstances can lead to apparent anomalies (e.g. relatively weak but respected Brahmins; relatively powerful Shudras), but usually status and power go together. Dumont explains all instances of ranking as either the rational manifestation of the hierarchical principle (ritual status), or contradictory and presumably irrational impositions of power (see 82). Those which accord with his theory are examples of the former; all others are examples of the latter. On the contrary, I would hold that in fact power and status are two sides of the same coin. Gonds, for example, are incorporated into the caste system as Untouchables except where, as a group, they

have retained power in the form of land; then they are Raj Gonds and adopt more or less suitable 'hierarchical' symbols of behaviour to justify that status. A case as good as that Dumont makes could be made for the primacy of power in caste relationships in India. He asserts that 'no doubt, in the majority of cases, hierarchy will be identified in some way with power, but there is no necessity for this, as the case of India will show' (20). Actually, the case of India can be used to show that *ideology* is primary (as Dumont does), or that *power* is primary, or that *both* are crucial and inseparable in the functioning of Indian caste. The logical and empirical difficulties in maintaining Dumont's position are suggested by the following summary statement:

The principle of hierarchy, completed by dominance, results in authority over a given caste being concentrated in the hands of castes which are superior to it either directly or in so far as they are dominant (183).

Dumont was grappling with a similar problem when, after asserting that criteria of rank are reducible to the purity/pollution opposition, he conceded that nevertheless

... there are factors on the level of observation which complicate or warp the status rankings and segmentation. These factors, though extraneous to the ideology, are operative empirically. . . . (45).

I would say that since caste does not exist except empirically —in the lives of people as they interact with one another—these factors can scarcely be dismissed as epiphenomenal. Again, one could as well make the opposite case, namely, that power relationships are sometimes (rarely) complicated or warped by ideological ones (e.g. the high status of weak Brahmans in some regions), but that the fundamental hierarchy is one of power. Dumont's argument is understandably thrown into utter confusion by the instances of Lingayat, Muslim and Christian castes in India which lack, as he admits (46), the ideological component of caste while nevertheless manifesting caste organization. I believe that there are fewer exceptions to be dealt with—that explanation of caste is simpler and more in accord with the facts of social life in India—if the basis of caste is regarded as lying in differential power which is expressed in ritual status terms, than if the reverse is assumed. Still better is to avoid the compulsive desire to find a single or transcendent basis for caste ranking, and to understand it instead in its full complexity with power and ritual factors combining, perhaps with others, to define caste and caste ranking.

Corporate rank is intrinsic to the caste system. It is made up of many components, sacred and secular, which vary by region, by historical circumstances, and by the social, economic and political characteristics of those being considered (see Berreman 1965). Ranking also varies by the social position of those making the judgement relative to those judged, and by the circumstances in which the ranking is applied: claimed rank is not the same as accorded rank. Untouchables define the rank of other groups in their category differently than do Brahmins. For example, ranking which is manifest at a ritual feast may be quite different from rank manifest in the bazar. Such is the complexity of caste and rank in India and it is scarcely reducible to the purity/pollution opposition.

My objection in this regard is not to injustice done by Dumont to the analyses of his academic peers, but to the injustice he does to the people of India. Two thousand years of struggle to escape the oppression of their status by those the caste system deprives cannot be dismissed as the projection of socio-centric Western scholars any more than that oppression can be justified by Sanskritic texts known only to elites. The oppression of caste, and attempts to overcome it, are not epiphenomenal to caste; they are integral and inevitable parts of it. Dumont fails almost totally to recognize caste for what it is on an empirical level: institutionalized inequality; guaranteed differential access to the valued things in life. Let there be no mistake. The human meaning of caste for those who live it is power and vulnerability, privilege and oppression, honour and denigration, plenty and want, reward and deprivation, security and anxiety. As an anthropological document, a description of caste which fails to convey this is a travesty in the world today; as much as would be an account of colonialism which ignored its costs to the colonized in glorifying its benefits to the colonizers.

When he chides Thomas O. Beidelman for confusing 'inequality' with 'exploitation', Dumont notes that he ' . . . failed to see that the system assures subsistence to each *proportionately to his status*' (32, Dumont's italics). That is indeed precisely what it does. It also assures life, comfort, health, self-respect, food, shelter, learning, pleasure, security, education, legal redress, rewards in the next life, and all of the other necessary and valued things 'proportionately to status'. And that is what exploitation is; that is what oppression is: providing for those at the top 'proportionately to their status', and at the expense of those at the bottom. This does not distinguish inequality from exploitation; it identifies their common characteristics; and caste systems in

India and elsewhere epitomize this relationship. That the relationship is described as paternalism—that it is rationalized as being for the benefit of all—is universal and hardly surprising since such descriptions are purveyed by the beneficiaries of the system, who arrogate to themselves the role of spokesmen for it.

(3) *The notion that caste occurs only in India and is not subject to cross-cultural comparison.* The theoretically weakest part of the book is where Dumont discusses and dismisses the notion of cross-cultural comparisons of caste organization. In this there is an anachronistic, romantic, and perhaps ethnocentric element partaking of the old stereotype of 'the mysterious East', reminiscent of the author's similarly held notion (discussed above) of the qualitative differences between wholistic, 'traditional' societies and individualistic, 'modern' ones. Not that Dumont is entirely wrong. It is true that caste in India is unique as, for that matter, is marriage, family, agriculture, government, and religion in India. This is hardly a convincing argument against comparison. Everything in the world is ultimately unique. Without denying the uniqueness of every culture, every institution, every object and every event, one can extract aspects, elements, principles or relationship which are (or are thought to be) common, for purposes of comparison. In fact this is the only way to determine what is specific to one culture, society or situation, and what is common to types or categories of social organization, or is common to recurrent processes and historical circumstances. Science, including social science, depends upon identifying and comparing common phenomena in the universe of unique elements. Whether and in what ways phenomena are 'the same' must be carefully specified but to require that they be in all respects identical is to deny the possibility of a science of society. In any case, to deny the possibility of comparison of caste in India with other social systems is a logical trap, for the thing called 'caste' varies widely within Hindu India by region and rank. It varies even more widely within India by religion, and it varies even more widely in South Asia from society to society, from culture to culture and from ideology to ideology. Yet even Dumont calls *these* variations 'caste'.

Unfortunately the theme of non-comparability of Indian caste is central to the argument of the entire book. Dumont is evidently unaware of the nature of conspicuously hierarchical, rigidly stratified caste-like systems outside of South Asia, and particularly of the value systems—the ideologies—underlying them. An even casual acquaintance with the systems of ranking, separation, repression and their accompanying value systems in the United States (see Pinkney 1969), in Japan (see DeVos and Wagatsuma 1966), and in Runada (see Maquet 1961), for example, would preclude most of his arguments about the non-comparability of hierarchy in India. One could only wish that Dumont knew as much—or a fraction as much—about race in America as he does about caste in India, just as one could wish the reverse for O. C. Cox, whose misconceptions about the differences between the two, Dumont cities approvingly despite Cox's innocence of contemporary knowledge about caste in India (see Cox 1945). Incomparability can only be deduced or refuted by knowledge of *both* phenomena, and the complementary ignorance of Cox and Dumont does not add up to a convincing argument. To say, for example, as Dumont does (225), that racism in America came after slavery, would be laughable if the subject were laughable. Slavery originated and flourished and died in an environment of racism, supported by a value system as coherent and convoluted, if not as complex, as that of India's caste system. Egalitarianism has always been irrelevant in that value system wherever race (for India read caste') differences have been relevant. The basis for the supporting value system lie in notions of shared hereditary status and differential intrinsic worth. Dumont unwittingly puts his finger on the central issue when, citing Talcott Parsons, he notes that hierarchy inevitably implies equality within the hierarchically ordered group (257). This is exactly the case in the American caste sytem. The ideology is equalitarian only as applied within the caste (white or black); it is hierarchical when applied without. To confuse this with equalitarianism is as inexcusable with reference to America as it would be with reference to India. It is worth noting in passing that contrary to Dumont's assumption, caste membership in America is not based on physical traits, important as they are, but as in India on birth—on putative heredity—of which physical traits are major, but not wholly reliable nor wholly dependant upon indicators. The crucial fact is that one is born black, not that one looks black. In both America and India the determinant of caste status is birth into a group with a particular status, not individual appearance or even behaviour. The last two are relevant only insofar as they are more or less reliable indicators of the first. Their display by those not properly born to them is deemed inappropriate and if detected will be met with stern sanctions rather than with affirmation of successful mobility.

(4) *The limited biased, albeit scholarly, sources of evidence upon which the arguments are based.* The nature of the sources upon which

Dumont relies in his analysis account for the book's other shortcomings to a large extent—shortcomings which I regard as fatal to its purpose: explication of the nature of caste in India.

Dumont relies heavily on some classical Sanskrit texts while ignoring others, a technique that is inevitable with such sources, but which enables one to 'prove' almost anything one wishes. He attends surprisingly little to the extensive empirical literature on village India and on caste in India which has emerged during the post-independence era, including much which appeared prior to the writing of the first edition of the book (in French, 1966c). The result is that he conveys a view of caste which is artificial, stiff, stereotypical and idealized. It is a view which conforms rather closely to the high-caste ideal of what the caste system of Hindu India ought to be like according to those who value it positively; it conforms well to the theory of caste purveyed in learned Brahmanical tracts. But it bears little relationship to the experience of caste in the lives of the many millions who live it in India, or to the feeble reflections of those lives that have made their way into the ethonographic, biographical and novelistic literature. And this, I insist, is a travesty. A frank talk with an Untouchable who knows and trusts one would be enough to make this clear. Hundreds of such talks would confirm it. A careful and empathetic reading of the recent empirical literature—supplemented by the epic and mythic literature from which we learn much of the social history of India— would do the same. Instead, we get from Dumont a view of caste in India analogous to the view one might derive of race relations in America if he were to consult the United States' Constitution, Declaration of Independence, Pledge of Allegiance, contemporary political party platforms, speeches of incumbent politicians, authorized textbooks, and editorials of major (and especially Southern) newspapers. The picture is not wholly false, but neither is it true; it is biased. In this case it amounts to a celebration of the rationale for a system of institutionalized inequality as advertised and endorsed by its architects and beneficiaries. It is not surprising that the system comes off well. Those who experience the system as oppression are hardly heard from in this book. Yet their view is pronounced loudly and clearly to anyone who takes the trouble to listen. It finds simple expression in contemporary social and political events as it has incidents and movements throughout India's history, from Buddhism to Sikhism to Arya Samaj to new Buddhism, all of which relied for their appeal largely on a promise of freedom from the burden of caste. These expressions, their causes and implications, are not communicated in Dumont's book (in fact, their very occurrence would seem inconsistent with Dumont's analysis), despite the fact that they are central to an understanding of caste in India.

In the relatively isolated, traditional, mountain village in which I did my initial Indian field research, I recounted to low caste people an explanation of caste almost identical to that which Dumont has since conveyed in this book (for it is a common one). They laughed, and one of them said, 'You have been talking with Brahmins'. And so I had. And so, it seems, has Professor Dumont.

The Caste System Upside Down

JOAN P. MENCHER

From the earliest writings on the subject until the present, with very few exceptions, the Indian caste system has been viewed—by law-makers, writers of all vintages and points of view, and, in recent times, sociologists and anthropologists—from the top down. (B.R. Ambedkar, the writer of the Indian Constitution—an Untouchable by birth—was one of the exceptions.) In this presentation, I want to view this system from a different vantage point and to show that there are important differences, both qualitative and quantitative, depending on one's perspective. Looked at from the bottom up, the system has two striking features. First, from the point of view of people at the lowest end of the scale, caste has functioned (and continues to function as a very effective system of economic exploitation). Second, one of the functions of the system has been to prevent the formation of social classes with any commonality of interest or unity of purpose. This latter function has clearly been one of the reasons for the persistence of the caste system and for the general failure of well-to-do leaders to do anything which would really break it down. I shall return to these points after presenting some views of Indian society expressed by social scientists (both Indian and Western) and discussing briefly the historical materials dealing with the Untouchable or slave castes.

The discussion here deals primarily with Untouchable labourers, focusing mainly on the state of Tamilnadu (formerly Madras), though some material from Kerala will also be included. Those groups traditionally regarded as Untouchable, now known generally as Harijans

Excerpted from Joan P. Mencher, 'The Caste System Upside Down or the Not-So-Mysterious East', *Current Anthropology*, Vol. 15, No. 4, December 1974.

('God's people'—a euphemism coined by Gandhi), are included with a few other groups of marginal status in the legal category of Scheduled Castes, constitutionally entitled to special considerations. . . . Every seventh Indian is a Harijan or member of the Schedule Castes— more than 85 million people. . . . This group makes up a little over 2 per cent of the total world population.

My interest in this subject derives from research on problems of change and development over the past five years. Any attempt to get a full understanding of the change process requires knowledge about the political, social, and economic class structure of India, both today and in the past, as well as the ways in which economic power has functioned and continues to function. The relationship between the Untouchables and higher castes and their attitudes towards each other appear to be of crucial importance in this context.

. . . .

Both the traditional system and the changes currently going on appear quite different from the vantage point of the lowest castes. Much has been said, for example, about the 'security' afforded by the caste system to each of the caste groups, but to a very large degree this argument looks at things from the viewpoint of the man at the top, or perhaps in the middle ranges. (The artisan castes, which are often pointed to, are all middle-range castes.) Furthermore, both today and in the past in much of India, all of the specialized castes taken together (Smiths, Washermen, Barbers, Potters, etc.) never constituted more than 10-15 per cent of the total population (see, for example, Tables 1 and 2) and their traditional services alone never sustained them (Parvathamma 1969: 58-60).

It is certainly correct to say that the lowest-ranking agricultural labourers could count on being employed (at least when there was work to do), but this is not to say that their position was secure or that they were content. We cannot judge past attitudes on the basis of people living today, but I frankly question the high-caste point of view often put forth, namely, that low-caste people have always accepted their position (expressed in such words as 'God has put me here, I must have done something bad in my past life, may be next time I will be born higher'). It is quite clear that it was the superior economic and political power of the upper castes that kept the lower ones suppressed.

The existence of numerous subcastes in some of the larger Untouchable castes and the existence of a fairly large number of exceedingly small Untouchable castes with limited specialized occupations

Table 1

Caste Census Figures, Chingleput District, Madras

Caste	Number (rounded figures)	Proportion per cent
Paraiyan	228,700	23
Vanniyar[1]	178,900	19
Vellalar[2]	175,400	19
Shepherds	46,500	5
Brahmins	34,300	4
Artisans[3]	23,800	3
Washermen	15,600	2
Toddy tappers	15,000	2
Barbers	9,400	1
Muslims	21,800	3
Others	92,300	19
Total	940,700	100

Source: Census of India, 1871.

Note : For the district as a whole, the three largest caste groups account for 61 per cent of the population. In any given village, between two and five castes normally account for 80 per cent or more of the population; the service castes, plus barbers, washermen *et. al*, form a very small percentage. This situation can be better understood by reference to the family's access to the means and results of production than by reference to caste alone.

[1] There are no significant subcastes among the Vanniyars. In the past (prior to 1800), the Vanniyars were called Naickers in the area of present Chingleput, Gounders in North Arcot, and Padiyatchis in most of South Arcot. There is a tendency for Naickers to marry only Naickers, but this primarily derives from the fact that one normally marries a person already related. Some marriages do occur, however, between members of the three named groups when they live in the same village and have known one another for a long time.

[2] The Vellalars include several subcastes, though it is rare to find more than one in a given village and usually attributable to migration during the British period or more recently.

[3] Artisians here include Blacksmiths, Goldsmiths, Carpenters, Stoneworkers, etc.

scattered around in the country-side have often tended to confuse analysis of the functioning of the socio-economic system in the past and today. Many observers have examined mainly the overt phenomenological level and thus have failed to see that, in broad terms, the system functioned to keep people separated from one another in a situation in which they were not allowed to own land (or at most, were given a few cents to cultivate). Several related facts that are often passed over need to be kept in mind. First of all, it is rare to find more than one subcaste of an Untouchable caste in any village, or often in any sub-region, and was even more so in pre-British times. Only a small number of castes accounts for by far the majority of the Harijan population in any given region (see Tables 1 and 2), and these tend to be concentrated in specific districts; thus the Pasi and the Chamar, the two main caste groups in Uttar Pradesh (representing 15 per cent and 57 per cent of the total Scheduled Caste population of the state, according to the 1961 census), are concentrated in different parts of the state.

In some parts of India, the different tasks performed by Untouchables are dispersed among a number of castes, whereas in other places, they are all performed by members of one caste. Thus in the area where I worked in Tamilnadu there is only one Untouchable caste, and members perform all of the various jobs, whereas in the area of Mysore State studied by Parvathamma these jobs are performed by members of three or four Untouchable groups.

The distribution of the Untouchable caste in India is quite uneven. Some of the groups are quite small and confined to specialized occupations like scavenging in small towns and cities or working as village mid-wives like the Hari in West Bengal. Others, like the Chamars, are very large and have numerous subcastes. The majority of Chamar subcastes, according to Briggs (1920: 7-8), are found in:

fairly well-defined areas, and these may be described as local groups. . . .

Some sub-caste names . . . are specifically local; while other sub-caste names . . . point to definite geographical origins. . . . There are good reasons for believing that the caste has received large recruitments from above. . . . The subjugation of tribe has been a recurring phenomenon in India. Local history fully illustrates this fact.

Thus, the present-day Chamars, scattered as they are over a vast area in northern India, have probably been recruited from a number of tribes, local castes, etc. Though known as leather workers, only a small proportion of the caste members actually do this work, and only a

Table 2
Caste Census Figures, United Provinces of Agra and Oudh[1]

Caste	Number (in thousands)	Proportion per cent
Chamar[2]	6,100	13.0
Brahman	4,700	10.0
Ahir	3,900	8.0
Rajput	3,700	8.0
Weavers[3]	2,254	4.7
Kurmi	1,900	4.0
Pasi[2]	1,300	2.8
Shaik	1,300	2.8
Bania	1,200	2.5
Lodha	1,100	2.3
Oil-pressers	958	2.0
Barbers	911	1.9
Washermen	724	1.5
Potters	725	1.5
Blacksmiths	588	1.2
Carpenters	600	1.2
Confectioners	301	0.6
Goldsmiths	267	0.6
Tailors	253	0.5
Brass-and coppersmiths	200	0.4
Carriers[2]	94	0.2
Others (Muslims and various small groups)	14,137	30.3
Total	47,212	100.0

Source: Census of India, 1911.

Note: Here again (cf. Table 1), the four largest castes account for a large proportion of the region's population (39 per cent). While these castes have many subcastes, they tend not to live in the same village unless the village is exceptionally large.

[1] Figures for Agra, Oudh, Dehra Dun, Jhansi, Jalaun, and Komaun. These areas are now for the most part incorporated into the state of Uttar Pradesh. We do not have caste-wise figures based on any of the modern states in north India.

[2] Untouchable.

[3] Includes three castes.

small proportion of their time has traditionally been spent in it,
especially in rural areas. Indeed, in rural areas, the major function
of the large Untouchable castes both in the past and today has been to
serve as a source of agricultural labour.

The greatest concentration of these large Untouchable castes was
and is to be found in the irrigated wheat and rice regions of the Indo-
Gangetic plain and in the coastal belts of the south. It is striking that
these are also the areas which support the densest populations. For
India as a whole, the percentage of Scheduled Castes was 14.69 per cent
in 1961, whereas for Madras State it was 18 per cent and only three
states ranked higher. As might be expected, the percentage of Untouchables is much lower in the dry regions of India, where there is less
need for a large number of extra hands at harvest time, and where either
owner cultivation or cultivation by tenant families is the main pattern.
. . . .

Untouchable Labourers in Present-Day Tamilnadu

At this point, it may be helpful to look at the status of Untouchables
in greater depth by focusing on one particular part of the country. For
this purpose, I have chosen Chingleput District of Tamilnadu. The
Untouchable group to be discussed here are the Paraiyans (source of
the English word 'pariah'), who along with the Pallans and Chakkilis
form the bulk of the Untouchable population of Tamilnadu. (According to the 1961 census, their proportions of the total Scheduled
Caste population of the state were Paraiyans 59 per cent, Pallans 21 per
cent, Chakkilis 16 per cent. The Pallans are mostly found in Tanjore
District in the south and the Chakkilis in Coimbatore District.) In the
southern half of Chingleput District, the Paraiyans as of 1871 made
up close to 26 per cent of the total population. According to a survey
of 94 villages made in 1967, they accounted for 26.7 per cent of the
population. In Tamilnadu, the highest percentage of Untouchables is
to be found in the biggest rice-producing regions. This is no coincidence; the majority are labourers in paddy fields. Of every 10,000
Paraiyans in Tamilnadu, 6,551 are in the four major rice-producing
districts (*Census of India 1961*).

The exact caste composition varies considerably from one village to
another throughout this region, though most villages have an
Untouchable *cheri*. In any case, there is always a colony within a mile
of the village site. The ratio of the total population of the villages to the
Paraiyan population also varies. One might except off-hand that this

ratio would affect the position of the Paraiyan within the village, but it is certainly not the sole consideration. Other significant factors are: (1) the amount of land owned by Paraiyans; (2) the degree of unity among the Paraiyans (which is of course sometimes affected by the ways in which they are manipulated by clever, well-to-do higher-caste-politicians; (3) the political position of the leading caste-Hindu landlords; (4) the degree of unity among the economically, and often numerically, dominant caste villagers *vis-à--vis* the Paraiyans; (5) the extent to which the Paraiyans are actively supported by leftist political parties on a day-to-day basis; and (6) the extent to which landless labourers of other castes see themselves in competition with Paraiyans, as opposed to recognizing common class interests.

A general picture of the current situation can be seen by looking briefly at some of the sample villages studied intensively as part of our current NSF project (Table 3). None of the villages is on a main road, though all have bus routes passing through them as a result of the vast expansion of bus services in rural Chingleput. In Manjapalayam, the Pariayans mostly work as day labourers for Naickers. In Paccaiyur and Perumalpuram, a few Paraiyan families have large enough holdings to be independent; furthermore, the higher-caste landowners there employ some Paraiyans as sharecroppers. In Paccaiyar, about 4 per cent of the land owned by the Mudaliars is cultivated by Paraiyans as sharecroppers on a 50-50 basis. Nearly 50 per cent of the Mudaliars hire Paraiyans on an arrangement under which the Paraiyan takes complete charge of the land, the owner supplying the bullocks, seeds, and fertilizers, and gets 1/6 or less of the crop. In Chinnavur and Annur, the majority of Paraiyans are agricultural labourers, though a few are sharecroppers for absentee Mudaliars.

Traditionally, Paraiyans dealt directly with members of higher castes (except for Brahmans), but they were expected to observe various proprieties in their presence. For example, they would not go beyond the veranda of a high-caste house, would not wear sandals or shirts in the presence of high-caste people, and in general would act obsequiously. This is now changing considerably, especially among the younger Paraiyan men and women, though there is considerable variation from village to village—depending on the degree of economic dependency of Paraiyans on the higher-caste villagers. To quote one of the students who worked on our project, comparing two villages in our sample :

The Harijans in Annur are different from other places, especially from Gendur. In Gendur, since it is a small village with a low *ayakat* [irrigated area], the

Harijans depend upon the villagers for their livelihood. Here it is a different case; since the village is big, with a bigger *ayakat* the village people have to depend upon the Harijans to carry out the agricultural work. So the Harijans need not depend upon a single employer. They are politically conscious. They even run a DMK-affiliated association in the name of M.G.R., a famous film star. . . . They ride a bicycle to see movies often and do not show any meek worship to the caste Hindus.

According to one of the rich men of this village,

Times have changed. The poor do not show any respect to the rich. I cannot dismiss my *padiyal* without any reason. If I do so, he would abuse me in filthy language face to face. . . . The poor are not ignorant as they were. The political parties have taught them they are equal to the rich in society. So they have started developing a contempt for us.

Though this represents a challenge to the caste system, in another sense the sysem is becoming stronger. There is an increased awareness of one's own group as a political entity and of the importance of 'group solidarity'. While the pollution complex may be weakening, people make a distinction between doing away with untouchability as such and any more profound changes in the caste system. The Paraiyan is still at the bottom, even though an individual Harijan may have more money than an individual Naicker. The poor Naicker, like the poor white in the American South, still has the superiority of his caste to cling to.

Certain changes were the direct result of government policies (e.g. Béteille and Srinivas 1969) thus, starting the year after Indian Independence, Paraiyan children were no longer expected to sit separately in the schools, though they still do not play freely with caste-Hindu children out of school. In some villages, for school festivals as well as on some other occasion, the Paraiyans and other village members sit together nowadays, but this is not true in all villages. In none of these villages do the Paraiyans enter the main caste-Hindu temples, though they are free to enter any urban temple and theoretically (by law) have the right to enter their village temple. Several of the Paccaiyur Paraiyans reported that, during the February 1967 election campaign, they were invited into the big Shaivite temple by the Congress Party candidate to hear a campaign speech by a former member of Parliament. This was told as a kind of ironically humourous incident, ending with the remark, 'well, we won't get in there again until 1972'. (When the election was held a year early, in 1971, they were not

Table 3

Percentges of Population and Land Ownership, by Caste in Southern Chingleput Villages

Caste	Village and Total Population				
	Manjapa-layam (1,362)	Paccai-yur (1,595)	Peru-Mal puram (1,597)	Chin-navur (617)	Annur (1,217)
Brahman					
population	9.0	-	-	-	-
land	23.0	-	-	-	-
Reddiar					
population	-	-	5.0	-	20.0
land	-	-	20.0	-	29.6
Mudaliar					
population	-	25.0	-	18.0	4.0
land	-	45.0	-	28.0	8.5
Vanniyar					
population	67.0	11.0	46.0	27.0	-
land	61.0	18.0	28.0	24.0	1.0
Yadava					
population	-	-	11.0	-	-
land	-	-	7.0	-	7.6
Nattar					
population	-	-	-	-	18.0
land	-	-	-	-	1.5
Paraiyan					
population	10.0	47.0	15.0	36.0	37.0
land	0.1	6.0	10.0	1.0	1.0

Note : These are five of the eight villages in our intensive study, and the figures are ours. All the villages have been given somewhat Tamil-sounding fictitious names; any resemblance to any villages that may exist bearing these names is purely coincidental. The land percentages do not add up for several reasons: (1) small amounts of land are owned by members of other small castes; (2) some land is owned by people in nearby villages (some of whom cultivate the land themselves); (3) some land is held by absentee landlords (primarily high-caste people), mostly in nearby or more distant towns; (4) land is held by temples or registered under the *bhoodan* board (mostly dry land, hard to cultivate); (5) we have not been able to account for all of the land. In Chinnavur, some has been taken over by the river.

invited back, presumably because the candidate in question did not run in this constituency.)

As may be seen from the example quoted above for Annur, the increase of freedom for the Paraiyans in many villages is related to the impact of the modern political system. While they recognize that they may have little or no influence on the village councils (*panchayats*), they are aware of having some influence as a group (though not as individuals) when it comes to voting. Just as the higher-caste people know that they must manipulate the Paraiyan vote, the Paraiyan voter knows that he has something others want, that he has some power at least in numbers. Thus, as one young man said:

All *cheri* people are going to vote for X this time. Last time we voted for Y, but didn't do any good. Only one well has been built in the past 19 years, and occasionally they give some house-site. Once government sent books to the *cheri* people and other poor people, but the *panchayat* president didn't give. He put them in a waste basket in his house. Once, the government offered cows to poor *cheri* people, but asked the *panchayat* for details and they said no one needs. In this way, they stop any help to us. So this time, we are not going to vote the same party. If any Paraiyan or poor Naicker on the *panchayat* tries to help us, they are made to keep quiet. But, we will get rid of the president by vote.

Such attitudes may lead to action which will eventually result in changes in the system; if not, they may ultimately lead to other forms of protest, possibly more violent. At present, most of the Paraiyans, certainly all the younger people, are looking to the DMK party to help them.

In the relationship between caste and politics in these villages, there are differences in the ways in which the politically important members of the caste group in power manipulate the Harijans in order to obtain benefits for themselves.

In Manjapalayam the Paraiyans are insignificant in numbers. The main danger from the point of view the Naicker politicians, especially the *panchayat* president, is that they might unite with the poor Naickers. The president has managed to stop this in a number of ways. For one thing, there is a group of Naicker landless labourers who serve him as henchmen for various political purposes (mainly intimidating those who oppose him), in return for a supply of illicit liquor and other small payments. Taking advantage of the movement among Vanniyars aimed at asserting their position as Agnikula Kshatriyas (Rudolph and Rudolph 1967: 51) he managed to make much of their superiority to Paraiyans and their need to keep together *vis-à--vis* others. He has further managed to keep the Paraiyans down by preventing them from obtaining any information about benefits available to them from the government. This only serves to raise his prestige among the poor Naickers. Although greater closeness has begun to develop between landless Naickers and Paraiyans, this has been held in check by the president's clever manipulation of Naicker sentiment.

In Paccaiyur, the Paraiyans form a near majority. Clearly, there is a possibility in such a situation that they might come to have political power. The Mudaliars have managed to keep this from happening in several ways. First of all, they have taken advantage of the fact that there are now two Paraiyan colonies in this village. The old colony was extremely overcrowded, and around 1960, under heavy pressure from the Paraiyans and the Community Development block, the Mudaliars agreed to let the Paraiyans build another colony at some distance from the traditional one. Though the Mudaliars were not eager at first to sanction the second colony, they have discovered that in some ways it has helped them to maintain political control of the village, since it is now easier to divide the Paraiyans. For example, recently the government gave two radios to the village, one for the main village and one for the Harijan colony. Since there are two colonies, the Harijans cannot agree on where it should be placed. As a result, the radio is still in the Block Development Office and the Harijans are fighting bitterly over it with one another instead of with the Mudaliars. Secondly, the Mudaliars have managed to buy off some of the potential Paraiyan leaders. (One was given a large loan from the agricultural bank, which he has never been pressed to repay.) Most significantly, they have managed to convince the Paraiyans that one cannot do anything politically without money or influence and that they (the Mudaliars of Paccaiyur) are very influential. To some extent this is true, but it has also served to keep Harijans from finding out what might be available to them from the government just for the asking. The Paccaiyur Mudaliars have been staunch supporters of the Congress Party; the Paraiyans, however, are politically fragmented. Those who believe the claims of the Mudaliars have supported Congress, whereas most of the younger men have joined the DMK in the hope that this more populist party will help them to escape the clutches of the Mudaliars. Of the few Paraiyans who have non-agricultural jobs in the nearby town of Kanchipuram, some have now decided that they cannot ever hope to get anything from the DMK and have become active Communists.

In Perumalpuram, the Paraiyans are not powerful. However, the Reddiars have used them in a sense to keep the poor Naickers down.

Since the Naickers form a large majority in the village, and also own slightly more land than the Reddiars, they have always been a serious threat to Reddiar power. By managing to keep the Naickers divided and keeping the Paraiyans on their side, the Reddiars were able for a long time to maintain a precarious political supremacy (though this was finally upset by the elections of August 1970). In the process, they have helped the Paraiyans to some extent, but it is very limited, short-term help. A Harijan may get land on a sharecropping basis from a Reddiar, but the Reddiars do not help the Harijans educate their children or gain in political power.

Some Views of Untouchables

There seem to be some important differences in the caste system, depending on the vantage point from which it is viewed. For one thing, those at the bottom appear to have a more explicitly materialistic view of the system and of their role in it than those at the top. This is not to deny that material and vested interests are the pivotal point for all, but simply to say that those at the bottom of the hierarchy have less need to rationalize its inequities. The notions of dharma and karma (or duty and fate) are more useful and rationalizations of the system from the viewpoint of high-caste people. Untouchables may accept these notions to some extent, but it is important to distinguish between the overt acceptance of such values and the holding of other values usually unexpressed to outsiders.

When questioned about various caste practices, some Harijans at first say things like 'It is their right. We are Untouchables'. But, when pressed, they offer explanations like 'They own all the land' or 'Even the poor Naickers have the support of the rich ones, none of us has much land', or as one girl put it, 'We can't ask them to do some work for us. No ! Instead of that those people only take work out of us, so naturally they are supposed to be higher than we are'. People also say, 'Previously, if we made any complaint, they would simply refuse to allow us to work on their land; and then what to do, we will simply starve'. Some of the older men do occasionally express the overt values of the higher castes. For example, one of the respected elder men of the Manjapalayam colony often expressed certain of these traditional notions. On one occasion, when he was going around the village with his drum making an announcement about an auction, and on another when he was drumming for a funeral, he said: 'This is our duty, it is the responsibility of Harijans to do this work'. Again, when seen taking a headload of paddy from fields at the harvest time, he commented that he was taking his accustomed small bunch from each acre of land to which he let the water from the irrigation channel. He went on to say, 'It is our right; we get rights in this, because we are *vittiyans*'. On the other hand, this same man, thirty-five years ago, led a successful six-month work stoppage among the village Harijans. This was done in part to stop a quarrel among the Naickers which was causing difficulties for the Harijans. (It was only after this strike that they got their new colony site.)[1]

I would like to suggest that, just as in any other situation of extreme economic oppression, one does not find recorded complaints by Untouchables from earlier times not only because the vast majority were illiterate, but also because it was simply too dangerous to express any but the 'official' line outside of one's own community. It is clear that within the traditional village community, and even today in many instances, no one outside the community has been willing to listen.

Food is another area where there is a clear dichotomy between the Untouchables' overt and covert values. In Manjapalayam, where Untouchables constitute a small minority, when I first asked about beef-eating, they tried to avoid the subject. After a long time, and when they were convinced that I ate beef and that in my country it was quite common, and when one elderly man commented that he had a friend who had worked for Europeans and had seen them eat beef, things changed. They started talking about how much they enjoyed a good beef curry—especially if there was plenty of meat, and they didn't have to use too much water. I was cautioned not to talk about it to the caste Hindus, and my Brahman assistant was taunted with such comments as 'I suppose you think we are bad, but see—she also eats it'. In some of the other villages I have worked in, however, where the Untouchables constitute a far more significant proportion of the population, they were much freer in talking about beef-eating. Many commented that beef was their favourite meat and talked with relish about how much one got for 8 annas in the market at Walajabad, and they were free in giving recipes for cooking beef. In one of the villages, about fifteen years back, there was one Paraiyan who had earned his living solely as a butcher of beef. He is now dead, and the cost of beef is sufficiently

---

[1] It is striking that this man changed his behaviour as he aged, but not that uncommon. The younger men in his colony resent his present stand, but rationalize it in such terms as 'what can you expect? He is old and he wants to please everyone. He had his time. But we do not accept these things.'

high so that no one in the village now can earn his living as a beef butcher. No one there feels bothered about eating beef, however, even though people will say that is one of the reasons higher-caste people look down on them. It has sometimes been said that their eating of carrion beef is the main reason for which Untouchables have been stigmatized, but in our data from Tamilnadu there is general agreement (1) that Paraiyans never ate beef from animals that had died of disease (except perhaps during a severe famine), but only from those that had died of old age or by an accident, and (2) that even such beef accounted for only a small part of the beef eaten. Caste Hindus are just as critical of Muslims who eat beef, but, as I have been told, 'We don't have any rules about them. The rules must have been made before there were Muslims'.

The free attitude of the Paraiyans to eating beef is illustrated by a story told me by a young man of this community with an M.A. in social work who helped me collect some of the Tamilnadu data. Because his father is a railway employee and they live in government quarters where 99 per cent of the people belong to higher castes, his immediate family does not eat beef. His father's sister, who lives in their native place, was amused at this and at his 'not keeping to their own ways'. One day she gave him a curry which tasted slightly strange, but she told him the flavour was that of a baby goat. He ate it and enjoyed it. Three days later, she told him he had eaten beef, and all his relatives seemed to be amused at this. The point is that, while high-caste values may be overtly sanctioned in the presence of powerful high-caste people this does not mean that they were ever held by low-caste people in private.

As noted above, the position of Untouchables in a village is subject to the political manipulations of members of the dominant caste, who often try to keep political and economic control by dividing Untouchables among themselves and maintaining the traditional barriers between Untouchables and poor higher-caste Hindus. For example, a well-to-do Naicker may flatter a poor Naicker about his caste, make comments to him that would make him jealous of anything given by the government to Untouchables, or give him preference in hiring. A variety of prejudices, accepted and often spread unconsciously by government officials, bolster up this preferential treatment. A typical example of this is the following rather ambivalent statement by an agricultural officer,

See, Harijans, of course, . . . they won't work hard. See, in any walk of life if one has got that hard-working nature, he can come up. . . . It is not the case of all the people. Especially poor Harijans. Why, we have another community people, called Naickers. Whenever we have those people for some job . . . the owners need not be there, whereas in the case of these Harijans they always expect the owner to be there to watch him. . . .

I don't think anything is wanting on the part of the government, especially for Harijans. They have all facilities. . . . Of course it will take some time. . . . Still, in some villages . . . these Harijans are slaves. . . . It will take some time, but government is giving all facilities.

The Harijans, on the other hand, especially those who have some education or work experience outside the village context, are now beginning to see that they may be able to gain some political power by virtue of their numbers, and political parties are beginning to take advantage of this. In the Kanchipuram area, where they are the main agricultural labour group, in 1969, an important state legislator belonging to the DMK party (which had not done too well in that region among higher-caste people) lent his support and indirectly that of his party to a successful strike for higher wages among the Untouchables (Mencher n.d.a).

The Untouchables are also beginning to take advantage of situations where they are in a numerical majority. Thus, in a village near one in our sample, in July 1970, a Paraiyan was elected president of the *panchayat*. (This was made possible in part by a change in the method for electing the president; formerly it had been done by the members of the council, but in 1970 the entire village voted directly.) This man, who with his brothers owned about 9 acres of land, was able to finance his own campaign. In his own words:

I do not depend upon others for my livelihood, that is why I was able to become the president. . . . Reddy community's cruelty towards my community has made me rebel against them. For the past ten years I used to oppose everything done by Reddiars. If at least one Harijan from a *panchayat* is like me in economic status, I am sure that every *panchayat* will have a Harijan president. Here the colony votes out-number the village votes. Some other caste people also worked for me. Some of the Harijans who were *padiyals* [permanent, tied labourers], though favouring me, voted against me under intimidation. . . . Being a staunch DMK man, I have helped some of my caste-people to get free *pattas* [titles to land] and house-sites.

In Tanjore, the largest rice-producing district in the state, in those *taluks* where almost all of the wage labourers are Harijans, it has been particularly easy for political parties, especially the Communist

Party of India, Marxist, to organize them against the landowners. Béteille (1972) notes that elsewhere they have not only found it difficult to isolate the pure wage labourers from sharecroppers and small owners, but having isolated the 'exploited class' they have been bedeviled by the distinctions within it between Harijans and caste Hindus.

Conclusions

....

As I have suggested, the caste system has functioned to prevent the formation of social classes with commonality of interests or purpose. In other words, caste derives its viability from its partial masking of extreme socio-economic differences. One of the most serious distortions in the understanding of Indian society has been the overriding importance given to the concept of caste. As Béteille (1969:18) points out,

When the basic groups in social system are defined as being non-antagonistic very little room is left, for the analysis of either conflict or change. In fact, this conception of Indian society is only one step short of the popular nineteenth century view of it as integrated, harmonious and unchanging. . . .

Béteille also notes (pp. 29-30) that what has been lacking in studies of Indian society is a comprehensive framework for the study of *interests* (such as the one Dumont has developed to study values), but that there is a certain utopian element in Dumont's insistence on the universal significance of dharma. Looked at from the bottom up, the system can be seen as having functioned primarily as one of economic exploitation and not one wherein 'every caste has its special privileges'. (It is true that an Untouchable was often referred to as an 'old son' of the landlord, but there does not seem to be any difference between this and the paternalism of the antebellum South in the United States.) Certainly there was in the traditional system some sort of harmony, but it was based on a balance of forces which kept the men at the bottom so isolated that they could not effectively unite for the purpose of changing the system. Those with greater wealth and political power could more readily unite whenever they deemed it necessary. The upper groups were all part of larger inter-regional communication networks. The lower ones had a much narrower range of contacts. Even today, higher-caste leaders in the areas where I have worked in Tamilnadu do their best to see that the Paraiyans have as little contact with non-village people (for example, Community Development

personnel) as possible. Even where a caste-Hindu *panchayat* president
has been elected by virtue of promises made to Paraiyans he is determined that none of the Paraiyans shall have any direct dealings with
the government (except possibly for people who are 'eating out of the
President's pocket').

I do not want to give the impresssion that Untouchables are the only
groups which have been subject to economic exploitation. Indeed,
what I am trying to show is that caste has functioned, both in the past
and today, to keep the Untouchables and the poor of other castes (who
might be equally exploited) from uniting for the purpose of seeking
improvements in their life.

The abundant attention given to caste, to the exclusion of class, is
emphasized in another article by Béteille (1970:138):

... there is a whole range of Bengali terms ... and their counterparts in
other Indian languages which are directly relevant to the analysis of what
sociologists understand by class. These ... constitute categories used by the
villagers to define a significant part of their social universe, to identify themselves and others and to act in a variety of contexts on the basis of these identities.

These are not new terms. As opposed to caste terms, however, they
have traditionally been used to denote groups that have no formal social
(or, more importantly, political) structure. The very existence of such
terms suggests that, at least on some level, there is an awareness of
class identities among various groups in India. On the basis of the
evidence given above, it seems reasonable to suggest that the great
emphasis placed on caste by people of wealth, power, or influence has
been in part an attempt to prevent the recognition, or even perhaps
the conscious development, of organized class-based groups in Indian
society.

Continuous Hierarchies and Discrete Castes

DIPANKAR GUPTA

Contemporary scholarship on caste continues to be influenced by the concerns of early European scholars who, in addition to being perplexed by this peculiar institution, also pondered over the possibility of India's entry into the modern age burdened as it was by the incubus of the caste system. India today has entered the modern age, without perhaps adequate streamlining, as the caste system refused to be steam rolled into a distant past.

The early scholars like the great Indologist Max Mueller, the scholar missionary Abbe Dubois, or even the sociologist Max Weber were not very certain if India would even succeed in modernizing itself as they felt that the caste system would continue to frustrate all attempts towards social and economic progress. But modern scholars do not generally see such a contradiction. They are willing to recognize that the institution of caste has not particularly blocked the development of democracy and adult franchise (Rudolph and Rudolph 1969). Nor has the caste system held up occupational mobility and economic innovations (Singer 1972). And what is more, it has also been discovered that the caste system provides for social mobility by an almost deliberate relaxation of rules.

However, while all this was empirically demonstrated, the lessons from these demonstrations rarely took wing to articulate a conceptual view of the institution of caste which would be in concinnity with the findings, and which, in the ultimate analysis, could alone validate them. We are thus faced with a somewhat curious situation. While empirical studies have disproved the traditional Indological-cum-sociological view of the strict and irreconcilable dichotomy between caste and modern social institutions or practices, the conceptual framework within which castes

Dipankar Gupta , 'Continuous Hierarchies and Discrete Castes', *Economic and Political Weekly*, Vol 19, No. 46, 17 November 1984.

in India have been understood has received no major reformulation. It is probably for this reason that studies which demonstrate the malleability of the caste structure and beliefs remain at the level of case studies and have not been able to provide an alternative conspectus on the issue of castes at a general level.

In other words, the belief that caste ideology over values 'karma'—a species of other worldlines; or that the caste system orders a hierarchy which universally legitimizes the position of each caste; or that the caste system looks down upon competition and conflict; or that the caste system differentiates on the principle of purity and pollution: are all closely interlinked and govern our conceptual understanding of the caste system. A quick reflection will at once reveal how much at odds the conceptual view of the caste system is with the dynamics of contemporary Indian reality. Our primary purpose in this paper is to suggest an alternative conceptual formulation on castes which can fully integrate many of these empirical findings.

The arguments put forward in this paper in a sense consummate some of the suggestions made by recent sociologists like Veena Das (1982) and Morton Klass (1980). There are however important differences. While Das begins her study by closely scrutinizing a Brahmanical Purana, we shall concern ourselves with the myths and traditions of the subaltern castes. Whereas Klass's main problem is to understand the origin of the caste system and its residual essence, we shall worry ourselves more with an investigation of how this essence is maintained without entering into a study of the origins of caste on which we maintain a point of view distinct from the theory put forward by Klass (see Gupta 1980). We have found it advisable for our purpose to build our contentions step by step, in direct opposition to the prevalent conceptual/theoretical view of the caste system. It is for this reason that we have taken on the most advanced and sophisticated proponent of the social anthropological mainline view of the caste system, viz. the author of *Homo Hierarchicus* Louis Dumont. Das too comes to many of her conclusions in conscious opposition to Dumont, but she only touches upon some of Dumont's positions: those that concern her more immediately.

Why Louis Dumont ?

Dumont not only is the most systematic exponent of the dominant conceptual view of the caste system, but he attains this distinction by undermining almost all the known, conceptual views on the caste system, either in terms of detail: in the case of those whose overall conclusions match his; or in terms of concept and methodology: in the case of those whose conclusions could perhaps be extended to refute his, to wit, those of Senart and Bouglé. When he refutes Bouglé, Senart or even Ghurye and Karve (Dumont 1970b : 66), he takes them up, not so much for what they say, but more for what they imply. As we find ourselves in sympathy with these implications, it is to Dumont that we must necessarily pay greater attention.

Even critics of Dumont, however, must accept his singular contribution to this subject. Right or wrong, Dumont's plea to undertake the macro level as the only legitimate level for Indian sociology has significantly altered the format of research on the caste system. Whereas the bare conclusions of Dumont sponsor a sense of *deja vu*, the methods by which he arrives at them are both novel and significant. Nearly all the major sociological/anthropological terms which give contemporary works on the caste system an academic ambience are significantly modified by Dumont. Terms such as stratification and hierarchy receive major renovations. Logical definitions and logic itself exercise a pervasive sway in his treatment of the caste system. The fact that this paper is addressed to logic and logical definitions is a measure of our indebtedness to Dumont.

It is true that before Dumont, Hegel had said that in order to understand caste, ideology should be considered as the primary level of reality. But Dumont, after specifically acknowledging Hegel's chronological priority in this matter (Dumont 1970b : 80), transformed the discourse by introducing modern structuralism with its notion of binary opposition as the critical clavis to his methodology and adroitly remarked that Marx before him had derived great advantage by distinguishing between the empirical and the logical levels in order to understand facts on the ground (ibid: 112). This led many Marxists to vigorously pursue the homology between caste and the Marxian notion of class. If Marxists could say with emphasis that the proletariat could only triumph once the bourgeoisie were vanquished, then by a homologous logic, it was possible to say, as Dumont in fact does, that unless the purity of the Brahman is itself radically devalued (ibid: 92) *hierarchicus castus* was here to stay, and thus the logic of the caste system would continue to constitute the primary level of social and political reality in India.

Objectives

In this paper we shall try to demonstrate that . . . Dumont's understanding of *hierarchy* is critically faulted in his application of the term to the caste system, and by his repeated assertion that the principle of *encompassment* can be extended from the sphere of the true hierarchy to the caste system as well. It is only at the end of this exposition that an attempt will be made to evaluate the political consequences of our criticism of Dumont where we shall more directly return to the question of caste and class and to the prospects and limits of caste and class mobilizations.

Without anticipating the discussion that follows it is well to mention that our primary purpose here is to demonstrate that caste cannot be looked at in terms of hierarchies but in terms of discrete categories or classes. The fact that it has been acknowledged almost universally in literate circles that castes can be hierarchically arranged with universal validity is, as we shall try to show, a reflection of our uncritical acceptance of the ideology of the privileged castes. If we are able to demonstrate the above then the logical corollary of our contentions should lead us to a position contrary to Dumont's view which holds that politics and economics are not constituents of the pure hierarchy of the caste system but enter its domains surreptitiously and that too only at the interstitial levels.

The Making of the 'True' Hierarchy

As Dumont is easily misunderstood it is best to outline his principal positions in his own words, as far as possible. For Dumont

A hierarchical relation is a relation between larger and smaller, or more precisely between that which encompasses and that which is encompassed (Dumont 1970b: 24).

With this definition of hierarchy Dumont proposes to shift the focal point of accounts that deals with the caste system.

In place of the isolation and the separation of the castes from one another, which have been found so prominent, we shall bring hierarchy to forefront (ibid: 30).

But the principle of the system has yet to be ascertained. How should one go about it? 'In this regard', Dumont writes, 'It is enough to observe that actual men do not behave: they act with an idea in their heads, perhaps that of conforming to custom' (ibid: 40). Finally '. . . the caste system is a state of mind, a state of mind which is expressed by the emergence, in various situations, of groups of various orders generally called "castes"' (ibid: 71). This state of mind provides 'the orientation towards the whole . . .' which in the eyes of those who participate in it legitimizes their respective positions . . . (ibid: 149). Moreoever ' to adopt a value is to introduce hierarchy, and a certain consensus of value, a certain hierarchy of ideas, things and people, is indispensable to social life' (ibid: 54).

It is therefore only *via* ideology that one can grasp the essence of castes and come to know the true principle behind the caste system. The 'single true principle' is 'the opposition of the pure and the impure' (ibid: 81).

This opposition underlies hierarchy, which is the superiority of the pure to the impure, underlies separation because the pure and the impure must be kept separate, and underlies the division of labour because the pure and impure occupations must likewise be kept separate (ibid: 81).

This hierarchical principle, Dumont concludes, is responsible for the 'linear order of castes from A to Z . . .' (ibid: 96). Caste A and Z must exist empirically, for the 'two poles are equally necessary, although unequal' (ibid: 93). For the sociologist, Dumont writes,

the decisive step is accomplished once a quality like impurity is attributed in a permanent manner to certain people. There to a great extent will be found the clue to Indian complexity (Dumont and Pocock 1957: 16).

This is so because Dumont believes that it 'is generally agreed that the opposition is manifested in some macroscopic form in the contrast between the two extreme categories: Brahmans and Untouchables' (Dumont 1970b: 84).

But what makes this hierarchy a true hierarchy? A true hierarchy 'cannot give place to power as such, without contradicting its own principle' (ibid: 117),

. . . but in concrete, we have seen that power, devalued to the advantage of status at the overall level surreptitiously makes itself the equal of status at the interstitial levels (ibid:197).

And yet it is not the interstitial levels or the median zone which is important if one is to appreciate a true hierarchy. Dumont categorically states, 'For us . . . what happens at the extreme is essential (ibid: 116). In a true hierarchy 'that which encompasses is more important than that which is encompassed' (ibid). 'For pure hierarchy to develop without hindrance it was also necessary that power should be absolutely inferior to status' (ibid: 114).

The caste hierarchy however is not merely a linear order but is 'a series of successive dichotomies and inclusions' (ibid: 106). For instance, the Shudra is opposed to the block for the first three, Vaishyas are opposed to the block of Brahman and Kshatriya, which finally divides into two (ibid; see also p. 79). In this manner Dumont demonstrates again the relationship between the encompassing and the encompassed.

The above, most briefly, are the essential methodological points of Dumont, which incidentally are also the sign posts in the developments of our position in this paper.

Facts Against Theory

In an earlier paper we had tried to demonstrate some of the factual inaccuracies in Dumont's work (Gupta 1981: 2093-104). But in this section we think it is worthwhile to mention certain facts which militate against Dumont's theory, and which are not comfortably positioned in Dumont's system. In fairness to Dumont it should be acknowledged that he is on all (or at least on most) of these occasions aware of the existence of these facts, but has a curious style of marginalizing their impact. Either such unpleasant things 'often' happen and are dismissed in a paragraph (Dumont 1970b : 98, 224), or they happen in relatively distant regions where the caste system is 'fluid' (ibid: 214), or they are simply characterized as variants and anomalies (ibid: 96). In this case then it is not so much for factual errors as it is for theoretical solecisms (made apparent by the so-called 'anomalies' and 'variants' which are, nevertheless, still facts) that Dumont is being faulted.

Dumont's starting posture is also a bit odd. He does not arrive at 'hierarchy' by dispassionate inductivism, but in his own words: 'we bet on hierarchy' (ibid : 258). Only subsequently does he realize that the choice is a good one. Our approach begins less adventurously. We have read Dumont. We are puzzled by the way he treats anomalies. We puzzle over these anomalies and non-anomalies. Unable to sort them out we look again into Dumont's definitions and his logical method. And it is here that we feel the problem can be located.

But what are these unpleasant facts? If power enters only at the interstitial levels, then how can a king—the supreme embodiment of the power of the Kshatriya principle— 'intervene directly' to refashion a caste hierarchy (ibid: 214)? Or why is a vegetarian merchant below the meat eating king (ibid: 114)? Or why do upper castes on occasions beat lower castes to 'uphold a symbol of subjection' even if it has nothing to do with pollution (ibid: 122)? Or why do Untouchables of Tanjore village believe that if a Brahman were to enter their village, pestilence and disease would strike it (ibid: 98)? Or why does a certain caste refuse to accept all types of food, both *kachha* and *pacca* from other castes? Why is this case 'absurd'—to use Dumont's adjective (ibid: 128)? Why do farmers 'pose' as puritans (ibid: 129)? Why is the Kshatriya model of Sanskritization 'shamefaced' (ibid: 130)? (Try asking a robust Jat to emulate a Brahman and the absurdity of the verdict 'shamefaced' will become apparent.) In short the major problem is: Why do people who believe in the caste system not follow the dictates of the true hierarchy? Or should the question be posed differently? Is there a true hierarchy at all in the sense in which Dumont has explicated it with reference to the caste system? Is it possible that contrary to Dumont's belief that traditional societies 'know nothing . . . of the individual (and) have basically a collective idea of man' (ibid: 42), the individuals in certain castes resent their position in the linear ranking as ordained by the 'true hierarchy'?

Redefinitions

Let us now indulge in our own variety of definitional purity and then try and abide by the logic of such a definition. A true hierarchy according to us is an unambiguous linear ranking on a single variable. Besides such criteria as wealth in cash, women, cattle, or land; authority can also be a valid criterion for a true and continuous hierarchy. For if one moves up or down, say on the authority scale within a particular organization, one's authority simultaneously increases or decreases. To illustrate, a foreman on the shop floor is not a manager, but is nearer to a manager than the ordinary worker. More importantly, within that particular organization the relative positions of authority are undisputed, and can only be disputed on the pain of transforming that organization.

Discrete classes on the other hand separate units into exclusive categories. One is either a Maharashtrian or not a Maharashtrian, a Brahman or not a Brahman. At the level of the mode of production in Marxism it would be similarly unwise to ask if one was less proletariat and more bourgeois. But this does not mean we are also trying to force a homology between Marxian classes and the Indian castes. The former are an analytical tool while the latter are popularly believed in entities.

Now let us remove some misunderstandings that are bound to arise at this stage. Continuous hierarchies are built around a single criterion which is shared to a greater or lesser extent by all those who occupy that hierarchy. Other factors need not be adduced to it to justify the ranking. Discrete categories are different. A proletariat is not merely not a bourgeois, but is made up of singular defining characteristic or characteristics not shared by a bourgeois. A Bengali is simply not a non-Maharashtrian, or a Bania is not simply a non-Brahman. Therefore, the criteria that separate discrete categories or classes cannot be simply understood by the presence or absence of any one criterion or attribute.

The above does not mean that systems can be distinguished solely on the basis of whether or not they subscribe to continuous hierarchies or discrete classes. Generally, most systems are amenable to either forms of differentiation, it is only a question of the level, or plane, at which one or the other form of differentiation becomes relevant. In a factory system, for instance, while it is possible to hierarchize on the basis of salary, or even power, the manager is simply not one who is not a worker, nor is the worker a person who is simply not an accountant. In this case we have to deal with social classes, the diacritical marks of which cannot be understood on the basis of a continuous hierarchy. Similarly in the agrarian system the sharecropper is simply not a person who is not a labourer or landlord. These social classes are discrete and exclusive. The separation between them is achieved and strengthened by a host of cohort features.

Even so, both in the factory system and in the agrarian system the continuous hierarchy can be significant on certain planes. Peasant movements in the countryside and economism in factories are sustained by the principle of continuous hierarchies: in one case on the basis of amount of land owned, and in the other case it is simply money. The principle of encompassment is overtly active. The 'they' can become the 'we' and *vice versa* without reworking the continuous hierarchy, or even without introducing an extraneous system of opposition. In the caste system, however, the 'they' never become the 'we', and the principle of encompassment and the process of linear inclusions and residual exclusions is never operative. One could say the same for linguistic entities, and also for social classes. The only problem with the last variant is that social classes are parts of different systems and are never unambiguously participants of any one system.

Much has been made about ranking on the principle of purity with respect to the caste system. It has also been accepted that this is a matter of ideology to which all those within the caste system subscribe. But as a matter of fact there are some problems with this too.

Rules and Ideologies

Rules are most nakedly an instrument of power hierarchy. Ideology, on the other hand, tries to mask this nakedness, or may even on occasions, unmask it. The caste rule in this sense, which holds that the subaltern castes must serve the privileged ones, is an expression of power and Brahman ideology attempts to cloak it. But what Brahman ideology also does is that it separates different castes, most fundamentally itself, from others. Naturally this principle is active in the case of other castes as well so that ultimately there is no one caste ideology, but multiple ideologies sharing some principles in common but articulated at variance and even in opposition to each other. In effect, therefore, the *rule* of caste is only obeyed when it is accompanied by the *rule* of power. Therefore, contrary to Dumont, it is the hierarchy of power and economics where we believe that hierarchy is naked. Ideology, on the other hand, introduces it 'shamefacedly' but only after effecting the separation between discrete classes.

There are two additional points to be made with respect to purity and pollution. From the vantage point of Brahmanical ideology Brahmans are the most pure and the level of purity decreases till we come to the other extreme who have no purity at all. Here Dumont quite unexpectedly helps us when he calls them actually polluted. Obviously at some point purity has undergone a dialectical change and is now a different category altogether, viz. pollution. What is not pure need not always be polluted and Dumont seems to be aware of this when he says that purity and pollution are categories in opposition. But very quickly he negates this insight by claiming that castes A to Z demonstrate the two poles of this opposition, with obviously castes B, C, D, etc., coming in between in an orderly and hierarchical fashion.

But if one were to set aside the hierarchy of purity and pollution and look instead at the ideology of purity and pollution, then one would find matters to be quite different. Ideology separates castes into discrete entities in a most self-centred way. Castes rarely, if ever, accept their biological fallibility and consequently reject the attribute of impurity which some other castes may impute to them. If they do abide on the ground by the ranking of purity inflicted on them by the ideology of some other castes then it is because of the conjoint working of the principles of economics and/or politics, both of which are amenable to hierarchical ranking but are unfortunately excluded by Dumont in his working out of the 'true hierarchy'. Ideology, in short, separates and muddles what a continuous and true hierarchy unites and encompasses.

It remains for us now to define caste. As we came to our definition not when we began this exercise, but after it was completed, we shall also present it towards the end of this paper. Additionally, as this paper is not really concerned with the definition of the caste system but seeks to clarify some of the conceptual problems involved in the discourse, we, at this stage, do not want definitional wrangles to deflect our primary purpose. We might however mention here that the task of defining caste is not an easy one, as many hitherto unassailable characteristics of it such as: (a) a uniform hierarchical ideology; (b) occupational specialization; and (c) the concept of purity and pollution as the principal instrument for separation ('repulsion') etc., dissolve under a more contemporary gaze.

One final clarification before we proceed any further. The terms caste and *jati* will be used synonymously in this paper. When we have to refer to whole caste groups like the Brahmans, Kshatriyas, Kaibartas, Mochis or Panchals, we shall simply use the term 'caste group'.

One Ideology or Many

A careful reading of Louis Dumont's several works on the caste system confirms that for Dumont the ideology of the caste system is all pervasive without exception in Hindu India. For the Hindus, Dumont avers, belief in God is secondary to belief in caste (Dumont and Pocock 1957: 20). But Dumont does not stop here. He goes on to argue that there is only one elaborated ideology based on these principles, and for the elaboration of this ideology he depends primarily on the ancient Brahman law giver, Manu. From the highest to the lowest caste everybody subscribes to this elaborated ideology, duly accepting as just his position in the ranking. It is possible for Dumont to say this for he believes that in traditional societies (as we mentioned earlier), there is only the idea of the collective man. It is therefore the duty of the Hindus, as they see it, to uphold this one supreme elaborated ideology. Some others who have also read Dumont may of course say that we are misinterpreting him, but then they would have to account for the complete omission by Dumont of what the subaltern castes think of their caste positions and of the caste system as a whole.

If one were momentarily to refuse to believe the prevalent Brahmanical ideology, then it would not be very difficult to accept that there can be many ideologies all of which adhere to similar values, but express the lived in situation differently and offer different guides to action. One should not, at this point, confuse values with ideologies. All caste ideologies value the need to separate caste groups from one another according to a mythical notion of biological differences as they also value the principle of endogamy.[1] And yet the manner in which these values are expressed can be vastly different and also opposed to one another. To draw an analogy, the racist ideology of say the National Socialist Party under Hitler shared certain values with the ante-bellum politics of those states which united to form the American confederacy in nineteenth century. Yet the ideologies of the ante-bellum southern confederacies and of the Nazi party were different and we might reasonably suppose that the segregationist policy in South Africa, and the ideology of 'the white man's burden' too are quite distinctive in character. All these articulations are racist as they have certain dominant values in common around which the different ideologies condense. Likewise, we believe that there can be different ideologies around certain common values which are shared by all who participate in the caste system. The fact that these ideological variations are limited to a defined geographical area, and occur nowhere else, and also because identical symbols are used and reused with different salience in diverse ideological articulations, often blind us to the fact that we are actually witnesses to not one ideology but to multiple ideologies. Ideologies translate pure values into empirical categories in order to provide definite guidelines on the ground (Schurmann 1971 : 38-9). They purport to explain the unhappy (or happy) circumstances in which the members of different caste groups are placed; what compromises they must effect to either consolidate or invalidate their positions; or what correctives they must adopt against real or imaginery challenges to their existence; and finally to assert their dignity and pride as separate groups.

It is in this context then of shared values that caste constitues a system of beliefs which has practical consequences. It is in this sense then that in spite of viewing castes as discrete classes we can still talk of a caste system and thus meet the charges that Dumont made against Bouglé or Senart somewhat unjustly. Neither Bouglé nor Senart were self-consciously espousing the cause that castes are discrete entities in the sense that we are, but their fault was that they did not consciously either use the word 'system' to which Dumont seems committed. If it had been possible for Bouglé or Senart to reply to Dumont they would have said that they were not anti-systemic because what made caste a distinctive system were the principles that were universally employed in separation, viz., hierarchy, occupation, and repulsion. Our view is, however, not identical to either Bouglé's or Senart's. In spite of the fact that castes are discrete

---

[1] See Kolenda's essay in this volume.

they form a system because each caste in spite of its own idiosyncratic articulation of the caste ideology nevertheless uses identical elements and positions itself with reference to a notion of hierarchy whose nodes appear and reappear in different ideological formulations. Generally, the *varna* system forms a reference to which each caste ideological formulation addresses itself, though very often the *varna* system is skipped, and the Gods of the Hindu pantheon are referred to. But both the primary and secondary symbols employed to differentiate one caste from the other occur in the context of a common reference particular enough to render this context non-referential in any other system of differentiation. The caste system is a system of condensed symbols, and like all symbols what is signified at one point makes sense within a referential context, and yet any particular signification does not limit the potentiality of the signifier. The signified, as the linguists tirelessly remind us, does not exhaust the signifier.

We shall leave this discussion here and take it up again towards the end of this paper when we try to attempt a definition of the caste system.

It is not possible for us to give a complete ethnographic account of how the discrete character of castes is maintained. We shall detail such ethnographic evidence as is available to us, but a more detailed ethnographic study should also bear out our contentions. However, there is not much use in asserting a position contrary to Dumont's if it does not yield some tangible benefits. We hope to demonstrate in the following pages that if one were to view castes as discrete classes or categories and follow our distinction between a caste rule that is imposed and caste ideologies that are believed in, many of the facts that Dumont marginalizes or ignores can be accounted for. Nor would it be necessary to be uncomfortable about the notion of politics and economics in order to understand the Indian caste system.

Discrete Ideologies: Tales of Origin

If ideologies separate the population and, surreptitiously at least, subvert or legitimize the rules of authority then caste ideologies should also contain these elements. Further as castes separate to maintain a distinct notion of their original heritage ontology becomes an important component of all discrete caste ideologies.

Like the Brahman who must go back to the original division in the Purusasukta, each caste has its own theory explaining its origins. Not always is the occupation aspect upper-most in these tales of genesis. But when in the tales of origin of the so-called lower castes the occupational aspect is stressed, as it is in the tales of the Telis and the Kumhars, then the occupation is not seen as a particularly degrading one by the members of these caste groups. In occupational valuations, and in other aspects too, individual caste ideologies differ markedly from the Brahmanical versions. We shall illustrate this difference by reproducing below the tales of origin of the lowly Chamars, the even lower Chandals, and of the upper caste Kayasthas as related by members of these castes. Note how pervasive the difference is between the Brahmanical view of the origins of these three castes and views that these castes have of their own genesis.

Case I: The Chamars: The orthodox view regarding the origin of Chamars is as follows:

According to the Puranas, the Chamars are descended from a boatman and Chandal woman; but if we are to identify them with the Karavara or leather worker mentioned in the tenth chapter of Manu, the father of the caste was a Nishada and the mother a Vaideha (Risley 1891, Vol 1: 175).

The Chamars view their origins as follows:

Chamars trace their predigree to Ravi or Rui Das, the disciple of Ramanada at the end of the fourteenth century. . . . Another tradition current among them alleges that their original ancestor was the youngest of four Brahman brethren who went to bathe in a river and found a cow struggling in quicksand. They sent the youngest brother in to rescue the animal, but before he could get to the spot it had been drowned. He was compelled therefore by his brothers to remove the carcass, and after he had done this they turned him out of their caste and gave him the name of Chamar (ibid: 176).

Case II: The Chandals: The orthodox view is as follows:

Manu brands them as the lowest of mankind; sprung from the illicit intercourse of a Sudra man with a Brahman woman, whose touch defiles the pure and who have no ancestral rites (ibid: 184).

The Chandals themselves, however, view their origins differently. 'Thus, according to a tradition of the Dacca Chandals, they were formerly Brahmans, who became degraded by eating with Sudras. . . .' (ibid).

Whereas the orthodox view claims that the Chandals have no ancestral rites, 'the Chandal celebrates the *Sraddha* on the eleventh day as Brahmans do, and the Gayawal priests conduct the obsequial ceremonies without compunction' (ibid).

Case III: The Kayasthas: 'The Kayasthas themselves reject the theory which gives them for an ancestor Karan, the son of a Vaisya father by a Sudra mother' (ibid: 438).

But the Kayasthas of Bengal go 'so far as to argue that the five Kayasthas of the tradition were political officers in charge as Kshatriyas, on a mission from Kannauj to the king of Bengal, and that the five Brahmans played quite a subordinate part in the transaction, if indeed they were anything more than the cooks of the five Kayasthas (ibid: 439).

These examples could indeed be multiplied *ad nauseum* but they would all point to one single fact. The elaboration of the pure hierarchy from the Brahmans' point of view is not shared by the other castes. The Kammalan caste which consists of artisans of five occupational sections, such as the goldsmiths, braziers, carpenters, stonemasons and blacksmiths, 'claim descent from Viswakarma, the architect of the Gods, and equality with Brahmans' (Hutton 1963: 12; see also Kramrisch, 1975:18). The Bhangis, who are as low as the Chamars, also partake of the myth that they were originally Brahmans (Blunt 1969: 4; see also Fuchs 1949: 235-6, with reference to the Balahi creation myth). Some other artisan castes like the Barhai, Bhatt and Lohar have sub-castes which claim descent from the Brahmans. The Nhavis (or barbers) of Deccan consider themselves superior to Brahmans because they claim descendence from

the serpent Shehsa who encircled Shiva's neck and was told to assume a human form at the time of the thread ceremony of the God Brahma (Enthoven 1975: 128).

The Mochis of Bombay Presidency claim Rajput descent for according to them one of their heroic and redoubtable ancestors made a pair of stockings (*moju*) out of a tiger's skin (ibid: 56)... and so on and on it goes. As discrete ideologies there is no embarrassment in accepting these facts for what they are without introducing the notion of Sanskritization, which in any case does not apply to all these cases.

In these tales of origin it is not always the Brahmans who are the models as the tale of the Kayasthas related above reveals. Those *jatis* that do not have a martial past and yet claim Kshatriya status are as varied as the well-to-do Chandraseni Kayastha Prabhus of Maharashtra, the Shimpis (or tailors) also of Maharashtra, the poor Kharwars of Bihar, or the Noniyas of north India. In all these cases the myth of Parasuram, the Brahman, who vowed to kill Kshatriyas so that Brahmans may have temporal power, is invoked to explain why their Kshatriya ancestors had to take to different occupations to escape Parasuram. In all these cases the Brahmans are viewed with a measure of hostility.

Discrete Castes and Muddled Hierarchies

The existencce of so many diverse and contrary tales of caste origin is not the only way by which discrete castes maintain their discreteness. If one were to look at the customs and traditions followed by different castes one would be hard put to force them into any grading system on the basis of purity and pollution. For instance, in the case of *kachcha* and *pacca* food it is not always the upper castes who are very particular in this matter. According to Blunt's classification, there is no relationship between the orthodox caste ranking and the severity of the cooking taboo. The Koiris and Kumhars are as rigid in their cooking taboos as the Brahmans, and belong to the same group in Blunt's classification. The Cheros and the Khatris also belong to one group and the Banjaras, Byars and Dangis are about as severe in maintaining the taboos relating to *kaccha* and *pacca* food as are the Kayasthas (Blunt 1969: 93). The Telis, or oil pressers of Orissa, not a front liner in terms of traditional caste aristocracy, nevertheless, are very particular about matters of food. Sometimes they can be more orthodox than the Brahmans as this delightful episode recorded by N.K. Bose reveals. At a ceremonial feast of the Telis somebody asked for water and used the words '*pani lao*' whereupon the Parichha (the traditional spokesman of the Telis),

lifted his hand, i.e he abstained from proceeding with his meals, as he complained that the sacramental social feast was defiled by the Urdu word '*pani lao* ' Everyone in the feast followed suit (Basu 1960: 15).

Similarly it is difficult to say according to any one ideology who is regarded as an Untouchable by whom. Though a Dhobi is higher than a Bhangi by orthodox valuations, sixteen castes will not touch a Dhobi but only eleven castes will avoid touching a Bhangi (Blunt 1969: 102). The low caste

Kuricchan of Malabar plasters his house with cow-dung if it is polluted by the entry of a Brahman (Hutton 1963: 78).

The Kurmi will not take any food from a Brahman unless he happens to be his guru (Risley 1891, Vol1: 536). The Sonar sub-castes of the Panchals will eat food cooked by Brahmans, but the other sub-castes of the Panchals such as the Lohars, Kansars, Sutars and Patharwats will not, as they consider themselves superior to Brahmans. The Sonars, on the other hand, consider themselves to be superior to the other four sub-castes among the Panchals (Enthoven 1975: 158, 369). The Meghavals or Dheds are a highly depressed caste group because carrion carrying has been their traditional occupation and yet they will not eat at the hands of the Kolis who are certainly superior to them by orthodox standards (ibid: 52). The Patidars of Gujarat earlier claimed Kshatriya (Rajput) status, but now claim Vaishya (Baniya) status, thus preferring a status which orthodoxy would hierarchize below the Kshatriya order (Srinivas 1975: 41).

Such inconsistencies and muddles in the hierarchy are also evident as we move from region to region. Consider, for instance, the following inconsistencies and hierarchical muddles in the cases of the Babhans, the Gareris, and the Goalas in different parts of East India. All these case are reported by Risley (1891, Vol 1):

(a) *The Babhans*: In South Eastern Behar they [the Babhans] rank immediately below Kayastha, but in Shahabad, Saran, and North Western Provinces they appear to stand on much the same level as Rajputs. The fact that in Patna and Gaya the Amashtha or Karan Kayasthas will eat *kachi* food which has been cooked by a Babhan, while the other sub-castes of Kayasthas will not, may perhaps be a survival from time when Bhabhans occupied a higher position than they do at the present day (ibid: 33).

(b) *The Gareris*. . . . the Gareri is reckoned higher in rank than the Ahir, and equal to the Majroti and Krishnaut Goalas, with whom, as has been mentioned above, Gareris will eat both *kachi* and *pakki* food and will smoke the same *hookah*. It is not clear, however, that this intercourse is reciprocal, and that the Goalas will accept food on the same terms from a Gareri, while the fact Gareris make wethers themselves must necessarily involve some measure of social degradation. In Bihar and Bengal this caste is generally reckoned a clean one from whose members a Brahman can take water; but in Puraniya, say Buchnan, it is impure (ibid: 273).

(c) *The Goalas* : In point of social standing the Goalas of Behar rank with Kurmis, Amats, and the other castes from whose hands a Brahman can take water. In Bengal they occupy a lower position, and are counted as inferior, not only to the Naba-Sakh, but also to the cultivating division of the Kaibartta caste. The Orissa Goalas, on the other hand, affect a high standard of ceremonial purity, and also look down upon the Behar and Bengal divisions of the caste (ibid: 290).

The principle of segmentation and inclusion cannot therefore be applied universally in the case of castes. This situation is noticeably different among tribes. Segmentalization in tribes follows a continuous hierarchy because the distance of a clan or sub-clan from the ancestor is clear and unambiguous. Characteristically, there is no muddling in this hierarchy. We, therefore, disagree with Dumont when he uses the segmental principle of tribal organizations to explicate encompassment in the caste system (see Dumont 1970b: 79).

Multiple Binding and Hypersymbolism

The discrete character of *jatis* and the pride that the members of each *jati* have in their own community are denoted by multiple observances and beliefs. These many denoters of separation are not linked by any precise convention and for this reason the notion of purity or pollution is not always active in the many rituals and symbols that separate *jatis*.

Occupational distinctions which have very little to do with any extended notion of purity and pollution are employed to maintain the separation between different *jatis* of the same caste group. Some years ago the Srivastavas broke away from the Kayasthas who were *patwaris* (keepers of village records) because the latter had earned a bad name for chicanery. The Srivastavas for this reason alone do not permit intermarriage nor observe commensality in matters of food with the *patwari* Kayasthas. This is especially true in the erstwhile Oudh region (Blunt 1969: 222). The Gacchua Teli and the Bhunja Teli no longer belong to the original caste of Telis, because they began to extract oil in a novel manner. The Gacchua Telis began

to extract oil by crushing the seed between wooden rollers; the second, or Bhunia Teli, parch the seed and then extract oil (Risley 1891, Vol 2: 306).

In neither of the two processes is there any association with any polluting substance and yet these two castes were excommunicated from the larger Teli caste group. Three new castes are emerging among the Mochis of western India on the basis of their newly acquired occupations. The Chandlagaras make lac bangles, the Chitaras are painters, and the Rasanis are electroplaters (Enthoven 1975: 57). While the separation of these castes from the original Mochi caste group can perhaps be explained on the basis of the notion of purity and pollution as these castes no longer do any tanning or skinning, however, the internal differentiation between these three *jatis* is not based on any polluting factor (see also Ghurye 1969: 83). There is yet another case; this time between whole caste groups. The Kaibartta and Tiyar fishing communities consider themselves superior to the Malos, another fishing caste group, because the

Kaibartta and Tiyar in netting always pass the netting needle from the above downwards, working from left to right; while the Malo passes it from below upwards, forming meshes from right to left. It is remarkable that the same difference is adduced to the Behar fisherman as a proof of the degraded rank of the Baj par (quoted in Risley 1891, Vol 2, 66).

Differences in marriage rites, jewellery, dress and other such factors also neutral to purity or pollution are adhered to rigidly by different castes, not always to show their superiority, but to emphasize their differences. These differences need to be made and emphasized. Ideologies thrive only when they are able to condense a large number of discrete phenomena in a comprehensive and total manner and it is through this process that ideologies attain their diacritical marks. There are certain features many castes share in common. The *nabashakhas* (originally 9 but now a group of 14 castes) have their ceremonies performed by the so-called 'orthodox' Brahmans. Their distinctiveness, however, does not become redundant because of this. The Baidyas, the Kayasthas, the Tantis, the Goalas— members of the *nabashakhas*—follow customs which also separate them comprehensively from each other. These differences are zealously guarded, and the depressed caste 'observe caste distinctions as rigidly as their social betters' (O'Malley 1975: 37; see also Briggs 1920). The Mahanayaka Sudras, a depressed agricultural caste, agree that 'Loyalty to one's own caste must be preserved even at the cost of life' (Bose 1960: 82). It would seem as if these caste distinctions are a matter of *aesthetic judgment*.

Within caste groups too the endogamous *jatis* are separated by divergent customs. The Mogers, traditionally fishermen, are divided into three endogamous *jatis*: the Aliyasantana who inherit through females, the Makalasantana who inherit through males, and the Raudesantana who allow their widows to remarry (Enthoven 1975: 60). The Maheshri Meghvals do not worship Mata but the Marwada, Gojra and Charanua Meghvals do, while the Marwada and Gojra Meghvals unlike the Charania Meghvals revere the saint Ramdev Puri. The Maheshri Meghvals do not have the *chori* or marriage alter, but the Marwada Meghvals do (ibid: 49). The Charania Meghval will not do any skinning and tanning while the others have no particular objection to performing these tasks (ibid: 59).

Jati differentiation through multiple rituals signifies not so much the different social histories of the various *jatis* as it does a natural history which separates *jatis* irreconcilably on a biological plane. This is the pre-eminent value to which all those who participate in the caste system subscribe. It is for this reason that endogamy is effective only at the *jati* level. The abundance of rituals, through social and aesthetized codes, guarantees that neither common social circumstances nor the absence of any visible biological variation among *jatis* sublates the rationale of endogamy.

The need to separate is accompanied by a certain reverence and pride in one's own customs and traditions which is not easily jettisoned just to fall in line with orthodoxy. The Dosadhs, a depressed agrarian caste group, insist on a high caste Hindu status, and in keeping with this claim have Maithil and Kannauj Brahmans officiate their ceremonies; yet they do not conform to the Brahmanical views. The Dosadhs particularly revere the deity Rahu even though this deity is considered a demon (*daitya*) by the Brahmans (Risley 1891, Vol 1: 255). Other castes like the Bhats—a pseudo Brahman caste—or the Kannapuria Rajputs revere distinctly tribal, even anti-Brahman deities (Blunt 1969 : 285). The items that enter into the making of the discrete character of castes are thus very varied in character, and some of them do not even have a Brahmanical or textual pedigree but are revered nevertheless by individual castes. To quote Guirand,

The greater the imprecision of the convention, the more the value of the sign varies according to the different users (Guirand 1975: 25).

The necessity to semaphore distinction between castes is done at several levels and junctions far exceeding what is strictly necessary for the purpose.

This abundance of symbols allows for the variation in salience given to different symbols and ritualized practices at different points of time. A primary symbol may at times become a secondary symbol, and *vice versa*. This is especially evident when castes enter politics, as we shall see a little later. Some symbols and practices may even be dropped if they come in the way of secular advancement of the members of a particular caste, or if they are seen by them to be unduly onerous. The so-called 'fallen Brahmans' who perform ceremonies for the depressed castes were forced, due to pecuniary pressure, to go against the Brahmanical ban against performing such services. Quite expectedly, they believe that their current degradation resulted from a chance occurrence in the remote past. The Dogras of Palampur in Himachal Pradesh consider themselves to be Rajputs and yet have, by and large, given up the practice of asking Brahmans to perform their ceremonies. They believe the Brahmans are too expensive and greedy. The Telis of Orissa have long valued child marriage, but are now asking their caste members to fall in line with the Sarda Act which prohibits child and infant marriage (Bose 1960 : 29). The many rituals and beliefs that have been dropped, or added on, to justify occupational change are too numerous to be recorded here. Even the expiatory rites which all caste Hindus had to religiously undergo if they interacted with aliens are now increasingly becoming a thing of the past (recall Milton Singer's description of 'ritual neutralization', Singer 1972; see also O' Malley 1975).

The Brahman as a Fiction

The discrete character of castes and individual caste ideologies as reflected in their tales of origin, make it possible for those belonging to the depressed and subaltern castes not to see themselves as intrinsically impure or despicable. They regard their current, rather unenviable position to the outcome of Brahman chicanery or of some chance misdeed of their ancestors (see Cohn 1975: 207). It is for this reason that they find it possible not only to believe in myths contrary to Brahman myths but are also capable of inviting Brahmans to perform their ceremonies even though this is contrary to superior caste injunctions. Theoretically, i.e. according to orthodox theory, the depressed caste members should not have dared to do this. In case Brahmans as a whole steadfastly refuse to service a particular caste then the caste itself comes up with its own caste priests. That the Lingayats of Mysore learned to do this is often recorded. But the Chamars too have their own Chamarwa Brahmans (Briggs 1920: 277), and according to Risley's report even Goalas have their own priests (Risley 1891, Vol 1: 289). In Orissa when the Brahmans boycotted the Gauras (or Gopalas) because the latter refused to be their palanquin bearers, the Gauras got hold of an unlettered and unattached Brahman to perform religious services for them. This Brahman assiduously attended the government sponsored Adult Education Centre and trained himself and successfuly ministered to the ritual needs of his Gaura clients. After three years the Brahmans broke their boycott (Bose 1960: 157). Today such low castes as the Koiris, the Bhars, the Pasis and the Dosadhs are served by Brahman priests. These priests are not given priestly status by the orthodox Brahmans, but are recognized as priests by the castes whom they serve, and therefore, it is eventually the caste itself that accords priestly status or otherwise in flagrant oppostion, if necessary, to orthodoxy. The low caste Mauliks of Bengal, like the powerful Lingayats of Mysore, also have their own priests and as a matter of fact revere them more than they do the so-called fallen Brahmans who occasionally serve them (Risley 1981: Vol 2: 83). The Maheshri Marwada and Gojra Meghvals have their own *jati* priests (Enthoven 1975: 50), and do not feel the absence of pure Brahmans. The Brahman therefore degenerates to a fiction on the ground whose exaltation as a putative reality is dependent on other castes. Only orthodoxy, and the Brahminical elaboration of the caste ideology can assert, as Dumont does when he writes, that 'Brahman could exist without Ksatra, not conversely' (Dumont 1970a : 63).

To quote a very revealing passsage from E. A. H. Blunt:

Eggeling, for instance, has asserted that: 'the cardinal principle which underlies the system of caste is the preservation of purity of religious belief and ceremonial usage. . . . All that need be said here is that if the caste system was devised with the object of preserving 'the purity of belief and ceremonial usage', it has been a singular failure (Blunt 1969: 37).

Consequences of the Above

In the preceding sections we attempted to make the following points:

1. Any notion of hierarchy is arbitrary and is valid from the perspective of certain individual castes. To state that the pure hierarchy is one that is universally believed in, or one which legitimizes 'the position of those, who participate in the caste system', is misleading.

2. The separation between castes is not only on matters which connote the opposition between purity and pollution. Distinctions and diacritical notches which are not even remotely suggestive of purity and pollution are observed as strictly. Obversely, distinctions relating to purity and pollution do not systematically affect caste status. The cultivating Amot caste solemnize their Goraiya festival with the sacrifice of a *pig* and yet Brahmans take water from them (Risley 1891, Vol 1: 18). Further, it is only after we accept castes as discrete are we in a position to understand why castes equally pure refrain from merging their identities. The *nabashakha* group of castes provides us with a telling example of this phenomenon. This also explains why inconsistencies in caste behaviour do not trouble the Hindus, as Srinivas noted while studying the Coorgs.

We are now in a position to quickly review the implications of the above for some major issues that dominate studies of the caste system.

The Jajmani System

The *jajmani* system, in theory, establishes, and indeed orders, religious protocol for the exchange of services between different castes specializing in different occupations. But in fact the *jajmani* system is a sporadic empirical reality. Even Dumont concedes this, but he is soon compelled to add that economic services and religious prestations are mingled together and 'this takes place within the prescribed order, the religious order' (Dumont 1970b : 147). But this is possible only if each caste follows its hereditary occupation which has been sanctified in the sacred texts. But surprisingly the sacred texts do not mention a larger number of *jatis* in existence today, and if it had been the job of sacred texts to clearly identify *jatis* with occupations then this was done very carelessly.

To begin with, let us examine the agricultural castes which are so numerous and are constantly increasing in number every day. In the prime sacredotal text, the Manusmriti, no prominence is given to . . . either landowning or agricultural castes or the corresponding occupations, though a large part of the population must then, as now, have consisted of cultivators, and their importance in the social system must have been great (Blunt 1969: 232). Further, castes who claim different origins, some like the Kurmis who claim Kshatriya status, others like Bhuinhars and Tagas who claim Brahmin status, are also 'traditionally landholders' (Ibid). The number of those castes whose caste names are clearly non-agricultural but who are moving into agriculture is constantly being enhanced (ibid: 251-2; Bose 1975: 192-3, 198; with reference to Untouchables see Desai 1976: 162). Even Brahmins, as Bouglé found, are not only ploughmen, but soldiers, tradesmen and cooks (Bouglé 1958: 19). The suggestion that a caste which follows an occupation which is not hereditary nor sanctioned in the texts is either degraded or excommunicated must necessarily be rejected. Even Brahmans such as the Tewaris, Ojhas, Upadhyayas or Jhas have engaged in agriculture without losing caste (see Risley 1891; Vol.1: 29). As one Brahman is reported to have confessed to Abbe Dubois: 'To fill one's belly one must play several parts' (Bouglé 1958: 19). If this is true for the Brahmans it should be equally true for the other castes as well. Ultimately the castes that cling to their traditional occupations the most are those 'which deal most with trade questions . . . the Bhangi, the Nai, the Bhishti, the Darzi' (Blunt 1969: 245), the drummer, the washerman, etc. (Dumont and Pocock, 1958: 47-8). Not surprisingly when any attempt is made to elucidate the *jajmani* system the authors invariably deal with these castes alone.

The *jajmani* system, in other words, is an idealization which in fact works out in a somewhat pure form only in a small minority of cases. This further strengthens our view that castes achieve their separation not primarily by the criterion of occupation as supposedly recommended in the texts, but in fact distinguish themselves from each other hyper-symbolically by a cluster of characteristics, the more important of which need not be recommended by the ideology of the true hierarchy. If certain members of a caste believe that they can forsake their traditional occupations because they do not regard them as prestigious then they promptly abandon them at the earliest opportunity. The development of the *helos* from among the erstwhile caste of Kaibartas is a case in point. At other times, as with the various Brahmans who turned to agriculture, it is a question of economic advantage. But even after these castes change their occupations they do not merge their caste identities with those who were from earlier times following that economic activity.

Sanskritization

The concept of Sanskritization very imperfectly understands the incongruence between deemed occupation and actual occupation. Any move on the part of the lower castes to appropriate life styles that were not traditionally theirs is interpreted as if these lower castes are ashamed of their identity. In some cases this might be true, but in fact when subaltern castes claim elevated caste status it is a phenomenon often independent of Sanskritization. Sanskritization is a reassertion in an extraverted form of what was till then an introverted expression of the caste's overall rejection of the position given to it by the hierarchical *rule* governed by the twin principles of economics and politics. But only in rare cases, if ever at all, do these castes want to give up their identity. They only seek to be relieved from the duress they were placed under in the prevailing hierarchical rule, by asserting demonstratively what they have always believed to be their rightful status. They are successful when they have access to the axes of economics and politics (Lynch 1968), as in the case of the Jatavas of Agra, or the Izhavas of Kerala, or the distiller caste groups of Orissa and Tamil Nadu. The importance of the economic factor cannot be overemphasized for very often the claims of the well-to-do sections of a depressed *jati* are accepted by the powerful and dominant castes, while the identical claims of their indigent *jati* brethren do not win such acceptance. The prosperous Noniyas, for instance, were accepted by the privileged castes as Chauhans but the poorer Noniyas were not accorded similar status. These poorer Noniyas nevertheless did not abandon their claim that they were really Cauhans.[2] Sanskritization seen thus is an extraversion of a long standing, deeply felt, and believed in judgement of their caste status which was hitherto privy only to members of that caste.

If Srinivas imperfectly understood this phenomenon through the optic of Sanskritization, Dumont did not understand it at all, for in his case the

---

[2] See Rowe's essay in this volume, pp. 326-38.

true hierarchy is paramount and castes have no business to believe otherwise. Dumont realized the difficulties his true hierarchy would face, so he introduced power and economics surreptitiously at the interstitial levels. But if castes are seen as discrete classes there is'no need to make this shamefaced concession. And in any case, mobility and transfer of occupation for economic and political purposes occurs both at the lowest level as also at the highest and not only at the interstitial levels. It is worthwhile to recall the case of the proud landowning Brahmans we mentioned earlier in this paper, as also the case of the so-called Untouchable claiming Brahman status.

If *jatis* can independently and idiosyncratically set up objects of veneration, then by equal facility they can also set up independent models for emulation, or Sanskritization. These objects of veneration and ritual practices are not always recommended by Brahmans but are devoutly adhered to, nevertheless, by both privileged and powerful *jatis* as well as by the subaltern ones. Likewise non-Brahmanical models of Sanskritization carry as much commitment as the Brahmanical model. It is not as if *jatis* choose the non-Brahmanical mode 'shamefacedly' as a second best choice (Dumont 1970b : 30). The Brahmanical life style and symbols do not excite universal favour among many *jatis*. As a matter of fact the Kshatriya, or Rajput, or Jat model contains an inbuilt hostility to Brahmans which is in line with the sentiments of these caste groups. This hostility is *sans* envy, as the Rajput Ikshwaku clan myth or even the myth of Parasuram demonstrates. The pride and the generic swagger that are built into the 'I-am-a-Rajput' syndrome (Hitchcock 1975: 10) cannot by a long stretch be considered shamefaced. Neither is the Patidars' transference of loyalty from the Kshatriya model to the Vaishya (or Baniya) model (Srinivas 1975: 41) an admission of their intrinsic inability to match up to the Kshatriyas as much as it is a consequence of the Patidars' devaluation of the Kshatriya life style and their concomitant over-valuation of the Bania one.

Caste and Politics

If castes are discrete classes (or categories) and if hierarchy is never universally acknowledged then alternative hierarchical rankings are not only believed in introvertedly but can also be asserted by political power. This does not happen only where castes are fluid, or in remote regions (Dumont 1970a : 214). But in point of fact it happens all over.

O'Malley describes the plight of some high caste subjects of one of the Orissa

Feudatory States who refused to accept the decision of their ruler in a caste case, and were themselves outcasted by him in consequence. No priest, barber or washerman could render them any service, with the result that 'they had long beards matted with dirt, their hair hung in long strands and was filthy in the extreme, and their clothes were beyond description for uncleanliness' (Hutton 1963: 95-6).

Perhaps, another illustration, this time from Bengal. Ballal Sen in the eleventh century is said to have divided the Kshatriyas into four castes according to locality, and not on the basis of purity and pollution, nor under the instance of the Brahmans (Risley Vol 1, 1891 : 440). In addition he also raised the positions of some castes and degraded others (Hutton 1963 : 94).

The principle that caste is ultimately a matter for the secular or political authority is to be seen carried so far that landlords at any rate in eastern India are apt to interfere in purely caste matters. . . . So clearly has the principle that the secular power is the final arbiter of caste been accepted in the past, that the Mughal rulers of Bengal and their British successors have in turn found themselves in the position of judges of such matters (Hutton 1963 : 96).

Significantly in keeping with our understanding of castes as discrete categories intra-caste matters are solved primarily at the level of the caste *panchayat*. The village *panchayat*, except in the hill regions, did not exist in pre-modern India, a fact that Dumont observes but fails to draw the proper conclusions from.

In modern politics too the principle of encompassment as detailed by Dumont is conspicuously absent. The principle of discrete caste is however upheld in a variety of situations. In Bihar, for instance, there has been no pattern at all when castes have aligned politically. In caste atrocities in Bishrampur the main issue was sharecroppers' right over cultivated land, and the Kurmis were the main attackers. But the Kurmis were aided by a variety of upper caste landlords to attack not only the Harijans, but also the Yadavs who are closer to them and traditionally considered to be of the same rank. But in Belchi their attack was on Brahmans, the kingpin of the true hierarchy (Dhar *et al.*, 1982: 110). In Gujarat the Bareyas and Kolis who are of the same rank often unite with the Rajputs to oppose one of their own kind, the newly ascendent Patidar caste (Shah 1982: 139). In Marathwada the Mahars were attacked by the powerful castes, but the Mangs, who are traditionally supposed to be lower than the Mahars, were left untouched. Neither did the Mangs stand by the Mahars as per the principle of encompassment (Gupta 1979: 12).

Rather than encompassment what one finds is deliberate and conscious linking between different *jatis* depending upon the exigencies of the situation. The so-called caste associations, like the Kshatriya Sabha or the Kayastha Samaj, also have members belonging to a variety of *jatis* and who independently decide, uninfluenced by the principle of encompassment, to participate in one organization or another. This is not only true of the so-called upper caste organizations, but, as Bose found, is also true of the Teli (oil pressers) association. Many members of this association in Orissa had nothing to do with oil pressing in Orissa or elsewhere (Bose 1960: 79).

It is true that 'to adopt a value is to introduce hierarchy . . .' (Dumont 1970b : 54), but it should also be noted that hierarchy is a consequence of adopting a value, and can therefore on occasions be shamefaced without disowning the symbols of separation. The Dhanuks, the Kurmis, and the Avadhis independently and internally position each other differently on a hierarchical scale, and yet they came together, in 1932, from Oudh to Bihar to form the Kurmi Association. Likewise in the peasant movement in Oudh (1919-22) where peasants from various caste groups came together, caste separation was strictly maintained without any overt antagonism or signification of inequality among them. The Ahirs fed the Ahirs, the Kurmis fed the Kurmis, the Pasis fed the Pasis, and yet they all united as equals on the political front, and that too, in the later stages of the movement under the leadership of the low caste Madari Pasi (Siddiqi 1978: 117).

Though hierarchy is consequent to separation, the former can, as we have seen, on occasions be suspended. Castes widely separated by orthodox hierarchization can unite irrespective of the vaunted principle of encompassment. While hierarchy becomes shamefaced and introverted on these occasions, the discrete character of castes is still upheld. The Telis of Orissa upheld sub-caste endogamy, and thus separation, while welcoming all Teli sub-castes as equals (Bose 1960: 11). As John Harriss observed in Tamil Nadu, the village people interpreted the notion of equality as meaning 'the removal of hierarchical distinctions' and did not find the principle of egalitarianism incompatible with the persistence of a strong caste identity so long as separation remained important (Harriss 1980: 58). Hierarchical notions in such cases become introverted and are forced to be shamefaced. Equally, as we illustrated with the Belchi and Bishrampur incident, when two caste groups are politically opposed, then hierarchy becomes strident. The opposed groups see each other as inferior, irrespective of the classical hierarchy. That each group itself is composed of discrete *jatis* widely separated further violates the orthodox hierarchy. Finally, in keeping with our contention that castes are, first and foremost, discrete entities, any unity between *jatis* is time bound and specific. These same *jatis* may on another occasion find themselves in opposition.

Caste, Class, and Social Class

In an earlier paper we had disputed the notion that caste is at the level of relations of production as Godelier and some other recent scholars on India have argued (Gupta 1981) and will not repeat those arguments here again. There is however only one clarification that needs to be added and which is possible for us to make at this stage.

In our understanding class in Marxism refers to the essentially antagonistic classes like the bourgeoisie and the proletariat in the capitalist mode of production. To understand and appreciate the analytical uses of the mode of production and the two classes in opposition is not to claim that the mode of production is all, and that it also informs us of the division of labour in society. Or, to be more specific, the mode of production does not immediately tell us of the exact positioning, distribution and proliferation of social classes in a given society. The caste system on the other hand, in its idealized form refers to the division of labour in society and is thus far from resembling the fundamental classes in Marxism. Moreover in Marxism the mode of production is an unconscious structure which constrains without prejudice different social classes. The caste ideology is not only a believed in and conscious structure, but there are almost as many believed in ideologies as there are castes in India. Significantly also a change of occupation does not automatically entail a change of caste. The proud landowning Brahmans remain Brahmans, nor do the traditional agrarian castes like the Dhanuks and Dusadhs cease to become so when they change their occupation. The Jatavs remained as Jatavs though they moved upwards economically. The Mahars remained Mahars even after many of them refused to do their traditional occupation. This, more than anything else, is the difference between caste and social class. When a worker becomes an accountant he leaves his former social class and becomes a member of another social class.

Flowing from this we may come to another conclusion. As castes and occupations do not coincide, so quite naturally there is no identity between the secular states of social classes and the caste identity of members who occupy these social classes. Blunt (1969: 251-2), Ghanshyam Shah (1982: 139), I.P. Desai (1976: 162-3), and Bose (1975: 192-3, 198), among many others, give ample documentation of this phenomenon which is widespread among all castes. In this situation to believe that caste ideology can be activated for economic or class war is fallacious. Caste ideology essentially separates castes, and consequently also separates social classes over and above the fundamental classes of Marxism. If caste divisions unambigously overlap with social class distinctions then some benefit might accrue in using the caste ideology. But if caste ideologies separate castes then the reliance on caste ideology, even the traditionally lower caste ones, will give only limited gains and will be counter-productive in the long run. All castes, high and low, secrete, propound and consolidate ideologies which separate them from their fellow beings in other castes. It is nearly embarrassing to mention such an obvious truth but it has become necessary in the face of the many confusions that persist among scholars in this field.

Defining Caste

Looking back at all that we have been through in this paper, we may, at this stage, attempt a definition of caste. History has liquidated many characteristics of the caste system and has offered us, without any conscious phenomenological effort, 'an imaginative variation of facts'. Hereditary occupational specialization is no longer active, the principles of purity and pollution do not invariably intervene to hierarchize, the notion of the encompassing and the encompassed can no longer summon the liege men. Only the principle of endogamy remains to ensure biological separation between different *jatis*. But as the biological separation can fall on no significant biological characteristics, *jatis* are forced to hypersymbolize their discrete character through a multiplicity of rituals.

The caste system is a form of differentiation. It cannot be subsumed under a system of *fundamentum divisionis*. For this reason caste cannot be seen as an extreme form of class, race or estates; and here Dumont is correct. And yet it is not within us to come up with an analytical definition of caste; the best we can do is to offer a definition that is traditionally known as a *definition per genus et differentiam*.

We will define the caste system as a form of differentiation wherein the constituent units of the system justify endogamy on the basis of putative biological differences which are semaphored by the ritualization of multiple social practices. The above definition according to us gives the essence of the caste system.

The phrase, 'ritualization of multiple social practices', however, needs further explication. By rituals we mean all those social practices that are followed because they are supposed to be inherently good irrespective of Weber's 'means-ends' rationality. For instance, to follow an occupation, and pursue it in a certain mode, regardless of means-ends rationality would also be considered by us to be a form of ritual activity. It is for this reason that we have not considered hereditary occupations *per se* to be an essential aspect of the caste system for it would have led to some misunderstanding. In any case, hereditary occupational specialization is not universal within the caste system, as has been argued earlier, nor is it a peculiarity of the caste system alone.

The caste system also exhibits two further characteristics which cannot be seen as its essence but may be understood as its *properties*. The two properties of the caste system are *hierarchy* and *hypersymbolism*.

(a) *Hierarchy*: The discrete character of *jatis* is maintained by the enhanced valuation that members of a *jati* place on their own customs, ritualized practices, and geneological heritage. This should, and does, imply a value loaded scale which places different *jatis* at different positions in the hierarchy. But .this hierarchical placement by virtue of being value loaded is extremely idiosyncratic, and different hierarchies exist at the subjective level. There are perhaps, as we have said earlier, as many hierarchies as there are *jatis*. But very often in practice we find one hierarchical order more in effect. This particular hierarchical order in effect is, however, not the essence of the caste system, nor the inevitable consequence of it, but an expression of political or politico-economic power. Logically, an alternative hierarchy can also effectively come into practice with a change in the political and economic strength of certain castes—a reshuffling, that is, of *jatis* on the secular plane.

(b) *Hypersymbolism*: Our definition tells us that the discrete character of *jatis* is maintained through a multiplicity of ritualized practices. These rituals are not to be lightly taken as they indicate to us the substantive and emotive content of *jatis*. The number of rituals and beliefs, and the plethora of diacritical marks that particularize individual *jatis*, do not follow any single rule. Neither are they restricted to the number necessary to differentiate one *jati* from another. Many of these rituals and beliefs are historical accretions and effects of past associations and contingent conditions. Members of a *jati* do not only value what separates them from other *jatis*. They also value those symbols and beliefs that are fairly widespread and held in common by a number of castes, leading to what we have called *hypersymbolism*.

The multiplicity of rituals in the caste system does not convey fresh information with every instance. Hypersymbolism and the consequent redundancy of rituals, on the other hand, heighten values characteristic of the caste system to invoke a passionate sense of belonging to one's caste. Contemporary semiology can legitimately stake its claim to clarify this domain. According to the semiologist Pierre Guirand:

The greater the redundancy, the more the communication is significant, closed, socialized and codified; the lower the redundancy, the greater the information and the more open, individualized and decodified the communication (Guirand 1975: 13).

Where would we place the question of purity and pollution? As we had recorded earlier (Gupta 1981), historical evidence tells us that untouchability is a later addition in the history of the Indian caste system. Till about the second century AD, certain castes, like the Ayogava, Paulkasas, and the Nishadas, were despised, but were not considered to be Untouchables. Untouchability is, therefore, an historical cohort of the caste system, but not its essence. The notion of purity and pollution, as Dumont correctly observed, is integrally linked with the institution of untouchability. But like untouchability, the notion of purity and pollution is also an historical accretion. Over time this notion freed itself from its specific and original task of separating Untouchables from the others and began to be operative at different planes of the caste system, thus providing additional gusto to the property of hypersymbolism. But it is in keeping with its character of being an historical accretion that the notion of purity and pollution does not subsume hypersymbolism: for, as we have been at considerable pains to point out earlier, purity and pollution are not universally employed to effect the diacritical marks separating different *jatis*.

Conclusion

Of the many scholars working on the caste system only one, as far as we are aware, consciously disputed Dumont's unilateral hierarchical principle. Veena Das in her insightful work, *Structure and Cognition* (1982), for the first time took serious note of Dumont's understanding of hierarchy and provided substantial theoretical and ethno-historical criticisms of it (ibid: 67-9). This is not the place to give a full account of Das's work. However, we would like to take this opportunity to express our disagreement with her when she attempts to conceptualize *jatis* on the basis of the relations between three separate poles, viz. the Brahman, the King, and the Sanyasi (ibid: 68). According to us each *jati* attains its distinctions on a variety of axes and the condensation principle whereby the manifold are encapsulated in one category is, for this reason, comprehensively and perpetually active. This, according to us, is the essence of *jati* distinctions. To give some examples as to why, neither singly nor collectively, the three poles mentioned by Das are sufficient to understand the discrete character of castes let us quickly look at the following two cases. The Bhats—a pseudo Brahman caste—in addition to worshipping Mahavir, also worship Bare Bir, a deified ancestor and Birtiya who is considered by them to be the protector of cattle (Blunt 1969: 285), and is obviously a non-Vedic deity. The Kanhpuriaya Rajputs worship such deities like the Mahisa Rakshasa or Bhainsaura, the buffalo demon. The Dais clan among these Rajputs worship Mathote, a tribal goddess (ibid). Probably, the three poles sufficed for Das as she was dealing only in the context of the Brahmans of a particular region on the basis of a single text, the Dharamaranya Purana. This difference between Das and ourselves could also arise because we believe that the content she gives to structural categories in her analysis of Dharamaranya Purana are exhausted within that context, and cannot be extrapolated outside it. The categories of structuralism are not empirical though the contents of these categories are, and therefore the latter are limited to that empirical context alone.

But apart from our partial, even minor, disagreement, considering our present preoccupation, we are in full agreement with her when she says that 'the difference in *jatis* is not seen as one of degree but of quality' (Das 1982: 69). From her case material Das is also able to show that fissions in *jatis* take place not only because a particular section of the *jati* has performed an impure act, but because of a disagreement over a particular issue which is more often than not political in character. But her more interesting comment is that even after the cause for the disagreement has been removed or forgotten, they are (recall the condensation principle) 'translated into separate diacritical marks of each group' (Das 1982: 7).

In insisting upon the diverse characteristic between continuous hierarchies and discrete classes a *propos* of the caste system we believe we have been able to accommodate facts without evasions and embarrasment. It is no longer necessary to surreptitiously bring in politics and economics as Dumont does as neither politics nor economics militate against the existence of a system composed of discrete categories. For if one were to conceptualize *jatis* as discrete entities, and see their difference as one of quality rather than degree, then this would account for the facility with which castes who occupy a very low position in the *varna* hierarchy, like the Shudras, find it possible to subsume political power ... (ibid: 89).

Neither do *jatis* as discrete categories exist in isolation. A *jati* is able to sustain itself only in the presence of other *jatis* in a clearly delimited referential context which give meaning to symbols, and indeed to hypersymbolism as well. A discrete caste lives in a world of discrete castes, and cannot exist where *only* social classes thrive. Castes do not form a system because they submit to the 'whole'—the true hierarchy (Dumont 1972-8)—but because they separate themselves only with reference to each other.

The relative freedom that each *jati* intrinsically possesses as discrete entities, allows its members to independently add, alter, or even drop rituals and beliefs if it helps them in their secular and economic spheres. This is not only logically possible, but has also been recorded by several studies, some of which were used in the preceding pages. The fact that even those who participate in the caste system are capable of reflection and action and not merely reflexive action is something that not many of us are quite used to, in spite of the growing evidence from many empirical studies by fellow anthropologists. Clearly a fresh conceptual effort is long overdue if one is to appreciate the vivacity and dynamism of castes in India.

Further Readings

Bose, N. K.,
1975   *The Structure of Hindu Society* , (translated with an introduction
by André Béteille), Orient Longman, Delhi.

An overall view of Hindu society from a dedicated field
worker whose thesis on the enveloping dynamic of the caste
system resulting in the absorption of tribals into the Hindu fold
is widely known and respected.

Klass, M.,
1980   *Caste: The Emergence of the South Asian Social System*,
Institute for the Study of Human Affairs, Philadelphia.

The most engaging part of this book is the author's critique
of the known contributions on the origin of the caste system
which includes a frontal attack on the popular views regarding
the 'Aryans'.

Kosambi, D. D.,
1988   *The Culture and Civilization of Ancient India in Historical Outline*,
Vikas, New Delhi.

This book draws deeply from archaeology and history to provide a profound Marxist alternative to idealist and culturological conceptions of Indian society and the caste system.

Leach, E. R., ed.,
1960   *Aspects of Caste in South India, Ceylon and Northwest Pakistan*,
Cambridge University Press, Cambridge.

An influential book which through case studies from India, Sri
Lanka and Pakistan focusses on the question of whether or not the
caste system is a peculiarly pan-Indian civilization phenomenon.

de Reuck, Anthony and Julie Knight, eds.,
1968   *Caste and Race: Comparative Approaches*, J. A. Churchill Ltd,
London.

This volume is very convenient as it contains precise position
papers from some of the best known authorities on the caste
system with whose help the reader can distinguish castes
from, and relate them to, other forms of social stratification.

II

Caste Profiles

This section hopes to give us an idea of the 'typical' caste situation as well as the not so typical ones. André Béteille's landmark monograph entitled *Caste, Class and Power* brought to light the traditional caste structure as well as the forces of change that were making their way into it. The excerpt from his book that is included here under the title 'Caste in a South Indian Village' however deals more with the synchronous dimension.

The other caste profiles included in this section are the so-called 'non-typical' cases. The fact that they are so understood is because in our general appreciation of the caste system we usually conjure the stereotypes of Brahmins, Warrior and the Untouchables. But in fact the caste system is abundantly unfaithful to this scheme. Thus if one is to think analytically on the caste system, then the so-called non-typical cases should be figured in the centre and the category 'non-typical' itself should perhaps be dissolved.

The caste profiles includ..d here hope to serve such a purpose. Joyce Pettigrew's essay on the Jats tells us of how valour, strength and agricultural prowess are all important hierarchical attributes of the Jats of Punjab. This is a far cry from the notion of purity associated with the Brahmanical view where priestly occupations are ranked highest. A Jat peasant is proud of being a Jat and considers a Brahmin to be an inferior, pot-bellied, lily-livered specimen of mankind.

S. N. Mukherjee draws our attention to the scenario in Bengal where education and attributional elements (as in Marriott) are essential for the attainment of *bhadralok* status. To be a part of the genteel folk (*bhadra* and *lok*) it is not enough to be a Brahmin, indeed many poor illiterate Brahmins may not be considered to be *bhadraloks* at all. Such valuations and hierarchies again go contrary to popular assumptions about the caste system.

The Untouchables too, as Khare points out, do not accept the Brahminical version of the world but have their own version of what makes an ideal ascetic. A study of the four square opposition to the Brahmanical version as provided by Khare is pregnant with analytical potentialities, many of which Khare himself is sensitive to. Interestingly, from this essay we learn, that not only do the Untouchables dispute their lowly status but that they also aspire to the status of a teacher/ascetic/sage. Such a status syndrome is usually reserved in popular conception for the Brahmins alone.

Imtiaz Ahmed and C. J. Fuller take us out of the Hindu fold into the Muslim and Christian domains respectively. The significance of their essays which have been excerpted here at length cannot be over-emphasized. The clear impact that the Indian caste system has had on stratification within the Christian and Muslim communities of India corrects the usual notion that castes are and can be manifested only among Hindus.

The diversities presented here invite analytical exercises of the kind mentioned in the earlier section. It is only when we are able to integrate these diversities can we hope to provide a rounded theoretical perspective of the caste system. We are able to bracket away for the time being the interactional nexus and get the attributional element of castes in greater depth. This in turn corrects some of our uncritical assumptions regarding the interactional dimension. One dominant assumption which needs correction is the belief that world views of different castes neatly dovetail into one another. But the Jats, the Brahmins, the Untouchables, and the *bhadraloks* all constitute their self-identity discretely and sometimes in contradiction to other identities.

A study of caste profiles also leads us to an examination of the principle of hierarchy and to ponder afresh whether it is advisable to keep alive, as Bouglé did, both hierarchy and repulsion. Of course, such caste profiles are strongly commendable as descriptive ethnographies, but as this brief introduction demonstrates, they raise lively theoretical issues as well.

Caste in a South Indian Village

ANDRÉ BETEILLE

I

In village Sripuram in the Tanjore district of South India the division of the community into a number of castes constitutes one of the most fundamental features of its social structure. In Hindu society, caste divisions play a part both in actual social interactions and in *the ideal* scheme of values. Members of different castes are, up to a point, expected to behave differently and to have different values and ideals. These differences are sanctioned by Hindu religion.

. . . .

II

Tamil society is characterized by a three-fold division into Brahmins, Non-Brahmins and Adi-Dravidas (or Untouchables). The importance of this division is reflected in the settlement pattern of the village in which each group of castes has its exclusive area of residence. The Brahmins live in brick and tile houses on a separate street known as the *agraharam*; the Adi-Dravidas live in thatched huts in their own hamlets which are called *cheris*; the Non-Brahmins' houses, which are of mixed type, are located in between.

The territorial division of the village are clear and social values are attached to them. The *agraharam*, for instance, is not only a cluster of habitations, but also the centre of social life for the Brahmins. During marriages, and on the occasion of temple festivals arranged by the Brahmins the customary processions go only through the *agraharam*, although it is generally said that such processions go around the village. To the Brahmins the *agraharam*, in more ways than one, is the village.

Adapted from André Béteille, *Caste, Class and Power: Changing Patterns of Stratification in a Tanjore Village*, Oxford University Press, Delhi, 1966.

The *cheri*, similarly, is not just another quarter of the village; it is a place which no Brahmin should enter. The concept of pollution attaches not only to groups and individuals, but also to places. The same is true of the concept of purity. The temple precincts are generally regarded as sacred. But not all of them have equal sanctity for every group in the village. Thus, for the Shri Vaishnava Brahmins, the venue of ceremonial gatherings during marriage or initiation is the Vishnu temple and not the Shiva temple, into which many of them will not even enter.

Brahmins, Non-Brahmins and Adi-Dravidas not only live in different parts of the village, but also in some measure regard themselves as having separate identities. Historically they have occupied different positions in the economic structure of the village, with Brahmins as landowners, Non-Brahmins mainly as tenants and Adi-Dravidas as agricultural labourers. These differences continue to exist, although a certain amount of levelling down has taken place in the last three decades. Politically there is some identification between these sections and the ideologies of certain parties. The three sections occupy different positions in the ritual hierarchy, the Brahmins at the top and the Adi-Dravidas at the bottom; the former are regarded as ritually the purest while the latter are considered as being in a permanent state of pollution.

In some ways the most striking difference between Brahmins on the one hand, and Non-Brahmins and Adi-Dravidas on the other, is in their physical appearance. The difference is summed up in various popular sayings, one of which runs as follows: ' *Parppan karuppum paralyan sehappum ahadu* ' (Dark Brahmins and light Paraiyas are not proper). In the popular image the Brahmin is regarded not only as fair, but sharp-nosed, and as possessing, in general, more refined features. Although some Non-Brahmins also have features of this kind, they are rare among the cultivating and artisan castes who constitute the bulk of Non-Brahmins in Sripuram. Among Adi-Dravidas fair skin-colour is so conspicious by its absence that normally a Brahmin would not be mistaken for a Palla or a Paraiya.

These differences are of significance because fair skin-colour and features of a certain type have a high social value not only in Sripuram, but in Tamil society in general, as indeed in the whole of India. The Brahmins are extremely conscious of their fair appearance and often contrast it with the 'black' skin-colour of the Kallas, or the Adi-Dravidas. A dark-skinned Brahmin girl is often a burden to the family because it is difficult to get a husband for her.

Traditionally, fair skin-colour has been associated with the 'Aryans' from whom the Brahmins claim descent and with whom they are now identified by leaders of certain separatist political parties. The *gotra* system, which is an essential feature of Brahmin social structure, links each one of them by putative ties of descent to one or another sage after whom the *gotra* is named. (The *gotra* is an exogamous division whose members are believed, particularly among the Brahmins, to be agnatically descended from a saint or a seer.) It is commonly believed that the Brahmins of an earlier generation, like the sages who were their forebears, were often endowed with *brahmatèjas*, a quality which gave to their appearance a peculiar glow and serenity. This is frequently constrasted with the coarse and undistinguished features of the Non-Brahmins.

It seems probable that a particular upbringing and style of life leaves some impress on the appearance of people. A college-educated and urbanized Kalla, following a sedentary occupation such as the practice of law, has a different bearing and appears different from the generality of Kallas who are peasants and cultivators. He looks more 'refined' and 'cultivated'. And refinement of a particular kind, both in appearance and behaviour, has a high social value among Brahmins.

No doubt the popular belief that the Brahmins consitute a separate race is fallacious and will not bear examination from the anthropological point of view. But social movements and political ideologies are often based not on technically correct, but on popular conceptions, and to that extent the latter are real and require to be understood. The real physical differences of the Brahmins, and the popular belief that they constitute a separate race, have led to their being isolated socially and politically to a much greater extent in Tamil Nadu and South India as a whole than in the north.

There are also typical differences in physical appearance between Non-Brahmins and Adi-Dravidas, as, indeed, there are between the different Non-Brahmin castes. On the whole the Pallas and Paraiyas appear to be darker, shorter and more broad-nosed than the Non-Brahmins, who, it must be remembered, constitute a very heterogeneous category both physically and culturally. These differences do not, however, have the same social significance as in the case of the Brahmins, for they have not generally been posed in racial terms or made the basis of any political ideology.

Dress also is in some ways distinctive of caste in the broader sense of the term. Among Brahmins, men are required by tradition to wear the eight-cubit piece of cloth or *veshti* after initiation. The traditional style of wearing the *veshti* by having the ends tucked at five places (*panchakachcham*) carries a ritual sanction among all Tamil Brahmins.

Non-Brahmins or Adi-Dravidas, at least at Sripuram, do not wear the *veshti* in this way.

The Brahmins are rapidly giving up their traditional mode of dress. They now wear the four-cubit *veshti* by simply wrapping it around the waist, or they wear the eight-cubit *veshti* in this way without any *kachcham*. On ritual occasions such as marriage and *upanayanam* (initiation), however, they are required to wear the *veshti* in the traditional style. Temple priests also, at least while they are officiating, are required to wear the *panchakachcham*, as are priests who officiate at domestic ceremonies. In Sripuram there are about a dozen men, mostly past the age of fifty years, who normally dress in the traditional Brahminical style.

Differences between castes are carried further in the matter of women's dress. The principal garment used by all is a long piece of unsewn cloth known as the *podaval*, but there are important differences in the length of the cloth and in the manner in which it is worn. Among orthodox married Tamil Brahmin women the *podavai* is eighteen cubits in length and is worn with the *kachcham*, the ends being tucked in various ways. Non-Brahmin women do not usually have the *kachcham*, and among them the length varies between ten and twelve cubits, the garment generally reaching down to the ankles as with the Brahmins. Among the generality of Adi-Dravida women the *podaval* is considerably smaller in size and reaches just below the knee, leaving the legs uncovered.

Among Brahmin women especially, wearing the *podavai* in a specific way symbolizes a particular culture or style of life. Minor distinctions of dress have been preserved with care and kept alive for generations, although, even in this, recent trends have been favouring a levelling down of differences. Tamil, Telugu, and Kannada-speaking Brahmin women have each their distinctive style of dress, and all these differences are in evidence even in a small village like Sripuram. Among Tamil Brahmins, again, a Shri Vaishnava (or Iyengar) woman will never wear her dress in the Smartha (or Iyer) style, nor will a Smartha woman adopt the Shri Vaishnava mode.

Today, however, there is a trend towards greater standardization of dress among women. Styles which were distinctive of particular castes are ceasing to be so, or are disappearing entirely. Married Brahmin women are slowly giving up their traditional mode of dress and beginning to take to the twelve-cubit *podavai* worn without a *kachcham*, as is common among Non-Brahmin women. It is true that in Sripuram such women constitute a small minority, but it is a minority which is increasing. The new style of dress blurs distinctions not only between Smarthas and Shri Vaishnavas, but also between Brahmins and Non-Brahmins. Yet even when married Brahmin women take to wearing the shorter, twelve-cubit garment, on ritual occasions they dress in the manner traditional to their caste. The more elaborate dress is called *madisaru* ('pure garment').

Among Adi-Dravida women, there seems to be a movement upwards, towards wearing longer garments like those worn by the Non-Brahmins. This is particularly true of the younger generation of Palla women in Sripuram. The older women continue to wear the shorter piece of cloth, especially while they work in the fields. The younger Adi-Dravida women have also started wearing blouses, whereas a generation ago the universal practice seems to have been to wear no separate upper garment. Thus in dress, and hence to some extent in outward appearance, differences between Non-Brahmin and Adi-Dravida women are tending to become smaller.

Whereas among Brahmin women the style of dress proclaims whether one is a Smartha or a Shri Vaishnava, the same purpose is served among men by the caste mark. Smartha men apply the *vibhuti*, which consists of three horizontal stripes made with consecrated ash, across the forehead and sometimes on other parts of the body as well. The *vibhuti* is an emblem of Shiva and its application has ritual significance. Similar ritual significance attaches among Shri Vaishnavas to the *namam*, which consists of a red (sometimes yellow) vertical stripe at the centre of the forehead, encased in a white U-shaped mark among the Vadagalai section and a Y-shaped mark among the Thengalai.

Although up to a point each subcaste, or caste, or group of castes maintains its distinctive identity, forces have been operating towards an ironing out of differences in dress and general appearance. In a large city like Madras it may be difficult to distinguish between a Brahmin and a Non-Brahmin, particularly if both are engaged in the same kind of occupation. But in a village such as Sripuram, in spite of the forces of secularization and the general influence of mass-produced consumer goods, broad distinctions are still maintained.

III

It would perhaps be an exaggeration to say that Brahmins, on the one hand, and Non-Brahmins and Adi-Dravidas, on the other, represent two cultures. None the less one cannot but be impressed by the differences between them while examining their speech and language. In Tanjore

District, particularly, Sanskrit has been a major influence on the Brahmins, both by way of enriching their thought and learning and by giving to their speech a particular character. It is well known that throughout Tamilnad Sanskritic scholarship has been a near monopoly of the Brahmins, while Non-Brahmins have specialized in Tamil studies.

The Brahmins of Sripuram are heirs to a long tradition of Sanskritic learning, whereas among the Non-Brahmins no such tradition has existed. Among the Adi-Dravidas literacy itself is a new phenomenon and is as yet confined to only a few persons. Some of the Vellalas, at least, have been familiar for generations with the devotional literature in Tamil, and perhaps it is no accident that the only professional Tamil *pundit* or teacher in Sripuram is a Vellala. It should, of course, be pointed out that virtually all adult Brahmins are literate in Tamil, which is, in fact, the language of their speech. The important point, however, is that even today they seem to attach greater value to Sanskrit, although only a few of them have more than a smattering of it.

The Brahmins are alive to the fact that the flow of events renders it increasingly difficult to transmit through the family their tradition of Sanskritic learning, and that ultimately it may become extinct. They require their sons and daughters to take up the study of Sanskrit in school, although it may be an optional subject. One of their principal grievances against the present educational system is that Sanskrit does not occupy within it the position of eminence which, according to them, it should.

A few years ago an informal school was started in the *agraharam* with a view to imparting some elementary knowledge of Sanskrit to the children and thereby keeping alive an ancient heritage. The school sits in the evening for about an hour on the veranda of one of the Brahmin residents who is a teacher in the Sanskrit College at Thiruvaiyar. He runs the school himself and charges only a nominal fee for the maintenance of petromax lanterns. The school is generally known as the *sahashranamam* class, but in addition to the *sahashranamam* (thousand names) of Vishnu, Lakshmi and so on, other *slokas* or verses in Sanskrit are taught. Both boys and girls between the ages of four and fourteen years attend the school, but it is open only to the Brahmin children of the *agraharam*.

Brahmins themselves regard their familiarity with Sanskrit as a sign of refinement, and a very high social value is attached to it. It sometimes enables them to engage in subtle arguments about abstract matters, since Sanskrit has a rich philosophical idiom. Moreover, the language of ritual among the Brahmins is almost entirely Sanskrit. This ritual is extremely elaborate in nature, even if one ignores entirely the complex temple rites and takes into account only those rites which the individual Brahmin is required to perform daily, monthly, annually and at various points of his life cycle.

There are minor distinctions of speech among Brahmins which the outsider, not familiar with the niceties of caste specialization, is likely to miss. Thus, the Iyers normally say *rasam* for pepper-water, whereas Iyengars have a special word, *sattumadu*. The Iyengars address the father's younger brother as *chittiya*, whereas among the Iyers he is called *chittappa*. The ceremony cf washing the idol is known among Iyers as *abhishekham*, and among Iyengars as *thirumanjnam*. These distinction, however slight they may appear, have been kept alive for generations, particularly in vocabularies of kinship and ritual. Today there seems to be a tendency for words to be interchanged a little more freely and easily.

The Tamil which is spoken by the Non-Brahmin peasants of Sripuram is different both in vocabularly and accent from the speech of the Brahmins. This difference is much wider than the difference between Smarthas and Shri Vaishnavas. Adi-Dravidas in their turn have their own forms of intonation, and it is not difficult even for a Brahmin to distinguish an Adi-Dravida from a Non-Brahmin by his speech. As more and more Adi-Dravida children go to school and come into contact with both Non-Brahmin and Brahmin boys and girls, difference in speech tend to be levelled out, at least to some extent.

As against the comparatively simple and unsophisticated Tamil used by the Non-Brahmin peasantry, there is the trend towards a revival of Tamil in its pure or classical form. This trend has been associated with the Non-Brahmin movement, and today it is kept alive by the DMK, the Tamil Arasu Kazhagam, the Nam Tamizhar, and other parties and associations. Tamil of this variety is consciously de-Sanskritized, and it is often abstruse and difficult to comprehend. It has been given vitality through the speeches of the many eloquent DMK leaders, and also in part through the films. The impact of this style on the Non-Brahmins of Sripuram has not been very significant, although the majority of them have been exposed to the influence of DMK speeches as well as Tamil films.

The differential importance of the two languages, Sanskrit and Tamil, with regard to the styles of living of the Brahmins and Non-Brahmins, can be seen in the choice of personal names. Brahmins almost always have Sanskritic personal names. In a sense this is inevitable because names of men and women are chosen from among names of deities, and the major deities of the Brahmins, particularly the Shri Vaishnavas, are all Sanskritic. Non-Brahmins take their names from Tamil saints, local deities and local heroes, as well as from certain popular Sanskritic deities. Among Brahmins, Shri Vaishnavas are more exclusive in their choice of personal names than Smarthas.

IV

Many of the important differences between Brahmins, on the one hand, and Non-Brahmins and Adi-Dravidas, on the other, are expressed in the sphere of rituals. Up to a point rituals can be regarded as standardized ways of expressing distinctive aspects of the style of life of a group or a category. Rituals serve to express in dramatic form not only the unity within a group, but also the cleavages between different sections of it. High points in the style of life of a particular community are often kept alive through ritual sanctions. Normally one group does not discard its particular rituals in favour of those of another unless it considers the style of life of the latter to be in some ways superior to its own.

The common meal has an extremely important social and ritual significance in Hinduism. When a large number of people gather together for a meal, ritual undertones are invariably associated with it. The common meal expresses symbolically both the unity of those who eat together and the cleavages between those who are required to eat separately. Ritual separation, having been elaborated to a high degree in Hindu society, serves to maintain the cleavages within the caste system. Generally two castes will not interdine unless the structural distance between them is small. Some castes are more exclusive in their commensal restrictions than others.

Broadly speaking, the higher the status of a caste, the more rigid it is in the matter of accepting food from the others. Thus, Brahmins do not accept cooked food from Non-Brahmins or Adi-Dravidas, although the latter accept it from them. This principle, however, is by no means a universal measure for the assessment of caste rank. Thus, orthodox Shri Vaishnavas do not accept food from Smarthas, or even sit for meals along with them, but the Smarthas are far less rigid in the matter of accepting food from the Shri Vaishnavas; yet it must not be inferred from this that Smartha Brahmins are lower in rank.

An examination of the manner in which the rules of commensality operate among the Brahmins of Sripuram will help us to gain some understanding of the nature of structural distance between different segments in the caste system. Since similar principles are operative in the case of Non-Brahmins and Adi-Dravidas, their part in the two latter cases will be indicated only briefly.

The Iyengars, who constitute the majority of Brahmins in Sripuram, are admitted to be the most exclusive in the matter of commensality. When a feast takes place in the *agraharam* on account of birth, marriage, death or some other occasion for ceremony, normally only Brahmins are invited to the meal. A few Non-Brahmins may be called, particularly if they are related to the family as servants or tenants, but they are given food separately in the backyard after the Brahmin guests have been served. Otherwise, particularly during marriage, a few influential Non-Brahmins may come to see the girl, and they are given betel leaves, areca nuts, bananas and coconuts, but not food in the proper sense of the term which includes cooked rice in one form or the other. Generally speaking, a Brahmin wedding at Sripuram, and the attendant feast, is a Brahmin affair; Non-Brahmins have very little to do with it, and still less Adi-Dravidas.

Brahmins do not dine at Non-Brahmin weddings. Generally they do not even attend, although the wedding may be taking place in the next street. If they go, they are given betel leaves, areca nuts and fruits—things which are not regarded as having any element of pollution attached to them. Orthodox Brahmins, particularly among Shri Vaishnavas, do not accept cooked food of any kind, including coffee, from Non-Brahmins. Some of the more 'progressive' and younger Brahmins, however, accept coffee and snacks when they visit their Non-Brahmin friends at Tanjore and elsewhere. For one thing, such Non-Brahmins, being town bred, are closer to them in their style of living than the peasants of Sripuram, and for another, social restrictions are more stringently observed in one's own village than outside.

When an important ceremony such as marriage takes place in the *agraharam*, it is obligatory on the part of the host to invite every family in the *agraharam* to the feast which forms a part of the occasion. Today, most of the Brahmins sit together and generally no distinction is made in the matter of serving. A generation or so ago, however, at wedding and other feasts Smarthas and Shri Vaishnavas sat in separate rows, although they were served at the same time. The fact that Smarthas and Shri Vaishnavas of the younger generation freely interdine is another indication of the lessening of structural distance between the two communities to which reference was made earlier.

In examining the rules of commensality we find that the whole of society is broken up into segments, each segment forming a unit within which commensality is more or less freely allowed. In the broadest sense, the Brahmins together constitute such a segment, since commensality is by and large confined within it so far as the individual member is concerned. The broad Brahmin category is further segmented into Smarthas and Shri Vaishnavas, and for the orthodox, and for a considerable number of people in the older generation, the bonds of commensality often stop short at the boundary of each of these subdivisions. The Smarthas are further segmented into Vadama, Brihacharanam and so on, but segmentation at this level does not seem, at least in the recent past, to have been associated with commensal restriction.

Commensal restrictions go hand in hand with a certain specialization of food habits which has been carried to a high degree by the Brahmins. Shri Vaishnavas, for instance, make use of silver utensils to a much greater extent than the others. In the Hindu scheme of values silver is considered to be, relatively speaking, 'pollution proof'; in other words, the pollution attached to a utensil by another person eating or drinking out of it can be more easily removed if it is made of silver rather than bell metal, aluminium or stainless steel. Orthodox Shri Vaishnavas offer water to their Smartha guests in silver tumblers and food in silver plates. Smarthas are generally less particular about the rigidities of pollution.

In the kind of food eaten also there is a good deal of variation. All Tamil Brahmins are vegetarians, and the eating of meat, fish or eggs is considered polluting. The Adi-Dravidas eat meat of various kinds and also fish and eggs. Non-Brahmins show a wide range of variation. Most of them in Sripuram eat meat of certain kinds, although not regularly. A few of the Shaivite Vellalas do not eat meat at all, and some avoid eating it on particular days. The eating of meat or otherwise among the Vellalas of Sripuram cannot be exactly identified with caste since it is largely a matter of personal choice, although there are some Vellalas who refrain from eating meat as a group.

Differences in food habits, which are so clear between the broad Brahmin, Non-Brahmin and Adi-Dravida divisions, are also perceptible, although on a reduced scale, between the smaller subdivisions. Thus, among Adi-Dravidas, the Paraiyas eat beef, or did so until recently, whereas the Pallas refrain from beef, but eat pork. In Sripuram the Pallas not only do not interdine with the Paraiyas, but do not take water from the Paraiyas' wells or allow the Paraiyas to use theirs; this seems to be the general practice in the area as a whole.

The avoidance of meat by Brahmins, of pork by Vellalas, and of beef by Pallas has ritual sanctions. Sometimes, however, food habits are specialized along caste lines without any apparent ritual basis. Vegetarian food among Non-Brahmins has a different taste from that of the

Brahmins, being generally more heavily spiced and hotter. Coffee is the most popular beverage among Brahmins, but Non-Brahmins, both in their homes and in restaurants, show a preference for tea. This is only partly explained by the fact that tea is less expensive.

V

We have seen that differentiation in styles of living has been developed to a very high degree within the caste system. Not only are there differences separating Brahmins from Non-Brahmins, but differences among Brahmins separate Shri Vaishnavas from Smarthas and, among Shri Vaishnavas, Vadagalai from Thengalai. The entire social world of Sripuram is thus divided and subdivided so as to constitute a segmentary structure in which each segment is differentiated from the other in terms of a number of criteria, major and minor. Further, in this structure the segments are not all equally separated from each other, but some are closer together and others further apart. For instance, the distance between Vadagalai and Thengalai Iyengar is smaller than the distance between either of them and any Non-Brahmin segment.

In the agrarian economy of Sripuram the three categories—Brahmin, Non-Brahmin and Adi-Dravida—have occupied rather different positions traditionally and are continuing to do so, by and large, even now. Very broadly speaking, one can characterize the Brahmins as landowners, the Non-Brahmins as cultivating tenants and the Adi-Dravidas as agricultural labourers. This characterization highlights only the typical positions. It holds true particularly with regard to Brahmins and Adi-Dravidas. Among the Non-Brahmins it admits of numerous exceptions since there are both landowners and agricultural labourers among them, and also there are Non-Brahmins of artisan and servicing castes who do not directly engage in agriculture.

Not all Brahmins are landowners, nor are all landowners Brahmins. The typical Brahmin in Sripuram is, none the less, a *mirasdar*,[1] and it is he who sets the pattern for other to follows. In addition to landownership, Brahmins traditionally have engaged in various priestly functions, either as domestic priests or as temple priests. In Sripuram, however, the majority of Brahmins have been *mirasdars* devoted to the pursuit of learning and have not engaged in priesthood as a profession or a means of livelihood. There are today only three families in the *agraharam* which have priesthood as the principal source of livelihood.

---

[1] As an alternative I have thought of the term 'mirasdar Brahmin', which seems to be equally unsatisfactory. The general meaning of *mirasdar* is landowner or rentier.

Brahmins in general can be classified into three broad categories according to their calling and social position. The first category includes those who have been traditionally associated with the pursuit of learning and have lived on grants made by princes and patrons. These include the Smarthas proper and the Shri Vaishnavas. The term 'Vedic Brahmin' will be applied to this category, although the choice is not altogether a happy one. The second category is made up of those who act as domestic priests for the Non-Brahmins; they are known as Panchan. gakkarans. The Panchangakkaran Brahmins in this area are Telugu-speaking. It should be emphasized that the Vedic Brahmins (the Shri Vaishnavas and the Smarthas proper) do not act as domestic priests for Non-Brahmins—at least, not in this area. The third category comprises temple priests or Archakurs; it is made up of Kurukkals, or priests who officiate at Shiva temples, and Bhattacharas, or those who officiate at Vishnu temples. These three categories of Brahmins constitute three endogamous divisions, each with further subdivisions.

The Brahmin has by tradition and scriptural injunction a number of roles: pursuit of learning; acceptance of alms; ministration to the spiritual needs of the populace. Although these roles may be combined in a single person, this is not always the case. The image of the Brahmin in the popular mind is of a person who lives by ministering to the religious needs of people. This image, as we have seen, is rather divorced from the real position of the Brahmins in Sripuram. In this village today there is only one Brahmin who acts as a *purohit*. But he ministers only to the religious needs of the *agraharam*, and only to the majority of Shri Vaishnavas, not to all the members of the *agraharam*. The Smarthas as well as certain other Shri Vaishnavas have *purohits* from among their own subcaste living at Thiruvaiyar and Tanjore.

The Vedic Brahmins of Sripuram do not today live by scholarship, although many of them can trace their descent from persons who did so in the past and were endowed with property for the purpose. Once a Brahmin scholar acquired property, it was handed down from generation to generation and the descendants became *mirasdars* by inheritance of ancestral property. It was not strictly obligatory on their part to keep up the family tradition, although many of them did so in practice. Thus, at the beginning of this century the Brahmins of Sripuram included a number of Sanskrit scholars pursuing their family traditions, and most of them owned at least a few acres of land. In course of the last sixty years the movement of population in and out of the *agraharam*, and the sale of land of many Brahmins, have reduced the number of *mirasdars* among them and, to some extent, disturbed the occupational homogeneity of the *agraharam*.

Today many Brahmins in the *agraharam* have taken up what may be considered new occupations. There are several clerks and school teachers among them. But one can easily see that in the choice of new occupations they have retained a certain continuity with the past and have not departed significantly from it. By and large, the most important element in their style of living has been preserved in their new occupations. No Brahmin has taken to any manual work in the real sense of the term. There is one person who has taken a job as a mechanic in a transport undertaking, but this is a recent occurrence and is regarded as exceptional.

Non-Brahmins, on the other hand, engage in various kinds of manual work. In Sripuram there are no big Non-Brahmin landowners, although there are absentee landlords among the Non-Brahmins living at Thiruvaiyar and Tanjore. The principal cultivating caste among the Non-Brahmins are the Vellalas, Padayachis and Kallas. Most of them are directly engaged in cultivation in one form or another. There is no ritual rule which prohibits the use of the plough by them as in the case of Brahmins; in fact, using the plough is their traditional occupation. There are some fairly prosperous Vellala and Kalla landowners who do not themselves till the soil, but supervise the work of agriculture. This practice, however, is exceptional rather than general; the Non-Brahmin cultivator in Sripuram adopts it only when he has acquired a good bit of land, and generally after he has passed a certain age.

In addition to these moderately well-to-do Vellala owner-cultivators, there are a few others who have taken to non-manual occupations. These include the Tamil pundit referred to earlier, and a few shopkeepers and clerks. Up to now the adoption of these occupations has been exceptional among the Non-Brahmins of Sripuram, and it does not appear to have significantly affected their styles of living. There is only one Non-Brahmin family which is significantly different from the others in this regard. This is the Maratha family which owned at one time a good proportion of the land in Sripuram and whose members in their ways and habits are clearly *mirasdars* rather than peasants.

The Non-Brahmins of Sripuram also include artisan castes such as Potters and Carpenters, and servicing castes such as Barbers and Washermen. The artisan castes do not all perform their traditional occupation today. But manual work enters as an important component in their style of living in the large majority of cases. Finally, there are many Non-Brahmins who are engaged as cartmen, masons and labourers of one kind or another within and outside the village.

If manual labour plays an important part in the lives of Non-Brahmins, it does so to an even greater extent among the Adi-Dravidas. The Pallas not only engage in manual work, but their work in general is non-specialized and unskilled, and less prestige is attached to it than to the work of the Non-Brahmin artisans. Occupations are graded by people in a more or less conscious manner, and the more degrading tasks such as hoeing, digging and carrying earth are reserved for Adi-Dravidas. Although there is a good deal of overlap between the work of Non-Brahmins and Adi-Dravidas, one can say, with some simplification, that the typical Non-Brahmin peasant in Sripuram is a sharecropper or a cultivator, whereas the typical Adi-Dravida is an agricultural labourer.

Occupation, however, is only one component, although an important one, in the style of life of a people. It has to be remembered that apart from the two families of temple priests there are no significant differences in traditional occupation among the Brahmins of Sripuram. Further, the new occupations adopted by them maintain a certain continuity with the past and seem to be more or less equally accessible to all varieties of Brahmins in the village. In spite of this, there are many differences among them, reflected particularly in their religious culture.

VI

Caste has often been viewed as the prototype of all hierarchical systems. Principles of caste rank rest essentially on conceptions of social esteem. Social esteem is attached to particular styles of life, and groups are ranked as high or low according to how or whether they pursue such styles. What is highly esteemed varies from one society to another and depends ultimately on the one society. In India ritual elements (and, in particular, the ideas of purity and pollution) have historically occupied an important place in styles of life which have enjoyed high social esteem.

Status in a caste hierarchy is based partly upon wealth, but not entirely. It is based upon wealth to the extent that the possession of a certain minimum of wealth is a necessary condition to the pursuit of a certain style of life. Beyond this minimum, however, it is not true that any caste which is in possession of more wealth is by this fact in a position of superior social rank.

Status, in addition to being associated with specific styles of life, has in every society a strong traditional bias. Hence it is not enough for a certain caste to adopt a particular style of life in order to achieve higher social rank. It has to legitimize its position by working this style of life into a tradition; it has to establish its association with the style over a number of generations.

Although it may be possible to list the different attributes which enter into styles of life that are highly esteemed, such listing would be of limited value. In the first place, people do not rank different castes in terms of a rational application of particular standards. Second, the standards themselves are ambiguous, variable, and subject to change over time.

Thus, although hierarchy is an important feature of the caste system, we must not assume that wherever there is segmentation we can rank the segments as higher or lower. There are conflicting claims to superior rank, and often it is impossible to speak of a consensus. It frequently happens that two castes put forward rival claims to superiority with regard to which members of other castes may be indifferent or may not regard themselves as competent to decide either way.

The important point to bear in mind about the hierarchy of the caste system is its ambiguities beyond a certain level. These ambiguities are essential in a system which seems always to have permitted a certain degree of mobility. These are further increased by the fact that the basis of social esteem, the entire value system on which the ranking of castes depends, has in recent times been undergoing important changes.

Ambiguities notwithstanding, one can say that the broad divisions, Brahmin, Non-Brahmin and Adi-Dravida, are associated with different degrees of social esteem. In the context of Sripuram, and perhaps of Tamilnad as a whole, there would be a wide measure of consensus that Brahmins rank higher socially than Non-Brahmins, who in turn rank higher than Adi-Dravidas. There are, no doubt, some Non-Brahmins who would challenge the relevance of such a system of grading; but most of them would accept it, and few would suggest a different order. Even though some Non-Brahmins may challenge the claim by Brahmins that they are superior in rank, this claim would certainly be acknowledged by the third party, the Adi-Dravidas. Thus, at the broadest level there is little ambiguity about social rank or the nature of the hierarchy.

Coming to subdivisions among the Brahmins, there would be fairly general agreement that the Smarthas and Shri Vaishnavas properly rank higher than the Panchangakkarans and the Kurukkals and Bhattachars. As between Panchangakkarans, on the one hand, and Kurukkals and Bhattachars, on the other, it is difficult to assign social precedence. The issue cannot in any case be decided with reference to Sripuram, since there are no Panchangakkaran Brahmins in the village.

The position of comparative inferiority of the Panchangakkarans and the Archakars (i.e. Kurukkals and Bhattachars) may be partly explained by the fact that their occupation makes them dependent for their livelihood on services rendered to Non-Brahmins. Services to Non-Brahmins in a specific way do not enter into the style of life of the Smarthas and Shri Vaishnavas proper. Rather, their style of life revolves around the cultivation of scriptural knowledge and the performance of individual and family rites, both of which are associated with high social esteem.

Shri Vaishnavas and Smarthas make competing claims to the highest social rank. The claims cannot be judged in terms of any fixed or objective standards. Shri Vaishnavas tend to be more orthodox and exclusive, and they may even refuse to take water from the hands of Smarthas. But this is not necessarily accepted as a sign of superiority, since Smarthas as well as other Brahmins regard it as an extreme example of bigotry and sometimes hold it up to ridicule. Shri Vaishnavas claim superiority on the ground that they are more rigorous and orthodox in their ritual observances and that they do not worship non-Sanskritic deities as the Smarthas do. Smarthas maintain that Shri Vaishnavas are not Brahmins at all, but descendants of assorted people converted by Ramanuja.

It should be recognized that the actual position of a caste in the village is not based merely upon certain absolute standards of social estimation, but depends also upon local factors. In Sripuram the Shri Vaishnavas are in a dominant position by virtue of their strength of numbers and their control over various aspects of social life in the *agraharam*, including control of the Vishnu temple. The Smarthas are in a position of relative weakness. But there are other villages where Smarthas are in a position of strength and the presence of Shri Vaishnavas in the *agraharam* is accepted only on sufferance.

Determination of caste rank among the Non-Brahmins suffers similarly from ambiguity and the absence of universally accepted criteria. Conflicting claims to higher social rank are often expressed among the Non-Brahmins in the idiom of the *varna* scheme. Some of them claim to be Brahmins, some claim to be Kshatriyas and some claim to be Vaishyas. But the presentation of a claim does not necessarily, or even generally, lead to its acceptance. Thus, although the Padayachis claim to be Kshatriyas, and the Vellalas do not generally go above the Vaishya level in their claims, it is the Vellalas rather than the Padayachis who are, by and large, accepted as superior.

Such claims to Brahmin, Kshatriya and Vaishya status cannot be used as a basis for deciding questions of rank among the Non-Brahmins, because they are rarely, if ever, fully accepted. In the absence of a uniform set of principles of ranking castes it would perhaps be more meaningful to give some idea of the actual rank order as it exists among the Non-Brahmins in Sripuram.

There is a popular saying in Tamil: *Kallan, Maravan, Ahamudiyan, mella mella wandu Vellalar anar.Vellalar ahi, Mudaliyar shonnar* (Kallan, Maravan, and Ahamudiyan by slow degrees became Vellala. Having become Vellala, they called themselves Mudaliyar.) This saying illustrates two important features of the system: (1) that there is a hierarchical order which can be ascertained in broad terms for any given area, and (2) that it is possible for individual castes to move up this order with some success.

Mobility in the caste system may be sought either through the *varna* idiom, which has an all-India spread, or through the idiom of the local system of *jatis*. When the Padayachis claim to be Kshatriyas, they try to make use of the *varna* idiom. When, on the other hand, the Ahamudiyas claim to be Vellalas, they make use of an idiom which has a more local character. Both kinds of idiom have been extensively used over the last several decades.

In the context of Sripuram the hierarchy of castes among the Non-Brahmins is clear up to a point; beyond this point there is a good deal of ambiguity. One can roughly determine the upper and the lower rungs, but in the middle regions ranking is uncertain. Thus it would be generally admitted that the Vellala (peasant) group of castes occupies a high position, and that the Vannans (Washermen) and Ambattans (Barbers) rank rather low. The Tattans (Goldsmiths) and Tachchans (Carpenters) also occupy high positions, while the Nadars (Toddy-tappers) would be ranked near the bottom. The bulk of the cultivating castes rank somewhat lower than the Vellalas. Beyond this, very little can be said with any measure of certainty.

The position with regard to the Adi-Dravidas is somewhat similar in Sripuram. The Pallas, who constitute the bulk of them, are regarded by reason of their occupation and their food habits to be less degraded than the Paraiyas, Thottis and Chakkiliyas. Conversion to Christianity does not seem to make a real difference as far as the social rank of the Paraiyas is concerned. What is important is the style of life with which they have been traditionally associated and which still persists among them without very serious modifications.

The Jats of Punjab

JOYCE PETTIGREW

Village Links

The pattern of settlement in the Punjab had traditionally testified to the lawlessness of the province. The population was clustered in large nucleated villages and there were few isolated houses. Defence against invading armies had historically been the principal reason for concentration. In the fieldwork area the villages were generally one or two miles distant from one another. Many of them had been founded by a number of Jat clan heads, who originally came from different areas and who had united for convenience against outsiders in order to defend the land they had seized. Village solidarity had traditionally depended on co-operation between these groups on the basis of mutual interest; it was not a matter of kinship.

....

The Jats, whether Hindu, Sikh or Muslim, have formed the backbone of the agricultural community in Punjab, the neighbouring provinces of Rajasthan and Sind, and in the western portion of the Gangetic Doab. They divide themselves into a number of clans known as *gots* each of which has the tradition of descent from a Rajput ancestor and of having come to the Punjab in the sixteenth century. The Jat section of the Sikh community is customarily endogamous but their clans are exogamous. There is no established hierarchy among the clans: they are unequal in size but not ranked, and which Jat clan is regarded as being superior has

Adapted from Joyce Pettigrew, 'Patterns of Allegiance I' and 'Patterns of Allegiance II', in *Robbers and Noblemen: A Study of the Political System of the Sikh Jats*. Routledge and Kegan Paul, London, 1975.

seemed to vary according to the criteria selected for differentiation by them. For example, at present, Garewals are admitted by other clans to be superior because a large number of them are in military service and administration. Traditionally their women have not worked in the fields, which is unique among the Sikh clans. Originally Garewals also considered themselves superior because of their tradition of descent from a Rajput prince. The oldest clan in the Punjab south and east of the Sutlej is that of the Sidhus. The premier Sikh prince—the Maharajah of Patiala—is a Sidhu, and his family traced its descent from 1526, while another Sidhu house in Majha—the Attari—traced its descent to the fourteenth century. Sidhus had played a prominent role in Sikh history, and the exploits of some Sidhu families were said to have raised the clan to a position of prominence in Sikh eyes. There was, however, a proverb which denied them their supremacy: '*Sandhu, Sidhu, ik baraabar, Gills tore uchera*' (Sandhus and Sidhus are equal but Gills are a bit superior to both). There was also a tradition that the clans of Maan, Chahal, Bhullar were '*asal Jats*', that is, genuine Jats, and that all others were degraded from Rajputs.

Thus among the Jats there is no universally accepted hierarchy of clans. The clans are also not arranged spatially. Not only are adjacent villages of different clan, but also in some areas, such as the fieldwork area, different sections within the same village are also of different clans. Jat clans are therefore, in many instances, not localized kinship groupings.[1] There is now no further division into smaller units within the clan, nor is there any conception of clan solidarity as such clans among the Jats are merely divisions which are recognized by the Jats themselves for marriage purposes. Some families concerned with the 'lineage' (a term synonymous simply with background) of another family might be interested in the 'blue blood' of the Sidhus. Simply being a Sidhu, however, counts for nothing. Likewise, the Garewals have become associated with high administrative and political position, but a man cannot 'get' anything out of merely being a Garewal.

Class

The Jats live in rural areas, in large compact villages. Almost a third of their villages were provided with an electricity supply at the time of my visit

---

[1] This differs from the pattern found among the Hindu Jats of Meerut Division in northwest Uttar Pradesh (Pradhan 1966) where each clan is associated with a definite geographical area.

in 1965-7. Most of the villages in central Punjab —i.e. in the districts of Amritsar, Ludhiana and Jullundhar—are connected to one another by some form of road. This area is the province's most intensively irrigated belt and hence its most prosperous part.

There is no difference in way of life between the categories usually called landlord, middle-class farmer and small proprietor. They ate the same food—a basic diet of wheat, raw sugar (*gur*), milk, butter (ghee), fresh vegetables, lentils (*daal*) and occasionally meat and rice, and oranges in season. In the villages, food was usually cooked in the open and eaten in the open. Frequently there was an equal lack of toilet facilities in their houses. The conception of a house was that it was a shelter. The house of a landlord Jat, i.e. a Jat owning upwards of 200 acres of land, was certainly larger than its neighbours, all its portions, including those where cattle were kept, being made of stone or brick. But even this was rapidly ceasing to be a differentiating factor, especially between the landlord and the middle-class farmer. In addition, many small proprietors had that part of the house in which they lived built of brick and cement. Also, in the houses of small proprietors and landlords alike there was a lack of decoration, and ornaments were not displayed but locked up in steel trunks. These three categories of landlord, middle-class farmer and small proprietors could not be clearly distinguished by their outside connections: it was not a pattern, for example, that small proprietors had some family members *only* employed as a bus conductor, lorry driver, in the ranks of the army, or as teachers, while those with large landholdings would have those of their family members working off the land in high administrative and political positions. Many of those in the latter positions had, indeed, small landholdings.

The main means of differentiating the middle-class farmer, i.e. a farmer owning between 50 and 100 acres of land, from the small proprietor was in the former's possession of a car and certain agricultural implements. Jats in the landlord category could be distinguished from middle-class farmers by the number of household servants they employed, as also by the finer clothes, design and quantity of jewellery, and finer looks of their womenfolk. Not infrequently, too, their sons and daughters were educated at boarding school. By virtue of his connections and his money, a larger landowner was also more likely to be able to remove himself from the monotony of village life whenever he wished, but again this was becoming a less exclusive privilege. Moreover, during the harvesting periods he participated in the same gruelling labour as did smaller landholders. The way of life of the Jats was essentially the same whether they were rich or poor.

Membership of these categories was, in any case, fluid, as the amount of land in a family's possession was not constant. It was specifically the system of land division on the death of the head of the family and the customary inheritance of equal shares by his sons that led to the difficulty in conserving wealth. If, for example, the four sons of a middle-class farmer who had 80 acres of land decided on inheriting their father's property to divide it, each would then have only 20 acres, i.e. they would have sunk to the category of small proprietors. The categories of landlord, middle-class farmer and small proprietor did not have anything like stable membership, and families were not securely in any one category. Ranking on the basis of the amount of land owned was also continually being disturbed by land disputes and land seizures, which were initiated by persons as soon as they had an affinal linkage or political connection to give them protection. One cannot, therefore, postulate three strata, each with definite characteristics, for the whole of the province. Moreover, each family had at least two or three important relatives whom they frequently used, and these relationships, often distant, may be said to have formed a link between the highest and lowest among the Jats. The links provided by affinal relationships stretched across the system and affinal links were especially nurtured when they offered possibility of a connection upwards in the political system. Active use of these ties may be associated with the lack of a firmly established class system. It was also believed by the Jats that they could all ultimately trace links with one another, an idea expressed in the proverb, '*Jat jatan dee salee wichhe ghale male.*' (Jats are all connected with one another through their wives' brothers.)

In the villages the significant economic division among the Jats was the division between those who were in a position to lend money and those who were dependent on these loans. To this I now turn.

Dependency Ties

Small landowning proprietors were often bound in so much debt to the landlord that they could not repay in their lifetime. Debt mainly affected small proprietors wanting to improve their general living conditions. They were often unable to seek supplementary sources of income because that would mean neglecting the land, causing yields to fall. Money was lent for such purposes as building brick houses or obtaining pumping sets and seed, and for expenditure on marriages. Litigation was also a major source of debt in central Punjab.

Technically, money could be borrowed from two sources. The first of these was the rural co-operative bank. All the rural co-operative banks of the area were under the Central Co-operative Bank in Ludhiana, and in villages were generally under the control of the *sarpanch* (head of the village *panchayat*). A man became a member of a bank by a deposit of Rs 100. A loan in excess of Rs 100 or in excess of what a man's deposit eventually became was given at the rate of 7 per cent. A member could only borrow up to Rs 2,000. For any amount in excess he therefore had to run to the landlord, who was the second source of money in the village. It was particularly to his friends that a landlord would lend from the co-operative bank; to those opposed to him or whom he disliked for some reason, he himself would give the loan. The landlord lent at the rate of 30 per cent and generally he lent up to the value of the borrower's land, the latter pledging his land as security. If small proprietors could not pay back the loan quickly enough, existing land assets were mortgaged. Most of the indebtedness of small proprietors in villages I was acquainted with had been running for over fifteen years. In many cases a landlord would not take over a small proprietor's land even when he was justified in doing so according to the terms of their agreement: he did not want to antagonize potential or actual supporters. Moreover, landlords often could not take over their clients' land formally because they already held land in excess of the prescribed 30 standard acres, thus if they did take the land, they shortly afterwards sold it and invested the money in some form of property elsewhere. In some cases, also, the landlord did not always have his eyes on the land. In one instance I know of, the landlord concerned, instead of taking to court the small proprietor who had defaulted on his interest payments—in which instance, while fighting the case he would have lost interest payments anyway, and maybe eventually also the case—struck a bargain with his client that he should vacate his house. From time to time he would allow default in interest payments as a favour. In one village in which I stayed for four months, a large landlord, who was also a *sarpanch* had, in the 1962 election, negotiated further loans for small proprietors at cheaper rates of interest from the Central Co-operative Bank, which could lend up to Rs 8,000. The local MLA, campaigning for re-election at the time, had been a director of the Central Co-operative Bank and agreed that loans be temporarily given at cheaper rates, since he knew that certain small proprietors, being indebted to the *sarpanch*, would vote the way the latter directed, i.e. for himself. There was no need to antagonize a set of small proprietors who could be used as a more or less permanent nucleus of support, and the landlord, one may say, obtained their gratitude for nothing.

The tie between a landlord and a small proprietor was a vertical tie. The horizontal ties of class and clan were noticeable by their absence, as also were strong horizontal relationships on the basis of caste.

The Jats and their Relationships to Non-Jats

In Punjab each major caste is broadly associated with an economic category. Broadly, the landowners are Jats; the middlemen, shopkeepers and businessmen are Aroras and Khatris; a high percentage of labourers in industry and on the land are Mazhbis (Scheduled Castes). Jats are, however, prominent in the transport industry and in the manufacture of machine tools, while Mazhbis, traditionally landless, *were* becoming tenants on government land and would eventually acquire this land. Caste did not necessarily determine occupation. But land tended to circulate among the Jats, and very little has in fact passed into non-Jat hands. Aroras and Khatris, for example, are legally excluded from the purchase of land by the Land Alienation Act, while the distribution of power in villages has effectively meant that Mazhbis have never had the resources to purchase land. No members of a caste in Punjab have aspired to 'jump into' the status of another, with the exception of certain members of the Mazhbi caste. They, in fact, aspired to become Jat, as was indicated by their adoption of Jat clan names.

(i) Jats and City Dwellers

The Jats considered themselves to be 'born Sikhs' and did not think other Sikhs deserved the title of *sirdar*. Each Jat felt tremendous pride that it was *his* section of community that had built up the military organization which led to the establishment of Sikh rule in the Punjab. He felt that prestige lay with the Jats because of this. The Aroras, who formed 9 per cent of the Sikh population and who generally supplied most of Punjab's petty traders and small shopkeepers, were spoken of as *kiraar* (coward) by the Jats. Originally the Arora section of the Sikh community had been principally found in West Punjab, in the districts to the west of Lahore. Jats from my fieldwork area, which was part of Malwa, often commented to me that, until 1947, they had never seen a Sikh who was shopkeeper by profession. This, they said, was the trade of Hindus, whom they despised, and generally they undoubtedly associated Sikh Aroras with their Hindu counterparts. They had traditionally, however, given respect to the Khatris, and particularly to those Khatri families to which the Sikh gurus belonged: the Bedis, Trehans, Sodhis and Bhallas. The Khatris until recently had exclusively provided the intelligentsia in the professions and education, and they were also prominent in business. An idea of essential nobility underlay the Jat ethos. Jat families had the longest tradition of adherence to Sikhism. In 1699, when Govind Singh had established the Khalsa, many non-Jat believers in the religion of Sikhism living in urban areas had not joined its ranks. They did not adopt the Sikh symbols until the period of Maharaja Ranjit Singh's rule, when they felt it prudent to identify themselves with the ruling class, which was Jat. Griffin (in *The Law of Inheritance to Chiefships...*) noted that the supply of candidates to become Sikh fluctuated with estimates of the advantage or disadvantage of joining the community. In the Punjab census report of 1881, another observer—a British commissioner of Amritsar District—reported that 'Sikhs decline in number in years of peace'. The 1931 census also mentioned that Hindu Jats become Sikhs to get their sons into the army, which during British rule showed a preference for them.

Jats pictured the townsman as lacking in physical bravery. They also had an image of him as grasping, greedy and lacking in dignity. Their outlook was epitomized in the proverb characterizing the city businessman as praying to God and saying, '*Jhooth vi bolney aan, ghut vi tolney aan, par tera naan vi taan laney aan* ' (We tell lies, we cheat, but we pray to you too). In the Arora-Khatri Sikh community of the towns, the ideal was that of the educated merchant and director of a large business firm who had travelled abroad and who bestowed money on gurudwaras; the aspirations of the Jats were towards military service, large landholding and high administrative position. They were people with a passion for dominance. More than three-quarters of the members of the Legislative Assembly are now Jats, and of the nine Sikhs representing Punjab in Delhi, eight are Jat. Of the nine Sikhs who were ministers before the general elections of 1967, seven were Jats. Similarly, of the six Sikhs who were secretaries to the government of Punjab at the same time, five were Jats. Jats also dominated in the Sikh percentage of the officer class of the Indian army.

Jat stereotypes regarding the Aroras and Khatris were a reflection of their economic antagonism to the urban section of the population, whether Sikh or Hindu. The clash of economic interest between the two had been brought into relief as far back as 1901, at the time of the Land Alienation Act, when large amounts of land were passing into the hands of moneylenders, who were principally Aroras and Khatris. Formerly, also, the army had recruited only Jats and had been closed as an occupation to Aroras and Khatris. More recently the opposed interests of the urban and rural sections of the population became evident when a predominantly Jat government came to power in February 1967 and fixed a stable price for wheat. This was in accordance with rural demands that middlemen in the food grains market, who were predominantly Khatris or Aroras, should not be allowed to take undue profit out of the small farmer's hard labour and that there should not be a wide yearly fluctuation in food grain prices, as small proprietors themselves had to buy from the market in the lean months from December to March.

It is clear that the Jats did not function on a caste basis with respect to the Aroras and Khatris of the towns and that their caste was not a basis of solidarity among them. Their interests, however, as the rural landowning section of the community were opposed to the interests of certain section of the business community (who happened to be of Arora-Khatri caste) in the cities.

(ii) *Jats and Labourers*

Labourers on the land of others were mainly members of Scheduled Castes, known as Mazhbis, who owned no land. Jats traditionally laboured only on their own land, and laboured for payment on the land of other Jats only in circumstances of extreme social and economic crisis. It is impossible to estimate the numbers of Jats that were 'servants' at any one moment in time. In the area where I worked, farms exceeding 30 acres in size were always worked with the help of a tractor. But irrespective of the size of landholding most Jats recruited landless labourers to work with them either on a daily basis (*dihari*) or on a yearly basis (*biit*). The relationship was purely contractual, and hereditary relationships between landlord and labourer or small proprietor and labourer were not customary. Daily labourers were hired on a sunrise-to-sunset basis and were given a fixed money payment at the end of each day. Labourers on a yearly basis were paid either in money or were given a certain percentage of the crop twice yearly at Lohri (13 January) and Nawani (13-14 June). The wives of these labourers were expected to give free service in the houses for which their husbands were working and they used to sweep out the courtyard, make dung cakes and collect vegetables for cooking. On a farm between 60 and 100 acres in size, which had high yields and a dependent family of nine, generally 15 per cent of the wheat crop and the same percentage of the maize crop would be given in payment to the labourers, with 5 per cent being kept for home consumption and 80 per cent of the farm's entire produce being sold for cash. Such a farm would be buying in from the outside only such food as a few vegetables, bananas and tea to supplement the basic diet built up on wheat, milk, sugar and home-grown vegetables such as spinach, potatoes and carrots.

The busy season was that between the beginning of October and the end of December, when wheat was being sown, cotton and maize were being harvested, and sugar cane was cut. Labour needs were never met at this time, and three to four hours' sleep at night was normal. There was a proverb that during this season it was permissible for a Jat even to refuse to attend his mother's funeral rites. January and February were free months with relatively little work to do. The Mazhbi population of any village, which apportioned itself out among the various Jat owners of land, could often only get work at harvest time. They sometimes tided over economic hardship by making shoes, which was their traditional occupation, and by selling them in towns, while a small percentage of them also had sons working in factories in the cities or, occasionally, in the ranks of the army.

Jats dominated relationships between themselves and the Mazhbis through control of the economic resources of the village and the *panchayat* system. Jats misused Mazhbi women when they got the opportunity, and they had been known to beat their Mazhbi labourers, though this was not a common occurrence. They could and did cause hardship to the Mazhbis if it was in their interest. For instance, they used to threaten that they would deprive them of the right to take sugar cane and spinach (an important item of diet during the winter) from Jat fields, and fodder for Mazhbi cattle, if the Mazhbis did not vote in a particular way at elections. The general pattern prevailing in these villages was that the Mazhbi labourers had to co-operate with the Jats to get themselves employed as permanent labourers and to gain access to the land for vegetables and fodder for their cattle. A labourer was automatically associated with the Jat proprietor who had his services; the interest of both was to get produce out of the land. Mazhbis were not organized on a caste basis but were divided, as were the Jats, according to the pattern of their ties of political and economic dependence.

Caste solidarity in Punjab rarely operated in practice. None of the castes discussed were politically organized on a state-wide basis. The only customs in which any solidarity was expressed among the Jats on a caste basis was that in the village they did not visit the houses of Mazhbis, take food from them, eat with them or intermarry with them. Jats, Khatris, Aroras, all ate with one another and there was also an increasing number of cases of intermarriage between them. In villages, neither Jats nor Mazhbis had any solidarity on a caste basis. Jat landlords, on antagonistic

terms with one another, forced those Mazhbis whom they had recruited
to work for them to support them politically. Allegiances were thus cross-
caste allegiances, and it is more helpful to look at them in terms of a patron
attaching himself to certain clients who, relative to him, are in an
economically depressed situation. For the same relationships that a
powerful Jat had with the Mazhbi labourers, he also had with small
proprietors who were in some way indebted to him, or with tenants.
Moreover, labourers, whether Jat or Mazhbi, were treated exactly alike
by their Jat employers. The core of the relationship was the same in all
these instances and unaffected by caste.

. . . .

Jats, during the 1960s, had developed a practical and active interest in
agriculture. Farmers had begun to be very concerned about land improvement and conservation. Fertilizers were widely used, and many farmers
visited the Agricultural University in Ludhiana to take courses on how to
improve their farming techniques.

Attachment to the land was glorified. It was a Jat's dearest possession,
which he was committed to secure and enlarge. This was his main
preoccupation, but connected with it were two other dominating concerns: the marriage of his sisters and daughters and the development of
influential contacts. All three were interrelated; all contributed to achieving family power, family honour.

Among the Jats the question was not that of survival to the next harvest
but of the threat felt from others to the security of life and possession,
whether these others be invaders from Pakistan or, more commonly, the
opposite faction in a village or particular rural area. It is in this context
that the concern of the Jats for family power has to be set. Family was to
be perpetuated, defended, made powerful and enriched by all the means
available. To this end, given the historic and still continuing conditions
of instability, power had to be achieved. Behind the emphasis placed on
achievement of some kind, whether in the form of material acquisition,
high rank in the army or high administrative position, was the concern to
improve family position by making it powerful. Power was the means by
which a man guaranteed not only the security of his family in certain
situational contingencies but also, when he was economically beyond the
stage of scarcity, by being a rich landlord or middle-class farmer, it was
the means by which he considered he honoured that family and made it
impregnable.

Family power was dependent on and achieved through the local
concentration of the family in one place, in combination with the

possession of a large landholding and a wide network of linkages outside the village built up through affinal connections and through factional contacts. In the first place, family power was related to keeping the men of the family physically concentrated in one place. Some of the power of the head of one of the factions in the fieldwork area was attributed to the fact that he had five brothers behind him, as the two following comments show:

Generally, if in one family in a village all are big, strong, healthy and living together, they manage to dominate that village (Panchayat officer, Doraha, March 1966).

When six tall, well-built brothers are living together and not mutually quarrelling they are a very powerful force. They can fight about a hundred men who are not brothers (General Mohan S., April 1967).

In the second place, a family's prestige was measured by the size of its landholding. Family was the unit which defended and extended rights in land. Strong families arose and were needed for this purpose. The amount of land in a family's possession, however, was never constant, because of the inheritance rules and because of disputes over and seizures of land. To protect landholding, therefore, alliances were formed through marriage with other families and by joining factions. Political links were sought primarily to give security in the possession of economic resources in the form of land, and possession of such resources enabled a man to disperse his daughters through a number of connections useful to him. Development of such connections was, indeed, not only a material necessity but also a duty. Marriage was an arrangement providing for the mitigation of the family's risks and the enhancement of its opportunities. A large progeny was therefore damaging to a family only if that family had little land. A large family on a large landholding allowed a wider network of useful ties through marriage to be built up. The political system operated on a patronage basis, and frequently much wealth flowed along affinal channels. Affinal relationships for the Jats were both a mode of securing influential contacts and a mode of dispensing the benefits of power.

....

The capacity of a family to dominate depended on control of men, economic resources and political institutions. In this struggle, violence was taken for granted and Jats often commented that it had a positive influence in that it kept up the martial spirit. It was accepted that depending on a man's successful or unsuccessful use of his coercive power and on his manipulation of outside ties, he might find himself with more possessions and influence tomorrow than he had today or, alternatively, with none at all. A proverb coined in the time of invasions of Ahmed Shah Abdali has certainly lost none of its relevance since: '*Khadda pitha lahada, Rehnda Ahmed Shahida.*' It means, only that which is eaten and drunk in one day is a man's own and can be said to belong to him, for the rest will be stolen by Ahmed Shah. It neatly epitomized the often variable fortunes of one man in his lifetime. Power was transient, possessions were transient, and the basis of both power and wealth was force. The ideology of the proverb remained to mirror the experiences of existent life, reflecting its quality of perpetual uncertainty.

Relationships of extreme friendship and hostility between families were actively involved with the philosophy of life embodied in the conception of *izzat*—the complex of values regarding what was honourable. If a Jat achieved power for his family he automatically enhanced family honour. Power was honour and honour was power. In a situation where a family had no power it was inconceivable that it could have 'honour', as it would not be able to defend the content of that honour from another family. The rise to power of a family into an 'honourable' position was inevitably accompanied by threats and litigation, and sometimes also by violence and murder.

That aspect of *izzat* according to which the relationships between families were supposed to be ordered emphasized the principle of equivalence in all things, i.e. not only equality in giving but also equality in vengeance. *Izzat* was in fact the principle of reciprocity of gifts, plus the rule of an eye for an eye and a tooth for a tooth. Giving was an attempt to bring a man of another family into one's debt, and acceptance of the gift involved the recipient in making a return, not necessarily in kind or immediately, but at the moment appropriate to the donor. Not making the return could break relationships and develop future hostility. *Izzat* enjoined aid to those who had helped one. It also enjoined that revenge be exacted for personal insults and damage to person or property. If a man was threatened he must at least threaten back, for not to do so would be weakness. The appropriate revenge for murder was likewise murder. *Izzat* was also associated with sanctioned resistence to another who trespassed into what was regarded as the sphere of influence of one's family. This 'other' might be other Jats belonging to the opposing faction; in the past it also applied to the state and foreign powers. The honour and pride of the Jats was expressed in opposition to their rivals within their own family and in other families, and in hospitality and co-operation to their friends.

In non-submission to threats they expressed their own dignity and their respect. Thus the concepts central to the Jat system of values, notably honour, respect, reputation, shame, prestige, which pertain to relationships between families and the status of these families *vis-à-vis* one another, can be seen as sustaining factional divisions.

It is important to note the feeling of the imminence and closeness of death, figuratively, often actually, and certainly potentially, to those families living in areas where there has been both a tradition of feuding and a high percentage of men enlisting in the army—namely the former PEPSU State, of which my fieldwork area had been a part, and the districts of Ferozepur and Amritsar. 'Death' for families living in these areas was within the range of the immediately possible. It was a tragedy only for sisters and for mothers. But for men, young and old, death was excitement, drama, a proof of their daring, their bravery, as true sons of the Khalsa. The legitimation of killing and violence was historical and cultural. Courage, the willingness to take risks, the absence in the ideology of any concept to defeat and submission and the capacity to impose oneself on others, were major values of the culture. The archetypes for such conduct were the two historical figures of Guru Govind Singh and Maharajah Ranjit Singh: on both personalities Jats had a fixation. Legitimation of killing and violence was, however, fundamentally based on power. Violence had always been the traditional accompaniment of dominance in a village or small local area and in the state. Moreover, the security achieved by dominance was conceived to be, and in fact often was, only temporary, and therefore required permanent guarding. This led to further violence. . . . Killing and violence were facts of existence that had to be lived with. [2] . . .

---

[2] This area continues to be without peace. I returned to Doraha in 1970, and during my two and a half year absence there had been four murders.

The *Bhadraloks* of Bengal

S. N. MUKHERJEE

Throughout this essay I have referred to the *bhadralok* as a social class. Although it is now fashionable in the academic world to discard the concept of class altogether I still find it a valuable intellectual tool in analysing the social and political development of modern India. Recently the *bhadralok* has been described as a 'status group', not a 'class'. It seems to me that to describe the *bhadralok* as a 'status group' or alternatively a 'mere category' is to ignore the economic changes and the social mobility in Bengal in the nineteenth century.

. . . .

In Calcutta, in the nineteenth century, class was one dimension of social stratification which determined social relationships in the city. If we use Marxian class analysis then Indian society in Calcutta was divided into two classes. There was the *abhijat bhadralok*, the big zamindars, merchants and top administrators, who were the owners of land and capital although as a capitalist class they were subservient to the British. Then there were the dockers, the builders, the workers, the domestics, the palanquin bearers and other wage-earners—a large migrant labour force, some of whom came from Orissa and the Up Country, formed the class of producers. The relationship between these two classes was contractual and economic, and was not determined by caste or custom.

Between these two groups there was already growing, as we have noticed, a middle class, the *grihastha bhadralok*, whom in 1829 the

Excerpted from, E. Leach and S.N. Mukherjee, *Elites in South Asia*, Cambridge University Press, London, 1970.

Bangadoot referred to as *maddhyabitto sreni*. The shopkeepers, small zamindars, small merchants and white-collar workers belonged to this group. However, this had not yet crystallized into a homogeneous social class. They accepted the leadership of the *abhijat* and imitated their life-style. They were dubbed together with the *abhijat* by the English officers as 'the educated natives' to distinguish them as a group from the old 'nobility' and the masses. The line of demarcation between the *abhijat* and the *grihastha* is not very clear; after all, the rich *bhadralok* emerged from a new 'middle class', who were considered as 'upstarts' by many. Although the *abhijats* were rich, enjoyed high status, and exercised considerable power in Calcutta, their subservience to the British and their imitation of the life-style of the colonial elite and the Mughal courtiers made them with the other *bhadraloks* rich and of the middle-income group, part of a 'new middle class'.

The class situation in Calcutta can be compared and contrasted with the class situation in England in the early nineteenth century. The Industrial Revolution [in England] brought about profound social and economic changes; the steam engine broke the eighteenth-century pyramidal structure of English society. . . . Before the rise of a politically conscious working-class movement, a class struggle was waged by the middle class against 'aristocratic tyranny' and 'hereditary opulence'. In contrast, in Calcutta, there was no Industrial Revolution, no large-scale introduction of the steam engine to break down the old social structure completely. Yet the market in land, trade and commerce brought about a significant social change, and Bengal witnessed the rise of a new middle class. This class was less aggressive and less homogeneous than its English counterpart but it was equally articulate in politics.

There was in fact in Bengal no conflict between trade and the land, nor between the 'old zamindars' and the 'new zamindars'. No doubt many old zamindaris were bought off by the *abhijat bhadralok*, and there was some resentment too against the *nouveaux riches*, but there was no class struggle between the *bhadralok* and the 'old aristocracy'. The tension between the family of Nubkissen and that of the Maharaja of Krishnagar, over the family idol, was a family feud not a class struggle. In fact the 'ancient families' were respected by the *bhadralok*. It was Radhakanta Deb, grandson of Nubkissen, who in 1838 proposed that the Maharaja of Krishnagar should be asked to be the President of the Zamindar Sabha, since he came from the 'most ancient lineage' in Bengal. In some areas the 'ancient families' still exercised considerable influence. If Ram Ram Bose is to be believed, the descendants of Raja Basanta Roy (uncle of Pratapaditya Roy, one of the Bengali chieftains

who fought the Mughals in the seventeenth century) were still respected
in Jessore, and were leaders (*Goshtipati*) of Bangaja Kayasthas in that
district.

Similarly the *bhadralok* had a deep respect for the Mughal nobility.
In 1842 Radhakanta Deb went to pay his homage to the Nawab Nazim
of Murshidabad on his way to Gaya. Rammohun Roy proclaimed his
allegiance to the family of Babar and accepted the title of Raja con-
ferred upon him by Akbar II.

However, there was some hostility towards the lower orders, the
dockers, palanquin bearers and other wage-earners in Calcutta, and the
tenants and the landless labourers in the rural area. . . . Many were afraid
that the spread of English education among the lower classes would hurt
the interests of the *bhadralok*; they would demand higher wages, equality and even the jobs dearly held by the *bhadralok*. *Samachar Chan-
drika* claimed that the demand for higher wages and the lack of washermen in Calcutta were due to the spread of education among the lower
classes (12 May 1830: 144-5). Thus, although there was no sharp class
struggle of the type England had witnessed under the impact of the
Industrial Revolution, and the interrelationship between classes was not
one of continuous conflict, many social conflicts and collective activities can only be understood in terms of class. Not all social relationships
in Calcutta were determined by class; society as a whole was not just
separated, as some of the missionaries thought, into two 'classes, the
borrower and the usurer, the industrious though exhausted poor, and the
fat and flourishing money-lender'. The people were also separated into
communities and castes. Nevertheless, the importance of class as one
dimension of social stratification in Calcutta cannot be denied.

The caste structure in Bengal during the pre-colonial period was less
rigid than it is supposed to have been in other parts of India. The Bengali
Brahmins, though enjoying a very high ritual status, never had that
exclusive high social and economic status which the Brahmins in South
India had enjoyed in the past (see Béteille 1965: 3-10, 191-2). The Brahmins had to share the economic and social power with other castes.
Traditionally, the Hindu community in Bengal was divided into two
varnas, Brahmin and Shudra. The Shudras were further subdivided into
three groups: clean, unclean and Untouchable. All *jatis* in Bengal were
fitted into these four broad categories, Brahmins, clean Shudras, unclean Shudras and Untouchables; there were at least forty-one *jatis* in
Bengal.

Two caste groups, Kayastha and Baidya, enjoyed a very high social
and political status along with the Brahmin, although their ritual status

was rather low. They had the monopoly of the educational system, and held important administrative posts; being landowners they controlled the agrarian economy. According to Abu-ul-Fazl in *Ain-I-Akbari*, the majority of the Bengali zamindars in the sixteenth century were Kayasthas. By the eighteenth century large zamindars were almost invariably Brahmins. A large number of the Brahmins were also employed as 'managers' of zamindaris belonging to other castes. They could obtain land leases on better terms and were exempted from various impositions and extortions to which the inferior classes are exposed. Thus in some parts of Bengal, in the eighteenth century, the Brahmins exercised considerable influence by combining their high ritual status with political and economic power. However, the Baidyas and Kayasthas were equally important, the majority of the administrative posts were held by them, many small zamindaris were under their control, and while the Kayastha monopolized the vernacular educational system the Baidyas shared the knowledge of Sanskrit with the Brahmins. It would seem that the Brahmin, Baidya, and Kayastha together formed a sub-elite group in the power structure of the traditional society; all rulers of Bengal, the Palas, Senas, Pathans, and Mughals, had to rely on their support.

Despite the social upheaval, the Brahmins, Kayasthas and Baidya continued to exercise considerable power in Calcutta. . . . Educational records of Bengal of this period also show that the majority of men who went for higher education came from these three castes. This factor has led many scholars, old and new, to believe that the *bhadralok* was a traditional elite, consisting of Brahmin, Baidya and Kayastha, which continued to enjoy high status and exercise power as junior administrators and landowners throughout the nineteenth century (Low 1968: 6 and 31; Seal 1968: 36-57). However, this view fails to recognize that, in contrast to caste, the *bhadralok* was an open *de facto* social group. Although the *bhadralok* was almost exclusively a Hindu group, caste had no part in the selection; men who held a similar economic position, enjoyed a similar style of living and received a similar education were considered as *bhadralok*. Men like Motilal Seal, a Subarnavanik (unclean Shudra) and Gaurchand Basak, a Weaver, although of very low ritual status, were leading *bhadraloks* of Calcutta. . . . Even L.N. Ghose included six Subarnavaniks, one Weaver, one Brazier, one Sadgop, one Tilu, and one Kaibartya (not to mention the Parsee, Khetri and Muslim families) in his list of eminent men of Calcutta. The lives of Bengali *abhijat bhadralok* proved, as the nineteenth-century biographer of Ramdoolal Dey put it, that ' there is an aristocracy which is not born but may be made' Those who could acquire enough wealth, English education, and high status through administrative service, belonged to this 'new aristocracy', and since a large number of Brahmins, Baidyas and Kayasthas had administrative skill, and economic incentives, they formed the bulk of the *bhadralok*. The majority of the Brahmins and Kayasthas, poor and illiterate, were not considered as *bhadralok*. . . .

In Calcutta, professions old and new, high and low, were open to all caste groups. The lists of *shroffs* (moneylenders) of Calcutta show that this old profession was not monopolized by any single caste group. The caste breakdown of the students of the Medical College given in Table 1 shows that only three out of fifty students in 1839 were Baidyas (whose traditional occupation was medicine).

Table 1
The Students of Calcutta Medical College

Brahmin	5	Goldsmith	2
Baidya	3	Bankers	8
Kayastha	15	Miscellaneous	10
Druggist	1		
Weaver	6	Total 50	

Source : 'General Committee of Public Instruction', *Report on the College and Schools for Native Education . . . in Bengal for 1838-9*, Calcutta, 1840, p. 42.

If castes in Calcutta could not be regarded as hereditary occupational groups then the intercaste relationships and the caste hierarchical order were also undergoing profound changes. The taboos regarding food and pollution could not be enforced rigidly, where the Brahmin had to share the same civic amenities along with other castes—often living in the same street—and when they had to work in an office all day or conduct business at the docks. In about 1821, a book called *Karmalochan*, was published, which listed the daily religious duties that a pious Hindu should perform. The publisher soon discovered that men in Calcutta were reluctant to purchase the work

as the instances of their religious ommisions were so numerously recorded in it, that they were afraid of being reduced to beggary, by imposition of fines from the Brahmins on account of neglect of religious rites.

In fact, it was widely believed outside Calcutta that the *bhadralok* had 'fallen from the approved usage' (*acharbhrasta*). It would also seem that no particular area was allocated to any particular caste as it had been in the traditional village society. In Pathurighata there were Radi Kulin Brahmins like Baidyanath Mukherjee, Kayasthas like Ramlochan Ghosh, Pirali Brahmins like Gopimohun Tagore, Subarnavaniks like Nilmani Mallick and Weavers like Radhakrishna Basak. Pathuriaghata was no exception; all areas in the Indian part of the town were adorned with large houses of multi-caste *abhijat bhadralok*.

In the new schools and colleges boys from different castes mixed freely. There was no caste privilege in the classrooms or in the playgrounds. In David Hare's school, Ramtoonu Lahiri, a poor Barendra Kulin Brahmin pupil from Krishanagar, used to be bullied by his class monitor called Aditya, who was a Washerman by caste. This free mixing left a deep imprint, which had a far-reaching influence outside the school compounds. The *Enquirer*, the mouthpiece of young Bengal, observed, 'boys of different castes can never long remain on an equal footing in a class without forgetting and giving up their distinctions'. Menfolk, like their sons, mixed freely at business, at school committees, at public meetings, in *sabhas*, and other public gatherings. The family functions of the *abhijat bhadralok*, marriages, *sradhs*, *pujas* were transformed into multi-caste social gatherings, and were celebrated with great pomp and splendour. The *barowaree*, or later the *sarvajanin pujas*, were invented in response to urban life. These *pujas* were not performed in temples or in family chapels but by 'subscription assemblies', annually formed for this purpose only. By the end of the nineteenth century almost every area in Calcutta had such multi-caste 'subscription assemblies'.

Castes, however, remained important, as we shall see, in relation to marriage and inheritance. The rich members of ritually low caste started to establish horizontal links with caste brothers outside their regions and began movements to improve their ritual status. The Baidyas were the first caste to take steps in this direction. In the eighteenth century, under the leadership of Rajballabh, some of them started wearing the 'sacred thread' and declared themselves 'twice born'. Since 1822, there had been a continuous pamphlet warfare between the Brahmin and the Baidya pandits of Calcutta over the ritual status of the Baidyas. In 1831, the Baidya doctors, under the leadership of Khudiram Bisliarad, who was a teacher of medicine at the Sanskrit College, formed the Baidya Samaj, to defend their caste privileges. Although it was primarily for the Baidya medical practitioners, the leading members of the caste like Ramkamal Sen gave the new Samaj their full support. The ritual status of the Brahmins was also challenged in Calcutta. In 1832, Dharma Sabha called a special meeting to discuss a crucial question concerning the Brahmin-Shudra relationship; they debated whether a Shudra (if he is a Vaishnava), can claim 'reverence' from the Brahmin. But despite the evidence of caste consciousness and the importance of caste rules in marriage and inheritance, class consciousness, breaking down the caste barriers, is noticeable. Although the *bhadralok* had yet to evolve a class ideology, they were conscious of their existence as a social group and had every confidence in themselves as an agency for change. They increased in number and in strength during the 1820s. In 1829, Nilratan Haldar wrote (*Bangadoot,* 13 June 1829) that the rise of this 'new class' (*nutansreni*), whom he earlier referred to as *maddyabitto*, would bring 'economic prosperity and political stability' in Bengal. . . .

The class of *abhijat bhadralok* was undoubtedly one of the most important agencies for change in nineteenth-century Bengal. It would be true to say that it was their class interest which stirred them most; the economic issues such as stamp duties, house tax, the resumption of *laki-raj* (rent-free) land, and the general fear that the government might interfere with landed property forced all *abhijat bhadralok*, of all shades of opinion, into agitational movements.

Many of their other public activities were also economically motivated: they were eager to introduce modern banking, steam navigation and tea plantation. Many invested money and took an active interest in the scheme to colonize Saugar Island. They were all in favour of the modernization and commercialization of the economy of Bengal. However, they were also inspired by ideas which reached them from Europe through books and personal contacts with some of the more enlightened European officials the missionaries and free traders. . . . The *bhadraloks* had faith in reform and in their ability to change their destiny. In this sense they were all agents of 'modernity'; rising above local and parochial ties, they felt that they had commitments to larger communities.

The Untouchable's Version:
Evaluating an Ideal Ascetic

R. S. KHARE

Ravidas exemplifies the medieval ascetic central to the formation of the Untouchable's ideology and at the same time illustrates some critical properties of a Hindu ascetic. The selection of Ravidas is culturally significant because he remains enigmatic, immediate, fresh, and most representative of the dilemmas and aspirations of contemporary Untouchables in northern, central, and western India. His occupation, domestic life, and subtle estrangement from Hinduism all reflect the Untouchable's dilemmas better (than perhaps Kabir), and he is more easily worshipped and politicized than stern Kabir. Though a house-holder-saint, Ravidas is now a temple-enshrined 'deity', a saint who is spiritual yet humane. Since he is unashamed to be an Untouchable, he immediately illuminates the depth of the Brahman-Untouchable divide. He is uniquely unexpected, regal, miraculous, moderate, and exceptional for the Untouchable, and also equivocal anomalous, and yet clearly an outstanding devotee (*paramabhakta*) of Rama (i.e. Rama as Vishnu's incarnation) for the caste Hindu. . . .

However as we consider this position further, it will be instructive to bring up the two distinctly different versions the Untouchable and the

Excerpted from R.S Khare, 'Evaluating an Ideal Ascetic', in *The Untouchable as Himself: Ideology, Identity and Pragmatism among the Lucknow Chamars*, Cambridge University Press, London, 1984.

Hindu award to Ravidas. The cardinal Hindu principles that the Untouchable ideologist variously refutes or rejects in his version are a faith in and/or the pursuit of (1) God as deified *Isvara*; (2) rebirth; (3) Vedas and subsequent Hindu law codes; (4) Brahman-presided personal and collective sacrifices, rites, and ceremonies; and (5) the 'divine' *varna* and *jati* (caste) order of social status and authority.

There are few readily available and reliable textual sources on the Hindu and Untouchable treatment of Ravidas. I select the reputable Nabhadas's *Bhaktamala* for the Brahmanic model; Jigyasu for the Untouchable's version; Briggs (1920) for an external perspective on this ascetic; and a popular, several-volume collection of devotional songs—*Bhajan Samgraha* (1972)—for cross-checking Ravidas's poems as shared among the ordinary Hindu. We will focus on the first two sources, giving special attention to the dominant patterns and meanings of value relationships.

Ravidas also gets the following entry, as an introduction, from Bhandarkar (1965: 74):

> Ravidas, a pupil of Ramananda, was a founder of a sect the followers of which are to be found in the caste of Chamars, or leatherworkers. Nabhaji in his *Bhaktamalas* tells many legends about him. Under the name of Rohidas he is known and revered even in the Maratha country, and Mahipati, the Maratha writer on saints, devotes a chapter to him.

On the other hand, Farquhar (1967: 328) mentions AD 1470 as the only approximate date in connection with the sect of Ravidas, giving very little historical or sectarian detail for this specific group. (Kabir received his primary attention.) Culturally, therefore, these sources are not very helpful, leaving little choice but to turn to the legendary and the mythical data on Ravidas.

Ravidas: The Bhaktamala Version

Nabhadas's text on Ravidas, as recorded in the current version of *Bhaktamala* (1969: 470-1), may be sequentially broken up in the following major cultural strands and their dominant values:

Cultural strand	Significance
1. Having pure (*vimal*) speech (vani)	Enlightened ('pure') word and speech
2. Being deft in resolving ('knots of') doubt	Truly knowledgeable (*jnanin*)

3. Uttering words in agreement with   Concordance with the Hindu
   Vedic and scriptural injunctions   tradition
4. Carrying deep, clear discrimination   Highest reflection, wisdom,
   (*nira-ksira-vivéka: or sarasara*)   and understanding
   emulated by the highest ascetic
   (*paramahamsa*)
5. Ascending into heaven with his   A celestial soul (*divyatma*)
   body by the grace of God
6. Announcing his *real* caste (*jati*)   Truthful, fearless, and successful
   even as occupying the throne
   (*rajasinghasana*; i.e., as a sect leader)
7. Receiving veneration from those   Highest veneration despite low birth
   of high varna (e.g., Brahman)
   and *asrama* (e.g., *Samnyasin*),
   who had to leave their pride behind

This list of cultural strands is sufficiently symbolic and representative for our purposes. It calls attention to a number of dilemmatic cultural relations that reflect the paradox Ravidas represents to the regular hierarchical order. He was socially low yet spiritually exalted. Thus, we cannot mistake the central structural issue, namely, how does a 'lowest' (*atisudra*) person acquire a position venerated by, and sought among, the Brahmans? Is asceticism alone, even of the best kind, sufficient to achieve this position? The *Bhaktamala* version offers us an interesting if indirect and equivocal cultural answer, one that cannot satisfy the Untouchable ideologist. However, examined in terms of the Hindu cultural system, the *Bhaktamala* version tries to offer a culturally consistent approach to the preceding two questions. Let us first see how this is done within the Hindu scheme, reserving for later a consideration of the Untouchable version.

In the foregoing list, items 3, 5, and 7 are worthy of special attention. If item 3 establishes the cultural backdrop against which to view Ravi das's life, mission, and work, item 5 accords him a mode of 'death' reserved for gods, demigods, and only liberated souls. Simultaneously, under the ascetic model, this very feature stamps Ravidas as superior as an ascetic can become: he is the ultimate Indian representation of the triumph of spirit over physical body, and of the perfect, 'unbounded' ascetic over social order. Items 1, 2, and 4 elaborate what is good for those following Ravidas; from the ascetic's point of view they reflect the properties of a celestial soul. Such a soul, the cultural assumption goes, effortlessly exudes deep wisdom, miracles, enlightened words, good deeds and exemplary life-style. Power and influence (see item 6) come automatically to such a person. We will see why (and how) Ravidas's lowest social status could become problematic, especially when items 6 and 7, probably the most crucial of all, clearly juxtapose the relations of the two important Hindu orders (i.e., *varna* and *asrama)* to the placement of the ascetic. Does the ascetic overpower the social order? Can he really do so?

An answer to the last question is found in the legends surrounding Ravidas. These are recorded by the commentators of *Bhaktamala* alongside the main entry by Nabhadas. Briggs (1920: 207-11) also mentions most of the same legends, but without catching the Hindu's dilemmatic approach to basic conflicts between the ascetic and the social order. In contrast, Jigyasu's (1968a) account of Ravidas carefully eschews Hindu apologetics as if it were either a totally irrelevant or superfluous 'concoction'. Several Chamar informants, drawn from each of the three Lucknow settlements, remarked repeatedly, 'They are the Hindu devices to treat Ravidas Saheb [note this long-standing honorific the northern Untouchables consistently apply to their leaders and heroes] in terms of the caste Hindu excuses'. 'He was not a Chamar ascetic but an ascetic Chamar', offered a reformer from Baudhabagh.

It is significant in the *Bhaktamala* narrative that Ravidas was, in his previous birth found to be a *celibate Brahman* disciple of Ramananda, a reputed saint-reformer of the Vishnuite sect. The disciple Ravidas had once committed an unpardonable lapse in his worshipping duties. He had collected alms in the form of uncooked food (*sidha* or *cutki)* from a Bania shopkeeper who kept business relations *(karbara)* with a Chamar, and offered it to the deity worshipped by Ramananda. The deity, Ramananda 'saw' in his meditation, did not 'eat' the food that day, leading to Ramananda's inquiry about the source of the food (for the impure source necessarily lends impurity both to the food and to its eater). When told the truth, he cursed Ravidas to be born a Chamar in his next life.

The culturological commentary hidden behind the legend is now clear: Ravidas was not 'really' a Chamar. He was instead a 'Brahman soul' (note how here the 'soul' is considered indivisible), given to asceticism and Vishnuite devotion continued from his previous life. He was neither truly a Chamar nor a Chamar ascetic but a Brahman ascetic in the temporary 'garb' (for a body is considered to be clothing for the soul) of a Chamar. If any doubts remain, the second legend, immediately following the first one, tries to resolve them.

Upon rebirth in a Chamar house, Ravidas, as an infant, would not suckle his mother's breast, thinking 'if for one lapse I am born a Chamar, what would become of me if I take her milk?' Ramananda, however, was instructed by his deity to be compassionate to his cursed disciple, now born a Chamar. Ramananda consequently initiated the infant, and the latter accepted his mother's milk.

What is sociologically important is the procedure of status reinstatement (again through food) in Ravidas's case. For what appears here occurs rather repeatedly in such cases in Hindu culture and society. We may observe that the two principles of karma and reincarnation weave a basic pattern from which these (or other such) 'corrective legends' derive their explanatory meanings. Notice how, for example, a bad karma in his previous life condemned him to the Chamar's status and how the cumulations of the good karmas in the low birth (beginning with rejection of the Chamar mother's milk) started his journey upward *in the same life*. If the principle of rebirth were subtracted, Ravidas would be a truly inexplicable cultural anomaly for the Hindu system. How else can one really explain a Chamar (a lowest-ranking person) becoming an ascetic of the highest order? The legend of his rebirth (from high to low) must, however, steal Ravi das's thunder as a Chamar saint: it compromises the ascetic's spiritual principle, making him fall within the established order of caste precedence. In the preceding list, items 3, 5, 6, and 7 describe Ravidas's position as a Hinduized ascetic: Here he obeys the Vedas and other scriptures, shows signs of a vestigial sacred thread on his body, is venerated by the Brahmans and the *samnyasins*, and bodily ascends to heaven. What initially seemed highly contradictory is now rendered ideologically tame and culturally understandable. It thus becomes apposite to Hindu cultural ontology.

Several other aspects are hidden in this legend, but we shall emphasize one aspect a little more: True to the Brahman's form, Ramananda's deity refuses to eat food obtained from a Bania shopkeepr who does business with Chamars. This indirect defilement of food is so strong that it meets refusal from the same deity who, later on, after the fulfilment of the curse, sends Ramananda to initiate the Untouchable infant (an abnormal case, of course) with a *mantra* most sacred to all the Rama-worshipping Vishnuites. And Ramananda, with no qualms, works as an 'instrument' of divine mercy (and boons) for a Chamar infant. (Note the Hindu ethic of spiritual and undeniable equalization.)

Untouchable thinkers (Jigyasu 1968a; and 1965, summarizing Bodhananda) characterize this response, whereby the deity on one occasion upholds the rigorous Brahmanic injunctions for food purity, and on another reverses itself by reaching out to the lowest to lift him up 'like a Brahman', as emotional and contradictory. ('Brahmans' deities are as

volatile as are the Brahmans', was the comment of one Chamar informant.) However, what is contradiction for the Untouchable is a subtle,
ultimate arm of 'justice'(*dharma-samgatanyaya*)) for the established
Hindu moral order. A Durkheimian sociologist, in yet another view of
the same property, may discover qualities of hierarchical interdependence and holism between those high and low. Alternative (but all singly
incomplete)cultural interpretations are perhaps at the heart of such a
story.

The *Bhaktamala* version of the Ravidas story contains several more
legends, classifiable in distinct ascetic themes. For example, Ravidas's
detachment from the world forms the core of one legend in which he,
rejected by his family, lived in poverty in a small hut with his wife and
followed his traditional occupation—shoe-making. Allured by God to
accept riches for himself, he remained undaunted until he was sure to
employ it in His service (i.e. on temples and devotees). But such a use
brought him repeated confrontations with Brahmans—the second theme
of these legends. They grew jealous of his devotion, fame, and riches
and either complained to a regional raja, refused meals from his
kitchen, or repeatedly and publicly tested his asceticism and devotion to
God. However, without exception, it was of course Ravidas who won.
How is this moral consequence to be justified?

Again, it is significant that the *Bhaktamala* commentator attributes
responsibility for this anomaly to the equivocating deity, who would,
for example, *test* Ravidas by offering him a philosopher's stone, force
him to handle conspicuous riches and social gatherings, and then turn
the Brahmans against him. Social resistance and opposition, we are told
by implication, are not without divine purpose. What looked like the
Brahman's ignorance is in fact a divine design.

A crisis for the caste ethic, for example, was reached when at the
invitation of a queen (named Jhali), Ravidas went to Chittaur (Rajasthan) and received her food offerings where the Brahmans, present for a
sacred occasion, were also eating. However, seeing Ravidas, they refused to accept even the fried (*pakka*; impurity resisting) food and asked
for only uncooked provisions so that they could separately cook and eat.
But the legend holds that when they sat down with their plates, they
found Ravidas sitting 'between every two Brahmans'. 'This opened the
eyes of these Brahmans . . . and several of them became his disciples'
(*Bhaktamala* 1969: 479). However, this could not properly be the climax, since 'for the reassurance of everybody', Ravidas also related the
story of his previous life and, 'peeling off his skin', showed his vestigial
'golden sacred thread' to all!

In this narrative, Ravidas is thus again selectively but variously (see items 3, 5, 6, and 7) incorporated into the Hindu fold. This process of successive cultural neutralization and incorporation, a process widely recognized as characteristic of Hinduism (though perhaps not unique to it), must aim to contain, deflect, and disperse oppositions to the established priority of Hindu values. Jigyasu (1968a : 88ff.) calls this process *Brahmanikarana* ('Brahmanization') and, as expected, he wants to see Ravidas freed from the applicability as well as results of this process, for it is, in his view, extraneous to the 'real identity and significance of Ravidas'. (Compare this handling of higher caste values of Srinivas 1966, for Sanskritization.) Jigyasu would be suspicious of any explanation fabricated for *prasthanatrayi* (i.e., Upanishads, Gita, and Brahmasutra). These were to him storehouses of contradicting personages and equivocating divinity.

Before we consider the Untouchable's version of Ravidas's story, let us note how the Untouchable thinker interprets the principles of karma and rebirth. These dominant Hindu principles may illustrate what the Untouchable reformer calls the 'heads-I-win-and-tails-you-lose' (*chit bhi apni our pat bhi apni*) reasoning. For if somebody is born low in this life but was high before, these devices offer a means, usually with the help of a network of curses and blessings in myths and legends, to prove, whenever necesary, 'that he is really not as low as he appears to be'. Additionally, if somebody is born high, the same devices may offer equally effective means to prove that his previous low birth need not matter. For example, if an Untouchable is born a Brahman in his present life, this is of course sufficient to make him a Brahman. But if a Brahman is born an Untouchable (and if there are circumstances as compelling as in Ravidas's case), birth alone will still be *insufficient* to wipe out the vestigial highness of the previous birth. In this way the supremacy of the top-down view of the hierarchical order must remain incontrovertible and completely dominant. Further, as Jigyasu remarked, somehow the 'souls' of upper-caste members are considered 'in-dividual' but divisible and scattered of those low.

Ravidas: The Untouchable's Version

Confining ourselves to the ideological level, we shall once again examine significant symbolic features the Untouchable ideologist awards to Ravidas. A caveat is necessary at this point. Since this ascetic is variously worshipped by the Ravidasi Chamars in northern India, and there are internal sectarian or localized interpretations, we do not intend to evaluate this empirical heterogeneity. Jigyasu (1968), Briggs (1920), and my Chamar informants from the three Lucknow localities, which include Ravidasis, will remain my main guides, lending uniformity to what has been and will be discussed.

One quick yet reasonably accurate way to characterize the Untouchable's Ravidas is to confute and reject those crucial items from the *Bhaktamala* list that we have already pointed out. For example, Ravidas did not obey the Hindu Vedic and scriptural constraints (item 3); he did not literally ascend to heaven with his mortal body but achieved the highly desired goal of nirvana, as provided in Buddhism (item 5); he revealed his real spiritual identity as a Chamar without any camouflage or pretext (item 6); and he encountered resistance and opposition from the Brahmans (and the caste Hindu)—householders and ascetics—throughout his life and overcame them like a true Chamar (item 7). On the remaining properties (items 1, 2, and 4, which award Ravidas exceptional intellectual penetration and powerful speech), the Untouchable version would agree, because these are the signs of any true ascetic, and the exclusive property of neither the Brahmans nor the Brahman ascetics.

As would be logical to expect, Jigyasu's (1968) profile of Ravidas significantly agrees with this reformulation. Actually, his first full chapter on Ravidas (chap. 6 of the book) is entitled 'Were Sant Ravidasji's Words in Agreement with Veda-Sastra?' and starts with the same quote from *Bhaktamala* discussed earlier. However, his translation differs in some important respects (especially item 5) from that of the *Bhaktamala's* commentator. He finds Ravidas unhesitatingly announcing his Chamar social status (p. 46). Jigyasu's several succeeding chapter headings are equally revealing: 'Was Sant Ravidasji an Idolator?' (chap. 7); 'Sant Ravidas on False Beliefs and his Contemporaries' (chap. 8), which is given to establishing a greater reliability and veracity of ascetic experiences (*anubhava*) over the Vedas; 'Four Sectarian Saints of Brahmanic Culture' (chap.9); which compares Hindu sectarian asceticism to that of the *adi* Hindu (illustrating it with four low-caste medieval saints in the succeeding chapter); 'Four *Panthiya* Saints of Ascetic Culture' (chap. 10); 'Opponents Burned the Sayings of Ravidasji' (chap.11); 'Ravidasji and the "Abode" of his Contemporary Saints' (chap. 12), which discusses yogic, philosophical, and sectarian distinctions within the ascetic culture; 'Rama of Ravidasji' (chaps. 13-16), which dispute the common notion that Ravidas worshipped the incarnation of Rama rather than the formless, attribute-free God through yogic practices; 'Fish, Ant, and Bird' (chap. 17), which analyses three successively superior paths of the yogi-ascetic (and shows Ravidas to be of the last—highest—kind); Jigyasu concludes with a discussion of Ravidas's death, anniversaries, and memorials. (chaps 18-19) and 'Ravidasji's [didactic] Sayings and Aphorisms' (chap. 20).

The foregoing is a thematic summary of the second of two volumes on Ravidas, which evaluates and carries forward to its ideological climax the biographical description of the first volume. The first volume is dedicated to establishing that Ravidas was *not* a disciple of Ramananda (also 1968a: 102); the second widens the base of its argument by presenting it in terms of the aforementioned chapters. The first theme of the second volume establishes a philosophical, mythical, historical, and sectarian dichotomy between the ascetic (*sramana samskrti*) and Brahmanic cultures. The second theme demonstrates that Ravidas belonged in word and deed to the first, not the second, culture and that the differences between the two cultures 'prove' to us that the ascetic culture has 'moral superiority' because it emphasizes spiritual equality in yoga as well as social life. The third theme presents 'the most complete' assembly of Ravidas's sayings (ten *Sakhis* and 102 *sabdas*), with an epilogue.

The Chamar ideologist converges on Ravidas either to discuss or controvert the following: idolatry, the order of the four sectarian (Panthi) saints, the disappearance of Ravidas's work, and his spiritual and yogic pursuit. Each of these features, we will see, either represents an important point of ideological difference with the Hindus or points towards a way of life that ascetic ideology envisages.

Idolatry, the hallmark of Hinduism, comes under particularly sharp attack by the Untouchable ideologist. Such a repudiation allows him to reject what the Hindus deny the Untouchable (e.g., temple entry) and to substitute Hindu devotionalism with the Buddhist doctrine of 'voidness' (*sunyavada*). In contrast, Hindu legends repeatedly depict Ravidas as one who showed his miraculous powers of devotion by being a devout idolator. Tested by the Brahmans for his idol worship, he is known to have publicly 'summoned the deity into his lap for accepting his food over that of the Brahman'. Jigyasu offers Ravidas's own sayings to refute this attribution. (We may note, however, that these sayings would be persuasive if Jigyasu were at the same time sure about what is genuinely Ravidas's work and what is not.)

Jigyasu (p. 55), in one place at least, notes that Ravidas may have kept up 'the idol worship more to secure a right [denied] than as a believer.' But he finally rejects this 'halfway formulation' as yet another Brahmanic invention and propaganda, and he offers in support of his own position *two* poems by Ravidas, appended with an ideological interpretation. One of these two, I have discovered, is also freely included in popular Hindi anthologies and demonstrates Ravidas's devotion to 'Rama' (*Bhajansamgraha* 1972: 107-8). Finally, it is quite revealing that Jigyasu (pp. 7, 149-50), although reviewing the varied modes of celebrating the Ravidas anniversaries and memorials, approves rather than condemns the idol of Ravidas himself in ornate and larger temples. He commends Ravidas's worship and 'Ravidas Katha' (i.e., recital of the Ravidas story), offering it in place of the popular *Satyanarayana* Katha (i.e., the story of the Hindu god Satyanarayana), which only a Brahman priest can recite.

This mode of treating and discussing idolatry in indic civilization has been endemic, and there seems to be little new that Jigyasu has been able to offer us in this context. It is probably the weakest segment of his argument. He yields most easily where he should have resisted most staunchly. However, this lapse, though important, is not sufficient to destroy the credibility of his ideological argument, especially since he confines Ravidas's deification to the less reflective, making the Ravidas temples a symbol of protest, religion and politics. He refuses to admit that Ravidas represents any ultimate cultural principle other than absolute, unqualified spiritualism. This axis also remains at the core of his criticism of the Hindu Sectarian philosophers like Samkara ('the one who crafted a new Brahmanic garb for the Buddhist ascetic values'; Jigyasu 1968a: 71), Ramanuja, Madhavacharya, and Vallabhacharya. He finds them torturing the selected ingredients of autochthonous asceticism to sustain the Brahmanic culture.

This Hindu exercise could not succeed in diluting the principles of the ascetic culture, argues Jigyasu; instead, the latter became more widespread. The four 'true ascetics' from the medieval period (Kabir, Ravidas, Dadu, and Nanak), observed Jigyasu, 'demolished the philosophical fort of the Brahman's culture by denouncing unequivocally the distinctions of caste, sect, sex, and special privileges, and by downgrading sacrificial rituals, temples, and bibliolatry.' Ravidas was on this difficult mission, according to Jigyasu, in the company of these three 'roughly contemporary' ascetics. He notes that three of the four came from low castes (Kabir, a Julaha; Ravidas, a Chamar; and Dadu, a Dhunia), substantiating the point that the notable ascetics of this period were most often drawn from the low or lowest caste groups (e.g., Namadeva was a Chipi; Nabhadas, a Doma; Bulla Saheb, a Kurmi; Parmesthia, a Darzi; Sena, a Nai; Dhana, a Jat; see Jigyasu 1968a: 50-1, 78, for more examples) and that they were highly influential reformers of the Indian society. He finds Kabir influencing and converting

Ramananda to his liberal view, controverting the usual information that Kabir was a disciple of Ramananda. Historically (whatever little is known), this position is untenable (Westcott 1953). But then we are not considering history alone, but rather an interpretation of the historical that must shape a whole range of notions from socially shared cultural innovations to untended meanings to mythic formulations.

Overview

In summary, a basic outline of the ideologist's argument is now clear. As he reflects on the dilemma of being the deprived and the lowest, he finds that his traditional cultural as well as social options must remain narrow, limited and ambiguous. If the task has been to propose a radical cultural alternative, the result, although structurally neither illogical nor symbolically inconsequential, is mixed. The tactic is logical in seeking the alternative from a quarter most promising—asceticism. Asceticism's unquestioned cultural depth and pervasion are the ideologist's best hope. Accordingly, he begins to piece together his version of ascetism and its immediate and remote implications. He also tries to cut through obstructions by emphasizing the spiritual (i.e., the symbolic and abstract) ideas and relations of the sacred. It is a movement basically opposite to the Brahman's, allowing the ideologist to try to limit and devalue the socially established Hindu icons, rituals, and institutions. The higher the stakes set by the concrete caste-Hindu relations, the more strongly felt is the ideologist's need to enunciate a contrasting spiritual scheme. From the outside, spiritualization may look like an escape, and perhaps the only one available, but from within, it is culturally the most direct, genuine, and powerful procedure to opt for. It is also the one that the caste Hindu can never dismiss or reject without damage to himself.

The foregoing evaluative argument progresses first by examining an ideological plank that stresses a sharing with, rather than exclusion from, mainstream Hindu values (e.g., of yoga, austerities, karma, and dharma); second, by recomposing the principal ideological categories and relations from within; and third, by trying to put Hindu ideology on the defensive. The post-Gandhi caste Hindu in India, for example, has increasingly shown a mixture of resistance and guilt, though this has to appear in response to a far more varied social condition than the preceding ideological formulations alone can point towards. Yet this slow change in conscience of the caste Hindu is now indeed a part of the new social reality. It shows, most of all, to the Untouchable thinker a way to

launch his own evaluative schemes by creating a relevant cultural platform for himself and his people.

The function of this ideology could either remain cathartic or mediat-
ing, or become antagonistic; the foregoing ideological exercise also
means engaging in comparative social judgment, that is, evolving one's
own cultural standards and measures, and evaluating others against
them. It is a procedure that violates an absolute of the hierarchical caste
ethic and promises potentially significant cognitive and practical consequences. To judge this way also means to claim freedom to plan, to
respond, and to learn from social experience; it is also to make such a
judgment serve one's own ultimate, as well as proximate, hopes for a
changed identity and existence. The Untouchable thus announces his
conscious entry into decision-making processes and his participation in
the domains of comparative social responsibility (especially as between
the Untouchable and the caste Hindu). It also means refuting the total-
dependence model.

Although we may not want to read too much at once into the comparative evaluation of Ravidas, it does encode, as we will see, such a
transition in a germinant form, and Ravidas is found to play a heroic part
in it. He is a medieval hero who, after Merleau-Ponty (1964: 183, and
his quotations of Hegel), would stand, in the Untouchable's view,
among 'the individuals of world history'. This hero has 'a presentiment
of the future' and strikes 'against the outer world as against a shell and
cracks it because such a shell is unsuited to such a kernel'.

Kerala Christians and
the Caste System

C. J. FULLER

Those who profess the Christian faith in Kerala are divided into three broad goupings—Syrian Christians, Latin Christians and New Christians—which are distinguished according to two main criteria: to which caste the original convert from whom the members of each grouping claim descent belonged, and the date of these original conversions (Alexander (1972) refers to the New Christians as 'Neo-Christians'; in Malayalam they are known as *putiya kristyani* —'new Christian' or as *avasa kraistava*—'backward Christian').

The Syrians, as I shall henceforth refer to them, have two legends about their origin. The first and most frequently quoted is that they are the decendants of Nambudiri Brahmins, the highest-ranking caste in Kerala, converted by St Thomas the Apostle after his arrival in India in AD 52. This legend has various versions which need no discussion here (see Ayyar 1926: 2-13; Brown 1956: 43sqq.). . . .

The second legend is that the Syrians are descended from families brought to Kerala by a merchant of Syria, Thomas of Cana, in the fourth or perhaps the sixth century, although this story does not exclude the possibility that a Christian community already existed in Kerala, as indeed it almost certainly did. This legend too has several versions (Ayyar 1926; Brown 1956). It has some interest in that it suggests that the Syrians were originally immigrants to India, like the Jews of Cochin (Mandelbaum 1970 : 560-3) or the Ashraf Muslims of north India. . . .

Excerpted from C.J. Fuller, ' Kerala Christians and the Caste System', *Man* , *JRAI* (n.s.), Vol. II, 1976.

However the Syrian Christian community originated, it is certain that by the sixth century at the latest there was a flourishing Christian community in Kerala; historians regard this as proven on the evidence of Cosmas Indicopleustes, the Egyptian monk whose wanderings are recorded in his Christian topography (Brown 1956: 66-9). It is indisputable that there were Christians in Kerala for many centuries before the arrival of the first European on the Malabar Coast. Marco Polo initially brought news of them to Europe—he visited India at the end of the thirteenth century. The first emissary from Rome, John of Monte-Corvino, sent by Pope Innocent III, is thought to have stayed in Kerala in 1291 and he was followed by various other priests and travellers from Europe (Brown 1956: 81-5; Atiya 1968: 360-1). It is thus not true, as some writers would have it, that Vasco-da-Gama, who landed on the Malabar Coast in 1498, was the first European to discover the Syrians. His landfall did, however, herald the rise of Portuguese power in Kerala, a historical development of the greatest significance for the region and especially for the Christians there.

In the wake of the Portuguese, St Francis Xavier visited Kerala in 1544 and again in 1549. His missionary endeavours led to the creation of the second major grouping, the Latin Christians. Most of his converts came from the fisher castes (Mukkuvans and Arayas) and even today, the vast majority of Latin Christians live on the Travancore coast where most of them are still fishermen. They are nearly all Roman Catholics with the Latin rite, hence their name. There were very few of them where I worked and I possess little first-hand knowledge of them. (They are discussed briefly in Ayyar 1926: 252-78; Klausen 1968, especially ch. 3, is the only modern ethnography in which they have a prominent place.)

The third gouping, the New Christians, is formed of the descendants of those converted in the missionary wave of the nineteenth and early twentieth centuries. These missionaries were inspired and often led by European Protestants from, for example, the Church Missionary Society and the London Missionary Society, as well as from Denmark and Germany, and like most other missionaries working during the British Raj, they concerntrated their attentions on the lowest castes. It is generally agreed that the appeal of Christianity to these people was the hope that they might be released from their degrading and humiliating station in life—a hope, of course, all too rarely realized in fact (Mandelbaum 1970 : 568-9). Some high-caste members underwent genuine religious conversions at this time, but the preponderant attitude of high-caste Indians to the missionaries varied from disinterest to contempt and opposition, which perpetuated itself by making it more and more the case that the missionary churches were Untouchables' churches and Christianity the 'religion of pariahs' (O'Malley 1941: 673). In 1857, the C.M.S. in Travancore reported that it probably had no more than ten Nayar converts among its 5,000-6,000 adherents. The attitude of most Syrians to the missionaries was identical to that of high-caste Hindus. But there were exceptions and some Syrian priests saw proselytism as a challenge to their churches and began their own efforts. One of the most prominent and successful of these Syrian priest-missionaries lived in the village where I worked, and many of the New Christians in the area are descended from those he converted in the late ninetneeth century. Although they attend the same church as Syrian Catholics in the village, they are not of the Syrian Christian grouping as understood here. As I shall explain later, some of these converts' descendants have now been accepted as members of the Syrian grouping. (On Syrian missionaries, see Arayathinal 1947.)

The Christian Groupings and Castes

In this section, I hope to show that the three Christian groupings may sensibly be regarded as castes.[1] The Christian groupings form part of the total segmentary caste structure and are ranked with respect to each other and to the Hindu castes in such a way that, if we wish to describe the caste system of Kerala or Travancore as a whole, we have to include the Christians in it. As I know most about the Syrian and New Christians, I shall mainly confine myself to them in the following.

Like other large castes in Kerala, the Syrians had and have no unique traditional occupational specialization, most of them are, and were even more so in the past, landholders and traders. There is some evidence that in the sixteenth century they were, in certain areas, powerful landlords and that they controlled a good part of the pepper trade, and also that many of them were soldiers, like the Nayars (Brown 1956:15). . . .

It is clear, though, that in the past there was certainly a higher proportion of Nayars than of Syrians who were large landlords and who held privileged positions in the tenurial hierachy, although during this century Nayar superiority in these respects has declined markedly. Along with their relative rise in prosperity has come a claim by

[1] The word 'sensibly' is cautiously used for only as an ideal type can 'caste' be defined.

the Syrians that they are of a rank equal to the Nayars in the caste hierarchy. This claim is not completely rejected by the Nayars themselves, although the latter probably still feel that they have the edge over the Syrians.

There are some Syrians who claim Nambudiri rank on the grounds of their descent from St Thomas's converts, and say that in the past they were accorded Nambudiri status by the Nambudiris themselves as well as by others such as the Nayars. This claim can be found in innumerable propagandist texts by Syrians and the main evidence adduced is that they and the Nambudiris shared various customs. Brown (1956:173) concludes that Syrians have generally been ranked equal to Nayars; both, he says, could formerly carry arms (1956: 15; Ayyar 1926: 55-7), both had similar roles in village organization inferred from the Syrians' role as 'protectors' of artisans, both had similar rights in land and both observed similar pollution rules (Brown 1956: 168-9; Ayyar 1926: 53-4). My evidence conflicts with Brown's conclusion, for I found it to be widely held, by both Nayars and Syrians, that the former had definitely ranked higher in the past, although today, maybe, the gap had narrowed. It may, perhaps, have been the case that in certain areas where Syrians enjoyed a decisive local dominance they ranked above or equal to Nayars; in most areas, however, I am certain that they ranked lower. As for Nambudiri status, the vast majority of Syrians accepts that they rank below them and there is little concern about the contradiction between this and their claimed Nambudiri ancestry. Nambudiris today react to the Syrian claim with little more than a wry smile.

The Syrian grouping is endogamous. Except for the very occasional 'love marriage' there are no marital unions between the Syrians and Latin Christians as marriage would be as unthinkable for a Syrian as would a marriage to a Harijan for a Nayar. Indeed, I have more than once heard it said by a Syrian that it would be preferable for one of their community to marry a Nayar or another high-caste Hindu than to marry a New Christian, and I feel sure that this is the popular senti-. ment. This is partially borne out by the example of a love marriage which took place between two Indian Administrative Service officers— a Brahmin man and a Syrian woman, both from a village near Changanacherry—and which was regarded by local Syrians as an exceptionally prestigious match for the woman. What would happen if a Syrian and a New Christian did wish to marry was regarded by most informants as so hypothetical a question that they could not answer it; it had never happened so far as they knew. But they thought that the priest would probably succeed in persuading such a couple to abandon the proposal.

Within the Syrian grouping, there is a division into Northists and Southists ('Nordist' and 'Sudist' in many writings); the division is said to stem from Thomas of Cana who had two wives of different status, one of whose children inherited his northern estates and the other the southern. The terms no longer have any territorial designation. The Northists are by far the more numerous, but they are ranked below the Southists and the two groups do not intermarry. The Syrians with whom I worked were Northists, but I have little information about the significance of the division today as my informants were not even aware of its existence. Presumably only in areas where there are Southists as well does it have any importance (see Ayyar 1926: 50; Brown 1956: 175).

The New Christians are mostly labourers on the land, on the roads or in factories. Very few of them possess land of their own. Economically, their position differs little from that of Hindu Harijans. They are regarded by the high castes, and by many of their own members, as being of a status more or less equal to that of the Harijans. Among the New Christians themselves, however, caste differences are of some importance. Many of my New Christian informants' families had been converted four or five generations previously and they claimed not to know from which caste they came, although they agreed that it was probable that they were from either the Pulaya or Paraya castes, the two largest Harijan castes in Travancore. But, they insisted, their caste of origin did not matter and they would marry any other New Christian. Those whose families had been converted more recently often did recall their original caste and usually said that they would not marry into a New Christian family of a different caste.

The question of 'forgetting' caste is problematic and not so simply explained as, for instance, 'forgetting' genealogies, given the importance of caste membership in India. The social conditions of the New Christians may have promoted this amnesia. In converting to Christianity, members of the lowest Hindu castes were motivated primarily by a wish to escape the indignities imposed on them by the caste system, but they then found that their condition was little changed in the Christian community. But here status is polarized—Syrians at the top, New Christians at the bottom—in a way which is but rarely found in the Hindu community, where there is a gradation of status from top to bottom through many castes. It may be that this polar situation, combined with frustrated aspirations, has promoted among the New

Christians a solidarity against the Syrians as a whole: a solidarity of the lowly which the Hindu system has, in the main, more successfully prevented. I certainly received the impression that many New Christians resented especially bitterly the Syrians' attitude towards them.

All Hindu Harijans are given Scheduled Caste status under the Indian Constitution. But New Christians converted from Hindu Harijan castes are classified only among the Backward Classes, a list drawn up by the state government and not guaranteed as inviolable by the President of India. Further, after four generations—the first being that of the original convert—Backward Class status is also lost in theory. However, as no records are kept of the original conversions, few New Christians are concerned about this. Many of them feel, though, that they deserve Scheduled Caste status as they claim, correctly in my opinion, that they are as under-privileged as Hindu Harijans. A considerable number of younger New Christians has actually re-converted to Hinduism, mainly in order to claim this status.[2]

I hope I have said enough for the reader to be able to accept that empirically the Syrian and New Christian (and also, though I have not discussed it, the Latin Christian) groupings can sensibly be regarded as castes. I have discussed the ranking of the Syrians *vis-à-vis* the higher Hindu castes, and mentioned that the New Christians are ranked with the Harijans. That the Christian and Hindu castes are ranked with respect to each other is some evidence for my assertion, which I shall try to substantiate more fully, that Christians and Hindus are members of one total caste system, not two separate ones existing side-by-side.

A possibly fruitful comparison with Indian Muslims is unfortunately not easy; while Ansari (1960: 67), for example, stresses the separateness of the two parallel Hindu and Muslim caste hierarchies in Uttar Pradesh, Mines (1972) shows that there is great variation in India. Some Muslims are practically integrated into the caste system while others are certainly not and between these extremes all variations are to be found. Dumont, in his important study of Hindu-Muslim relations, insists on the 'lasting social heterogeneity of the

---

[2] In the Indian Constitution, Scheduled Castes (Harijans) are given privileges such as reserved posts in government, reserved places in public education and jobs in the public sector, special welfare provisions, etc., designed to ameliorate their lowly economic and political position. The Backward Classes, the list of which is drawn up by the state government, are given an extensive range of privileges.

two communities' (1970a : 95); 'The crucial point is that co-existence has produced no general ideological synthesis' (1970a : 96). I shall try to show below that there is such an 'ideological synthesis between the Hindu and Christian communities in Kerala and this, I would argue, is correlated with the empirical fact that the castes of both communities are mutually ranked and form parts of a single caste system. Possibly Dumont's argument applies more strongly to Uttar Pradesh than it does to other areas. Almost certainly, the fact that the Ashraf Muslims of that region\ see themselves as invaders from outside India and were in actuality, rulers over the Hindus is significant, as is also the existence of a pan-Islamic consciousness. Miller (1950: ch. 4), in a comparison of Muslims and Christians in Kerala, shows how the Muslims, originally integrated like the Christians into the caste system, developed an Islamic consciousness during the Muslim Mysorean invasions of Malabar (1760s to 1790s) which continued to grow until independence and beyond. But the Syrians stress their 'Indian-ness' and Brahmin origins, they have never ruled over Hindus except, perhaps, temporarily and locally and they have developed no strong pan-Christian consciousness. There was no campaign for a Christian Pakistan nor, within Kerala, for a Christian equivalent of Mappillastan, demanded by Malabar Muslims (known as Mappillas) after 1947.

Christian Sects

The history of the Kerala Christian sects is long, complicated and controversial and a detailed account is unnecessary. . . . Briefly, it is generally agreed that before the arrival of the Portuguese there was one church in Kerala which probably adhered to the Nestorian doctrine. The Portuguese, through the procedure of the Inquisition which began in Goa in 1560, tried to eradicate the Nestorian heresy and switch the allegiance of the Syrian church from Antioch to Rome. When the Portuguese power ebbed, a part of the Christian community repudiated Rome. Those that did not, then the minority but now the majority, are known as Syrian Catholics or Romo-Syrians, and theirs was the most numerous sect in the Changanacherry region. The Syrian Catholics recognize the authority of the Pope and although their mass was until recently said in Syriac, not Latin—it is now said in the Malayalam vernacular—they followed the standard Roman Catholic order of service. The part of the church which repudiated Rome became the Jacobite church. (In the nineteenth century, Syrian Catholics were sometimes known as *pazhayakutukka*—'old division' and Jacobites as *puttankut-tukkar* —'new division'.) So between the sixteenth and nineteenth centuries, there were two predominantly Syrian Churches in Kerala—the Catholics and the Jacobites—plus the separate Latin Catholic church. Foreign missionary influence promoted further fission in the nineteenth and early twentieth centuries. Strongly influenced by Protestant teaching, a section of the Jacobite church split off to form the Mar Thomite church, whose first Metropolitan was consecrated in 1842. Later fissions produced the Syro-Malenkara church, a branch of the Catholics, in the 1930s and the Syrian Orthodox, another branch of the Jacobites, which finally separated between 1909 and 1912. In 1958, however, partial reconciliation was effected between the main Jacobite church and its Orthodox branch. Besides these major sects, there exist many minor ones with a few adherents situated in different localities and further divisions and also reunifications still occur sporadically. There are also many distinct Protestant, predominantly non-Syrian sects.

Are the sects castes or subcastes? Dumont (1970b : 203) implicitly, and Mandelbaum (1970 :565) explicitly, have assumed that they are castes: mainly it seems the basis of Ayyar's statement (1926: 60) that:

Each division among the Syrian Christians has become, as in a Hindu caste, an endogamous sect, with no inter-marriage between the members of one sect, and those of another, though no objection is made to inter-dining.

But endogamy is an insufficient criterion, for many religious sects throughout the world—European Catholics being until recently an obvious example—are endogamous. The crucial criterion is not endogamy but recruitment. Is recruitment ascriptive by birth (caste) or by voluntary affiliation (sect)?

As it stands, my question is naive and no simple answer can be given. But we may conceive of two ideal types: an ideal caste in which recruitment is exclusively by birth and an ideal sect in which recruitment is exclusively by affiliation. All the sects, or rather cults at this stage, which have grown up within Hinduism appear to have been formed initially by voluntary affiliation. Early examples of such sects are the Jains and the Lingayats, both starting in the way I have mentioned. But it is plain that there is a general tendency for a sect to 'degenerate' into a caste (Dumont 1970b: 187-91; 1970b: 57-9; Mandelbaum 1970: 524-44). The social conditions under which the sect

develops are evidently important but, equally clearly, time by itself
is one of the most significant factors. We find that sects such as those
of the Jains or the Lingayats (founded in the fifth to sixth centuries
BC and the twelfth century AD respectively) are now practically
indistinguishable from castes, whereas modern cults such as the
Radha-Krishna cults in Madras (Singer 1966) are still quite distinct
from castes and recruitment to them is still principally by voluntary
affiliation. In other words, the history of Hindu sects demonstrates
that there is a tendency over time, without in any way denying the
relevance of other social factors, for a group to move from a position
close to that of the ideal sect towards that of the ideal caste. Though it
may sometimes be impossible precisely to place a group on this
continuum, it is clear that analytically the distinction between caste and
sect can be made and that it may be important.

The observations I have made about Hindu sects may be applied to
the case of the Christians. Although the children of a Syrian Catholic,
say, are likely to be baptized as Catholics, they may freely alter their
beliefs later and become communicants of another church. Such
changes are not particularly frequent, but they are by no means rare and
I know of instances. Hence we may conclude that the Christian sects
are, at least now, very much nearer to our ideal sect than they are to
our ideal caste and that we should not regard them as castes or subcastes, although it is true that they do have a structural role in defining the
village similar to that of castes or subcastes, a question which cannot be
elaborated here.

There is a further point to be made. When a Hindu joins or leaves
the Radha-Krishna cult, say, his caste membership remains unaltered
and his status, in so far as it derives from his caste, also remains
the same. This is equally true among the Christians; if a Syrian leaves
the Catholic and joins the Jacobite chruch, he is still Syrian and has
the same caste status. Status only attaches to a sect in so far as a sect
is associated with either Syrians or New Christians. For instance,
the various Protestant churches in Kerala are regarded as low in
status because almost all their members are converted Harijans; this
does not mean, however, that the few members of these churches
who are from high castes are regarded as low-caste members or as
having low-caste status. Similarly, when, as has happened quite often
in the village where I worked, a New Christian has left the Protestant
church and joined the Catholic church to which most of the local
Syrians belong, his status has not risen through his being a member of
a predominantly Syrian church; it has remained the same.

Criteria for Membership of the Christian Castes

The principal criterion for membership of the Syrian caste, as I shall now term it, is that one can claim descent from St Thomas's Nambudiri converts and that the claim is accepted by others. This claim, or rather the status which attaches to its acceptance, is transmitted through the patrilineal clan. Thus membership of the Syrian caste is acquired ascriptively by birth although, as we shall see, there are exceptions. Of course, not all Syrians really believe that they are descended from St Thomas's converts. There are as many cynics in the community as in any other and the cynics are supported by most of the evidence. The claim is essentially similar to that of the claims of innumerable other castes in India; for example, in Kerala, the claim of the Nambudiris that Parasurama, the sixth incarnation of Vishnu, settled them in the land. Caste origin myths of this type are familiar to all anthropologists of India, and that of the Syrians has exactly the same social function as any other; the only difference, which does not affect its function, is that it could be historically true. St Thomas might have come to Kerala, whereas the exploits of Parasurama are more difficult to credit.

Many Syrians almost certainly do belong to families which have been Christian for centuries. But others quite definitely do not. One informant explained to me at great length how he knew he was descended from one of the Apostle's converts. Later, I was reading the 1908 Land Settlement Report which gives along with the name of each landowner his caste. In the Report, I discovered that the members of the clan to which my informant belonged were listed as recently converted from a Hindu low caste. There were in fact several such families in the village. They all had two features in common: they owned land and they were fair-skinned. I did not discuss the cases of these particular families with informants in the village as it was an embarrassing topic. But it was generally agreed by informants that if a new convert acquired land and had a fair complexion, his descendants would probably be accepted, publicly at least, as Syrians after two or three generation.

The ownership of land was regarded as a virtual *sine qua non* for aspiring to Syrians status and it is a clear example of how, among the Christians, material wealth can be transformed into a form of status supposedly independent of economics. At the same time, one of the most effective ways of 'putting down' the *nouveaux riches* is to accuse them of being recently converted from a low caste and of attempting to purchase Syrian status with their new wealth. The best example of this that I came across was a very rich family in a local town. They were merchants and had become wealthy over the last fifty years or so. They were widely accused of attempting to buy themselves Syrian status by offering enormous dowries to men who would marry their daughters. In 1971, they set a new record for the area when one of their daughters took a dowry of Rs 125,000 (approx. £ 6,500). 'Genuine' Syrians who had not been so fortunate in their daughters-in-law's dowries were ever quick to pour contempt on this family's alleged lowly origins and their blatant attempts to buy status, as well as on the renegade Syrians prepared to sell their status for cash. Fair skin is required in order to pass as a Syrian because of the stereotyped belief of almost all Syrians that they are fair like the Nambudiris, considered to have the lightest skins in Kerala. In fact, most Syrians are relatively fair, especially when compared with the Harijan castes, the majority of whose members have typical 'Dravidian' features, including dark skins and woolly hair. Izhavas, though, are generally lighter in complexion and are thus better able to pass as Syrians and my data suggest that most of those new converts whose descendants have become Syrians were formerly Izhavas.

The above evidence demonstrates that individual mobility between castes, under certain conditions and over a certain time, can occur within the Christian community. Membership of the Syrian Christian caste is thus not completely ascriptive and the Syrian caste does not approximate so closely to our ideal caste as does the Hindu caste. A similar conclusion evidently applies to the New Christian caste. Conversions are rare today and thus recruitment to the latter is mainly ascriptive. But the possibility of conversion always exists and, therefore, there is a direct parallel with the sect, and unambiguous incorporation into the caste is likely to be attained not by the convert but by his descendants. I do not wish to underestimate the importance of this question of mobility. Nonetheless, when the total context remains in view, I consider that the use of them term 'caste' to describe the Christin groupings remains justified (cf. Mines 1972: 348 on Muslims). (Individual mobility is also found among Muslims and I briefly return to the problem below.)

Rules of Caste and Pollution

In their relations with other castes, in so far as these are defined by the rules of purity and pollution, Christians behave just like local Hindus with certain exceptions. In the past, when distance pollution was observed by the Hindus, it was observed by Christians too. (In Kerala, pollution could traditionally be transmitted not only by touch, but also through the air if the difference in caste rank was sufficiently great; the latter was known as distance pollution.) In the past again, they would not have sat down to eat with persons from other castes. (Evidence for the above may be found in Ayyar 1926: 216; Brown 1956: 173-4.) This traditional pattern of caste behaviour has, however, disappeared in contemporary central Travancore.

In the nineteenth century, New Christians were not permitted to worship in the same churches as Syrians and separate ones had to be built for them, although Izhava converts were allowed into Syrian churches in some areas. It was not until 1914 that a Catholic church permitted New Christians to worship with Syrians (Arayanthinal 1947: 245-7; cf. Ayyar 1926: 215). In the late nineteenth century, the Syrian Catholic missionary from the village where I worked, whom I mentioned earlier, did encourage some of his Pulaya converts to worship in the same church as the Syrians. After the service, according to his diary, all the Syrians purified themselves in the nearest tank. Eventually, he was forced to construct a separate church. His missionary endeavours were opposed not only by Hindus but also by many Syrians, for both groups felt that new converts might refuse to work or to obey pollution rules. One of the solutions adopted by this missionary to quell opposition was to instruct his new converts that they must continue to serve their masters and observe all rules concerning caste and pollution. He then asked them to repeat three times that they would not leave their masters, after which he informed them that, were they to break their promises, they would be beaten not only by their masters but also by the priests. Such an explicit acceptance of the cast system was, of course, virtually impossible for European missionaries, who not infrequently had to call on British power to protect their converts from the threats of high-caste landlords and other powerful personages.

Although Chiristian behaviour regarding caste and pollution was, in most respects, identical to that of the Hindus, the Syrians did have a rather bizarre role outside the pollution system as well. In the past, they used to be considered by high-caste Hindus as capable of acting as pollution neutralizers in some contexts. For example, if certain objects were handed by a low caste person directly to a high-caste person, then the latter would be polluted—to use an electrical analogy, the pollution would have been 'conducted' through the objects. But if the low-caste person handed the objects to a Syrian who then passed them on to the high-caste person, the latter would suffer no pollution, for the Syrian would have 'earthed' it and the pollution would have drained away. A Malabar Syrian, Joseph (1928: 29) relates: '. . . the present writer himself in his boyhood about thirty years ago, used to be asked by Hindu temple servants to touch conventionally polluted provisions intended for the temple about a stone's throw from his house.' This was a standard practice for temple provisions, according to Joseph. Brown (1956: 172) tells the story of a Syrian who, in about 1890, had purified a temple which had accidentally been polluted and Aiyappan (1944: 41) says that oil, touched by an Izhava, can be purified by a Christian for the use of a Nayar, although cooked food cannot. Until quite recently, I was told, the brass lamps in Changanacherry temple were always cleaned by Syrians to avoid the possibility of pollution but, so far as I am aware, Syrians never act as pollution neutralizers nowadays. Pocock (1972 : 44) reports that in many parts of Gujarat, Muslims were able to act as pollution neutralizers in an identical manner. For non-Hindus to act in this way may be quite a common phenomenon in India, although I know of no other cases. The 'elasticity' of Hinduism and the way in which pollution rules can be 'bent' has often been remarked upon; this would appear to be an instance of such a 'bending', taking advantage of the presence of a group defined as marginal in appropriate circumstances.

In this section, I have discussed Christian behaviour with respect to purity and pollution. It has long been recognized that Hinduism distinguishes radically between, and evaluated differently, belief and behaviour. As O'Malley put it (1932: 20): 'Hinduism is elastic as regards belief but rigid as regards practice'. The essential correctness of this judgment will not, I think, be challenged. It underlies the important distinction between 'orthopraxy' and 'orthodoxy'. In the sphere of caste and pollution, it matters little what the ordinary Hindu thinks; it is what he does that counts. I have said that in their relations with other castes, Christian behaviour was almost identical to Hindu behaviour. More generally and conclusively, this may be re-expressed by stating that Christians and Hindus share, for the most part, a common orthopraxy and, therefore, at this level at least, we are concerned with a single social system, not two more or less separate sub-systems.

Unlike Hindus, however, Christians—like Muslims (Mines 1972: 339) —have no concept of bodily pollution consequent on birth, death, menstruation or other bodily conditions, nor do they observe pollution for them. Dumont has argued that the same concept of hierarchy is continuous throughout Hindu society. By this is meant that the

hierarchical notion, based on purity and pollution, which order
relations *between* castes are the same as those ordering relations
within the castes. There is no discontinuity in the hierarchical ordering at the boundary of the caste—an assertion which becomes less obscure when it is realized that the caste system has a segmentary structure (Dumont 1970b : ch. 2). One of the principal differences between
the Christians and the Hindus is, therefore, that among the Christians the hierarchy is discontinuous. Within the Christian community,
purity and pollution rules have only a very restricted application
and, in particular, birth, death and menstrual pollution—central features
of Hindu society—are absent. The shared orthopraxy operates only between the Christian and Hindu castes; within the Christian castes, behaviour differs from that within the Hindu community.

The Question of Ideology

The subject matter of this final section is unquestionably difficult
and, despite many re-draftings, I do not pretend that I am satisfied with
it. Some of the problems arise from inadequacies in my data; others
from the inherent complexity of the theoretical problem. Since Dumont,
however it has become imperative that the question of ideology be
confronted and those of us working on caste cannot afford to ignore it.

One problem can be dealt with immediately: the apparent contradiction between Hindu hierarchy and Christian egalitarianism. The
significance of this contradiction can be greatly exaggerated. Although
certain forms of Christian teaching have, at various times, given some
prominence to egalitarianism, it is historically the case that its dogma
has not emphasized this aspect and that hierarchy, as exemplified by
the concept of the 'chain of being', has been a constant and fundamental
element in Christian thought (Lovejoy 1953). Further, Christianity has
almost always been the religion of profoundly unequal societies and
has had little difficulty in adapting to them. Often, of course, it has
provided support for them. I do not think that this topic needs further
discussion, although we may note that the egalitarian aspects of
Christianity, as of Islam and Buddhism, have had negligible effect on
the Hindu way of life.

In analysing the importance of Hindu ideology, there have been two
principal, and distinctly different, approaches. The first of these,
which I shall only outline, concerns itself with the classical explanation
and justification of the caste system in terms of the concepts of dharma
and karma. According to dharma 'the divinely ordained norm of good

conduct, varying according to class and caste' (Basham 1971 :114), one should carry out the duties enjoined on one at birth as a consequence of having been born into a particular caste or role; to paraphrase the Bhagavad Gita's words (xviii, 47), 'it is better to do one's own duty imperfectly than to do another's well. Karma, 'the result of the deeds of one life affecting the next' (1971: 244), with the associated concept of samsara, i.e. continual transmigration of souls, explains why one has been born into a particular caste in this life. If one has behaved meritoriously, i.e. if one has adhered to the laws of dharma, then one will be reborn in a higher caste; if one has not so behaved, then one will be reborn in a lower caste. This is a very brief and over-simplified summary, but it will suffice for our purpose. The theory of dharma and karma is quite clearly antipathetic to all Christian teaching.

Weber is the most important sociologist to have placed emphasis on this aspect of Hindu ideology. Weber's ideas warrant an extended discussion, but this is impossible here. Very briefly, I think that serious doubt must be cast on them by the ethnographic evidence that many ordinary Indians are either ignorant or scornful of the doctrines of dharma and karma or alternatively do not employ these concepts as they are used in the classical texts (Sharma 1973 : 362-4). This paragraph, I must insist, does not purport to contain a refutation of Weber's theories but merely an indication of the direction in which I would begin.

The second approach to Hindu ideology is that of Dumont, who traces his intellectual descent from Bouglé. Here the emphasis is on the ideology of purity and pollution, together with the separation of the religious from the politico-economic. The ideology of caste, for Dumont, takes the 'first and foremost' place, for it 'orders and logically encompasses' (1970b : 37) the secondary politico-economic aspects of society. According to him, we must

first take lessons from the Hindus, Hindus of today and of times past, in order to see things as they do. They see them very systematically and it is not impossible to isolate the principle behind their view. . . . Some eight centuries perhaps before Christ, tradition established an absolute distinction between power and hierarchical status . . . .

Not only is the existence of this latter distinction necessary for the development of the purity-hierarchy, it is also imperative for this development that power should be absolutely inferior to status (1970a: 74). Without outlining Dumont's theories in any detail, I think it is reasonable to assert that the ideological distinction between power

and status is a cardinal point in his analysis and indeed the very definition of a caste system is ultimately dependent on the presence or absence of this distinction (1970a : 215).

Dumont states (1970b : 72) that the Brahmanas tell us about the distinction between status and power 'with extreme clarity' and elsewhere (1970a : 62-88), he has discussed these texts at greater length.
The question is, however, whether all Hindus, or even many Hindus,
of times past or present, see things 'very systematically' and make
the distinction between status and power which Dumont attributes to
them. Surely not; the notion that ordinary Hindus think with the clarity
and in the same manner as the authors of the Brahmanas is inherently
implausible. Dumont does not, of course, make such an assumption
explicitly but, I would suggest, it is present implicitly. . . .

I would contend that the ideology of ordinary Hindus in central
Travancore, as elsewhere in India, does not contain as a central feature
the concept of an absolute distinction between status and power. On
the contrary, this ideology recognized an intimate connection between the two and ordinary Hindus see politico-economic factors as
highly significant in the attribution of status. One piece of evidence
that this is so is the data on ordinary Hindus' explanations of caste
rank, which, as Sharma (1973 : 362-3) points out, are often couched
in secular or historical terms. This is hardly clinching evidence and I
admit that such evidence, whether from my own fieldwork or elswhere,
is not available. On the other hand, there is no evidence to support the
contrary view. It is fairly clear that ordinary Christians do not make an
absolute ideological distinction between status and power—nor does
Christian theology—and thus if my arguments about Hindu ideology
be admitted, it can be seen that both Christians and Hindus, at least in
this respect, share a similar ideology. The relation between status and
power is a crucial component of the caste system and, therefore, what
I am arguing is that the ideological conceptualization of caste is common, in its fundamental element, to both Christians and Hindus. Overall, therefore the conclusion is that not only do Christians and Hindus
share, at least in inter-caste relations, a common orthopraxy, they
also share a common ideology. An 'ideological synthesis' has taken
place.

In one place (1970b : 211) Dumont hints at an approach resembling mine. Writing of Hindus and Muslims, he refers to the development of a 'hybrid type' of society 'which we are scarcely in a position
to characterize, except by saying that, lying beneath the ultimate or Islamic values are other values presupposed by actual behaviour'. But

he presses no further and the reader remains unclear as to what exactly is implied by this passage.

To resolve completely the problems of this final section would involve an analysis of the relations between orthopraxy and ideology, on the one hand, and between theology and ideology, on the other. Such an analysis would, of course, also lead to a conclusion about the relation between orthopraxy and theology. Such a total analysis is probably impossible. However, to pose the problem naively, there clearly are basic differences between Hindu and Christian teachings and these presumably have their effect both on what ordinary Hindus and Christians think and on what they do. For example, there is a greater stress on the concept of the individual in Christian than in Hindu thought. Dumont has noted this more than once (e.g. 1970c: 33-5)—though he is not the first to have done so—and he is, in my judgement, correct. Christianity, of whatever persuasion, tends to stress the importance of the individual, as opposed to the group, as the 'normative subject' (Dumont 1970b : 9) more than does any variety of 'orthodox' Hinduism, although—significantly—the individual is given greater stress in many Hindu sects and cults (Dumont 1970a: 50-60). This point must not be exaggerated for it is a matter of relative emphasis only; Hinduism does not totally devalue the individual and Christianity does not totally devalue the group. Nonetheless, the difference is there and may have some significance.

I am tempted to relate the difference to the fact that individual mobility between castes is empirically possible within the Christian community, whereas it is not, except perhaps in some circumstances arising out of modern socio-economic changes in Hindu communities, where social mobility is a group phenomenon only. However, stating such a correlation between theological or ideological and behavioural levels is inadequate without a more precise demonstration of the connection. Among the Muslims too, individual mobility between castes within the community occurs (Mandelbaum 1970: 544-59). Mandelbaum (1970: 547) attributes it to the fact that 'ritual criteria' are 'not as weighty'in the Muslims as in the Hindu ranking system—a remark which also seems applicable to the Christian system. However, like my own hypothesis, it merely states a correlation between levels without any explanation or demonstration of the connection. Mines (1972: 345-9) agrees with Mandelbaum, but also points to the Muslim stress on personal independence (an individualist trait). But he too fails, I think, to demonstrate the connection between the behavioural and ideological levels, while his remarks about an ideological emphasis on equality and the dignity of work are inapplicable to the Kerala Christians or to most Muslims, as he is aware. Clearly, these problems require for their solution both more data and more powerful analysis.

Conclusion

This article is offered as a contribution to the understanding of the place of a non-Hindu community in the caste system. I have argued that Christians and Hindus share a common orthopraxy—i.e. behave *in* accordance with the same set of rules concerning caste and pollution—in respect of relations between castes, although the Christians also had a role as pollution neutralizers in certain contexts. Within the Christian community, however, pollution rules only operate restrictedly and thus there is a discontinuity in hierarchical ordering which is absent among the Hindus. I have further suggested that Christians and Hindus, for the most part, share an ideology of caste and that in this ideology, in contradistinction to Hindu theology, politico-economic power is not absolutely separated from religious status. Christians and Hindus thus form one total community, for they are integrated, albeit with some qualifications, at both the behavioural and ideological levels. In the course of my argument, I have been forced to reject Dumont's use of the concept and term 'ideology'. A more extended analysis of the problem of this article would demand a much stronger and deeper critique of Dumont's theories together with more comparative data on other non-Hindu communities in India only some of which appear to resemble closely the Kerala Christians in their place in the social system. Such a study should end in a better understanding both of Indian society and of the relation between ideology and behaviour.

Endogamy and Status Mobility among the Siddique Sheikhs of Allahabad

IMTIAZ AHMAD

One of the characteristic features of the caste system has been said to be the regulation of marriage. Each caste is characterized by the obligation to marry within the group, by endogamy. No doubt, there are numerous exceptions to the rule of endogamy as is clearly demonstrated by the Nambudiri Brahmans and Nayar castes in Malabar, by the Kulin Brahmans in Bengal, and by the Patidar caste in Gujrat, but castes are generally associated with rules which require endogamy. Wherever infringement of the rule of endogamy is allowed, as it seems to be the case in the instances just cited, the approved degrees of marriages outside the caste are usually hypergamous. . . .

In this essay, I shall describe how a Muslim social group successfully used endogamy to build up its distinctive group identity as well as to transform it suitably and subsequently employed both endogamy and hypergamy to raise its social standing within the hierarchy of Muslim groups. The group is the Sheikh Siddiques of Allahabad District. It is today divided into two 'marriage circles' one of which is strictly endogamous while the other has followed a pattern of selective hypergamy. I shall show that social mobility centring around recognition of their status as Sheikh Siddiques has been a primary concern of members

Excerpted from Imtiaz Ahmad, ed., *Caste and Social Stratification among the Muslims*, Manohar Bookservice, Delhi, 1973.

of both these marriage circles but their approaches to the problem have diverged. . . .

Endogamy among the Muslims

Even though endogamy has been frequently reported to be a characteristic of Muslim social groups, there seems to be some difference of opinion about the level at which the principle of endogamous marriage alliance operates among them. Dumont, for example, has asserted that

among the Ashraf there is no (absolute) endogamous grouping in the sense in which we have given the term . . . the Ashraf are contaminated by caste spirit although they have not succumbed to it (Dumont 1970b : 207).

He then distinguishes the so-called Ashraf groupings from the non-Ashraf and concludes:

These groups indeed seem to be endogamous in the Hindu sense of the term, and quite a large number of Hindu customs which they have preserved have been mentioned, some to do with marriage (Dumont 1970 b : 208). . . .

The Ashraf as a general category is composed of four major groups called the Sayyads, Sheikhs, Pathans and Mughals, and the widespread belief is that these four groups are the Muslim proto-types of castes. Ghaus Ansari, thus, characterizes these four groups as castes and attempts to discuss their relative positions into a hierarchy. But closer scrutiny of empirical facts suggests that the Sayyad, Sheikh, Pathan and Mughal are not castes at all; they are rather categories somewhat similar to the Hindu categories like Brahman and Kshatriya. Just as Brahmans and Kshatriyas actually represent categories rather than castes, so are the Sayyad, Sheikh, etc., categories including large numbers of people who identify themselves as members of different groups. For example, to take only one example, the Sheikhs are divided into a series of still smaller groups which share a common name, trace their descent from a common ancestor and, while they all characterize themselves as Sheikhs, scrupulously distinguish themselves from other groups of like order. These groups are secondary divisions while the division of the Ashraf category into Sayyads, Sheikhs, Pathans and Mughals, is a primary status division.

The secondary divisions are not castes either, or at least they cannot be characterized as such. On the contrary, they are sub-categories. For instance, the Sheikhs are often divided between three or four major sub-categories. One would find the members of the same sub-category claiming the name of that sub-category lived in different cultural regions or occasionally in different parts within the same cultural regions. This does not, however, mean that they either interact as members of one caste-like grouping or are regarded as such. On the contrary, members of the same named sub-category are often divided further into segments on the basis of marital links and geographical identification. Firstly, the members of a particular segment are identified, or identify themselves, with a particular region. In the rural areas, this identification assumes the form of the geographical areas identified with a particular segment as being referred to by the name of that segment. Thus, the set of villages which are identified with the sub-category of Kidwai Sheikhs is known as Kadyana. No doubt, Kidwai Sheikhs may be found to live in other regions but they are treated as members of a different group.

The second basis of segment separation is marriage link. All the members of a segment are endogamous, showing a greater emphasis or preference for marriage within the segment. Marriage of the segment members with members of other segments which may bear the same generic name, such as Sheikh Siddique or Ansari, are not approved. In effect, then, the segment is not merely a local unit but is also endogamous. This is also the real unit of endogamy and should be considered the Muslim equivalent of Hindu endogamous castes. But generally the sub-category or the primary category (e.g. Sayyad, Mughal and Pathan) have been regarded as real units of endogamy. The real units can be identified only on the basis of local enquiry, and there have been few empirical studies of Muslim social groups. Small wonder, then, that it should appear that there is no endogamous grouping among the so-called Ashraf Muslims.

Once it is recognized that the real unit of endogamy is not the primary or the secondary category, but a further segment of the latter defined by marriage and geographical location, it would also become clear that the character of the endogamous grouping among the Muslims is not particularly different from that among the Hindus. The Hindus are broadly divided into four *varnas*: Brahman, Kshatriya, Vaishya, and Sudra. The Kshatriya category is again divided into two sub-categories called the Suryavanshi Kshatriyas and Chandravanshi Kshatriyas. Each one of these sub-categories lives in several areas, but it does not mean that all the Chandravanshi and Suryavanshi Kshatriyas necessarily constitute single homogeneous castes. On the contrary, the Suryavanshi

Kshatriyas living in any one particular geographical area consider themselves a separate group and confine their marriages within it. Like the segments referred to among the Sheikhs, this geographical unit would appear to be the real endogamous grouping rather than the category Kshatriya or the sub-categories Suryavanshi and Chandravanshi.

It is clear, then, that the distinction which Dumont and others draw between the Muslims belonging to the Ashraf category on the one hand and the non-Ashraf groupings on the other does not conform to actual empirical facts (1970b : 282-8). On closer scrutiny, what appears to be the case is that a more meaningful distinction can be drawn between the higher Hindu castes and the so-called Ashraf Muslim groups on the one hand and the lower Hindu castes and non-Ashraf Muslim social groups on the other. . . .

The Sheikh Category

. . . .

Literally the word 'Sheikh' means chief or leader and is used in its Arabic form as an honorofic title for the head of a tribe, lineage or family. However, in India the term has come to enjoy a somewhat specific meaning and connotes a status group. It is used throughout the subcontinent to refer to persons who claim to have descended either from the Arab tribe of Koraish, the tribe to which Prophet Muhammad belonged, or from one of the close associates or friends of Muhammad. Such persons are generally supposed to be persons of noble birth in India and, along with the Sayyads, Pathans, and Mughals, are distinguished from the converts of indigenous origin. Like the Sayyads, Pathans, and Mughals, the Sheikhs also occupy a fairly high social position within the idealized scheme of social hierarchy among the Muslims. Alongwith the Sayyads who claim to have descended directly from the Prophet Muhammad through his daughter Fatima and Ali, and the descendants of the Afghans and Mughals, the Sheikhs are considered to constitute a category of social groups somewhat analogous to the *dwija* castes among the Hindus and these four groups are collectively referred to as the Ashraf.

The Sheikhs are widely dispersed throughout the whole subcontinent with a somewhat heavier concentration in the Indo-Gangetic plains. . . . They do not constitute a single homogeneous caste at all, but represent instead a congeries of a large number of separate sub-groups each of whom shares certain characteristics of a caste. For example, the Sheikhs are divided into a number of sub-groups based on descent and source of origin and their members not only identify themselves as members of separate groups but also try to preserve and highlight their separate group identity through a careful use of surnames. Ghaus Ansari (1969: 38-41) has noted that the members of each separate sub-group within the general Sheikh category suffix a particular title or name, such as Qureshi, Ansari, Kidwai, Usmani, etc., which serves to indicate the source from which they trace their descent and distinguish them from members of other groups within the Sheikh category. Of course, this does not mean that these distinctions are necessarily reckoned or recognized by outsiders. Generally speaking, the members of two or more sub-groups rarely live in the same locality, except in urban centres and the distinctions are not directly relevant. Whenever members of more than one Sheikh subgroup live within the same locality, the different groups maintain their distinct identity, but also outsiders see them all as a single group, that is as Sheikhs. This is to be expected, especially since the internal divisions within any social category are likely to be irrelevant to outsiders.

The different Sheikh subgroups are distinguished on a number of criteria. At least four principles can be easily identified: (a) they are based on affiliation with an Arab tribe, (b) they are based on descent from a person of definite and distinctively Arab origin whose close ties with the Prophet Muhammad are known, (c) they are based on names of places in Arabia or Persia, and (d) they are based on someone who is said to have been of foreign origin and who is supposed to have come with the invading Muslim armies in the early phases of the expansion of Islam into India. The essential point about these sub-groups is that they are always regarded as foreign and their members emphasize their foreign origin either by tracing their link to one of the historic personages or tribes of early Islamic Arabia, or by identifying themselves with a place which lies in Arabia or Persia, or by claiming descent from a person who supposedly came from the heartlands of Islamic civilization into India.

Each of the sub-groups within the Sheikh category is hierarchically arranged, ranking being based on descent and the source of derivation of the group. The criteria of ranking is the same that applies in determining the relative standing of the different categories within the Ashraf stratum. Thus, the degree of distance from the Prophet serves to define the relative standing of the sub-groups. Highest in the hierarchy of Sheikh sub-groups are the Qureshis who trace their descent from the tribe of Koraish to which, as indicated earlier, the Prophet Muhammad himself belonged. Next in order of precedence are the descendants of the three Caliphs, Abu Bakr Siddique, Usman and Umar.[1] There is a hierarchy, however, even within the descendants of the first three Caliphs. The highest in rank order are the descendants of the first Caliph, Abu Bakr Siddique, who was also a close and trusted friend of Muhammad, followed by the descendants of the other two succeeding Caliphs. Following the descendants of the Caliphs are the descendants of close associates or friends of Muhammad, especially those who accompanied him to Medina. Lastly, below these groups are the descendants of those who are supposed to have been of Arab or Persian origin and supposedly came with the invading Muslim armies. However, the hierarchy of the sub-groups of the Sheikhs is largely theoretical and idealized. It has already been indicated that the members of the different Sheikh groups do not live in the same locality. There is, consequently, no interaction among them that could serve to indicate their relative standing. Secondly, each group is largely endogamous. Under the circumstances, disagreement among the Sheikh sub-groups about relative standing is quite common, especially among groups which claim descent from persons of supposedly foreign origin who came with the invading armies.

Even the Sheikh sub-groups described above are not castes though popular usage treats them as such. Communities bearing the same sub-category name are often dispersed in several districts, but this does not mean that they are all members of the same caste. On the contrary, they distinguish themselves from one another both verbally and through endogamy. Occasionally, the distinctions are also expressed through clearly marking off the villages where the members of the group sharing a common notion of group identity live in a separate area. Thus, the area adjoining Rasulpur* has a population of Siddique Sheikhs who are distributed in thirteen villages over a radius of approximately thirty miles. These Sheikh Siddiques marry among themselves and consider themselves to be members of the same group. Sheikh Siddiques also live in other villages and in Radauli town, about seventeen miles away, but Sheikh Siddiques of the circle of fourteen villages collectively called Sheikhana neither recognize these other Sheikh Siddiques as members of their caste nor inter-marry among them. From the point of

---

[1] The fourth Caliph, Ali, was the son-in-law of the Prophet and his descendants are regarded as Sayyads rather than as Sheikhs.

* *Rasulpur is a village in U.P., where the author initially conducted an enquiry on the nature of stratification among the Muslims. Editor.*

the Sheikh Siddiques themselves, the Sheikh Siddiques of the area called Sheikhana and Sheikh Siddiques of these other areas regard themselves as members of different sub-castes.

....

The Sheikh Siddiques

The Sheikh Siddiques of Allahabad District today claim themselves to be the descendants of Abu Bakr Siddique and this claim is recognized by others. But this recognition has come only within the last quarter of a century. In fact, the Sheikh Siddiques are converts from the Kayastha caste among the Hindus. Over the generations, the group has succeeded in completely obliterating its Hindu ancestry and create a new social identity for itself as descendant of Abu Bakr Siddique. This has been aided by certain historical developments which came in the wake of British rule, urbanization and the gradual movement of the members of the caste from their original location in Allahabad District to urban centres in Uttar Pradesh and Pakistan, the economic and occupational differentiation within the caste, and the ability of a section of the caste to contract marriages into social groups of supposedly Sheikh status. Nevertheless, systematic and sufficiently persistent enquiries within the area of their original residence does still yield information that shows that these Sheikhs were originally Kayasthas and their Sheikh status is a matter of recent acquisition.

The Sheikh Siddiques originally lived in the Chail Tehsil of Allahabad District. It is said that they were distributed in over thirty villages at the time of their conversion to Islam and the entire area comprising those thirty villages is still collectively referred to as Kaethana, probably a corruption of the word 'Kayasthana' meaning the home of the Kayasthas. Legendry accounts preserved by the local Bhats and occasionally confirmed by the settlement records suggest that the Kayasthas were land record keepers before their conversion to Islam. The precise circumstances of the conversion of the Sheikh Siddiques to Islam are not known. It is, however, known that when they converted to Islam they were allowed to retain their traditional occupation as land record keepers, a fact which is also attested to by the fact that the members of the caste often served as *patwaris* well after the annexation of the area by the British. Today, the occupation is no longer a monopoly of the Sheikh Siddiques partly because it is no longer considered very attractive and partly because the educated members of the caste have moved out to urban centres and taken up employment in government offices. This movement is said to have commenced at the time of the establishment of the provincial capital at Allahabad. It opened up new employment opportunities and the Sheikh Siddiques cashed in upon those new opportunities because, apart from the financial advantages, they aided their search for a new status identity.

Today the Sheikh Siddiques are not associated with any single occupation, traditional or modern. On the contrary, they are distributed among a variety of different occupations: some are still agriculturists, some are employed as under civil servants in administration, some work as teachers, accountants, and salesmen, etc. It is, however, noticeable that the Sheikh Siddiques have a definite bias in favour of lower administrative jobs. For example, a survey of the families who could be contacted showed that 67 per cent of the Sheikh Siddiques in the present generation on whom data were available work as clerks in government offices while the remaining are distributed in other lower jobs. Until the creation of Pakistan, the Sheikh Siddiques did not, with a few notable exceptions, occupy senior administrative jobs. However, since the creation of Pakistan several members of the caste have migrated to that country and have succeeded in securing senior administrative positions by virtue of their educational qualifications. Such occupational mobility was particularly made possible by the dearth of educated and experienced personnel in the initial stages of the creation of Pakistan.

The conversion of the Sheikh Siddiques to Islam was a group process. The whole of the Kayastha caste was converted rather than individuals who might have become Muslims. The conversion of the whole group made the transition from Hinduism to Islam and the accompanying positional changes somewhat easy for the members. Some marginal adjustments were required, especially with the other Hindu castes with whom the Sheikh Siddiques must have interacted closely, but their adjustments could be made without any great difficulty as the corporateness of the group remained inact. Moreover, since the area was already inhabited by certain other Muslim groups, especially those who enjoyed land grants under previous rulers, whatever was lost by way of social intercourse among the Hindus for the group was eventually gained among the Muslims.

Convert groups to Islam are generally characterized as New Muslims and they are looked down upon by the social groups which are known to be desendants of foreign sources or who have succeeded in eliminating the stigma of recent conversion. This gave rise to certain differentiations in the adjustment of the Sheikh Siddiques after their conversion to Islam in the different villages. In villages which were

largely or predominantly Hindu, the Sheikh Siddiques were excluded
from the framework of interaction with the Hindu castes but they
continued to enjoy a somewhat superior status as a Muslim group. But
in villages where there were numerous other Muslim groups of superior
status, the Sheikh Siddiques were not merely excluded from the social
hierarchy of Hindu castes, but were also relegated to a somewhat lower
position even within the hierarchy of Muslim castes.

. . . .

New Status Identity

The Sheikh Siddiques who received Western education and moved into
urban based occupations at the begining of this century eventually
grew dissatisfied with the stigma of Hindu ancestry that continued to be
attached to their caste and their status as neo-Muslim. They wanted to
shake off their Hindu ancestry and wanted to be recognized as Sheikhs.
There were, however, two major difficulties in their getting recognition
of their aspirted status identity as Sheikhs. Firstly, their Kayastha antecedents were quite well known in the area and many of their caste customs and practices betrayed their Hindu ancestry and origin. Secondly,
their caste was entirely endogamous and they could not cite any instances of marriage alliances with groups of accepted Sheikh status, or
even with groups who might previously have been Hindu converts but
had succeeded over the generations in establishing a Sheikh identity for
themselves. Therefore, in order to overcome the first difficulty, it was
necessary that the caste should discard some of its more obvious Hindu
customs and practices and adopt those customs which were characteristic of proper Sheikh groups. Equally, in order to support and reinforce
the claim to Sheikh status, it was essential that caste members should
selectively enter into marriage alliances with groups of known Sheikh
origin so that it could be shown that the group was actually Sheikh and
its members had formed marriage alliances with Sheikh groups whose
high birth was recognized.

The first of these difficulties of the Sheikh Siddiques in search for a
new status identity was comparatively easily resolved. Self-conscious
members of the caste who had received Western education and had
consequently succeeded in raising their economic and political positions through working for the government started a movement for the
abandonment of Hindu caste customs and practices for the more Islamic
customs and practices associated with the Sheikh style of life. This
change was specifically directed towards the twin practices of *pankti*

and *cherava*.* On the one hand, the practice of sitting in a separate row consisting exclusively of Sheikh Siddiques at inter-caste dinners was abandoned and the members of the Sheikh Siddique group began to sit with other castes of comparable social status. Since the decision to sit in a separate row had been taken by the Sheikh Siddiques themselves and it had not been imposed upon them by other castes as a status differentiating mechanism, the attempts to sit in a common row with castes of comparable status aroused some comments but no apparent opposition. On the other hand, the practice of sending offerings of clothes and dry fruits to the bride's house on the occasion of marriage was also modified; instead of earthen pitchers previously used for the purpose the caste adopted the use of large brass trays as is customary among the Muslims of recognized Sheikh standing in the region and elsewhere. Simultaneously, certain other changes in dress and religious rituals were undertaken and a more rigid and orthodox observance of religious prescriptions and rituals was adopted.

. . . .

Prior to their Islamization, the Sheikh Siddique women usually wore *saris* as their normal dress. However, the *saris* were regarded by the Sheikh Siddiques as a Hindu dress and it was gradually replaced by the tighter and more uncomfortable *churidar pyjamas*. The members of the caste thought that the *churidar pyjamas* were a more typical Islamic dress suited to a caste that claimed to belong to the Sheikh status category. There is nothing in the Koran which says that the *saris* constitute any less Islamic form of dress than the *churidar pyjamas*, but the members of the caste felt that the *churidar pyjamas* reinforced their image as Muslims of high social position. It is clear, then, that the question whether a particular item adopted as part of Islamization is truly Islamic or not is decided not on the ground that it enjoys a sanction in the Shari'at, but rather on the ground that the Islamizing group considers it as basic to its self-definition as a Muslim group of high social standing.

Side by side with the gradual Islamization of their caste customs and practices and the style of life generally, the Sheikh Siddiques also pressed the claim to be recognized as Sheikhs. Its members, and particularly the more self-conscious ones amongst them, emphasized that they were descendants of the first Caliph, Abu Bakr Siddique, through a priest who had accompanied the Ghaznavid army and was known to

---

*Pankti *refers to the manner in which different castes sit in rows in inter-caste dinners and* cherawa *is the offering of dry fruit and sugar to bride's house at the time of marriage. Editor.*

have descended from the Caliph. In the course of time a genealogy was suitably fabricated which showed the Sheikh Siddiques to be the descendants of Abu Bakr Siddique through this priest in the Ghaznavid army.

The Sheikh Siddiques were a locally influential and well-off group and their attempts to claim Sheikh Siddique status do not appear to have given rise to any serious opposition from other castes. As a matter of fact, the other caste groups in the area remained indifferent to the Sheikh Siddique claim as it made very little difference to them what status claim the Sheikh Siddiques preferred. Commensal relations between the Sheikh Siddiques and other high Muslim castes of the area were reciprocal and they were not affected by whether the Sheikh Siddiques retained their Hindu origin or discarded it. On the other hand, as far as marriages were concerned, each caste was endogamous in the area and there was no change in the pattern of marriage alliances by the Sheikh claim on the part of the Sheikh Siddiques. Clearly, social protest would have arisen if the Sheikh Siddiques had tried to break into the endogamy of other castes, but this they were not in a position to do. Consequently, the Sheikh Siddique claim to be recognized as the descendants of Abu Bakr Siddique apparently produced no serious opposition from other high castes of the area.

Islamization certainly helped to elevate the prestige of the Sheikh Siddiques within the hierarchy of local Muslim castes, but it failed to bring about the recognition of their status as Sheikhs. There still remained the fact that the Sheikh Siddiques had not been successful in forming marriage alliances with recognizeable Sheikh groups and other high Muslim castes of the area refused either to give their daughters or to accept girls from the Sheikh Siddiques in marriage. Unless the Sheikh Siddiques could demonstrate definite marriage links with groups of recognized Sheikh status either within their original home area or outside, their claim to Sheikh status could be accepted tentatively but not necessarily taken as established. And, this was especially so because the group was known to have descended from the Kayastha caste among the Hindus and its Hindu antecedents were a matter of common knowledge in the area.

Ideally the Sheikh Siddiques would have preferred to form suitable marriage alliances with groups of recognized Sheikh status and to cite that fact in support of their claim to be recognized as Sheikh Siddiques. But this presented difficulties both because the Hindu ancestry of the group was commonly known in the area and the groups of known Sheikh status were unwilling to give their daughters in marriage to, or to take girls from, the Sheikh Siddiques. Consequently, the Sheikhs had to try to make a virtue of the fact that they had failed to form marriage alliances with groups who were recognized to be Sheikhs. Unable to form marriage alliances with other groups of high rank, the Sheikh Siddiques claimed that their failure to form marital links with other groups of high status did not arise from their Kayastha ancestry and the reluctance of castes of high status to enter into marriage alliances with them. On the contrary, they asserted that it was so because they themselves refused to marry into other castes. Its members claimed that their group was characterized by a special ritual quality which was said to be inherent in the blood and bone of the caste members (*har-gor*). This ritual purity of the blood and bone was supposed to be best preserved when marriages were confined within the group. Marriages with outsiders, whether hypergamous or hypogamous, were supposed to adversely affect this ritual quality of the caste. Thus, the Sheikh Siddiques argued that their caste was endogamous not because the other high castes refused to marry with them but because they themselves did not marry into other castes as a mechanism for the preservation of their purity of the blood and bone.

The belief in the ritual purity of the blood and bone was symbolized through the caste genealogy (*Shijra*). It has already been mentioned that along with the rise of mobility aspirations, caste members fabricated a genealogy of the group which traced its origin to the descendants of Abu Bakr Siddique and showed that the ritual purity of the blood and bone had been preserved through a somewhat strict adherence to endogamy. The genealogy, thus, became a symbol through which the status of the caste as Sheikh Siddiques was made public. . . .

Recently the attitudes of the Sheikh Siddiques belonging to both the marriage circles have been undergoing change. They allege that there is a great dearth of eligible Muslim boys nowadays as Muslim youngmen frequently migrate to Pakistan in search of employment and the few Muslim boys who prefer to stay on in India are easily 'roped in' by families of better economic and social status. Consequently they no longer place much emphasis upon ritual purity of blood and bone or on descent and are willing to marry off their daughters to eligible boys of comparable rank. For the same reason, however, the marriages of eligible Sheikh Siddique boys can now be arranged into families of recognized Sheikh descent and are often used to raise their social status and to reinforce their claim to Sheikh status.

Further Readings

Berreman, G.D.,
1963   *Hindus of the Himalayas*, University of California Press, Berkeley and Los Angeles.

This work presents an atypical case of the Hindus of the Kangra region whose observance of the caste system is not nearly as rigid as compared to the Hindus of the plains.

Dumont, Louis,
1986   *A South Indian Subcaste: Social Organization and Religion of the Pramalai Kallar*, Oxford University Press, Delhi.

This study is recommended not simply because of its grinding detailed presentation of the material, technological and cultural aspects of the Pramalai Kallar, but also because this monograph is the basis for Dumont's better known theoretical positions on marriage and alliance, and on the character of Indian society.

Madan, T. N.,
1989   *Family and Kinship: A Study of the Pandits of Rural Kashmir*, Second Enlarged Edition, OUP.

A close-up of the Kashmiri Pandit household bringing out in detail the ideas and beliefs that sustain their patrilineal kinship system.

Risley, H.H.,
1981   *The Tribes and Castes of Bengal*, Firma Mukhapadhyaya, Calcutta.

An eye-opener for all social anthropologists for the detailed ethnographic information on the castes of what is today India's West Bengal, Bihar, East U.P. and Orissa.

Shah, A. M. and I. P. Desai,
1988   *Division and Hierarchy: An Overview of Caste in Gujarat*, Hindustan Publishing Corporation, Delhi.

A lively debate between the two authors on the portrayal of the Banias and Rajputs of Gujarat.

III

Class

There are several ways in which class is understood in sociological and social anthropological literature. The reader is recommended to read Appendices I to III in this connection to get a view of the principal ways in which this term has been understood. It is worthwhile therefore to clarify the ground and be aware of the fact that the term class does not mean the same thing to different scholars.

To begin with it must be kept in mind that the different usages of the term arise because of different theoretical perspectives. Marx used the term class as in 'class struggle' to signify the contradiction, inherent between the principal classes in different historical epochs. In bourgeois societies the principal or determinate classes in contradiction are the bourgeoisie and the proletariat. In feudal societies, on the other hand, the determinate classes are constituted by the lords and the serfs.

This however should not be taken to mean that Marx thought that there were only two classes to each kind of society and nothing more. Marx indeed visualized a large number of other classes too, like the professionals, the apprentices, the journeymen, the traders, and so on, but in his view the scope of these classes was determined by the essential contradiction between the determinate classes in that society. So while traders are a class that has existed through history from the earliest of times, nevertheless the historic role of this class has been conditioned and constrained by the class contradictions in different social formations. This is why the merchant class in capitalist societies is quite different from the merchant classes in feudal societies.

Weber as is well known (see AppendixIII) felt the use of the term class to be appropriate only in capitalist, market-oriented societies. In such societies one's economic fortunes were dictated by the principles of the capitalist market place. This view of class is quite dominant in the social sciences and has won several adherents. Classes are viewed as economic categories which function independently according to capitalist market rules. The rewards of the market are unprejudicially bestowed for no consideration other than pure market factors determine the outcome of classes.

The selections in this section however do not represent either pure Marxian or pure Weberian views. Instead we find imaginative exercises which help us to explore the potentialities within different perspectives. Morris D. Morris raises the problem of whether or not precapitalist ties restrict the formation of a working class emerging in a capitalist industrial city like Bombay. The role that factors outside of the market play in the formation of the working class cannot be underestimated. At the same time, as Morris and Holmström demonstrate, there are hard economic factors too that separate different orders among the working class. Holmström draws our attention to the differentiation between the organized and unorganized sectors of the working class. In this connection Holmström brings out the market forces which separate these two classes. The fact that the market does not play fair and that there are different levels at which different classes and strata enter the working class category reveal to us the diversities within the working class and the prestige hierarchy that operates among them.

Both Marx and Weber paid scant attention to agrarian classes. From Weber this was to be expected because for him classes existed only in capitalist market societies. Marx too paid little notice to agrarian classes. Even though he accepted that there were lords and serfs, apprentices and moneylenders, and peasants huddled together like potatoes, none of these classes were understood in detail. This is probably because Marx felt that with the development of capitalism the countryside would soon reflect the profile of the industrial classes.

However appealing this may appear at first sight, sociologists and anthropologists working in India and other developing countries have to take stock of agrarian classes because of the sheer preponderance of the agrarian population in these societies. India's population is not only primarily rural, but the rural countryside is far too complex to be lightly dismissed with the analogy of a sack of potatoes, as Marx did. Contemporary scholarship has righted much of the neglect that classes in the countryside were subjected to by the early masters. Analytically too these studies have furthered our understanding of class which was hitherto limited to the urban experience.

To a large extent classes in the agrarian sector are classified on two axes. The first axis is whether or not land is owned, and the second is whether self or hired labour is expended on land. Different combinations arise from the presence or absence of attributes along these two axes. Some may own land and not work on it, some may work on land and not own it, and then again some may own land and work on it. In addition to the above one can think of more categories based on the amount of land owned and on the work put into one's own land as a proportion of work done on other's lands. Daniel Thorner's essay on the agrarian structure brings out these features. In this work Thorner depends on the native categories in use to flesh out the diversities extant in agrarian classes. D.N. Dhanagare goes further along this route and weaves in Maoist insights into the understanding of rural classes.

Kathleen Gough provides an empirical display of classes in rural Thanjavur. She also brings out the varying fortunes these different rural classes have faced over the last several decades. Quite clearly her analysis shows that the rural poor have been hit the worst. . . . Finally, we have Ghanshyam Shah's illuminating study telling us about the extent to which even tribes are internally differentiated along class lines. Tribes in this sense do not exist as a pure category outside the ambit of class forces. Tribes are drawn into the mainstream economy and are not immune to its effects. Tribes may popularly present themselves as status groups, but as Shah argues, the inegalitarian character of the capitalist economy leaves its impress quite clearly on these communities. Both Gough and Shah attempt to place their empirical material in the context of a wider theoretical perspective which is significantly informed by Marxism.

Undoubtedly literature on the class structure in India is not as conceptually rich or plentiful as material on the caste system. This is of course to be expected. Unlike castes classes exist all over the world. This is probably why it seems more challlenging to test, apply and dispute received theoretical formulations on the subject on the basis of empirical evidence. The selections presented here attempt such an engagement and at the same time encourage independent analytical assessments.

The Emergence of an Industrial Labour Force in India

MORRIS, D. MORRIS

Although there is complete agreement that in India today unemployment both overt and covert is widespread, there has been almost equally uniform agreement among industrialists, officials, and scholars that industrial development in India before 1947 was seriously handicapped by the difficulty of mobilizing a stable, disciplined labour force of adequate size. This was the considered judgement of the Indian Factory Labour Commission (IFLC) of 1908:

The position of the operative has been greatly strengthened by the fact that the supply of factory labour undoubtedly is, and has been, inadequate; and there is, and has been, the keenest competition among employees to secure a full labour supply (IFLC 1908 I:19).

The classic statement on the subject appeared in 1931 in the report of the Royal Commission on Labour (RCL) in India:

Throughout the greater part of its history, organized industry in India has experienced a shortage of labour. A generation ago, this shortage was apt at times to become critical. . . . [After 1905] the position became easier in the

Adapted from Morris, D. Morris, 'Nature of the Problem' and 'Supply of Labour', in *The Emergence of an Industrial Labour Force in India: A Study of the Bombay Cotton Mills, 1854-1947*, Oxford University Press, Bombay, 1965.

factory industries, but even in these, before the [first world] war, few employers were assured of adequate labour at all seasons of the year. . . . Perennial factories . . . have now reached a position in which most of them have sufficient labour at all seasons and there is a surplus of factory labour at several centres. . . . Speaking generally, it would be true to say that the turning point came during the last five years. Up to that stage, labour tended to have the upper hand in that there was competition for its services; since then the tendency has been for the workers to compete for jobs (RCL 1929, Report : 21). . . .

. . . . Not only is this purported shortage of labour supposed to have affected directly the rate of industrial growth in an adverse way; it is supposed to have shaped also the behaviour and attitudes of workers coming into industry. Put briefly, the behaviour pattern is described in one of two ways. One line of analysis suggests that, labour being short in industry, employers had to scramble for their work force and make all sorts of concessions which weakened their hold on the workers. The employees, because of absence of effective employer-imposed discipline, were able to indulge in the luxury of all too frequent returns to the villages to which they were unyieldingly devoted.

The alternate and essentially contradictory hypothesis recognizes the potential surplus of labour in the country-side that was available for urban employment. It argues that as a consequence of this surplus employers were able to abuse workers unmercifully. Since working conditions in the factories were intolerable, labour tended to remain in the villages or was very quickly forced back to the land by utter exhaustion (Gadgil 1942 : 127-30). Whatever the specific line of causation accepted by scholars, the general conclusion is that workers retained their rural links to an extent which limited the supply of labour for industrial development. As a consequence, disciplined urban-industrial (i.e., proletarian) types of behaviour did not develop. The failure of a proletarian outlook to appear was accompanied by the purported high rates of absenteeism and labour turnover and the slow growth of trade unions in Indian industry. . . .

I think there is a great deal that can be contributed by a historical study. Careful analysis will throw quite a novel light on the whole process of labour force creation. The evidence will show that contrary to the canonical view the supply of labour for industrial requirements was not hard to get. The material will also indicate that the level of labour force performance was almost entirely set by the nature of industrial organization and operation. (In other words, the basic quality of labour performance as it emerged in the cotton textile industry was the

result of employer policy and responses to market forces and not the consequence of labour force psychology or social structure.)
. . . .

In order to discuss the supply of labour, it will be useful briefly to consider the rural sector from which the majority of the work force initially came. There have been no satisfactory studies of the economic relationship of the country-side with the growing urban centres of nineteenth- and twentieth-century India. This is not the place to undertake such an analysis, but there are important interpretive consequences which flow from certain traditional notions about the rural areas. Let me, therefore, point to three features which are almost always ignored.

First, we must recognize that the historic balance between men and resources in most areas of the subcontinent was always precarious, and equilibrium was sustained only by the systematic working of the checks of war, famine, and epidemic. Such vitality as has been claimed for the traditional order before the nineteenth century tended, on the whole, to be the vitality of no alternatives.

Second, we must also recognize that even before the establishment of British rule a significant proportion of the population was already landless or cultivated plots which yielded submarginal incomes. These groups, apparently present in all areas of the country, had to eke out their existence by working for others. Finally, and as a partial consequence of the two features already mentioned, there were movements of people from one district to another during the traditional period (Habib 1963: 116-17, 120-2):

The point of all this is to suggest that the European Industrial Revolution did not burst upon India in the first half of the nineteenth century and smash a primitive utopia in which all owned land and where the population was immobile because of high levels of well-being. This was a society which historically had been making Malthusian adjustments to its environment; the existence of a quasi-proletariat and population migration were two socio-economic manifestations of this historic condition.

Western India was no exception to these generalizations. A careful reading of the innumerable settlement reports for districts in the Bombay Presidency yields hints of the existence of a rural proletariat or quasi-proletariat at mid-century. An official report, attempting to grapple with the allegations that are frequently made as to the poverty and want of the lower classes, produced evidence which leads me to the conclusion that in the 1880s at least 30 per cent of the rural population of Bombay Presidency was in continual economic difficulty, being forced to engage in at least some wage labour to eke out an existence. The greater bulk of these, perhaps 15 to 20 per cent of the rural population, had no significant claim to any land.

Patel claims that the proportion of agricultural labourers to the total agricultural population of Bombay Presidency was increasing, that by 1901 this group totalled more than 30 per cent, and it continued to increase during the twentieth century (Patel 1952: 21-5). There are serious doubts about the accuracy of his estimates, but the evidence is clear that during the whole of the nineteenth century and the early twentieth century a substantial population in the rural areas was landless or nearly so and was dependent for survival on various forms of wage labour. These groups of landless labourers and submarginal peasants constituted a large part of the potential labour force for the Bombay cotton mills.

The next question that has to be answered is whether or not there were geographical or social barriers inhibiting the flow of labour into Bombay. With regard to the geographical issue, it is true that western India did not possess adequate land-transport facilities until the spread of railways after 1854. In the absence of adequate feeder lines, even these affected only limited areas. But long before the building of railways there was a large and growing land trade between Bombay and the rest of western India. Where there was great commerce there had to be a great movement of people, if only by foot.

Sea transport was far easier, and passenger as well as freight traffic was extensive. Some regular coastal ferries were operating at the end of the eighteenth century, and in the early 1850s steam and sailing vessels were hauling passengers to and from Bombay by the thousands each year. By the 1880s even the most isolated parts of the Ratnagiri District had been brought into contact with Bombay through the elaborate development of water transport. All the evidence indicates that there were no significant physical barriers to movement to Bombay from the countryside during the nineteenth century.

A great deal has been written about the stabilizing effects of Indian rural social structure—joint family, caste, and village organization—and how social relationships acted as barriers to population mobility. There is no evidence that bears out this proposition. It is probably safe to say that the Indian population historically has been as mobile as, for example, the populations of western Europe at equivalent stages of economic development.

If we look at the evidence from the Bombay end, where economic alternatives to rural existence were available, it seems clear that the Indian social structure cannot have been a decisive barrier to the flow of population needed for urban economic expansion. The growth of Bombay's population is, itself, the best evidence of rural mobility and, as has been indicated elsewhere, all the evidence suggests that the rate of movement of people from the country-side was a more or less direct function of employment opportunities. For example, the population in Bombay City increased very rapidly between 1830 and 1864, from 229,000 to nearly 817,000. It seems clear that this enormous increase was directly linked with the city's economic expansion and the demand for labour it induced. What is particularly noteworthy is that this same period is one during which there seems to have been a general improvement in the state of the agricultural sector of western India (Sovani 1954: 868).

It is true that some of this migration to Bombay was seasonal, reflecting a search for work during the slack periods in the country-side. But it is equally important to recognize that much of the temporary migration was certainly a function of the seasonality of Bombay's labour force requirements. A large proportion of employment opportunities on the island during this period as in later years stemmed from construction and shipping demands which were markedly affected by the monsoon. In other words, the strong seasonal element of much of this migration was caused not only by the nature of economic activity in the country-side but also by the seasonal fluctuations in demand for labour in the city (Edwardes 1909: 57-8).

The census data after 1864 also seem to point conclusively to the fact that migration was responsive to the economic opportunities available on the island. When these sources of employment and income dwindled, the flow of labour into Bombay slowed up and could even be reversed, as the 1872 census showed. It was not the call of opportunity or 'traditional ties to the land' that lured labour back to the countryside, for the collapse of commercial activity in Bombay after 1865 was accompanied by the disintegration of rural prosperity as well. The return to the rural areas after 1865 was the only recourse, a counsel of despair (Gadgil 1942: 24-32). . . .

Where did the Bombay mill work force come from? We have no explicit information for the first half century but the census reports of 1911, 1921 and 1931 give us some fairly detailed information.

Table 1
Place of Origin of Cotton-Mill Work Force, 1911-31

Place of origin	Per cent of total mill hands		
(miles from Bombay)	*1911*	*1921*	*1931*
1-100	7.48	5.13	3.62
101-200	63.44	50.07	38.26
201-300	2.68	4.98	4.71
301-400	3.37	2.67	1.30
401-500	0.62	3.46	1.98
501-750	0.28	1.50	0.99
751 and more	3.05	10.65	14.62
Unidentified migrants	8.16	2.67	8.19
born in Bombay	10.92	18.87	26.33
Total	100.00	100.00	100.00

Table 2
Districts Providing Main Supply of Cotton-Mill Work Force, 1911-31

District	Distance from Bombay (miles)	Per cent of total mill hands		
		1911	*1921*	*1931*
Ratnagiri (Konkan)	(101-200)	49.16	35.53	25.37
Satara (Deccan)	(101-200)	7.27	6.63	5.15
Kolaba (Konkan)	(1-100)	6.22	4.47	3.04
Poona (Deccan)	(101-200)	5.65	6.18	5.72
Kolhapur (Deccan)	(301-400)	3.07	1.85	0.51
Ahmednagar (Deccan)	(201-300)	1.46	2.99	2.01
United Provinces	(Over 750)	3.05	9.42	11.82
Total of above districts		75.88	67.07	53.62

At least three interesting features are exhibited by these two tables. First, the largest proportion of mill hands came from the 100 to 200 mile circle. The vast majority of these came from the Ratnagiri District and, generally speaking, the bulk of the immigrant work force came from the Konkan districts south of Bombay and the Deccan plateau east of Bombay. The Gujarat districts north of Bombay seem to have contributed only a very small proportion of the textile workers. Non-statistical evidence suggests this general pattern from the beginning of the industry's history.

The second feature is that with the passage of time there was a tendency for mill hands to be drawn from a greater number of districts and from increasingly distant areas. If one looks at Table 2, it appears that in 1911 the six most important Bombay Presidency districts contributed 72.83 per cent of all mill hands in Bombay. By 1921 the proportion from those districts had fallen to 57.65 per cent and by 1931 to 41.80 per cent. Other regions were contributing a rising proportion to work force (Gokhale 1957: 117-18). As part of this phenomenon, mill hands were coming from districts farther away, notably from areas 751 miles and beyond which included virtually all districts of the United Provinces (now Uttar Pradesh). It was in the United Provinces that the BMOA (Bombay Mill Owners' Association) attempted to recruit labour in 1897 and failed. Yet without any formal effort this particular region began to contribute an increasingly large supply of labour to the mills. In 1911 the United Provinces districts furnished at least 3.05 per cent; in 1921 the proportion rose to 9.42, and in 1931 to 11.82 per cent of total mill hands.[1] Put more generally, the census data indicate that between 1911 and 1931 the proportion of mill hands coming from distances 501 miles and more rose from 3.33 per cent to 15.61 per cent. And the BMOA surveys suggest that the trend continued, with 19.29 per cent in 1940 and 22.4 per cent in 1954 coming from distances of more than 500 miles (Gokhale 1957: 87-9).

These figures should put an end to the frequently argued view that Indian workers could not move long distances, that the ideology of the society and its social institutions tended to keep the population restricted to the neighbourhood of its traditional residence.

The third important feature, suggested in Table 3, is the increasing proportion of the mill work force born in Bombay. This occurred despite the fact that the mill labour force was expanding rapidly until 1922. And in the interval 1911 to 1921 it occurred in contrast to the declining proportion of Bombay-born in the city's total population.

---

[1] The Bombay Mill Owners' Association (BMOA) 1940 survey suggests that this trend continued.

Table 3
Proportion of Total Bombay Population
and Mill Hands Born in Bombay
1911-31[2]

Year	Total population (Per cent)	Total mill hands (Per cent)
1911	19.6	10.92
1921	16.0	18.87
1931	24.6	26.33

There is no consistent series that shows the changing sex and age composition of the mill work force. I, therefore, have attempted to construct one from the data that are available.

The most striking feature, especially when compared with the sex and age distributions of textile work forces in other countries during the nineteenth and early twentieth centuries, is the relatively limited use of women and children. Even in the earliest years for which we have evidence adult males never constituted less than 69 per cent and women never more than a quarter of the total work force. Children, legally defined, never exceeded 5.6 per cent.

The proportion of female mill hands seems to have remained remarkably constant at between 20 and 25 per cent of the work force until 1931 when the figure began to decline. The reduction can be attributed to the widespread adoption of night-shift working after that date. Prohibited by law from working nights, women could not be added to the second and third shifts. Another factor contributing to the diminishing significance of women in the work force may have been the increasing use by Bombay mills of their yarn in the production of cloth, thus reducing the need for reelers, a predominantly female occupation.

Right from the inception of the industry women seem to have been employed predominantly in the cotton cleaning, winding, and reeling departments—schemes in which power equipment was not generally

[2] *Census 1931*, IX, Part I, p. 14, gives figures on the Bombay-born part of the total Bombay population. Information on the Bombay-born part of total mill-hand populations is taken from Table 1.

Table 4

Average Daily Employment of Men, Women, and Children in
Bombay Cotton Mills (All Shifts), 1884-1947
(Per cent)

| Year | Adults | | | Year | Adults | | |
	Men	Women	Children		Men	Women	Children
1884	76.50	22.20	1.30	1919	77.47	20.33	2.20
1892	69.80	24.63	5.57	1920	77.72	20.38	1.90
1893	69.22	25.87	4.91	1921	77.96	20.49	1.55
1894	70.47	24.74	4.79	1922	79.50	19.68	0.82
1895	71.01	24.74	4.25	1923	79.09	20.46	0.45
1896	71.11	25.38	3.51	1924	78.10	21.49	0.41
1897	72.91	23.30	3.79	1925	77.66	22.15	0.19
1898	73.81	22.37	3.82	1926	77.34	22.62	0.04
1899	73.54	23.54	2.92	1927	77.88	22.10	0.02
1908	74.02	22.23	3.75	1928	78.23	21.77	.....
1909	75.12	21.36	3.52	1929	78.56	21.42	0.02
1910	75.35	21.00	3.65	1930	77.11	22.86	0.03
1911	76.09	20.34	3.57	1931	78.01	21.96	0.03
1912	75.62	20.69	3.69	1934	81.06	18.94	....
1913	75.46	20.61	3.93	1937	84.08	15.92	....
1914	75.45	20.37	4.18	1939	85.07	14.93	....
1915	75.86	19.65	4.49	1944	87.86	12.14	....
1916	76.03	20.59	3.38	1947	88.83	11.17	....
1918	78.04	19.89	2.07				

used until well after the end of World War I. Some were employed as sweepers and on spinning frames. They never seem to have been employed as weavers. . . .

The next issue we must examine is the degree to which caste influenced specific occupational patterns. There is a tendency to argue that industry is caste-blind for a number of reasons. It may be because no single caste can provide an adequate supply of labour, because it is impossible to determine specific caste affiliations in an industrial situation, because employees are uninterested in caste affiliation, or

Table 5

Untouchables as a Proportion of Bombay City
Population and of the Bombay Mill Labour Force,
1872-1941

Year (1)	Untouchables as a proportion of total Bombay population (2)	Untouchable mill hands as a proportion of total mill labour force (3)
1872	4.86	0.99
1881	6.36	2.11
1891	n.a.	n.a.
1901	9.38	n.a.
1911	9.09	9.05
1921	11.53	11.91
1931	8.88	11.28
1941	8.15	13.81

because all castes are willing to do all work in industry. It is not infrequently suggested that some or all of these features result in the
mixing of workers in such a fashion as to lead to the ultimate undermining of the caste system. Kingsley Davis advanced an extreme
version of this view, saying: 'If industrialization proceeds rapidly [in
India] . . . the caste system will have essentially disappeared by the
end of this century' (Davis 1951:176).

Although such propositions suggest something, right or wrong,
about the ultimate impact of factory employment, they tell us nothing
about caste groups as they have existed in industry. They contribute
nothing to our understanding of why, in the early decades of the Bombay mill industry's career, the proportion of Untouchables was insignificant and why that proportion gradually increased. It is possible
that this trend was the result of purely accidental factors, but I think
that what little evidence there is suggests that it was not. If accident is
ruled out as an explanation, we must try to determine the degree to
which caste affiliation tended to determine the general chances of
being hired and the specific jobs for which hiring was done. If caste had
any effect, we must explore the extent to which access to occupational
opportunities was determined by the social attitudes of employers and
their agents or stemmed from the labour force itself.

But first, we need statistical evidence of the extent to which the phenomenon of caste clustering was, in fact, found in the cotton mills. There is only one study available, the BMOA 1940 survey of 37,639 workers in nineteen Bombay mills (Gokhale 1957:116). The survey shows that Marathas constituted more than half (51.8 per cent) of all male workers. They were found in large proportions in all departments. Of the other important groups, Bhayyas contributed 13.8 per cent to the total male labour force. Unlike the Marathas, they tended to cluster in certain departments. 53.8 per cent were in the 'mixing to speed frame' departments and 17.2 per cent in the weaving sheds. But only in the former did they represent a large part (46.8 per cent) of departmental employment.[3] Harijans (Untouchables) contributed 11.9 per cent of all male employees. 72.5 per cent were employed in the ring-spinning departments where they made up 39.5 per cent of all male workers. Muslims, the only other large group distinguished, made up 5.2 per cent of total male workers. The 52.2 per cent employed in the weaving sheds constituted 6.9 per cent of the weaving operatives.[4]

Looking at the survey data somewhat differently, were there any departments in which any of these groups was not found? As I have already suggested, Marathas were extremely important in all sections.[5] Bhayyas, though concentrated in certain sections, could be found in all departments as could the Muslims. Only the Harijans showed a restricted pattern of participation. Clearly, the most distinctive feature is that of a total of 1,240 workers in the weaving sheds only eighty (0.6 per cent) were Harijans, and they represented only 2.2 per cent of all Harijans in the work force.

In spite of this fact, we have to recognize that this survey really tells us very little about caste-clustering in the mills. I do not think it necessary to set down a precise definition of caste, but it is essential to recognize that I am using the term to refer to what are more precisely called subcastes (*jati*), endogamous and interdining groups which exist in territorially confined areas of the country-side. For any analysis

---

[3] In the weaving sheds they represented only 6 per cent of the male work force.

[4] Women mill hands were much more restricted occupationally. Of all women, 85.9 per cent were employed in winding and reeling, and Marathas and Harijans were the dominant groups by far. Of all Maratha women, 92.4 per cent worked in this department, and 73.5 per cent of all Harijan women were employed there.

[5] In five of the six departmental classifications of the survey, Marathas were a plurality or a majority of the workers. In the 'mixing to speed frame' section, Bhayyas supplied more labour (46.8 per cent) but Marathas provided 31.5 per cent of the total in that section.

of labour recruitment and the study of the behaviour of rural recruits in an industrial environment, we must begin our study with those social groups which exhibit homogeneity and cohesive behaviour in the country-side. It is entirely inappropriate to lump into larger groups because of similarity of name, function, social status, or region subcastes that are not endogamous.

I am not necessarily arguing that village subcaste (*jati*) relationships will ultimately prove to be the most relevant categories of social behaviour inside the factory. In fact, it may well be that *jati* relations were irrelevant there. But when one is concerned with the historical process of creating an industrial labour force, analysis must begin with the existing social relationships in the villages from which the work force comes. This is crucial when the specific problem is the influence of caste on the process of recruitment and disciplining of rural migrants to urban-industrial employment. If these social groupings, so decisive in the villages, ceased to have relevance or were transformed in the factory environment, this does not diminish the original significance of *jati* as a category for the problem with which I am here concerned. It is , precisely the transformation from *jati* to something else that becomes important to describe and evaluate. Unfortunately, research has not yet gotten this far. My difficulty is that investigators have tended to use the concept caste (*jati*) to mean one thing in the description of village social structure and function and something quite different when describing industrial socio-economic behaviour. In fact, the sources on the Bombay situation have systematically confused *jati* with district, region, language, occupation, or religion.

The 1940 BMOA survey poses grave difficulties precisely in these terms. Apart from serious questions about the representativeness of the sample, the so-called 'caste' categories are really not that at all. The Hindu group, representing 92.4 per cent of all workers, was divided into six 'caste' categories—Marathas, Kunbi, Bhandari, Bhayya, Kamathi and Harijan. Of these, only one—Bhandari—seems fairly clearly to represent a *jati*, and the employees so identified constituted only 2.7 per cent of the entire work force.

Neither Marathas nor Kunbis are single interdining, intermarrying entities. Both are clusters of endogamous groups. Moreover, Kunbis of various sorts have gradually incorporated themselves within the Maratha designation. Bhayya is not a caste designation at all but a regional term referring to all groups from what is now Uttar Pradesh. Kamathi also seems to be a regional rather than a *jati* classification. And Harijan, of course, is an euphemism comprehending all depressed castes. In Bombay there were at least six major Untouchable caste group—Bhangi, Chambhar, Dhed, Mahar, Mang and Mochi—and a number of minor ones. Since these groups are mutually exclusive in the country-side, it is inappropriate to lump them together. These conglomerate categories are impossible to justify analytically if the basic issue is not only the functioning distinctiveness of the groups which ultimately become part of the industrial labour force but also the possible consequences of such exclusiveness inside the mills. On the other hand, the fact that the BMOA used the general categories it did, raises the possibility that these broader distinctions were of greater operational significance than *jati*. If so, then it was not 'caste' in the technically precise sense that was crucial in the industry.

The BMOA survey does suggest some regional—linguistic and religious—as well as caste-clustering in the mills of Bombay. But the data also seem to indicate that the enclaves of workers were not preclusive. With the exception of Untouchables in the weaving sheds, we find all major regional and religious groups and Hindus of all castes in every department.[6] This 1940 evidence seems to be supported by nineteenth-century reports. For example, in 1864 the Census Commissioner of Bombay wrote:

It is supposed that at one time caste determined the occupation that a Hindu was to follow. Now it is but a limited influence, and there are few castes of which the members will not engage in any occupation, and few occupations in which the persons of any caste will not seek a livelihood (xviii).

Seventeen years later (*Census 1872 :* 42) another census commissioner, making the same point, added the comment: 'Hindus have a very great capacity for adapting themselves to circumstances and necessities.' And in 1892 a factory inspector stated that the 'refusal of men of one caste to work with those of the other has been singularly rare in the textile trade' (RCL 1892:136). These judgements seem to be borne out by the absence of any substantive contradictory evidence.

The weaving sheds apparently were the only historically significant exception to the generalization that whatever the situation in

---

[6] We actually cannot be certain of the almost complete exclusion of Untouchables from the weaving sheds. Lumping all migrants from the Uttar Pradesh region under the 'Bhayya' designation ignores the possibility that some, at least, of these people employed in the weaving shed may have been Untouchables. Moreover, 4.6 per cent of weaving shed employees were lumped into a Hindu 'miscellaneous' category which also may have included Untouchables.

the country-side, nothing prevented the employer from selecting freely from the Bombay labour market and assigning his recruits in any way he saw fit. The explanation widely given for the situation in the weaving sheds is that whenever a weft bobbin was replaced, yarn had to be sucked onto the shuttle. If Untouchables were employed, other groups working with the same shuttle would have been ritually defiled.

Reasonable though the explanation may be, it is not possible to tell whether this is a complete explanation of the fact. After all, the mills apparently had little trouble getting Hindu and Muslim weavers to work together. But even if the phenomenon has been correctly explained, it stands as a clear exception to the situation in every other department where caste people and Harijans are found working promiscuously . . . side by side without religious stigma. . . .We would still have to answer the question: why here and nowhere else ?

There is one aspect of the situation which has been largely ignored, the fact that historically the weaving department tended to be the highest paid section in the industry, with its relative advantage increasing over time. In effect, the situation in the weaving sheds pitted all 'clean' groups (including Muslims) against all Untouchable groups. We must at least raise the possibility that the exclusion of Untouchables was not entirely a caste phenomenon but was also a device to preserve the monopoly of particularly advantageous but very limited economic opportunities against newcomers.

The weaving shed represents the one possible case where workers would not permit the employers to use certain groups. To continue looking at the labour supply problem in terms of worker attitudes, there is one additional question to be raised. Were there any occupations in the mills which would not be accepted by all groups? There were none in the ritually degrading tasks—sweeper jobs—which were accepted only by Untouchable castes. There is, however, no statistical evidence bearing on this point. The 1940 BMOA survey throws no light on the subject. But apart from this, certain problems are involved. To the extent that over time the flush toilet replaced the honey bucket in the mills, it is possible that the issue of ritual contamination became irrelevant. However, even if we accept the fact that these tasks continued to exist, we are in no position to say that it was, in fact, only Untouchable castes which were taking them. And even if we could document the fact, we still could not be certain that this caste-clustering was a result of selection by workers rather than the selection of members of these castes for these jobs by the employers.

I have already implied that not only those who seek employment but also those who employ are intimately involved in the caste system and are as largely affected by its demands. The employer as a caste-affected person may seek to give employment to his caste brethren. If true, this would have made for the tendency for specific companies, if not in the industry itself. Although the evidence is not clear, such a pattern is not suggested.

But even if the employer did not recruit labour from his own particular subcaste, he may still have had views and prejudices as to the appropriate distribution of jobs among available castes in terms of purported caste skills, appropriate mixing of groups and the like. On this point there are some scattered facts. There is no question that many employers at various times had specific notions about the adaptability of special groups—not necessarily caste groups—to specific types of work. For example, many early mills seem to have sought out Julahas, a traditional group of Muslim handloom weavers, to employ in their weaving sheds. It has been said that these people were brought from long distances in the early years—from Upper India, Madras, and Calcutta—as well as recruited from among the group permanently resident in Bombay (ITJ 1907, XVII, No. 96:106).

There is also evidence that some of the early mills refused to employ Untouchables. In 1874 the manager of the United Spinning and Weaving Mill reported: 'No low-caste operatives are allowed to be employed in the mill.' In 1908 the manager of the D. Petit Mill not only stated that 'There were no low caste men in the weaving shed', but he also made the point that 'When a man applied for work, his caste was enquired into. Caste, in fact, was a great consideration' (IFLC 1908, II: 82). And one of the reasons the Tata scheme of 1897 to recruit labour in the Uttar Pradesh region seems to have foundered is that the Untouchable caste weavers—Kosto Mahars—who were available at the wages offered under the scheme were unacceptable to the millowners who sponsored the enterprise.

But whatever the specific examples, they are exceedingly few in number. For the industry as a whole there seems to have been no generally formulated and explicitly maintained policy of caste selection. It seems fairly safe to conclude that most of the changing pattern of group concentrations by department and mill had nothing to do with any clearly defined employer policy but were linked with the general methods of hiring labour and the preponderant power of the jobber in the process. ... It is sufficient at this point to indicate that the jobber played a decisive role in the selection and retention of labour and thus very clearly must have been responsible for much of the specific caste or other group concentrations that existed in individual mills.

This does not in itself explain the tendency, particularly of Untouchables, to increase their share in mill employment before 1921. It is possible that the rapid growth of employment opportunities at various times contributed to this in one special way. As the industry increased its emphasis on cloth production, weaver wages rose relatively, and there seems to have been a shift of 'clean' castes from spinning into the weaving sheds. Though there is no evidence on this point, it is possible that the lower paid employments, particularly ring spinning, then became more easily accessible to Untouchables. Strikes and the opportunity for strike-breaking apparently also offered Untouchables a channel for employment.[7] Once having established a foothold in the industry, they seem to have consolidated their position.

On examining the historical evidence as a whole, there seems little basis for arguing that any of the traditional features of the caste system as it may have functioned in the country-side affected the employer's ability to recruit labour as he saw fit. Whatever caste distinctions did persist in industry seem not to have imposed any obstacles to efficient utilization of workers or to profitable operation of the enterprises. Moreover, many of these institutional carryovers from the rural sector seem to have broken down over time. It was, after all, a fact that the refusal of men of one caste to work with those of the other has been singularly rare in the textile trade (RCL 1892:136).

There were, it is true, a few examples of employers providing separate welfare facilities based upon 'caste' distinctions. For example, in the 1920s one mill had set aside a separate playing field for its Untouchable workers. In some of the few cases where employers established canteen or dining facilities, separate arrangements were made for Untouchables. There is one report that 'clean' caste women refused to use a creche because an Untouchable *ayah* was employed to operate it. But the same source indicates how quickly and easily the company was able to eliminate the opposition. In fact, the inescapable conclusion from the evidence is that whatever distinctions did persist in the mills survived only because employers found it unnecessary to eliminate them. Whenever and wherever industry operations required the disruption of these traditional distinctions, they crumbled.

---

[7] For example, during the 1929 general strike, it is claimed that B.R. Ambedkar, leader of the Untouchables, undertook to supply strike breakers for a number of mills. It is possible that the strike breaking role of Untouchables has been exaggerated.

Let me make one final point. To the limited extent that group distinctions of a caste type did persist, they were clearly not based on *jati* prescriptions of the traditional sort but, as in the weaving sheds, on much wider elements—on a division between all Untouchables and all other workers. The persistence of this phenomenon seems to be more easily explicable in terms of limited job opportunities rather than on the basis of ritualized hostility of one *jati* towards another. In a society of enormous poverty and very restricted employment opportunities there was an overwhelming tendency for groups to preempt for themselves the monopoly of whatever jobs were available. Intruding groups, whatever their character, were a threat to the tenuously held advantages which did exist.

Who Are the 'Working Class'?

M. HOLMSTRÖM

People commonly refer to industrial workers, and sometimes other kinds of wage-earners and self-employed workers, as the 'working class'. Usually this means a group who share a similar economic situation, which distinguishes them from others, like property-owners, employers and managers. It suggests common interests and a shared consciousness of these interests. When left-wing people not just Marxists use the term, it implies that the working class work not for themselves, but for those who control the means of production and live off other people's labour.

Alternatively one could argue that it is misleading to lump together, as 'working class', people who share few interests and are not conscious of any; and that there is an important class line to draw between organized and unorganized sector industrial workers (Joshi 1976a), or between an urban class, which includes all industrial workers, and the mass of rural poor (Lipton 1977). In either case, well-paid organized sector workers are allied with the privileged or exploiting class, though the sections of this class fight among themselves for the spoils. That is what trade unions are for.

Are organized and unorganized sector industrial workers two classes with different or conflicting interests? On the face of it they seem to be, and I half implied that they were in *South Indian Factory Workers* (Holmström 1976); those inside the citadel of permanent

Excerpted from M. Holmström, 'Who are the "Working Class"?' *Industry and Inequality, Social Anthropology of Indian Labour*, Cambridge University Press, London, 1984.

employment, together with their close relatives; and those outside trying to get in, with little chance of success.

Do these two kinds of workers think and act as if they were classes with distinct interests, either in their everyday lives at work and at home, or when they become involved in joint action organized by unions or parties or more short-lived movements? And if they are sometimes aware of common interests do these cut them off from other people like casual general labourers, the self-employed and small peasants? ...

This [article] matches objective evidence; working and living conditions, careers, family economics to what I know about workers' experience and thinking, according to what they told me or others, unionists, sociologists and jornalists: workers' mental maps of society, built up from their experience of everyday problems.

In the end, everyone has her or his view of the world, which we may hope to understand but cannot reduce to a mere expression of self-interest. or to 'culture', values and perceptions which each person learns without question. People's motives and thoughts are more complex. But members of a group share ideas and assumptions, which reflect their common experience without being determined by it. How far do these workers see society as divided into those inside and outside the citadel? To the extent that there really is a citadel wall and people receive it, how much movement takes place across the wall, and what links remain between people on opposite sides of it? Do organized and unorganized sector workers live in separate social worlds? What links are there between all industrial workers and other people, especially peasants: for example, is there really an alliance between industrial workers and rich farmers which bolsters 'urban bias' in Indian planning and politics?

Wages

To start with the most obvious difference: big firms usually pay much more than small ones, at least to permanent employees. The bigger the firm the higher the pay, especially within the same industry, thus a 1973 settlement between engineering employers and unions in West Bengal laid down different minimum wages for firms employing over 50, 250 and 1000: firms with under 50 workers to be dealt with separately. Whether a small firm is technically in the organized sector does not seem to make much difference, though the presence of a union does : for many firms near the borderline, laws on bonus and overtime payments are a dead letter. Where there is a legal minimum wage it applies in theory to all local firms in an industry.

Some of the reasons why big firms pay best are clear: the law, the unions, economics of scale; often they take their pick of the skilled workers; many small employers are marginal and cannot afford to pay more, while the others take advantage of workers' weak bargaining position. . . .

However there are glaring exceptions to the rule that big firms pay best. I mentioned a Faridabad engineering factory where the minimum unskilled wage was Rs 600 a month, and a bigger one where it was Rs 230 (p. 152). These figures for 1976-7 include Dearness Allowance (D.A.), added to a national basic wage in large firms: the distinction no longer matters except as a bargaining counter. In one Bombay factory the minimum basic wage is Rs 40 + Rs 460 as D.A.! Multinationals generally pay best, private firms better than the public sector; so communist workers and union officials prefer the firms and managements which are ideologically the most suspect. Some small firms pay factory wages—without the security—to get skilled labour. . . .

Most big factories pay[1] well above the minimum: in the old Bombay textile mills, Rs 500 a month upwards as against Rs 200 for powerloom workers in small firms, or Rs 50-65 for children : in the biggest engineering or pharmaceutical factories, Rs 800 or more. Some car workers take home Rs 1200-1500 including overtime. The rates do not include the bonus, which varies between 8 and 20 per cent and is seldom paid in small firms. In some cases temporary workers get the same rates as permanent ones doing the same work, without the security or chance of promotion. Otherwise temporary, casual or contract workers earn less, sometimes a fraction: Rs 150 for contract cleaner, working beside factory cleaners who earn Rs 600.

The legal minimum varies between industries, but this does not make much difference in practice. Thus in Bombay the minimum forplastic workers is lower than in engineering, but unskilled workers in small firms get about the same, though with far less chance of learning a skill and raising their market value: the same in pharmaceuticals. The legal minimum can however serve as a rallying-point or target in campaigns to raise wages. I mentioned (p.160) a Bombay plastic firm where an agreement to pay the legal minimum would raise the women's daily

---

[1] Some wages are normally expressed as daily rates, some especially in larger firms as monthly salaries. I have not standardized them all. In some factories the distinction between 'daily-rated' and 'monthly-rated' employees is important, for status and security.

wage from Rs 4 to Rs 8.60: the men already earned as much at piece-work rates, and though the union was against piecework it had to go slowly.

In Bangalore, on the other hand, the legal minimum is below the market rate for most kinds of work, and the wage gap is even wider than in Bombay. Workshops employ labourers at Rs 3 a day (Rs 78 a month) upwards and semi-skilled workers from Rs 4 (Rs 104), while wages in the big factories are as high as in Bombay....

Working Conditions and the Experience of Work

Some people work in safer, more pleasant conditions, with less accidents, discomfort, fatigue, noise and monotony; more space, shorter hours, bearable or even pleasant work rhythm and personal relations, freedom from harassment or close control; interesting varied work with a chance to learn something that could lead to a better career.

Some of these things are easy to observe, like safety measured by accident rates or work space, canteens, creches, lavatories and wash-rooms. Others are more subjective: their importance depends on workers' own preferences and other things in their lives outside work.... How closely do these differences in working conditions go with other diferences in terms of employment, between organized and unorganized sector workers, or between large and small firms? Do the best paid (and most secure?) work in the best conditions? Is there little relation, or even a trade-off, as there is for many English working-class people who, unlike the middle class, face 'the dilemma . . . of having to *choose between* work which offers variety, scope for initiative and relative autonomy, and work which, for any skill level, affords the highest going rate of economic return'? (Goldthorpe *et al.* 1969: 64).

Conditions in many small workshops are appalling by any standards: the cramped dirty rooms on the private 'multi-storey 'industrial estates' of Bombay, or worse conditions in many slum or back street workshops. There is no trade-off here: people work here only because they cannot get anything better, though they might get something worse—casual building work; making *bidis* at home until their fingers are too numb to continue; or the walled and guarded stone quarries outside Bangalore:

Thirty-five families, all in debt to the contractor, worked in a quarry. A mother of five who escaped to another quarry was hunted down, brought back and branded on the breast. At one quarry, whole families were never allowed out together, in case they should escape.

(Based on *Indian Express*, 7 Nov. 1975.)

In city workshops the problem is not atrocities on this scale (apart from the occasional use of *goondas* or thugs to deal with unrest) but rather the blatant disregard of safety precautions, required by law in small firms as well as large, and the resulting accidents and occupational diseases. In Bangalore, men earning Rs 4 a day are in danger from the belts connecting their lathes to one overhead drive shaft, which saves electricity and the cost of separate motors. Presses, polishing wheels and machines to cut out tin cans have no guards. Welders and lathe operators work without goggles; men handle hot metal without protective clothing. Workers with burns, lost or injured fingers or splinters in the eye complain they have been sacked, or laid off without compensation until their injuries heal. Men working with chemicals complain of acid burns, weakness, pain and long-term illness. Yet several small employers told me they paid all medical bills for workers and their families, who were better served than they would be by Employees' State Insurance.

Conditions are just as bad in many larger factories. The Factories Act, including the safety and health provisions, is enforced by the grossly understaffed and overworked Factory Inspectorate. In most states it is the policy to avoid prosecution wherever possible, and to persuade factory owners to put right any violations. The owners have nothing to lose by waiting until an inspector puts in an adverse report, which is unlikely. Very unpleasant conditions may be legal and unavoidable: the intense heat of foundries and heat treatment sheds, especially in hot weather; the dust in a cement factory, even with extractor fans, the deafening noise in a weaving shed or bicycle factory. Some managements, large and small, try to improve conditions because they think it is wrong to employ sweated labour, and a false economy; but the best enforcement agency is a strong union, which can protest about conditions and press the claims of sick or injured workers for compensation. Though unions care very much about working conditions, they are bound to put job security and wages first.

. . . .

One should not romanticize small industries—small employers have an obvious interest in the theory that labour relations are closer, more personal and relaxed than in factories—but it is *sometimes* true that physical conditions in small firms are at least as good as in factories, the pace of work easier and relations between the employer and his workers based on trust and long familiarity. Workers have security as long as the firm stays in business: only the pay is low. . . .

Working conditions—health and safety precautions, space, venti-
lation, working hours, leave and weekly rest days, access to
medical care for the worker— are all regulated by laws which apply
to factories, not small workshops. Conditions in some big modern
factories are better than those required by law. Whether the law
is observed elsewhere depends on the factory inspectors' zeal,
employers' attitudes, 'modern management', old-fashioned paternalism or cold calculation and especially the strength of the unions:
also the importance workers attach to working conditions, and
how far they are prepared to go in demanding better conditions
rather than, for example, higher wages or security.

Jobs, Careers and Security

A permanent factory worker not only has a job, but a career. His
working life is not just a list of things that happened to him—jobs
he got and lost—but a line leading somewhere. When he tells the
story of his life, it has a plot—each stage led to the next in some
rational intelligible way; and although job finding and promotion
depend largely on luck, his actions affected the outcome, even
if it was only the negative action of hanging on to his job, never
moving forward without a secure base to fall back on.

His career extends into the future. Assuming he keeps his job, he may
plan to improve it by learning a skill and getting promotion; to change
it for a better one; to improve pay and conditions through union action; to start his own workshop; to earn his long-service gratuity and
then to farm or keep a shop; or simply to use his steady income to support and educate his family. . . .

Ideally a permanent job is secure. A worker can look forward to
gradual promotion, more or less reflecting skill and experience; or at
the least, yearly pay rises until he reaches the top of his grade. Job
changes are voluntary; he moves from one safe job straight into another. In the end he retires comfortably.

In practice, factories close down or lay off workers in bad times.
Workers are dismissed for bad work or making trouble. They fall ill,
their sick leave and Employees' State Insurance run out, and they lose
their jobs. They resign for personal reasons, perhaps because they cannot bear the work any longer. These are the accidents in the plot, which
one has to allow for. One plans one's life on the assumption that these
things will never happen.

When the disaster strikes, itt can hit very hard , because it is un-expected and the worker has long-term commitments, like children to educate:

The Labour Bureau 1971b (summarized in Labour Bureau 1978: 123-4) shows that the great majority of retrenched industrial workers in the sample had no other earner in the family, they borrowed from shopkeepers, relatives and friends, took their children out of school, gradually lost hope and spoke of their fear of destitution. 'The shopkeeper, however, refused to give him goods on credit when he came to know about his lay off. Had not the shop-keeper been merciful and promised to help him in his hard days, he would have joined the rank of beggars. Shri Ganga Ram, however, was constantly under fear lest the shopkeeper change his mind and withdraw the help' (4; 'Profiles of Hard Cases'). Those interviewed were not yet destitute, unlike ex-factory workers who join the pavement-dwellers of Calcutta.

A Bangalore worker, struggling to etablish a union in his engi-neering factory, said that uneducated workers are the most easily in-timidated by the management because they are terrified of losing their jobs. A highly skilled or well-connected worker may know he has a good chance of finding a new job quickly; yet some skills, though hard to learn, are over-supplied or too specialized.

The most prized possession of the Coimbatore mill worker is his job. Consid-ering the level of skill there is almost no other employment around which would pay him as well. Nor is there much chance of his being able to shift from one mill to another. . . . It is only by remaining in his employment that the worker can hope to maintain a valued standard of living. The mill worker is in much the same position as the craftsman who jealously restricts entry into the trade to protect the conditions of his employment. His job is to the worker what the craft is to the craftsman. The important difference between the two is that the mill worker is unskilled and cannot hope to find an alter-native job with comparable pay whereas the craftsman is so highly skilled that he does not want to incur the cost of giving up his trade and moving to another (Ramaswamy 1977: 69).

One man told me his skill would only be useful in a foam rubber factory: there are few in Bangalore, none as good as his present place. Some skills are specific to one firm, for example in the telephone industry.

Office workers, supervisors and managers, who may have savings or property but whose relatives expect them to keep up a middle-class life-style, may feel the blow worst of all.

. . . .

The point is that 'permanent' workers in big factories assume they have, or ought to have, jobs for life or until they choose to leave. They see this security as a necessary condition for the chance to make plans and advance their careers. The search for security explains both immobility (when workers think they have security) and mobility (when they move to get it).

. . . .

The main threat to security in small firms is from factors beyond the employers' control: falling orders, seasonal demand, or the end of a single large contract, which force the employer to close the firm or lay off workers (if they are only laid off, the employer may keep in touch until he needs them again). If orders fall, workers—and their unions, if any—know there is little they can do, except wait for better times. . . .

If orders can fall abruptly, they can rise. Big factories have a core of skilled labour which they can expand by taking on temporaries or putting out work to small firms. The small firms are much more vulnerable to sudden shortages, not only of skilled workers like toolmakers, but even semi-skilled workers used to particular machines: they may not take very long to train, but the employer must start on the new order at once if he is not to lose it. While factory managements complain, frequently, that their work force is too stable, too secure, small employers have to entice workers to stay: building up close personal relations if they can, offering loans to workers in times of need, turning a blind eye to absence and spoilt work, sometimes even paying factory wages without factory security.

The large modern factories have a formal promotion structure. Movement up the ladder depends on skill, years of service, manager's assessment of individuals, and union pressures. Some men enter the factory already trained and skilled. The others either learn a skill over time, or are likely to be promoted to a 'skilled' grade in recognition of long service, rationalized as experience. In factories of an older type, there is security but little promotion. In small firms, there is no formal classification of skills: the wide variations in pay reflect the manager's present need for each worker. In workshops, much more than in factories, there is wide gap in wages and prospects between workers with a skill in real demand, and the rest, the 'helpers', who may pick up a marketable skill if they are lucky.

Some of these 'helpers' and unskilled labourers are always moving from job to job, with periods of unemployment when they depend on relatives. Others are on good terms with an employer whose business is stable, and this gives them enough security to rent two rooms, keep their families in the city and send their children to school. They are the more fortunate part of the mass of urban poor that Breman writes about: 'The poor try to increase their security within the urban system by entering into dependency relations with social superiors'—employers or brokers: 'For this part of the urban population, work is not the basis for a more or less independent existence, but the outcome of a comprehensive dependency relationship' (1976:1906). But an important minority of unorganized sector workers have real bargaining power. Unemployment has costs for them, but no terrors. If you can acquire a marketable skill in the unorganized sector, it is unlikely to get you into a big factory, but it frees you to a large extent from personal dependence on employers, brokers and contracts. It allows you to plan some kind of career strategy for yourself and, if you choose, to call in a union to help you and your fellow workers.

Let me modify my simple image of the organized sector as a citadel. A small number of workers have real security: almost, not quite, jobs for life if they choose. All their other projects depend on this, whether these concern their career, family life, friendships, political and religious activities, or anything else. The thought of losing this security is terrifying.

Then there is a much larger group of factory workers who know that no job is safe, and plan accordingly. Security comes before income or good conditions; unions sometimes have to make this choice, but individuals seldom do when job hunting, because the safest jobs are generally the best paid.

In the smaller factories as well as the whole unorganized sector, the ideal of job security becomes more and more unrealistic. A job saved may not be saved for long. Unions will fight dismissal, but as part of a strategy to win the best immediate advantage for their members; workers will talk of a strike for higher wages as a success, although it meant sacrificing a few jobs. These people do not *expect* security, but they work hard to get it, through relations with employers which can be seen sometimes as one-way dependence, sometimes as mutual need; by keeping their friendships in good repair; or for those who have the chance, by learning a skill and keeping it up to date.

. . . .

Social Worlds

[The] simple dualistic image of Indian society, at least in towns . . . . those with safe well-paid jobs inside the organized sector citadel, and those outside trying to get in . . . is too simple. The labour market appears to separate people into at least three groups, or perhaps to continue and reinforce a separation which existed already, before these people came into industrial work. These three kinds of people have different chances in the job market, different earnings and working conditions, often live in different places and have different friends; though kinship and friendship can cut across these boundaries.

First there are permanent organized sector workers, including factory workers as well as government and office employees; though there is an enormous gap between the best factories and the worst. This group shades into workers with fairly regular employment unprotected by law, including all workers in small firms and 'temporaries' etc. in large ones. A sharper line separates both kinds of regular workers from unskilled casual labourers.

That covers most people whose living depends on manufacturing industry, though there is also a fourth group: the self-employed, ranging from those depending on one or a few customers who can dictate terms, to independent craftsmen like carpenters who have a real market for their work. . . .

There is no point in classifying for the sake of classifying, but these distinctions refer to important differences in people's situation and perhaps to conflicts of interest, which they may or may not be aware of How separate are these groups, both in reality and in people's minds, and what relations cut across the dividing lines? There are really three sorts of questions: about real differences in economic conditions and life chances, which depend on large-scale economic forces and the job market: about social maps—the differences and alignments that people think are important; and about the social worlds they live in—whatever they think or say, who do they spend their time with, depend on, and help or oppose or avoid?

Evidence from the labour market, from families and from areas where industrial workers live is sometimes contradictory, especially about the relations between 'organized sector' and other regularly employed workers. There are instances of solidarity and mutual aid; of dependence, where factory workers profit in one way or another from acting as patrons or brokers to their less fortunate neighbours; of movement across the line by able or lucky individuals, who may or may not help their relatives to follow; separation into different groups with their own kinship and job-finding networks, living apart and not aware of any common interests; and sometimes, tension and open hostility.

. . . John Harriss finds that few Coimbatore workers have relatives employed in another sector. He concludes that

the labour market in Coimbatore is strongly segmented, and current trends in factory employment may be strengthening this segmentation even further. We refer to systematic exclusion of people from low caste backgrounds from employment in some of the big mills (1982 : 99).

Now that labour is abundant, the dominant caste millowners exclude low-caste people where they can.

Employment in workshops is not neccessarily a route into factory employment, and . . . petty commodity producers and traders are generally from different backgrounds than casual workers, or factory and workshop employees. . . . Connections between 'sectors' or parts of the labour market—within families or even within wider circles of kin—are not much developed. The principal exception to the general picture of separation is that of the PCPs [Petty Commodity Producers] in 'new' activities who are often people who have had experience of employment in workshops or factories.

The historical existence of a strong relationship between certain occupations and membership in particular communities of caste or kin has provided an ideological context for this strong differentiation within the labour market; and the way in which large numbers of people are continually deprived of access to means of earning their livelihoods now supplies a firm basis for the persistence of caste identities—when these identities constitute one of the few 'resources' that many people possess (1982: 999).

In other words, there are almost separate social worlds, from the top to the bottom of the social scale, and an ideology of difference which keeps each little world closed to outsiders. This is truer in Coimbatore, or for example in Calcutta, than in places like Bombay and Bangalore where there are better chances to move up and less rigid ideological barriers to movement, and to some extent one can put the difference down to local cultural factors and historical accident.

    Things are just as bad at the bottom; for the 'informal sector' which provides some sort of a living is not the bottom. The foulest, most dangerous and badly paid work may be hard to break into. There is no reason to think the lines between factory and workshop employees, or between both and casual workers like building labourers, are any sharper than these divisions among the very poor, and a good deal of evidence—for example, in Deshpande's 'Bombay labour market'—to suggest the opposite: that people at the bottom live in little closed boxes, competing fiercely with very poor people in other closed boxes. Once you break out and gain a foothold, however insecure in small industry where you can get experience with machines and make useful friends, your chances of better-paid regular work improve gradually. The first step is the hardest.

Everywhere it seems that those at the bottom generally stay there. Migration to town may make them less poor and blunt the edge of prejudice and discrimination, but they occupy roughly the same space on other people's social maps.

. . . .

Generally a worker in a big modern factory earns two or three times as much as a worker with the same title, like a turner, in a small organized sector factory or a workshop; and he has security and fringe benefits. Some of this difference reflects skill, and experience on machines which only the big factories have. I asked low-paid workers why there was this difference. The usual explanation was simply that big factories naturally paid more, they were 'limited companies', there were economies of scale and stronger unions. They did not imply that these high wages were at their own expense, they just wanted to get into the same situation themselves: either individually by getting a better job or collectively, by forcing their employers to give higher pay and security. To do either of these things, they need the better-paid workers' help: to get a job, one needs friends in the firms where the jobs are: to organize effectively, it is essential to get the help of unions based in large firms, which are only now beginning to take an interest in the smaller companies and workshops. Since it is now clear to unorganized sector workers that the old avenues of upward mobility are closed except for a few with special skills, the low-paid workers on both sides of the organized/unorganized boundary now see their best chance in militant union action, though they do not appear to see this as a confrontation with the better-paid workers. . . .

My image of the 'citadel' was too simple. The organized/unorganized boundary is not a wall but a steep slope. Indian society is like a mountain, with the very rich at the top, lush Alpine pastures where skilled workers in the biggest modern industries graze, a gradual slope down through smaller firms where pay and conditions are worse and the legal security of employment means less, a steep slope around the area where the Factories Act ceases to apply where my wall stood, a plateau where custom and the market give poorly paid unorganized sector workers some minimal security, then a long slope down through casual migrant labour and petty services to destitution. There are well-defined paths up and down those slopes, which are easiest for certain kinds of people.

Whether the boundary is a wall or a slope, the important question is whether the whole organized sector exploits the unorganized. Michael Lipton (1977) believes there is a Grand Alliance of industrial owners and workers unions, big farmers and intellectuals who maintain urban bias in planning (though it is not always clear whether he is writing about urban rural differences or differences between rich and poor). Heather and Vijay Joshi (1976) show some sympathy for the argument that the whole organized sector workers, unions, owners managers and related interests form a privileged upper class, making luxury goods for an upper class market: we should revise our view of the unorganized sector as rifraff without productive potential. However the trend is now to go to the opposite extreme; to subsidize small firms because they are small and assumed to be labour-intensive and to develop 'appropriate' technology as if suitable technologies were not available already for any economic strategy worth choosing.

Those who are sceptical about 'the philosophy of small-scale industries' are on the defensive. A good counter-attack is in Jan Breman's article (1976), where he argues that it is a mistake to think of the 'informal sector' as a thing in itself, a separate economic compartment or labour situation. There are no separate markets, no dual economy, and the informal or unorganized sector has little growth potential of its own. The different criteria for distinguishing between waged and self-employed, formal and informal, organized and unorganized, security and insecurity, etc. do not add up to any clear stratification. I implied that they did (Holmström 1976) and I was wrong. . . .

Agrarian Structure

DANIEL THORNER

In returning to India in 1952 my aim was to carry forward research on the country's changing agrarian structure. When I tried to find usable data on such basic questions as who actually *worked* the land, what was the product of the land, what was the division of that product among those who *owned* and those who worked, I became somewhat discouraged. There was indeed available a welter of published material in the form of reports of agrarian inquiry commitees, texts of land reform laws, revenue department statistics, and the like. But the content was more often than not either incomplete or out of date or not sufficiently trustworthy. From these materials I could not puzzle out a satisfactory picture of the structure of land ownership or of the pattern of cultivation.

The decision which I somewhat reluctantly reached was that, for the time being, I would have to put aside the books, periodicals, and documents with which I was accustomed to working. I would have to desert the libraries and proceed into the villages to see for myself what agrarian relationships actually existed, and how they operated. That is just what I have been doing since 1952: going to one village after another in all states and regions of India, and asking questions directly of the villagers as to who owns the land, who works it, what is the product, and who gets what share of that product.

I have no illusion that in the villages I have visited, somewhere between 75 and 100 in all, I have been told the truth, the whole truth, and nothing but the truth. Rather I hope that by asking the same question in

Excerpted from Daniel Thorner, 'Agrarian Structure', *The Agrarian Prospect in India*. Allied, Delhi, 1973.

different ways and of different men I have been able to set up a rough form of checking on the answers. Perhaps my working procedure could be characterized as a series of hit-and-run raids into the country-side.

Clearly every conclusion arrived at by such methods must be treated as tentative and provisional. Any results are at best prelimi-nary. If I should seem at times to be putting things forcefully, or, Heaven forbid, dogmatically, please do not be misled. The apparent confidence on my part will be merely an effort to make as plain as I can precisely how I view the situation at this stage of my knowledge. I am only too painfully aware of the contours of my ignorance.

Let us start, then, with an attempt to define our field of concern. We can say that our aim is to describe and analyse the network of rela-tions among the various groups of persons who draw their livelihood from the soil. We are also concerned with the consequences of this pattern of relationships for the economy of the country as a whole.

In order to describe the relations among classes, we must agree on the nature of classes. Or, more correctly, in order to describe the nature of the classes, we must set forth the relationships obtaining among them. The agrarian structure is, after all, not an external framework within which various classes function, but rather it is the sum total of the ways in which each group operates in relation to the other goups. We will find that some of these relations are defined and enforced by law. Others are customary. Still others are of a flexible or fluctuating character. I might observe in passing that the agrarian history of India is replete with instances of efforts to change these relationships by law, efforts which have almost always fallen far short of their goals or had effects other than those intended.

What, then, are the basic differences of interest in the rural scene today? We all know that there are landlords, tenants, and labourers. But are these terms sufficiently precise? Cannot one and the same man belong simultaneously to all three of these categories? Let us suppose that he owns a few acres of land. Part of this he cultivates himself, and part, perhaps in another village, he lets out to a tenant or cropsharer. He may also rent in another bit of land for his own cultivation. And, from time to time, he may work as a field labourer for one of his more substantial neighbours. Thus he is a landlord and a tenant, a 'cultiva-tion owner' and an agricultural labourer.

Some parts of India, as, for example, Andhra, Tamilnad, and Bihar, have to this day large absentee landlords, whose holdings are let out to tenants. In Bengal there are known to be several layers of tenants and subtenants between the zamindars and the men who actually till the soil. The former princely states still contain a great variety of *jagirdars*, *imamdars*, and other holders of large estates under specially privileged tenures. In Bombay, where the landholders are *raiyats*, we find many instances of cultivation by *halis* (debt-slaves), and a large amount of cropsharing. Punjab is generally thought of as the home of sturdy self-cultivators of small and medium-sized farms; in practice both Punjab and Pepsu have large numbers of *siris* (attached servants), paid in kind with a share of the produce, and *muzara* (particularly insecure tenants). Malabar has its characteristic quadruple structure of *janmis*, *kanamdars*, *verumpattamdars*, and *cherumas*. From Tamilnad, historically a *raiyatwari* area like Bombay, we hear frequent stories of conflict between the aristocratic *mirasdars* and the lowly *pannaiyals*.

Let us try to set up criteria which will help us marshall these divergent systems of tenure and cultivation into usable categories. We can begin by asking in what form the income from the soil is obtained. Is it received as rent, as the fruit of cultivation, or as payment for labour? We can then ask what type of rights in the soil are enjoyed, and just how much land is held under these rights. Finally we can inquire to what extent the individual actually performs the required fieldwork, or whether others are hired to do it for him.

If we look at the rural position today with these questions in mind, I think we will find that, despite wide regional variations, we can trace a common pattern. Roughly speaking there are three principal groups, whom we can call proprietors, working peasants, and labourers. Or, better, we could use the terms *malik*, *kisan*, and *mazdur*. By *malik* or proprietor we will refer to a family whose agricultural income is derived primarily (although not necessarily solely) from property rights in the soil. That is to say that whatever other sources of family funds may exist, such as from a profession or business, the main agricultural income is derived from a share of the produce of lands belonging to the family. Typically, this share will be realized in the form of rent. Usually the rent will be taken in money, but it may be in kind if the tenants are on a cropsharing basis. Instead of renting out his lands, however, a proprietor may hire labourers to cultivate them for him. He may manage these hired labourers himself, or he may hire someone else as manager. He may actually go into the fields and perform some of the work alongside of his labourers, although this is far from typical; but, even so, we would class him as a *malik* if his agricultural income from that part of his holdings which he cultivates with his own hands is less than the amount he receives from renting out the rest

of his lands, or having them tilled by hired labourers. You will note
that I am making no distinction here between proprietors who rent out
their land and those whose fields are cultivated by hired labourers.
Some of you, I know, will raise your eyebrows at this. May I ask you
to accept this grouping tentatively for the time being. In the course of
[this paper] the reasons for lumping the two together will become
clearer. At this point I may simply observe that many proprietors
today exploit their holdings simultaneously in both of these ways, i.e.
they give out part to tenants or cropsharers, and reserve part to be
worked by hired labourers. We may recall that in the history of economics the distinction between income derived from the performance
of labour and income derived from the possession of property is older
and more fundamental than the classical division of income into
wages, rent and profits.

Usually, but not necessarily, the *malik* or proprietor will enjoy a
high type of property right in the soil. He may hold directly under the
government, or he may be a superior tenant with rights of occupancy,
transfer, mortgage, and inheritance protected by law. He may hold various lands under more than one type of tenure. The total amount of land
held is such that the income serves to meet the major shares of the
family's expenses (or, at least, the expenses of those members of the
family resident in the village). One or another member of the family
may act as manager or supervisor, but none is required to work with
his hands in the fields in order to assure the family's sustenance.

Within this group or class of *maliks*, it is possible to separate out two
subgroups. One consists of large absentee landlords who typically have
holdings in more than one village. The second consists of smaller
proprietors who reside personally in the village in which they own
land, and usually exercise some degree of management and control
over its cultivation. It must be emphasized that the distinction here is
not one of formal tenure. Either of these two types of proprietors may
have the highest type of property rights. Either may be an occupancy
tenant. Both have the same basic economic interest in keeping up the
level of rent payable to them by lesser tenants, subtenants, or cropsharers; and keeping down the level of wages of farm servants and
other old labourers. For it is the *maliks*, large and small, who are the
receivers of rural rent and the chief employers of rural labour.

The members of the second class, whom we will call *kisans*, or
working peasants, have also a recognized property interest in the land.
They may be small owners, or tenants with varying degrees of security.
By and large (but not in every state) their legal and customary rights

will be somewhat inferior to those of the *maliks* in the same village. The chief distinguishing feature, however, is the amount of land held. In the case of the working *kisan*, the size of the holding is such that it supports only a single family and then only if one or more members of the family actually perform the field labour. In fact, the produce from the land owned by the *kisan* may not even provide the entire income required by his family, but at least it provides a larger share than whatever funds he may receive from other agricultural sources, such as doing labour on other people's lands. *Kisans*, as defined here, are those villagers who live primarily by their own toil on their own lands. They do not employ labour, except briefly in the ploughing or harvest season, nor do they commonly receive rent.

The third rural class, that of labourers or *mazdur*, comprises those villagers who gain their livelihood primarily from working on other people's land. Families in this class may indeed have tenancy rights in the soil, or even property rights, but the holdings are so small that the income from cultivating them or from renting them out comes to less than the earnings from fieldwork. Wages may be received in money or in kind. If the latter, they may be fixed or in the form of a crop share. In practice the lower ranks of croppers and tenants-at-will are almost indistinguishable from *mazdur*; they will tentatively be included in this category.

I have suggested, by these definitions, that we may divide rural India into three main classes: the *maliks* or proprietors, the *kisans* or working peasants, and the *mazdur* or agricultural labourers. The key to the division is the amount of actual labour contributed to the production process and the share in the product. The extent to which income is received despite lack of participation in agricultural work may well be an index to the severity of the agrarian problem.

In order to receive agricultural income without performing field labour, one must have property rights in land. Just what are these rights, what responsibilities and privileges do they entail, how have they arisen? At this stage of a discussion of the Indian agrarian scene, it is customary to give a brief disquisition on the differences between zamindari and *raiyatwari* types of tenure, the historical background of the two, and the superiority of the latter over the former. Thus we all know that when the British came into control of substantial tracts of India in the eighteenth century, they made arrangements to receive the benefits of empire in the form of the land revenues. For this purpose, as we have often been told, they transformed the tax-gatherers of the defeated local dynasties into near replicas of English landed gentry, and the actual cultivators into their tenants. Thus, runs the oft-repeated story, was private property in land introduced into India.

If we re-examine the record a bit more closely, I think we will agree that (the establishment of private property in land) was precisely what Cornwallis and his successors did not do. Like the Mughals before them, and the Guptas and the Mauryas before the Mughals, the British insisted on the right of the imperial power to the first share of the fruits of the soil. But this type of a claim was already centuries out of date in England itself, and belongs properly to a stage of economic development where there is, in effect, no other principal source of State revenue. The key fact about all the British land settlements of the late eighteenth and nineteenth centuries, whether zamindari, *raiyatwari, ualwari, taluqdari,* or *malguzari,* whether permanent or temporary, so that the new rights in the land were invariably subordinate to the rights of the State. To *no* holder was granted the exclusive right to occupy, enjoy, and dispose of land which, *in practice,* is the hallmark of western private ownership. Without this quality of exclusiveness, real private property cannot be said to exist.

Some of the rights normally associated with private property in land (e.g., transfer, mortgageability, heritability) were indeed accorded to the new 'owners'. But their privileges were restricted by the simultaneous recognition of rights both superior and inferior to their lies in the same land. The State, as a super-landlord, claimed a share in the rents; while the actual tillers exercised a traditional claim to occupancy.

Under the various pre-British regimes, land revenues collected by the State were simply the State's share of the produce, the right to which was unquestioned. The early British officials assumed that since the State collected what *appeared* to them as a *rent,* the State must be the owner of all the land. Accordingly, as they took over territorial power from the various rulers, they established the right of the British rule as the supreme or ultimate landowner; and with this justification they continued to collect revenues at the former or, more commonly, enhanced levels.

What the British established in India might be described, in fact, as an imperfect or *kaccha* kind of private ownership of land. To this date there has not emerged in India a fully developed or *pakka* private property in agricultural land. It was the British insistence upon the State's prerogative as ultimate owner, which has given India's land tenures their distinctive character.

Below the State's claim, elaborate sets of inferior claims were for the first time precisely defined and put into writing. A body of written laws, regulations, and rules was brought into being. Far-reaching administrative and judicial machinery was set up for enforcing property relations and collecting the State's revenues from the land. The countryside was systematically divided up and placed under the jurisdiction of the several ranks of Commissioners, Deputy Commissioners, Collectors, Deputy Collectors, Magistrates, Deputy Magistrates, Mamlatdars, Zaildars, Tehsildars and the like.

We are all well acquainted with the layering of rights in the land which resulted in the Permanent Settlement areas (Bengal, Bihar, Orissa, and part of Madras) where several ranks of non-working rent-collecting intermediaries came to fill the gap left between the fixed revenue obligations to the State and the growing value of the land. Actually, all over India, a similar development can be traced to a greater or lesser degree. Whatever the particular form of land system that was followed, it served to confirm the right of one group of holders to a share in the produce of the land, whether or not they participated personally in the productive process. Whether this right (i.e., the privilege of receiving agricultural income without necessarily performing agricultural labour) was retained by the descendants of the original holder, or, as happened even more frequently, purchased and enjoyed by others, it tended to become increasingly separated from the actual tilling of the soil, and even from residence in the village.

As the evils of this system became apparent, legislation was introduced with the aim of restoring the traditional rights of the actual cultivators. Largely, this legislation took the form of tenant protection. Thus the group who held directly *under* the zamindars or landlords (i.e., the group of the *sub*-penultimate owners) were confirmed in lifetime and even heritable occupancy of their lands, or given rights of sale, mortgage, and transfer of their *tenancies*. But in time even this group of enhanced-right holders followed the path charted out by their predecessors in the imperial favour, the private landlords or penultimate owners. They found it more profitable to rent out their holdings to sub-tenant and retired from the active practice of agriculture. Or else they sold out completely to newcomers, typically merchants, moneylenders, or other non-agriculturists interested less in cultivation than in collection of rents.

Of course, the original settlements and the subsequent legislation constitute only one of the several factors to which the development of agrarian structure during the British period can be attributed.

We have already mentioned that there was a rise in the price of land. This resulted in part, I suspect, from the fact that, in the new setting, land has been made more of a commodity than ever before in Indian territory. With the opening up of railways and ports, which made possible much better access to overseas markets, it became profitable to put more land under crops and the demand for land increased. A later factor was the growth of the population and the lack of alternative employment. This had the effect of weakening the bargaining position of the agricultural labourers and the would-be tenants or croppers in their relations with the holders of land rights. The high price of land showed a steep threshold over which few labourers or petty tenants were able to climb in order themselves to become landholders.

The shift from food crops to cash crops attendant upon the opening of paths to the world markets increased the need for credit. At the same time the rising value of agricultural land, the legal provision for mortgageability, and the administrative machinery available to back the collection of debts made it worthwhile for more⁻ moneylenders to operate in the rural field. In many cases individuals who had made the start as moneylenders were in the best position to buy up or foreclose the ownership and tenancy rights which the British land action had made transferable, and thus to establish themselves as agricultural proprietors. Even where landholdings were not transferred outright to the moneylenders, the smaller tenants and owners fell increasingly under their power. Debts, increasing from year to year at compounded interest rates, were often so high that the petty landholder could not hope to pay them off in his lifetime. The obligation to the moneylender was thus inherited along with the property right. Holders who might appear in both the official records and the census returns as independent proprietors were in effect little more than bondservants of the credit-suppliers. Thus the moneylenders, if they did not actually become proprietors themselves, came to share with the proprietors the privilege of drawing income from agriculture—or, more precisely, from agriculturists—without doing agricultural work.

Socially, the resident *maliks* and moneylenders form a small and quite distinctive group within the village. A handful of six or a dozen families, they typically belong to Brahman, Thakur, or other high ranking castes; alternatively, as in Andhra, they may be members of respectable cultivating castes like the Kammas, Reddis, or Raos. They live in larger houses, wear finer clothes, and eat a better diet than the rest of the villagers. They may send their children to higher schools, subscribe to newspapers, listen to battery radios, or own bicycles—all luxuries usually quite beyond the compass of the debt-ridden *kisans*, to say nothing of the landless *mazdur-log*.

Between these last two groups, although the community of economic interest may appear very large, there is a steep social barrier. The *kisans* are drawn primarily from cultivating or artisan castes; the *mazdur-log* primarily from Harijans, Scheduled, depressed or 'backward' classes. Certain types of work locally considered degrading, such as ploughing in eastern U.P., are reserved for these lowly servitors. The rare Chamar, Mahar, Panchama, or other Untouchable who prospers economically and attempts to secure a foothold for his family by buying land may find insurmountable obstacles in the way of the purchase. For he is up against the deeply entrenched tradition of rural inequality — a tradition which goes back centuries, if not millennia. To a considerable extent, the belief that low castes are born to labour with their hands, and high castes to enjoy the fruits of other's labour, is accepted by the former as well as the latter. The separation between proprietorship and physical cultivation both draws sanction from and serves to reinforce the caste structure of rural society.

What we have here in India today, then, is an unique agrarian structure. It represents a blending of remnants from the pre-British economic order (including, above all, the claim of the State to a share of the produce of the land), together with modern Western concepts of private property. The result has been a layering of rights from those of the State as super-landlords (or ultimate owner) down-through those of the sub-landlords (penultimate owners) to those of the several tiers of tenants. Both the State and the superior holders exercise the right to draw income from the soil in the form of rents. Wherever possible the tenants also try to subsist by collecting rents from the working cultivators with rights inferior to their own.

The maintenance of this hierarchical structure of interests in the land has required, in effect, that quite a substantial proportion of the produce be reserved for persons who perform no agricultural labour. What was left to the actual cultivator, after the claims of the various superior right holders were satisfied, might still be subject to collection as unpaid debt by the moneylender. The mechanism for the enforcement of this withdrawal of the great bulk of the product from the primary producers was provided by the new body of written law, the courts, the police, the promulgation of ordinances, and so forth. In the end, the working *kisan* was left with no surplus to invest in better implements, improved seed, or fertilizer, and in any case no real incentive to increase his productivity. Since his tenure was in most cases insecure, it was scarcely worth his while to think of undertaking long-term improvements. For the landless *mazdur*, there was even less point to any attempt to raise his efficiency.

Both the harassed small-holder and the downtrodden labourer, seeing before them little prospect of a betterment of their condition, concentrated rather on warding off a worsening. So far as any changes might be proposed, their attitude was typically one of a stubborn and suspicious conservatism. The superior right holders, from whom a more progressive approach might have been expected, were interested in agriculture only to the extent that they might continue to draw their incomes from it.

Typically they found it more profitable to rent out their lands than to manage them personally. Clearly it was not worth their while to invest capital in agricultural operations so long as these operations were to be left in the hands of the most backward and ill-educated villagers. On the other hand, as members of higher castes, they preferred not to think in terms of undertaking the 'degrading' fieldwork themselves. The primary aim of all classes in the agrarian structure has been not to increase their income by adopting more efficient methods, but to rise in social prestige by abstaining in so far as possible from physical labour.

This complex of legal, economic, and social relations uniquely typical of the Indian countryside served to produce an effect which I should like to call that of a built-in 'depressor'. Through the operation of this multi-faceted 'depressor' Indian agriculture continued to be characterized by low capital intensity and antiquated methods. Few of the actual tillers were left with an efficacious interest in modernization, or the prevention of such recognized evils as fragmentation. The pattern of landholding, cultivation, and product-sharing operated to hold down agricultural production. From the 1880s to the 1940s total output rose so slowly that it would not be too strong to speak of stagnation. The income of the *kisans* and *mazdur-log* (i.e., the overwhelming bulk of the rural population) remained at or below the subsistence level. For the newly developing urban manufacturing sector, this in turn constituted a serious handicap in the form of a severely restricted Indian home market. It is difficult to see how India's current plans for economic development can get very far without a concerted effort to remove the 'depressor'.

The Model of
Agrarian Classes in India

D. N. DHANAGARE

The agrarian social structure varies from one region to another; the relations among classes and social composition of groups that occupy specific class positions in relation to land-control and land-use in India are so diverse and complex that it is difficult to incorporate them all in a general scheme. . . . Here the attempt is to set out a workable conceptual model that would enable us to deal with apparently diverse sets of social groups and compare them in order to arrive at broader empirical generalizations of some theoretical relevance.

Despite the diversity of social arrangements on land in different parts of India, Daniel Thorner has attempted to reduce them into well-defined and precise social categories on the basis of the three following criteria:

(1) Type of income obtained from the soil: (a) rent (b) fruits of own cultivation, or (c) wages. (2) The nature of rights: (a) proprietary or ownership (b) tenancy (with varying degree of tenurial security), (c) share-cropping rights, or (d) no rights at all. (3) The extent of fieldwork actually performed: (a) absentee who does no work at all (b) those who perform partial work (c) total work done by actual cultivator with family labour and (d) where work is done entirely for others to earn wages (Thorner 1956: 4).

Excerpted from D. N. Dhanagare, 'The Model of Agrarian Classes in India', in *Peasant Movements in India, 1920-50*, Oxford University Press, Delhi, 1983.

Taking these criteria Thorner has outlined the following model of agrarian class structure in India:

I. *Maliks* whose income is derived *primarily* from property rights in the soil and whose common interests is to keep the level of rents up while keeping the wage-level down. They collect rents from tenants, sub-tenants and share-croppers.

a. *Big landlords*, holding rights over large tracts extending over several villages; they are absentee owners/rentiers with absolutely no interest in land management or improvement.

b. *Rich landowners*, proprietors with considerable holdings but usually in the same village and although performing no fieldwork, supervising cultivation and taking personal interest in the management and also in the improvement of land if necessary.

II. *Kisans*, working peasants having property interest in the land but actual rights, whether legal or customary, inferior to those of the *maliks*.

a. *Small landowners*, having holdings sufficient to support a family, who cultivate land with family labour and who do not either employ outside labour (except in harvest) or receive rent.

b. *Substantial tenants*, tenants holding leases under either Ia or Ib; tenurial rights fairly secure; size of the holding usually above the sufficiency level. The rest is as IIa.

III. *Mazdoors*, those earning their livelihood primarily from working on others lands/plots.

a. *Poor tenants*, having tenancy rights but less secure; holdings too small to suffice for a family's maintenance and income derived from land often less than that earned by wage labour.

b. *Sharecroppers*, either tenants-at-will, leases without security; cultivating land for others on share-cropper basis, and having at least agricultural implements.

c. *Landless labourers*, Thorner's three major categories, designated by the current Indian vernacular terms, are based on the relations of production or are in relation to the means of production and in this sense represent a Marxian model of agrarian classes, although Thorner himself does not specify the theoretical assumptions underlying the model. In defining the sub-categories, however, he takes into account 'the kinds of rights and kinds of services' which are in fact typical Weberian concerns. Although Thorner's sub-categories are nearer the realities of the Indian agrarian social structure, he does not relate the specificity of the internal differentiations within Indian agrarian society to broader and more widely used conceptual models in contemporary sociology. There is, therefore, a need to readjust or regroup Thorner's sub-categories into such a broader and more comprehensive model and redesignate them by more commonly used concepts and criteria in the study of peasant societies. Such a model can be drawn from the works of Lenin and Mao, especially those relating to analyses of agrarian classes in the Russian and Chinese societies respectively.[1]

I.	Landlords:	This class broadly subsumes Thorner's Ia.
II.	Rich peasants:	IIa. i.e. Thorner's Ib.
		IIb. Rich tenants who have substantial holdings, enjoy secured/occupancy rights and have to pay a nominal rent to their landlords (Thorner does not account for this class-situation at all).
III.	Middle peasants:	IIIa. Landowners of medium size (i.e. self-sufficiency) holdings (Thorner's IIa).
		IIIb. Tenants who have substantial holdings (although not as large as IIb) but have to pay higher rent than those paid by IIb. (This corresponds to Thorner's IIb category.)
IV.	Poor peasants:	IVa. Landowners with holdings that are not sufficient to maintain a family; and therefore forced to rent others' land. (Thorner does not account for this class situation.)
		IVb. Tenants with small holdings but with some tenurial security (Thorner's IIIa).
		IVc. Tenants-at-will or share-croppers. (Thorner's IIIb).
V.	Landless labourers:	(Thorner's IIIc).

While using this model of agrarian classes in the Indian context some caution is necessary. First, all the five class situations and their sub-categories are regionally specific. Secondly, more often 'rich', 'middle' and 'poor' peasant categories can be distinguished from each

[1] This model consisting of five class categories has been taken from Lenin (1946: 57-9, 1960: 70-87) and Mao Tse-tung (1967:138).

other only in qualitative rather than in quantitative terms. Adjectives like 'substantial', 'medium' or 'small', that are often used to differentiate between landholdings, cannot be defined with precision and accuracy in terms of acreage, etc., partly because of regional variations and partly because of lack of uniform data and statistics on different regions of India in different periods. What one could possibly do is take into account the comparability of relative positions of agrarian classes in different regional structures. Finally, although the class categories of the model are analytically separable, their boundaries are sometimes blurred in reality. There is considerable overlapping between categories III and IV, and also between IV and V, but there is no satisfactory way of resolving this problem, particularly at macro-level analysis. All that an analyst can do is broadly identify the class situations from which came the leaders and principal participants of the peasant movements in question.

Obviously then there is some risk in using a 'class' model in analysis of an agrarian social structure in a traditional society such as India. But the risk must be taken if any meaningful historical and comparative sociology of peasant movements in India is to be attempted. When we discuss some specific peasant revolts and resistance movements that occurred at different times in different regional structural settings, we shall relate specific strata of a regional agrarian hierarchy to the general class catergories of our model.

. . . .

The social composition of these agrarian classes in terms of specific status-groups like castes, religious or ethnic groups, etc., is far too complex in different regions of India to reduce into any simplistic formulae. Members of a status-group (e.g. caste) often belonged to different classes while those who, in terms of their relations to the means of production, belonged to the same class-situation, came from different status-groups. Nonetheless, certain broad patterns are descernible, and social groupings that are more likely to occupy certain class positions than others are generally identifiable. For example, landlords and rich landowners (including non-cultivating urban moneylenders/owners) belonged to the upper castes such as Brahmin, Thakur, or Bania in northern India. In Andhra the Kammas, Reddis and Raos, in Mysore the Okkaligas and Lingayats, the Patidars in the Gujarat region while the Kunbi Maratthas and Deshmukhs in Maharashtra could be cited as more examples of the locally dominant landowning castes. At the village level these landowning classes often only formed a small nucleus.

The middle and poor peasantry, mostly debt-ridden, came primarily from the traditional castes of cultivators, artisans and so on. The landless labourers belonged mostly to Untouchable castes, the Harijans. For example in Uttar Pradesh, the great bulk of agricultural workers was, and is even now, recruited from the Untouchable Chamars—the most populous caste there. All the same, members of a single caste or religious or tribal community could be found spread vertically, some owning patches of land here and there, others holding tenures, either permanent or year-to-year leases, and still others working as unattached farm labourers.

This vertical spread was, however, more likely to appear in the upper than in the lower castes although it was not totally absent even in the case of some lower castes traditionally engaged in cultivation and craftsmanship. Such a vertical spread often ensured that peasant classes found a developed class awareness hard to come by. Thus, the co-existence of agrarian classes and status-groups of a non-economic nature is the most fundamental fact about the Indian agrarian social structure to be reckoned with. The status-groups bound men by an essentially non-economic sentiment or identity, and frequently served to sustain subjugation and exploitation of those in the lower strata. In India these structural linkages and anchorages tended to maintain the *status quo*, to keep the simmering discontent and conflicting class interests within the 'boiling point' and to prevent the struggle for economic and political power from assuming a revolutionary form, but not always. Whenever the exploited sections of the peasantry felt that they were being unjustly treated, deprived or oppressed, they did erupt and resist whenever conditions were favourable.

Class and Economic Structure
in Thanjavur

KATHLEEN GOUGH

The Indian Big Bourgeoisie

... The Indian big bourgeoisie ... lived entirely outside Thanjavur in 1951, being composed of the owners of oligopolistic corporations each involved in a great variety of enterprises ... having family incomes of more than one million rupees a year and owning substantial investments in mills, banks, and landed estates. Three big landlords ... as well as one other well-known landlord house, were in this category. The landlords came from ranking Kallar and Moopnar castes. The merchants and industrialists were mainly Nattukkottai Chettiars or Muslims.

Apart from these people, Indian big business operations in Thanjavur were mainly directed from outside the district, and their profits largely removed from it. As in the case of foreign big business, these profits derived from industry, trade, banking, transport, agriculture, services, communications and power production. Together with the foreign bourgeoisie and the Union and State governments, the Indian big bourgeoisie made most of the decisions affecting Thanjavur's economic life, yet were largely invisible to its people.

The Medium Bourgeoisie

I include in this category Tamil business families and small joint stock companies engaged in only one or two types of enterprise,

Adapted from Kathleen Gough, 'The Propertied Classes', 'The Manual Working Classes', and 'Economy and Class Structure', in *Rural Change in Southeast India: 1950s to 1980s*, Oxford University Press, Delhi, 1989.

mainly or entirely with Thanjavur, employing a dozen or more workers, and in 1976 earning more than about Rs 18,000 per household per year. Also included in this class are the upper ranks of salary earners or 'bureaucrat capitalists', the independent professionals such as doctors and lawyers, the state and national level politicians, and the landowners possessing more than about 20 acres of mainly wet rice land. Apart from landowners the businessmen included independent bankers, moneylenders, mill owners (chiefly of traditional, medium-sized rice mills), owners of bus, truck, or taxi firms, or of hotels, restaurants, garages or stores, and also a variety of commission agents for foreign and Indian big business firms. Most of the medium bourgeoisie came from the middle and upper castes. They included Hindus, Muslims, Christians and Jains, probably roughly in proportion to the size of these religious groups in the total population.

....

The Independent Entrepreneurs

This class comprises the petty commodity producers and traders, that is, those who run family businesses without the aid of wage labour, or with only occasional or seasonal labour. It includes the middle peasants, small cultivation families who own, or lease as occupancy tenants, about 1 to 4 acres and work the land themselves, employing casual labour only at the peak seasons of transplanting and harvest.

Among the nonagriculturalists, the independent entrepreneurs include a great variety of individual or family traders—dealers in paddy, coconuts, milk, or other farm products; tea, coffee, and grocery shopkeepers in villages; small store-owners in towns; and various itinerant peddlers.

By 1976, many former village servants such as barbers, washermen, household priests for life crisis rites, carpenters, builders, and blacksmiths, belonged to the class of independent entrepreneurs. Instead of serving a village or other designated areas in return for shares in the harvest and living under the authority of the dominant landlord caste as formerly, they worked independently for clients in their own or nearby settlements in return for private cash payments, plus, sometimes, a small harvest donation. Some former village servants were prosperous enough to employ regular labourers and so must be counted as petty bourgeoisie. Others still served the landlord or rich peasant group of one village in a subordinate relationship and must be classed together with the semiproletariat. The majority of village servants, however, were probably independent entrepreneurs by the mid-1970s.

....

The Semiproletariat

This class consists of people who are not lifetime workers solely reliant on cash wages, yet who work mainly or solely for one or more masters and surrender most of their surplus product to their employers. The semiproletariat is divisible into two categories according to the degree of independence of the worker.

The higher category, in prestige and usually in income, is relatively unsupervised in its daily work and may own a small amount of equipment. I would place in this category the poor peasants or tenants-at-will. In 1976 they lacked a document certifying their permanent occupancy of the land, surrendered virtually all their surplus to the landlord, and usually worked for wages for a few weeks each year. Yet they leased some land for a season or a year and worked on it independently, usually with their own ploughs and oxen. Other relatively unsupervised semiproletarians included village servants or putting-out craftsmen (some weavers, washermen, barbers, etc.) who worked regularly for particular masters and were under their authority, yet carried on their work at home or at another private workshop and owned the tools of their trade.

This upper layer of the semiproletariat was declining in numbers with the modern eviction of tenants and the loss of their traditional work by craftsmen. Thus, many weavers, potters, oilmongers, goldsmiths, wagon builders, and even blacksmiths had lost their trades as a result of industrialization, and in most cases had become wage workers.

The lower, and much larger, layer of the semiproletariat consists of manual unskilled workers who own little or no equipment and work under regular supervision by their employers. At the same time, they are not strictly speaking 'pure' proletarians, for they have small sources of income or subsistence beyond their wage work. Semiproletarians also often receive part of their wages in kind; although payments in cash became more common between 1951 and 1976.

In 1976, by far the largest group in the semiproletariat class was the agricultural labourers. . . . Yet all of them obtained most of their living from wages while also having access to other, minor sources of subsistence, such as edible roots, rats, fuel, or crabs from the village domain. Between the early 1950s and the 1970s agricultural labourers greatly increased in numbers and as a percentage of the total workforce.

. . . .

The Class Profile

. . . In Kirippur . . . there was a decline in the percentage of men who were petty bourgeois, . . . yet the number of petty bourgeois men remained roughly constant. . . . There was a substantial decline in the number of percentage of petty bourgeois agriculturalists, and a large increase in the number and percentage of petty bourgeois men who, having lost their land, relied on white collar salary work.

. . . There was relatively little change in the percentage of independent entrepreneurs. In Kirippur . . . the number of agricultural entrepreneurs (middle peasants) had declined because of distress sales of land by small owners. Probably because of its lower productivity . . . more middle peasants . . . had been obliged to sell to bigger owners. Correspondingly, the number and percentage of nonagricultural independent entrepreneurs had increased considerably in Kirippur.

[The] village showed a significant decline in the number and percentage of tenant cultivators as a result of the eviction of tenants resulting from the Land Reform Acts and the introduction of green revolution technology. In both periods Kirippur . . . had few or no nonagriculturalists working in dependent relationships but with little supervision, for Kirippur's artisans and other village servants were mainly independent entrepreneurs, not supervised by the village's landowners.

. . . There was some increase in the number and percentage of labourers having some leased land. This resulted from the loss of some of their land by tenant cultivators, who were obliged to do part-time wage work for others. Such labourers were few in Kirippur, where, even traditionally, there were fewer absent rentier landlords and therefore, fewer tenants. . . . In 1976, there was a small number of men who worked as labourers but also owned about one-third to one acre of land. This category did not exist in 1952. In Kirippur . . . this category of persons arose partly as a result of the government's distribution of small plots to a few formerly landless people, but more commonly, because a few former peasants had lost almost, but not quite, all their own land and worked as labourers.

The category of landless agricultural labourers (those working for wages and possessing no land or only a tiny house site) had grown most spectacularly . . . in Kirippur by 65 per cent, from 89 to 147. In addition to the landless labourers, the beggers, sick, and unemployed (almost all of them former agricultural labourers) had also increased. . . .

Table 1

Class Affiliations of Men Over 15 Years in Kirippur, Showing
Agriculturalists and Nonagriculturalists, 1952

	Class	No. of agric.	% of Total agric.	No. of Nonagric.	% of Total nonagric.	Class Total	% of Total Men
1.	Petty Bourgeoisie	48.0	26.4	4.0	9.1	52.0	23.0
2.	Independent Entrepreneurs	25.0	13.7	18.0	40.9	43.0	19.0
3.	Semiproletarians & Proletarians						
(a)	Tenants, etc., with control of equipment, under little supervision	17.0	9.3	-	-	17.0	7.5
(b)	Labourers with some leased land	3.0	1.7	-	-	3.0	1.4
(c)	Labourers with some own land	-	-	-	-	-	-
(d)	Landless Labourers	89.0	48.9	17.0	38.6	106.9	16.9
4.	Mendicants, Unemployed, etc.	-	-	5.0	11.4	5.0	2.2
	Total	182.0	100.0	44.0	100.0	226.0	100.0

Note: Students have been placed in the classes of their father.

Table 2

Class Affiliations of Men Over 15 Years in Kirippur, Showing Agriculturalists and Nonagriculturalists, 1976

Class	No. of agric.	% of Total Agric.	No. of Non-agric.	% of Total Nonagric.	Total in Class	% of Total Men
1. (a). *Medium Bourgeoisie*	4	1.8	—	—	4	1.2
(b). *Petty Bourgeoisie*	29	12.8	21	21.0	50	15.4
2. *Independent Entrepreneurs*	20	8.9	35	35.0	55	16.9
3. Semiprolet-arians and Proletarians						
(a) Tenants, etc., with control of equipment, under little supervision	11	4.9	1	1.0	12	3.7
(b) Labourers with some Leased Land	6	2.6	—	—	6	1.8
(c) Labourers with some own land	9	4.0	4	4.0	13	4.0
(d) Landless Labourers	147	65.0	22	22.0	169	51.8
4. *Medicants Unemployed, etc.*	—	—	17	17.0	17	5.2
Total	226	100.0	100	100.0	326	100.0

Note: Students have been placed in the classes of their fathers.

Finally, the nonagricultural male workforce had increased more rapidly than the agricultural workforce. . . . This change was . . . marked in Kirippur because, being near the coast and the export trade, it had more locally available wage work in rice mills and other small factories. . . . Even so the category of landless agricultural labour formed a *cul-de-sac* into which most of the dispossessed villagers had fallen. This category had increased from . . . 39.4 per cent to 45.1 per cent in Kirippur. As percentages of the agricultural workforce, landless agricultural labourers had increased . . . from 48.9 per cent to 65.1 per cent in Kirippur. Agricultural labourers as a whole had increased from . . . 50.5 per cent to 71.1 per cent in Kirippur.

Caste and Class

Table 3 presents the adult men and women of Kirippur in terms of both caste and economic class. . . . There were more adult women than men because some men were absent in the army or in urban work. Table 4 presents the same information for Kirippur in 1952. . . .
From these tables I have calculated the degrees and strength of the association between caste and class memberships in each village and period, using Goodman and Kruskal's Coefficient of Ordinal Association (gamma or G). This measure is a ratio of the amount of predominance of agreement or inversion between two sets of rankings to the maximum possible agreement or inversion, that is:

$$\frac{\text{Number of agreements - Number of inversions}}{\text{Number of agreements + Number of inversions}}$$

Perfect agreement would produce a coefficient of ordinal association of 1.00; perfect disagreement, of -1.00.
The . . . tables show very strong and significant associations between caste and class in both villages and periods. Taking the working adults and omitting the unemployed, we find the strongest association between caste and class in Kirippur in 1952, and the second strongest . . . in 1976.
. . . .

In Kirippur, the increase in wage labourers, even in relatively high and middle ranking castes such as Seiva and Choliya Vellalars and Padaiyacchis, slightly weakened the caste-class association over the 24-year period. It however has stronger caste-class association . . . mainly because of more independent entrepreneurs (the middle class) in its middle ranks.

Table 3

Class and Caste Affiliations of Men and Women Over 15 Years in Kirippur. 1976

Caste	Medium Bourgeoisie		Petty Bourgeoisie		Independent Entrepreneurs		Tenants Village Servants		Supervised Labourers		Mendicants Unemployed	
	M	F	M	F	M	F	M	F	M	F	M	F
Brahman	-	-	-	-	-	-	-	-	-	-	-	-
Non-Brahman	-	-	7	6	-	-	-	-	-	-	-	-
Tondaimandalam												
Vellalar	-	-	9	9	1	1	-	-	-	-	2	-
SeivaVellalar	-	-	-	-	1	3	-	-	2	5	-	-
Choliya Vellalar	3	3	8	8	7	10	1	1	4	8	1	1
Naidu	-	-	8	7	5	4	-	-	-	-	1	0
Pandaram	-	-	-	-	1	1	-	-	-	-	-	-
Sengunda Mudaliar	-	-	10	12	19	21	-	-	5	3	1	-
Agambadiyar	-	-	-	-	2	1	-	-	-	-	-	-
Kallar	-	-	-	-	1	1	-	-	1	-	-	-
Padaiyacchi	4	4	5	10	5	10	7	5	1	-	-	-

Vanniyar	–	–	–	2	1	1	1	1	–
Porayar	–	–	–	–	1	2	5	4	1
Muslim	–	–	–	1	1	1	–	–	–
Konar	–	–	–	–	–	–	1	2	–
Kammalar	3	2	3	5	–	–	1	1	–
Vaniyar	2	–	2	2	–	–	–	–	–
Nadar	2	2	4	6	–	–	10	15	–
Vannar	–	–	2	2	–	–	–	–	–
Ottar	–	–	–	–	–	–	1	1	–
Harijan									
Pallar	–	–	1	1	3	3	39	40	1
Paraiyar	–	–	–	–	–	–	39	34	1
Total	52	39	43	59	17	21	109	109	5

Note: Women and students have been placed in the classes of their fathers or husbands.

Gamma = .75237   Sig. = 0.0

Table 4

Class and Caste Affiliations of Men and Women Over 15 Years in Kirippur, 1952

Caste	Petty Bourgeoisie		Independent Entrepreneurs		Tenants and Village Servants		Supervised Labourers		Mendicant, ill, Unemployed	
	M	F	M	F	M	F	M	F	M	F
Brahmin	4	3	-	-	-	-	-	-	-	-
Non-Brahmin										
Tondaimandalam										
Vellalar	15	8	-	-	-	-	-	-	-	-
Seiva Vellalar	-	9	5	4	1	1	1	2	-	-
Choliya Vellalar	11	4	1	1	1	1	-	1	-	-
Naidu	7	7	2	1	-	-	1	-	-	-
Poosari	-	-	1	3	1	-	-	-	-	-
Sengunda Mudaliar	6	7	17	22	-	-	3	3	1	-
Agambadiyar	-	-	-	-	1	1	1	1	2	1
Padaiyacchi	1	2	4	3	9	9	4	4	19	17

	1	2		3	4		5	6		7	8		9	10		11	12
Vanniyar	-	-		-	2		6	11		1	-		2	5		-	-
Porayar	-	-		-	-		-	-		-	1		9	9		-	-
Chettiar	-	-		-	-		1	1		-	-		-	-		-	-
Konar	-	-		-	-		-	-		-	-		5	5		-	-
Kammalar	-	-		3	4		2	1		-	-		1	3		1	-
Nadar	-	-		1	3		-	-		1	1		29	22		1	-
Vannar	-	-		-	-		1	1		-	-		-	-		-	-
Harijan																	
Pallar	-	-		-	-		-	-		2	2		67	61		6	5
Paraiyar	-	-		-	-		1	-		2	2		43	45		2	-
Total	4	5		50	54		55	64		12	12		188	184		17	7

Note: Women and students have been placed in the classes of their fathers or husbands
Gamma = 0.79501 Sig. = 0.0

Despite these minor differences, the association between caste and class remained extremely strong and significant . . . in rural Thanjavur generally inspite of land reform, increased commoditization, and green revolution techniques. This pattern had scarcely changed since independence.

Tribal Identity and Class Differentiations: A Case Study of the Chaudhri Tribe

GHANSHYAM SHAH

Thanks to the ritual hierarchical order of the caste system, several scholars have categorized castes in terms of upper and lower as equivalent to class divisions. It is assumed by many—and demonstrated by a few studies—that upper castes not only hold higher ritual status but also higher economic status in terms of occupation and income. Lower castes on the other hand are poor. Significant correlation between caste and class hierarchy exists. Such analysis is important so far as it goes, but essentially they remain studies on caste rather than on caste-class relationships. They do not lead us beyond 'socio-economic hierarchy' which tells us about economic conditions of different castes. Relationship among the classes cutting across castes has hardly been discussed; instead, what is discussed is ritual relationship. They overlook the fact that all the members belonging to a particular caste do not enjoy equal economic status; in other words, castes are not homogeneous from an economic point of view. Economic differentiations within most of the castes—high as well as middle and low—exist, or have been developing during the last two decades. Intra-caste economic differentiations vary from caste to caste. Even studies of single castes do not pay sufficient attention to this aspect.

For a meaningful understanding of the complexity of relationships between caste and class, it is necessary to go beyond mere socio-economic hierarchy. Two questions are pertinent in this context. First, what

Adapted from Ghanshyam Shah, 'Tribal Identity and Class Differentiations: A Case Study of the Chaudhri Tribe', in *Caste, Caste Conflict and Reservation*, Ajanta, Delhi, 1985.

are the economic differentiations within a caste and how do they cut across various castes both vertically and horizontally? Second, to what extent does the ritual status of a caste and a sense of fraternity among caste members blur economic differentiations, or to use a popular phrase, sustains false conciousness? This paper is an endeavour to explore these questions with the help of empirical data. However, the unit of our observation is a tribe and not a caste. . . .

While discussing the tribe (caste)-class issues two factors which influence the overall relationship need to be mentioned at the outset. One, India follows the path of capitalist economy, and competitive polity. Capitalist economy develops differentiations in society on class lines, and competitive polity compels politicians to widen their support structure across the narrow boundaries of kinship and caste. Secondly, political ideology and practice ignore the growing economic differentiation within and between tribes. All the tribes are clustered into one group described as Schedule Tribes by the Indian Constitution. This practice ignores differentiations among tribes, and also legitimizes a tribe as tribe with distinct social and cultural identity. Social workers and administrators working among tribals treat them as economically homogeneous groups and carry out the programmes for tribal development accordingly. Political parties address tribals as one undifferentiated group. This is true of communist parties too. Furthermore, studies on tribals by social scientists also treat them as one homogeneous egalitarian group. They have used concepts like 'tribal economy' etc. How these factors—capitalist economy and political ideology and practice—operate and influence tribal society is the subject of the present exercise which is confined to one tribe in Gujarat.

Economic Differentiations

Scheduled Tribes constitute 14 per cent of the total population of Gujarat. The major tribes in the state are : Bhil, Dhodia, Gamit, Varli, Dubla, Kotwaliya, Chaudhri and Rathwa. Some of the tribes like the Dubla and the Rathwa are economically very poor and educationally backward. They are mainly landless labourers. There is 6 per cent literacy among Rathwas. On the other hand, Dhodias and Chaudhris are economically advanced. Literacy among the Dhodia is 31 per cent.

The Chaudhri tribe is mainly found in Surat District, south Gujarat. In 1971, its population was 188,273. Almost all of them are found in villages. Chaudhris can be divided into four economic strata on the basis of occupation and ownership of land. These are : (1) Agricultural labourers and poor cultivators; (2) Middle cultivators; (3) Rich cultivators and (4) White-collar employees. The first three strata constitute more than 92 per cent of the Chaudhri working population. The white-collar employees are less than 3 per cent.

Labourers and Poor Cultivators

Labourers and poor cultivators are at the bottom of the occupational hierarchy. It is the single largest stratum, constituting 61 per cent of the cultivators, of which 24 per cent are almost landless and 37 per cent have land between 1 and 5 acres. Their main source of livelihood is manual labour. The cultivators falling in this category do not have enough infrastructural facilities to make their land economically viable. Their soil is rocky and barren. Most of them do not have a pair of bullocks or even a well, let alone an electric or diesel pump for irrigation (Table 1). Of these 41 per cent use chemical fertilizers whenever they are available at subsidized price from the government. Often they do not get it in time and they do not have enough money to buy in the open market. In this situation, their lands produce very little. Whatever they produce is barely enough for their own needs. They hardly employ labourers. During the harvest season, they help each other by way of mutual exchange of labour. They work on their own and daily wages on other cultivators' farms. Those who do not have land work as manual labourers. A labour gets anything between Re 1 and Rs 3 per day, depending upon the nature of the work and availability of labour. Labourers do not get work on the farms all round the year. During the off season, they and poor cultivators take up wood cutting or road construction work, or migrate to nearby towns in search of manual work. Or else, they starve, or eat certain edible roots to mitigate their hunger.

Middle and Rich Cultivators

Of the Chaudhri cultivators 33 per cent own land between 5 and 15 acres. They may be classified as middle cultivators. Of them 20 per cent have wells on their farms for irrigation, and half of them have diesel or electric pumps. A majority of them use chemical fertilizers. On an average each household of the middle cultivators has 1.7 bullocks : or, to put it differently, 70 per cent of the households have a pair of bullocks. They produce surplus to sell in the market if they have infrastructural facilities.

Table 1

Agriculture Infrastructural Facilities

(Percentages)

	Poor Cultivators*	Middle Cultivators	Rich Cultivator
Well on the farm**	5.0	11.0	9.0
With pumpset	2.0	9.0	25.0
Using chemical fertilizers	41.0	60.0	81.0
Average bullock	1.1	1.7	2.8
Total N	1250.0	1098.0	165.0

* This excludes labourers.
** Percentage in all cases are calculated for the total (N) in respective stratum.

Rich cultivators who own more than 16 acres of land are at the apex of the economic ladder. They constitute 5 per cent of the Chaudhri population. One-third of them have irrigation facilities, and 25 per cent have an electric or diesel pumpset. They use chemical fertilizers. On an average, they own 2.8 bullocks (Table1).

Middle and rich cultivators employ labourers during the harvest season. The members of their families work on their own farms but they rarely work as wage-earners on others' farms. The few rich cultivators grow more than one crop on their irrigated land and the members of their families, particularly women and children and educated boys and girls, do not work even on their own farms. They employ tribal labourers.

Earlier, middle and rich Chaudhri cultivators· did not produce any marketable surplus. They were in the clutches of non-tribal moneylenders who were also absentee landlords. Their condition has however changed, thanks to certain progressive land legislations and to the spread of infrastructural facilities such as irrigation, roads etc. They have changed their cropping pattern. With the availability of irrigated water and the use of fertilizers and improved seeds, they produce cash crops, and a surplus of food crops for sale. Those who can take advantage of the irrigation facility prefer to cultivate Kolam IR 22 paddy, because it gives a higher yield, and this means more money, though for personal consumption they either buy low quality paddy from the market, or cultivate it in a small area.

They are no longer ignorant of price fluctuations in the market. They try to sell their products at a competitive price. An Adivasi, who owned about 16 acres of land energized by a pumpset, said, 'Our village is on the road and connected with Unai, Buhari, Valod and Vyara (all *taluka* business centres). We enquire at all the places and sell at the place where we get the best price. We get a good price for groundnut at the Vyara Co-operative Ginning Factory. Baniyas do not give such a good price; so we sell it to the co-operative society'. Some of the prosperous cultivators have now started lending money on interest as high a rate as 144 per cent, to poor tribals. Also, they purchase land from fellow tribals or take their land on mortgage.

White-Collar Employees

About 3 per cent of the Chaudhris are engaged in white-collar jobs. The first nonagricultural white-collar job that the Chaudhris got was teaching in primary schools. It may be mentioned that Sayajirao Gaekwad III of Baroda started a school in Songadh in 1885. A few of those who were trained in this school became teachers in other schools started by the Gaekwad and later by the British Government. After the twenties, some Chaudhris were trained to become teachers under Gandhian education schemes. The process has continued. About 50 per cent of the primary school teachers in Surat District, according to one survey, were Adivasis between 1947 and 1967. The Chaudhris topped the list among the Adivasis. Out of 1943 Scheduled Tribe teachers in the district, 739 (44 per cent) were Chaudhris (Jadeja 1971).

Some others are clerks, postmen, *talatis, gramsevaks,* extension officers, etc., in government departments. A few are secretaries, accountants or clerks in co-operative societies or such other organization. Such office jobs require formal education. Earlier, one could be a primary school teacher with a vernacular seventh standard certificate; but now an aspirant for such a job is required to have passed the SSC with 55 per cent marks. Similarly, 10 years ago, one with fourth standard education could get the job of a peon in a government office. But now, the minimum qualification required is seventh standard. In this sense, the office-goers are educated.

Middle and rich cultivators dominate the stratum of educated white-collar employees. Sixteen per cent and 12 per cent of rich and middle cultivators, as against only 7 per cent of poor cultivators' households have someone serving in government or semi-government offices. The lower positions in government offices are occupied by Chaudhris coming from poor cultivators' households, whereas higher positions are occupied by the persons coming from middle and rich cultivators' households.

White-collar employees who earn regular salaries save some amount from the salary and send a part of it to their families in the village. A few of them invest their savings in developing agriculture. Moreover, thanks to their exposure and contact with non-Adivasis, they grab opportunities offered to them by different government agencies. They also look after agriculture. From their savings, a few of them purchase land from fellow Adivasis. Some lend money to the needy villagers on interest. Their rate of interest is as high as that of the non-Adivasi moneylenders.

Fission in Social and Religious Life

The Chaudhris are divided into five endogamous groups: Nana, Mota, Valvai, Tekaria and Bonda. Nana and Mota Chaudhris form the largest groups in terms of numbers. The Chaudhris are further divided, cutting across endogamy, into Varjela, those who renounced traditional customs and the Sarjela, destined 'to suffer and be exploited'. The divisions began with the Gandhian social reform activities in the twenties. The Gandhians adopted the approach of Hindu reformists, who believed in maintaining a flexible structure, in giving up expensive social customs and introducing simplicity in marriage and such other rites, emphasizing vegetarianism and teetotalism. This coincided with the influence of Varjelas and Sarjelas within each Bhakti movement. Divisions between endogamous groups have become very sharp recently. The Varjelas look down upon Sarjelas and avoid social relations with them. They prefer to marry their children to Varjelas. One of the Varjelas, a Gandhian activist, told us that 'in the near future, we Chaudhris will not bother about the sub-groups such as Nana or Mota, but there are going to be two distinct major groups, that is, Varjelas and Sarjelas'. This opinion is indicative of the new social divisions that are emerging among the Chaudhris. It may be added that the Varjelas largely come from the strata of middle and rich cultivators and the white-collar employees.

Though some of the traditional marriage and other customs have continued, white-collar employees and the Varjela rich and middle cultivators follow certain Hindu customs. They invite Brahmin priests to perform marriage ceremonies. Instead of playing *dobru*, the indigenous traditional musical instrument, they have devotional choral groups singing hymns or a brass band playing Hindi film tunes. The *dobru* is condemned because according to them the tunes played by it are obscene. . . . Further, instead of oral and symbolic invitation called *punj mukavi*, they send printed invitations. Interestingly enough, though the poor Chaudhris do not follow these 'new' customs, they do not disapprove of them either. Of the poor Chaudhris 81 per cent felt that reforms in marriage rites and other social changes followed by a few were good and desirable. They do not adopt them partly because they cannot afford them and partly because they find it difficult psychologically to change over to the new customs. But they consider that the new customs do add to the prestige of the family. Thus, values and norms of upper caste and class—Brahmins, Baniyas and Patidars—of the larger society are increasingly being adopted by the white-collar workers as well as the middle and rich Chaudhri cultivators.

In the religious sphere, Chaudhris worship various gods. Ahindo Dev, the god of the hills, Himario Dev, protector of fields, Kansarimata, the goddess of corn, Kaka Balia and Shilimata, the god and goddess of chickenpox and smallpox respectively, Vag Dev (tiger), Nag Dev (snake), etc., are some of their important gods. Some of the Hindu gods and goddesses have entered the Chaudhris' religious life. It is difficult to draw a line between 'Adivasi' and 'Hindu' gods. Some deities like Kaka Balia or Nag Dev have been commonly worshipped for many decades by both. What is significant, however, is that some Chaudhris now mainly worship Ram, Krishna or such other Hindu gods, and they rarely pay a visit to the shrine of the traditional Adivasi gods. Stratumwise the differentiation is reflected in their religious beliefs. White-collar employees are prone to Hindu gods or they do not visit any temple, and a large number of the poor Chaudhris still worship traditional Adivasi gods (Table 2). Sixty-four per cent of the poor as against 5 per cent of the white-collar employees and 40 per cent of the rich Chaudhris worship only traditional Adivasi gods.

There is a striking difference in the life-style of different strata. An educated office-going Chaudhri dresses himself in a manner which is similar to that of other non-tribal office-goers. Varjela rich and middle cultivators are closer to non-tribals in their dress than the poor Chaudhris. Their food habits are also undergoing changes. Generally, *jowar* and *dal* are used in their daily diet by all Chaudhris. Wheat is not regularly consumed by the poor. But 43 per cent of the white-collar Chaudhris consume wheat almost daily. Rice is also an important cereal used by Chaudhris. But since rice is costlier than other cereals, only 9 per cent of poor Chaudhris as against 38 per cent and 74 per cent of rich and white-collar Chaudhris respectively consume rice regularly.

Table 2
Pattern of Worship

(Percentages)

	Labourers and poor Cultivators	Middle Cultivators	Rich Cultivators	White-Collar Employees
Adivasi god	64	48	40	5
Hindu god	16	24	21	48
Both Adivasi and Hindu god	6	20	24	
No one	13	8	14	48
Total N	67	50	43	42

cultivators and labourers do not consume milk regularly—not even with tea. Ghee is rarely used except by the white-collar employees. But edible oil is used by many. However, the frequency of its use varies from stratum to stratum; only 39 per cent of the poor Chaudhris as against 83 per cent and 93 per cent rich and white-collar Chaudhris use edible oil most of the time. Except for the poor, the majority of the rich and middle cultivators and white-collar employees use sugar regularly. However, in the case of meat and eggs the order is reversed. Forty-five per cent of the white-collar as well as rich Chaudhris are vegetarians, thanks to the influence of Gandhian and Bhakti movements. Their number is small in the case of the poor and middle cultivators (Table 3).

Further, the Chaudhris of the different strata own different household articles. Though most of the Chaudhri households do not have a piece of furniture like a chair, a table or a bench, stratumwise the difference is sharp. Only 12 per cent of the poor as against 55 per cent of the rich Chaudhris have furniture. Or take the case of stoves. Only 3 per cent of the poor against 17 per cent of the rich Chaudhri households possess stoves. A similar pattern is also found in other household items (Table 4). Data about white-collar employees' households are not available, but it can be safely said that most of them have all these items.

Thus, the Chaudhris as a social and religious group are losing their identity. Their so-called pristine 'tribal' social and religious beliefs and life-style are disintegrating. The differentiations among the different strata are becoming sharp. The labourers and poor cultivators are following the traditional life-style, social customs and religious rituals. On the other hand, the rich and educated Chaudhris follow social and religious life-s.,ies of the middle and upper classes and castes of the non-tribal society.

Table 3
Main Foodstuff Regularly Consumed

(Percentages)

	Labourers and poor Cultivators	Middle Cultivators	Rich Cultivators	White-Collar Employees
Rice	9	28	38	74
Tuver	40	64	79	86
Mung	16	32	19	40
Jowar	93	98	98	95
Wheat	15	26	19	43
Milk	13	22	31	48
Mutton	3	4	2	2
Eggs	1	10	2	12
Vegetable	54	68	79	81
Ghee	1	2	7	24
Oil	39	64	83	93
Sugar	31	62	81	93
Total N	57	50	43	42

Table 4
Household Items

(Percentages)

Household Items	Labourers and Poor Cultivator	Middle Cultivators	Rich Cultivators
Stainless steel utensils	10	27	48
Furniture	12	30	55
Watch	9	21	42
Radio	4	10	28
Stove	3	6	17
Total N	2039	1098	165

Vocal Section

Middle cultivators and educated white-collar employees constitute a vocal section of the Chaudhri tribe. They are politically more active than the poor and rich cultivators. About 20 per cent of the middle cultivators and white-collar employees, as against 12 and 9 per cent of the rich and poor cultivators respectively, take some interest in politics. A similar pattern is also found regarding attendance at public meetings, and participation in processions. While 54 and 40 per cent of white-collar employees and middle cultivators attended public meetings, in the case of poor and rich Chaudhri cultivators, such attendance was confined to only 29 and 25 per cent of them respectively. Similarly, a majority of the poor Chaudhris (52 per cent) have not yet visited any *taluka* office. Among those who visited, there were those who needed the help of others—an educated person or a village leader—to approach an official. Only 9 per cent of them visited the *taluka* office alone. The middle cultivators are the largest in number (74 per cent) who have visited *taluka* office either alone or with someone else.

The members of the middle cultivators and white-collar employees occupy various positions in government and political organizations. One of them was a member of Parliament between 1971 and 1977. He is now the Chairman of the Tribal Development Corporation, Gujarat. Another was a minister in Gujarat Government for two years. He is now the secretary of the district Congress (I). Still another is the president of the district *panchayat*. Besides them, half a dozen other Chaudhris occupy important positions in different political parties and district level organizations. They are graduates, largely coming from middle cultivator families. They were or they still are government servants or professionals like engineers or pleaders.

What are the problems of the Adivasis that are uppermost in the mind of this section? Do they give voice to the problems of the majority of the Adivasis? In order to know their perception of the problems regarding their community, we asked them the question: 'According to you, what are the problems of your community?' This question was addressed to the members of all the sections. Most of the poor Chaudhris reported :

We do not have sufficient bullock, if some have, they do not have fodder to feed them.

Moneylenders do not lend us money and co-operative societies do not assist us when we are in need.

We do not get work throughout the year; wages are too low.

There is no food, not enough clothes.
Agricultural implements are not sufficient.

The middle and rich cultivators complain:

Government has increased land revenue.
Government collects levy.
There is the problem of good roads.
State Transport system is not adequate.
There is no electricity in our villages.
Canal water for irrigation is not available.
Enough loans from banks are not forthcoming.
We have to go a long distance to buy clothes,
kerosene, diesel, etc.
The educated are not getting jobs.
Scholarship for higher studies is not adequate.

White-collar employees reported the following:

Canal water is not available.
There are the problems of electricity . . . roads . . . and   transport.
People are lazy and they waste their energy in drinking.
Jobs are not available.
There is discrimination against us.
Our people are not given jobs.

The above responses show quite clearly that poor and better-off Chaudhris perceive the problems of their community differently. They perceive the problems of their stratum to be the problems of the entire tribal society. Moreover, as far as the perception of the problems is concerned, there is no difference between the middle and rich cultivators. We have, therefore, combined them into a single category. Not only that, the educated white-collar employees also share common problems with middle and rich cultivators. This is obvious as the white-collar employees come from middle and rich cultivator households. They, therefore, talk about irrigation, transport and marketing facilities, about educated unemployment and inadequate quota of scholarship to tribal boys. In social and cultural matters also, these three strata feel closer to each other. They may be called the better-off tribals.

The better-off tribals also obtain larger chunks of benefits provided by the government. This is evident from Table 5, which reports the answers to the question: 'What benefits have you received from the government?' The table shows that quite a large number of respondents fall in the 'do not know' category. This is probably because they do not know whether the government had given them any assistance. Since they do not know anything about government's assistance, we can assume that they have not received any assistance Stratumwise the breakup of responses leads us to the conclusion that the poor Chaudhris who constitute 61 per cent of the population are deprived of the government benefits the most. Thirty per cent of them are still untouched by any government assistance. If we include 'do not know' answers, the percentage rises to fifty-five. The white-collar employees, though a small section, have benefited the most, compared with other sections of the community. For education, they have received scholarship and other assistance. And because of education, they are in the know of government schemes. They pursue their cases and get things done. Besides, a large number of rich cultivators not only got benefits but they also obtained more benefits than the middle cultivator Chaudhris. This is significant in view of the fact that though many rich cultivators do not hold a political position, they are not deprived of benefits. In other words, middle cultivators and white-collar employee Chaudhris do not hesitate to serve the interests of the rich. So far, there is no clash of interests between the rich and the middle cultivators, or the rich and the white-collar employees.

All the three together, that is, the better-off Chaudhris, join with other better-off Adivasis belonging to different tribes. They have developed a certain commonness, cutting across tribal boundaries, in social and cultural matters and in life-styles. They participate together in government and non-government organizations. They aspire for certain positions. They want to use and control resources.

But the divisible and undivisible resources in society are limited, and the number of contenders among Adivasis has increased recently. This creates competition among themselves. In such a situation, the competitors get divided on tribe lines such as Chaudhri, Dhodia, Bhil and so on. The Chaudhri leaders blame the Dhodias for taking undue advantages and *vice versa*. For instance, when one Chaudhri became a president of the Surat District *panchayat*, vocal sections of the Gamit tribe protested that Gamits were neglected. Sometimes in the assembly and the parliament elections, political leaders of different tribes—as it happens in the case of castes—try to mobilize the tribesmen on tribal lines. Thus there is a competition among the members of the vocal strata of different tribes. But, at the same time, the vocal sections of all the tribes together bear a grudge against and exploit the labourers belonging even to their own tribe. They do not give them even the 'minimum' wages. They charge very high interests on the money that they loan out to them. They share common stereotype views regardings the poor tribals—that they are lazy, they drink too much, they are ignorant and illiterate, etc.

The better-off vocal Adivasis, on the other hand, identify their interests with those of the non-tribal middle and rich cultivators and the urban middle class. For instance, the middle and rich Adivasi cultivators in south Gujarat supported the Khedut Samaj (rich and middle peasant organization of the state) against paddy levy and land ceiling in 1973-4. College-going Adivasi students joined the Nav Nirman movement led by urban middle class against corruption in 1974. They organized demonstrations and processions in tribal villages. Thus the better-off non-tribal cultivators and the middle class are the reference group of vocal Adivasis.

There is thus an informal alliance between the two relatively better-off non-tribals (middle and rich cultivators as well as the middle class) and better-off tribals. In this alliance, the latter have the place of junior partners, due to various historical reasons. Unequal partnership often creates clashes between the two. The better-off tribals want to be at par with the non-tribals of the same stratum but they suffer from certain constraints. They are new entrants in agricultural development; therefore, their know-how is limited. They lack a tradition of enterprise. Moreover, new development programmes are taken advantage of first by the better-off non-tribals who dominate administrative and political machinery. Better-off tribals also face certain ecological disadvantages—their soil is rocky and rainfall is scanty. On the other hand, non-tribal middle and rich cultivators grudge any left-over or special development programmes allotted to the tribal cultivators. They feel this cuts into their resources and advantages. Their grudge is not only against the tribals but against any one including their own caste members with whom they are compelled to share a part of the cake.

Similarly, educated tribals aspire for white-collar jobs. They want to be equal to non-tribal *babus*; therefore they want quick promotion. But they are handicapped by their traditions and family socialization from competing with non-tribal high caste white-collar employees. Non-tribal high or middle castes resent the fact that the jobs which they monopolized for many years are now to be shared with the tribals by virtue of the reservations. They dislike the entry of the new group in their economic activities. They use resources at their command to create obstacles in the way of educated tribals—which the latter resent.

In order to sustain the competition with the better-off non-tribals, the vocal sections of the tribals use ethnic symbols and idioms to seek the backing of a larger number of their owner. They mobilize poor tribals whose class consciousness is subdued by talking euphemistically of 'tribal development' and 'tribal culture', or by raising issues of 'tribal backwardness', 'injustice to tribals', etc. The leaders of the vocal sections pressurize the government for more and more 'tribal development'. Needless to say, this means the development of their own class in the tribal society as against the poor Adivasis. They are interested in seeing a middle or rich cultivator or an educated person from among them as a cabinet minister in the state, to get more reservations in white-collar jobs, to organize co-operative banks which can support Adivasi entrepreneurs to get irrigation facilities, fertilizers, improved seeds and so on. They make these and other demands in the name of the Adivasis, but in practice, their concern for an ordinary Adivasi is not only secondary but also instrumental. This has been possible because they are conscious of their interests whereas the poor Adivasis are docile and apolitical as far as class interests are concerned. The poor Adivasis are mobilized in politics by the vocal tribal on tribal and non-tribal rather than on class lines. Moreover, the vocal strata of the tribals instil 'tribal-ness' in terms of tribal culture which tranquillizes the poor. But vocal tribals themselves discard the so-called 'tribal culture' in their day-to-day life because it is against their own aspirations and interests.

The foregoing data make it clear that differentiations based on wealth and occupation have taken place within the Chaudhri tribe during the last three decades. These differentiations are reflected in their social and cultural life too, weakening the traditional tribal identity. . . .

Further Readings

Béteille, André,
1974   *Studies in Agrarian Social Structure*, Oxford University Press,
          Delhi.
          A useful up date of the state of the art on agrarian sociology
          with special reference to the specifics of the Indian situation.

Joshi, Heather and Vijay Joshi.,
1976   *Surplus Labour and the City : A Study of Bombay*, Oxford Uni
          versity Press, Bombay.
          This detailed study examines the relationship between the
          segmented labour market and the vast and differentiated labour
          force in Bombay to highlight our understanding of the
          organized and unorganized sectors of the economy.

Levkovsky, A.I.,
1972   *Capitalism in India: Basic Trends in its Development*, Peoples'
          Publishing House, Delhi.
          This book incorporates in its historical sweep both the
          industrial and the agrarian sector to illustrate the colonial
          origins of contemporary Indian economy.

Mukherjee, Ramkrishna.,
1987   *The Dynamics of a Rural Society : A Study of the Economic Struc-
          ture in Bengal Village*, Akademie Verlag, Berlin.
          A concise modern classic whose persuasive presentation
          of the evolution of contemporary agrarian classes made it a
          trend-setter for later studies on rural exploitation and agrar-
          ian conflict.

Rosen, George.,
1966   *Democracy and Economic Change in India*, Vora and Co., Bom-
          bay.
          A competent all-India portrayal of rural and urban classes
          and their emergent trends in post-Independence India.

IV

Caste, Class And Conflict

Following Max Weber (see Appendix III) sociologists have examined social stratification under three major categories, viz. class, status and power. All known forms of social stratification belong to one or the other category. Income or occupational strata can easily be classified under economic stratification; hierarchies of prestige and life-styles can be grouped as species of status stratification, and finally, the hierarchies of power and authority, of superordination and subordination, can be placed under the rubric of power stratification.

While there is little to dispute with regard to the Weberian scheme mentioned so far it must still be noted that Weber himself glossed over the intersection between these three domains of stratification. Scholars after Weber have realized that while stratification can be analytically separated into these three types, and in many cases they are also manifested as such, nevertheless class, status and power often also

interact densely. In such cases of interaction the units of the stratification system cannot be studied as if they solely belong to one category
or another, but rather an effort needs to be made in order to delineate the linkages between the economic, status and power dimensions
within a perspective sensitive to conflict potentialities.

This section opens with a conceptional essay on the dominant caste
by M.N. Srinivas. This concept won wide acclaim when it first appeared in Srinivas's monograph on Rampura. The concept of the
dominant caste brings together the three dimensions of status, class
and power. The members of the dominant caste must belong to a respectable caste, they must be economically well off, and finally they
must be politically well represented in terms of numbers.

In the next essay Srinivas examines the scope of mobility in the caste
system where he draws our attention to the areas of non-conformity
and change within the traditional structure. Here too we find that when
caste, class and power interact the sources of social dynamism and
change are activated. In later sections of the same paper he brings out
the more contemporary changes that have been politically induced
into the caste system and which have had economic consequences for
the castes concerned. Though Srinivas is not known for his open advo-
cacy of a dynamic frame of analysis, his empirical material and logic of
argumentation open up the field for those who are specifically interested in issues like organizational and structural change.

Rowe's study of mobility among the low caste Noniyas is important
as it clearly illuminates the various obstructions that lie in the path of
a caste seeking upward mobility. In particular Rowe demonstrates how
important an economically viable status is for such castes which seek
upward mobility. Those Noniyas who are economically well off have
successfully claimed Chauhan status while their poorer brethrens have
failed to do so.

The interaction between caste, class and power in terms of how
supra-local changes affect a village's economy and polity is brought
out in the next paper, by André Béteille. Caste in Béteille's understanding is an aspect of status differentiation (following Weber), but
in my opinion he goes further to demonstrate how caste, economic
class and power interact. Béteille examines this interaction at the
village level. He, however, does not limit himself to local politics
alone but goes on to study how supra-local politics involving the DMK
and the Congress have made their presence felt in the village. He
documents the shift in traditional power alignments from the traditional elite to the non-Brahmins.

Bandopadhyaya and Von Eschen pursue the interaction between caste, class and power in the context of economic backwardness and inequality. The authors after an elaborate and detailed field study, come to the conclusion that the more affluent classes and castes thwart and impede developmental projects because of their superior informal access to sources of power. The poorer sections in rural West Bengal are unable to compete with the more affluent classes because of their poor economic position. Apart from developmental projects, the poor also find it hard to take advantage of the opportunities provided by the green revolution techniques. Many of these conclusions are perhaps familiar to most of us. What many of us are not fully aware of, however, and would want to know, is the precise reasons that lead to such a denouement, and this is why this essay is so helpful.

Even though the incidents of caste-based politics find their most extreme manifestation in Bihar, one is still hard pressed to find a sufficient number of detailed academic analyses on the subject. Pradip Bose's view of caste politics in Bihar, is under the circumstances, perhaps best suited for the purposes of this volume. In this essay Bose takes us through the various twists and turns that have characterized politics in Bihar. His particular emphasis is on the alignment of caste and class factors in Bihar. Interestingly enough, caste alignments do not follow established lines of hierarchy, nor are caste alignments durable. They keep changing depending upon existential conditions. Bailey's study of village disputes alerts us to a similar situation because in the two cases that he examines he finds political and economic factors crucial for understanding why the two disputes took two different directions. Awareness of the caste system alone is not sufficient, Bailey argues, if one is to comprehend these disputes in their totality.

From Bihar and Orissa we go on to Gujarat with Breman's study of mobilization among the landless labourers or Halpatis. These Halpatis are not really Adivasis, nor are they accepted as full-fledged Hindus. They have traditionally occupied the lowest rung in the agrarian hierarchy of Gujarat. The extreme poverty of the Halpatis make them easy prey for rival political contenders. True, there has been a strengthening of horizontal solidarity among them, especially after the earlier ties of patronage fell into desuetude, and yet this has not helped them to establish their independent political status. A major part of this essay details the live structural constraints that inhibit the development of class-oriented political activism among these Halpatis of south Gujarat.

The last paper in this section has to do with state formation in the Chota Nagpur tribal region. It is interesting to learn that political and economic differentiation has been going on among the tribals of Chota Nagpur for several centuries. The stratification here may not be as deep or pronounced as it is in non-tribal regions, but the authors leave no doubt about the fact that economic and political forces have been impinging on tribal India from pre-British days. This helps us to understand the contemporary tribal situation better by erasing the popular and romantic impression that the tribes of India have always been vigorously egalitarian.

Finally, it is probably quite in order to remember that caste, class and power can interact only if they are not fully bound by their respective hierarchies (as, for instance, in Weber). Order and conformity are the characteristic features of a hierarchy and that is why any true hierarchy cannot comfortably admit extraneous factors. This is also why, it may be recalled, Dumont believes that the true caste hierarchy can allow economics or politics to enter only surreptitiously. If our understanding of social stratification is governed principally by such notions of hierarchy then the whole area of social conflict involving caste, class and politics will remain outside the purview of social stratification.

The Dominant Caste in Rampura

M. N. SRINIVAS

The concept of the dominant caste is crucial to the understanding of rural social life in most parts of India. Whether analysis is to be made of the hierarchy of a multi-caste village, the settlement of a dispute at the level of village or caste, or the pattern of Sanskritization among the several castes of an area, a study of the locally dominant caste and the kind of dominance it enjoys is essential. Occasionally a caste is dominant in a group of neighbouring villages if not over a district or two, and in such cases, local dominance is linked with regional dominance. Such linkage also exists when the caste which is locally dominant is different from the caste which is regionally dominant.

I stumbled on the importance of the idea of dominant caste only in 1953, after I had made two field trips to Rampura, a multi-caste village about 22 miles southeast of Mysore City in South India, and the present analysis is based on material which was collected previously. A full understanding of the dominance which a caste such as the Peasants (Okkaligas) enjoy needs a study of the entire region over which they are dominant, and over a period of time. I regret that I do not have the data for such an analysis. My analysis would have been even sketchier but for the fact that in 1952 the headman of the Peasants in the neighbouring village of Kere loaned me several documents which related to the settlement of disputes in the Kere area over a period of forty years. These documents referred to villages in Kere *hobli* (an administrative division referring to a group of 20-50 villages) which is different from the *hobli* to which Rampura belongs. But as Peasants are dominant in

Excerpted from M. N. Srinivas, 'The Dominant, Caste in Rampura', in *The Dominant Caste and Other Essays*, Oxford University Press, Delhi, 1987.

both the areas, and as culturally the two areas are quite close to each other, I have made use of the Kere documents in order to clarify the concept of the dominant caste. I define a dominant caste in the following words :

A caste may be said to be 'dominant' when it preponderates numerically over the other castes, and when it also wields preponderant economic and political power. A large and powerful caste group can be more easily dominant if its position in the local caste hierarchy is not too low.

However, the above definition omits an element of dominance which is becoming increasingly important in rural India, namely, the number of educated persons in a caste and the occupations they pursue. I have called this criterion 'Western' since Western and non-traditional education is the means by which such dominance is acquired. Villagers are aware of the importance of this criterion. They would like their young men to be educated and to be officers in the Government. As officers they are expected to help their kinsfolk, castefolk and co-villagers.

When a caste enjoys all the elements of dominance, it may be said to be dominant in a decisive way. But decisive dominance is not common; more frequently the different elements of dominance are distributed among the castes in a village. Thus a caste which is ritually high may be poor and lacking strength in numbers, while a populous caste may be poor and ritually low.

The Peasants in Rampura enjoy more than one element of dominance. Numerically they are the largest caste with a membership of 735, while the next largest is the Shepherd with 235, followed by the Muslim, 179, and the Untouchable, 125. The biggest landowners are among the Peasants, and the Peasants together own more land than all the other castes put together. There are also more literates and educated men among Peasants than among the others. In 1948 there were three Peasant graduates and a single Lingayat lawyer employed by the Government. The three most important patrons in the village were also Peasants. All of them owned land and loaned money. The official Headman of the village was one of these; he was the biggest landowner, owned two buses, and had built a few rental houses in a nearby town. The second was Nadu Gowda,[1] who had kept two shops and a

---

[1] Here Nadu Gowda is the name of a Peasant; it is usually the name of the hereditary headman of the Peasant caste in a hobli-capital.

small rice mill. The third was Nadu Gowda's agnatic cousin Millayya, who owned a big rice mill.

The ritual rank of Peasants is not very high. While they do rank above the Untouchables and such low castes as the Swineherd, they are well below Brahmins and Lingayats. In terms of *varna* they are Shudras, the fourth category in the all-India hierarchy. But this does not mean much in Rampura, as there are no 'genuine' Kshatriya or Vaishyas. (The local trading castes of Banajigas are not accorded the status of the 'twice-born' Vaishya.)

While it is true that Peasants are not ritually high, they command respect from everyone in the village including the priestly castes of Brahmins and Lingayats. The members of the latter castes consult one or another of the Peasant patrons on important occasions. Even on ceremonial occasions, outside pollution contexts, Peasants are shown respect by Lingayats and Brahmins. Everyone is aware of the dominant position which Peasants occupy in Rampura.

Over the last fifty years or more, the dominance of Peasants has increased in Rampura. The available evidence indicates that in the early years of this century Brahmins owned a considerable quantity of irrigated land in the village. The Brahmins were the first to sense the new economic opportunities opened to them through Western education, and they gradually moved to the towns to enter the new white-collar professions. Urban living, the cost of educating children, and the high dowries which the new education and economic opportunities had brought about, gradually caused the Brahmins to part with their land. Much of this land passed to non-Brahmins, especially the Peasants, during the years 1900-48.

In the different parts of South India shortly after World War I there began what may be called the Non-Brahmin Movement. At the end of World War I, most of the important posts in the Government of Mysore were held by Brahmins, and non-Brahmin leaders realized that they must get Western education if they wanted position and power. Agitation was started for the institution of scholarships to help non-Brahmin youths study in schools and colleges, for reservation of seats for non-Brahmins in medical and technological colleges, and for preference in appointments to government posts. The non-Brahmin agitation succeeded, and gradually a number of rules discriminating against the Brahmins were evolved by the Government of Mysore. As a result of these measures there has come into existence since the late thirties a Western-educated non-Brahmin intelligentsia.

This Non-Brahmin Movement is relevant to the understanding of the situation in Rampura. It was in the thirties that the leaders among Peasants in Rampura and the neighbouring villages began to think of higher education for their sons. Contact between the Peasants in Rampura and Peasant politicians and officials outside increased in the forties; furthermore, contact with the towns increased generally, and a few Peasants and Lingayats frequently went to Mysore and Bangalore to secure permits and to buy machinery and other goods.

The Brahmins and Lingayats in Rampura provide an instance of ritual dominance existing by itself, unaccompanied by the other forms of dominance. Neither caste is numerically strong nor is it wealthy. But some families in these two castes, namely, the Brahmin priest of the Rama temple and the Lingayat priests of the Madeshwara and Basava temples, are quite well off by village standards. The main source of income for these families is from the land with which the temples have been endowed, while a subsidiary but not unimportant source is the gifts in cash or kind which the devotees make to the priests whenever they visit the temples or during harvest. The eldest son of the Rama priest is employed in the Integral Coach Factory in Perambur (Madras) while, as mentioned earlier, one of the Lingayat priests practices as a lawyer in a neighbouring town.

But when a caste enjoys one form of dominance, it is frequently able to acquire the other forms as well in course of time. Thus a caste which is numerically strong and wealthy will be able to move up in the ritual hierarchy if it Sanskritizes its ritual and way of life, and also loudly and persistently proclaims itself to be what it wants to be. It is hardly necessary to add that the more forms of dominance which a caste enjoys, the easier it is for it to acquire the rest.

What I have said above applies only to caste Hindus; Untouchability constitutes a serious obstacle to group mobility. Untouchables in Rampura are either landless labourers, tenants, or very small landowners. They started going to school only in the thirties. In 1948, Untouchable leaders from outside were going around asking Untouchables in the Rampura area to try to shake off the symbols of Untouchability. In the neighbouring village of Bihalli, for instance, Untouchables decided to give up performing services such as removing the carcasses of dead cattle from the houses of the higher castes, beating the tom-tom at the festivals of village deities, and removing the leaves on which the high castes had dined during festivals and weddings. The Bihalli Peasants became annoyed at this and beat up the Untouchables and set fire to their huts. A similar attempt by the Kere Untouchables was nipped in the bud by the local Peasants.

The dominant caste of Peasants in Rampura is plainly opposed to the emancipation of Untouchables. Government efforts to improve the position of Untouchables are often frustrated by the leaders of the locally dominant caste. Thus, in 1948, the Government of Mysore sanctioned a sum of money to enable Untouchables in Rampura to have tiled roofs instead of thatch. The grant was administered through the Headman. The Untouchables later complained that the Headman did not readily give the money, and then only a small part of what he should have given. The Peasants, on the other hand, said that the Untouchables had spent the money given to them on toddy, and that this showed that Untouchables could not be improved.

Thus, while the Government of India and Mysore want to abolish untouchability, and the Untouchables themselves want to improve their position, the locally dominant caste stands in the way; its members want the Untouchables to supply them with cheap labour and perform degrading tasks. They also resent the idea that Untouchables should use their wells and tanks, and worship in their temples. They have the twin sanctions of physical force and boycott at their disposal. It is true that the Untouchables can enforce their rights with the aid of the police and law courts, but there are many considerations which come in the way of taking such a drastic step.

Mobility in the Caste System

M. N. SRINIVAS

While traditional, that is, pre-British, Indian society was stationary in character, it did not preclude the mobility, upward as well as downward, of individual castes in the local hierarchy. This fact, however, has not received sufficient emphasis nor have its implications been commented upon by the analysts of caste.

The two most potent sources of mobility were the fluidity of the political system, especially at the lower levels, and the availability of marginal land which could be brought under the plough, itself the result of a static demographic situation. I shall consider each of these sources briefly.

It was the establishment of British rule over the Indian subcontinent that closed the door finally to families and bigger groups achieving mobility through warfare. Until then, it was always possible, though not easy, for an official or soldier, or the head of a locally dominant caste, to acquire political power and become a chief or king. Thus, even during the heyday of the Mughal empire, Shivaji (1627-80), the son of a *jagirdar* or fiefholder of the Muslim kingdom of Bijapur in South India, was able to found a large and powerful kingdom (Majumdar 1963). Shivaji's was no doubt an exceptional case, but it illustrates, though with some exaggeration, the fluidity or openness of the pre-British political system. . . . Recent detailed studies

M.N. Srinivas, 'Mobility in the Caste System', in *The Cohesive Role of Sanskritization and Other Essays*, Oxford University Press, 1989.

of this system in such different parts of the country as eastern Uttar Pradesh (Cohn 1962) and Central Gujarat (Shah 1964) make clear how ambitious and unscrupulous tax collectors and officials could take advantage of periods of confusion to found their own chiefdoms or kingdoms.

Political fluidity in pre-British India was in the last analysis the product of a pre-modern technology and institutional system. Large kingdoms could not be ruled effectively in the absence of railways, post and telegraph, paper and printing, good roads, and modern arms and techniques of warfare. A ruler, however able, had to delegate his authority to his subordinates. Succession to political office followed the rule of primogeniture, and this posed a problem to kings who had uncles (father's younger brothers) and younger brothers who had to be kept out of mischief. Fratricide and patricide were deemed to be great sins, and a man was indeed expected to show affection for his brothers and his father's brothers who stood in the social relationship of fathers. Appointing uncles and younger brothers to posts was one way of solving the problem, though it was not without its risks. Where the kingdom was big, they could be posted to jobs far away from the capital.

The life of ordinary folk was regulated by such institutions as caste and village community, and the elders of the locally dominant caste punished violators of the social and moral code. This suited the rulers, even Muslim rulers, excepting those whose proselytizing zeal was stronger than their political wisdom. Warfare was endemic, and frontiers as well as loyalties changed frequently. A great ruler brought a brief period of order to the kingdom. The death of a great king was often followed by efforts on the part of tribute-paying chiefs to declare themselves free and stop paying tribute.

Opportunities for seizing political power were more likely to be available to the leaders of the dominant castes, and even tribes, than to others. This is why in South India dominant peasant castes such as the Marathas, Reddis, Vellalas, Nayars, and Coorgs have been able to claim Kshatriya status. Numerical strength and the prestige and power coming from ownership of land put them in a strategic position for capturing political power in periods of uncertainty, which were only too frequent. This situation, however, does not seem to have been confined to South India. The medieval Pala dynasty of Bengal was 'Shudra' in origin (Panikkar 1955: 9). The Patidars of Gujarat, in origin a peasant caste, became politically powerful in the eighteenth century, when they claimed to be Kshatriyas. Arvind Shah has written:

The Patidars were the principal local supporters of the Gaekwads [Maratha rulers of central Gujarat]. Some Patidars had taken to arms, and a couple of them had established petty principalities. All this had led the Patidars to claim the status of the Kshatriya varna and to adopt many, 'kingly' customs and manners' (1964: 94).

Historically, the Kshatriya *varna* was recruited from a wide variety of castes all of which had one attribute in common, that is, the possession of political power. According to Athelstane Baines:

There is, in fact, no section of the Brahmanic hierarchy into which the recruitment from outside has been more extensive or to which the claims to membership have been more numerous (1912: 30).

The historian K.M. Panikkar has stated that ever since the time of Mahapadma Nanda in the fifth century BC, every known royal family has come from a non-Kshatriya caste (1955: 8). Even the upper levels of tribes, such as the Bhumiji, Munda and Gond, established their claims to be Kshatriyas.

When a leader of a dominant caste or small chieftain graduated to the position of a raja or king, acquiring, in the process, the symbolic and other appurtenances of Kshatriyahood, he in turn became a source of mobility for individuals and groups living in his domain. A necessary concomitant, if not precondition, of such graduation was Sanskritization, that is, the acceptance of the rites, beliefs, ideas, and values of the great tradition of Hinduism as embodied in the sacred books. For instance, a king who did not have the requisite number of Brahmins for performing an important ceremony did not hesitate to raise members of a lower ranking group to the status of Brahmins (Baines 1912: 27). Where, however, there was an entrenched group of Brahmins, the king had to recognize their power and make the necessary adjustments.

By virtue of his position as the head of the social order, the Hindu king had the responsibility to settle all disputes with regard to caste and the power also to raise or lower the ranks of castes as a reward or punishment. Muslim kings, and even the British in the early days of their rule, exercised at least the first function. Most of the Hindu maharajas ruling over the larger native states during the British period allowed their jurisdiction in caste matters to lapse only at the beginning of the twentieth century.

I shall now consider the second source of mobility, that is, the 'open agrarian system' of medieval India. According to Burton Stein, a historian of mediaeval South India, 'marginally settled lands suitable

for cultivation' were always available, and this 'permitted the establishment of new settlements and even new regional societies'
(1968: 79). This situation was not, however, confined to South India,
but was true of the country as a whole. Irfan Habib has written:

The *Ain-i-Akbari* and Rennel's Atlas (1780) show that down to the eighteenth
century large cultivable tracts still lay behind the forest-line. The medieval governments attempted to encourage extension of cultivation and improvement in cropping by grant of revenue concessions and loans to finance
[the] purchase of seeds, cattle, or excavation of wells by the cultivators
themselves (1963-2).

In other words, there was a premium on human labour, initiative and
skill, and rulers offered incentives to individuals to open up new frontiers. Such a situation imposed a check on the authority of chiefs and
kings, who had to treat their rural subjects reasonably well in order to
keep them. The ability of citizens to flee to frontier areas provided a
sanction against excessive oppression by rulers.

Burton Stein has argued that the modern phenomenon of competition
among castes for enhanced status within a narrow, localized ranking
system is inappropriate for understanding medieval mobility. Social
mobility in medieval India involved spatial mobility, and the units of
mobility were individual families; the need as well as the facilities for
'corporate mobility' did not exist. Stein has pointed out that the various subdivisions which now exist among the Tamil peasant caste of
Vellalas arose out of their former mobility (1968: 79). Similar subdivisions also exist among several other peasant castes.

While the sources of mobility lay in the political and economic systems, Sanskritization provided a traditional idiom for the expression
of such mobility. This is not to say, however, that all cases of Sanskritization in traditional India were always preceded by the possession of
political or economic power, or even that Sanskritization always had a
mobility aspect.

The British Period

The establishment of British rule resulted, on the one hand, in closing
the traditional avenues to mobility and, on the other, in opening several
new ones. More important, it set forces in motion which altered fundamentally the overall character of society; Indian society ceased to be
stationary and became mobile, and the quantum of mobility increased
as the years went by.

I shall now mention briefly, and in a grossly oversimplified form, the factors directly bearing on the new mobility which came into existence as a result of British conquest. For the first time in Indian history there was a single political power straddling the entire subcontinent, and this was made possible by the new technology as well as by certain forms of administrative and military organization which the British brought with them to India. The land survey and settlement work of the nineteenth century, the introduction of tenurial reforms, the application of British concepts of ownership to land which made it saleable, and the availability of new economic opportunities in the port cities and capitals, all had far-reaching effects on mobility. Land could be sold to anyone who had money, even members of low castes (Bailey 1957:49). There came into existence a class of men, recruited generally from the upper castes, who resided in urban areas but who had a *pied-a-terre* in villages. Land ownership was a symbol of security as well as high social status even for them, and there was, in addition, a sentimental attachment to ancestral land and village. But gradually the high cost of urban living, including the education of sons, and later, daughters, celebrating expensive weddings, performing funeral and other rituals, and fulfilling obligations to a large number of relatives, forced this class to sell their land to peasant and other rural castes.

The British were instrumental in bringing modern knowledge to India and Indians and also such new values as the equality of all citizens before the law, the right of every man not to be imprisoned without resort to due legal process, and the freedom to practice as well as to propagate one's religion. So also there was a new humanitarianism or, rather, the extension of humanitarianism to new areas, resulting in the abolition of suttee, human sacrifice, and slavery. Western rationalism appealed quite early to the Indian elite, and by 1830 there was a small but articulate body of rationalists in Calcutta (O'Malley 1941: 70, 309, 314).

I should make it clear that I am not concerned here with the argument that the British belief in the equality of all human beings was far from being unequivocal, and that some of them were indeed racists; that in their desire to remain in power they supported reactionary sections of Indian society such as the princes and the landlords, and indeed, even resorted to the time-honoured principle of divide and rule. My main concern here is with the understanding of the changes in social mobility brought about by British rule and their implications for Indian society as a whole.

European missionary effort was a significant factor in the modernization of India. Spurred by an evangelizing zeal, missionaries highlighted the evils of indigenous society, quite unmindful of the bitter hostility which their criticisms roused among Indians. One of the causes of the Indian Mutiny was 'a genuine fear that government intended to Christianize Hindus and Muslims alike. This idea seems to have been entertained chiefly in north India, where missionary propaganda was active and recent' (ibid.: 78). Untouchability, suttee, human and animal sacrifice, idolatry, ritualism, polytheism, polygyny, infant marriage and the ban on widow marriage among the higher castes, all were subjected to sharp and persistent criticism.

The missionary onslaught was particularly significant inasmuch as it threw the new, Western-oriented Indian elite on the defensive and made them address themselves to the immense task of reforming their society and reinterpreting their religion. This reaction was more prominent among Hindus then among others for a variety of reasons which are not relevent here.

Missionaries were also active in humanitarian work and education. They ran hospitals, orphanages and schools, concentrating their attention on the poor and the lowly, that is, Untouchables and others from the low castes, tribal folk living in remote areas, and women behind the *purdah*. They stimulated the growth of regional literatures by setting up printing presses, cutting types for various Indian scripts, printing books and founding journals, writing dictionaries and grammars, and translating classics in the regional tongues into English.

New economic opportunities came into existence as a result of the establishment of law and order, removal of internal customs barriers, and the extension of communications linking, first, the different parts of the country into a single economy and, second, the country with the world outside. The building of railways, digging of canals and roads, introduction of such plantation crops as indigo, tea, cotton, coffee, and jute, and the growth of towns and factories, provided employment for thousands all over the country. However, English education was indispensable for an Indian who wished to take advantage of the better-paid and more prestigious occupations, such as the higher levels of the administration and commerce, and the professions. The new opportunities, at least at the higher levels, were usually taken advantage of by the high castes, resulting in a considerable overlap between the traditional and the new elites. This had the twin effect of increasing the cultural and ideological distance between the high and the low castes, as well as making the new opportunities doubly desirable. In the first place, they were well paid and prestigious, and in the second, only the high castes had access to them. Eventually, this gave rise to the Backward Classes Movement.

Less frequently, in some areas, a few low castes had access to new trading or employment opportunities. Bailey mentions how the prohibition policy of the government of Bengal (of which Orissa was then a part) resulted in a relative prosperity for the Ganjam and Boad Distillers (1957:160-1). Oilmen (Telis) all over eastern India benefited from the enlarged market for trade in oil and pressed oilseeds brought about by the improved communications and population growth. The Noniyas of eastern Uttar Pradesh, Kolis of the Surat Coast in Gujarat and members of several other groups benefited from the new employment opportunities resulting from the railway, road, and canal construction. In all such cases, the wealthier families or sections became possessed by the desire to move up in the caste hierarchy by acquiring the symbols and ritual of the higher castes. The absence, in British India, of legal barriers to donning the sacred thread and chanting Vedic hymns (*mantras*) on ritual occasions, both symbolic of 'twice-born' status, was certainly an important factor in this process. But everywhere the locally dominant castes were antagonistic to the mobility aspirations of the low castes, and they used physical violence as well as economic boycott to prevent them from Sanskritizing their style of life. They did not, however, always succeed. An ambitious low caste had a new remedy at its disposal. It could appeal to the police and law courts against dominant caste violence. The twentieth century has indeed witnessed a great increase in the quantum of mobility in the caste system, and Sanskritization played an important role in this mobility by enabling low castes to pass for high.

The mobility of a few low castes had a 'demonstration effect' on all the others in the region. The latter felt that they were no longer condemned to poverty, oppression, and lack of esteem. They could also move up if they tried hard enough. Social horizons suddenly expanded for them. It is probable that this widening of social horizons contributed to the vigour and strength of the Backward Classes Movement of the twentieth century.

The Backward Classes Movement was widespread in the Indian subcontinent as a whole and was particularly strong in peninsular India, where it had a distinctive ideology and pervaded every area of social life. The importance of the movement is beginning to be appreciated by Indianists, particularly in the context of the significant changes occurring among the Harijans. But it is necessary to stress that the movement affected not only the Harijans but also a wide variety of castes and, in South India, all castes except the Brahmin.

The conversion of the so-called low castes to Islam and Christianity in many parts of India, and to sects such as Sikhism and the Arya Samaj in the Punjab and western Uttar Pradesh, was often motivated by a desire to shed the odium attached to being low. But the converts found that it was not at all easy to shake off their caste and that, in fact, they carried it with them to their new faith or sect. Indian Islam and Christianity both bear the stamp of the caste system; this is not to say, however, that the caste system among the Indian Christians and Muslims is the same as the caste-system among the Hindus.

The Backward Classes Movement

Speaking broadly, the Backward Classes Movement passed through two stages; in the first, the low castes concentrated on acquiring the symbols of high status, whereas in the second the emphasis shifted from the symbols to the real sources of high status, that is, the possession of political power, education, and a share in the new economic opportunities. The leaders of the Backward Classes Movement realized clearly that all three were interelated and that one could not be secured in full measure without the others. Thus, political power was necessary to introduce the principle of caste quotas for jobs in the administration and seats in technological, medical and science courses, and, later, to secure the licences and permits necessary for trading in a variety of goods and for undertaking other economic enterprises. Education, on the other hand, was indispensable for obtaining the higher categories of posts in the administration and even for the effective exercise of political power.

It is this emphasis on power that led to such seeming inconsistencies as a caste claiming to be 'backward' in official and political contexts and of high rank in traditional context. Classification as 'backward' enabled the members of a caste to obtain preference as a matter of right in the matter of seats in educational institutions, scholarships, and jobs in the administration and this was not counted against it in evaluating its rank in the traditional hierarchy.

The 'low' castes realized clearly that, once they had the necessary power, the acquisition of the symbols of high ritual rank would be easy and also meaningful. It also meant that they were aware that a new prestige system had emerged, in which education, political power, and a Westernized style of life were important ingredients, and which in principle were open to all. Acquisition of power became necessary in a situation in which the high castes, which had a head start over the others with regard to the new sources of power and prestige, would otherwise continue to remain on the top. The kind of situation depicted by Harold Gould for a few villages in eastern Uttar Pradesh for the mid-1950s (1961) belongs, properly speaking, to the first phase of the Backward Classes Movement and not to the more sophisticated second phase.

In the first phase, the traditional aspects of the caste system were still strong and the high castes resented the appropriation of the symbols of high rank by the low. They could no longer rely on the political authority to punish the pavenus who dared to appropriate those symbols. The latter, however, had to overcome their own resistance to such appropriation, and, even when they did, the high castes had enough 'moral authority', if that is indeed the proper term, to ostracize and even physically punish them. Equally important was the fact that the new opportunities thrown up by the British rule were taken advantage of mainly by the high castes: Brahmin, Baniya, Vaidya, and Kayastha. It was in this context that the institution of the decennial census, introduced by the British, came unwittingly to the aid of ambitious low castes. Sir Herbert Risley, the commissioner of the 1901 census, decided to make use of the census investigations to obtain and record the exact rank of each caste. Not unnaturally a number of castes decided to seize this occasion to claim high rank. They seem to have felt that, if they succeeded in getting themselves recorded as high in the census, an official document of the Government of India, no one would indeed be able to dispute their rank. In other words, the census became the equivalent of the traditional copper-plate grants of Indian kings declaring the rank and privileges of a caste, highlighting the role of the political authority in the caste system. There was a widespread move among castes to assume new and high-sounding Sanskritic names generally ending with suffixes indicating 'twice-born' rank. Mythology, traditions, and particular customs were also cited in support of the claim to high rank and no distinction was made between mythology and history. Not infrequently, the different sections of a single *jati* living in different areas claimed to belong to different *varnas*, and ambitions also changed from one census to another. Over the years, an increasing number of castes assumed new names in their desire to be recorded as high castes, and this was one of the factors which made inter-census comparisons of castes impossible.

The coming into existence of caste *sabhas* or associations was an important factor in the spread as well as the acceleration of mobility. Initially, their aims were to reform caste customs in the direction of Sanskritization, to lay claim to high rank, to undertake such welfare activities for caste fellows as building hostels, houses on a co-operative basis, colleges and hospitals in some areas, founding journals and endowing scholarships. With the gradual transfer of power from the British to Indians, caste associations tended to become political pressure groups demanding for their members electoral tickets from the principal political parties, ministerships in state cabinets, licences for undertaking various economic activities, jobs in the administration, and a variety of other benefits. I may add here that castes performed these functions even where they were not organized into formal *sabhas* or associations.

Caste and Class

According to Burton Stein, the modern phenonmenon of competition among castes for enhanced status within a narrow, localized ranking system is inappropriate for understanding medieval mobility (1968: 80). The need as well as the facilities, such as the printing press, for 'corporate mobility' did not exist in medieval India. The units of medieval mobility were individual families, and the 'open agrarian system' favoured spatial mobility, which, in turn, facilitated social mobility. Burton Stein has certainly enhanced our knowledge of Indian society, but in his analysis of mobility processes in medieval South India he has ignored the need which has always existed in the caste system to translate familial mobility to caste mobility. Mobility does not otherwise obtain public recognition. Whom will the sons and daughters of the mobile family marry? Marriage within the old caste group, the most natural solution, would be the negation of such mobility. Another solution would be hypergamy, by which the parent group continue to give its girls in marriage to the mobile family, while the girls born in the latter either married into a higher caste or remained unmarried. The connubial drag on mobility was far less severe in South India where cross-cousin and cross-uncle-niece marriages were, and are, more preferred than elsewhere. Ideally, in South India a simple, nuclear family could in the course of two generations achieve connubial self-sufficiency. However, in every part of India it was necessary for the mobile family or section of a caste to break with the parent caste and claim a new identity. To that end it was necessary to form a separate endogamous unit. Having hypergamous relations with the parent caste was only the second best solution. Further, even apart from marriage, a mobile family or section had to become a caste, for only then could its relations with other castes be defined.

The new opportunities created by the British rule resulted in greater spatial mobility and increased economic disparity among the members of the same local caste group. These two effects became heightened as the Indian economy developed and political power was gradually transferred to the people from the rulers. An important feature of social mobility in modern India is the manner in which the successful members of the backward castes work consistently for improving the economic and social condition of their caste fellows. This is due to a sense of indentification with one's caste, and also to a realization that caste mobility is essential for individual or familial mobility. Thus, a rich distiller or butcher had to get the name, customs, and style of life of his caste changed in order to shed *his* identity as distiller or butcher and acquire another that was more esteemed. Herein came the enormous usefulness of the traditional avenue to mobility, Sanskritization. However, it had to cope now with a far greater number of castes than before.

The kind of mobility I have described above may be regarded as typical. There was, however, another kind of mobility which was much less common in the past, but which might become more common in the future. In the big cities of India there are small numbers of rich people who are educated and have a highly Westernized style of life. These may be described as living minimally in the universe of caste and maximally in that of class. The occupations practised by them bear no relation to the traditional occupations of the castes into which they were born. They ignore pollution rules, their diet includes forbidden foods, and their friends and associates are drawn from all over India and may even include foreigners. Their sons and daughters marry not only outside their own castes but occasionally also outside region, language and religion. The introduction, in independent India, of universal franchise at all levels of the political system has placed before vast sections of the populace new opportunities of mobility through the acquisition of political power. This is particularly true of the dominant peasant castes and even the non-dominant castes which are numerically strong. There are highly influential political leaders from the Harijan and other backward castes and there exists a wide cultural and economic gulf between the leaders and the rest of the caste members. The style of life of the leaders tends to be Westernized, and their associates and friends are not restricted by caste and regional considerations. Political leaders, however, have to maintain their links with their castes and regions if they wish to stay in power, whereas members of the professional elites need not.

Competition among Castes

Edmund Leach recently stated that 'wherever caste groups are seen to be acting as corporations in competition against like groups of *different caste*, then they are acting in defiance of caste principles' (1960: 7). Again,

People of different castes are, as it were, of different species—as cat and dog. There can therefore be no possibility that they should compete for merit of the same sort.

According to him, the caste system is distinct from class, only the dominant castes, who are always numerically in a majority, compete for the services of individual members of the lower castes (ibid: 6). There is also competition between members of different *grades* of the same caste: 'the grades would not exist unless their members were constantly in competition one against the other'(ibid.:7). According to Leach, then, the position of each caste is fixed, while the *grades* within each caste are in a relation of competition with each other. If such competition results in mobility, the position of the mobile *grade* ought not to be higher than that of the caste of which it was a *grade*, for that might result in competition between different castes.

I have tried to show earlier that the traditional or pre-British political and economic systems favoured the mobility of particular castes, especially the dominant peasant castes. Several of them claimed, some successfully, to be Kshatriyas. Indeed, as many observers of the Indian scene have noted, the Kshatriya category has been a very popular one, and all kinds of castes have claimed to be Kshatriyas. This would run counter to Leach's statement that there can be no possibility that different castes 'should compete for merit of the same sort'.

Again, it is a commonplace observation that the caste system, in any given area, is not a clear-cut hierarchy with the position of each caste defined precisely, but that vagueness characterizes the position of many castes. This is the position today, and there is no reason to think that the situation was radically different in pre-British India. This lack of clarity is not accidental but an essential feature of the system, inasmuch as it makes for the mobility of individual castes (Srinivas 1962). It is relevant to note here that during the traditional period the ultimate authority for settling disputes with regard to the rank of a caste was the king, who could also, incidentally, raise or lower the rank of castes. All this is not consistent with a situation in which different castes are in a non-competitive relation with each other.

If Leach's 'principles' are not applicable to the caste system in traditional or pre-British India, they are even less applicable to the situation obtaining today. In independent India competition between different castes seems to be the normal situation. With the passing of political power to the people, castes have become pressure groups and are competing for power and for the fruits of power.

Burton Stein's characterization of mobility in modern India as 'corporate', in distinction from medieval mobility, which was familial, is important. While the existence of modern means of communication facilitates 'corporate mobility', the motive force for corporateness comes from the prospect of obtaining political power and using that power to benefit caste fellows. This tendency has become stronger in independent India, where every adult has the vote, and the government pursues the policy of providing special facilities and concessions to backward castes with a view to enabling them to catch up with the advanced castes in education and economic position. Numbers means strength, and divisions which previously seemed important are now ignored. As Béteille has pointed out,

Competition for power and office requires a certain aggregation of segments. The thousands of minimal segments in a given region cannot compete individually in the struggle for power. When they come together they follow alignments inherent in the traditional structure of caste. That is why the larger segments which compete for power today regard themselves as castes or *j atis* and are so regarded by others (1964: 134).

However, the political need for aggregation is so great that sometimes distinct caste groups occupying different positions in the regional hierarchy manage to come together. As an example, I may mention the Gujarat Kshatriya Sabha, in which Rajputs are admitting the populous but low-status Kolis to the rank of Kshatriya in order to capture power in Gujarat State. The Yadavs of north India provide an even more egregious instance of a large number of castes from different linguistic areas coming together and trying to form a single caste-category in order to strengthen their political power (Rao 1964). It is likely, however, that aggregations attempting to span great social and cultural distances are apt to be less stable than those which only bring together the different segments of the same caste or even structurally neighbouring castes.

The situation may be summarized by stating that mobility in medieval India was based on *fission* and, in modern India, on *fusion*. But the fusion of like units has had consequences for the entire system. For instance, it contributes to the weakening of the ideas of pollution, and it is also a result of such weakening. The unit of endogamy is beginning to widen to include adjacent segments or *grades*. In other words, in the process of exploiting the new opportunities, significant changes are occurring in the caste system. This is why Bailey's formulation that 'Castes still exist: but they are used as building blocks in a different kind of system', is unsatisfactory inasmuch as it ignores the changes which have occurred in the individual 'building blocks' (1963:123).

The New Cauhans: A Caste Mobility Movement in North India

WILLIAM L. ROWE

Mobility within the Hindu system of caste stratification has always existed, although it has fluctuated in accordance with the varieties of sociocultural time and place. Historical records of such movement are perhaps deficient, but glimpses of the self-conscious direction of caste mobility movements appear in abundant detail throughout the Indian census reports of the late nineteenth and early twentieth centuries. Reference to specific movements is frequently limited to sparse, terse comments, such as the remarks of a census official who states:

A section of Luhars (blacksmiths), known as Panchal Luhars, claimed to be returned as Panchal Brahmans; some Baria Kolis claimed to be Thakores; and Kayatia Brahmans wanted to be returned as Acharyas. The idea of raising themselves in the social scale, by adopting new caste names, had occurred also to the Hindus converts to Islam. Those known as Puijara (cotton carders) wanted to pass themselves off as *Dhunak Pathans*; and Tais (weavers) wanted to be Panni (shuttle cock) Pathans *(Census 1911*, XVI: 237).

Many of the caste movements described in the census materials are expressed, as in the above example of the Panchal Brahmins, in the attempt to change the group name to one more hallowed in Hinduism. Through a process of social fantasy the caste alleges that it has been 'incognito' for a period of time well beyond historical verification and

Excerpted from William L. Rowe, 'The New Cauhans: A Caste Mobility Movement in North India', in James Silverberg, ed., *Social Mobility and the Caste System in India: An Interdisciplinary Symposium*, Mouton, The Hague, 1968.

that it has now rediscovered its real identity. Census reports from 1891 through 1931 contain copious references to such attempts at name-changing. Frequently these data are economically listed in tables informing us of the present caste name, the claimed name, and the geographical location of the caste. The volume of such petitions may be appreciated if we consider the statement of one harried census official who, writing in the Bengal census of 1911, states:

Hundreds of petitions were received from different castes—their weight alone amounts to 1½ maunds (120 pounds)—requesting that they might be known by new names, placed higher in the order of precedence, be recognized as Kshatriyas, Vaisyas, etc. (*Census 1911*,V; 1: 4401).

Name-changing is of at least three types. Some castes, as in the example of the Baria Kolis, choose the name of a known higher caste. Others choose to append the name of a *varna* higher than their own after the usual caste appellation. In this way, the Kurmis (Sudra cultivators) petition to have their name changed to Kurmi Kshatriya or the Saini caste claims the title of Saini Kshatriya. Still another type of petition urges a change from a functional Sudra caste name such as Teli (oil manufacturers and vendors) to Vaishya, the *varna* of traders, not a caste name at all. One official, bemused by the frequency and insistence of such requests, comments to the effect that petitioners seem not to realize that the claims in themselves do not alter the actuality of the caste's position in the hierarchy (*Census 1931*,VII1: 265). The relationship of such movements to and the changes taking place in Hindu society were not the concern of census officials.

Another type of caste mobility movement operating on a different level attempts merely to reform caste practices. In this case the caste name is retained but claims are made for a rank higher than that usually accorded the caste. In such a mobility movement, the direction of change may well be towards a Western or 'modern' model rather than the Sanskritic one (Srinivas 1956: 481-96). The active and prosperous Agarwal community, for example, in its recent caste association meetings urged such reforms as banning of dowry and support of higher education.

When a caste wishes to change its name the movement seems always to focus on reforms emulating the traditional, Sanskritic model of social and ritual custom. The change of name is ordinarily to a caste of a higher *varna* and the most common *varna* for north India is that of Kshatriya.

The meaning and function of these social movements in Hindu society changes radically as we trace them from the Victorian era, through the First World War, and into the independence struggle. A survey of the Indian census reports indicates that, in all probability, movements expressing themselves in caste petitions for census recognition of caste-name changes reached their apex in the 1920s. Today the caste *sabhas* (organizations) that persist tend to have other directions. They are now less concerned with traditional caste hierarchy and more involved in political action directed toward the acquisition of gains and special privileges for the caste community (Rudolph and Rudolph 1960: 522).

The Cauhan Movement

One north Indian caste mobility movement which appears in the nineteenth century, and whose persistence today is at least partially successful, is that undertaken by the Noniyas, a Sudra caste found in Madhya Pradesh, Uttar Pradesh, and Bihar. They claim the status of a well-known warrior clan, the Cauhan Rajputs. The data reported here on this movement were collected both on a regional basis and through a two-year study of one Noniya Cauhan community located about 25 miles north of Banaras.

The inquiry began with the focus on Noniya Cauhan mobility within the Kshatriya dominated multicaste village of Senapur. It was eventually extended to include interviews with Noniya Cauhan leaders in several north Indian cities as well as a significant elite group in Bombay. Also, Senapur Noniya Cauhans residing and working in the Bombay slums were studied to determine the nature and impact upon them of the urban experience.

In both urban and rural settings, a wide range of rank may be observed. Some rural Noniya communities are almost entirely landless, economically and politically dependent upon a local landlord class. In such villages, Noniyas frequently perceive the Cauhan movement as a distant and not very real entity. However, in Bombay I found an organized group of about twenty-five Cauhans who would appear to the superficial observer as well-established middle-class professional men of a Kshatriya caste. In both the rural and urban setting interaction between the relatively small group who have 'passed' as Cauhans and the mass of those who have been largely unsuccessful in establishing that status, is very infrequent, uncomfortable and difficult.

Noniya rank in the hierarchy of the twenty-four castes which comprise the village Senapur has demonstrably risen over the past fifty years. Village Kshatriyas now place the Noniyas well above the Untouchable line at number nine or ten from the top in the hierarchy of castes. Elderly Kshatriyas claim that in their own childhood the Noniyas were 'almost Untouchable'.[1] There is quite general verbal consensus among all castes of the village on the Noniyas place in the hierarchy and observation of caste interaction confirms this. However, among the Noniya themselves there is great dissensus. When asked to rank the castes of the village hierarchically by arranging a group of cards (each card having the name of one caste on it) my Nonia Cauhan informats responded in terms of their 'Cauhan' claim by placing that card either second or third from the top. If they placed the 'Noniya' card at all in the hierarchy, they placed it much lower than was justified by social reality (as measured either by actual caste interaction or by verbal statements by other castes of the village). Some denied the existence of a caste named 'Noniya' or else claimed that it was a 'very low caste', not locally represented. Still other informants were angered by the very sight of the 'Noniya' card and two men tore up the 'Noniya' card.

The Noniyas

The caste name Noniya, is derived from the Hindi word for salt, *non*. An alternate form of the caste name is Loniya from the word *lon*, which also means salt. The caste is known in North India as Noniya, Nuniya, Loniya, or Luniya.

Sherring, reporting on Banaras and Mirzapur Districts in 1872, states:
. . . . The name, Nuniya designates the original occupation of the caste, that of manufacturing salt. But this occupation had given place to others, and now in some parts of the country . . . . The Nuniya, finding no scope for his business (salt and saltpeter making), has wisely taken in hand other species of labour. He digs water courses, ponds, wells and tanks. He also makes bricks and tiles (Sherring 1881: 347).

[1] The most defiling of the pre-Cauhan practices (from the viewpoint of Hindu food regulations) of the Noniyas was their custom of eating field rats. In village tradition, the Noniyas and the Musahars (literally, those who hunt and eat rats) were coupled as related castes. Currently the social distance between these two castes is very great, for the Musahars are Untouchables, landless and poor, while the Noniyas are prosperous and have improved their ritual rank. Village Kshatriyas frequently would disparage the Noniya pretensions (out of their hearing) with such statements as 'Oh yes, they are Cauhan Rajputs now, but only yesterday they were eating rats'.

This description is still quite accurate for the majority of Noniya communities in eastern Uttar Pradesh, with the important addition that they are now primarily agriculturalists. In isolated places they may still process alkali or saltish soils but for the most part they are farmers and earth-workers. The Indian census of 1981 lists 412.822 Noniyas in the North West Province while the 1931 Census records a population of 471,000. Subsequent census reports do not record population by caste distribution.

During the last half of the nineteenth century an increasing number of Noniya acquired considerable wealth through contracting for earth work, brick-making, and other traditional caste work for the British government. These Noniya contractors found a profitable business in road and bridge building and in the general expansion of public works during the period after the 1857 movement and before World War I. A changing opportunity structure was emerging and a caste such as the Noniya was partially emerging from its close ties to the rural community into the economy of the wider world. At the crest of this structure a small Noniya elite emerged. They were increasingly dissatisfied with the noticeable discrepancy between their customary low ritual rank and their newly acquired economic rank. Although this group was, and continues to be, quite small it has constituted an upper-class elite segment within the Noniya Cauhan caste. For the low status rural Noniyas the average distance from which brides are taken is 12 miles whereas the elite members of the caste invariably report marriage relations at distances of 50 to 300 miles(Rowe 1960: 299-311). The changing opportunity structure in colonial society, with the emergence of a newly prosperous group within the caste and the resulting incongruence of their ritual and economic ranks led to the founding and financing of a self-conscious caste mobility organization.

The Rajput Advancement Society

In 1898, Lalla Mathura Prasad Singh, a Noniya of Pratapgarh District, who had recently acquired wealth through his career as a contractor for construction and public works, founded an organization with the purpose of encouraging members of the Noniya (or Loniya) caste to claim their rightful status as Cauhan Rajputs. Characteristically, after having made his fortune in Patiala, the princely state, he returned to his home in Pratapgarh where he settled into the life of a newly rich zamindar. Joining with others of the newly created economic elite of the Noniya caste—professionals such as school teachers, postmasters, as well as contractors—he founded. the Cauhan organization, the Sri Rajput Pracarmi Sabha (Rajput Advancement Society). Although formed at the turn of the century, most informants claimed that the organization did not appreciably grow until after World War I.

The Cauhan organization moved eastward into the districts of Allahabad, Banaras, Mirzapur, Jaunpur, and Azamgarh, making gains wherever a group of Noniyas existed whose wealth enabled them to attempt social emulation of the Rajput style of life. The movement seems to have followed economic advancement rather than having preceded it. That caste mobility movements tend to filter through rural areas in relation to the general economic level of specific caste communities is verified by at least one incidental reference in the Indian census reports. Referring to a caste mobility movement in Bengal, the 1901 Census states that the claim is limited to certain sections of the province and that '. . . the lower sections of the community are still but imperfectly acquainted with their new name and the improvement in their status which it is intended to connote' (*Census 1901*, VI, 51: 380). The economic level of the community appears to be a very significant variable in the spread of such movements.

In Jaunpur, a relatively backward and underdeveloped district, the spread of the Cauhan movement has taken several decades and it still remains most effective only in the western portion of the district. In 1924 a meeting was called at Sanghaipur in Jaunpur District at which leaders of Noniya communities ritually donned the sacred thread, the symbol of twice-born status for males of the Brahmin, Kshatriya, and Vaishya *varnas* of Hinduism. More than any other symbol, the assumption of the sacred thread is the 'symbolic justification' par excellence in caste mobility movements. The choice of meeting place provided another kind of symbol. Sanghaipur was chosen because it had been the scene of a historic fight betwen the British and a group of Noniyas during the 1857 movement.

During the 1920s and 30s, the expanding sabha provided still another visible symbol for the New Cauhans—a body of literature which functionally served as a social charter to authenticate the claims of Noniyas to Rajput status. By 1935 the organization had been able to found an all-India sabha which exists in much the same form today with its headquarters located in Katni, Madhya Pradesh. An active branch exists in Jaunpur City composed of lawyers, teachers and petty officials who meet informally as the New Cauhans.

To the Noniyas of Village Senapur, the memory of their becoming Cauhans is a vivid part of local history. They relate that in 1936, a prosperous contractor of Kerakat, the nearby market and tehsil town, took the initiative in calling a meeting of the caste brotherhood. In a mango grove at the edge of the town the responsible leaders of Noniya communities throughout several tehsils listened to speeches by educated Cauhans and Arya Samaj leaders from Jaunpur City.[2] Following the speeches, a Brahmin priest invested all of those present with the sacred thread. Each of these leaders was enjoined to spread the message of the Cauhan movement to the caste brotherhood and to arrange for all Noniya males to don the sacred thread.

Twenty years after this meeting, every child in the Noniya settlement of Senapur knew the story of their Rajput lineage and of their claim to recognition as Cauhans, one of the oldest and most respected clans of Kshatriyas. Although I recorded the story many times, the main elements of the tale remained quite consistent.

Cauhan Myth and Literature

In the twelfth century, Prithviraj Chauhan, the last Hindu king of Delhi, bravely defended his kingdom and faith against the Muslim hordes. Eventually, through treachery, he was defeated and killed by Mohammed Gouri, the Muslim leader. Because the Cauhans opposed the invaders with the greatest of heroism and valour and with a ferocity beyond that of other Hindus, they were punished more severely by the triumphant conquerors. Cauhans were hunted down and slaughtered wherever possible. Village informants talk of the 'maunds of sacred threads' taken from the dead Cauhan warriors. In disarray and desperation the remaining Cauhans left their traditional homes in Western India and proceeded eastward in a state of great poverty and persecution. In various localities they were allowed to settle, but being landless and without wealth they had no source of livelihood. They were allowed to enter the occupation of salt-making and through countless generations of poverty they came to forge their Cauhan identity and customs.

[2] The Arya Samaj, a Hindu reformist organization, was founded at Bombay in 1875 by Swami Dyananda Saraswati. The Samaj had its most profound impact in the Punjab and Uttar Pradesh, where it first attracted support from 'modernist' elements of the educated middle classes (largely middle and upper caste). Since the Arya Samaj had as one of its most important programmes the abolition of costly, Brahman-dominated Sanskritic ritual, it is something of a paradox (perhaps explained by selective perception) that the New Cauhans were helped and assisted to Sanskritize themselves by an organization noted for its opposition to these same 'reactionary' forms.

Because they made salt, they were incorrectly called Noniyas, or Loniyas. Now, my village informants claim, they are prepared to resume their rightful status as Cauhan Rajputs. In the flight from Western India they removed their sacred threads to conceal their twice-born status from the pursuing Muslim armies.

A subsidiary element in the story is sometimes introduced which describes defilement of the caste and explains their low ritual status. In the flight from the scene of battle a Muslim officer chases some Cauhans to the house of an Untouchable. In this tale, the Untouchable claims that the Cauhan refugees are in fact his kinsmen. The Muslim officer demands as proof that the 'kinsmen' take food from the hands of the Untouchable. In accepting the defiling food, the Cauhans secure their lives but lose their caste rank.

The elements of this tale as well as an elaborated caste 'history' are contained in the principal book of the movement, published in 1925 under the auspices of the Cauhan Sabha (Agnihotri 1925). The author traces the development of the Cauhans from the inception of all human history through the downfall of the clan at the time of Prithviraj Chauhan's death. The largest and, in some ways most functionally significant, portion of the book deals with tracing the various clans and sub-clans of the Cauhan Rajputs. After describing the traditional home of each social grouping, he then indicates the area in eastern India where each group settled following the exodus. In this way Noniya Cauhans living throughout Uttar Pradesh and Bihar can obtain a social charter or genealogical link to a specific Cauhan sub-group which reputedly settled in local areas following the migration from western India in the 12th century.

In dealing with the fall of the Cauhans and their subsequent style of life, the author relates the ways in which the caste became associated with salt-making and with the names Noniya and Loniya.

The people, who are called Loniyas in west Marwar and Mehwar, are known also by the name Khaural or Kharwal. Research and diligent work have shown that Loniya is not the name of any caste, but is only a trade name. When the origin of the 'Loniyas' was traced, it was found that they were Rajputs in the beginning, but because they had assumed the occupation of making the salt, they became known as 'Loniyas', *Lon* means salt (ibid). The summation of the volume reasserts the claims of the movement and, in much the same manner as villagers report the speeches at Cauhan meetings, exhorts the community to action:

What a change of circumstances! The descendants of those who were once respected as kings and warriors are now struggling for their very existence, and are called people of low caste.

Those living in Pratapgarh, who are actually Rajputs, have forgotten their past, and poverty has led them to even worse situations. They have left their work according to the varnas.

Evidence has been given above that these people [Loniyas and Noniyas] are none other than the Rajputs, who centuries ago found shelter in Oudh and in the Districts of Benaras and Pratapgarh. With the passing of time, and having forgotten their ancestral work they have also forgotten their origin and began to be called by local names. However, there is no doubt that these persons are in fact Rajput descendants. The sun of their fate is hidden under the shade of clouds. They are crushed by their work, and because of mean-minded persons, they are unable to earn their just profits. Thus they are without hope of performing their duty[dharma]. Seeing this state of the Rajputs, I pray to the Aryan people that not everything has been broken or perished. Let us forget that which has happened and save the Rajputs in the present. This is our hope, and it is our main duty, also (ibid).

Implications of the Movement

Noniya communities adopted the Cauhan movement as they became prosperous. It provided a mechanism which allowed them to reduce the discrepancy between their contrasting positions in the ritual and economic hierarchies. The changing opportunity structure in Indian society had allowed them to achieve this discrepant economic position, first through money earned outside the village context, and then through the acquisition of lands. Wealthy contractors seem to have been the first to adopt the Cauhan claim and their sons and grandsons are now successful lawyers, teachers, and government officials. This small elite has promoted the spread of the movement through publication of various caste histories and the organization of such meetings as described above. They interact with one another, have their own network of marriage relations apart from the majority of the caste.

Although the impact of dynamic changes in Indian society is felt by all in the caste, it is among the elite that the impact is most strongly felt. This group is most actively involved in the Cauhan Sabha, a movement which does not challenge but rather upholds the traditional stratification system. At the same time, many of the younger generation of the elite are becoming involved and committed to the newer message of political egalitarianism for modern India. They have been subjected to the same secularizing influences as have the wealthier, more educated, high castes. As Bernard Cohn has demonstrated (Cohn 1955: 53-77), the dominant high-caste groups now look more frequently to a model of Western or modern values. Members of the Jaunpur City Cauhan Sabha, for example, are also active in the Arya Samaj, a socio-religious organization which opposes the ritual and caste orthodoxy which is so basic to the Cauhan movement. These same men have more recently become active in the Congress Party and in the association of Scheduled Castes, organization stressing political equality, anti-casteism, and special concessions for the underprivileged castes. The contradiction inherent in these dual loyalties does not seem to trouble the younger elite informants, men in their late twenties and thirties.

I would predict that this young elite will increasingly devote its energies to the 'modern' and directly political activity rather than to the caste mobility that was characteristic of the last generation. In this sense, then, we see the fundamentally different form which mobility striving is begining to assume. As members of the new elite, the Cauhan lawyers, school teachers, clerks, etc., who become active in anti-caste political movements—for example, the Republican Party of Uttar Pradesh[3] — are in essence challenging the stratification system itself. Scheduled Caste associations and anti-caste political movements appeal to individually mobile members of the new elite in class terms and in a way that denies the very importance of the traditional stratification system.

In contrast, older men who were interviewed, especially retired postmasters and school teachers prefer to continue indulging in the social fantasy of being Cauhans. For most of them, the throwing aside of that which they see as the fruit of a long and frequently bitter struggle, would be too difficult a step.

[3] 'This party' composed of Backward and Scheduled Castes and drawing heavily upon Muslim support (especially in western Uttar Pradesh) has had significant success at the polls in its chosen role as an anti-caste minority party opposed to high-caste domination and exploitation. In 1962, the Republican Party returned eight members to the State Assembly and three members to the Lok Sabha in New Delhi. Caste association movements of the Cauhan sort are said to consider the Republican Party as the dirtiest party in India (i.e., in its opposition to caste it encourages interdining of castes and intercaste marriage, and would favour a plan whereby a bonus would be paid by the government to each couple undertaking an intercaste marriage). However, leaders of the Republican Party feel that increasingly the young elite of the mobile lower-caste groups are becoming interested in their movement. (Interview with Sri B.P. Maurya, Republican Party member, Lok Sabha, Aligarh, U.P. constituency, Berkeley, California, 8 July 1963.)

Turning to the development of the Cauhan movement among the Noniyas of Senapur, we note a somewhat delayed series of reactions, probably because of their relatively modest economic position and because of the dominance of the local socio-political scene by the caste of Kshatriya landlords. Following the historic meeting at Kerakat in 1936, the Noniya leaders of Senapur returned to the settlement wearing the sacred thread. As enjoined by their caste leaders, they arranged for all adult Noniya males to assume the sacred thread. In reprisal, the affronted Kshatriya landlords beat the Noniyas, tore off the sacred thread and imposed a collective fine on the caste. Some years later, the Noniyas again began to wear the sacred thread but were unopposed. Their first attempt had been a direct, public challenge, but on the second occasion the Noniyas assumed the sacred thread quietly and on an individual basis.

Local Brahmans are few in numbers and are entirely dependent upon the dominant Kshatriya landlord caste in all but ritual matters. Although Brahman priests scoff at the high-caste pretensions of the Noniyas, they are not loathe to officiate at Noniya Cauhan weddings, life-cycle rites or Satya Narayan *kathas*, when newly affluent families wish to enhance their prestige through such forms of conspicuous consumption. The two Brahman priests most frequently called by Noniyas to officiate at their rites are, however, men of dubious background and from another village. Both of these men tend to have a low-caste clientele. Since the Brahmans in this particular area are so very much overshadowed by the dominant Kshatriya caste, they apparently do not attempt to uphold orthodoxy too stringently.

During the period of my field research, I discovered that actually most men of the very oldest Noniya generation do not wear the sacred thread, that a very considerable number of the middle generation do, and that among the youngest generation there is a decreasing interest in this symbol of high ritual rank. This has occurred at the very time when high-caste opposition has disappeared or at least decreased partly because of the secularizing influences among the young elite mentioned earlier. An important factor in understanding the disinterest of the younger generation of Noniyas in the sacred thread is that, to a very great extent, they have been exposed through urban employment to a society where class and not caste is the crucial measure of social rank.

Also some Noniyas have become disillusioned with attempts to observe a more Sanskritized ritual life. Bachila Devi, the goddess who protects the caste, has herself been Sanskritized and no longer wishes blood sacrifices in her honour but demands instead the more Brahmanical offerings of flowers and fruits. Sanskritized ritual is more expensive, involves paying for the services of a Brahman priest, and one senses among many of the Noniyas that they are unsure about Bachila Devi's *true* wishes. In at least one instance, a secret blood sacrifice to her was made by a prosperous family following a new, Sanskritized ceremony. And in several ritual matters, many Noniyas find that after all they are not economically able to validate their Cauhan claim for they cannot afford the costly rituals of the traditional Sanskritic model.

Meanwhile, the Noniyas have developed ambivalent feelings about the Cauhan claim itself. Their assertion in itself has not helped them to raise themselves economically, while the society in general values economic or class success much more than in the past. A growing attitude of the sophisticated, urbanized Cauhan lawyers and teachers is expressed best in the words of one city informant: 'What is the use of calling yourself "Singh" [the appellation of Kshatriya rank, whereas Ram is the appropriate name for a Sudra person], if you cannot be Singh'?

Persons of this persuasion point to the preferences given to Depressed or Scheduled Castes, to the scholarships available to children of these castes and they conclude that being a New Cauhan is a liability. Although the trend is strongest among the small urban elite, it is also observable in the village setting.

Regardless of this nascent trend toward class rather than caste values, caste endogamy remains unshaken. Consequently, there has been no generalized apostasy with regard to the New Cauhan movement. So long as it is required that potential marriage partners conform to the Cauhan code, that bridegrooms wear the sacred thread (at least during the marriage ceremony), that proper Sanskritized marriage rituals be utilized, and so long as there is the necessity for conforming to the Cauhan dietary reforms and for partial seclusion of women,[4] the movement will remain strong. Through the powers of social control exercised by affinal connections and by the local caste community, Cauhan standards are maintained.

---

[4] That the caste views purdah, or seclusion of women, as desirable, is attested to by the comment of one elderly Noniya women who responded to an inquiry on social change in her lifetime, with the statement 'Now we [the Noniyas] are more advanced than when I was a bride: now we keep our brides in purdah'.

There may be confusion regarding the real achievements of the movement and other castes in the village usually do not use the Cauhan designation in reference to them, but the leaders of all castes point to the Noniyas as having risen in the caste hierarchy.

Caste, Class and Power

ANDRÉ BÉTEILLE

The popular leaders of the village Sripuram today are not necessarily big landowners. The *panchayat* president who is a key figure in village politics owns some land, but this is not his principal source of power. We have seen how his power depends upon a plurality of factors, among which his contacts with politicians and party bosses outside the village and his position in an elaborate system of patronage are important ones.

Two factors have contributed in a big way to changes in the distribution of power in the village. The first of these is the decline in the influence of the old *mirasdar* class for a variety of reasons. The second is the growth of an elaborate political machinery, linking MLAs, party bosses, and village leaders and making it possible for people to acquire power in ways which were not open before the introduction of adult franchise and Panchayati Raj.

The power of the big landowners in Sripuram (and, to some extent, in Tanjore District as a whole) has been progressively curbed over the last several decades. It is not unlikely that this weakening of power has been confined to the old *mirasdar* or rentier class of landowners, and that the farmer and owner cultivator classes have held their own or even strenghtened their political position. Since Sripuram has been dominated in the past by rentiers and absentee landowners, it is to this class that we now turn our attention.

The power of the *mirasdars* in Sripuram was considerable at the beginning of the present century. These were several among them who each owned more than 30 acres of land. Most of them lived in the *agraharam*, and they were united by bonds of kinship and caste

Excerpted from André Béteille, 'Conclusion', in *Caste, Class and Power: Changing Patterns of Stratification in a Tanjore Village*, Oxford University Press, 1967.

and by a common style of life. The rest of the village looked up to them for their livelihood and for help and guidance on a variety of matters. In addition to agriculturists, the artisan and servicing castes also depended to a large extent on the patronage of the *mirasdars*.

Several factors were responsible for the power and influence of the old landowning class in Sripuram. There was, to begin with, a greater measure of unity among them as a class than there is today. Landowners were united, not only in terms of economic interest, but by a common style of life. In a majority of cases they were born in the village, had grown up there, and had known each other from childhood. Their relationships with each other, as well as with their tenants, were of a close, intimate, personal character.

Today not only has the proportion of landowners resident in the village gone down, but fragmentation has greatly reduced the size of individual or family holdings. Together with this, the cost of living has gone up, since landowners have very often to support one or more children studying outside. This makes it very difficult for the *mirasdar* to meet his traditional obligations to tenants and to artisans and servicing groups. Formerly at festivals such as Deepavali and Pongal, as well as on other occasions, landowners were expected to give liberally to a host of dependents. Today most of them cannot easily afford to do this. As their ability to distribute patronage becomes weakened, their power and influence over tenants and dependents also tend to wane.

Along with this, one has to consider the fact that a large section of landowners have left the village and settled elsewhere. Absentee landowners do not generally have either the opportunity or the interest to maintain control over affairs in the village. They do not have any close or enduring ties with their tenants. They do not distribute patronage or in any appreciable way influence political life in the village. Many of them know the village, and are known by its inhabitants, only superficially.

Thus, the landowners as a class have become fragmented and scattered. Some of them cling to the traditional ways of life and continue to reside in the village. Others have acquired Western education, secured urban employment, and developed interests outside the village. The former unity of the landowners — and, along with it, a part of their strength — has been destroyed.

Political and legal factors have further undermined the position of the old class of rentier *mirasdars*. Earlier, the landowner had a fairly free hand in fixing rents, as well as in evicting tenants. Land legislation in recent years has considerably strengthened the position of tenants at the same time as it has curbed the powers of landowners. A tenant can no longer be evicted at the pleasure of the *mirasdar*. The latter is, thus, deprived of one of the most powerful weapons in his armoury. The political climate in the state as a whole is changing, and the class of rentier *mirasdars* in Sripuram has begun to feel that the tide is against them.

The emerging leaders of the village are, thus, not members of the old landowning class. They generally belong to the class of small owner-cultivators. Their power is, to a large extent, based upon numerical support within the village and political contacts outside it. These two factors, as we have seen, tend to reinforce each other.

Members of the old *mirasdar* class feel ill at ease in the face of changes in the ideological climate. The introduction of democratic forms of government, and more particularly of adult franchise, has created in the minds of people a new consciousness of their own political importance, irrespective of caste, class, and other social factors. Villagers, however low their social or economic position, have by now had the experience of being courted during elections by important political personalities from towns and cities. The support of the masses can no longer be taken for granted. And in this matter the new political leaders, the contact men, have an edge over *mirasdars* of the older type.

There is always a certain barrier which deters the old *mirasdar* from approaching his tenants and servants for votes in an attitude of supplication. There is a sense of pride which keeps him from competing for popular support with people who had till recently taken his superiority for granted. The campaign for popular support demands many compromises which do not come easily to the rentier *mirasdar*, who still preserves a very keen sense of personal prestige.

There is a feeling of estrangement between the old elite of the village and the masses. The *mirasdar*, who is often a Brahmin, cannot go to the *cheri* to canvass votes from the Pallas. The new Non-Brahmin leaders have an advantage over him in this regard. Non-Brahmins in general have long had much closer contacts with the Adi-Dravidas in the village. It is easier for them to assume an air of equality when approaching the latter for votes or political support in general. The very structure which in the past ensured the superiority of the *mirasdar* by keeping others at a distance from him now acts as an obstacle when he is faced with the demands of an egalitarian ideology.

Popular leaders of the kind who now dominate the village *panchayat* began to come to the forefront after 1942. As the Congress developed more and more into a mass movement, young people with initiative and drive, and with the ability to organize support, moved into the limelight. Gradually the skill to organize people became an important factor. The self-esteem of members of the old *mirasdar* class often stood in the way of their developing such a skill. Particularly today there is a distinct tendency on the part of the college-educated *mirasdar* to regard local politics as something dirty, requiring the prospective leader to rub shoulders with people of all descriptions.

The new popular leader in his turn began to expand his contacts both within and outside the village. Lack of funds was not always a very serious handicap, since the party as well as various agencies of the government could be tapped for money. The development of democracy, with its elaborate paraphernalia of parties and local self-government, has made politics a paying business for those who have initiative, drive, and popular support. Being a part of this elaborate political machinery gives to the individual a certain standing, irrespective of his caste or class position.

As more and more specialized political agencies develop, the political system itself tends to acquire a weight of its own. In the traditional system there were no parties, legislatures, or Panchayat Union Councils in and through which the individual could acquire power independently of his position in the class or caste structure. No doubt, membership in the party, the Legislature, of the Panchayat Union Council is even today largely dependent upon caste and class. But the relations between caste, class, and power have become more complex and more dynamic in contemporary society, and the introduction of adult franchise in particular has opened up new avenues for the acquisition of power.

Thus, there is a certain divergence between economic and political power in the village today. The big *mirasdars* are no longer the ones who are politically the most powerful. Those in whom political power is vested in the village today cannot accurately be described as big landowners. To what extent are the ones who have acquired political power also on the way to acquiring control over land? This is a question to which no satisfactory answer can be provided under the terms of the present analysis. Although it would be useful to view the relationship between political and economic power in terms of dynamic criteria, there is no doubt that there may be considerable lags betwen the two over a particular period of time.

One should not, however, emphasize too much the divergence between political and economic power. In order to acquire and retain political power it is necessary for a person to have some economic standing. Although political power has shifted from the class of rentier *mirasdars*, it has not gone into the hands of landless labourers. The latter are still largely in a state of subordination. In the *panchayat* and outside they have very little say in matters which affect the village as a whole.

Although not big *mirasdars*, most of those who enjoy political power in the village have some land or other source of income. A person who is politically influential has to distribute patronage to his followers. He has to entertain guests from outside and keep up a certain standard of living. It is not possible for a landless labourer, or for one whose income is very small and uncertain, to meet the demands which are made by followers on a leader and a man of influence.

While a moderately secure economic position is an important condition for the acquisition of power, political power, in its turn, brings certain economic advantages. The *panchayat* president receives funds from the party, or from leaders higher up, and part of this he can divert to this personal use. He also has certain discretionary powers in the use of *panchayat* funds, and it is widely believed in the village that he is able to use these powers to his own personal advantage. Members of the *panchayat* and, particularly, of the Panchayat Union Council have authority to give contracts for jobs of various kinds, and the giving of contracts usually brings in its wake reciprocal benefits.

Contacts with officials in government departments is an important source of economic advantage for the villagers today. One can obtain credit facilities for various purposes and an increasing range of benefits through government departments. Political connections often help to break through the rigid demands of a bureaucratic structure. The *panchayat* president of Sripuram, who has contacts with important political leaders, is in a position to use these contacts to gain many administrative advantages.

Although numerical strength has become an increasingly important basis of power, by itself it does not count for very much. What is required, in addition, is organization, and in this regard people with some social and economic standing play an important part. Small tenants and landless labourers, and those who are on the border line between them, have as yet very little power. Far from being able to manoeuvre for benefits and privileges, they are generally not even able to get for themselves what they are entitled by law.

. . . .

In the traditional set-up political power in Sripuram was in the hands of the Brahmins. The Non-Brahmins, with the exception of the Maratha family, did not enjoy much political power. Major decisions affecting the village as a whole were in general taken and implemented by the Brahmins. This, as we have seen, has changed considerably. Power has now gone into the hands of Non-Brahmins, and Brahmins tend to play a smaller part in deciding the fate of the village.

One of the most important political phenonmena of the past three decades, in Sripuram as well as in Tamilnadu as a whole, has been the shift of power from Brahmins to Non-Brahmins. This has not necessarily or always meant a shift from landowners to tenants or cultivators. The new men of power in Sripuram cannot adequately be characterized as tillers of the soil. More important, they owe much of their power to connections with influential Non-Brahmins outside the village who in many cases happen to be big landowners.

In Sripuram the transfer of power from Brahmins to Non-Brahmins was symbolized by the shift of the *panchayat* office from the *agraharam* to the Non-Brahmin quarters. This was associated with the replacement by a Non-Brahmin of the Brahmin *panchayat* president in the mid-forties. Today guests of the *panchayat*, including state ministers, are received in the new *panchayat* office and do not have any occasion to visit the *agraharam*.

The relationship between caste and political power has to be examined in the context of change, because change has been an important feature of this relationship over the last few decades. Further, such changes as have been taking place within the village are, in many cases, reflections of shifts in power in regional society. It is necessary, therefore, to undertake a broad survey of the changing role of caste in the politics of Tamilnadu over the last forty years in order to place in their proper perspective the events which are taking place in Sripuram today.

The Brahmins have occupied a rather ambivalent position in the politics of Tamilnad since the end of nineteenth century. Their changing fortunes in Sripuram reflect their general decline in the state as a whole. Yet the superior position which Brahmins enjoyed in traditional society had been further strengthened during the earlier years of British rule, when they added Western education to the high economic position and ritual status which was already theirs.

Till the outbreak of World War I, Western education in Tamilnad was almost a monopoly of the Brahmins. This was particularly true of the Tanjore Brahmins. It had the consequence, at least initially, of further widening the gap betwen Brahmins on the one hand and Non-Brahmins and Adi-Dravidas on the other. . . . The Brahmins turned themselves towards urban life, and there was corresponding loss of interest in agriculture. The Non-Brahmins, on the other hand, remained firmly rooted to the village and its agrarian economy.

Western education not only brought social prestige on its own right, but also opened the way to new economic opportunities. The new urban jobs—clerical, executive, and professional — became a virtual monopoly of the Brahmins. Brahmins in important executive and managerial positions used the ties of caste and kinship to recruit more Brahmins. The Non-Brahmins found themselves virtually excluded because of their belated start.

Western education, and employment in important managerial and administrative positions, brought the Brahmins close to the new rulers of India, the British. Brahmins entered the highly prestigious and powerful Indian Civil Service, and government bureaucracies of all kinds became their strongholds. They also dominated the professions of law, medicine, and education. Since nationalist awakenings first found expression among members of the professions and the urban middle classes in general, the leadership of the Congress party came to be dominated by the Brahmins.

The Non-Brahmins, however, did not for long remain reconciled to their inferior position. Those among them who were able to acquire Western education soon set about organizing themselves politically and appealing to the British for a more equitable distribution of opportunities. *The Justice* newspaper, a vehicle of Non-Brahmin demands, was launched in 1917, and at about the same time the Justice party. The stage was set for the struggle for power between Brahmins and Non-Brahmins.

In the early decades of the present century in Tamilnad the Brahmins dominated the Congress party, by far the most influential national political organization. The Non-Brahmins, including Muslims and Christians, rallied round the Justice party. The latter gained important advantages by co-operating with the British over the Government of India Act of 1919, which the Congress decided to boycott. The struggles betwen Brahmins and Non-Brahmins were initially confined largely to the urban middle classes, but they soon pervaded wider areas of society.

The leaders of the Non-Brahmin movement expressed the fear that the transfer of power for which the Congress was agitating might lead to the domination of the people by a small elite composed of Brahmins. They argued, therefore, for preferential treatment of Non-Brahmins to make up for the advantages which the Brahmins had secured over them in the field of education and employment.

After the Congress boycotted the Government of India Act of 1919, the leaders of the Justice party managed to have discriminatory measures favouring the Non-Brahmins built into the administration. Posts in the government as well as seats in the institutions of higher learning came to be reserved for Non-Brahmins. For those aspiring to pass into the new middle classes it became important at every stage whether they were Brahmins or Non-Brahmins. Discrimination continues against Brahmins to this day and is a major factor in their feeling and consciousness of unity.

In the twenties the Brahmins began to lose ground in education and administration. In the thirties the Self-Respect movement started carrying anti-Brahmin feelings to the masses. Newspapers were started in English (*The Liberator*) and in Tamil (*Swaya-mariyadai*) in which Brahmins were denounced for their arrogance and the pursuit of their narrow group interests. Brahminism as a way of life came in for attack for its bigotry and duplicity, and for the exploitation which it practised and encouraged.

Attempts were made to do away with the service of Brahmin priests. The Purohit Maruppu Sangam (Association for the Elimination of Priests) was formed, and Self-Respect marriages (without the service of Brahmin priests) began to be performed. A general attitude of hostility towards Brahmins came to be built up on the social plane, and feelings ran high against them.

The leading figure in the attack against Brahmins over the last thirty-five years has been the one-time Congress leader, E.V. Ramaswami Naicker. In the thirties and early forties he spearheaded the Self-Respect movement and trained a band of educated young men with idealistic fervour as his disciples. In the forties he formed the Dravida Kazhagham (DK), a militant organization devoted to anti-Brahmins and anti-north Indian activities. In 1949 some of the ablest young men split from the DK and formed a separate party, the Dravida Munnetra Kazhagham (DMK), which has now emerged as the leading opposition party in the state. Though also rooted in anti-Brahminism, the DMK is more moderate in its programmes, even admitting Brahmins within its folds. It claims to be hostile not to

Brahmins as such, but to the elements of obscurantism and exploitation in the Brahminical way of life.

The wave of anti-Brahmin feeling which swept through the state found its echo in Sripuram. At Thiruvaiyar leaders of the DK burnt copies of the Ramayana and threatened violence to the Brahmins in political speeches. Films preaching the DMK ideology and heaping scorn on Brahmins drew large audiences from the village at cinema halls in Thiruvaiyar and nearby places. The Brahmins found themselves politically isolated and the target of attack from forces of various kinds, some of them politically organized.

The Congress itself, which in the early decades of the present century was largely dominated by Brahmins, gradually passed under the control of Non-Brahmins. In 1942 the 'August movement' provided a major breakthrough for the Non-Brahmins, whose support became increasingly important, if for no other reason than the strength of their numbers. After independence the political influence of the Brahmins dwindled rapidly. Today in Tamilnad the ministry and the Legislature as well as the Congress party are dominated by Non-Brahmins. The Congress has to some extent been forced to transform the character of its leadership in order to hold its own against parties with a Non-Brahmin background such as the DK and the DMK with the replacement of C. Rajagopalachari by K. Kamraj in the fifties, the political influence of the Brahmins has been more or less effectively neutralized.

Political events of the last forty years have given the Tamil Brahmins a strong feeling of identity as a minority. The traditional quarrels between Smartha and Shri Vaishnava, let alone Thengalai and Vadagalai, have been largely forgotten. In general the feeling is strong among the Brahmins of Sripuram that they should be united if they are to survive. This feeling of unity among the Brahmins, their consciousness of a common destiny, is in considerable measure a response to the political challenge of the last forty years.

In the village the Brahmins have gradually come to accept their social and political isolation. They have been singled out for attack by leaders of the DK and the DMK, through the press and the films. Their social exclusiveness, once jealously guarded in the interest of 'culture', refinement, and ritual purity, has now been turned against them. Although there has been bitterness against landowners and moneylenders, it has never been organized in the way in which hostility towards Brahmins has been. The anti-Brahmin movement is not in its practice an attack against a particular economic class, but against

Brahmins in general, whether they are landowners, school-teachers, clerks or temple priests.

It is the anti-Brahmin movement rather than class conflict between the landowners and the landless that has dominated political life in this area over the last forty years. No doubt, the anti-Brahmin movement has been viewed by many in the idiom of a class struggle. And, in fact, the Communists in the early fifties drew the support of the DK to lauch their attack against the landowners, who in the Thiruvaiyar area often happened to be Brahmins.

The Brahmins have not fared very well in the hands of the Congress party, or the government either. We have seen that discriminatory measures against the Brahmins have been built into the administration since the twenties. The Congress party, when it came into power after independence, continued with the policy of preferential treatment of the background communities. A Brahmin today, as before, finds the odds against him when applying for a job in the state government or a seat in some technical institution.

The Brahmins, thus, are in a political situation which is, in many ways, unique. From being a political elite in the first part of the present century, they now find themselves in the position of a political minority. The forces of democracy have turned the tables upon them. What has happened in Sripuram is only one instance, and to some extent it follows from what has been happening in the state as a whole. But although the Brahmins have lost much political ground, they have not entirely withdrawn from political activities within the state. We shall examine presently the changing relationships between the Brahmins and a variety of political parties.

The political fortunes of the Non-Brahmins have also been rather varied, and perhaps even more complex that those of the Brahmins. We have noted that the Non-Brahmins first organized their political interests around the Justice party. The Justice party, however, was a platform for only a small section of the Non-Brahmins - the urban, educated middle classes among them. Its impact on the rural masses was negligible, and it became virtually extinct after its rout in the 1937 elections.

The Justice party served one importance purpose. It served to bring into focus the conflict of interests between Brahmins and Non-Brahmins, and to organize this conflict politically on a state-wide basis.

The Non-Brahmins had, in the meantime, found a new sense of identity and a new ideology in the Self-Respect movement. This movement called upon Non-Brahmins to rid themselves of their ritual dependence on Brahmins and to stand on their own feet. It tried to create for the first time a feeling among Non-Brahmins that they were equal to the Brahmins, if not superior. And the Self-Respect movement was not confined to the cities; it spread to the rural masses. Even as late as 1961, Self-Respect marriages were being conducted in Sripuram, among both Non-Brahmins and Adi-Dravidas, without the service of Brahmin priests.

The political fate of the Non-Brahmins was not decided by the defeat of the Justice party in the elections of 1937. The Congress, which was successful in the election, began to draw increasingly upon the Non-Brahmins for its leadership. We have seen how in Sripuram the 1942 movement paved the way for the emergence of Non-Brahmins to positions of influence in the Congress. What happened in Sripuram was taking place in the state as a whole. Independence in 1947, and the first General Elections in independent India in 1951-2 saw the Non-Brahmins forge further ahead in their control of the Congress and of politics in Tamilnad as a whole. By the mid-fifties the Non-Brahmins were in a commanding position in the Congress party, the State Legislature, and the cabinet. They have more or less effectively maintained their control till now.

Non-Brahmin control is not confined among political parties to the Congress alone. New parties, which arose as successors to the Justice party, made their appeal to Non-Brahmins in particular..The Congress, at least, has expressed itself in a universalistic idiom, and has not come out explicitly for any particular community, however much it may have been favoured or controlled by that community in practice, and neither has it come out openly against any.

In the mid-forties the DK emerged as a champion of Non-Brahmins and Adi-Dravidas. It has been militant in its approach, openly preaching violence and directing its attack and virulence against Brahmins in particular. By the mid-fifties, however, with the Non-Brahmins gaining effective control over the Congress, the DK had become a spent force as a separate political entity. In 1951-42, when the veteran Brahmin leader C. Rajagopalachari was still at the helm of Congress affairs, the DK supported the Communists. In 1957 and 1962 the DK joined hands with the Congress, taking active part in its campaigns, particularly in the districts of Tanjore and Trichy.

Although the DK has become politically a spent force, this is by no means true of its offshoot, the DMK. The DMK separated from the DK in 1949. It has been, on the whole, less militant than the parent body and less aggressive in its attitude towards Brahmins. In theory, at least, membership is open to Brahmins, although they have not shown much keeness to join the party.

. . . .

In spite of the relatively moderate policies of the DMK, its anti-Brahmin background must not be lost sight of. Many of the present leaders of the party had their apprenticeship under Ramaswami Naicker and have a number of anti-Brahmin activities to their credit. Through the medium of films the party leaders have made attacks on religious orthodoxy and on the Brahminical social order with which orthodoxy has been associated. Sporadically the party members are known to have participated in outrages against the Brahmins. In practice the leadership of the DMK has been almost entirely Non-Brahmin.

In Sripuram the relationship of the Brahmins to the Congress party is now a purely negative one. It is, nevertheless, important, because their attitude towards the Congress has led them to support parties to which they would be otherwise hostile. We have noted that in the 1962 elections, the Brahmins of Sripuram voted for the DMK candidate for the Assembly seat. This support was based explicitly on hostility towards the Congress and not on any appreciation of either the policy or the leadership of the DMK.

The importance of caste loyalties among Brahmins manifested itself in an increasing manner in the 1962 elections. The Brahmins of Sripuram, for the reasons just mentioned, had taken a more or less collective decision to vote against the Congress. For the Assembly seat they voted almost *en masse* for the DMK candidate, who, like all the other candidates for the seat, was a Kalla by caste. For the Parliamentary constituency, however, the Congress had put up a Brahmin candidate, C.R. Pattabhiraman, the son of a very distinguished Tamil Brahmin, Sir C.P. Ramaswami Iyer. In spite of their firm resolve to vote against the ruling party, a large section of the Sripuram Brahmins changed their mind at the last moment and voted for the Brahmin Congress candidate.

Non-Brahmins have a choice of associating themselves with a number of political parties. In Sripuram and the surrounding area, the most important of these are the Congress and the DMK. The Swatantra party has made practically no headway among them, although it has done so in other areas. The DK has a number of sympathizers, but since it does not contest elections on its own, it is not always possible to separate its supporters from those of the Congress.

In Sripuram during the 1962 elections Non-Brahmin support was divided between the Congress and the DMK. But it is very difficult to infer any pattern on the basis of this. Those who voted for the Congress, or even took part in its election campaign, might in many cases switch over their support to the DMK, depending upon a variety of personal and local factors. Political opinion among the Non-Brahmins of the village is not as sharply defined as it is among the Brahmins. This is, no doubt, due largely to the much lower proportion of literacy and education among them, and to their greater diversity.

Class differentials among the Non-Brahmins of Sripuram do not today play a very important role in determining party support, although they may do so elsewhere. There seems to be a generational difference, but this, too, is not very sharp. On the whole, the older, better-established Non-Brahmins in the village tend to support the Congress. The DMK is run by younger people, some of whom are sons of fairly well-to-do farmers and owner-cultivators.

The Adi-Dravidas are, on the whole, supporters of the Congress. Thus, Congress support cuts across both caste as well as class. Support of the Congress by the Adi-Dravidas is closely related to the policies which the ruling party has been following. Indeed, there is some criticism by both Brahmins and Non-Brahmins that the Congress has been nursing the Adi-Dravidas at their expense and with the political objective of keeping itself in power by ensuring massive support from the Adi-Dravidas.

By virtue of their position as Scheduled Castes, the Adi-Dravidas enjoy a number of privileges which are embodied in the Constitution of India. In addition, they are believed to enjoy certain political advantages in Tamilnad in particular. Both Brahmins and a section of Non-Brahmins think that Congress ministers and MLAs are generally more easily accessible to the leaders of the Adi-Dravida community and that they tend to take a more sympathetic view of its grievances. This attitude is often interpreted in terms of political motivation. To what extent the sympathetic attitude of the Congress leaders at the top actually benefits the rank and file among the Adi-Dravidas is, however, open to question.

Although it is quite likely that the government will continue to provide benefits to the Schedule Castes irrespective of the party in power, these benefits tend, in practice, to be attributed to the Congress party. Leaders of the Congress, in their turn, do not hesitate to claim for themselves the credit for improving the position of Adi-Dravidas. The latter, being largely illiterate, are not always able to see the finer distinction between the government and the ruling party, and tend to support the Congress. In the 1962 elections most of the Adi-Dravidas in Sripuram voted for the Congress.

It should be reiterated that the Adi-Dravidas enjoy their special position by virtue of their caste, and not their class position, although it is true that the two overlap to a considerable extent. Adi-Dravidas who own land, although they are few in mumber, enjoy special benefits in spite of their economic position; a landless Non-Brahmin is not entitled to these benefits. It is thus caste, and not class, which is decisive in shaping the political attitudes of the Adi-Dravidas.

It will have been noted that political attitudes and party support are least clearly defined among Non-Brahmins. This is, to some extent, explained by the fact that they constitute the largest and the most heterogeneous of the three principal divisions. Whereas Brahmins as well as Adi-Dravidas evince a degree of political unity and cohesiveness, internal conflicts are common among the Non-Brahmins. Power tends to be divided between several dominant castes which operate at the district level, or at the level of the Assembly constituency. These dominant castes today all belong to the Non-Brahmin division.

. . . .

The distribution of power has acquired a very dynamic character over the last two decades. In some ways the traditional relationship between caste and power has been reversed. Whereas in the past power was concentrated in the hands of Brahmins, today the village *panchayat* is controlled by Non-Brahmins and the traditional elite is being pushed into the background.

Power has also become independent of class to a greater extent than in the past. Ownership of land is no longer the decisive factor in acquiring power. Numerical support and a strategic position in the party machinery play an important part. Adult franchise and Panchayati Raj have introduced new processes into village society. The struggle for power has become a pervasive phenomenon. This may partly be due to the fact that today much more power is accessible to the common man than was ever the case in the past. Mobility in the caste system has always been an extremely slow and gradual process. To acquire land and move up in the hierarchy of class also takes a generation or two. Shifts in the distribution of power under the new set-up are, by comparison, quick and radical in nature.

Agricultural Failure: Caste, Class and Power in Rural West Bengal

SURAJ BANDOPADHYAY AND DONALD VON ESCHEN

This paper has been divided into three parts. The first reveals that rural society in the study area is highly stratified and fragmented. The second demonstrates that these features are heavily responsible for the failure of a more rapid agricultural progress. It is important to stress that this second proposition need not follow from the first. It can be quite plausibly argued that an unequal distribution of resources is essential for economic progress. Therefore, only empirical data can determine whether steep stratification inhibits or generates growth. It is in part for this reason that the discussion of the existence of steep stratification is separated from a discussion of its impact. Finally, in the third section, it is argued that while government policies and practices are significantly rooted in rural stratification and fragmentation, so that the former explanation can be partially reduced to the latter, nevertheless, these policies and practices probably also have certain independent roots, and are themselves partly responsible for rural social structure. In short, it is argued that the administrative explanation probably has some empirical autonomy as an explanation,

Adapted from Suraj Bandopadhyay and Donald Von Eschen, 'An Extended Summary of the Conditions of Rural Progress in India', ISI, Calcutta, 1981' (Mimeo).

and is not only a consequence of rural stratification and fragmentation, but also a cause.

The Prevalence of Rural Stratification and Fragmentation

It is common in studies of stratification to distinguish three static or cross-sectional dimensions—economic class, status (or prestige), and power—and one temporal or dynamic dimension—social mobility. It is quite possible for a system to be stratified along each of the static dimensions. But these dimensions can cross-cut one another in such a way that a person's lowly position on one dimension is compensated by a higher position in another, resulting in the overall system not being highly stratified. Similarly, it is possible for the system to be highly stratified in terms of the static dimensions (in that they all tend to coincide), but for there to be substantial social mobility over time, so that the system cannot be regarded as being highly stratified.

The data for the study area, however, indicate that rural society is highly stratified in all respects. There is steep stratification on each of the three static dimensions of class, status, and power; these three dimensions closely coincide; and social mobility over time is quite low.

Economic Stratification

In terms of economic stratification, there is a real puzzle. Census data often fail to show a high degree of economic stratification in the country-side. This is frequently true of survey data, as well. Anthropological village studies, on the other hand, often do indicate substantial inequality. The solution to this puzzle lies in several striking features of village life. First, studies of land concentration often fail to take into account whether or not the land is irrigated. . . .Our study shows that irrigated land is worth much more than that which is unirrigated. When land is appropriately weighted by irrigation, the data show a high degree of land concentration. Not only do half of all fami-'ies own no land whatsoever, but among those who do, the top (6 families) own as much land as the bottom 50 per cent (264 families). Second, over one-third of the farmers simultaneously hold an off-farm job; such multiple job-holding is particularly frequent among the larger farmers; and these larger farmers virtually monopolize the most desirable, best-paying non-agricultural jobs (doctor, lawyer, large shop owner, head school master, etc.). In short, the top landholders often supplement their farm income with income from top non-farm jobs, thus further strengthening their economic position. Census or survey data which fail to pick up this multiple job holding under-estimate the amount of inequality involved. Third, the largest land-holders tend to have joint families, whereas most other families in these villages are minimally extended, at best. In these joint families, there are generally several adult male job holders in addition to the head. The data indicate that these, too, usually hold relatively good jobs. Thus, these families collectively occupy an immense economic field, a fact that is, again, often not picked up in surveys or census data. Fourth, not only do the top families tend to hold a very dispro-portionate share of the land and monopolize the best non-farm jobs, sometimes several to a family, they have important additional sources of wealth, often inherited. Among these are jewellery, all weather housing, furniture, work animals, carts, skills of literacy, and educa-tion, all factors which further distance them from the rest of the popu-lation. Furthermore, many possess significant numbers of debters; often in the form of tied labourers who must work for them free of charge to pay off past debts. In contrast, at the bottom of the society are a mass of villagers (at least one-fourth of all families) who are desperately poor, generally own no land, often are employed less than half the year, without two meals of rice a day (that is, living in a state of semi-starvation), virtually without access to any major source of protein (such as milk), living in lean-tos insufficiently high to stand up in and open on one or more sides to the weather. In short, in a truly desper-ate condition. And even among those at the bottom of the society who do 'own' land, this ownership often takes the form of bonded cultiva-tion, a state of semi-servility, in which the cultivator owes debts to a local wealthy family which go back over a generation, and where the land has *de facto* become that of the lending family, so that the cultiva-tor is, in reality, only an agricultural labourer on 'his' land. This semi-servile status characterizes about one out of every eight cultivators in the villages. In short, whatever might seem to be indicated by normal census data, or sample surveys that fail to examine the situation closely, rural society in this area is highly stratified economically.

Status Stratification

As for stratification by prestige, these villages are steeply stratified by the caste system. The central question here, therefore, is how closely this system coincides with economic stratification. One might expect the association to be only loose, for the caste system is ostensibly based on religious criteria. Furthermore, however close the association may have been in the past, one might expect it to have been substantially undermined in recent times by changes in the overall occupational structure in India. Castes have historically been associated with occupational groups. . . . But the last century has seen considerable changes in the occupational system, with a considerable increase in the non-agricultural sector, and a change in the latter's occupational composition. Many writers have argued that this new occupational system is based more on achievement and less on ascription, with the result that lower caste persons have had greater opportunities for advancement, thus weakening the association between caste and economic class. Nevertheless, however plausible these arguments may sound, the data show them to be false. Class and caste, these data show, are very strongly associated in the study villages. Why is this so? Inheritance is inevitably a major determinant of economic position in a rural area, since wealth is heavily based on land, buildings, and jewellery, all of which are largely inherited. Nevertheless, inheritance can be dissipated over time, and the occupational system has substantially changed in the non-agricultural sector, even in rural areas. Two additional processes are, therefore, critical. One is that a high caste position brings a disproportionate access to those occupations within the new occupational structure that are well paying. The second is the tendency of a caste in maintaining a correlation between its economic position and ritual status.

The upper castes have traditionally possessed skills of literacy and education, and these give differential access to well paying non-agricultural jobs; and, employers tend to discriminate in favour of the upper castes. The income earned in these non-agricultural jobs is often, in turn, used to purchase land, which can then be passed down over generations as inheritance, thus maintaining the association between caste and class.

The association between caste and class is maintained in the face of a changing occupational structure because the villagers tend to bring a caste's prestige into line with its changing economic attainments. This takes two forms. In the short run, the villagers re-rank the prestige of the caste in spite of its recognized religious position. In the long run, they actually change the religious position of the caste, by assenting to new legends about its origins, which often involves a new name for the caste. Thus, over time, a very strong association between caste and economic class is maintained.

Stratification of Power

Here again we find an extraordinarily steep system of stratification. Most villages contain highly structured, pyramidical patron-client networks, in which most villagers are tied as clients to a few top cliques of families, each of which tends to be well organized internally, while the mass of villagers tend to be disorganized, having few informal ties with one another, and little membership in any common formal associations, such as co-operatives. The top families tend to control all village institutions, including the *panchayats*, and are on good terms with government officials to the point where many feel they can engage in illegal acts without fear of sanction. In contrast, the mass of villagers barely participate in politics at all, and often fear not only the politically powerful families in their villages, but government officials as well, often seeing the latter as self-interested, and even corrupt.

Power tends to be very closely associated with class and caste. That is, those who feel they have power, . . . are generally both wealthy and belong to upper caste. One striking indication of the disproportionate power of wealthy, upper-caste villagers is that virtually all of the drinking wells that have been sunk by the Community Development Programme in the area were sunk in the wealthy, upper-caste neighbourhoods, in spite of the fact that most of these already had access to sanitary drinking water, whereas it was the lower class, lower caste neighbourhoods that were without such sources and in real need of the wells.

The causes of the close association between power, class, and caste are diverse and complex, and they run in both directions; that is, high class and caste position not only bring power, but power brings wealth and, even, in the long run, high caste position. Among the mechanism generating *power out of class* are the poverty of the mass of the villagers, giving them a desperate need for petty favours from the well-to-do, thus tying them to the latter as clients. The ability of only the well-to-do to afford court costs and lawyers, and, thus, their access to the use of threat of legal suits as a sanction against other villagers is usually real. The well-to-do are able to supply services (such as transportation vehicles) to local community development officials, which the latter need to get their work done. The income advantage of the local well-to-do over government officials, gives them the ability to bribe. Government officials are often integrated into the local elite either by their recruitment from this group itself, or by the (illegal) purchase of land. The ability of the well-to-do to travel to government offices to gain information, shepherd applications through bureaucratic channels, are additional factors that help to make them powerful, and pressure officials. There is finally almost an unbridgeable gap in culture between the mass of villagers, the majority of whom have little education and are often illiterate, and government officials, most of whom are educated and often have cosmopolitan (urban) backgrounds. It becomes very difficult therefore for the latter to empathize with the former. This gives the local elite a monopoly on culture and local recreational facilities, from which they are able to exclude recalcitrant government officials. Among the mechanisms generating *power out of caste* are the possession by the upper castes of houses (through inheritance) in which government officials must stay when visiting the countryside, since there are no inns (again, a consequence of poverty), and since most other villagers do not have adequate housing. Most government officials besides, are upper caste and, thus, are differentially sympathetic to that stratum. The upper castes also have wider contacts due to their pattern of marriage, giving them greater access to knowledge and an increased ability to travel to urban areas where government offices are located. Among the mechanism generating *class and caste out of power* are the ability of those with power to encroach on the land of others without fear of legal sanction; the ability to monopolize water from government irrigation works; and the ability of numerically dominant and wealthy castes to compel villagers to re-evaluate their status position.

In sum, then, rural society in the study area is steeply stratified along all three dimensions of class, status, and power, and these closely coincide. Might not this system, however, be at least somewhat moderated by social mobility over time? According to the empirical evidence the answer is negative. Using mobility data, which are almost unique in quantitative studies of the Indian countryside, three principal conclusions emerge. First, until recently, there has been very little mobility in the villages. Secondly, what recent mobility there has been has largely been not exchange but structural mobility. Exchange mobility is where some persons fall and other rise to replace them, and is the most accurate measure of the openess of a stratification system. In contrast, structural mobility is that resulting from a change in the structure of positions; that is, from an expansion or contraction in the relative proportion of desirable and undesirable slots. Most mobility in the villages has been only of the latter sort. Third, what exchange mobility there has been has strengthened rather than weakened the close association of class, caste, and power; for it consisted principally of the upward mobility of upper-caste families and the downward mobility of lower-caste ones, as the former use their differential access to well-paying non-agricultural jobs and to government services (such as irrigation and modern agricultural inputs) to improve their position. This latter type of mobility has had some importance in recent years, and is leading to a dangerous economic polarization between castes in rural society. It is exactly opposite to the process predicted by many writers, who saw the rise of a new occupational structure as weakening the association between caste and class. In fact, in the one quantitative mobility study we have been able to locate, the author is so strongly influenced by the received theory that he misinterprets his data, which are similar to ours. Modernization is not breaking up the caste system in the study area, but consolidating it.

Let us now turn to village fragmentation. Many writers, and the founders of the Community Development Programme, while sometimes recognizing that most villages are characterized by sharp economic inequalities and by caste, nevertheless felt there was considerable potential for social cohesion. Their arguments run somewhat as follows: most villages are relatively small (consisting of, at most, a few hundred families, so that cohesion-promoting face-to-face interaction is both possible and likely. Most villagers share a common religion, Hinduism, which can bind them together. They are related by ties of kinship to many other members, and wealthy kin feel obligated to help their poorer brethren. While the caste system does partially divide the villages, within castes people feel strong ties and non-kin are strongly motivated to interact across kin boundaries, so that well-to-do caste members help poorer ones. Caste is itself a method of establishing a functional division of labour necessary to the village's health, and upper caste families recognize and appreciate this, thus feeling some obligation to give aid to the lower castes. The very steepness of the economic divisions can promote cohesion by isolating the top families, thus forcing them to interact across kin and caste lines, and by creating a community of poverty among the rest of the villagers, thus eliminating conflicts of interest that might divide them. What we have earlier identified as patron-client relations are in this view relations of unilateral aid by the rich to the poor. And one should expect to find considerable informal interaction among the mass of villagers, including ties of mutual help, and there should be substantial willingness to participate in common community action.

This image of the solidarity of village life in the light of our data is completely false. Religious sentiment is too weak to bind villagers together. In spite of the small size of most villages, villagers do not interact in ways reflecting mutual trust. The villagers told us that such interactions are only those of mutual aid, friendships, and social invitations (excluding invitations to marriages, where all kin and most villagers are invited). In most villages, such interactions are very limited. Furthermore, the factors of class, caste, and kinship do not promote interaction across these boundaries. The contrary is shown by the sciometric data. Thus, class and caste, instead of each giving villagers a basis on which to interact across the boundary of the other, fragment the villagers into a set of segments defined by their intersection and, then, within these segments, barriers of kinship further confine interaction. Furthermore, the data indicate that not even ties of kinship are sufficient to bind persons together. Typically, most kin groups are fragmented into mutually exclusive cliques (in so far as interaction is sufficiently dense to even produce this level of informal organization). The result is that the ties between most villagers are very tenuous, and little mutual aid occurs. Nor do the patron-client relations reflect a feeling of obligation by the well-to-do; the amount of aid given in this manner is very small, and is regarded by those receiving it as based almost entirely on self-interest. Finally, participation in community projects has been very low indeed, and declining. In short, these villages are highly fragmented.

There is, in fact, only one source of cohesion in these villages, and it is radically different from that envisioned by the theorists of cohesion; what one might call cohesion by power. While most villagers are highly disorganized, typically elite families are not, but instead have informal ties of mutual aid, social invitations, and the like, with various other elite families. And these families tend to have large numbers of clients as well. When these elite families are unified on some action, they can, by mobilizing their clients, give a certain uniformity of direction to a community; a cohesion, in effect, based on power. However, even this type of cohesion is rare, for in most villages, the informal ties of elite families do not bind them into a single group. Instead, they tend to be informally organized into two or more competing groups, or factions, hostile and at cross-purposes with one another. For most villages, cohesion even by power does not exist. Fragmentation is absolute.

What accounts for this extreme fragmentation? This is a critical question, not only for the understanding of fragmentation, but of stratification, as well: for were the mass of the villagers to have some cohesion, their organization would permit them to break the monopoly of power held by top families, since they could make up in numbers and collective resources what they lack in individual ones; and this power, in turn, could be used to force a redistribution of access to sources of income and a shift in prestige.

The data so far analysed in the study do not give a complete answer. They do indicate, however, that a large part of the answer lies in the system of stratification itself: in the economic and political inequalities, in the associated poverty of most villagers, and in the caste system. The importance of poverty is shown in part by the fact that informal organization in terms of ties of friendships, social invitations, and the like, systematically decline as one goes down in the class system, with the poorest villagers being virtually without such ties. The importance of economic inequalities is shown in part by the fact that a comparison across villages indicates that informal organization is much lower in highly than in less stratified villages; and the importance of inequalities in power is shown by the frequent cases where the powerful deliberately interfered with attempts of other villagers to organize. The importance of caste is shown, in part, by the fact that of all three sources of division—class, kinship, and caste—caste has the most powerful impact in confirming interaction within its boundaries.

The mechanism through which poverty, economic and political inequality, and caste generate fragmentation are many. Poverty throws most villagers into acute competition with one another, as desperate short-run needs override the long-run advantages of co-operation. It means many villagers have neither the time for friendships, the housing facilities to extend social invitations, nor the means to give aid to others. When combined with economic inequalities, it means most villagers are dependent on the well-to-do for petty favours, a factor further dividing them as they are caught up in the factional in-fighting of the wealthy. The factional in-fighting itself is partly due to these patron-client networks, for they, along with other factors discussed earlier, mean top families can assemble immense power, a fact tempting them to use power as a central method of advancement, thus bringing them into conflict with other elite families. In addition, the inequalities and the associated poverty create an immense cultural gap inhibiting interaction. And finally, the caste system by its very nature is divisive, for by its marriage rules it restricts one of the strongest ties

among people, which is kinship. Besides this, its ritual pollution rule
formally discourage other forms of interaction across caste lines

In sum, rural society in the study area is both highly stratified an
fragmented. Each of the elements of the stratification system—class,
status, power, and mobility—reinforce each other. The stratification
system, in turn, is heavily responsible for the high degree of fragmentation. And the latter, in turn, helps support the steep system of stratification.

The Inimical Impact of Stratification and Fragmentation on Agricultural Progress

This system of social relations clearly hurts the short run welfare and
level of production of the poorer cultivators. It is not possible, however, to jump immediately from this fact to the conclusion that it is
detrimental to agricultural progress.

It can plausibly be argued that such progress may initially require
fairly steep stratification. If adequate resources of land, irrigation,
and capital are required for the adoption of modern inputs and practices, and if these resources are scarce, their equitable distribution
among all villagers could mean that none would have them in sufficient
amounts for meaningful agricultural modernization to take place. If
the modern inputs are themselves scarce—as they, in fact, currently
are— and if an important goal is to maximize agricultural production,
stratification may be necessary to ensure that they get into the hands of
those most able to use them productively. In addition, a growing and
productive urban sector is probably important for agricultural progress. A productive urban sector is important to absorb surplus rural
population and thus prevent debilitating partitioning. A productive
urban sector is important in order to provide ever cheaper consumer
and producer goods (e.g., clothes, implements) for cultivators, thus
freeing their income for investment in other inputs. This is also important for advances in basic science that underlie long-run technical advances in agriculture. But if resources and inputs are too equitably
distributed, farms might be too small and unproductive to do more than
feed their operators, thus leaving no surplus for the urban sector.
Finally, as these arguments show, even though detrimental to the
short-run welfare of the rural poor, stratification may be necessary
for their long-run welfare. In the long run, poorer farmers can benefit
from cheaper goods produced by the urban sector and more powerful
agricultural technology. Poor labourers might likewise gain from

cheaper food (their main consumer good), and increasing number of jobs in agriculture as it becomes intensified through the adoption of better inputs and practices. They can also migrate to urban jobs.

In short, it is by no means obvious that stratification (in so far as it is an inescapable concommitant), and fragmentation, are damaging to agricultural progress. Only empirical investigation can throw light on the reality of the situation. The steep system of stratification and fragmentation, according to empirical evidence in the study area, has a purely negative effect. Furthermore, each of the components of the stratification system—class, status, power, and mobility—individually contribute to this, as does, also, fragmentation. Each of these elements, therefore, shall be taken up separately, with power reserved for last, since in some sense its impact is the most detrimental of all.

Class

The central conclusion here is that not only are economic resources much more unequally distributed than can be justified by their scarcity. The poorer cultivators are unnecessarily deprived of the resources they need, to adopt modern inputs and practices. Besides, this unequal distribution is itself partly responsible for the scarcity which already exists, and creates a situation in which not only those at the bottom of the system but those with the most assets also fail to use scarce inputs productively.

The conclusion rests on the following propositions, each demonstrated by the data.

The resources of land, irrigation, and capital are all critical to adoption, with each being especially important for certain items. Land is particularly important for crop diversification, since, where plots are too small or few, crops compete with one another for space, and there is insufficient diversity of soil conditions. Irrigation is particularly important for HYV seeds. Savings, or the ability to borrow at reasonable interest rates, are also important for chemical fertilizers which are expensive. Carts are important both for crop diversification and fertilizer, since many crops are bulky and must be transported to market by the cultivator himself, and fertilizer is heavy, and must be transported from town to field.

Nearly one-third of the cultivators have so few of these resources as to be virtually incapable of adopting modern inputs and practices, and many more are sufficiently deprived to find adoption very difficult. This, then, is a major reason for the low level of adoption.

The deprivation of resources cannot be justified by their scarcity. Land, irrigation, and capital are all somewhat scarce in the study area. Thus, it is probably true that their equitable distribution among all villagers—including the landless—would yield farms too small for adoption and surplus production for urban areas. However, their more equitable distribution among those currently with land—that is among the cultivators alone—would not. A farm of 10 unirrigated or 5 irrigated acres (hereafter termed an 'economic size' farm) is sufficiently large to permit both adoption and a substantial surplus; the sale of the latter helping to finance the former. Currently, only one farm in three attains this size. Such is the extreme degree of concentration on land and access to irrigation that an equitable distribution of these resources among the cultivators would bring virtually all farms up to this standard; a near tripling. This, furthermore, assumes no expansion in the amount of irrigated land. But irrigation, unlike land, cannot be regarded as a fixed resource. The resource on which irrigation is based—water—is not scarce in the study area. Rainfall and the water table are such that most land could be irrigated. At present only half the land is irrigated and much of that, poorly. Were all land irrigated, not only could all current cultivators have economic size farms, but one-third of the landless families, as well. Such an extension of irrigation depends on making the necessary investments in tubewells, river pumps and the like. That is, it is essentially a matter of capital. How scarce, then, is capital? The answer is that while it is somewhat scarce, it is considerably less scarce than might appear from the prevailing high interest rates. These rates are less a result of capital scarcity than of the stratification system itself, which by depriving so many cultivators of adequate resources, makes production loans to them risky. This forces many villagers to desperately borrow for consumption and to accept whatever rate is charged. That capital is not as scarce as it appears to be was demonstrated during a peasant uprising when just three families in one village deposited, for safety, enough funds in a regional bank to have irrigated the total village. More generally, were resources redistributed so that all cultivators could have economic size farms, much of the capital needed could have been generated from within their own operations, and the sustained viability of their farms would mean that the rest could be raised from loans with low interest.

The existing highly unequal distribution of resources has the paradoxical effect of lowering the level of adoption not only of those cultivators at the bottom of the stratification system, but of those at the top, as well. A critical feature of this system is that many of the larger farmers either simultaneously hold an elite non-farm job, or engage in money lending, or both. These activities distract them from agriculture. As a result, they exhibit low levels of adoption of HYV seed and crop diversification, as these require considerable attention. They concentrate instead on chemical fertilizers, which can be used in a casual fashion with traditional crops. The failure to adopt HYV seeds is a major depressant on production, since elite job holders and money-lenders between them hold nearly half of all irrigated land, the land on which HYV seeds can be most productively used. These persons are, also, holders of some of the largest plots of land, on which crop diversification can best be practised. As for fertilizer, the fact that they do adopt this simply means that this scarce input is used not where it would do the most good—that is, in combination with HYV seeds and multiple crops, but on traditional rice. This distraction from agriculture, also, means that where these large farmers do not yet have access to irrigation (true for over 40 per cent), either because they are not on the canal system, or because a traditional pond has silted up, they fail to use their sizeable capital to invest in tubewells, thus holding down the level of irrigation. In some cases, the attraction of elite non-farm jobs in the towns has led larger farmers to abandon agriculture altogether and migrate without, however, selling their land. Where these farmers have been owners of traditional ponds, from which other villagers have drawn water, the tendency has been to let the ponds deteriorate, again adversely affecting the level of irrigation. In addition, moneylenders often acquire bonded cultivators as *de facto* labourers (one out of every eight cultivators were in this category). This type of work force inhibits the adoption of modern inputs and practices for several reasons. For instance, it cannot be trusted to cultivate carefully, and to use rather than to sell fertilizer, or to turn over crops to the moneylender-landlord, rather than covertly selling or consuming them. Thus, the moneylender-landlord is motivated to have his bonded cultivators grow only traditional crops, since they require less care; only one or two crops, so he can keep account of them; and to do so without expensive inputs. A natural choice is traditional rice, cultivated without chemical fertilizers. Finally, moneylenders and elite job holders are among the best educated elements of the population, and those with the greatest managerial skills. All these processes, thus, mean that scarce inputs are diverted from, rather than directed to, those with the greatest potential capacity in terms of land, irrigation, capital, and skills.

Status

The caste system strongly biases community development personnel toward upper caste cultivators, both in terms of contact, and in terms of access to modern inputs, loans, and direct financial aid. The result is that upper caste cultivators with low motivation to efficiently use advice and modern inputs, or with inadequate resources to do so, nevertheless often get these, while lower caste cultivators with high motivation and adequate resources often do not. In addition, the caste bias in contact combines with an equally strong bias by economic class to confine the contact of officials to a very narrow segment of village society, with the result that officials mis-perceive the motives of the bulk of the villagers with the negative consequences for agriculture.

Social Mobility

Mobility process is one in which upper caste persons use differential access to good non-agricultural jobs to purchase land. Land is in this way increasingly placed in the hands of those whose non-agricultural experience distracts them away from agriculture, thus lowering adoption.

Fragmentation

Fragmentation hurts agricultural progress in two principal ways. First, many studies have shown that adoption is often the outcome of a process of diffusion through friendship and other personal networks. Fragmentation, by breaking such networks, inhibits this type of diffusion. Second, in a situation of scarce resources, these resources can be expanded through co-operation. This is a central purpose of credit co-operatives, to purchase river pumps, and the like, as well as many community projects, etc. thus, expanding human capital. Fragmentation has been a major barrier to successful co-operative efforts of these sorts. This is shown by the fact that formal co-operative efforts went farthest in those villages where fragmentation (in terms of informal networks of friendships, social invitations, and the like) was least, or where a 'cohesion by power' existed. Only rarely, however, was fragmentation sufficiently absent in even these villages for co-operative efforts to be carried forward to successful completion.

Power

This dimension has been left to the last because in some sense it is the most fundamental. To begin with, to an important extent, income in the study area is earned through the exercise of power. As a result, among the very top farmers, those with the most irrigated land, over half have turned to almost full time political work, with the result that they have adopted almost no modern inputs or practices. Next, the qualitative data is permeated with examples where those with local power have unwarrantably denied others access to crucial resources and inputs, for instance, by persuading fertilizer dealers to deny fertilizer to members of rival factions; by failing to share the fertilizer they had been given by community development officials to transport to their villages for distribution; by refusing to permit water to flow through irrigation channels to cultivators legally entitled to that water; and the like. Closely related to this, is the fact that those with power have repeatedly appropriated for their own use funds generated by co-operatives, thus destroying them, and rendering villagers increasingly cynical about the possibilities of common action. There are also instances where they have deliberately prevented even the initial efforts of villagers to organize, for fear that such organization will undermine their power. Finally, and most fundamental of all, this concentration of power is heavily responsible for the failures in government policies and practices, that is, for the failure of the government to provide an adequate infrastructure for agriculture. The process here is straightforward. First, village elites do not find the absence of this infrastructure particularly onerous, for they have the capita to independently acquire irrigation (in the form of tubewells), if they want it; they have the power to acquire modern inputs even if they are scarce; they have the vehicles permitting transportation even if roads are poor; and many have no special commitment to agriculture, for reasons already given. Second, not only is the absence of this infrastructure not particularly onerous, but in certain ways, they benefit from it. It permits the earning of high income through moneylending; the monopolization of skills permitting privileged access to top non-farm jobs; the acquisition of land as smaller cultivators fail; and the maintenance of local political power in part by collusion with or by control over government officials. Third, as the only persons with much capital and income, it is they who would largely have to pay (in the form taxes) for the necessary changes. In short, their interests do not lie with a massive effort to provide an adequate infrastructure; neither with the expenditures it would take to finance it, nor with the correction of the deficiencies in the government bureaucracy—in terms of efficiency, competehce, honesty, and impartiality—that would be required to maximize the impact of these expenditures. Fourth, and last, the concentration of power in their hands means that they have the ability to see that their interests are realized. Thus, the failures of government policies and practices are, in fact, partly reducible to the steep system of stratification and fragmentation itself.

In sum, this system is absolutely deterimental to agricultural progress. Not only are resources not as scarce to justify sharp inequalities in their distribution, but the impact of these inequalities is to lower the adoption of those at the top of the system, as well. Not only does the system fail to ensure that scarce inputs get into the hands of those most able to use them productively, it hasa powerful negative impact. . . . The absence of adequate infrastructure also means inadequate agricultural research, and an inadequate network of roads to connect cultivators to urban markets. The steep system of stratification and fragmentation, thus, means not more adoption of modern inputs, but less; not more production, but less; not more surplus to urban areas, but less; not more technical progress in agriculture, but less; and it hurts not only the short-term welfare of the rural poor, but their long-term welfare as well.

Mobility and Conflict:
Social Roots of Caste Violence in Bihar

PRADIP KUMAR BOSE

The incidence of caste violence in recent times have not been confined to rural areas only, but have taken place in urban areas as well. While the recent incidents of caste violence in Gujarat and Maharashtra took place predominantly in urban localities, in Uttar Pradesh and Bihar, for example, it occurred mostly in rural regions. In other words, for different reasons, the incidence of caste violence cuts across the boundaries defined as rural or urban. The structural dimensions of caste violence have been discussed quite extensively in the recent literature on caste and class. Factors like social stratification, mutual reinforcements of social and economic inequalities, and culture and ideology of repression in promoting and aggravating tensions, are by now quite well known. In this paper we shall try to focus on one significant aspect of rural caste violence, namely, the course of mobility different castes have adopted and its relationship with caste violence, by taking the case of Bihar as an example.

The occurrences of urban caste violence, as for example in Gujarat and Maharashtra, were related to the mobility of the Scheduled Castes. As studies have shown, violence was associated with the increasing urbanization, literacy, and entry into government services by a particular section of Scheduled Castes like the Vankars and the Mahars and it

Excerpted from Pradip Kumar Bose, 'Mobility and Conflict: Social Roots of Caste Violence in Bihar', in *Caste, Caste Conflict and Reservations*, Ajanta, Delhi, 1985.

was these castes who were the main targets of attack during the caste riots. In the rural areas of northern and eastern India, caste violence, as we shall try to show in this paper, is associated with the mobility of the backward castes and especially in the case of Bihar, with the mobility of castes like the Yadavs, the Kurmis and the Koeris.

In Indian sociological literature, the various mobility courses that castes, lower in the hierarchy, have adopted for improving their status are characterized as Sanskritization. But there seem to be at least two distinct courses, which need to be differentiated. In the one, caste mobility depended upon gaining access to some source of wealth, substantiated by a plausible genealogy and also by mobilizing caste groups by forming caste associations and by petitioning and appealing to the colonial administrators to change the status of castes in the decennial census. The attitude of these caste groups was totally loyalist to colonial rulers because their primary intention was to *consolidate* their social status after improving their economic position. As a result these caste groups maintained their separation from equivalent castes whose economic status was lower. . . . In Bihar, examples of such castes are the Kayasthas and the Bhumihars.

Figure 1
Two Types of Mobility Courses

Due to improved economic status	Due to deteriorated economic status
Loyalty to the ruling class	Antagonistic towards the ruling class
Perpetuation of existing economic relations	Removal of existing economic relations
Separation from other castes	Association with other castes
Consolidation of social status	Assertion of social status

The other mobility course has its roots in exploitation. These caste mobility movements represented economic grievances and deprivations. Here the caste groups favoured association with other equivalent caste groups, were antagonistic to colonial rulers and wanted to change the existing economic relations. In contrast to our emphasis on 'consolidation' for the first group, we can call this mobility movement, a movement of *assertion*. In Bihar, the movements by the Yadavs, Kurmis and Koeris are examples of such a mobility course. Figure 1 represents in a schematic fashion, the two mobility courses.

Mobility for Consolidation

Bihar is the second largest state in the country in terms of population and density of population. Around 8.7 per cent of the total population live in villages and the percentage of urban population is only 12.5 per cent. The caste-wise distribution of the population is shown inTable 1, which shows that altogether the backward castes constitute about 51.3 per cent of the state's population of which about one-third (18.7 per cent) are Yadavs, Kurmis and Koeris—who can be called the upper backwards on the basis of their political and economic successes in contrast to the lower backwards. Taking a rough guide from the 1911 Census, we find that only in a few areas of Bihar are the upper castes, namely, the Brahmins, Bhumihars, Rajputs and Kayasthas in sizeable numbers; they form over 25 per cent of the total population only in parts of Bhojpur, Saran, Aurangabad, Patna, Rohtak and Siwan Districts. For the most part, however, they collectively amount to between 5 and 15 per cent of the population. Instead it is backward castes that form a majority group in most of the states, and the Yadavs alone account for over 25 per cent of the population in districts like Bhagalpur, Gaya, Hazaribagh, Patna, Saharsa, Saran and Vaishali. Taken together with the Kurmis and Koeris, they amount to over 30 per cent in larger pockets of Giridih, Nalanda and Rohtas Districts, in addition to those just named.

If the Rajputs, Brahmins and Bhumihars were identified as the zamindari caste of Bihar in the past, the Ahirs, Kurmis and Koeris could be categorized as the tenants and small cultivating castes, and other Untouchable and depressed castes (especially the Chamars and the Dusadhs) as providers of menial and agricultural labour. The Bhumihars have been landholders in Bihar and most of the big zamindaris of Bihar, namely, Bettiah, Amawna, Hathwa, Tekari, Maksudhpur, Madhnaan, Sursand, etc., were under the Bhumihars. The percentage of landless labourers among them was quite small. Though the Bhumihars were economically powerful, they never enjoyed a very high rank in the social hierarchy.

The Census of 1901, while classifying the castes according to the four *varnas*, recorded the Bhumihars and the Kayasthas as equivalent to the backward castes like the Yadavs, Kurmis and Koeris, making them socially lower than the Rajputs and Brahmins. This was immediately resented by the Bhumihars and the Kayasthas and the richest among them began agitating for the upliftment of their caste status. To substantiate the higher ranking of the Bhumihars, Swami Sahajanand

Saraswati scanned Sanskrit texts to show that the Bhumihars were actually Brahmins by *varna*. In the annual session of Akhil Bhartiya Bhumihar Brahman Sabha in 1914, he played a leading role and declared that the agriculturist Bhumihars were superior to priestly Brahmins and

Table 1
Major Caste Groups in Bihar

	Caste	*Per cent of Total Population*
Upper Castes	Brahmin	4.7
	Bhumihar	2.9
	Rajput	4.2
	Kayastha	1.2
	Sub Total:	13.0
Upper Backwards	Bania	0.6
	Yadav	11.0
	Kurmi	3.6
	Koeri	4.1
	Sub Total:	19.3
Lower Backwards	Barni	1.0
	Dhanuk	1.8
	Hajjam	1.4
	Kahar	1.7
	Kandu	1.6
	Kumhar	1.3
	Lohar	1.3
	Mullah	1.5
	Tatwa	1.6
	Teli	2.8
	Others	16.0
	Sub Total:	32.0
Scheduled Castes		14.4
Scheduled Tribes		9.1
Muslims		12.5
	Grand Total :	100.0

Source: Adapted from Blair (1980 : 65).

wrote in 1916 a voluminous book *Bhumihar Brahman Parichaya*. After some time, around 1924, he revised his views and exhorted the Bhumihars to take up priestly functions. He called this movement *Purohiti Andolan*. The caste association of the Bhumihars in the beginning was confined to the big landlords and it championed their cause. It was loyal to the colonial rulers and the higher-ups in the government attended and addressed its annual sessions. This movement towards higher social ranking among the Bhumihars resulted during the 1931 Census in the transfer of a significant chunk of the Bhumihar population to the fold of the Brahmins and this caste recorded an actual decrease of 8.5 per cent during 1921-31 period. According to the census reports the loss sustained was unreal and was caused by a wholesale transference of the Bhumihars to the Brahmin caste.

The mobility course adopted by the Bhumihars has all the elements described in the foregoing section: strong economic position, claim supported by evidence from the Shastras of higher status, loyalty to the ruling class, and compliance with the colonial administrators in continuing the economic relationship which made them acquire wealth. The leadership of the caste association was in the hands of the English educated elites supported by zamindars and they made their best efforts to make their association pro-British in which they received encouragement from the British Government. For instance, the Bhumihar Brahmin Sabha was addressed by the Viceroy in 1922, and in the same meeting tenancy reform moves were opposed. In this context it is useful to mention that by viewing caste categories as units of patronage and proscription, for the award or denial of favours (e.g. public employment and political representation), the colonial administration evoked a predictable response from these castes. Those seeking patronage or protesting proscription had to speak in the name of a bureaucratically recognized category; favour had to be courted and attempts to project a favourable image had to be launched in the name of the category. For instance, like the Bhumihars, the Kayasthas also realized quite early their total dependence upon the goodwill of the government for favours to come. Following the 1894 conference session, 'A Kayastha' wrote to the *Pioneer*.

The Kayastha conference held during the last Christmas week at Benaras, was a monument of that community's loyalty to the British Government. . . . [The Kayasthas] have, as a nation, kept aloof from sedition and agitation. The Kayasthas have invariably been the foremost in supporting the Government. May I therefore ask whether the Government does not think it advisable to order a more extended employment of this community in positions of trust and responsibility, which is surely second to none in its allegiance to the British throne (cited in Caroll 1978 : 245).

The government's mediation in the distribution of patronage through caste categories was also an important factor which enabled these caste groups to elevate themselves in status ranking. . . . A small section of the elite, besides attempting to consolidate its position in terms of social ranking, was also claiming political posts and jobs, to further consolidate itself in the bureaucracy and politics. The dominance of upper castes in the economy and in politics continued in the thirties and forties and as long as the Congress ministry remained in power, there was no attempt to weaken the economic power of the landlords. The landlords of two castes, the Bhumihar and the Rajput, fought between themselves for power and patronage. During the early phase of the post-independence era, the government of Bihar had been either comprised of or strongly influenced by, shifted coalitions of landholding castes (notably Brahmins, Bhumihars and Rajputs) who had little incentive to pursue reforms that might limit their own rights and prerogatives. It is these castes, as we shall see below, who took the lead in suppressing the struggles of the backward castes in the 1920s.

Mobility for Assertion

The causes and nature of the mobility course of the backward castes like the Yadavs, Kurmis, Koeris were vastly different from that described above. As we have mentioned earlier, most of the members of these castes were tenants. Previously the relationship between zamindars and tenants was mainly governed by the upper-caste backward-caste social relations. By the end of the last century, tenancy acts were passed recognizing the rights of tenants *vis-à--vis* the zamindars, and in consequence, the zamindars

turned more hostile to the cause of the tenants. A large number of zamindars, turned absentee and were interested only in the realization of rents. Irrigation facilities in villages stopped functioning because of the lack of maintenance. Subinfeudation and rack-renting worsened the plight of the tenants. The zamindars and their employees let loose an orgy of repression. As a result, the tenants lost their respect for the zamindars and . . . the upper castes (Sengupta 1979 : 89).

The mobility movement of the backward castes in the twenties was in essence an expression of their resentment against their pitiable

socio-economic condition. Through these mobility movements the
tenant farmers attempted to abolish the local authority and the economic tyranny of the landlords who over and above the legal rent
demanded *abwabs* (extra-legal cesses), *nazrana* (tribute for renewal of
tenancy), *begar* (forced labour) and various other non-economic privileges. The Ahir (Goala) movement which developed around 1914 was
described in 1921 as the most important of the lower-caste associations
and movements for social upliftment that had arisen in Bihar. A report
from the Patna Division mentions various instructions that the Goalas
had laid down for their community at a series of meetings. These included the wearing of sacred thread, an end to the practice of early
marriage, refusal to perform *begar* for zamindars, to open shops of
their own, discontinuation of the sale of *chipris* (cow-dug cake), milk,
curds, etc. except at bazar rates to their landlords and the maintenance
of unity among themselves (Jha 1977 : 550). This movement was not
confined to the Yadavs alone but embraced gradually other backward-
castes who also began agitating for reform. As a report of 1923 notes,

Inside the Hindu community, the efforts of the lower castes to improve their
status led to considerable friction, and occasional disturbances. Goalas,
Koeris and Boviasis [*sic*] in the Muzaffarpur District attempted to assume
the sacred thread, while in Mankhum the Kurmi Mahtos combined with a
view to the advancement of their caste. The only movement which had any
organization, however, was that of the Goalas who sought to improve the education and prospects of their members, and secure representation of their interest in local bodies (cited in Das 1983 : 71-2).

The claims of the backward castes to upper caste status, their refusal
to render any unpaid labour and sell their products at reduced rates to
landlords and moneylenders, their demands for occupancy rights over
their land, stoppage of menial services and payment of *abwabs*, etc., led
to violent reactions on the part of landlords and moneylenders mostly
belonging to upper castes and resulted in caste riots. The landlords
started a counter or anti-Goala movement and sought the co-operation
of other high castes on the plea that the Goalas had taken to wearing the
sacred thread. Though the pretext of the anti-Goala movement was the
violation by the Ahirs of the existing ritual norm, steps taken against
them were aimed at crippling them economically. As one report
mentions,

The reprisals taken against *Goalas* by the landlords were (1) to deprive them
of the Khud Kast Lands and to turn them out of their houses on the ground

that the houses belonged to the landlords (2) refusal to allow their cattle to use the ordinary grazing grounds and to take water at the ordinary drinking tanks, and (3) complete social boycott . . . . (Jha 1977: 551; emphasis in original).

The opposition only served to make the Goalas more determined than ever. For instance, in Kiul, when the Bhumihar landlords refused to allow the Goalas to hold a meeting a riot broke out. The report by a DIG of Bihar notes,

The *Babhans* (Bhumihars) intended to break it up ostensibly because the *Goalas* were conspiring to adopt certain privileges peculiar to the higher castes as for instance the wearing of the sacred thread. This was the ostensible motive. The true motive is that there is a movement amongst the Goalas to resist certain reaction's of their *zamindars* (Jha 1977: 552; emphasis in original).

In other words, the mobility course attempted by the backward castes was a means to get rid of social and economic oppression and to assert their legitimate rights. Such attempts were resisted by the upper caste zamindars mainly to protect their own vested interests. The efforts of the backward castes to ascent the social scale threatened the economic and social interests of the upper caste zamindars and their appropriation of social surplus. Jha (1977: 557) rightly notes that

It was the economic and social oppression, rather than the economic prosperity, that led to peasants of lower castes in general and Yadavs in particular in Bihar during the early 1920s to start the process of Sanskritizing themselves.

Of Bihar of the 1920s which was precapitalist in nature, we can say following Lukacs (1971: 55),

. . . class interests in precapitalist society never achieve full (economic) articulation. Hence the structuring of society into castes and estates means that economic elements are inextricably joined to political and religious factors.

Therefore the mobility movement was linked to ritual purification as well as to social oppression.

As the thirties drew to a close the Ahirs, Kurmis and Koeris were bridging their social distance and joining together in a broader unity.

Subsequently, in 1934, the Triveni Sangh was formed, which symbolized the unit of the Ahirs, Kurmis and the Koeris. Its aims were broad and comprehensive:

fostering solidarity among different sections of the caste community, participation in democratic politics, opposing and retailing upper caste tyranny like *corvee, begar,* rape and social ostracisms (Mukherjee and Yadav 1980: 27-8).

Within two years the Triveni Sangh became a sizeable force with membership of around 10 lakhs of backward caste people. Class themes began emerging in the organization when the ideologues defined the Sangh as an organization incorporating the aspirations of *kisans, mazdoors* and small traders. This horizontal extension of localized caste segments, and the formation of associations comprising different *jatis*—the Ahirs, Kurmis and Koeris as in the case of Triveni Sangh in Bihar—were elementary forms of class organization. Colonialism thus created the material base for class formation, but the same colonialism, having arrested the organic growth of the economy, could not transform fully the nature of interest articulation. As a result, caste identities got dominance and caste associations flourished. The Triveni Sangh, instead of launching militant struggles against the landlords, chose to take part in elections and lost in the 1930-1 district board elections. In the 1937 elections it again tried to form a coalition with the Congress, but after being ditched by them, it decided to fight elections alone and lost again. In the next eight years,

Triveni Sangh-Congress conflict took its toll. The composition of the Sangh leadership did considerable damage. Most of its leaders came from an educated, propertied class which could only elicit a limited caste response despite its secular character. In the eyes of other backward-caste sections it slowly came to be viewed solely as an Ahir-Koeri-Kurmi syndicate. A caste response to an essentially class problem—the underlying theme of *abwabs, begar,* landlessness (*bakasht*) and social ostracism—thus failed to unhinge the Congress from its base of support. By 1946, its absorption in the Congress was nearly completed (Mukherjee and Yadav 1980: 31-72).

This elementary form of class organization failed to take off also because the Kisan Sabha movement could not draw the peasants belonging to the backward castes to its fold. Hauser (1961) has mentioned that, 'socially, the Kisan Sabha leadership was predominantly Bhumihar. . . . Economically, the Kisan Sabha leaders were primarily from landholding families'(cited in Jha 1977 : 558).

In 1944 Swami Sahajanand, the founder of the Kisan Sabha, himself admitted that the middle and big cultivators

are using the Kisan Sabha for their benefit and gain, while we are using or rather trying to use them to strengthen the Sabha, till the lowest strata of the peasantry are awakened to their real economic and political interests and needs and have become class conscious. . . . It is they, the semi-proletariat or the agricultural labourers . . . who are the Kisans of our thinking . . . and who make and constitute the Kisan Sabha ultimately (cited in Das 1983 : 137-8).

This, however, did not happen in his lifetime. During this period there took place a number of conflicts among cultivators, landless labourers and landlords on the question of occupancy rights, sharecropping and the *bakast* land. As the Kisan Sabha movement was not well organized and failed to bring all sections of the peasantry into its fold, the only alternative the peasants could resort to was to express their grievances through their respective caste associations.

The struggle launched by these backward castes as a subaltern group in the pre-independence period, changed its course in the post-independence era. As we shall show below, the main perpetrators of violence against the Harijans in the seventies and eighties were these backward castes who had themselves followed a mobility course which included violence. It is a section of these backward castes who became politically and economically powerful during the sixties and it was those who became rich peasants from tenant farmers and had consolidated their economic position who were most aggressive against the labourers.

The Backward Castes and the Upper Castes after Independence

We have mentioned above that in the pre-independence period power within the Congress remained in the hands of the landholders who were not prepared to commit themselves to far-reaching agrarian reforms. Even after independence radical language on-land policy followed by conservative action became standard practice followed by the Congress especially in Bihar. Bihar assumes special significance because it was the first state to initiate agrarian reforms through the enactment of a legislation to abolish the zamindari system, and possibly least successful of all in implementing that and other agrarian reforms. As Jannuzi writes : "Nowhere in contemporary India is the gulf

between articulated ideas with respect to agrarian reforms and solid ac-
complishment more conspicuous than in Bihar' (Jannuzi 1977: 209). He
shows that reforms in Bihar have not led to redistribution of land resources in a significant manner nor reduced the number of landless
agricultural labourers. Nor have the reforms contributed to a lessening
of tensions between the landowning peasants and landless labourers
(Jannuzi 1974). The green revolution benefited the *raiyats* having operational holdings of 15 acres or more. This was clearly evident in
Bihar in 1970 where government officials made no effort to disguise the
fact that landholders with 24 acres or more had been deriving the major
part of benefits from the state's agricultural development activities.
At the same time the conditions of the agricultural labourers deteriorated sharply. Jannuzi writes:

During field investigations in Bihar, in regions . . . experiencing increases in
agricultural output attributed to 'new technology in agriculture' the author
noted numerous instances in which wages for labour had remained static since
1957. Increased wages for labour, when reported, generally reflected the
prevailing inflated market price for wage in kind, and did not represent an
increase in real income for agricultural labourers living at subsistence levels
(Jannuzi 1974: 166).

Within these limitations of land reform and development programmes, a new section of rich peasants and urban bourgeoisie emerged
from the Yadavs, Kurmis and Koeris. The class of capitalist landlords and rich farmers in Bihar, as a result, contains disparate elements
evolving from *both* of what Lenin considered as the two alternative
historical forms of agrarian development (what he called the 'American' and the 'Prussian' paths): upwardly mobile peasant farmers who
have had a long history of direct cultivation (often as tenants) and now
expanding through buying and leasing in land from absentee or small
landowners, and erstwhile non-cultivating landlords converting themselves—somewhat in Junker-style—into a group of active farmers as
the new technology and pliant government policies (of low taxation,
high support prices and liberal provision of credit and subsidized inputs) made cultivation a more profitable proposition than rack-renting.
While the Yadavs, Kurmis, Koeris belong to the first group of landlords, the Bhumihars and Rajputs belong to the second. Again, these
backward castes improved their positions because with the development
of transport and communication, vegetable growers, dairy farmers and
sellers of milk and milk products among them could make money. They

built cold storages, opened shops in towns and cities, purchased land and entered into trades.

The rising economic power of the backward castes was gradually reflected in the political arena as well. On the one hand the backward castes competed for a greater share in bureaucracy and for the job market with the upper castes; on the other hand they attempted to establish their hegemony over the agricultural labourers belonging mostly to the Untouchable castes whose discontent was rising.

Before 1952 voting rights in Bihar were based on property or educational qualifications and political power was the monopoly of the upper castes, particularly the Kayasthas, Rajputs and Bhumihars. With the adoption of adult franchise, backward castes became politically important because of their numerical superiority. The Socialist party founded by Ram Manohar Lohia first realized the importance of the backward castes and mobilized them into the party. The Congress party also started sympathizing with the backward caste sentiments. The articulation of the sentiments of the backward castes during the tenure of Chief Minister K.B. Sahay in the 1960s and, more especially, since the time of the distribution of Congress tickets for the general elections of 1967 helped to mobilize the backward castes of the state. Naturally the Yadavs, Kurmis and Koeris being more advanced economically and better organized were first to respond to such opportunities and were able to gain important leadership posts, but still there was a good deal of time lag between political awakening and the acquisition of real political power. Though in the late 1960s and early 1970s, several chief ministers belonged to the backward castes, they were primarily compromise candidates of the various factions, and behaved as such. It was not until the late 1970s that these backward castes became really powerful politically and Karpoori Thakur was able to unite them on the basis of a common policy, that of reservation.

This is also evident from the election figures. Caste breakdown of the general seats in the Bihar Legislative Assembly over the 1962-7 period depicts

the familiar story of upper caste domination in the early years, when well over half of the MLAs from non-reserved seats belonged to the four 'twice-born' castes. The pattern maintained itself through the 1967 and 1969 elections, and even down to the period of Emergency, when fully 54.8 per cent of the MLAs from general seats were Forwards [i.e. upper castes] as against 16.5 per cent of the non-Scheduled population. The 1977 election meant a noticeable decline in the Forwards' representation, to 48.6 per cent. ... As the

Forwards declined in strength, the Backwards grew (Blair 1980 : 67), and the Yadavs by 1977 became the second largest group in the assembly next only to the Rajputs.

On the issue of reservation for backward castes, as we have already mentioned, the three backward castes were competing with the upper castes for greater power and privileges. In Bihar the backward community consists of 51.3 per cent of the state's population, of which about one-third (18.7 per cent) are the Yadavs, Kurmis and Koeris. The list of backward classes was first prepared in 1951, which contained a list of 128 castes. However, due to the dominance of upper castes in Bihar politics the backward caste issue was never taken seriously by the powers that were at that time. In the 1970s this issue could no longer be ignored. The government of Bihar appointed a new commission in December, 1977 headed by Mungeri Lal. The new body submitted its final report in February 1976 settling on a new list of 128 castes. Essentially the 128 castes were the same ones as in the earlier version, augmented by some Christian groups. Promulgated in the autumn of 1978 by Karpoori Thakur the reservation policy asserted that in addition to the quotas on government employment already reserved for the Harijans and Adivasis (24 per cent if taken together) 26 per cent of new government positions would be reserved for the backward classes. This reservation policy caused widespread violence and riots and was protested against strongly by the upper castes. Through the reservation issue Karpoori Thakur attempted to make the point that the backward castes had displaced the upper castes as the dominant force in Bihar politics and that the old days of dominance were gone forever and that his government would be one based on the support of the backward castes. The upper castes also interpreted things this way fearing that their days of dominance might indeed have departed and responded with a volatile mixture of fear and rage.

The government recognition of caste as a category for privileges and concessions in the post-independence period, added a new dimension to the caste-based association. For instance, the Awadhias of Patna, the Dhanukas of north Bihar and the Mahatos of Chota-Nagpur are distinct castes and intermarriage among them is not the practice. But as Sengupta (1979: 86) writes,

While participating in politics they regard themselves as a single caste named 'Kurmi' or a still more broadbased one— 'Backward'. The Kurmi in the political arena is a very different entity from the traditional Kurmi caste, and it

is as much a caste grouping as it is 'Backward'. In consecutive caste Mahas-
abhas and conferences the Kurmis widened their group by including others
like Mahatos of Chotanagpur, Marathas, or Kunbis, some of whom were not
even aware of one another. Today they are described as subcastes of Kurmis.
Yadavs constitute another important example of such grouped caste.

In other words, caste became a category with no specific limits and
could be expanded and contracted according to the needs of the time.
It was used more as a mobilizer for gaining economic and political
privileges by the backward castes. The fall-out of this government
policy of mediation in distribution of benefits through caste categories
was the same as during the colonial rule, only the contending castes
were different.

The Backward Castes and the Harijans

While the backward castes struggles against the upper castes were
mostly confined to the electoral arena, legislative assembly, etc., for
the enforcement of certain policies beneficial to them, at the village
level, a more violent repression was perpetrated by them to suppress
the discontents and grievances of the agricultural labourers, of which
nearly half belonged to the Scheduled Castes. According to the census figures, the proportion of agricultural labourers rose from 28 per
cent in 1951 to 39 per cent in 1971. In absolute number the increase
was from 31 lakhs to 68 lakhs. No wonder, the struggle of this class has
become so frequent of late. The backward castes in the recent past have
burnt the Harijans alive, murdered vocal leaders among them, killed
their sympathizers, and razed their dwellings to tighten their own hold
on the castes which were below them to get absolute control over
their labour power. Table 2 shows that in most of the cases of major
caste violence that occurred in the recent past in Bihar, it was mostly
the Yadavs and Kurmis who were the perpetrators of violence against
the Harijans. For instance, in Bishrampur, where several landless agricultural labourers were burnt alive by the Kurmis in 1978, the rich peasantry is comprised of the Kurmis. Some of the Kurmi landlords possess
more than 100 *bighas* of land, maintain tractors and own impressive
houses. As Sachchidananda (1979: 32) points out,

The overall socio-economic position of the Kurmis can be compared to
that of the upper castes such as the Rajputs and Brahmins in the neighbouring villages. The only distinction between the higher castes and the Kurmi

landlords is that the latter have not yet given up manual work in the field. However, this has led to a harsher attitude towards the Harijans while at work during the agricultural operations. It is one of the reasons why the Harijans do not like to work with the intermediate caste households.

Similarly in Belchi, where eight Harijans were burnt alive by the Kurmis in May 1977, the Kurmis were the rich landlords. As one report mentions, in Belchi

the Kurmis have prospered through the cultivation of potatoes and onions. They have accumulated wealth : apart from engaging in farming, they are also government contractors and owners of transport services and cold storages (Bhushan 1977 : 974).

When Mahavir Mahto, the central figure among the assassins in Belchi, was arrested, the backward castes in a demonstration demanding reservation of jobs, also shouted slogans like 'Release Mahavir Mahato' (Sengupta 1979: 92). . . .

The violence against the Harijans was visible in those places where the Harijans as agricultural labourers were getting organized and becoming politically conscious. Singheshwar Paswan, who was a leader of the Harijan labourers in Belchi, belonged to the Dusadh caste. The Dusadhs are, as such, known to be militant people. They used to be employed in earlier times by upper caste landlords for the protection of their life and property. In the 1970s the Dusadhs were at many places in the forefront of the struggle against the oppression of the Harijans by backward castes. . . .

The repression only reflects the attitude of this class of capitalist landlords towards the growing class consciousness amongst the agricultural labourers of Bihar. In this the landlords get tacit support from the state and from the administration. The attitude of this class has so hardened that even women and children are lynched and burnt alive, as happened in Pipra in February 1980. The landlords, to counter the defiance of the agricultural labourers, now recruit musclemen, give them arms and money in order to defend themselves. These groups of armed men are given a name, Bhoomisena, or the soldiers of the landlords. Today the Bhoomisena is an accepted fact and almost any landlord, who has a rebellious group of farmers on his hands and wants to teach them a lesson, gives a contract to the local unit of the Bhoomisena. The Bhoomisena is also used increasingly in times of elections when their muscle power is needed to win votes. . . .

The backward caste landlords, by exploiting caste sentiments, have tried to rally their castemen for their own cause even by raising slogans and demanding the release of anti-socials like Mahavir Mahato. Their role today is the same as that of the Bhumihar-Rajput landlords of yesterday. These are the castes who have improved and consolidated their positions from tenant farmers to rich peasants in the course of the last fifty years and they want to hold on to them at any cost.

The class dimensions of these conflicts and atrocities are quite obvious. Even Table 2 shows that in almost all the cases the primary cause of conflict was wages, proper share of the crops, or land dispute. . . . It would be wrong to assume, however, that the agricultural labourers and poor peasants of all the castes are free from caste loyalties and express their solidarity as a class. For instance, in Bhojpur, where a fierce struggle is on between the landlords and the lower classes, which includes agricultural labourers and poor peasants, there are many Rajputs and Bhumihars who are themselves small or even poor peasants, but as Sinhà (1977: 6) points out, 'The experience as yet has been that the poorer Rajputs or Bhumihars have fanatically supported the landlords of their own caste in the face of Naxalite organization.' On the other hand, the lower castes, as we have shown above, are emerging out of their narrow caste confines and have taken a more militant posture as a class. It is this growing militancy of the lower classes, that threatens the vested interests of the backward caste landlords who retaliate by more repressive measures. These landlords, after having improved their economic status, want to hold on to it at any cost and have let loose an orgy of violence in the countryside. They are engaged in a bitter fight against the old feudal classes consisting of the upper castes. However, at the same time they also want to tighten their own hold on the classes which are below them. The growing awareness among the Harijan labourers is bound to escalate more violent confrontations in the future. So far it was the backward caste landlords who were the aggressors and the Harijans remained the victims, but will the Harijans continue to remain victims?

Table 2
Caste Violence in Bihar

Place	Aggressor		Victim		Issues
	Caste	Economic Status	Caste	Economic Status	
1. Bajitpur	Bhumihar	Landlord	Harijan	Agricultural labourers and sharecroppers	Wages, sharecroppers right over land
2. Belchi	Kurmi	Landlord	All caste	Poor peasants, agricultural labourers and sharecroppers	Social oppression
3. Beniapatti	Kurmi	Landlord	Harijan	Agricultural labourers	Wage
4. Bishrampur	Kurmi	Landlord	Harijan	Agricultural labourers sharecroppers	Wage, sharecroppers right
5. Chandadano	Kurmi	Landlord	Harijan	Agricultural labourers	Wage

6.	Dharampuri	Brahmin	Landlord	Harijan	Agricultural labourers and sharecroppers	Wage and sharecroppers' right
7.	Dohija	Yadav	All Class	Bhumihar	Poor peasants and one big landlord	Retaliation
8.	Gopalpur	Kurmi	Landlord	Harijan	Agricultural labourers	Wage
9.	Jarpa	Bhumihar	Landlord	Yadav	Poor peasants and sharecroppers	Land dispute
10.	Kalia	Kurmi	Landlord	Harijan	Agricultural labourers	Wage
11.	Khijuria	Brahmin	Landlord	Harijan	Sharecroppers	Sharecroppers' right
12.	Parasbigha	Bhumihar	Landlord	Yadav	Sharecroppers	Sharecroppers' right
13.	Pathada	Yadav	Landlord	Harijan	Agricultural labourers	Wage
14.	Pipra	Kurmi	Landlord	Harijan	Agricultural labourers	Wage
15.	Pupri	Kurmi	Landlord	Harijan	Agricultural labourers	Wage and possession over land

Source: Adapted from Hiranmay Dhar (1980: 4).

Two Villages in Orissa

F. G. BAILEY

Bisipara

On the outskirts of the Oriya village of Bisipara there is a temple. This temple is built on Bisipara land, and the Brahmin and other officials who care for it are Bisipara men, but the temple belongs to all Hindus in the Kondmals, and an annual excursion is made by the priest and his assistants to collect contributions for its upkeep.

The Bisipara Pans, a caste of Untouchables, hearing of the Temple Entry Act,[1] organized a procession to the temple and announced that they would go inside, since they now had a legal right to do so. When the Pans came to the temple they found it guarded by the clean castes of Bisipara, headed by the Warriors.[2] The police were then called by the Pans, who demanded that their right to enter the temple should be enforced. The Warriors asserted that they, as men of Bisipara, were merely the custodians of the temple and not its owners, they would stand aside and permit the Pans to enter, providing that all other clean-caste Hindus in the Kondmals were first consulted. After a few days tempers cooled; the police went away; the Pans made no further efforts to enter the temple.

Excerpted from F.G. Bailey, 'Two Villages in Orissa', in Max Gluckman, ed., *Closed Systems and Open Minds*, Aldine, Chicago, 1964. The title of the original essay is 'Two Villages in Orissa (India)'.

[1] This Act makes it an offence to exclude people from places of worship on grounds of untouchability.

[2] For a fuller description of these cases, see Bailey (1957). The caste there called Boad Outcastes is here called Pan.

Some time afterwards the village council, on which clean castes alone sit, announced that the Pan privilege of music-making and licensed begging on ritual occasions had now been withdrawn and would be allowed to a different Untouchable caste. The Pans did not, to my knowledge, make any formal protest against this decision. Instead they did two things which seem to me implicitly to accept, and even to welcome, the withdrawal of their traditional privilege. They met in council and announced a series of measures which in effect denied their Untouchable status. They would no longer act as scavengers for the village and they would not cart away and flay dead cattle. They would no longer drink alcohol. They would be vegetarian. From that time onwards they were no longer Pans but Harijans—'children of god—the name by which Gandhi dignified Untouchables. Finally, as another gesture of independence and equality, they built their own temple in their own street.

In 1953 an elderly Pan was returning in the evening from the market. His path lay through the centre of the village and along a narrow track on a bank above the water-logged rice-fields. On this track he met a youth of the high Warrior caste, returning from fishing in the fields. They came face to face on the pathway; there was a scuffle; the youth fell into the muddy field. The youth ran home, roused the village, and a council meeting was called. This meeting summoned the Pan. A message came back that he would attend in the morning. During the night the Pans sent an appeal to the police, eight miles away, saying that their houses had been attacked by the clean castes. The police came in the early morning and took statements from both sides. That same day a Minister from the Orissa Government happened to be touring in the area, and the Bisipara Pans intercepted his party and asked for his protection. This resulted in a second police enquiry by a higher official. The police decided that there was no case to answer. The Pans then appealed to the Magistrate. The case was heard in 1954 and the Magistrate ordered both sides to keep the peace.

In the closing months of 1953 (I left the village at the end of that year) the tension between the two sides seemed to me curiously compartmented. Everyday economic relationships— casual labour hired by clean castes from among Pans to work on the farm or about the house—went on as usual, and there was nothing that I could distinguish in the behaviour of master and servant to indicate communal tension. But the village council behaved as if it was in a state of siege. Pans were no longer allowed to lounge outside the meeting-house and hear what was going on. There were frequent warnings against careless talk, and threats to fine any clean-caste person who revealed to a Pan—even inadvertently—what the council had decided to do. Money was levied to pay the expenses of witnesses at court, and there was even talk of hiring a lawyer. I was told many times that the Pans no longer knew their place; allegations that they were unfit to be received in decent human society were bolstered by stories of their nauseating personal habits; in short, the incidents of 1953 brought into the open great bitterness and the emotions which we associate with racial conflict.

Baderi

In 1955, in the Kond village of Baderi, which is half an hour's walk from Bisipura, some Baderi Pans sat down at a wedding feast beside the visiting Pan musicians who came with the bride's escort.[3] A Baderi Kond, named Liringa, abused the Baderi Pans and drove them away. That night the Baderi Pans slashed the skins of the visitors' drums. The visitors complained, and the Konds of Baderi, who hold in that village a position analogous to that of the clean castes in Bisipara, met in council and summoned their Pans. The Baderi Pans attended, and at once complained that when they were driven away from the wedding feast, their caste had been publicly insulted. In a very short time Liringa and the Pan elders were shouting at one another. Then one of the Pans struck Liringa and another Kond who stood at his side. Both men were struck across the face, openly, and in full view of the council. The Pans then fled and the council broke up in disorder.

The Kond council met again at the instigation of Liringa and decided to impose an economic 'lock-out'. Pans would no longer be employed as labourers or retained as clients. Land or any other form of property given to them must be resumed. The village would no longer employ them as musicians. All this was written into a document together with the reasons for the lock-out: the Pans no longer obeyed or respected their Kond masters: 'since the Government started calling them Harijans', and they therefore would no longer be granted the privileges of servants. The names of all present were written on the document together with an agreement to pay a fine of Rs 25 if they broke its provisions.

In fact the document came to nothing. No one dismissed a Pan; no one resumed his property; a few months later, when the agricultural season began, the Baderi Pans were working as labourers in Kond

[3] For a more detailed description of this dispute, see Bailey (1960: Ch VI).

fields, as they had always done. Even before that, at a ceremony held in one of the hamlets which constitute Baderi village, they had appeared with their drums and provided music and had been paid for it.

The attitudes of the Konds towards Untouchables differs from the attitude of the clean castes in Bisipara. It is true that they put forward many of the same reasons to explain the behaviour of their Pans, especially they insisted that this kind of conflict was caused by the 'Government using the term "Harijans". But some of them said that in Baderi there was no real Harijan problem. The fault was Liringa's, with a little more tact he might have smoothed the whole thing over. Whatever was happening elsewhere, this argument ran, there was no real problem in Baderi, the Pans could be kept in their places.

After they assaulted Liringa, the Pans made no further move to protect themselves or to assert their rights. They did not call in the Administration, as the Bisipara Pans did. They made no proclamations about reforming themselves. They continued to behave in a manner of the traditional Pans.

Within a few days the excitement died down, and the incident appeared to have been forgotten.

The Problem

In some ways the events in these two villages resemble one another. Both cases arise from an encounter between individuals, and both immediately mobilized groups on each side of the barrier of untouchability. Both in Baderi and in Bisipara an Untouchable assaulted a person of clean caste, and in both villages this breach of the rules of ritual avoidance was the occasion, but not the sole cause, of the conflict. In both cases the village council met, first as a judicial body summoning the Pans to stand before it as before a court. These summons were ignored or frustrated, and when the councils met again later, they met as councils of war, determining how to deal with an opponent whose equality they thus implicitly acknowledged.

There are also differences, not so much in the actions of the clean castes, but in the way in which the two sets of Untouchables conducted their case. The Baderi Pans, after their two acts of violence (damaging the drums and assaulting Liringa), did nothing to embarrass the Konds and quickly resumed their normal posture of subservience. The Bisipara Pans, on the other hand, were defiant: they made several appeals to the Administration and one to a Minister, and by doing so they kept the Bisipara clean castes on the defensive for a year. They made vociferous claims that their rights, as citizens of India, should be respected. They made a general issue out of the assault case, and used it to demonstrate that they were no longer subservient to the clean castes, and in particular to the Warriors. The consequences of this was that the dispute in Bisipara was much more bitter and more protracted than the dispute in Baderi.

These cases pose two questions. Firstly, why did these disputes occur at all? This is not the historical question: Why did these particular unique events occur at that time? Rather it is the question: Can these events be understood as aspects of regular behaviour, as social regularities, as part of a system? Secondly, how can a sociologist explain the differing course of the two disputes, the greater initiative shown by the Bisipara Pans, and the relative lack of political enterprise apparent among the Baderi Pans?

Explanations from Culture

In the first place there are certain cultural items, the significance of which must be known if one is to understand why the actors behaved as they did. One must, in other words, have some knowledge of Hinduism and of the symbolic values which Hindus attach to certain places and certain forms of behaviour.

One has to know that an Untouchable is so called because if he comes into contact with persons of clean caste he pollutes them, and some form of ritual cleansing becomes necessary before the polluted person is fit again to carry out his normal tasks.

Knowing this, one better understands why the assaults, neither of which did apparent bodily harm, nevertheless caused such an uproar—and that among a people who readily use violence to gain their ends. In each case the blow was struck by an Untouchable on a person of clean caste, and the effect upon clean-caste public opinion was much the same as when we read of attacks on women and children. The incidents were seen by the clean castes not so much as assaults on individuals, but rather as attacks on a fundamental principle of morality.

The attempt of the Untouchables to gain entry to the Bisipara temple has the same significance. The temple is an object of ritual purity; the Untouchables are polluting. Knowing this, one better understands what the trouble was about. The same point comes up again in the fact that Pans are not members of the village council in Bisipara, although they are permitted in normal times to stand outside the meeting-house and listen to what is going on. But the meeting-house itself is also a shrine, which would be polluted by the presence of Pans.

Another point which would be obscure without a knowledge of Hindu culture is the significance of the methods employed by the Bisipara Pans to make themselves respectable. Vegetarianism and the avoidance of alcohol are habits which bring spiritual merit; they are also the habits of the much respected priestly caste, the Brahmin. Conversely, any form of violence to the cow, including the handling of dead cattle and hides, is a sin. Forms of behaviour [stated above] are indices not only of spiritual merit, but also of social prestige.

These are cultural values which Hindus hold, and if we know them, we understand better the significance of various ways of behaving in the two disputes. But there arise further questions:

(a) Does a knowledge of these cultural items answer the two questions posed above? By understanding Hindu culture, do we understand sociologically why these disputes occurred? And can we account, in this way, for different behaviour in the two villages?

(b) Do we need to explain these cultural items, and if so, how is the explanation to be made?

It seems to me that a knowledge of the culture is only the beginning of the effort to understand sociologically why these disputes occurred. In each case the cultural description poses, at a higher level of abstraction, a sociological problem. A knowledge of Hindu values helps us to understand that when the Bisipara Pans imposed on themselves a ban on eating meat and drinking alcohol and handling dead cattle, they were making an attempt at social climbing. But cultural symbolism will not explain *why* they were trying to better themselves. By knowing the meaning of 'untouchability' and the symbols associated with it, we also know that in trying to enter the temple, and in striking a person of clean caste, the Pans were making an attack on the established social order. But we do not know yet what is that social order, nor why the Pans were attacking it. A knowledge of Hindu culture will not help us to understand why these disputes took place; that knowledge only helps us to realize that there is a problem.

. . . .

The nuances of social relationships only become apparent to one familiar with the culture in which those relationships are expressed. The better one is able to absorb Hindu values and Hindu culture, the more penetrating is likely to be one's insight into social relationships. Yet the Hindu culture which helps us to sharpen the dissecting knives of sociology is not, on the whole, the distillation and systematization which appears in the sacred books in the Sanskrit language. There is a link, as Marriott and others argue, between the 'great tradition' and the 'little tradition' of the village: but they are nevertheless separable when we regard a knowledge of culture as a tool which helps us to frame particular sociological problems. Our knowledge of the 'little tradition' we acquire partly from reading about the manners and customs of the people of India, and partly (and more satisfactorily) by seeing how people behave and listening to the explanations they give of that behaviour. If one ventures very much further into the literature, it is because one is interested, not because familiarity with the more academic side of Hinduism is required for the understanding of peasant social relations.

To many this will seem the attitude of a Philistine. But it is not; it is merely specialization. To explain culture traits in a village by relating them, either genetically or through morphological similarity, to traits described in the sacred literature or found in the courts of kings or in the great religious centres, is another problem, different from the one with which I am concerned. It is a cultural problem which is left behind, unanswered and not needing to be answered, in the process of abstracting a system of social behaviour. In the language of this book, it is a problem about which one can afford to be naive, just as Marriott, in his discussion of festivals and deities, could afford to abstract away, or ignore, or be naive about, the social relations involved in those festivals and in the worship of those deities.

Structural Explanations: Internal

Neither dispute would be in the least comprehensible unless one traced out the alignments of the protagonists, and realized that only in the beginning were these disputes between individuals; in one case about who was to have priority on a narrow pathway, and in the other case about who was to share in a feast. In both disputes groups immediately mobilized behind the protagonists. These groups were not simply gathered to prosecute the quarrel, but possessed a relative degree of permanence, existing apart from this situation. They were, in other words, part of the structure of social relationships.

An elementary knowledge of Hindu culture and Hindu values was indispensable, as I showed in a previous section, to understand what was going on, although it did not help us to understand why the disputes took place, nor why they followed different courses in the two villages. Does an analysis of the roles of the people concerned, and a comparison of social relationships in the two villages explain why the disputes took place, and why they developed differently in the two villages?

Baderi consists of nine nucleated hamlets dispersed in, and at the mouth of, a valley. The greatest distance between any two hamlets is about 2 miles, but three-quarters of the population live within a mile of one another. Bisipara has a single 'suburb' about half a mile from the main village; the rest of the village live in a compact settlement, which is divided into streets, roughly on the basis of caste. Bisipara contains 700 people; Baderi 500. In Bisipara, Pans are 21 per cent of the population; in Baderi, Pans are 17 per cent. Of the clean-caste group in Baderi, Konds are 84 per cent : but in Bisipara the clean-caste group is divided into eighteen different castes, two of which contain half the clean-caste population.

In none of this information is there any fact which would explain why the disputes arose, nor why they followed different courses in the two villages. The proportion of Pans in the population of each village is roughly the same, and the villages themselves do not differ greatly in size. We might seem to have a clue to the different behaviour of the clean-caste groups in the fact that the Baderi group is virtually one caste and one lineage, and might therefore need less institutionalized efforts to display unity in the face of the Pan threat. The division of the Bisipara group into different castes might require greater organization to achieve unity. On the other hand, the Baderi clean castes are dispersed over different settlements, while those of Bisipara live compactly. These clues might help later, but it would be premature to attribute the difference in the two disputes to structural differences of this kind. In any case, in these structural differences there is no hint why the disputes broke out in the first place.

If the explanation does not lie in the gross structural difference between the two villages, it might lie in the roles which the different protagonists play in sub-systems within the village. The different course of the disputes might be accounted for if, for instance, an unimportant man had been assaulted in Baderi, and a person of standing and influence attacked in Bisipara. Exactly the reverse is true. The victim in Bisipara was a youth, and the alleged assault was committed by an elder. Youth owes respect to age, and had the two persons belonged to the same caste, the older man would have had every right to cuff the youngster out of his way. In Baderi the victim was one of the leading men of the village. In Bisipara the assault took place in the dusk out in the fields, with no witnesses, and could easily have been dressed up as an accident. In Baderi the blow was struck, deliberately and openly, in full view of the village council, and in no circumstances could anyone have pretended that it was an accident. In this situation one would have expected the Baderi dispute to be the more bitter and to be fought out more strenuously. In fact, the opposite happened.

One could explore various other roles and attributes of the protagonists—their economic activities, their education, the offices which they held, and so forth—in an effort to explain the different course of the two disputes, but there is no space to do so here, and in any case it would be to explore blind alleys. In the end, one would be brought to the conclusion that the significant role in both cases is caste membership, and the structural relationship which might throw light on what happened is the relationship of the two groups across the barrier of pollution: the relationship between the clean castes and the Untouchables.

The nature of this relationship is well known and I have described it, with reference to these disputes, in the books noted earlier; here I can be brief. The traditional relationship—and from the point of view of the high castes, the proper relationship—lies in the political, economic, and ritual subordination of the Untouchables. The Pan families should be attached to families in the clean castes, in particular to the Warriors in Bisipara and to the Konds in Baderi. The Pans work for their clean-caste masters about the house and on the farm, and they themselves own only such property as their masters choose to give them. They achieve political representation only as the servants of their masters, for they themselves may not sit on the village council; and if they wish to bring a matter before the council, their masters must act for them. Their humble position is symbolized by ritual behaviour, in particular by the usages of Untouchability, by their habit of eating and drinking substances which are degrading in the views of Hindus, and by their exclusion from places of ritual importance in the village.

In this outline of groups and institutions are contained some of the clues which explain the behaviour of the disputants. Hindu ideas about pollution explain why the blows which were struck were not simple assaults, but were also attacks on a fundamental moral principle, governing the relationship between a clean caste and an Untouchable. This ritual relationship is now seen as one part of a complex in which political and economic interests are also involved. The blows now appear not only as an offence against village morality, but also as an attack on the established political order of the village. Given that the rituals of Untouchability symbolize also political inferiority, these assaults were tantamount to a revolution. So also was the attempt by the Bisipara Pans to enter the Kondmals temple.

A structural analysis, carried out to this depth, and confining itself to the two villages concerned, tells us, putting it briefly, only what is the normal expected behaviour between a clean caste and an Untouchable, and what issues are involved in that behaviour; it tells us who are the actors, how they are expected to act, and what political, ritual and economic interests lie between them. It also shows what village institutions come into action when there is a breach of these rights and obligations: in both the disputes the village council was concerned to restore equilibrium and to sanction correct behaviour.

But such an analysis of village groups and village institutions cannot explain why these institutions failed to restore the balance. In Bisipara, institutions which do not appear in a structural analysis of village relations, in the end prevented the dispute from becoming more violent; in Baderi, the action taken by the village council failed, and normal relations were restored in spite of, rather than because of its intervention.

In both disputes the action taken by the Pans was tantamount to a revolution. It is obvious, from the course of the two disputes, that the Bisipara Pans wanted a revolution and the Baderi Pans did not. In order to explain this, one has to take into account the relationships which the villagers have with persons and groups outside the village, and which are not part of the village structure; and one has also to take into account institutions which do not belong within the village system.

External Relationships

In neither village does this structural description fit the reality of political and economic relationships. The Pans of Bisipara number among them several schoolmasters, and this profession, by the standards of wealth in the Kondmals, is well paid, and, money apart, carries a high social prestige. There are also several men who make a good living through trade, and the land owned per head of the Bisipara Pans is not so very much less than that owned by the Bisipara Warriors. Even the poor Pans are not, as a rule, tied as clients in a serf-like bond to individual Warrior families, but usually sell their labour in an open market. In short, they are not, in any sense, the complete economic dependants of the Warriors and the clean castes.

The Pans of Baderi are by no means so advanced, and can boast of no men in the professional classes. But they depend for much of their living on outside sources. Some make a precarious living by weaving for the market. In the summer many find work as casual labourers on the roads. And they too, like the Pans of Bisipara, are seldom tied as clients, but in almost every case sell their labour on a day-to-day basis.

In the traditional structure of the village, the Pan had no political role except as the client of his master. This master had to speak for him in the village council and had to be prepared to defend him against other people. But the reality now is different. Both the Pan and his master stand equal as citizens of India. The Pan can (in practice, with many difficulties) enforce his rights in the government courts, and he can enforce them even against the Warriors of his own village. Or at least he can try to do so, and the Warriors can no longer legally use force against their Pans. In other words, many of the political functions of the village council have been taken over by the government courts, and the locus of ultimate power has certainly shifted from the council to those of courts and to the Administration.

In Bisipara at least, the Pans have political and economic privileges superior to their former masters. They owe this to the policy of the government which has been trying for many years to improve the lot of Untouchables. Untouchables have preference over clean-caste men for appointment to certain jobs in the Administration; there are special scholarships for them; they are the favoured wards of government. There is not this difference in Baderi, since the Konds too, having the status of Adibasis (members of primitive tribes), are qualified to receive similar privileges.

By taking into account the political and economic relationships which the people of the villages have with the world outside, and the effect of these relationships on village structures, we can explain why the Untouchables of both villages made their protest. We can understand why a quarrel between individuals quickly became generalized into a conflict between castes. Since the Pans are no longer politically entirely subordinate and no longer economically entirely dependent on their clean-caste masters, they were unwilling—in Bisipara at least—to follow out the usages of ritual subservience. Earlier I said that the Bisipara Pans wanted a revolution; it would, perhaps, be more correct to say that they want recognition of a revolution that has already taken place. They want to be acknowledged, or, more accurately, their leaders want to be acknowledged, as the political and economic equals of the clean castes. That is one reason why they tried to enter the Kondmals temple; that is the reason why they threw off customs—drinking alcohol, meat-eating, scavenging—which are associated with an inferior status; that is the reason why they were so ready to call in the police, and it is also the reason why the clean-caste council tried to keep the matter within the village and have it settled by the village council. Both sides knew that in the village council an assault by an Untouchable on a person of clean caste is a heinous offence, but that in the courts the caste status of the persons involved would be considered irrelevant. That is why the Pans refused to come before the village council, and planned to get the case heard outside the village.

By taking into account relationships going outside the village, we can explain also why the dispute in Bisipara was so much more bitter than in Baderi. The Baderi Pans were less wealthy, relatively to their own clean castes, than were the Bisipara Pans; they had no men of influence; they had no educated men and no one in touch with outside political movements, while among the Bisipara Pans there was a Congress agent and two men who were candidates for the Orissa Legislative Assembly. In short, there had been no revolution in Baderi: the Pans were still very much dependent for their living on the Baderi Konds, and they were too ignorant of their constitutional rights to exploit these rights efficiently.

We have now reached a third level of understanding. The values of Hinduism—vegetarianism, untouchability, and so forth—explain the emotional significance of various actions. An analysis of groups and their interrelationships within the village sorts out the actors, provides a picture of normality, and enables us to see what is at stake—that is, what interests (political, economic, and ritual) are involved in these relationships. Finally, by looking at relationships outside the village, we see how these enabled certain groups within the village to challenge and, to some extent, to overthrow, the established order.

I have used a phrase 'levels of understanding'; but I do not mean by this that the three explanations are arranged in order of profundity, nor that any one gives us 'deeper' understanding than any other. For instance, with events outside the village, examining their effects on the structure of the village, and coming finally to the 'given' of Hindu values. These three explanations are complementary to one another: one is not discarded and rejected when another is taken up.

Mobilization of Landless Labourers: The Halpatis of South Gujarat

JAN BREMAN

Halpatis, a Tribal Caste of Landless Labourers

The majority of the population of south Gujarat* is concentrated in the central plain, the backbone of Bulsar, Surat, and Broach Districts. This old and fertile agricultural belt is also the area where the Halpatis live. They particularly inhabit the first two districts where, with over 3,30,000 caste members, they form about 12 per cent of the total population.

The division into *ujliparaj* and *kaliparaj*, light and dark-coloured, is the main feature of the social structure in south Gujarat. Half the district population consists of Scheduled Tribes, and the Halpatis are also registered as such. There are, however, marked differences among the tribal communities. Unlike the Halpatis, who were accommodated at the bottom of Hindu society long ago, the tribals living in the eastern parts—where the country becomes increasingly infertile and hilly—succeeded in maintaining a position of semi-independence well into the nineteenth century. Only gradually were they subjugated as sharecroppers and tenants by penetrating caste Hindus. While the Halpatis form a substantial minority in the central belt, the tribal communities in the eastern region make up 80 per cent or more of the local population.

Jan Breman, 'Mobilization of Landless Labourers: The Halpatis of South Gujarat', in Arvind Das and V. Nilakant, ed., *Agrarian Relations in India*, Manohar, Delhi, 1979.

*My fieldwork during 1971-2, which forms the basis for this paper, was sponsored by the Netherlands Foundation for the Advancement of Tropical Research.

Consequently, tribal elements are more pronounced in their social structure and culture. It is, therefore, hardly surprising that tribal emancipation movements, which arose in the eastern parts of the districts during the last decade, have not found much support among the Halpatis of the plains.

The Halpatis are not really Adivasis; on the other hand they are not considered by the caste population of the central belt to be full-fledged Hindus. The ambivalent way in which the Halpatis are ranked in the social order indicates their dependent and inferior position. Most probably, their low level of existence has prevented a more rapid process of Hinduization in their case.

Halpatis have no recorded past as peasant owners. It is true that, locally, individual members of this caste own small pieces of land, but the majority has worked as agricultural labourers since long. According to the 1961 Census, this was still the main, if not the only, source of livelihood for 73 per cent of them.

Condition of Agricultural Labourers: Past and Present

Agricultural labourers have usually been in the employment of the bigger landowners. Their masters are nearly always Anavil Brahmins or Kanbi Patidars, members of the dominant caste of Bulsar and Surat Districts. The dependence of the labourers was institutionalized in the *hali* system. Elsewhere I have described this pattern of relationships between landlords and their Halpati labourers in terms of bondage and patronage (Breman 1974).

Extension of scale during the last few decades before independence resulted in the disintegration of the *hali* system. Intervention in local affairs by the colonial bureaucracy only played a limited role in this process of change. A more important factor was the commercialization of agriculture. Increasing market production put an end to the traditional arrangements that were based on widely varying mutual obligations of economic, political, cultural, and social nature. The relations between *dhaniamo* and *hali*, landlord and labourer, gradually became more contracted and impersonal. The daily grain allowance which, together with other daily and seasonal perquisites, guaranteed a subsistence livelihood for the Halpatis, was transformed into a wage paid in cash, in exchange for a more specific labour performance. The firm and intimate bonds between the households of landlords and their labourers, often continued from generation to generation, dissolved to be replaced by loose and limited contacts. The percentage of casual wage earners rapidly increased. To the extent that farm servants are still required, they are hired nowadays on a contractual basis.

The abolition of the *hali* system was pursued by Gandhi and his followers in south Gujarat. The struggle against colonial rule was, in their view, justified only if bondage within the country's own social order was also done away with. 'Halpatis'—literally, 'holders of the plough'— became the name of honour given by Gandhi to this caste of agricultural labourers in replacement of the name 'Dublas', which was regarded as pejorative. Since the thirties, voluntary social workers have been devoting themselves to the improvement of the Halpatis' social position, working from the Swaraj *ashram* in Bardoli, and later from similar social action centres elsewhere in Surat and Bulsar Districts.

The activities of the Gandhian movement were, however, directed at convincing the landlords of the injustice of *halipratha* rather than at mobilizing the agricultural labourers towards discontent. But the Kanbi Patels did not even keep to the conditions—unfavourable for the Halpatis though they were—of an agreement that was reached in Bardoli in 1938 through the arbitration of Sardar Patel, and with the approval of Gandhi, for the purpose of putting an end to the *hali* system. Nor did a new attempt, undertaken by the political leader, Morarji Desai in 1948, meet with success. The change in the relationships between landlords and landless labourers in south Gujarat was, in my opinion, only marginally due to the efforts of the social workers.

From 1962 to 1963 I collected a great deal of data on the condition of the Halpatis in a few villages, and during a second period of fieldwork in 1971-2, I used the opportunity to supplement and actualize my previous analysis.

On the basis of my first investigation I had arrived at the conclusion that the disappearance of the *hali* system was primarily due to the depatronization of the relationships between the parties concerned. My opinion in this respect was strengthened by developments in the past few years. One of the most drastic changes in the labour market of south Gujarat is, undoubtedly, the fact that rural labour has become mobile over large distances. This large-scale migratory labour—it was one of the objects of study during my recent fieldwork—has a wage-depressive effect, and facilitates replacement in cases of so-called insufficient performance or 'impertinent behaviour' on the part of the Halpatis.

Labour is available in large supply and the fierce competition for work is enhanced by the enlargement of scale, so that labour comes into the market at prices far below subsistence level. In 1972 the daily wage for agricultural labour fluctuated between Rs 1 and 2. The labourers' dependence on landowners has not disappeared, but the humanizing features of dependence under the *hali* system have. In the present relationship pattern, the exploitation of the Halpatis is more evident. Deterioration of the socio-economic condition of the agricultural labourers preceded the Green Revolution in south Gujarat and was, as a matter of fact, more a pre-condition than an effect of this technological breakthrough in agriculture. Social intercourse with labourers has been reduced to an absolute minimum.

Considerations of profitability are not the only explanation of why landowners changed to more capital-intensive agricultural techniques in recent years. They have come to dislike personal contacts with their labourers and try to avoid them as much as possible by using jobbers and foremen. The Halpatis have become increasingly isolated.

Pauperization is usually regarded as an economic phenomenon but in the case of Halpatis the social dimension might be even more important. This paper deals with the political effects of this process of change. The eclipse of the vertical ties that formed an integral part of *halipratha* undoubtedly facilitated the emergence of a common stand among the labourers; in other words, it made for reinforcement of horizontal solidarity. The poverty and exploitation to which the majority of Halpatis are exposed are now nothing but a breeding ground for political unrest. Spontaneous outbursts do occur, but they are local and incidental. Organization is a necessary pre-condition for any sizable and durable protest movement to emerge.

As is shown below, it is precisely in a situation of pauperism that the chances of such a development are severely limited. It has been argued by many observers that, in the present Indian situation, political awareness among the landless proletariat can only be fostered by organized action. But even if such actions were provided from outside, social emancipation would not follow as a matter of course.

Obstacles in the Path of Self-mobilizations

The impression that one is left with, after talking to Halpatis in their peripherally situated village quarters, is one of utter defencelessness in all respects. Their inability to find a way out of the misery and insecurity of their daily life leaves most of them with no scope at all for any ulterior thought or action.

In the present social system there are simply not enough means of existence for the rapidly growing number of Halpatis. In the rural districts the labour supply far exceeds the demand; nor do the Halpatis easily find employment outside agriculture. They cannot be absorbed by the urban economy of the region. In the rivalry for the slowly expanding employment opportunities outside agriculture even the urban Halpatis barely come into the picture. As an unskilled category they are only considered for the lowest paid, least valued, and most irregular work, and most of them lead lives nearly as forlorn as those of their fellow caste members in the villages.

In a never-ending cycle the surplus is thrown out of the rural system. After the rainy season, about October, men, women, and children migrate in large numbers—in the Bulsar villages more than half the Halpatis may go—to the brickyards and salt pans near Bombay and other cities, to return only towards May, before the beginning of the monsoon. Year after year this seasonal migration is repeated. The splitting up of households—some members stay behind, others are put under contract by one or different jobbers—fits into the picture of pauperization. The yearly exodus does not really enhance the employment opportunities for those who stay home: in the slack season the agrarian labour market remains saturated, partly on account of the influx of migrants from other regions looking for work. The Halpatis have become redundant in society. Many of them are drifting and have all but lost their roots in both village and family life.

A coalition with castes of petty cultivators (notably Kolis, Dhodhias, and Chaudaris) might invalidate the Halpatis' isolation, but it is not likely to occur. In a very general sense the land reforms have stabilized the position of the small landowners and most of them have few interests in common with the Halpatis. Although many small-holders have not profited much by the Green Revolution—if their position has not deteriorated—the social, economic, and political advantages attendant on caste membership operate against their early identification with the powerless agricultural labour proletariat. That the demoralizing situation, in which the Halpatis are placed, manifests itself in political inertia is only natural. Their need of security and protection, essential in the former *hali* system, is not met by the government.

The huts of the Halpatis used to be on the land of the land owners, but in many villages they now live together in separate quarters. They have usually been allotted the worst parts of the terrain, difficult of access and far from the village centre, where they live as Untouchables. Compulsory education has been introduced, but very few Halpati children attend school. About nine out of every ten caste members are illiterate, the highest proportion in the central plain of south Gujarat. In the second half of 1972, after years of delay, the minimum daily wage for agricultural labourers was at last fixed at Rs 3, a considerable rise! Efficient control is lacking, however, and in practice employers do not abide by the law. But if they did, the amount would still not be enough for the Halpatis to meet the sharply rising cost of living.

The majority of Halpatis believe the only thing they owe the government is obedience, and try to avoid all further contact with its officials. The benefits put at the disposal of Scheduled Tribes do not reach them. 'For that you need influence', they say resignedly. The time is past that the votes of the agricultural labourers were returned through their masters, but that does not mean they are now politically emancipated. They lack the awareness that, collectively, they generate power. During the campaign for the State elections in 1972, I found that many Halpatis were not registered in voting lists. Often they had no idea of the differences between the parties; but then, such differences if any were scarcely relevant if seen from their position. Their votes were for sale for a few rupees, and especially among the higher castes colourful tales were told about it. An often heard opinion among members of the social upper layer, who feared the strength of their number, is that only literates should be allowed to vote.

The Halpatis' passivity is closely bound up with their ignorance. They often turn out to be only vaguely, if at all, aware of slogans such as 'Garibi Hatao', although these were raised in their name. Illiteracy deprives them of a great deal of information. The combination of indifference and ignorance, both indissolubly bound up with poverty, underlines their exclusion from society. Those of them who have the greatest trouble have the least capacity to articulate their point of view.

These drawbacks are partly due to the fact that the members of the caste of landless labourers are not accustomed to function within frameworks which stress collective aims. Their experience with group activities is very limited. The traditional caste *panch* in the village operates only incidently, and then it is a question of one or more persons (Patels) meeting to settle divorce or other disputes among households. Probably more important as a new organizational form are the *bhajan mandlis* which, stimulated by workers from the *ashrams*, have been set up in the past few years. They are groups that gather one evening a week to sing devotional and Gandhian songs. Finally, group experience is gained by working in gangs, initially composed for semi-industrial work, but now also for agricultural operations.

The Halpatis themselves explain their backwardness due to a lack of leaders. It is true that there are no figures among them who are known and prominent in the region as is the case with most other tribal castes

in the plain of south Gujarat. Even at the village level there is very
often no leader recognized by all Halpatis. Influence seems to be
exerted by individuals only within their own hamlet and jealousy is a
complaint heard on every part. Outsiders and experienced social workers too assert that Halpatis are not capable of collaborating with one
another.

It should, however, be borne in mind that landless labourers do not
form a homogeneous mass as such. The interests of farm servants, casual wage-earners, gang labourers, piece-workers, and seasonal migrants
are partly opposed. Moreover, all of them are, to varying extents, dependent on landowners and jobbers, their principal employers. The
competition for the few favours to be had in a situation of continuous
scarcity in each and every respect invalidates any strengthening of horizontal solidarity.

Dependence has, finally, been internalized by the Halpatis. In the
households of the high castes, one Halpati said, our women are daily
injected with poison. In conversations with Halpatis, references to their
own backwardness are not at all uncommon. Those few that have been
educated may speak bitterly of their fellow caste members' lack of culture, but many of the others have a low opinion of themselves too. What
other caste, they wonder, lends itself to cleaning the stables and performing the dirty housework for the landlowners?

Does the above suffice as an explanation of the passivity among agricultural labourers? Apathy, ignorance, and feelings of inferiority fit too
well into theories of a culture of poverty to be altogether acceptable as
the sole or even the main reasons.

The Halpatis are certainly aware of the structural conditions that
obstruct the betterment of their lot. They show a deep grudge against
the high castes in general, and the Anavil Brahmins and Kanbi Patels
in particular. 'They are the ones who oppose us: not only in the villages, but also in the government offices, where they have to put their
signatures and stamps on papers that are important for us.' Agricultural
labourers used to be able to count on the intercession of their masters,
but now they often meet with opposition on the masters' part, inspired
by vexation over their labourers' insufficient work performance. To
prevent the Halpatis from becoming too independent, the landowners may use their influence with the district officials against them.
They often succeed. Aside from this, the Halpatis have their dependence rubbed into them in more direct ways.

As I said above, the agricultural labourers are especially open to the
various sanctions that the rural elite has at its disposal, particularly

that of demoralizing their potential leaders—those who understand their own situation and adopt militant attitudes. The police, too, is an instrument of oppression. Although the days of individual violence are gone, when every landlord felt entitled to give his farm servant a good thrashing for 'misconduct' other kinds of arbitrary behaviour are still common. Accusations of drinking or crop theft, false or otherwise, are an effective way to call Halpatis to order, and maltreatment of the accused by members of the local police force, the hated 'brown dogs', is not exceptional.

Under the circumstances, submissiveness and avoidance is an obvious reaction. A group of agricultural labourers who had been granted permission to build their huts in a village on government land, concurred with a petition, composed by the large landowners who were afraid to lose their grip on them, in which they cancelled their request. Examples such as this are the order of the day. Their fear of committing themselves is evident, and this explains why only shopkeepers, artisans, and others who enjoy a measure of independence and security, emerge as leaders in the Halpati neighbourhoods. Yet even these self-styled representatives of their own caste are not altogether to be trusted. All too often they have turned out to be agents for outside interest.

The investigator's contacts with Halpatis do not run smoothly. His questions are answered vaguely, evasively, or not at all. The informants are fully alive to their own vulnerability and have learned to put no trust at all in outsiders. They pretend to lead an extremely atomized existence; a striking number of Halpatis denied to me having friends or maintaining social contact with neighbours or others in their hutment area. To some extent this is true, no doubt, but at the same time statements like these indicate the defensive attitude they have adopted. It is the contacts in their own neighbourhood that enable them to form closer mutual ties. And, in fact, they sit together in groups in front of their huts at night, and thrash out among themselves the forms and degrees of exploitation they suffer at the hands of landlords, shopkeepers, government officials, police, and social workers. The cumulative weight of economic, political, and social dependence invalidates the view that class feelings do not occur among pauperized categories. For them to show any such feelings is imprudent; to act accordingly, impossible.

My conclusion is that this combination of structural and cultural conditions, intra-caste and inter-caste contradictions, is at the bottom of the Halpatis' inability for self-mobilization. I hope to show below that not every outside attempt to mobilize them is successful either.

Organized Action: Gandhian Approach

The role played by the Gandhian movement in the disappearance of the *hali* system has been touched upon above. In the early twenties, some of Gandhi's close collaborators made themselves leaders of a reform programme that was to bring about the emancipation of the Adivasis in south Gujarat. But the activities undertaken by these people, working from the Swaraj *ashram* in Bardoli and one of its branches in Vedcchi both in Surat District, were mainly directed at the tribal castes whose members led a semi-independent existence as petty cultivators. Already then there were a few *ashramites* who took interest in the Halpatis, but under pressure from the local landlords they gave up their attempts to run night classes for the agricultural labourers in a number of villages. Serious work among the Halpatis only started after independence, partly inspired by a report written about them in 1946 entitled *Halpati Mukti*, by Jugatram Dave, the oldest and most prominent protagonist of the movement.

The *ashrams*, most of which have also become educational institutions, function as action centres that aim at changing the rural system in a Gandhian direction. Apart from this, Gandhi's ideas have penetrated among the population of south Gujarat in a more direct way. In many villages there are persons who perform social work on an individual basis in accordance with the doctrines of Gandhi. They advocate social reforms such as the material and cultural improvement of the tribal castes, abolition of untouchability, prohibition, women's emancipation, or village uplift in a general sense. For the *ashrams* these social workers are key figures, through whom they maintain their contracts with the local population. The chief task of these social workers is mediation. Their aim is to advance neglected interests and to speak for deprived categories. They try to gain access to those who take decisions or have favours to distribute in government offices. Most of these voluntary workers are inspired by a mixture of social awareness and political ambition. On the one hand their influence on the regional level is needed to gain advantages for the people under their care, while on the other hand they are attractive to political parties, owing to the votes they can control.

The older social workers are mostly members of higher castes and, if only for that reason, not acceptable to the Halpatis as confidential agents, even if they are apt to describe themselves as such. In the last few years, increasing numbers of young Adivasis, trained in *ashrams*, have succeeded in establishing themselves as social workers. They are practically all Dhodias or Chaudaris, that is, members of landowning castes, that form the majority of the population in their tribal constituencies. They see to it that the benefits distributed on behalf of the Scheduled Tribes in the way of employment, education, agriculture, and so on, go to their fellow caste members. The Halpatis are given the go-by.

The Halpatis live scattered over a large area in which they form a minority and, as I said above, they have no supra-local leaders of any importance. More than half the *taluka* seats for the state assembly in Ahmedabad have been reserved for tribal candidates, but not one of these seats is occupied by a Halpati. Nor does the weight carried by Halpatis in the district councils correspond in any way with their proportion in the total population. In Bulsar District, for instance, no member of the important social welfare committee, through which the benefits for 'backward communities' are channelled, belongs to this second largest tribal caste of the region. The Dhodhias, on the other hand, who are only slightly more numerous, command an absolute majority in this committee.

Whereas some decades ago the voluntary social workers in the villages followed Gandhi in stressing their spiritual guidance, they have since independence narrowed down their role to that of local-level politicians. In a slightly different way the Gandhian movement itself has undergone professionalization. I. P. Desai, in a very interesting study, has described this process of change and its implications (Desai 1969). Referring to the *ashrams'* staff workers of today, he says, 'The social worker is likely to be a paid worker and organizer, committed to fixed, assigned duties, rather than the Gandhian missionary type, which is becoming a historical type.' The transition outlined by him from movement to organization is very pronounced in the case of social work among the Halpatis.

Halpati Seva Sangh Organization and Programme

In 1961, social work among the Halpatis was given an organizational basis in the Halpati Sewa Sangh (HSS). As early as 1946 a *mahajan* had been founded, an association that aimed at the emancipation of this caste on the principles of truth, non-violence, and arbitration. Those who took this initiative continued to operate from the *ashrams*, especially those of Bardoli and Vedcchi. Jugatram Dave acted as the chairman of the HSS in an honorary capacity. Thus, although the tie with the institutions was preserved after 1961, that year saw the beginning of a new phase. In Bardoli a head office was established, in which an ever growing administrative staff now co-ordinates all activities among the Halpatis of south Gujarat. During the years that followed, twenty local branches were founded in *talukas* where Halpatis form a substantial part of the population. In the survey published on the occasion of the organization's tenth anniversary,[1] it is said that in 1972 almost 20,000 Halpatis were registered with HSS: they theoretically pay a subscription of 10 paise a year. Apart from the nearly 500 paid staff members, the organization comprises about 2,000 unpaid helpers and contributors, for the most part non-Halpatis. There are *taluka* and district boards, composed of members of the various categories, which discuss the activities once a year. The subscription fees are, of course, negligible as a source of income. The broadly conceived programme, aimed at the social abolition of the caste of agricultural labourers in south Gujarat, is practically wholly financed by the government.

The most important HSS activities are:

Mediation in the allocation of land to Halpatis to build their huts on, so that they depend less on the landlords. The striking of wells or pumps in the new quarters. The founding of co-operative housing societies to enable them to build better huts The government has only granted subsidies for this purpose since the great floods of 1968, and until now on a limited scale.

Foundation of schools of their own, to make up for their backwardness in education. In the new village quarters over a hundred kindergartens have been opened. Distributed over the districts, there are also five primary residential schools and four secondary schools. In spite of the provision of free books, clothing, food, and accommodation, the schools do not generally attract many Halpati pupils. To avoid losing the government subsidies they therefore accept children from other tribal castes, who in some schools account for more than half the total number of pupils. This also applies to the seven hostels that accommodate boys and girls who attend the ordinary village schools.

Employment opportunities. A limited number of young people are enabled to be trained as artisans. After completion of their training they are given a modest amount of equipment needed to practise their skills. The *khadi* household industry, much less propagated now than it used to be, has failed to take root among the Halpatis. The establishment, after years of preparation, of eighty-five agricultural labour

[1] Halpati Seva Sangh, Bardolini Jhamki, Bardoli, 1971.

co-operatives seems to be more promising, but none of these has as yet developed into a going concern.

A wide range of socio-cultural activities. Propaganda is carried out for prohibition, till now without much success. It is encouraged indirectly by *bhajan mandlis,* which spread Hindu values. Young people's clubs compaign to attract pupils for the schools. Women's group are formed, to learn *garba* and other high-caste dances. To prevent crippling expenditure for marriage festivities —often the beginning of increasing indebtedness—garlands are presented to couples in substitute marriage ceremonies. In case of illness, Halpatis are entitled to either medicines or the cost of medicines. Agricultural labourers who are in serious conflict with the police or their landlord can count on legal aid. A few times a year, *sibhirs* are held, meetings of one or more days to which Halpatis with leadership qualities are invited. To widen their horizon, they occasionally go on tours to other parts of south Gujarat.

Although on paper this looks impressive enough, various components of the programme are only moderately successful. Criticism, however, should not be directed at the shortcoming in implementation but rather at the ideology underlying the programme and the policy of the organization.

To begin with, it may be stated that the HSS has become the executive body for all provisions and regulations intended to benefit the Halpatis. Besides the activities enumerated above, the salaries of the staff members and other overhead costs are paid by the government. This means that the organization is an extension of the bureaucratic apparatus without, however, possessing its authority. In the circumstances, any real consideration of the Halpatis interests is an illusion. The HSS, as a semi-government body, cannot possibly act as a pressure group which is a *sine qua non* for winning the confidence of the people whom the workers are supposed to represent.

Secondly, the work of the HSS has aggravated the isolation of the agricultural labourers rather than relieved it. According to the law they cannot be evicted from the land on which they built their huts. Instead of supporting the valid claim of the Halpatis in this respect, the organization promotes their removal to separate village quarters. In remote and often badly drained neighbourhoods, deprived of the most elementary public facilities, the Halpatis live together with a stain of Untouchability. Separate educational provisions contribute to their apartheid. Young people who have been educated in these schools complain that the Gandhian bias in the curriculum damages their chances, which are weak to begin with, in the labour market.

Thirdly, the HSS is above all a welfare organization. Most of its activities are ameliorative in character. They are aimed at relieving the worst distress, and at the same time, at educating the Halpatis to be better Hindus. This, especially, seems to be the nature of the emancipation the HSS strives after.

The HSS advocated higher wages for the landless proletariat. But when agricultural labourers go on strike somewhere to reinforce their claims, the social workers intervene in order to prevent rising tensions and to reach a compromise. Self-respect and class-consciousness are not taught. On the contrary, the organization does not aim at making the Halpatis capable of standing up for themselves, aware of their exploitation and oppression, but envisages their adjustment to the social system without any fundamental change in their dependence. It is true that the rural elite does not take very kindly to the existence of the HSS, even if no threat to the *status quo* emanates from it. But, says the present leader meaningfully, it is due to the absence of communist influence among the Halpatis that the organization is assured of support by the government and does not meet with more obstruction on the part of the landlords.

The mobilization of the labourers is non-antagonistic in nature. The Gandhian principles of arbitration, compromise and avoidance of open clashes between the parties concerned form the basis of this policy. In the Gandhian ideology, the class struggle is not so much strategically unjustified as immoral. In conservative south Gujarat, to speak of an unbridgeable cleft between rich and poor is nearly viewed as sinful.

In the strongly harmonious Gandhian view of the social order, the landlords are placed as guardians of the rural riches, ideal patrons, who are expected to take good care of their subordinates. There are, of course, contrasts, but these should be neutralized by persuasion and reconciliation. Capital and labour should co-operate. In spite of disappointing past experience, the HSS persists in this approach. But in the prevailing, sharply polarized socio-economic system, such an ideology plays the game of the landlords. Attempts to persuade them to treat their labourers better are of no avail. Yet the labourers are invariably urged to be patient and moderate in their demands. The HSS, in short, is a movement of accommodation rather than emancipation.

Political Leadership

Ever since its foundation, the HSS has been a stronghold of the Congress party. As early as 1963 I attended a meeting, at which Morarji

Desai, who is from the region, announced that times were changing for
the Halpatis. Now that, after the disappearance of the *hali* system, the
labourers' votes can no longer be controlled through their employers,
the existence of the HSS makes it possible for a party that serves the
interests of the landlords to acquire the support of the labourers.

The 1969 split in the Congress party seemed to initiate a more radical course. The majority of the HSS top, and most of the voluntary
social workers, fairly soon declared themselves for Indira Gandhi's
party, while the regional government was still solidly in the hands of
Morarji Desai's supporters. Promptly the subsidies to the HSS were
stopped. But the time of adversity did not last long, for in 1972 the
Congress (R) came to power in the region, and the interests of the HSS
and the ruling party ran parallel again.

The split has further strengthened the tendency towards polarization. The HSS leaders became very prominent in the Congress (R) of
south Gujarat. Fearing that the Halpatis would take the 'Garibi Hatao'
slogan seriously, and follow Indira Gandhi's supporters in a body,
members of the Congress (O) founded a new organization, the Halpati
Vikas Sangh. They put forward a number of discontented Halpatis as
figureheads. One of them, whom they suspected of having political
aspirations of his own, was already sent home before the election, the
others were dismissed afterwards. In none of the *talukas* of Bulsar and
Surat Districts were locally influential Halpatis put forward as candidates. They were only required for canvassing among their fellow caste
members.

The HSS is an organization for the Halpatis, but not of them. The
leadership is solidly in the hands of members of high castes. Among a
delegation visiting Indira Gandhi early in 1972 to request her to allocate
more money for the work among the Halpatis, only six of the thirty
members belonged to this caste. The hierarchical order is also evident
at the meetings that are held in the districts. The senior social workers
sit in the front rows with the local notables. They address the agricultural labourers, who stand at some distance. The social workers from
the higher castes attach great importance to excessive drinking, lack of
self-discipline, etc. as explanations for the Halpatis' poverty. In fact,
they agree with the translation of the Halpatis' former name of Dublas
as 'weaklings'. As one of them remarked, 'You can always see
which of them are landlords bastards: they have more courage and intelligence'.

The Gandhian veteran Jugatram Dave entrusted the daily management of the HSS to Arvind Desai. The transition from semi-religious

to political leadership could not be better illustrated. The aged spiritual leader Jugatram Dave is held in great veneration. Those who meet him derive moral inspiration from the contact. He is above party politics. The contrary is true of Arvind Desai, a 'boss' if ever there was one, who leads the organization with a strong hand. His word is law, and he leaves no doubt about it. His attitude is recognizably that of a member of the dominant Anvil caste. Not afraid to evoke the wrath of the landlords, paternalistic in his behaviour towards the labourers, he acts like a *rajal* in his domain. When, for instance, the rendering of the song of welcome by the pupils in honour of our visit to a Halpati school was not wholly perfect, he gave vent to his displeasure in no uncertain terms.

The HSS cadre—the local staff members and teachers—consists for the most part of Halpatis. They are generally young people who have been educated at secondary schools, some of them even at the Gandhian Vidyapith College in Ahmedabad. The organization is strongly centralistic, keyed to one-head leadership. The staff members at that level are not authorized to take decisions on their own; they have to refer for the smallest details to the directives issued by the Bardoli head-office, where policies are determined. Those who act on their own authority run the risk of being instantly dismissed. The lack of security—in the lower echelons, the staff members do not hold permanent appointments—virtually enforces submissiveness and unconditional obedience. One of the workers described the HSS succinctly as *halipratha* with Arvind Desai in the role of *dhaniamo*. They have to take second place, and regard this as a conspiracy of the high castes, of which they are able to quote many examples. They are not always right, but figments of the imagination may be quite as illustrative of the prevailing social relationship as facts. These staff members dream of taking over the leadership of the organization, or discuss plans to form groups in secret, in order to offer resistance to the established interests inside and outside the HSS. There were vague references to the Naxalite movement and—very topical at the time of my fieldwork—the Mukti Bahini fighting groups in Bangladesh. But most of the staff members in the lower echelons have resigned themselves to powerlessness and dependence, are under no illusion as to the power of their number, and also show little compassion for the miserable lives led by their fellow caste members. They cling to their jobs in the certainty that they cannot find any other employment.

Contacts with Halpatis

The local workers represent the HSS in the villages. The contacts with the agricultural labourers are indirect, that is to say, through those who have come to the fore as leaders in one or more neighbourhoods (*phalias*). They are visited in the village or asked to come to the small office of the local branch in the *taluka* for consultation.

As I said above, this informal leadership can only be fulfilled by Halpatis who are not directly dependent on the landlords.[2] Another condition is that they must have enough time to maintain their contacts. A Halpati is not recognized as a leader either inside or outside his village until he proves that he is functional to both levels. Since communication is nearly completely verbal he has to be out most of the time, keeping up with the news, maintaining and extending his channels of information. Some ability to read is a real asset, and he must at least be able to put his signature. Finally, all my informants asserted that a certain amount of 'culture' was required: a leader must know how to behave in his contacts with outsiders.

The leadership in question is of a different kind from that exerted by the Panch Patel and the Bhagat (medicine man). Their roles have traditionally been attuned to the needs of the Halpatis themselves, whereas the mediation of the leaders in the village quarters is primarily a question of dealing with outside influences. They themselves have none of the scarce resources at their disposal, but they know how to get access to them. Their intervention is badly needed, especially since the landlords have come to refuse to promote the interests of their subordinates. Through these intermediaries the isolation of the agricultural labourers is somewhat mitigated.

The leading position of the local influentials finds recognition by and through the HSS. They are invited to meetings at which social workers of a higher level lecture on the abuses of alcohol, or propagate education. All those present are asked to introduce themselves and tell something about their own backgrounds. In this way they get acquainted with each other, and a loosely structured network of supra-local relationships grows. The HSS staff keeps them posted on the various activities; the distribution of possible benefits—allocation of land for huts, issue of scholarships, the striking of wells—takes place through their intermediacy.

[2] Among the fifteen local leaders I met, there was not a single agricultural labourer; some have a shop in the Halpati neighbourhood of artisans (carpenter, mason), and others work outside their village as office peons, tiffin carriers, etc.

These local leaders form the backbone of the HSS. In the last election campaign they functioned as the real mobilizers of the Halpatis. But, as it turned out, their political preference was inspired by very pragmatic considerations: they selected the candidate who stood the best chance of winning. There was no question of any ideological motivated choice. Most of them were inclined to regard the differences within and between the parties as conflicts between persons and factions of the elite. Being aware of the fluctuating course of coalitions, these Halpatis tried to behave politically as neutrally as they could.

Are they recognized by the Halpatis as their spokesmen? They are, as I said above, the only channel through which the labourers can obtain benefits. But very clearly they have their own interests, and these do not always run parallel to those of the labourers. They are often blamed for being agents of those in authority. It would, therefore, be incorrect to believe that the Halpati influentials enjoy the confidence of their fellow caste members. This goes even more for the workers of the HSS, who are in fact identified with government officials and scornfully called *chamchas* (lackeys) of the high castes. The local staff members also behave like minor officials. Dressed in terylene trousers, shoes, socks and shirts, and armed with plastic briefcases and with fountain pens in their breast pockets, they address the Halpatis on their rounds through the villages. Reprimandingly, because they do not send their children to school, or encouragingly when it is a question of *bhajan mandli*s to be formed, but always as their superior. Their audience is silent, smiles diffidently or shows signs of muted agreement. Behind their backs the Halpatis—those at least who know about the existence of the HSS—complain of the carelessness, arrogance, and also the corruption of the cadre. The Halpatis are as wary of them as they are themselves of voluntary social workers and politicians from the higher castes.

The Halpatis do not have much cause to regard the HSS as an organization that fights for their interests. For them, it is an obscure body, affiliated with the government and representing external interests. It is, therefore, doubtful whether the HSS may be called an emancipation movement at all—its aims and methods rather seem to prevent mobilization.

Conclusions

With the above, the HSS would seem to stand condemned, but any such judgement should be modified by an appraisal of possible alternatives.

First of all the situation of pauperism as such prevents the agr. &ural labourers from reaching solidarity on a class basis. In a situation of such extreme scarcity, how could we expect them to mobilize on their own? To be sure, dissatisfaction among them is clearly growing. But it still expresses itself in disconnected incidents, particularly in strikes that flare up suddenly but remain limited to one village and soon fall flat when the landlords engage labourers from elsewhere. There is, further, little likelihood that the bargaining power of agricultural labourers will be strengthened by their joining forces, on their own initiative, with *castes* of small landowners. Their economic interests differ too much for that, and their social distance is too great.

What possibilities of organized social action other than by the HSS are there? The political left has barely found a foot-hold in south Gujarat. The Praja Socialist party is as good as liquidated. The cadre of this party had collectively gone over to the Congress party in the early sixties, in exchange for the promise that the large grassland area in the south of Bulsar District, which was in the hands of big landowners, would be distributed among the petty cultivators of tribal castes (the Pardi Grassland Movement).

The Communist movement, which has always been weak in the region, lost even more power after the split in the Congress party. Its most prominent leaders went to the party of Indira Gandhi, taking part of the rank and file with them, and they adjusted themselves without difficulty. Only in the cities of Surat and Bilimora there are small CPI nuclei left. The section in Bulsar District has less than a hundred members. They are practically all urban factory workers, an exceedingly privileged category in comparison with the landless paupers. In the rural regions the CPI is not very active. Bulsar and Surat Districts have never known a strong *kisan* movement. A handful of members in a few villages of Chikhli Taluka—red flags fluttering from long poles over their huts does not make them difficult to trace—led the illegal occupation of some fields belonging to big landowners at the time of the Land Grab movement which took place all over the country in the middle of 1970. Some hundreds of Halpatis joined in the short-lived, badly prepared action. The HSS staff had received orders not to support them, nor were they allowed to aid the victims of the ensuing police terror. Rumour has it that the recent murder of a CPI cadre member in this region was staged as a drunken brawl. The CPI leader of Bulsar District stated that the factory workers are much less militant than the landless Halpatis for fear of losing their jobs. In explanation of the lack of political awareness among the peasant population in the area he said, echoing the words of a national party leader, that Gujarat was the Taiwan of India!

Nor is it to be expected that the Halpatis will join the tribal movement, which reached a peak towards the end of the sixties. The chances of a religious revival based on simple Hindu doctrines, however, are much greater. Literate Halpatis feel strongly attracted to the popular devotional tracts that are distributed on a large scale. The rise of sectarian movements——for which the *bhajan mandlis,* too, prepare the way——is to be explained as a protest against the social discrimination of the Halpatis, but also as an escape from the misery of daily life. It does not look as if the situation of the landless proletariat will improve soon. What are the prespectives for betterment envisaged by the Halpatis themselves? They are not expressed collectively. In any case they should not be measured by those of the HSS. It is believed that pauperized categories tend to hark back nostalgically to the past, and to some extent they do. They claim that they are entitled to the security that was inherent in the *hali* system. Does this mean that they long for the old order to be resorted? Not at all. They value security of enough work at a wage that enables them to keep alive. But they are certainly not interested in a return to the dependence and bondage that formed the basis of the relationship of former times. Landlords show boundless irritation over the fact that agricultural labourers no longer know their place, that is, no longer wish to behave obsequiously. It would seem that precisely the hopeless situation in which the Halpatis now find themselves enhances their militancy. But mobilizing agricultural labourers requires more than that. An increased capability to organize themselves is crucial, and this is done, alberit with other ends in view, by the HSS. The establishment of agricultural labourers, co-operatives, and the leadership training courses for Halpatis who, owing to the efforts of the HSS. , have been elected village headmen, widens the organizational experience of a growing number of Halpatis It is an experience which may in the future be used in a way that leads to real progress.

From this point of view, the growing impatience of a number of social workers inside and outside the HSS is equally promising. Disappointed in the unwillingess of the lanlords to offer the Halpatis a decent existence, they are inclined, in imitation of some movements based on Gandhian ideology elsewheere in India, to set a different and more radical course. It is the course of so-called non-violent direct action in which, if necessary, a confrontation with the landlords is not avoided. The supporters of this view may succeed in adapting in this way the Gandhian strategy to the actual situation, that of a polarized rural system. An important fact in this connection is the organized radicalization of the rural elite. Their representation in the political arena till now was mainly based on caste, but their dominant position is gradually changing in quality. They are increasingly manifesting themselves as a class, and the emergence of economic-interest organizations—such as the rapidly growing Khedut Samaj in Surat District—confirms this tendency. The landlords are opposed to any movement, however moderate, that aims at improving the condition of the agricultural labourers. The aggression of the large farmers is heightened by the organized pressure they exercise nowadays, and this in turn leads to a further escalation of conflicts.

The situation is ripe for an explosion; in fact, it has been ripe for a long time. Not because things can be worse still; there are limits to the absorption capacity of a demoralized proletariat. Organization of the latent unrest is the lacking factor. It will probably be after the event that we will know at what moment the optimal combination of factors came into being. But it would be frivolous to assume that on account of their pauperism combined with Gandhian conditioning, the Halpatis cannot be mobilized in a more antagonistic way. How this will come to pass, and what will be the outcome cannot easily be predicted. In view of the present situation in India, however, there is little reason to be optimistic about an early emancipation of the agricultural labourers.

Tribals in History:
The Case of Chota Nagpur

ROMILA THAPAR AND MAJID HAYAT SIDDIQI

Among the many generalizations made about Chota Nagpur, there are
two which have a bearing on the question of ethnic group relations
in the area. The first is that the Chota Nagpur plateau in eastern India
was cut off from the mainstream of Indian history until the last couple
of centuries, and the second, that the tribal institutions have remained
virtually untouched since their early beginnings with history regularly
superimposing layers of immigrants but leaving the autochthons relatively intact. (A popular misconception holds that the tribal system was
a hunting and gathering one, plough agriculture being a recent innovation.) Both these generalizations probably stem from a colonial histori-
ography which placed unfamiliar cultures outside of what was considered to be the mainstream. There was a distinct cult of the preservation
of earlier forms in such areas and familiarity with these areas is looked
upon as a journey back in time. This chapter sets out to evaluate these
generalizations. Such an exercise involves an attempt to reconstruct the
history of the early period, particularly in terms of the changes
introduced once the State system came to be imposed on the earlier
tribal once. We are concerned with the problem here only as it relates
to the Munda tribes. . . .

Munda society was structured on the basis of the *Khunt Katti* system
which was also adopted by the Oraons. Land was owned by a lineage of

Excerpted from Romila Thapar and Majid Hayat Siddiqi, 'Chota Nagpur: The Pre-
colonial and Colonial Situation', in Roger Batra, ed., *Trends in Ethnic Group Relations in
Asia and Oceania, Race and Society*, UNESCO, 7 place de Fontenoy-75700, Paris 1979.

khunti and rights over land required lineage membership: the argument being that it was the lineage's ancestors who first cleared the land and settled on it. The cultivated area was expanded through the clearing of new land and the setting up of new villages by segments or branches of the main lineage. The heads of these patrilineal clans or *kili* were the powerful *mundas, pahans* and *mahtos*. The *munda* was regarded as the secular chief, while the *pahan* was considered to be his 'spiritual' counterpart. Gradually, both offices became hereditary and had their own lands attached to them. In addition, some land was also set aside as service land dedicated to various spirit cults—the *bhutakheta*. This was distinct from the *sarna*, the sacred grove in which the god resided, and near which, in the *Sasandiri* (burial ground), members of the village lineage or lineages wished to be buried. *Sasandiri* membership was an important proof of the claim to kinship rights in the *kili* or clan. Professional services were provided by craftsmen who were outside the lineage. Lineage landowners (*khuntkattidars*) collected a tribute or a kind of rent from the affinal relatives (*praja*) living in the village.

With the growth of the cultivated area came the need to demarcate village boundaries as well as to organize units of villages for services and administration. Groups of villages—often twelve—were formed into a unit called the *patti* (the *parha* of the Oraons) and the chief of the *patti* was the *manki*. The village chiefs swore allegiance to *manki*, promising him military services and certain gifts which, inevitably, as the *manki's* power increased became regularized as dues. The *manki* often had one village for his personal maintenance and his office was hereditary.

Thus, the emergence and need for the *manki*, the hereditary character of the offices of *manki, munda, pahan* and *mahto*, the hierarchical arrangement and the gradual transformation of the gifts into dues, all encouraged a hierarchical arrangement of power based on access to land and its produce which ran counter to the original lineage system with its stress on egalitarianism. British Indian reports of the nineteenth century have made much of the system as 'the non-Aryan village commune' but it would seem that the egalitarian aspect had been declining for quite some time. The tribal system was giving way to chiefdoms, bringing in the complexities of a ranked society.

It is against this background that the beginnings of a State emerged. Whether the development was internally evolved or imposed by aliens is still a subject of controversy. It has been argued that State-formation occurs particularly among the 'Dravidian' elements who had come from central India (Singh 1971: 170 *et seq.*), but it seems more worth while to look for other preconditions since presumed familiarity with the institution of the State cannot be a sufficient cause. The formal symbol of the emergence of the State was the establishment of the Chota Nagpur Kingdom under the Nagavamsi dynasty. The origin myth of the Nagavamsis is similar in structure to a large body of such myths incorporated with the *Vamsavalis* or dynastic chronicles. These frequently relate how a number of formerly obscure families came into prominence in the early medieval period (from about the eighth century AD onwards) and ultimately established independent kingdoms. Such origin myths cannot be accepted as authentic history in their details but do provide some historical assumptions in their structuring of events.

A characteristic feature of the agrarian system of northern and eastern India in the first millennium AD was that of kings making grants, initially of land and later of villages, to either religious or secular grantees. The grant carried the rights of ownership and revenue from the land and, in the case of villages, the rights of administrative authority at various levels and the collection of taxes and dues. Grants to religious beneficiaries such as Buddhist monasteries and individual Brahmins predated those to secular grantees. These became more common in the later half of the millennium and were frequently made to officers in lieu of salaries for services. In addition, when senior administrative offices became hereditary it was possible for families to use these grants to build a base for themselves and eventually emerge as independent rulers.[1] Such families used origin myths to acquire *ksatriya* status.[2]

From about the eighth century AD the frequency of the grants increased. Improved irrigation techniques, such as the Persian wheel, in some areas increased the productivity of land already under cultivation and, in others, made possible the utilization of hitherto uncultivable land. There was therefore a search for new land. The period from AD 1000-1200 has been described as the heyday of land grants in northern and eastern India with an increasing tendency to grant whole villages. The Gahadvalas, based in western Uttar Pradesh, had feudatories as far

---

[1] One such example was the Maitrakas of Vallabhi in western India. These officers of the Gupta kings moved up the ladder from generation to generation in the post-Gupta period from *senapati* (army, commander), *samanta* (feudatory) to raja and finally maharaja.

[2] Such myths are referred to briefly in the inscriptions, particularly land grant charters and donatory inscriptions, of the newly established kings. Further details on the myths and the acquisition of status are to be found in the various Vamsavalis of the kingdom.

away as Palamau in Chota Nagpur, such as the Khayaravalas of Japla who were themselves sufficiently well off to make grants of villages to others, thus encouraging the process of subinfeudation. In Bhagelkhand to the north-west of Chota Nagpur, the system of grants was well established by the Kalacuri Kings. Brahmins migrated from Uttar Pradesh, Bihar and Bengal to Orissa and other parts of the subcontinent and were in great demand in these areas. Orissa records a heavy number of grants to Brahmins, particularly during the reign of the Tunga dynasty, which claimed to have come from Rohtas. In the earlier part of this period, records relating to the granting of villages did not define village boundaries clearly, thus suggesting the availability of land. Twelfth-century records however indicate these boundaries very precisely. This has led to the suggestion that by the thirteenth century the colonization of new land was exhausted in Uttar Pradesh, Bihar and Bengal. If this was so then a search would have to be made further afield for less optimum areas. Possibly at this point Chota Nagpur came into the search for new lands.

Brahmin grantees settled on their estates and either introduced or strengthened the influence of Brahminical, Sanskritic culture in the region. Before the period of extensive subinfeudation they were also the innovators of improved agricultural techniques. Secular grants were made either to existing village headmen or chiefs who would remain in their own areas but would indicate their new status by acquiring the trappings of Sanskritic culture and courtly norms in immitation of the more powerful courts of their overlords; or the grants were made to officials who, as aliens, took up residence in the new area and brought the courtly life with them and used the area to create their political base. The emergence of the Nagavamsis in Chota Nagpur seems to have followed one of these patterns.

Some clues are provided by the origin myth of the Nagavamsis (Haldar 1928:259-93), whose significant features are that the founder of the dynasty, Phani Mukut Rai, is of Naga origin and does not claim the higher status of a *suryavamsi* or *candravamsi ksatriya* (i.e., of either the solar of lunar lineage, or even the *agni-kula* or fire lineage, all of which were accorded a high rank). As is often the case, his mother is of Brahmin descent and his father a serpent in human form explaining the name *naga* (serpent), as well as giving him a supernatural ancestry. The child is born and abandoned soon after when the parents are returning from a pilgrimage to Orissa. The orphaned child is protected by a sun-worshipping Sakadvipi Brahmin, a category which was looked upon as distinctly inferior until the medieval period when it rose in status and became particularly influential in Orissa. The child is adopted by a *manki* thus securing his local status. The problem of succession is then raised and the Munda and Oraon clan chiefs jointly decide to put him to the test. He proved his superiority over the *manki's* own son and was therefore given precedence over him. Eventually, he became the first raja of Chota Nagpur, although the myth glosses over the intervening steps from *manki* to raja.

Clearly, Phani Mukut Rai was not a Munda but an adopted alien. The coming of the family to Chota Nagpur may have been due to one of two possibilities. Either a Sakadvipi Brahmin family had been given a grant of villages and had gradually built up a political power base through appropriating revenue collecting rights and taxes, possibly marrying into a local *manki* family, after investing it with the appropriate caste rank and ultimately established a kingdom; or a member of a Nagavamsi family was similarly granted villages in the region and used the same technique to acquire a kingdom. The territory of the kingdom was probably quite small at this stage. Nagavamsi families were known in various parts of the subcontinent but among the more prominent ones in the medieval period was that of the Chakrakottas (the Bastars in the Madhya Pradesh). In the eleventh and twelfth centuries, this dynasty successfully campaigned against the Kalacuris in Dakshina Kosala (to the west of Chota Nagpur) extending its territorial control to the borders of Chota Nagpur. A campaign against Orissa is also on record as is the existence of a Nagavamsi dynasty in that region.[3] Possibly a branch of one of these families established itself through a series of grants in the north-west part of Chota Nagpur, in about the thirteenth century or even later.

Thus, validation of a dynasty came through the origin myth, marriage alliances and ritual symbols. Its formal symbol was expanded into other observances and rites associated with the Great Tradition and State-formation in medieval India (Sinha 1962:35-80). The Brahmins presided over rituals especially those connected with 'rites of passage', and marriage alliances with *ksatriya* families from elsewhere

---

[3] The connection with Orissa appears to have been fairly close during this period since the Panchpargana area south of Ranchi displays traces of Oriya influence in its icons and temple architecture. D.P. Patil, *Antiquarian Remains in Bihar*. The Surya icon in the *sarna* and Buradih bears a striking resemblance to the Surya image from Kiching. A systematic study of the icons and shrines of this area could provide valuable evidence on chronology and contacts. Perhaps the river valleys of the Subarnarekha and Baitarni acted as routes inland from the coastal areas.

buttressed status.[4] There was a conspicuous display of wealth in imitation of a 'Hinduized' life-style as manifested by the construction of temples and palaces, while elements of the literature of the Great Tradition, the spices, and the Puranas filltered down to the levels beyond the court and so on.[5]

Not that these symbols were entirely alien. Local cults and customs were incorporated into the elite culture but presented as manifestations of the Great Tradition. Thus, local goddesses came to be worshipped as the consorts of Siva and were invested with the correct attributes, iconic forms and Puranic myths.[6] The link with Sivaism reflects the earlier phase of contact.[7] More intensive Hinduization occurs with the arrival of Vaisnavism. The saint Chaitanya is said to have travelled from Orissa through Chota Nagpur in the fifteenth century with some evident impact, for from the seventeenth century onwards, Vaisnavism acquired substantial royal patronage.

The more fundamental changes however related to rights over land. The axis shifted from clan to territory: tenurial rights based on kinship were encroached upon by those based on professional services. The raja granted lands and villages on perpetual tenures for military, administrative and personal services— the services required by the infrastructure of a State. The grantees attempted to appropriate the maximum rights. A distinction was made between the lineage lands or *bhuinhari* (the remnant of the old *khuntkatti*), the lands held directly by

[4] This is reflected in the Nagabansi Annals when Phani Mukut Rai wishes to marry the daughter of the Sikhar raja. The latter belonged to the high-ranking Parmara'*ksatriya* of the *agni-kula* (fire lineage) and was naturally hesitant about giving his approval. We are told that Phani Mukut Rai's father appeared before the messenger of the Sikhar raja in his natural form of a snake and declared the parentage of his son whereupon the bride's father agreed to the marriage.

[5] The Nagabansi Annals are based quite clearly on the genealogical sections of the Puranas and the Mahabharata. A more widespread influence can perhaps be observed in the significance of the flood in Munda cosmology where it plays the same structural role as in the Puranic tradition.

[6] These influences were not limited to Saiva cults alone as is evident from the occasional Buddhist icon from the medieval period which turns up in the western areas of the Chota Nagpur plateau. A striking example of what seems to be an Avalokitesvara figure is to be found in a *devta jhumra* (sacred grove) near the village of Majhgaon, not far from the shrine of Tanginath. This again ties in with the existence of a particular sect of Buddhism in eastern India mostly during the early medieval period, as well as indicating a growth in the agricultural base in this region.

[7] The story of Tanginath, whose shrine is located in the Chainpur subdivision, shows evident borrowing from Puranic tradition, Tanginath himself echoing Parasurama in the association with the axe. The rituals reflect a mixture of the two traditions; Puranic and

the grantee or the *manjhas* lands and those from which the produce was collected and given to the grantee for the raja, the *rajhus* lands. Quite clearly, the original *khuntkatti* had been dealt a severe blow and was further weakened when the grantee acquired the *bhuinharis* of those who had died intestate or had migrated. Later, with the giving of villages or even *parganas* to such members or the raja's family as the Kanwars, Thakurs and Lallas as maintenance grants, a further erosion of lineage rights took place especially when they, in turn, granted land to their retainers. Thus, the tendency towards social stratification which had already begun with the *khuntkatti* system was not only intensified and accelerated under the State, but was also made more complex with the interpolation of various levels of intermediaries. The breaking down of the tribal mode of production related not merely to the loss of lineage rights over land and the redistribution system according to lineage, but also to the loss of politico-juridical rights invested in the lineage. These rights now passed into the hands of professionals outside the lineage, and often from outside the region. With the resultant strengthening of the correlation of social status with landholding and power, the earlier lineage connections became less important although they did not disappear.[8] The situation has been described as the superimposition of a feudal State on tribal society. To some extent this is true. But had the tribe been converted into a caste or had the State evolved through a process of internal development, it is likely that tribal identity would have still been eroded.

The question as to how tribal identity (albeit in a battered form) survived, needs an answer. Perhaps the availability of wasteland or forest with a relatively sparse population provided the continuing

---

...bal. The shrine is served by Kherwar priests *(baiga)* who now call themselves Ahira-...nkhi Kherwars, but the ritual is Brahminical. The shrine, although well-endowed with ...ons of the medieval period, seems not to have been a major centre of Brahminism. Inter-...stingly, local opinion associates the shrine with the *sadhus* of the Nath-sampradaya—an ...nfluential, popular, pan-Indian movement, not always acceptable to the orthodox.

[8] This is again reflected in the Nagabansi Annals where we are told that Phani Mukut Rai invited all the Munda and Oraon chiefs to a feast and plied them with liquor. In an ensuing drunken brawl they began killing one another. Only a few survived and the Kols were put down. Among those who survived were the two *mankis* (in some versions only one is mentioned) who had reared Phani Mukut Rai as an orphaned child. Permitted to ask for a favour, they requested to become Bhuinharas and be permitted to take this title. Perhaps this account proves that the accession of the Nagabansis was not as peaceful as it is often made out to have been.

possibility of new *khuntkattis*, at least in the period prior to the seventeenth century. Inevitably, the new *khuntkattis* would be swallowed up in the State system but the grantees may have encouraged them initially as a means of bringing more land under cultivation. Given the generally low yield of the land and lack of agricultural innovation Chota Nagpur was not to experience intensive colonization during this period. The best land would slowly be acquired by the hierarchy of grantees, but the less fertile areas and the uplands would not arouse great interest among the new landowners.

State formation requires the availability of a substantial surplus of a kind which the tribal land cannot provide. Presumably there was some improvement in agricultural technology and irrigation facilities which helped in the generation of a surplus. Yet the Saradkel excavation would suggest that plough agriculture was known prior to the coming of the State. Irrigation technology could have meant the introduction of the water-lifting system or the Persian wheel, both of which would have reduced dependence on rainfall. Whereas the former appears to have been widely used, the opposite seems to be the case for the latter, possibly because it was not very suitable for the terrain. Perhaps the surplus was produced not by a system of intensive agriculture but by extending the acreage under cultivation.

As we have suggested, the preservation of tribal identity was in part due to the nature of land relations. In addition, the cultural legitimization of the elite was in terms of a wider Indian context, i.e. the world of Sanskritic courtly culture, however watered down its expression may have been in areas at a distance from the nucleus. Integration existed at the court level for the *jagirdars* and possibly some clan chiefs, but did not permeate much further. Elite culture was, therefore, a Sanskritic culture thus deepening the differentiation between the Munda and Oraon, on the one hand, and those who represented the State, on the other. The arrival of Vaisnavism, perhaps the most assimilative of current religious movements, was late, requiring and encouraging as it does a well-established agricultural base and a network of trade connections. . . .

. . . If the major trade routes continued to bypass the area, the incidence of trade would then be restricted to local markets and small-scale traders. Commodity production does not flourish in tribal economies; but here even the non-tribal appear to have been unconcerned with commodity production. Apart from some agricultural produce, there was little to attract the trading entrepreneur. Iron production was frequently a State monopoly and diamonds did not offer opportunities for large-scale trade. In such a situation the trader would be the alien simply bringing in goods from the outside world to bolster the life-style of a local élite. Trading activities would increase and reach the non-élite levels only after the introduction of money. It is perhaps not altogether surprising that the term '*diku*' (outsider/alien) was initially applied to the moneylenders. Commodity production on any appreciable scale may well have weakened tribal identity.

The pressure on the land would appear to date from the seventeenth century when the area was drawn into the orbit of Mughal influence; up until then the court at Delhi showed little interest in the Argaon. We are told that in the fourteenth century Firoz Shah Tughlaq, returning from a campaign in Orissa, passed through Jharkhand—the forest land, as Chota Nagpur came to be called. Incursions into the adjoining areas by adventurers and others from the courts of northern India are also on record for this period. It would seem that the accommodation of outsiders as retainers was in full swing even in Chota Nagpur. It was the Mughal Emperor's interest in diamonds mined in the area which led the Mughal army into Khokhara (Abul Fazl, *Ain-in-Akbari*). The Mughal action resulted in the demand for a regular revenue from the raja and this, in turn, necessitated a fuller exploitation of the land.

The memoirs of the Mughal Emperor Jehangir record how a region called 'Khokhara' in the south of contemporary Bihar and ruled over by a petty chief was brought under Mughal rule after its diamond mines had attracted the emperor's attention. Jehangir's military commander, Ibrahim Khan, was ordered by the Emperor in 1616

to go and take the province out of the possession of that unknown and insignificant individual [Raja Durjan Sal]. As soon as he arrived in the province of Bihar, he assembled a force and went against that Zamindar. According to former custom he [the raja] sent some of his men with a promise to give some diamonds and some elephants. . . . (Beveridge 1968 : 315-16).

But Ibrahim Khan could not be persuaded to withdraw and pursued Durjan Sal to the jungle area of the plateau where the raja took refuge in a cave. Elephants and diamonds worth several thousands of rupees were extorted from Durjan Sal who was captured and taken to the Mughal court. After a few years of captivity and the payment of some more tribute, Durjan Sal was released. From that time on, while continuing as a part of the larger province of Bihar, and later of Bengal, and tech-

nically a tribute-paying subordinate chieftainship of the Mughal Empire, Khokhara was a quasi-independent kingdom in the heart of the
empire. It was not an exceedingly productive area and as such was
never really coveted by Mughal feudalism which survived for over two
centuries on the produce from the more fertile and better cultivated
areas. As mentioned earlier, the point to remember in all this is that the
autonomy of the quasi-independent Chota Nagpur was not absolute.
In terms of the nature of the existing relations of production and exchange in the region surrounding Chota Nagpur, this small isolated
chieftainship was surrounded and assailed by an economic system in
which the cash-nexus prevailed (Habib 1963). Consequently, the regular revenue payments which had to be made after the inclusion of Chota
Nagpur in the British East India Company's dominions changed the
internal tribal social structure composed primarily of the original
Munda and Oraon settlers to one of increasing landlordism during the
first and second stages of colonial rule. This led to social dislocations,
i.e. tribal revolts, the most important of which were those of 1831-2,
and between 1895 and 1900.

Further Readings

Chakravarti, Anand,
1975   *Contradiction and Change: Emerging Patterns of Authority in a Rajasthan Village*, Oxford University Press, Delhi.
         By concentrating diachronically on a single Rajasthan village, the author demonstrates the analytical importance of examining changes in local power alignments within a larger and more inclusive political structure of the country.

Mahar, J. Michael, ed.,
1972   *The Untouchables in Contemporary India*, University of Arizona Press, Tuscon, Arizona.
         A very useful reader, focussing on the political and cultural means employed by Untouchables in different parts of India to socially uplift themselves from their traditional degraded status.

Omvedt, Gail, ed.,
1982   *Land, Caste and Politics in Indian States*, University of Delhi, Delhi.
         The essays in this book draw upon empirical data from different provinces of India to demonstrate the variations possible in caste and class alignments in situations of conflict.

Kothari, Rajni, ed.,
1970   *Caste in Indian Politics*, Orient Longman, New Delhi.
         Though this book carries an interesting collection of papers it is best known for the editor's introduction which argues that we replace the notion of 'casteism of politics' by one of the 'politicization of castes' if we are to grasp the reality of caste and politics in India.

Sharma, K.L., ed.,
1986   *Social Stratification in India*, Manohar, Delhi.
         This book attempts to open up the field of social stratification by including essays which relate conflict, class and caste to sub disciplines such as agrarian sociology, industrial sociology, sociology of professions, sociology of ethnicity and migration.

Appendices

I

The Use of the Marxian Method
of Class Analysis

GAVIN SMITH

I

Class analysis is less concerned with breaking down society into discrete groupings of people with bundles of common characteristics
than with trying to examine the whole social structure as a system of

Excerpted from Gavin Smith, 'The Use of Class Analysis', in D. H. Turner and G. A
Smith, eds, *Challenging Anthropology*, McGraw-Hill Pyerson Limited, Toronto, 1979.

classes. So the problem of slotting particular individuals into certain categories called 'classes' is a second order concern. What is of primary importance is to assess how the working of a particular social structure acts to push people towards one another in one direction, and against others in another direction. So the kinds of classes existing in a society are essentially linked to the kind of social structure the society has. It follows from this that the first task of a class analysis is to ascertain the nature of the social structure being examined.

So before saying anything about *class*, I must say something about what I mean by social structure. In fact, I prefer the expression *social formation*, because it helps to remind us that societies are engaged in an endless dynamic of forming and re-forming the essential relationships which give them a particular character. This view of society needs clarifying before we can go on.

Let us suppose that societies can be seen as factories which are in the business of producing social relations. Let us go further and suggest that, while this is their ultimate task, in order to undertake it successfully they have to produce many other things besides social relations. In fact, they have to produce people, and goods to satisfy the desires of those people. In a sense then, societies are the mirror image of our common-sense view of a factory: a car factory serves to maintain and reproduce a certain set of social relationships—between shareholders, managers, workers, and sales people—in order to produce its end product: a car. A society has to reproduce goods and people in order to produce its end product: a particular set of social relationships.

If this analogy seems a little far-fetched, let me re-examine what I have just said about the car factory. It is at least possible that the car factory exists not so much to produce cars, but to provide dividends to its shareholders and a wage for its managers and workers; should the production of cars become unprofitable, shareholders, managers and employees may all be agreeable to changing the end product to something else. The product changes in order to maintain the factory (strictly speaking, the set of social relationships which we have called a 'factory'). Whether or not you find this second view of the factory acceptable, you will, I hope, agree that, as social scientists, it might be useful to look at factories in this light.

Anyway, whether we are talking about factories or social formations, the key concept is that of *producing*. In looking at a particular social formation, the question that matters is, 'How does this social formation produce and reproduce through history the social relations contained within it?'

Social anthropologists answer this question by suggesting that it is done through the interaction of people, mediated through things. There are in fact two processes involved here, which are so closely intertwined that it is impossible to think of one without holding in our minds at the same time our concept of the other. Nevertheless, for the purpose of analysis we have to try to separate them out. On the one hand, people act upon the material of the world in order to produce the goods which society deems necessary for its survival (in its present form). On the other hand, it is impossible to conceive of people doing this without entering into relationships with one another. In fact, I have already suggested that, in the *social* world we live in, it is the needs of these social relations which call forth and then give form to the former activity of work.

The reason why there is this reversal, in society, of what appears to our common sense (i.e., work leads to social relations) is that the act of appropriating goods from nature (i.e., work) involves not only the input of labour, but also access to essential things: tools and raw materials. And in any given society access to these things is laid out by the social relations of the society: men have axes, women baskets; the tiger clan have the river bank, the leopards the forest, and so on. In order to emphasize my interest in society as a system of production, I shall refer to these relationships as the *social relations of production*.

The actual work of putting out energy in order to appropriate goods from nature, I shall refer to as the *forces of production*, and besides the combination of labour with tools and raw materials, I shall also include under this rubric the actual *way* in which these are combined as a function of the skills of the producers and the technical development of tools which pevails in the society. This will give us the technological division of labour for producing a certain good in the society: a loaf of bread, a suit of clothes or whatever. (It is important to note, at this point however, that this easily visible set of technical relations arising during the production of a paiticular good must not be confused with the often far less discernible *social relations of production*.)

In any particular social formation being studied, it is possible to examine the way in which the *forces* and *social relations* of production are intertwined, the one determining and constraining the development of the other. For example, the introduction of the production line in the U.S. (i.e., and instrument in the *forces* of production) had a significant influence in modifying the social relations of North American society. This was so because of the impetus it gave to economies of scale, thus allowing a very few, very large, firms to control production (an element in the *social relations* of production). On the other hand, existing social relations of production in contemporary North America mitigate against the development of efficient public transport systems, partly because of the threat they would be to existing social relations of production and partly because the social relations of production in a capitalist society make it difficult to develop a communications network within the framework of 'free enterprise'. From this latter point of view then, social relations influence the development or not of the forces of production. I shall refer to this twofold process as *reciprocal causality*.

To say that these two elements are intertwined, however, is not to say that their interrelationship is complementary. In many social formations the relationship between forces and relations of production is one of endless tension and contradiction. This becomes clearer if you reflect that control over the resources of a society (social relations of production) is of little use to those who have control unless the resources can be given value by being put to work (by the forces of production). Your control over a tractor, for example, may not be especially advantageous to you, if nobody is willing or able to drive it for you. By the same token, it makes no odds if you are the straightest ploughman in the neighbourhood; if you have neither plough, nor oxen, nor tractor you will go without work unless you can gain access to these necessary instruments. Here I am stressing the ties between those who offer labour and skill and those who control resources; it can be referred to as a relationship of dependency.

But where the control over resources is separated from the input of the human energy that makes them work (as in the example I have just given), there is likely to be latent tension in the society, and this I shall call a relationship of conflict.

It is here that we move from a discussion of the general characteristics of a social formation to the question of *class*. What gives class interaction its dynamic quality is the coexistence of these two relationships: dependency and conflict. As a political strategist, you would have to reflect hard on what the implications would be for political tactics if you found a relationship of conflict but no crucial dependency, or one of dependency but no conflict. In neither case would you be looking at relations between two *classes*.

If the social anthropologist can locate the points in the social formation where this kind of structural tension is inherent to the way the society is put together and made to work, then he or she can begin to discover the social forces behind the development of that society. This is because, where the elements of a system are not perfectly compatible, they are subject to constant reformulation. Their total destruction and replacement by new relations between the elements will, in the last analysis, take the form of a conflict between classes: interests representing preservation versus interests representing structural change. It is for this reason that class analysis of a society is important.

II

We can now look at the essential features of class. I shall do this by bringing the discussion on a statement made by Lenin in 1919, when the understanding of the important classes in Russia was crucial for the direction of a revolution.

Classes are large groups of people differing from each other by the place they occupy in a historically determined system of social production, by their relation (in most cases fixed and formulated by law) to the means of production [i.e., tools and raw materials], by their role in the social organization of labour, and consequently by the dimensions of the share of social wealth of which they dispose and the mode of acquiring it. Classes are groups of people one of which can appropriate the labour of another owing to the different places they occupy in a definite system of social economy [in our terms: social formation] (1971: 486).

According to this formulation, classes are determined by both the social relations of production and the forces of production. In terms of the social relations of production, we are talking about people who can either control the important resources of the society (the means of production) or not. And in terms of the forces of production, the organization of labour is such that either the controllers themselves work the tools and raw materials (you drive your own tractor), or people separated from control do it (somebody else drives your tractor).

Two points arise at this stage. Firstly, it is impossible to understand what a class is without placing it in the context of the working of the whole society. And secondly, a class arises out of a relationship and must therefore be understood by reference to other classes which act to define and confine it. As the angle of a triangle cannot be thought of without reference to its position *vis-à-vis* the other two angles, so too with classes in society.

Emmanuel Terray has suggested that we can formulate four types of essential classes:

1. Producers controlling the means of production.
2. Producers separated from the means of production.
3. Nonproducers controlling the means of production.
4. Nonproducers separated from the means of production.

At a very schematic level what we have is as follows. In the first case you have a hypothetical society with only one class: those who produce also control. There may be a few people, such as old people and children, who fall into the fourth kind of class in such a society, but these people hardly constitute a class since they are not related to the means of production in any way (according to Terray's breakdown). In essence then, this would be a classless society: the producers may put aside some surplus in order to maintain the nonproducers in the fourth kind of class, but it is they (the producers) who can decide what this should be, since they also control the means of production.

In the case of (2) and (3), we are talking about a conventional class society of some kind, consisting of producers and controllers. The controllers' command of the means of production puts them in a position to be able to demand some surplus from the producers. Because the producers, in this kind of society, must rely on the controllers in order to get the necessary tools and raw materials in order to produce at all, they are obliged to relinquish some of what they produce over and above what they require for their own sakes alone. Conversely, by dint of having control over the valued resources of the society, the controllers do not themselves have to work productively in appropriating goods from nature (after Terray, 1975: 87-8).

This gives us the essential configuration of what is involved in a class analysis, while at the same time raising a number of problems. The most important of these are: 'How is control over the means of production by a particular class exercised in any given society, i.e., what form does it take? What other elements in the social formation such as ideology and politics are brought into play as part of this control?' 'How is this control used as a means for extracting surplus from the direct producers?' 'How does the controlling class reallocate this surplus in such a way as to ensure its own continued survival?' and finally, 'What are the varying roles of the fourth type of class which Terray suggests, in the differing kinds of societies we study?'

We can best answer these questions by turning the spotlight onto different kinds of societies which interest social anthropologists.

III

Limitations of space make it impossible to dwell at any length on a class analysis of 'tribal' social formations. What I can do is suggest the kinds of questions which would be relevant for establishing the power of class relationships as a social force in any such society.

Despite the fact that very little class analysis of the kind I have been discussing has been undertaken for 'tribal' societies, two things immediately become obvious when attempting such an examination of these societies. Firstly, it is impossible to come up with any universally valid criteria of what establishes class relationships in all societies; and secondly, since class has to do with access to valued resources, so many other elements in the social formation may be brought into play—such as the ideology of kinship, or the use of physical might (power)—that it would be misleading to restrict class analysis to an examination solely of the forces and relations of production. Such an analysis may give you the beginning of class relationships without allowing you to see how those relationships were expressed in the specific society you were looking at.

Let us imagine a society in which both agricultural and animal husbandry takes place. Agricultural land is divided into two categories: there is land which is farmed by the group as a whole supposedly for the benefit of the community and its gods; and there are smaller plots farmed by each household unit. Labour on communal land and the distribution of the small plots to households are supervised by the elders of the group. Livestock are held by individual households; pasture is held by the community, but the location of flocks on the land is again supervised by the elders.

The questions which concern us are whether or not there is a group in this society with a capacity to exclude and hence control certain important resources, what these resources are, and, if such control does exist, from what does it derive?

In our rather abbreviated example, it is clear that the elders do appear to have some control. In some cases, they may only have discretionary control over the distribution of the final product: their authority may simply be limited to distributing the products of labour on community land. If this is so, then the actual power to retain some of this surplus for themselves will be severely restricted. If, however, the elders control this *distribution of the social product* as a function of their *prior control over some of the essential means of production*, as is the case in the example given here (they not only supervise the labour on the communal fields and the distribution of the harvest thereafter, but they also *control* the distribution of individual household plots and pasture), then the possibilities for them to retain surplus for themselves are clearly much greater.

So it is necessary, then, to distinguish between *control over the distribution of the social product* (in this case the harvest on communal land) from *control over the distribution of the means of production*. The first is essentially functional for social production; when this includes some supervision of the labour process itself, as in our case, we may refer to it as *the management function*. The second is at least potentially exploitative, by which I mean that control over the means of production may allow the elders to hold back some of the surplus in order to use it for the continued reproduction of their position of power.

Nevertheless, this may not be the only way by which elders can retain surplus. Where control over the distribution of the social product does not derive quite so overtly from control over such obvious means of production as the land, domination may be retained through the use of ideology: the maintenance of myths about reciprocity, for example, and the control of important symbols. This, however, is likely to lead to the allocation of certain surpluses into the ideological apparatus—shrines, priests, etc.—and insofar as this apparatus is used for the maintenance of dependency relationships, it is not true to say that the surplus used to cover such 'costs' is being redistributed entirely for the benefit of the direct producers.

All I have done here is raised the questions relevant for a class analysis of 'tribal' societies. It seems to me at least, that while we have avoided the danger of presenting producers in classless societies as all equal controllers of the means of production, we are not necessarily referring to class relationships in quite the nice way suggested by the scheme laid out in section II. To begin with, the elders are not recruited on the basis of their relationship to the means of production, but rather on the basis of their position in the system of kinship, and possibly other criteria more ascribed than achieved. Secondly, while what Rey refers to as 'the power of function' (management) may be turned to 'the power of exploitation' (1975: 29), it remains the case that at least *some* surplus must be disbursed outside the dominant class, in what Sahlins (1966) refers to as 'the politics of generosity'. This would seem to mitigate against the possibility of any real class-like formation among one group. Thirdly, we must be careful to distinguish between 'managers' and 'controllers' between a *technical* process and a *social* relation. It would seem that the two kinds of class (2) and (3) in my earlier schema, do not quite work here, because elders may in fact not necessarily be either real controllers (in the sense of exclusive possessors) nor entirely nonproducers, insofar as they are performing an essential management function on behalf of the direct producers (Hindess & Hirst 1977: 67-72).

One final point should be made. These remarks about pre-state social formations seem to call into question just what can be referred to as *means of production*. It would seem that particular symbols in some societies are vital for the process of production—certain totemic emblems for example. Does control over these constitute a form of control over the means of production? If this is so, then class analysis must concern itself with far more than the purely 'economic' narrowly conceived.

The question of the role of 'class' interaction in the historical development of 'tribal' societies must remain unanswered, as long as ethnography continues to concentrate on the effect of status relationship on the functioning of 'tribal' societies, rather than on the way in which differential control over valued resources and variations in position in the process of social production gives a class-like characteristic to such social formations. Until class analysis is undertaken, the question of transition from classless to class societies will likewise remain a matter of conjecture.

II

Some Principles of Stratification:
The Functionalist Position

KINGSLEY DAVIS AND WILBERT E. MOORE

In the present paper a further step in stratification theory is undertaken—an attempt to show the relationship between stratification and the rest of the social order. Starting from the proposition that no

Kingsley Davis and Wilbert E. Moore, 'Some Principles of Stratification', *American Sociological Review*, 10, No. 2, April 1945.

society is 'classless' or unstratified, an effort is made to explain, in functional terms, the universal necessity which calls forth stratification in any social system. Next, an attempt is made to explain the roughly uniform distribution of prestige as between the major types of positions in every society. Since, however, there occur between one society and another great differences in the degree and kind of stratification, some attention is also given to the varieties of social inequality and the variable factors that give rise to them.

Clearly, the present task requires two different lines of analysis—one to understand the universal, the other to understand the variable features of stratification. Naturally each line of inquiry aids the other and is indispensable, and in the treatment that follows the two will be interwoven, although, because of space limitations, the emphasis will be on the universals.

Throughout, it will be necessary to keep in mind one thing—namely, that the discussion relates to the system of positions, not to the individuals occupying those positions. It is one thing to ask why different positions carry different degrees of prestige, and quite another to ask how certain individuals get into those positions. Although, as the argument will try to show, both questions are related, it is essential to keep them separate in our thinking. Most of the literature on stratification has tried to answer the second question (particularly with regard to the ease or difficulty of mobility between strata) without tackling the first. The first question, however, is logically prior and, in the case of any particular individual or group, factually prior.

The Functional Necessity of Stratification

Curiously, however, the main functional necessity explaining the universal presence of stratification is precisely the requirement faced by any society of placing and motivating individuals in the social structure. As a functioning mechanism a society must somehow distribute its members in social positions and induce them to perform the duties of these positions. It must thus concern itself with motivation at two different levels: to instill in the proper individuals the desire to fill certain positions, and once in these positions, the desire to perform the duties attached to them. Even though the social order may be relatively static in form, there is a continuous process of metabolism as new individuals are born into it, shift with age, and die off. Their absorption into the positional system must somehow be arranged and motivated. This is true whether the system is competitive or non-competitive. A competitive system gives greater importance to the motivation to achieve positions, where a non-competitive system gives perhaps greater importance to the motivation to perform the duties of the position; but in any system both types of motivation are required.

If the duties associated with the various positions were all equally pleasant to the human organism, all equally important to societal survival, and all equally in need of the same ability or talent, it would make no difference who got into which positions, and the problem of social placement would be greatly reduced. But actually it does make a great deal of difference who gets into which positions, not only because some positions are inherently more agreeable than others, but also because some require special talents of training and some are functionally more important than others. Also, it is essential that the duties of the positions be performed with the diligence that their importance requires. Inevitably, then, a society must have, first, some kind of rewards that it can use as inducements, and second some way of distributing these rewards differentially according to positions. The rewards and their distribution become a part of the social order, and thus give rise to stratification.

One may ask what kind of rewards a society has at its disposal in distributing its personnel and securing essential services. It has, first of all, the things that contribute to sustenance and comfort. It has, second, the things that contribute to humour and diversion. And it has, finally, the things that contribute to self-respect and ego expansion. The last, because of the peculiarly social character of the self, is largely a function of the opinion of others, but it nonetheless ranks in importance with the first two. In any social system three kinds of rewards must be dispensed differentially according to positions.

In a sense the rewards are built into the positions. They consist in the rights associated with the position, plus what may be called its accompaniments or perquisites. Often the rights, and sometimes the accompaniments, are functionally related to the duties of the position. Rights as viewed by the incumbent are usually duties as viewed by other members of the community. However, there may be a host of subsidiary rights and perquisites that are not essential to the function of the position and have only an indirect and symbolic connection with its duties, but which still may be of considerable importance in inducing people to seek the positions and fulfil the essential duties.

If the rights and perquisites of different positions in a society must be unequal, then the society must be stratified, because that is

precisely whatstratification means. Social inequality is thus an unconsciously evolved device by which societies insure that the most
important positions are conscientiously filled by the most qualified
persons. Hence every society, no matter how simple or complex, must
differentiate persons in terms of both prestige and esteem, and must
therefore possess a certain amount of institutionalized inequality.

It does not follow that the amount or type of inequality need be the
same in all societies. This is largely a function of factors that will be
discussed presently

THE TWO DETERMINANTS OF POSITIONAL RANK

Granting the general function that inequality subserves, one can specify
the two factors that determine the relative rank of different positions.
In general those positions convey the best reward, and hence have the
highest rank which (a) have the greatest importance for the society
and (b) require the greatest training or talent. The first factor concerns
function and is a matter of relative significance; the second concerns
means and is a matter of scarcity.

Differential Functional Importance

Actually a society does not need to reward positions in proportion
to their functional importance. It merely needs to give sufficient
reward to them to insure that they will be filled competently. In other
words, it must see that less essential positions do not compete
successfully with more essential ones. If a position is easily filled, it
need not be heavily rewarded, even though important. On the other
hand, if it is important but hard to fill, the reward must be high enough
to get it filled anyway. Functional importance is therefore a necessary but not a sufficient cause of high rank being assigned to a position.[1]

---

[1] Unfortunately, functional importance is difficult to establish. To use the position's
prestige to establish it, as is often unconsciously done, constitutes circular reasoning from
our point of view. There are, however, two independent clues (1) the degree to which a
position is functionally unique, there being no other positions that can perform the
same function satisfactorily (2) the degree to which other positions are dependent on
the one in question. Both clues are best exemplified in organized systems of positions
built around one major function. Thus, in most complex societies the religious, political,
economic, and educational functions are handled by distinct structures not easily inter-
changeable. In addition, each structure possesses many different positions, some clearly

Differential Scarcity of Personnel

Practically all positions, no matter how acquired, require some form of skill or capacity for performance. This is implicit in the very notion of position which implies that the incumbent must, by virtue of his incumbency, accomplish certain things.

There are, ultimately, only two ways in which a person's qualifications come about through inherent capacity or through training. Obviously, in concrete activities both are always necessary, but from a practical standpoint the scarcity may lie primarily in one or the other, as well as in both. Some positions require innate talents of such high degree that persons who fill them are bound to be rare. In many cases, however, talent is fairly abundant in the population but the training process is so long, costly, and elaborate that relatively few can qualify. Modern medicine, for example, is within the mental capacity of most individuals, but a medical education is so burdensome and expensive that virtually none would undertake it if the position of the MD did not carry a reward commensurate with the sacrifice.

If the talents required for a position are abundant and the training easy, the method of acquiring the position may have little to do with its duties. There may be, in fact, a virtually accidental relationship. But if the skills required are scarce by reason of the rarity of talent or the costliness of training, the position, if functionally important, must have an attractive power that will draw the necessary skills in competition with other positions. This means, in effect, that the position must be high in the social scale—must command great prestige, high salary, ample leisure, and the like.

How Variations are to be Understood

In so far as there is a difference between one system of stratification and another, it is attributable to whatever factors affect the two determinants of differential reward—namely, functional importance

---

dependent on, if not subordinate to, others. In sum, when an institutional nucleus becomes differentiated around one main function, and at the same time organizes a large portion of the population into its relationships, the key positions in it are of the highest functional importance. The absence of such specialization does not prove functional unimportance, for the whole society may be relatively unspecialized; but it is safe to assume, that the more important functions receive the first and clearest structural differentiation.

and scarcity of personnel. Positions important in one society may not be important in another, because the conditions faced by the societies, or their degree of internal development, may be different. The same conditions, in turn, may affect the question of scarcity; for in some societies the stage of development, or the external situation, may wholly obviate the necessity of certain kinds of skill or talent. Any particular system of stratification, then, can be understood as a product of the special conditions affecting the two aforementioned grounds of differential reward.

Major Societal Functions and Stratification

Religion

The reason why religion is necessary is apparently to be found in the fact that human society achieves its unity primarily through the possession by its members of certain ultimate values and ends in common. Although these values and ends are subjective, they influence behaviour, and their integration enables the society to operate as a system. Derived neither from inherited nor from external nature, they have evolved as a part of culture by communication and moral pressure. They must, however, appear to the members of the society to have some reality, and it is the role of religious belief and ritual to supply and reinforce this appearance of reality. Through belief and ritual the common ends and values are connected with an imaginary world symbolized by concrete sacred objects, which world in turn is related in a meaningful way to the facts and trials of the individual's life. Through the worship of the sacred objects and the beings they symbolize, and the acceptance of supernatural prescriptions that are at the same time codes of behaviour, a powerful control over human conduct is exercised, guiding it along lines sustaining the institutional structure and conforming to the ulimate ends and values.

If this conception of the role of religion is true, one can understand why in every known society the religious activities tend to be under the charge of particular persons, who tend thereby to enjoy greater rewards than the ordinary societal member. Certain of the rewards and special privileges may attach to only the highest religious functionaries, but others usually apply, if such exists, to the entire sacerdotal class.

Moreover, there is a peculiar relation between the duties of the religious official and the special privileges he enjoys. If the supernatural world governs the destinies of men more ultimately than does the real world, its earthly representative, the person through whom one may communicate with the supernatural, must be a powerful individual. He is a keeper of sacred tradition, a skilled performer of the ritual, and an interpreter of lore and myth. He is in such close contact with the gods that he is viewed as possessing some of their charactertics. He is, in short, a bit sacred, and hence free from some of the more vulgar necessities and controls.

It is no accident, therefore, that religious functionaries have been associated with the very highest positions of power, as in theocratic regimes. Indeed, looking at it from this point of vew, one may wonder why it is that they do not get *entire* control over their societies. The factors that prevent this are worthy of note.

In the first place, the amount of technical competence necessary for the performance of religious duties is small. Scientific or artistic capacity is not required. Anyone can set himself up as enjoying an intimate relation with deities, and nobody can successfully dispute him. Therefore, the factor of scarcity of personnel does not operate in the technical sense.

One may assert, on the other hand, that religious ritual is often elaborate and religious lore abstruse, and that priestly ministrations require tact, if not intelligence. This is true, but the technical requirements of the profession are for the most part adventitious, not related to the end in the same way that science is related to air travel. The priest can never be free from competition, since the criteria of whether or not one has genuine contact with the supernatural are never strictly clear. It is this competition that debases the priestly position below what might be expected at first glance. That is why priestly prestige is highest in those societies where membership in the profession is rigidly controlled by the priestly guild itself. That is why, in part at least, elaborate devices are utilized to stress the identification of the person with his office— spectacular costume, abnormal conduct, special diet, segregated residence, celibacy, conspicuous leisure, and the like. In fact, the priest is always in danger of becoming somewhat discredited—as happens in a secularized society—because in a world of stubborn fact, ritual and sacred knowledge alone will not grow crops or build houses. Furthermore, unless he is protected by a professional guild, the priest's identification with the supernatural tends to preclude his acquisition of abundant wordly goods.

As between one society and another it seems that the highest general position awarded the priest occurs in the medieval type of social order. Here there is enough economic production to afford a surplus, which can be used to support a numerous and highly organized priesthood, and yet the populace is unlettered and therefore credulous to a high degree. Perhaps the most extreme example is to be found in the Buddhism of Tibet, but others are encountered in the Catholicism of feudal Europe, the Inca regime of Peru, the Brahminism of India, and the Mayan priesthood of Yucatan. On the other hand, if the society is so crude as to have no surplus and little differentiation, so that every priest must also be a cultivator or hunter, the separation of the priestly status from the others has hardly gone far enough for priestly prestige to mean much. When the priest actually has high prestige under these circumstances, it is because he also performs other important functions (usually political and medical).

In an extremely advanced society built on scientific technology, the priesthood tends to lose status, because sacred tradition and supernaturalism drop into the background. The ultimate values and common ends of the society tend to be expressed in less anthropomorphic ways, by officials who occupy fundamentally political, economic, or educational rather than religious positions. Nevertheless, it is easily possible for intellectuals to exaggerate the degree to which the priesthood in a presumable secular milieu has lost prestige. When the matter is closely examined the urban proletariat, as well as the rural citizenry, proves to be surprisingly god-fearing and priest-ridden. No society has become so completely secularized as to liquidate entirely the belief in transcendental ends and supernatural entities. Even in a secularized society some system must exist for the integration of ultimate values, for their ritualistic expression and for the emotional adjustments required by disappointment, death, and disaster.

Government

Like religion, government plays a unique and indispensable part in society. But in contrast to religion, which provides integration in terms of sentiments, beliefs, and rituals, it organizes the society in terms of law and authority. Furthermore, it orients the society to the actual rather than the unseen world.

The main functions of government are, internally, the ultimate enforcement of norms, the final arbitration of conflicting interests, and the overall planning and direction of society; and externally, the handling of war and diplomacy. To carry out these functions it acts as the agent of the entire people, enjoys a monopoly of force and controls all individuals within its territory.

Political action, by definition, implies authority. An official can command because he has authority, and the citizen must obey because he is subject to that authority. For this reason stratification is inherent in the nature of political relationships.

So clear is the power embodied in political position that political inequality is sometimes thought to comprise all inequality. But it can be shown that there are other bases of stratification, that the following controls operate in practice to keep political power from becoming complete:

1. The fact that the actual holders of political office, and especially those determining top policy must necessarily be few in number compared to the total population.
2. The fact that the rulers represent the interest of the group rather than of themselves, and are therefore restricted in their behaviour by rules and more designed to enforce this limitation of interest.
3. The fact that the holder of political office has his authority by virtue of his office and nothing else, and therefore any special knowledge, talent, or capacity he may claim is purely incidental, so that he often has to depend upon others for technical assistance.

In view of these limiting factors, it is not strange that the rulers often have less power and prestige than a literal enumeration of their formal rights would lead one to expect.

Wealth, Property, and Labour

Every position that secures for its incumbent a livelihood is, by definition, economically rewarded. For this reason there is an economic aspect to those positions (e.g., political and religious) the main function of which is not economic. It, therefore, becomes convenient for the society to use unequal economic returns as a principal means of controlling the entrance of persons into positions and stimulating the peformance of their duties. The amount of the economic return therefore becomes one of the main indices of social status.

It should be stressed, however, that a position does not bring power and prestige *because* it draws a high income. Rather, it draws a high income because it is functionally important and the available personnel is for one reason or another scarce. It is therefore superficial and erroneous to regard high income as the cause of a man's power and prestige, just as it is erroneous to think that a man's fever is the cause of his disease.

The economic source of power and prestige is not income primarily, but the ownership of capital goods (including patents, goodwill, and professional reputation). Such ownership should be distinguished from the possession of consumer goods, which is an index rather than a cause of social standing. In other words, the ownership of producers' goods is, properly speaking, a source of income like other positions, the income itself remaining an index. Even in situations where social values are widely commercialized and earnings are the readiest method of judging social position, income does not confer prestige on a position so much as it induces people to compete for the position. It is true that a man who has a high income as a result of one position may find this money helpful in climbing into another position as well, but this again reflects the effect of his initial, economically advantageous status, which exercises its influence through the medium of money.

In a system of private property in productive enterprise, an income above what an individual spends can give rise to possession of capital wealth. Presumably such possession is a reward for the proper management of one's finances originally and of the productive enterprise later. But as social differentiation becomes highly advanced and yet the institution of inheritance persists, the phenomenon of pure ownership, and reward for pure ownership, emerges. In such a case it is difficult to prove that the position is functionally important or that the scarcity involved is anything other than extrinsic and accidental. It is for this reason, doubtless, that the institution of private property in productive goods becomes more subject to criticism as social development proceeds toward industrialization. It is only this pure, that is, strictly legal and functionless ownership, however, that is open to attack; for some form of active ownership, whether private or public, is indispensable.

One kind of ownership of production goods consists in rights over the labour of others. The most extremely concentrated and exclusive of such rights are found in slavery, but the essential principle remains in serfdom, peonage, encomienda, and indenture. Naturally this kind of ownership has the greatest significance for stratification, because it necessarily entails an unequal relationship.

But property in capital goods inevitably introduces a compulsive element even into the nominally free contractual relationship. Indeed, in some respects the authority of the contractual employer is greater than that of the feudal landlord, inasmuch as the latter is more limited by traditional reciprocities. Even the classical economics recognized that competitors would fare unequally, but it did not pursue this fact to its necessary conclusion that, however it might be acquired, unequal control of goods and services must give unequal advantage to the parties to a contract.

Technical Knowledge

The function of finding means to single goals, without any concern with the choice between goals, is the exclusively technical sphere. The explanation of why positions requiring great technical skill receive fairly high reward is easy to see, for it is the simplest case of the rewards being so distributed as to draw talent and motivate training. Why they seldom if ever receive the highest reward is also clear: the importance of technical knowledge from a societal point of view is never so great as the integration of goals, which takes place on the religious, political, and economic levels. Since the technological level is concerned solely with means, a purely technical position must ultimately be subordinate to other positions that are religious, political or economic in character.

Nevertheless, the distinction between expert and layman in any social order is fundamental, and cannot be entirely reduced to other terms. Methods of recruitment, as well as of reward, sometimes lead to the erroneous interpretation that technical positions are economically determined. Actually, however, the acquisition of knowledge and skill cannot be accomplished by purchase, although the opportunity to learn may be. The control of the avenues of training may inhere as a sort of property right in certain families or classes, giving them power and prestige in consequence. Such a situation adds an artificial scarcity, to the natural scarcity of skills and talents. On the other hand, it is possible for an opposite situation to arise. The rewards of technical position may be so great that a condition of excess supply is created, leading to at least temporary devaluation of the rewards. Thus 'unemployment in the learned professions' may result in a debasement of the prestige of those positions. Such adjustments and readjustments are constantly occurring in changing societies; and it is always well to bear in mind that the efficiency of a stratified structure may be affected by the modes of recruitment for positions. The social order itself, however, sets limits to the inflation or deflation of the prestige of experts: an over-supply tends to debase the rewards and discourage recruitment or produce revolution, whereas an under-supply tends to increase the rewards or weaken the society in competition with other societies.

Particular systems of stratification show a wide range with respect to the exact position of technically competent persons. This range is perhaps most evident in the degree of specialization. Extreme division of labour tends to create many specialists without high prestige since the training is short and the required native capacity relatively small. On the other hand it also tends to accentuate the high position of the true experts—scientists, engineers, and administrators—by increasing their authority relative to other functionally important positions. But the idea of a technocratic social order or a government or priesthood of engineers or social scientists neglects the limitations of knowledge and skills as a basis for performing social functions. To the extent that the social structure is truly specialized the prestige of the technical person must also be circumscribed.

VARIATION IN STRATIFIED SYSTEMS

The generalized principles of stratification here suggested form a necessary preliminary to a consideration of types of stratified systems, because it is in terms of these principles that the types must be described. This can be seen by trying to delineate types according to certain modes of variation. For instance, some of the most important modes (together with the polar types in terms of them) seem to be as follows:

(a) The Degree of Specialization

The degree of specialization affects the fineness and multiplicity of the gradations in power and prestige. It also influences the extent to which particular functions may be emphasized in the invidious system, since a given function cannot receive much emphasis in the hierarchy until it has achieved structural separation from the other functions. Finally, the amount of specialization influences the bases of selection. Polar types: *Specialized, Unspecialized.*

(b) The Nature of the Functional Emphasis

In general when emphasis is put on sacred matters, a rigidity is introduced that tends to limit specialization and hence the development of technology. In addition, a brake is placed on social mobility, and on the development of bureaucracy. When the preoccupation with the sacred is withdrawn, leaving greater scope for purely secular preoccupations, a great development, and rise in status, of economic and technological positions seemingly takes place. Curiously, a concomitant rise in political position is not likely, because it has usually been allied with the religious and stands to gain little by the decline of the latter. It is also possible for a society to emphasize family functions—as in relatively undifferentiated societies where high mortality requires high fertility and kinship forms the main basis of social organization. Main types: *Familistic, Authoritarian* (Theocratic or sacred), and *Totalitarian* or secular *Capitalistic.*

(c) The Magnitude of Invidious Differences

What may be called the amount of social distance between positions, taking into account the entire scale, is something that should lend itself to quantitative measurement. Considerable differences apparently exist between different societies in this regard, and also between parts of the same society. Polar types: *Equalitarian, Inequalitarian.*

(d) The Degree of Opportunity

The familiar question of the amount of mobility is different from the question of the comparative equality or inequality of rewards posed above, because the two criteria may vary independently up to a point. For instance, the tremendous divergences in monetary income in the United States are far greater than those found in primitive societies, yet the equality of opportunity to move from one rung to the other in the social scale may also be greater in the United States than in a hereditary tribal kingdom. Polar types: *Mobile* (open), *Immobile* (closed).

(e) The Degree of Stratum Solidarity

Again, the degree of 'class solidarity' (or the presence of specific organizations to promote class interests) may vary to some extent independently of the other criteria, and hence is an important principle in classifying systems of stratification. Polar types: *class organized, class unorganized.*

EXTERNAL CONDITIONS

What state any particular system of stratification is in with reference to each of these modes of variation depends on two things: (1) its state with reference to the other ranges of variation, and (2) the conditions outside the system of stratification which nevertheless influence that system. Among the latter are the following:

(a) The Stage of Cultural Development

As the cultural heritage grows, increased specialization becomes necessary, which in turn contributes to the enhancement of mobility, a decline of stratum solidarity, and a change of functional emphasis.

(b) Situation with Respect to Other Societies

The presence or absence of open conflict with other societies, of free trade relations or cultural diffusion, all influence the class structure to some extent. A chronic state of warfare tends to place emphasis upon the military functions, especially when the opponents are more or less equal. Free trade, on the other hand, strengthens the hand of the trader at the expense of the warrior and priest. Free movement of ideas generally has an equalitarian effect. Migration and conquest create special circumstances.

(c) Size of the Society

A small society limits the degree to which functional specialization can go, the degree of segregation of different strata, and the magnitude of inequality.

COMPOSITE TYPES

Much of the literature on stratification has attempted to classify concrete systems into a certain number of types. This task is deceptively simple, however, and should come at the end of an analysis of elements and principles, rather than at the beginning. If the preceding discussion has any validity, it indicates that there are a number of modes of variation between different systems, and that any one system is a composite of the society's status with reference to all these modes of variation. The danger of trying to classify whole societies under such rubrics as caste, feudal, or open class is that one or two criteria are selected and others ignored, the result being an unsatisfactory solution to the problem posed. The present discussion has been offered as a possible approach to the more systematic classification of composite types.

III

Class, Status, Party

MAX WEBER

1. *Economically Determined Power and the Social Order*

Law exists when there is a probability that an order will be upheld by a specific staff of men who will use physical or psychical compulsion with the intention of obtaining conformity with the order, or of inflicting sanctions for infringement of it. The structure of every legal order

Excerpted from Max Weber, 'Class , Status, Party', in *From Max Weber: Essays in Sociology*, edited and translated by H.H. Gerth and C. Wright Mills, Oxford University Press, Inc., New York, 1946.

directly influences the distribution of power, economic or otherwise, within its respective community. This is true of all legal orders and not only that of the State. In general, we understand by 'power' the chance of a man or of a number of men to realize their own will in a communal action even against the resistance of others who are participating in the action.

'Economically conditioned' power is not, of course, identical with 'power' as such. On the contrary, the emergence of economic power may be the consequence of power existing on other grounds. Man does not strive for power only in order to enrich himself economically. Power, including economic power, may be valued 'for its own sake' Very frequently the striving for power is also conditioned by the social 'honour' it entails. Not all power, however, entails social honour: The typical American Boss, as well as the typical big speculator, deliberately relinquishes social honour. Quite generally, 'mere economic' power, and especially 'naked' money power, is by no means a recognized basis of social honour. Nor is power the only basis of social honour. Indeed, social honour, or prestige, may even be the basis of political or economic power, and very frequently has been. Power, as well as honour may be guaranteed by the legal order, but, at least normally, it is not their primary source. The legal order is rather an additional factor that enhances the chance to hold power or honour; but it cannot always secure them.

The way in which social honour is distributed in a community between typical participating in this distribution we may call the 'social order'. The social order and the economic order are, of course, similarly related to the 'legal order'. However, the social and the economic order are not identical. The economic order is for us merely the way in which economic goods and services are distributed and used. The social order is of course conditioned by the economic order to a high degree, and in its turn reacts upon it.

Now: 'class', 'status groups' and 'parties' are phenomena of the distribution of power within a community.

2. Determination of Class-situation by Market-situation

In our terminology, 'classes' are not communities; they merely represent possible, and frequent, bases for communal action. We may speak of a 'class' when a number of people have in common a specific casual component of their life chances, in so far as, this component is represented exclusively by economic interests in the possession of goods and opportunities for income, and is represented under the conditions of the commodity or labour markets. These points refer to 'class situation,' which we may express more briefly as the typical chance for a supply of goods, external living conditions, and personal life experiences, in so far as this chance is determined by the amount and kind of power, or lack of such, to dispose of goods or skills for the sake of income in a given economic order. The term 'class' refers to any group of people that is found in the same class situation.

It is the most elemental economic fact that the way in which the disposition over material property is distributed among a plurality of people, meeting competitively in the market for the purpose of exchange, in itself creates specific life chances. According to the law of marginal utility this mode of distribution excludes the non-owners from competing for highly valued goods; it favours the owners and, in fact, gives to them a monopoly to acquire such goods. Other things being equal, this mode of distribution monopolizes the opportunities for profitable deals for all those who, provided with goods, do not necessarily have to exchange them. It increases, at least generally, their power in price wars with those who, being propertyless, have nothing to offer but their services in native form or goods in a form constituted through their own labour, and who above all are compelled to get rid of these products in order barely to subsist. This mode of distribution gives to the propertied a monopoly on the possibility of transferring property from the sphere of use as a 'fortune' to the sphere of 'capital goods'; that is, it gives them the entrepreneurial function and all chances to share directly or indirectly in returns on capital. All this holds true within the area in which pure market conditions prevail. 'Property' and 'lack of property' are, therefore, the basic categories of all class situations. It does not matter whether these two categories become effective in price wars or in competitive struggles.

Within these categories, however, class situations are further differentiated: on the one hand, according to the kind of property that is usable for returns; and, on the other hand, according to the kind of services that can be offered in the market. Ownership of domestic buildings; productive establishments; warehouses; stores; agriculturally usable land, large and small holdings—quantitative differences with possibly qualitative consequences; ownership of mines; cattle; men (slaves); disposition over mobile instruments of production, or capital goods of all sorts, especially money or objects that can be exchanged for money easily and at any time; disposition over products of one's own labour or of others' labour differing according to their various distances from consumability; disposition over transferable monopolies of any kind—all these distinctions differentiate the class situations of the propertied just as does the 'meaning': which they can and do give to the utilization of property, especially to property which has money equivalence. Accordingly, the propertied, for instance, may belong to the class of rentiers or to the class of entrepreneurs.

Those who have no property but who offer services are differentiated just as much according to their kinds of services as according to the way in which they make use of these services, in a continuous or discontinuous relation to a recipient. But always this is the generic connotation of the concept of class: that the kind of chance in the *market* is the decisive moment which presents a common condition for the individual's fate. 'Class situation' is, in this sense, ultimately 'market situation'. The effect of naked possession *per se*, which among cattle breeders gives the non-owning slave or serf into the power of the cattle owner, is only a forerunner of real 'class' formation. However, in the cattle loan and in the naked severity of the law of debts in such communities, for the first time mere 'possession' as such emerges as decisive for the fate of the individual. This is very much in contrast to the agricultural communities based on labour. The creditor-debtor relation becomes the basis of 'class situations' only in those cities where a 'credit market', however primitive, with rates of interest increasing according to the extent of dearth and a factual monopolization of credits, is developed by a plutocracy. Therewith 'class struggles' begin.

Those men whose fate is not determined by the chance of using goods or services for themselves on the market, e.g. slaves, are not, however, a class in the technical sense of the term. They are, rather, a 'status group'.

3. Communal Action Flowing from Class Interest

According to our terminology, the factor that creates 'class' is unambiguously economic interest, and indeed, only those interests involved in the existence of the 'market'. Nevertheless, the concept of 'class-interest' is an ambiguous one: even as an empirical concept it is ambiguous as soon as one understands by it something other than the factual direction of interests following with a certain probability from the class situation for a certain 'average' of those people subjected to the class situation. The class situation and other circumstances remaining the same, the direction in which the individual worker, for instance, is likely to pursue his interests may vary widely, according to whether he is constitutionally qualified for the task at hand to a high, to an average, or to a low degree. In the same way, the direction of interests may vary according to whether or not a *communal* action of a larger or smaller portion of those commonly affected by the 'class situation' or even an association among them, e.g. a 'trade union', has grown out of the class situation from which the individual may or may not expect promising results. Communal action refers to that action which is oriented to the feeling of the actors so that they belong together. Societal action, on the other hand, is oriented to a rationally motivated adjustment of interests. The rise of societal or even of communal action from a common class situation is by no means a universal phenomenon.

The class situation may be restricted in its effects to the generation of essentially *similar* reactions, that is to say, within our terminology, of 'mass actions'. However, it may not have even this result. Furthermore, often merely an amorphous communal action emerges. For example, the 'murmuring' of the workers known in ancient oriental ethics: the moral disapproval of the work-master's conduct, which in its practical significance was probably equivalent to an increasingly typical phenomenon of precisely the latest industrial development, namely, the 'slow down' (the deliberate limiting of work effort) of labourers by virtue of tacit agreement. The degree in which 'communal action' and possibly 'societal action' emerges from the 'mass actions' of the members of a class is linked to general cultural conditions, especially to those of an intellectual sort. It is also linked to the extent of the contrasts that have already evolved, and is especially linked to the transparency of the connections between the causes and the conseuquences of 'class situation'. For however different life chances may be, this fact in itself, according to all experience, by no means gives birth to 'class action' (communal action by the members of a class). The fact of being conditioned and the results of the class situation must be distinctly recognizable. For only then the contrast of life chances can be felt not as an absolutely given fact to be accepted, but as a resultant from either (1) the given distribution of property, or (2) the structure of the concrete economic order. It is only then that people may react against the class structure not only through acts of an intermittent and irrational protest, but in the form of rational association. There have been 'class situation' of the first category (1), of a specifically naked and transparent sort, in the urban centres of antiquity and during the Middle Ages; especially then, when great fortunes were accumulated by factually monopolized trading in industrial products of these localities or in foodstuffs. Furthermore, under certain circumstances, in the rural economy of the most diverse periods, agriculture was increasingly exploited in a profit-making manner. The most important historical example of the second category (2) is the class situation of the modern 'proletariat'.

4. Types of 'Class Struggle'

Thus every class may be the carrier of any one of the possibly innumerable forms of 'class action' but this is not necessarily so. In any case, a class does not in itself constitute a community. To treat 'class' conceptually as having the same value as 'community' leads to distortion. That men in the same class situation regularly react in mass actions to such tangible situations as economic ones in the direction of those interests that are most adequate to their average number is an important and after all simple fact for the understanding of historical events. Above all, this fact must not lead to that kind of pseudo-scientific operation with the concept of 'class' and 'class interest' so frequently found these days, and which has found its most classic expression in the statement of a talented author, that the individual may be in error concerning his interests but that the 'class' is 'infallible' about its interests. Yet, if classes as such are not communities, nevertheless class situations emerge only on the basis of communalization. The communal action that brings forth class situations, however, is not basically action between members of the identical class; it is an action between members of different classes. Communal actions that directly determine the class situation of the worker and the entrepreneur are: the labour market, the commodities market, and the capitalistic enterprise. But, in its turn, the existence of a capitalistic enterprise presupposes that a very specific communal action exists and that it is specifically structured to protect the possession of goods *per se*, and especially the power of individuals to dispose, in principle freely, over the means of production. The existence of a capitalistic enterprise is preconditioned by a specific kind of 'legal order'. Each kind of class situation, and above all when it rests upon the power of property, *per se* will become most clearly efficacious when all other determinants of reciprocal relations are, as far as possible, eliminated in their significance. It is in this way that the utilization of the power of property in the market obtains its most sovereign importance.

Now 'status groups' hinder the strict carrying through of the sheer market principle. In the present context they are of interest to us only from this one point of view. Before, we briefly consider them, note that not much of a general nature can be said about the more specific kinds of antagonism between 'classes' (in our meaning of the term). The great shift, which has been going on continuously in the past, and up to our times, may be summarized, although at the cost of some precision: the struggle in which class situations are effective has progressively shifted from consumption credit towards first, competitive struggles in the commodity market and, then, towards, price wars on the labour market. The 'class struggles' of antiquity—to the extent that they were genuine class struggles and not struggles between status groups—were initially carried on by indebted peasants, and perhaps also by artisans threatened by debt bondage and struggling against urban creditors. For debt bondage is the normal result of the differentiation of wealth in commercial cities, especially in seaport cities. A similar situation has existed among cattle breeders. (Debt relationships as such produced class action up to the time of Cataline.) Along with this, and with an increase in provision of grain for the city by transporting it from the outside, the struggle over the means of sustenance emerged. It centred in the first place around the provision of bread and the determination of the price of bread. It lasted throughout antiquity and the entire Middle Ages. The propertyless as such flocked together against those who actually and supposedly were interested in the dearth of bread. This fight spread until it involved all those commodities essential to the way of life and to handicraft production. There were only incipient discussions of wage disputes in antiquity and in the Middle Ages. But they have been slowly increasing up into modern times. In the earlier periods they were completely secondary to slave rebellions as well as to fights in the commodity market.

The propertyless of antiquity and of the Middle Ages protested against monopolies, pre-emption, forestalling, and the withholding of goods from the market in order to raise prices. Today the central issue is the determination of the price of labour.

This transition is represented by the fight for access to the market and for the determination of the price of products. Such fights went on between merchants and workers in the poutting-out system of domestic handicraft during the transition to modern times. Since it is quite a general phenomenon we must mention here that the class antagonisms that are conditioned through the market situation are usually most bitter between those who actually and directly participate as opponents in price wars. It is not the rentier, the share-holder, and the banker who suffer the ill will of the worker, but almost exclusively the manufacturer and the business executives who are the direct opponents of workers in price wars. This is so in spite of the fact that it is precisely the cash boxes of the rentier, the share-holder, and the banker into which the more or less 'unearner' gains flow, rather than into the pockets of the manufacturers or of the business executives. This simple state of affairs has very frequently been decisive for the role the class situation has played in the formation of political parties. For example, it has made possible the varieties of patriarchal socialism and the frequent attempts—formerly, at least of threatened status groups to form alliances with the proletariate against the 'bourgeoisie'.

5. *Status Honour*

In contrast to classes, *status groups* are normally communities. They are, however, often of an amorphous kind. In contrast to the purely economically determined 'class situation' we wish to designate as 'status situation' every typical component of the life fate of men that is determined by a specific, positive or negative, social estimation of *honour*. This honour may be connected with any quality shared by a plurality, and, of course, it can be knit to a class situation: class distinctions are linked in the most varied ways with status distinctions. Property as such is not always recognized as a status qualification, but in the long run it is, and with extraordinary regularity. In the subsistence economy of the organized neighbourhood, very often the richest man is simply the chieftain. However, this often means only an honorific preference. For example, in the so-called pure modern 'democracy', that is, on devoid of any expressly ordered status privileges for individuals, it may be that only the families coming under approximately the same tax class dance with one another. This example is reported of certain smaller Swiss cities. But status honour need not necessarily be linked with a 'class situation'. On the contrary, it normally stands in sharp opposition to the pretensions of sheer property.

Both propertied and propertyless people can belong to the same status group, and frequently they do with very tangible consequences. This 'equality' of social esteem may, however, in the long run become quite precarious. The 'equality' of status among the American 'gentlemen', for instance, is expressed by the fact that outside the subordination determined by the different functions of 'business' it would be considered strictly repugnant—wherever the old tradition still prevails—if even the richest 'chief', while playing billiards or cards in his club in the evening, would not treat his 'clerk' as in every sense fully his equal in birthright. It would be repugnant if the American 'chief' would bestow upon his 'clerk' the condescending 'benevolence' marking a distinction of 'position', which the German chief can never dissever from his attitude. This is one of the most important reasons why in America the German 'clubby-ness' has never been able to attain the attraction that the American clubs have.

6. *Guarantees of Status Stratification*

In content, status honour is normally expressed by the fact that above all else a specific *style of life* can be expected from all those who wish to belong to the circle. Linked with this expectation are restrictions on 'social' intercourse (that is, intercourse which is not subservient to economic or any other of business's 'functional' purposes). These restrictions may confine normal marriages to within the status circle and may lead to complete endogamous closure. As soon as there is not a mere individual and socially irrelevant limitation of another style of life, but an agreed-upon communal action of this closing character, the 'status' development is under way.

In its characteristic form, stratification by 'status groups' on the basis of conventional styles of life evolves at the present time in the United States out of the traditional democracy. For example, only the resident of a certain street ('the street') is considered as belonging to 'society' is qualified for social intercourse, and is visited and invited. Above all, this differentiation evolves in such a way as to make for strict submission to the fashion that is dominant at a given time in society. This submission to fashion also exists among men in America to a degree unknown in Germany. Such submission is considered to be an indication of the fact that a given man *pretends* to qualify as a gentleman. This submission decides, at least *prima facie*, that he will be treated as such. And this recognition becomes just as important for his employment chances in 'swank' establishments, and above all, for social intercourse and marriage with 'esteemed' families, as the qualification for dueling among Germans in the Kaiser's day. As for the rest: certain families resident for a long time, and, of course, correspondingly wealthy, e.g., 'F.F.V., i.e., First Families of Virginia,' or the actual or alleged descendants of the 'Indian Princess' Pocahontas, of the Pilgrim fathers, or of the Knickerbockers, the members of almost inaccessible sects and all sorts of circles setting themselves apart by means of any other characteristics and badges . . . all these elements usurp 'status' honour. The development of status is essentially a question of stratification resting upon usurpation. Such usurpation is the normal origin of almost all status honour. But the road from this purely conventional situation to legal privilege, positive or negative, is easily travelled as soon as a certain stratification of the social order has in fact been 'lived in' and has achieved stability by virtue of a stable distribution of economic power.

7. 'Ethnic' Segregation and 'Caste'

Where the consequences have been realized to their full extent, the status group evolves into a closed 'caste'. Status distinctions are then guaranteed not merely by conventions and laws, but also by *rituals*. This occurs in such a way that every physical contact with a member of any caste that is considered to be 'lower' by the members of a 'higher' caste is considered as making for a ritualistic impurity and to be a stigma which must be expiated by a religious act. Individual castes develop quite distinct cults and gods.

In general, however, the status structure reaches such extreme consequences only where there are underlying differences which are held to be 'ethnic'. The 'caste' is, indeed, the normal form in which ethnic communities usually live side by side in a 'societalized' manner. These ethnic communities believe in blood relationship and exclude exogamous marriage and social intercourse. Such a caste situation is part of the phenomenon of 'pariah' peoples and is found all over the world. These people form communities, acquire specific occupational traditions of handicrafts or of other arts, and cultivate a belief in their ethnic community. They live in a 'diaspora' strictly segregated from all personal intercourse, except that of an unavoidable sort, and their situation is legally precarious. Yet, by virtue of their economic indispensability, they are tolerated, indeed, frequently privileged, and they live in interspersed political communities. The Jews are the most impressive historical example.

A 'status' segregation grown into a 'caste' differs in its structure from a mere 'ethnic' segregation: the caste structure transforms the horizontal and unconnected coexistences of ethnically segregated groups into a vertical social system of superordination and subordination. Correctly formulated: a comprehensive societalization integrates the ethnically divided communities into specific political and communal action. In their consequences they differ precisely in this way:

ethnic coexistences condition a mutual repulsion and disdain but allow each ethnic community to consider its own honour as the highest one; the caste structure brings about a social subordination and an acknowledgement of 'more honour' in favour of the privileged caste and status groups. This is due to the fact that in the caste structure ethnic distinctions as such have become 'functional' distinctions within the political societalization (warriors, priests, artisans) that are politically important for war and for building, and so on. But even pariah people who are most despised are usually apt to continue cultivating in some manner that which is equally peculiar to ethnic and to status communities: the belief in their own specific 'honour'. This is the case with the Jews.

Only with the negatively privileged status groups does the 'sense of dignity' take a specific deviation. A sense of dignity is the precipitation in individuals of social honour and of conventional demands which a positively privileged status group raises for the department of its members. The sense of dignity that characterizes positively privileged status groups is naturally related to their 'being' which does not transcend itself, that is, it is to their 'beauty and excellence'. Their kingdom is 'of this world'. They live for the present and by exploiting their great past. The sense of the negatively privileged strata naturally refers to a future lying beyond the present, whether it is of this life or of another. In other words, it must be nurtured by the belief in a providential 'mission' and by a belief in a specific honour before God. The 'chosen peoples' dignity is nurtured by a belief either that in the beyond 'the last will be the first', or that in this life a Messiah will appear to bring forth into the light of the world which has cast them out the hidden honour of the pariah people. This simple state of affairs, and not the 'resentment' which is so strongly emphasized in Nietzsche's much admired construction in the *Genealogy of Morals*, is the source of the religiosity cultivated by pariah status groups. In passing, we may note that resentment may be accurately applied only to a limited extent; for one of Nietzsche's main examples, Buddhism, it is not at all applicable.

Incidently, the development of status groups from ethnic segregations is by no means the normal phenomenon. On the contrary, since objective 'racial differences' are by no means basic to every subjective sentiment of an ethnic community, the ultimately racial foundation of status structure is rightly and absolutely a question of the concrete individual case. Very frequently a status group is instrumental in the production of a thoroughbred anthropological type. Certainly a status group is to a high degree effective in producing extreme types, for they select personally qualified individuals (e.g., the Knighthood selects those who are fit for warfare, physically and psychically). But selection is far from being the only, or the predominant, way in which status groups are formed. Political membership or class situation has at all times been at least as frequently decisive. And today the class situation is by far the predominant factor, for of course the possibility of a style of life expected for members of a status group is usually conditioned economically.

For all practical purposes, stratification by status goes hand in hand with a monopolization of ideal and material goods or opportunities, in a manner we have come to know as typical. Besides the specific status honour, which always rests upon distance and exclusiveness, we find all sorts of material monopolies. Such honorific preferences may consist of the privilege of wearing special costumes, of eating special dishes taboo to others, of carrying arms—which is most obvious in its consequences—the right to pursue certain non-professional dilet-tante artistic practices, e.g. to play certain musical instruments. Of course, material monopolies provide the most effective motives for the exclusiveness of a status group; although, in themselves, they are rarely sufficient, almost always they come into play to some extent. Within a status circle there is the question of intermarriage: the inter-est of the families in the monopolization of potential bridegrooms is at least of equal importance and is parallel to the interest in the monopoli-zation of daughters. The daughters of the circle must be provided for. With an increased inclosure of the status group, the conventional pref-erential opportunities for special employment grow into a legal monop-oly of special offices for the members. Certain goods become objects for monopolization by status groups. In the typical fashion these in-clude 'entailed estates' and frequently also the possessions of serfs or bondsmen and, finally, special trades. This monopolization occurs positively when the status group is exclusively entitled to own and to manage them; and negatively when, in order to maintain its specific way of life, the status group must not own and manage them.

The decisive role of a 'style of life' in status 'honour' means that status groups are the specific bearers of all 'conventions'. In whatever way it may be manifest, all 'stylization' of life either originates in status groups or is at least conserved by them. Even if the principles of status conventions differ greatly, they reveal certain typical traits, espe-cially among those strata which are most privileged. Quite generally, among privileged status groups there is a status disqualification that operates against the performance of common physical labour. This disqualification is now 'setting in' in America against the old tradition of esteem for labour. Very frequently every rational economic pursuit, and especially 'entrepreneurial activity', is looked upon as a disqualification of status. Artistic and literary activity is also considered as degrading work as soon as it is exploited for income, or at least when it is connected with hard physical exertion. An example is the sculptor working like a mason in his dusty smock as over against the painter in his salon-like 'studio' and those forms of musical practice that are acceptable to the status group.

9. Economic Conditions and Effects of Status Stratification

The frequent disqualification of the gainfully employed as such is a direct result of the principle of status stratification peculiar to the social order, and of course, of this principle's opposition to a distribution of power which is regulated exclusively through the market. These two factors operate along with various individual ones, which will be touched upon below.

We have seen above that the market and its process 'knows no personal distinctions': 'functional' interests dominate it. It knows nothing of 'honour'. The status order means precisely the reverse, viz.: stratification in terms of 'honour' and of styles of life peculiar to status groups as such. If mere economic acquisition and naked economic power still bearing the stigma of its extra-status origin could bestow upon anyone who has won it the same honour as those who are interested in status by virtue of style of life claim for themselves, the status order would be threatened at its very root. This is the more so as, given equality of status honour, property *per se* represents an addition even if it is not overly acknowledged to be such. Yet if such economic acquisition and power gave the agent any honour at all, his wealth would result in his attaining more honour than those who successfully claim honour by virtue of style of life. Therefore all groups having interests in the status order react with special sharpness precisely against the pretensions of purely economic acquisition. In most cases they react the more vigorously the more they feel themselves threatened. Calderon's respectful treatment of the peasant, for instance, as opposed to Shakespeare's simultaneous and ostensible disdain of the *canaille* illustrates the different way in which a firmly structured status order reacts as compared with a status order that has become economically precarious. This is an example of a state of affairs that recurs everywhere. Precisely because of the rigorous reactions against the claims of property *per se*, the 'parvenu' is never accepted, personally and without reservation, by the privileged status groups, no matter how completely his style of life has been adjusted to theirs. They will only accept his descendants who have been educated in the conventions of their status group and who have never besmirched its honour by their own economic labour.

As to the general effect of the status order, only one consequence can be stated, but it is a very important one: the hindrance of the free development of the market occurs first for those goods which status groups directly withheld from free exchange by monopolization. This monopolization may be effected either legally or conventionally. For example, in many Hellenic cities during the epoch of status groups and also originally in Rome, the inherited estate (as is shown by the old formula for indiction against spendthrifts) was monopolized just as were the estates of knights, peasants, priests, and especially the clientele of the craft and merchant guilds. The market is restricted, and the power of naked property *per se*, which gives its stamp to 'class formation', is pushed into the background. The results of this process can be most varied. Of course, they do not necessarily weaken the contrasts in the economic situation. Frequently they strengthen these contrasts, and in any case, where stratification by status permeates a community as was strongly the case in all political communities of antiquity and of the Middle Ages, one can never speak of a genuinely free market competition as we understand it today. There are wider effects than this direct exclusion of special goods from the market. From the contrariety between the status order and the purely economic order mentioned above, it follows that in most instances the notion of honour peculiar to status absolutely abhors that which is essential to the market; higgling. Honour abhors higgling among peers and occasionally it taboos higgling for the members of a status group in general. Therefore, everywhere some status groups, and usually the most influential, consider almost any kind of overt participation in economic acquisition as absolutely stigmatizing.

With some over-simplification one might thus say that 'classes' are stratified according to the principles of their *consumption* of goods as represented by special 'styles of life'.

An 'occupational group' is also a status group. For normally, it successfully claims social honours only by virtue of the special style of life which may be determined by it. The differences between classes and status groups frequently overlap. It is precisely those status communities most strictly segregated in terms of honour (viz. the Indian castes) who today show, although within very rigid limits, a relatively high degree of indifference to pecuniary income. However, the Brahmins seek such income in many different ways.

As to the general economic conditions making for the predominance of stratification by 'status' only very little can be said. When the bases of the acquisition and distribution of goods are relatively stable, stratification by status is favoured. Every technological repercussion and economic transformation threatens stratification by status and pushes the class situation into the foreground. Epochs and countries in which the naked class situation is of predominant significance are regularly the periods of technical and economic transformations. And every slowing down of the shifting of economic stratifications leads, in due course, to the growth of status structures and makes for a resuscitation of the important role of social honour.

10. Parties

Wheras the genuine place of 'classes' is within the economic order, the place of 'status groups' is within the social order, that is, within the sphere of the distribution of 'honour'. From within these spheres, classes and status groups influence one another and they influence the legal order and are in turn influenced by it. But 'parties' live in a house of 'power'.

Their action is oriented towards the acquisition of social 'power' that is to say, toward influencing a communal action no matter what its content may be. In principle, parties may exist in a social 'club' as well as in a 'state'. As over against the actions of classes and status groups, for which this is not necessarily the case, the communal actions of 'parties' always mean a societalization. For party actions are always directed toward a goal which is striven for in planned manner. This goal may be a 'cause' (the party may aim at realizing a programme for ideal or material purposes), or the goal may be 'personal' (sinecures, power, and from these, honour for the leader and the followers of the party). Usually the party action aims at all these simultaneously. Parties are, therefore, only possible within communities that are societalized, that is, which have some rational order and a staff of persons available who are ready to enforce it. For parties aim precisely at influencing this staff, and if possible, to recruit it from party followers.

In any individual case, parties may represent interests determined through 'class situation' or 'status situation' and they may recruit their following respectively from one or the other. But they need be neither purely 'class' nor purely 'status' parties. In most cases they are partly class parties and partly status parties, but sometimes they are neither. They may represent ephemeral or enduring structures. Their means of attaining power may be quite varied, ranging from naked violence of any sort to canvassing for votes with coarse or subtle means: money, social influence, the force of speech, suggestion, clumsy hoax, and so on to the rougher or more artful tactics of obstruction in parliamentary bodies.

The sociological structure of parties differs in a basic way according to the kind of communal action which they struggle to influence. Parties also differ according to whether or not the community is stratified by status or by classes. Above all else, they vary according to the structure of domination within the community. For their leaders normally deal with the conquest of a community. They are, in the general concept which is maintained here, not only products of specially modern forms of domination. We shall also designate as parties the ancient and medieval 'parties', despite the fact that their structure differs basically from the structure of modern parties. By virtue of these structural differences of domination it is impossible to say anything about the structure of parties without discussing the structural forms of social domination *per se*. Parties, which are always structures struggling for domination, are very frequently organized in a very strict 'authoritarian' fashion . . . .

Concerning 'classes', 'status groups', and 'parties', it must be said in general that they presuppose a comprehensive societalization, and especially a political framework of communal action, within which they operate. This does not mean that parties would be confined by the frontiers of any individual political community. On the contrary, at all times it has been the order of the day that the societalization (even when it aims at the use of military force in common) reaches beyond the frontiers of politics. This has been the case in the solidarity of interests among the Oligarchs and among the democrats in Hellas, among the Guelfs and among Ghibellines in the Middle Ages, and within the Calvinist party during the period of religious struggles. It has been the case upto the solidarity of the landlords (international congress of agrarian landlords), and has continued among princes (holy alliance, Karlsbad decrees), socialist workers, conservatives (the longing of Prussian conservatives for Russian intervention in 1850. But their aim is not necessarily the establishment of new international political, i.e. *territorial*, dominion. In the main they aim to influence the existing dominion.

IV

Hierarchy, Status and Power:
The Caste System and its Implications

LOUIS DUMONT

Castes and Ourselves

The caste system is so different from our own social system in its
central ideology that the modern reader is doubtless rarely inclined to
study it fully. If he is very ignorant of sociology, or of a very militant

Excerpted from Louis Dumont, *Homo Hierarchicus: The Caste System and its Implications,* Oxford University Press, Delhi, 1988.

turn of mind, his interest may be confined to wanting the destruction or the disappearance of an institution which is a denial of the rights of man, and appears as an obstacle to the economic progress of five hundred million people. It is a remarkable fact that, quite apart from the Indians, no Westerner who has lived in India, whether the most fervent reformer or the most zealous missionary has ever, so far as is known, attempted or recommended the abolition pure and simple of the caste system, either because of an acute consciousness of the positive functions fulfilled by the system, as in the case of the Abbé Dubois, or simply because such a thing appeared too impracticable.

The reader, even on the assumption that he is more moderate in his opinions, cannot be expected to consider caste other than as an aberration, and the very authors who have devoted books to it have more often tried to explain the system as an anomaly than understand it as an institution.

If it was only a question of satisfying our curiosity and forming some idea of a social system which is as stable and powerful as it is "opposed to our ethics and unamenable to our intellect, we would certainly not devote to it the effort of attention which the preparation of this book has required, and which I fear the reading of it may also require to some extent. More is necessary: the conviction that caste has something to teach us about ourselves.[*] Indeed, this is the *long term* ambition of works of the type to which this book belongs, and it is necessary to stress this point in order to indicate the nature and context of this endeavour..... Anthropology, by the understanding it *gradually* affords of the most widely differing societies and cultures, gives proof of the unity of mankind. In doing so, it obviously reflects at least some light on our own sort of society....

To anticipate in a few words: the castes teach us a fundamental social principle, hierarchy. We, in our modern society, have adopted the principle contrary to it, but it is not without value for understanding the nature, limits and conditions of realization of the moral and political egalitarianism to which we are attached. There is no question of reaching this point in the present work, which will stop in substance at the discovery of hierarchy, but this is the prospect to which the study is directed. There is one point to be made clear. The reader may, of course, refuse to leave the shelter of his own values; he may lay it down that for him man begins with the Declaration of the

---

[*] *Meaning the French or more generally the Europeans. Editor.*

Rights of Man, and condemn outright anything which departs from it. In doing so he certainly limits himself, and we can question not only whether he is in fact 'modern', as he claims, but also whether he has the right to be so-called. In actual fact, there is nothing here like an attack, whether direct or oblique, on modern values, which seem in any case secure enough to have nothing to fear from our investigation. It is only a question of attempting to grasp other values *intellectually*. If one refused to do this, it would be useless to try to understand the caste system, and it would be impossible, in the end, to take an *anthropological* view of our own values.

It will be readily understood that the inquiry, defined in this way, forbids us to adopt certain facile approaches. If, like many contemporary sociologists we were content with a label borrowed from our own societies if we confined ourselves to considering the caste system as an extreme form of '*social stratification*', we could indeed record some interesting observations, but we would by definition have excluded all possibility of enriching our fundamental conceptions: the circuit which we have to travel, from ourselves to caste, and back again from caste to ourselves, would be closed immediately because we would never have left the starting-point. Another way of remaining shut in upon ourselves consists in assuming from the outset that ideas, beliefs and values — in a word, ideology — have a secondary place in social life, and can be explained by, or reduced to, other aspects of society. The principle of equality and the principle of hierarchy are facts, indeed they are among the most constraining facts, of political and social life. There is no space here to dwell upon the question of the place of ideology in social life: as far as methodology is concerned, all that follows, both in outline and in detail, aims to answer this question. The clear recognition of the importance of ideology has an apparently paradoxical consequence: in the case of India it leads us to make much of the literary heritage and the 'superior' civilization as well as of 'popular' culture. . . .

For the moment, our first aim is to come to understand the ideology of the caste system. This ideology is directly contradicted by the egalitarian theory which we hold.
. . . .

The Place of Ideology

We have said that we shall be concerned first and foremost with a system of ideas and values. We have also in passing acknowledged territory or locality as an example of a factor which, while not figuring directly in the ideology, intervenes at the level of the concrete manifestations of the caste system. It is as well to throw some light on this duality. First let us note that the two kinds of aspects are perceived in different ways, so that the distinction between them expresses our position in relation to the object. On the one hand it is the indigenous theory which provides us with the name: when we say 'caste' we are more or less translating an indigenous concept (*jāt, jāti,* a word of Indo-European root but which is probably encountered everywhere); if we were to speak of '*social stratification*' we would introduce the following arbitrary judgments: (1) that *caste* and *social class* are phenomena of the same nature; (2) that *hierarchy* is incomprehensible; (3) that in the Indian system the separation and the interdependence of groups are subordinated to this sort of obscure or shamefaced hierarchy. On the other hand, in so far as we are able to detect in the facts a dimension other than that contained in indigenous consciousness, this is thanks to comparison, thanks first and foremost to the implicit and inevitable comparison with our own society. This must be obvious.

We must therefore proceed in two phases: first take lessons from the Hindus, Hindus of today and of times past, in order to see things as they do. They see them very systematically and it is not impossible to isolate the principle behind their view. Indeed, we shall realize that they have largely done the work for us. Some eight centuries perhaps before Christ, tradition established an absolute distinction between power and hierarchical status, and this is a cardinal point which modern research has not been able to elucidate by its own means. Yet on certain points we shall take the liberty of completing and systematizing the indigenous or orthogenic theory of caste — not without employing empirical aspects in a secondary capacity -- by postulating that men in society behave in a coherent and rational manner, especially in such an important matter, and that it is possible to recover the simple principle of their thought. Naturally we make these modifications at our own risk, the touchstone always being what the people themselves think and believe. There is nothing new in all this, of course: it is what the ethnologist or social anthropologist has

always tried to do. But the itinerary is made longer and more complicated, but at the same time more certain, by the fact that we are
dealing with a great and ancient civilization. It is only recently that the
premature generalizations of sociology, in the restricted sense of the
term, have offered specious short-cuts in this lengthy journey.

But ideology is not everything. Any concrete, localized, whole,
when actually observed, is found to be decisively oriented by its
ideology, and also to extend far beyond it. This poses the fundamental
problem of these studies in general. Currently several solutions are
offered: nowadays, ideology is often sacrificed to the empirical
aspect, but sometimes the reverse is done, or else the two may be
opposed absolutely to each other. We shall give some examples. Let
us observe in passing that the fact is universal: if it reflected only the
data, and reflected it completely, the system of ideas and values would
cease to be capable of orienting action, it would cease to be itself. In
our case, in every concrete whole we find the formal principle at work,
but we also find something else, a raw material which it orders and
logically encompasses but which it does not explain, at least not
immediately and for us. This is where we find the equivalent of what
we call relations of force, political and economic phenomena, power,
territory, property, etc. Those data which we can recover thanks to the
notions we have of them in our own ideology may be called the
(comparative) concomitants of the ideological system. Certain
authors select them for study without noticing that the devaluation
which they undergo in the present case alters them profoundly. The
specialist steeped in modern ideology expects everything from these
phenomena, but here they are bound by the iron shackles of a contrary
ideology. To confine ourselves to these is — to take a local simile —
to entrench oneself in an inferior caste. On the contrary they must, in
our opinion, be set in their place and related to the ideology which
they accompany in fact, it being understood that *it is only in relation
to the totality thus reconstructed that the ideology takes on its true
sociological significance.*

. . . .

Starting from our current view of hierarchy we tend at first to
picture the caste system, or a concrete set of castes, as a linear order
going from the highest to the lowest, a transitive non-cyclic order:
each caste is lower than those which precede it and higher than those
which follow it and they are all comprised between two extreme
points. It will be objected that this is too simple a picture: in the

middle region in particular it is often difficult to rank one of two given castes absolutely in relation to the other. Further, an order of this sort, should we have to content ourselves with it as a final datum, is scarcely convenient. Happily, things change if one considers the *principles* whereby the castes are ranked in a more or less exact order. Underlying this order is found a system of oppositions, a structure.
. . .

The Fundamental Opposition

. . . For the moment it is a question of the formal system. We shall try first to grasp its principles and then to reduce it to a structure. Though Hutton cannot serve as our starting point, Hegel can, for he, as long ago as 1830, went further than many a more recent author. Hegel saw the principle of the system in abstract *difference* (and indeed *jāti*, caste, is also 'species' in the botanical or zoological sense). True, Hegel seems at first to bring caste close to the modern individual in the way we have criticized, but one very soon realizes that he ascribes this 'difference' to the whole and to hierarchy: it is a question of a differentiation of functions, which could not come from the outside, and culminates in the universal.

More recently, Bouglé says nothing very different, though his language is more precise. His *Essai**, dating from the beginning of the century, is still topical. The work has not made the mark it deserved for two reasons. First it was written in French, while few Indians read French; English is of necessity the main language of these studies. Secondly, the work was in advance of contemporary ideas, it moved away from the dominant empiricist and materialist tendencies of these studies, and as the author had acquired no direct knowledge of India it passed all the more easily for a manifestation of French intellectualism. Bouglé's *Essai* provides us with the best initial definition; it is indeed a work relying exclusively on secondary sources, though Bouglé was a sociologist of Durkheim's school who had devoted his thesis to egalitarian ideas, and who was careful to reduce things to their principles while omitting nothing essential. According to him, the caste system is composed of hereditary groups (the castes, except for the segmentary aspect which will be mentioned again later) which

---

* *See Bouglé's essay in this volume, pp. 64–73. Editor.*

are both distinguished from one another and connected together in three ways:

(1) by gradation of status or hierarchy;

(2) by detailed rules aimed at ensuring their separation;

(3) by division of labour and the interdependence which results from it.

Bouglé sometimes tends to separate these three aspects from one another. However, it is obvious that all three are given together and that their separation is an analytic distinction introduced by the observer. Indeed, Bouglé himself recognizes this in certain passages of his book. The three 'principles' rest on one fundamental conception and are reducible to a single true principle, namely the opposition of the pure and the impure. This opposition underlies hierarchy, which is the superiority of the pure to the impure, underlies separation because the pure and the impure must be kept separate, and underlies the division of labour because pure and impure occupations must likewise be kept separate. *The whole is founded on the necessary and hierarchical coexistence of the two opposites.* One could speak of a 'synthetic *a priori*' opposition: it is unprofitable to atomize it into simple elements just to gratify our logic, and in any case it should not be analysed without being subsequently recomposed.

This fact is of extreme importance, since it transports us at once into a purely structural universe[.] . . .* [T]wo sorts of facts appear crucial: on the one hand a sectarian group like the Lingayats (who may or may not be classified as Hindus depending on the definition adopted) can formally deny impurity, and on the other hand the Muslims and the Christians have nothing in their official religion other than the opposite of the notion, yet all, at first sight at least, certainly have castes. . . . Hence it is true that the ideology in which we see the conscious centre of caste can be lacking here or there *within the Indian world*, and observation of these cases is of the greatest interest, to show us to what extent and in what conditions institutions of this kind can survive the weakening or disappearance of their ideological aspect. (In point of fact intensive study is needed to throw light on this.) In short, one must distinguish the basic ideology present in the society at large, and which observed systems demand for their intelligibility, from what is encountered by way of ideology in each particular observation. One may say that the basic

* *Section II of this book on Caste Profiles specifically addresses this issue. Editor.*

ideology is incontestably very widespread and powerful in most of the actual cases: it does not spring from the imagination of the inquirer, and it is not a purely literary or 'cultural' matter. The fact that it is lacking in extreme cases and that it is weakened in a large number of cases — increasingly so nowadays — poses a problem, and requires an inquiry of a finer degree of precision than we can reach here; but it does not throw doubt on the elementary level with which we must be content for the moment.

Pure and Impure

General view. Here we propose to specify the nature of the opposition between pure and impure by successive approximations. At first sight, two main questions will probably come to mind: why is this distinction applied to hereditary groups? And, if it accounts for the contrast between Brahmans and Untouchables, can it account equally for the division of society into a large number of groups, themselves sometimes extremely subdivided? We will not answer these questions directly but will confine ourselves to some remarks in relation to them. It is generally agreed that the opposition is manifested in some macroscopic form in the contrast between the two extreme categories: Brahmans and Untouchables. The Brahmans, being in principle priests, occupy the supreme rank with respect to the whole set of castes. The Untouchables, as very impure servants, are segregated outside the villages proper, in distinct hamlets (or at least distinct quarters). The Untouchables may not use the same wells as the others (barring recent local relaxations), access to Hindu temples was forbidden them up to the Gandhian reform, and they suffer from numerous other disabilities. (It must be said that the situation has been somewhat modified since the Gandhian agitation, and that independent India has declared Untouchability illegal; this is an important step, but it cannot transform overnight the traditional situation which concerns us here.)

Why, it may be asked, this separation of the Untouchables? May it be supposed, for example, that it is due to the nauseating smell of the skins they are accustomed to treat? Hygiene is often invoked to justify ideas about impurity. In reality, even though the notion may be found to contain hygienic associations, these cannot account for it, as it is a religious notion. . . . The immediate source of the notion is to be found in the temporary impurity which the Hindu of good caste contracts in relation to organic life. Starting from this, we shall see that it is specialization in impure tasks, in practice or in theory, which leads to the attribution of a massive and permanent impurity to some categories of people. Ancient literature confirms that temporary and permanent impurity are identical in nature. But one must not lose sight of the complementarity which exists between pure and impure, and also between the social groups in which these ideas are expressed. One can subsequently trace not only the multiple derivations of the notion, but also the multiplication of the criteria of distinction and the extreme portioning out, so to speak, of hierarchical status between a large number of groups. . . .

On Hierarchy in General

We have encountered hierarchy but we have not defined it. Hierarchy must be our starting-point for two connected reasons: first, it is none other than the conscious form of reference of the parts to the whole in the system; secondly, it is the aspect of the system which escapes modern writers.

For modern common sense, hierarchy is a ladder of *command* in which the lower rungs are encompassed in the higher ones in regular succession. 'Military hierarchy', the artificial construction of progressive subordination from commander-in-chief to private soldier, would serve as an example. Hence it is a question of systematically graduated authority. Now hierarchy in India certainly involves gradation, but is neither power nor authority; these must be distinguished. We can already do so within our own tradition. Thus the Shorter Oxford Dictionary says under *hierarchy*: '(1) Each of the three divisions of angles . . . . (2) Rule or dominion in holy things . . . . (3) An organized body of priests or clergy in successive orders or grades. (4) A body of persons or things ranked in grades, orders, or classes, one above another.' It can be seen that the original sense of the term concerned religious ranking. We shall keep to this sense here, making it somewhat more precise. We shall admit that, any idea of command being left aside, the religious way of seeing things requires a classification of beings according to their degree of dignity. Yet the presence of religion is not indispensable, for the same applies whenever the differentiated elements of a whole are judged in relation to that whole, even if the judgment is philosophical as in Plato's Republic. So we shall define hierarchy as the *principle by which the elements of a whole are ranked in relation to the whole*, it being understood that in the majority of societies it is religion which provides the view of the whole, and that the ranking will thus be religious in nature. . . .

We are concerned in this case with concepts which have become totally foreign to us, for our egalitarian society adopts their opposites, as Tocqueville has shown us. In the modern age, hierarchy has become 'social stratification', that is, hierarchy which is shamefaced or non-conscious, or, as it were, repressed. The notion has become incomprehensible even to many of the Indian intelligentsia, brought up as they are in the European tradition and subjected to the influence of modern political ideas for more than a century. Consequently, it is not surprising that hierarchy should be the stumbling block for modern writers studying the caste system, as has been seen in the case of the earlier writers, and as will be seen in the case of the more recent.

Once hierarchy has been isolated as purely a matter of religious values, it naturally remains to be seen how it is connected with power, and how authority is to be defined. In the previous chapter, we linked the principle of hierarchy with the opposition between the pure and the impure. Now we cannot but recognize that this opposition, a purely religious one, tells us nothing about the place of power in the society. On this question, we must resort to a traditional Hindu theory which, while not dealing with caste (*jāti*) *stricto sensu*, yet has an intimate bearing on it, I mean the classical theory of the varnas. In any case, one cannot speak of the castes without mentioning the varnas, to which Hindus frequently attribute the castes themselves. Thus there are good reasons for studying the varnas, even in ancient India, and then specifying the relationship between varna and caste, especially from the angle of the relationship between hierarchy and power. This will enable us to consider some regional or local examples of caste ranking.

The Theory of the Varnas: Power and Priesthood

There is indeed in India a hierarchy other than that of the pure and the impure, namely, the traditional hierarchy of the four varnas, 'colours' or estates (in the sense the word had in France in the *Ancien Régime*), whereby four categories are distinguished: the highest is that of the Brahmans or priests, below them the Kshatriyas or warriors, then the Vaishyas, in modern usage mainly merchants, and finally the Shudras, the servants or have-nots. This is only a preliminary enumeration, and we shall have to specify the content of these categories in historical terms. There is in actual fact a fifth category, the Untouchables, who are left outside the classification. Now the relationship between the system of the varnas and that of the jati or castes is complex. Indologists sometimes confuse the two, mainly because the classical literature is concerned almost entirely with the varnas. Following Senart, one must certainly keep the two distinct.

On the other hand, it seems that recent anthropological literature does not give the importance of the traditional schema its full due, even from the point of view of castes in the strict sense. There has been too great a tendency to consider the classification of the varnas as nothing but a survival without any relation to contemporary social reality, as Hocart observed. Nearer our own time, it has been recognized that the theory of the varnas has certain functions in the modern age but there has been little attempt to account for this fact. In this connection one must first draw attention to a similarity in the constitution of the hierarchy of the varnas and that of the castes.

Thanks to Hocart and, more precisely, to Dumézil, the hierarchy of the varnas can be seen not as a linear order, but as a series of successive dichotomies or inclusions. The set of the four varnas divides into two: the last category, that of the Shudras, is opposed to the block of the first three, whose members are 'twice-born' in the sense that they participate in initiation, second birth, and in the religious life in general. These twice-born in turn divide into two: the Vaishyas are opposed to the block formed by the Kshatriyas and the Brahmans, which in turn divides into two. I comment elsewhere on this last feature, as first encountered in the Vedic ritual commentaries called Brahmanas (800 BC?) .... Let me simply say here that the lot of the Shudras is to serve, and that the Vaishyas are the grazers of cattle and the farmers, the 'purveyors' of sacrifice, as Hocart says, who have been given dominion over the animals, whereas the Brahmans-Kshatriyas have been given dominion over 'all creatures'. We shall return to the solidarity between the two highest classes and the distinction between them: the Kshatriya may order a sacrifice as may the Vaishya, but only the Brahman may perform it. The king is thus deprived of any sacerdotal function. It can be seen that the series of dichotomies on which this hierarchy rests is formally somewhat similar to caste hierarchy, and it also is essentially religious; but it is less systematic and its principles are different.

It seems that this fourfold partition of later Vedic society can be regarded as resulting from the addition of a fourth category to the first three, these corresponding to the Indo-European tripartition of social functions (Dumézil) and to the triad found in the first books of the Rig-Véda: *brahman-ksatra-vis* or: the principle of priesthood, that of *imperium*, and the clans or people. The Shudras appear in a late hymn of the Rig-Véda and seem to correspond to aborigines (like the *dāsa* and *dasyu*) integrated into the society on pain of servitude. It must be noted that the Brahman is the priest, the Kshatriya the member of the class of kings, the Vaishya the farmer, the Shudra the unfree servant. This classification has remained identical in form throughout all the literature right up to modern times, though naturally with shifts and modifications in the contents of the categories. In particular, this is the only conceptual scheme which is made use of by the classical texts of Hinduism in order to characterize persons and their function *in* society, even though actual groups do appear otherwise in these texts, and sometimes have an ambiguous place in the scheme. In all likelihood these texts are contemporaneous with the development of castes in the strict sense of the word, yet they always refer castes to the varnas, and see them, as it were, as varnas. First and foremost, these texts were to mask the emergence, the factual accretion, of a fifth category, the Untouchables, each emulating the others in proclaiming that 'there is no fifth . . . .'. Note that this amounts simply to applying the existing scheme: the Untouchables are outside the varnas just as the Shudras were outside the 'twice-born'. . . .

There are some details to be noticed in connection with the hierarchy of the varnas in classical Hinduism. The Brahman naturally has privileges, and these are listed in the literature. He is inviolable (the murder of a Brahman is, with the murder of a cow, the cardinal sin), and a number of punishments do not apply to him: he cannot be beaten, put in irons, fined, or expelled. The learned Brahman (*śrotriya*) is in theory exempt from taxes, and the Brahman is specially favoured by the law about lost objects, which generally, when they are found, revert mainly to the king, and which only a Brahman finder may keep in part or whole; similarly, if a man dies intestate, only if he is a Brahman do his goods not accrue to the king (here one can see a certain mixing of the two functions).

It should be recalled that although the Brahman is characterized in the Vedic period by his sacrificial function, in the Hindu period, in harmony with the decline of sacrifice in favour of other rites, the Brahman is, above all, purity. Further, the Brahmanic varna became segmented, even in the classical period, and the priests in charge of public temples, the *devalaka*, were despised by their colleagues. Today the Brahman lineages are graded in virtue of the rank of the castes they serve as domestic priests (*Panjab Census Report*, 1911, I, 310), the highest being the learned Brahmans who do not serve at all.

Generally speaking, the hierarchy of the varnas is expressed in many ways by the differentiated treatment that each is accorded. The punishment of Brahmans just mentioned is an example of this. Whilst there is generally privilege or immunity, at the same time *noblesse oblige*, and a Brahman thief, for example, is punished more severely than his inferiors. Some points are difficult to interpret. Thus Manu lays down that a Shudra may not carry a Brahman's corpse (V, 104), which is incomprehensible from the point of view of purity. But above all, starting from the Dharmasutras of Gautama and Vasistha, one finds seemingly illogical injunctions, which later became very widespread. These are those which prescribe, all other things being equal, an increasing period of impurity for a decreasing status: in the case of death, close relations are impure for ten days for Brahmans, twelve for Kshatriyas, fifteen for Vaishyas and thirty for Shudras. Even nowadays, where orthodoxy prevails, the proportion goes in the same direction (the longest periods are often reduced). But, going by the nature of the system, we would expect the contrary, for impurity is more powerful than purity, and the higher the degree of purity to be regained, the more severe should be the effect of impurity. Either we have not yet managed to enter into the spirit of the system, or else the Brahmans have here transformed into a privilege what ought to be a greater incapacity. This view is reinforced by the fact that, while other prescriptions go in the same direction (for example, how far water must reach to purify someone, Manu II, 62), we find the gradation reversed in certain cases: thus in the case of stillbirth, Brihaspati (*Āsauca*, 34–5) prescribes respectively ten, seven, five and three days for the Brahmans and the following varnas. . . . the same goes for expiations.

We have said that the classical texts described in terms of varna what must surely have been at that time a caste system in embryo. The word *jāti* does occur, but it is generally confused with varna (except in Yajñavalkya, II, 69, 206) and, according to Kane, the emphasis is on birth rather than function. Moreover, concrete names of reference groups are encountered, as in the case of the Chandala already mentioned, and so are names of other groups, either equivalent in status (placed outside the village, Manu, X, 36, 51) or else of distinctly superior status. Although from a very early epoch the Buddhist texts confirm the actual existence of despised castes and inferior occupations, the normative Hindu texts mostly present the groups they name as if they were products of crossing between varnas. This is the very detailed theory according to which the 'mixing of varnas' gave birth to mixed categories, inferior and more or less hierarchized. It is generally admitted that this theory was used to refer real *jāti* to the varnas. It is difficult to say how these groups come into the classification of the varnas. At least the lowest of them seem outside it, and yet it is repeated that 'there is no fifth (varna)', and there is a tendency to associate them with the Shudras. Already in Panini (500 BC) this produced a distinction among the Shudras, since one hears of 'excluded' (*niravasita*) Shudras. Later, expressions like 'the last', 'the outsiders' etc., increase, and the word 'untouchable' (*aspṛśya*) is not quite unknown. The distinction which people had for so long refused to make in theory finally compelled recognition: the Shudras have acquired rights, they have become in fact members of the religious society, and those excluded are now the fifth, the Untouchables.

A point which must be emphasized in connection with the varnas is the conceptual relationship between Brahman and Kshatriya. This was established at an early date and is still operative today. It is a matter of an absolute distinction between priesthood and royalty. Comparatively speaking, the king has lost his religious prerogatives: he does not sacrifice, he has sacrifices performed. In theory, power is ultimately subordinate to priesthood, whereas in fact priesthood submits to power. Status and power, and consequently spiritual authority and temporal authority, are absolutely distinguished. The texts called the Brahmanas tell us this with extreme clarity, and, whatever has been said to the contrary notwithstanding, this relationship has never ceased to obtain and still does. For example, the obligation of the powerful and rich to give, as is prescribed in the texts, has not been a dead letter. On the contrary, sovereigns have always supported the Brahmans — and their equivalents in this respect — by endowments of land which, as the inscriptions show, may be under two different rubrics (donations to the temples, and the establishment of Brahman settlements). The difference with the West, let us say Catholic Christianity, seems to consist in the fact that in India there has never been spiritual *power*, i.e., a supreme spiritual authority, which was at the same time a temporal power. The supremacy of the spiritual was never expressed politically.

Thus in the theory of the varnas one finds that status and power are differentiated, just as the general consideration of hierarchy seemed to require. This fact is older than the castes, and it is fundamental to them in the sense that it is only once this differentiation has been made that hierarchy can manifest itself in a pure form. . . . This is not all, for we must remember that these two entirely distinct principles are nevertheless united in their opposition to the other categories which constitute the society. As early as the Brahmanas, these are 'the two forces', represented by the men who, according to Manu, have been given dominion over 'all creatures'. In submitting to priesthood, royalty shares in it.

CASTE AND VARNA

We must try to indicate the main features of the relationship between jati, caste, and varna, category or estate, or more precisely, the relationship between the caste system as it can be directly observed, and the classical theory of the varnas. This task is necessary if we remember that the classical authors scarcely speak of anything other than the varnas, and that even nowadays Hindus often speak of castes in the language of the varnas.

In the first place this transition is quite comprehensible, not only in virtue of the traditional prestige of the varnas, but also in view of the homology already mentioned between the two systems, both of which are structural, and both of which culminate in the Brahmans, either as a varna or as a particular caste or subcaste of Brahmans which may be regarded as the representative of the varna in a given territory (the highest if several are found there). In the second place, the varnas have the advantage of providing a model which is both universal throughout India, and very simple compared to the proliferation of castes, subcastes, etc. Consequently it is a model which can among other things facilitate the comparison between different regions. . . . Something of the kind is found in Marx: on the one hand there is the antithesis between the bourgeoisie and the proletariat, as described in his political writings, and on the other the more complicated picture of social classes which emerges in his historical works. There is a tendency to sort the many castes in a given territory into the four classical categories (and the fifth, traditionally unnamed). However, there are regional peculiarities. Thus in the south there are scarcely any castes intermediate between Brahmans and Shudras; the warrior castes themselves are considered as part of the Shudras, and scarcely worry about this at all.

So this provides a very convenient form of classification, distinct from, or supplementary to, the criteria of purity whose complexity we have mentioned. Has its importance increased in modern times, with the improvements in transport, and, even more, with the registration of castes in the decennial Censuses made by the government in the last part of the nineteenth century, and that of 1901 which sought to achieve a status ranking for each province? Srinivas thinks so. Certainly many castes took advantage of these Census Reports to present claims aiming to make the public authority sanction a higher status than their real status, and these claims, sometimes vindicated in published memoranda, were expressed, with greater or lesser plausibility, in terms of the varnas. Here the varnas were an instrument for mobility, but to make a claim is one thing, and for it to be accepted is another. Furthermore, the circumstances were exceptional. . . .

Far from being completely heterogeneous, the concepts of varna and *jāti* have interacted, and certain features of the osmosis between the two may be noticed. The notion of the varnas which prevails nowadays, even among anthropologists, is influenced by caste. Thus it is often said that the true Kshatriyas have been long extinct, and that the Rajputs, though having the function of the Kshatriyas in modern times, are not real Kshatriyas. It is thought that in ancient India the accession to the throne, and to the dignity of Kshatriya, by dynasties of a different origin, was an irregularity. This assumes that heredity is more important than function, which is true of caste but not of the varnas. So far as the varnas are concerned, he who rules in a stable way, and places himself under the Brahman, is a Kshatriya. Moreover, these categories were not strictly endogamous either. Probably the Kshatriyas have always been rather lax in this matter. The particular place given to power in the system has had notable and lasting results: in the first place, the pattern of polygyny and meat diet, which does not correspond to the Brahmanic ideal, has been quietly preserved at this and lower levels until quite recently; in the second place, since the function is related to force,* it was easier to become king than Brahman: Kshatriya and Untouchable are the two levels on which it is easy to enter the caste society from outside.

Conversely, it is not enough to say that the caste system is influenced by the theory of the varnas. In the first place, the existence of the theory of the pure and the impure presupposes at least the relationship established in the varnas between priesthood and royalty. It is correct to say that the opposition between pure and impure is a religious, even a ritualistic, matter. For this ideal type of hierarchy to emerge it was necessary that the mixture of status and power ordinarily encountered (everywhere else?) should be separated, but this was not enough: for pure hierarchy to develop without hindrance it was also necessary that power should be absolutely inferior to status. These are the two conditions that we find fulfilled early on, in the relationship between Brahman and Kshatriya.

In the second place, we shall maintain that the theory of castes resorts implicitly or obliquely to the varnas in order to complete its treatment of power. Indeed, in the theory of purity a vegetarian merchant ought logically to have precedence over a king who eats meat. But this is not the case, and to understand this fact it is necessary in particular to remember that the theory of the varnas, whilst it subordinates king to priest, power to status, establishes a solidarity between them which opposes them conjointly to the other social functions. This is a subtle and important point and requires special discussion.

HIERARCHY AND POWER

Most contemporary authors see things differently. In previous generations, with the exception of the aristocratic tendency which took for granted the existence of status ranking, hierarchy was often overlooked as the central feature of the system, but the better of the materialist writers tried to explain it in terms of other features . . . . Nowadays hierarchy, or rather the existence of an order of precedence, a status ranking, usually compels recognition, but it is seen only from the outside ('social stratification'), and leaves a residuum which is not reducible to the clear and supposedly basic notions of power and

* Force in French. Pouvoir, meaning legitimate force(§71), is translated as 'power'. —Translator

wealth. This unresolved duality, which has not even been properly characterized, hangs like a millstone round the neck of the contemporary literature.

Usually, those who study the status ranking of the castes of a definite region distinguish between what happens 'at the extremes' and what happens in the 'middle zone' of the ranking. The extremes, where the pure and the impure are in evidence, are said to be less important than the middle zone, where the operation of power is rightly recognized. Such authors conclude, in short, that their categories are sufficient for the understanding of the system: according to them, the distribution of power (and wealth) is in the, last analysis congruent with (ritual) status, except, naturally, at the 'extremes', where questions are raised by the lowly place of the Untouchable, and particularly by the precedence taken by the priest over the master of the land. Emphasis is often placed on situations in which the priest is to a striking degree materially dependent on the masters of the land, but the more this is done, the more the claimed congruence is destroyed. In short, it is laid down as a principle that hierarchical status is of small importance when it does not simply validate an economic-political situation. To describe this attitude is enough to pass judgment on it: it raises the question of whether our task is to provide a semblance of confirmation for our sociocentric prejudices or to do scientific work. Here is an illustration:

There was a high degree of coincidence between politico-economic rank and the ritual ranking of caste. This is a reflection of the general rule that those who achieve wealth and political power tend to rise in the ritual scheme of ranking. It is what is meant by saying that the ranking system of caste-groups was validated by differential control over the productive resources of the village. But the correlation is not perfect, since at each end of the scale there is a *peculiar rigidity* in the system of caste . . . in between these two extremes, ritual rank tends to follow their economic rank in the village community. [Bailey, 1957: 266-7]

I have italicized a particularly delightful expression: here a basic feature of the caste system is reduced to a 'peculiar rigidity' at the extremities of the social order. It will be understood why we prefer another approach.

For us, on the contrary, what happens at the extremes is essential. We must free ourselves from familiar ideas: we tend to put the essential at the centre and the rest at the periphery. Here, by contrast, because it is a question of hierarchy, and more generally of ideas, and of sociology, that which encompasses is more important than that which is encompassed, just as a whole is more important than its parts, or just as a given group's place in the whole governs its own organization. Our approach is quite unlike the preceding one and, as we have said, involves two stages: first we shall be concerned with the ideology, which easily accounts for the overall framework; secondly, finding the concrete factor, power, in the 'middle zone', a factor not immediately accounted for by the theory of purity, we shall consider it in its turn.

The controversy is exemplary from the epistemological point of view, for, by keeping to the level of power, one is prevented from understanding the essential characteristic of the Indian system. This characteristic is the subordination of power, which, as we shall shortly see, is both intellectually absolute and practically limited. The alternatives must be clearly stated: one may either start from conscious ideas and move from the whole to the parts, while bringing out the important and unnoticed fact that power in India became secular at a very early date; or else one starts from behaviour, in which case one can neither account for the whole nor finally build a bridge between Indian concepts and our own.

Two approaches to the question of the relationship between hierarchy and power have just been contrasted. For us, the question only arises for the present in connection with the relationship between varna and caste. Anticipating the study of actual observable status rankings, we admit in advance that they give power a place which is not allowed for by the theoretical hierarchy of the pure and the impure. At first sight it is an example of that 'residual' component which should normally be brought out by the confrontation of ideology with observation. Then we would have to take notice of it as accurately as possible and be content with that. However, when the king or a man of royal caste, an eater of meat, takes precedence over a vegetarian merchant or farmer, it is not that the hierarchy of relative purity is simply complemented—that one could accommodate—rather it is contradicted. Must it be said that the ideology is false in the 'median zone' of the status ladder, or should it be admitted that an extraneous factor counterbalances ideology at this point, once the extremes are located?

To start with it must be observed that, although very important, hierarchy or its concrete and incomplete form, status ranking, is not everything. It leaves out power and its distribution, but given the fact that it does not attack or negate power, should it not reflect power within itself in some manner? Otherwise, and in general, the ideology provides an orientation or ordering of the datum rather than a re-production of it, and the act of becoming conscious of something in fact always means making a choice of one dimension in preference to others: one can only see certain relationships by becoming, temporari-ly at least, blind to others. Then this sort of complementarity can lead to a real contradiction when it is a matter of completely ordering the datum in accordance with a single principle. In our case, power exists in the society, and the Brahman who thinks in terms of hierarchy knows this perfectly well; yet hierarchy cannot give a place to power as such, without contradicting its own principle. Therefore it must give a place to power without saying so, and it is obliged to close its eyes to this point on pain of destroying itself. In other words, once the king is made subordinate to the priest, as the very existence of hierarchy presupposes, it must give him a place after the priest, and before the others, unless it is absolutely to deny his dignity and the usefulness of his function. Brahman authors have had a feeling of this sort, as can be seen from the way in which they consider royalty within the theory of the *dharma*. As Lingat shows in his fine work on the relationship between *dharma* and the law, the king tends in this tradition to appear as a quasi-providential instrument whereby the theoretical world of the dharma is linked with the real world here below. Although they lay down an absolute rule, these authors are keenly aware of its transcendant nature and of the impossibility of introducing it into the facts just as it is. Thanks to the king, and in particular to the king as the supreme judge, as the link between Brahmanic wisdom represented by his counsellors and the empirical world of men as they are, the dharma rules from on high, but does not have to govern, which would be fatal.

Thus it can be seen that there are internal reasons for the contradic-tion in question. The remaining task is to understand how it has been possible for this contradiction to be accepted, and it is here, in my opinion, that the theory of the varnas must be taken into consideration. Indeed this theory from the outset sees in the first two varnas 'the two forces' which, united in their particular way, must reign over the world; in this way it enables the prince to share to some extent in the absolute dignity whose servant he is. It should be observed, moreover, that there is no contradiction in the classical authors, for they speak only of the varnas, even when we may suppose that they have the caste society in mind. In this sense, it is we who distinguish a hierarchy of purity as a distinct social principle. In the minds of these authors, as soon as government or secular matters in general are involved, this view unceasingly relies for external support on the varnas. All the more reason for us to avoid incorrectly dissociating the two views, and to recognize their implicit connection as reflected in actual status rankings, when power in some way counterbalances purity *at secondary levels*, while remaining subordinate to it at the *primary or non-segmented level*.

As the mantle of Our Lady of Mercy shelters sinners of every kind in its voluminous folds, so the hierarchy of purity cloaks, among other differences, its own contrary. Here we have an example of the complementarity between that which encompasses and that which is encompassed, a complementarity which may seem a contradiction to the observer. Before becoming familiar with this phenomenon through concrete examples, it must be stressed that we have made a first step out of the dualism of the 'religious' and the 'politico-economic', of idealism and materialism, of form and content. Let us admit at once that the tendency we have criticized has been a considerable help to us: by its onesided insistence on power it has made it impossible for us to overlook it. . . .

References

AGNIHOTRI, 'PANDIT RAMBHAROSA'
1925   *Bans Prabodhni*, Chauhan Sabha, Kanpur.

AIYAPPAN, A.
1944   *Iravas and Culture Change, Bulletin Madras Government Museum*, 5, 1.

ALEXANDER, K.C.
1972   'The Neo-Christians in Kerala' in J.M. Mahar, ed., *The Untouchables in Contemporary India*, University of Arizona Press, Arizona.

ANSARI, GHAUS
1959   *Muslim Caste in Uttar Pradesh: A Study in Culture Contact*, Ethnographic and Folkore Society, Lucknow.

————
1960   'Muslim Caste in Uttar Pradesh: A Study of Culture Contact', *Eastern Anthropologist*, 13, 5-58.

ARAYATHINAL, T.
1947   'The Missionary Enterprises in the Syrian Catholics of Malabar', *Eastern Churches Quarterly*, 7, 236-51.

ATIYA, A.S.
1968   *A History of Eastern Christianity*, Methuen, London.

AYYAR, L.K.A.
1926   *Anthropology of the Syrian Christians*, Cochin Government Press, Ernakulam.

BAILEY, F.G.
1957   *Caste and the Economic Frontier*, Manchester University Press, Manchester.

————
1960   *Tribe, Caste, Nation*, Manchester University Press, Manchester.

494   *References*

BAINES, A.
1912   *Ethnography*, Trunber Verlag, Strassburg.

BASHAM, A.L.
1971   *The Wonder that was India*, Fontana, London.

BERREMAN, GERALD D.
1963   *Hindus of the Himalayas*, University of California Press,
            Berkeley and Los Angeles.

———

1965   'The Study of Caste Ranking in India', *Southwestern Journal
            of Anthropology*, 21, 115-29.

———

1966   'Caste in India and the United States', *American Journal of
            Sociology*, 66, 120-7.

———

1970   'The Brahmanical View of Caste', *Contributions to Indian
            Sociology* (n.s.), 5, 16-23.

———

1979   *Caste and Other Inequities*, Folklore Institute, Meerut.

BÉTEILLE, ANDRÉ
1964   'A Note on the Referents of Caste', *European Journal of So-
            ciology*, 5, 130-4.

———

1965   *Caste, Class and Power: Changing Social Stratification in a
            Tanjore Village*, University of California Press, Berkeley
            (Oxford University Press, Delhi, 1966).

———

1972   *Inequality and Social Change*, Oxford University Press,
            Delhi.

———

1977   *Inequality Among Men*, Basil Blackwell, Oxford and London.

BETEILLE, ANDRÉ (ed.)
1970   *Social Inequality: Selected Writings,* Penguin, Harmondsworth.

BEVERIDGE H.(ed.)
1968   *The Tuzuk-i-Jehangiri,* vol.1, Munshiram Manoharlal Reprint, Delhi.

BHAHAN SAMAGRAHA
1972   26th. Hindi ed., compiled by Viyogi Hari, Gita Press, Gorakhpur.

BHAKTAMALA
1969   5th. Hindi edn., compiled by Nabhadasa, Teja Kumar Press, Lucknow.

BHANDARKAR, R.G.
1969   *Vaisnavism, Saivism and Minor Religious Sects,* Indological Book House, Varanasi.

BHUSAN, SHASHI
1977   'The Belchhi Killings', *Economic and Political Weekly,* 12, 974.

BLAIR, HARRY W.
1980   'Rising Kulaks and Backward Classes in Bihar: Social Change in the late 1970s', *Economic and Political Weekly,* 15, 64-74.

BLUNT, E.A.H.
1960   *The Caste System of Northern India with Special Reference to the United Provices of Agra and Oudh,* S. Chand and Co., Delhi.

BOSE, NIRMAL KUMAR
1960   *Data on Caste, Orissa,* Anthropological Survey of India, Calcutta.

————
1975   'Some Aspects of Caste in Bengal', in Milton Singer, ed.,

Traditional India: Structure and Change, **Rawat** Publications, Jaipur.

BOUGLE, C.
1958   'The Essence and Reality of the Caste System', *Contributions to Indian Sociology*, 2, 7-30.

_____

1971   *Essays on the Caste System*, Cambridge University Press, Cambridge.

BREMAN, JAN
1974   *Patronage and Exploitation: Changing Agrarian Relations in South Gujarat*, University of California Press, Berkeley.

_____

1976   'A Dualistic Labour System? A Critique of the "Informal Sector" Concept', *Economic and Political Weekly*, 27 Nov., 4 Dec. and 11 Dec., 1870-8, 1905-8, 1939-44.

BRIGGS, GEO W.
1920   *Chamars*, Oxford University Press, London.

BROWN, L.W.
1956   *The Indian Christians of St. Thomas*, Cambridge University Press, Cambridge.

BROWN, LUCY
1956   'Colonial Perceptions of Indian Society and the Emergence of Caste(s) Associations', *Journal of Asian Studies*, 37,2.

COHN, BERNARD S.
1955   'The Changing Status of a Depressed Caste', in Mckim Marriot, ed., *Village India: Studies in Little Community*, University of Chicago Press, Chicago.

_____

1962   'Political Systems in Eighteenth Century India: The Banaras Region', *Journal of American Oriental Society*, 82, 312-20.

COX, O.C.
1945   'Race and Caste: A Distinction', *American Journal of Sociology*, 50, 360-8.

DAMLE, Y.B.
1968   'Reference Group Theory with Regard to Mobility in Caste', in J. Silverberg, ed., *Social Mobility and the Caste System in India: An Inter-disciplinary Symposium*, Mouton, The Hague.

DAS, ARVIND
1983   *Agrarian Unrest and Socio-Economic Change in Bihar, 1900-1980*, Manohar, New Delhi.

DAS, VEENA
1982   *Structure and Cognition:Aspects of Hindu Caste and Ritual*, Oxford University Press Bombay.

DAVIS, KINGSLEY
1951   *The Population of India and Pakistan*, Princeton University, Princeton.

DESAI, I.P.
1969   'The Vedechi Movement' (Mimeo), Centre for Regional Development Studies, Surat.

———
1976   *Untouchability in Rural Gujarat*, Popular Prakashan Private Ltd., Bombay.

———
1988   'Critique on Division and Hierarchy', in A.M. Shah and I.P. Desai, eds., *Division and Hierarchy: An Overview of Caste in Gujarat*, Hindustan Publishing Corporation, Delhi.

DEVOS, GEORGE AND H. WAGATSUMA (eds.)
1966   *Japan's Invisible Race: Caste in Culture and Personality*, California University Press, Berkeley.

498   *References*

DHAR, HIRANMOY
1980   'Bihar: Caste and Class Tangle', *Frontier*. 10, 21-4.

DHAR, HIRANMOY, *et al.*
1982   'Caste and Polity in Bihar', in Gail Omvedt, ed., *Land Caste and Politics in Indian States*, Authors' Guild Publication, Delhi.

DUBOIS, ABBE, J.A.
1981   *Hindu Manners, Customs and Ceremonies*, Oxford University Press, Delhi.

DUMONT, LOUIS
1970a.   *Religion, Politics and History in India*, Mouton, Paris and The Hague.

1970b   *Homo Hierarchicus: The Caste System and its Implications*, Weidenfeld and Nicholson, London.

1970c   'Religion, Politics and History in the Individualistic Universe', in *Proceedings of Royal Anthropological Institute*, pp. 31-41.

1972   *Homo Hierarchicus: The Caste System and its Implications*, Paladin, London.

1988   *Homo Hierarchicus: The Caste System and its Implications*, Oxford University Press, Delhi.

DUMONT, LOUIS AND D. POCOCK
1958   'A.M. Hocart on Caste, Region and Power', *Contributions to Indian Sociology*, 2, 7-30.

DURKHEIM, EMILE
1964   *The Elementary Forms of Religious Life*, Allen and Unwin, London.

EDWARDES, S.M.
1909   *The Gazetter of Bombay City and Island*, 3 vols., The Times
       Press, Bombay.

ENTHOVEN, R.B.
1975   *The Tribes and Castes of Bombay*, 3 vols., Casmo Publica-
       tion, Delhi.

FARQUHAR, JOHN NICOL
1967   *An Outline of the Religious Literature of India*, Oxford Uni-
       versity Press, Oxford.

FRIED, MORTON
1967   *The Evolution of Political Society: An Essay on Political An-
       thropology*, Random House, New York.

FUCHS, STEPHEN
1949   *The Children of Hari: A Study of the Nimar Balasis in
       Madhya Pradesh*, Thacker and Co. Ltd., Rampart Row, Bom-
       bay.

GADGIL, D.R.
1942   *The Industrial Evolution of India in Recent Times*, Oxford
       University Press, London.

GHURYE, G.S.
1950   *Caste and Class in India*, Popular Prakashan, Bombay.

_____

1969   *Caste and Race in India*, Popular Prakashan, Bombay.

GOKHALE, R.G.
1957   *The Bombay Cotton Mill Worker*, Millowner's Association,
       Bombay.

GOLDTHORPE, J.H., *et al*.
1969   *The Affluent Worker in the Class Structure*, Cambridge Uni-
       versity Press, Cambridge.

GOULD, HAROLD A.
1961   'Sanskritization and Westernization: A Dynamic View', *The Economic Weekly*, 13, 945-50.

GUIRAND, PIERRE
1975   *Semiology*, Routledge and Kegan Paul, London.

GUPTA, DIPANKAR
1979   'Understanding the Marathwada Riots: A Repudiation of Eclectic Marxism', *Social Scientist*, 82, 3-22, Trivandrum.

————
1980   'From Varna to Jati: The Indian Caste System from the Asiatic to the Feudal Model of Production', *Journal of Contemporary Asia*, 10, 249-71.

————
1981   'Caste, Infrastructure and Superstructure', *Economic and Political Weekly*, 16 Dec. 2093-104.

HABIB, IRFAN
1963a   *Agrarian System of Mughal India*, Asia Publication House, Bombay.

————
1963b   'An Examination of Wittfogel's Theory of 'Oriental Despotism', *Enquiry*, 6, 54-73.

HALDAR, R.D.
1928   'An Abstract of the Annuals of the Rajbansi Family of Chota Nagpur', *Man in India*, 7, 259-93.

HARRISS, JOHN
1979   'Why Poor People Stay in Rural India', *Social Scientist*, 85, 20-47.

————
1982   'Character of an Urban Economy, Small Scale Production and Labour Market in Coimbatore', *Economic and Political Weekly*, 5 and 12 June, 945-54, 993-1002.

HINDESS, B. AND PAUL Q. HIRST
1975   *Pre-Capitalist Modes of Production*, Routledge and Kegan
        Paul, London.

1977   Mode of Production and Social Formation: An Auto-Critique
        of 'Pre-Capitalist Modes of Production', Macmillan, London.

HITCHCOCK, JOHN T.
1975   'The Idea of the Martial Rajput', in Milton Singer, ed., *Tradi-
        tional India: Structure and Change*, Rawat Publication,
        Jaipur.

HOLMSTRÖM, MARK
1976   *South Indian Factory Workers: Their Life Cycle and Their
        Work*, Cambridge University Press, Cambridge.

HUTTON, J.H.,
1963   *Caste in India: Its Nature, Function and Origin*, Oxford Uni-
        versity Press, Bombay.

IFLC
1908   *Indian Factory Labour Commission*, Report of the Indian
        Factory Labour Commission, 2 vols., Government of India,
        Central Press Branch, Simla.

ITJ
1908-   *Indian Textile Journal*, The Indian Textile Journal Limited,
1951   Bombay.

JADEJA, Y.D.
1971   *Primary School Teachers of Surat District: Adivasis and
        Non-Adivasis* (Mimeo), Centre for Social Studies, Surat.

JANUZZI, TOMASSON
1974   *Agrarian Crisis in India: The Case of Bihar*, Sangam Books,
        New Delhi.

JANUZZI, TOMASSON
1977 'An Account of the Failure of Agrarian Reforms and the Growth of Agrarian Tensions in Bihar', in R.E. Frykenberg, ed., *Land Tenure and Peasants in South Asia*, Manohar, New Delhi.

JHA, HETUKAR
1977 'Lower Caste Peasants and Upper Caste Zamindars in Bihar (1921-5): An Analysis of Sanskritization and Contradiction Between the Two Groups', *Indian Economic and Social History Review*, 9, 4.

JIGYASU
1968 *Santapravara Ravidas Saheb*, 2 vols, Janata's Welfare Publication, Lucknow.

JOSEPH, T. K.
1928 'Malabar Miscellany', *Indian Antiquary*, 57, 24-31.

JOSHI, HEATHER AND VIJAY JOSHI
1976 *Surplus Labour and the City: A Study of Bombay*, Oxford University Press, Delhi.

KETKAR, S. V.
1909 *The History of Caste in India*, vol. I, Taylor and Carpenter, Ithaca.

KLASS, MORTON
1980 *Caste: The Emergence of the South Asian Social System*, Institute for the Study of Human Issues, Philadelphia.

KLAUSEN, A.M.
1968 *Kerala Fishermen and the Indo-Norweigian Project*, Allen and Unwin, London.

KRAMRISCH, STELLA
1975 'Traditions of the Indian Craftmen', in Milton Singer, ed., *Traditional India: Structure and Change*, Rawat Publications, Jaipur.

LEACH, E. R. (ed.)
1960   *Aspects of Caste in South India, Ceylon and North West Pakistan*, Cambridge University Press, Cambridge.

LENIN, V.I.
1946   *Capitalism and Agriculture*, Little Lenin Library, New York.

———
1960   *Collected Works*, vol. 3, Progress Publishers, Moscow.

———
1971   *Selected Works*, vol. 1, Progress Publisher, Moscow.

LIPTON, MICHAEL
1977   *Why Poor People Stay Poor: A Study of Urban Bias in World Development*, Temple Smith, London.

LOEWENSTEIN, KARL
1966   *Max Weber's Political Ideas in the Perspective of our Time*, University of Massachusetts Press, Massachusetts.

LOVEJOY, A.O.
1957   *The Great Chain of Being*, Harvard University Press, Cambridge.

LOW, D. A. (ed.)
1968   *Soundings in Modern South Asian History*, University of California Press, Berkeley.

LUKACS. G.
1971   *History and Class Consciousness*, Merlin Press, London.

LYNCH, OWEN
1963   'The Politics of Untouchability: A Case from Agra, India', in Milton Singer and Bernard Cohn, eds, *Structure and Change in Indian Society*, Aldine Publishing Co., Chicago.

MACLEAN, A. J.
1971 'Syrian Christians', in *Encyclopaedia of Religion and Ethics*, 12, T. and T. Clark, Edinburgh.

MADAN, T. N.
1970 'On the Nature of Caste in India: A Review Symposium on Homo Hierarchicus, Introduction', *Contributions to Indian Sociology* (n.s.), 5, 1-13.

MANDELBAUM, DAVID G.
1970 *Society in India*, University of California Press, Berkeley.

MAO, TSE TUNG
1967 *Selected Works*, Foreign Languages Press, Peking.

MAQUET, JÁCQUES J.
1961 *The Premise of Inequality in Ruanda*, Oxford University Press, London.

MARRIOTT, MCKIM
1951 'Social Structure and Change in a U.P. Village', *Economic Weekly*, 4.

———

1959 'Interactional and Attributional Theory of Caste Ranking', *Man in India*, 39, 92-107.

———

1973, 'Caste Systems', in *Encyclopaedia Brittanica*, vol. 3, 982-91.

———

1976 'Hindu Transactions: Diversities Without Dualism', in B. Kapferer, ed., *Transaction of Meaning*, Philadelphia Institute for Studies of Human Issues, Philadelphia.

MARRIOTT, MCKIM AND RONALD B. INDEN
1977 'Towards a Ethnosociology of the South Asian Caste System', in Kenneth A. David, ed., *The New Wind: Changing Identities in South Asia*, Aldine Publications, Chicago.

MARX, KARL AND FREDERICK ENGELS
1959 *First Indian War of Independence*, Progress Publishers, Moscow.

1969   *Selected Works* (3 vols.), vol. 1, Progress Publishers, Moscow.

MAYER, ADRIAN C.
1960   *Caste and Kinship in Central India: A Village and its Region*, Routledge and Kegan Paul, London.

MERLEAU-PONTY, MAURICE
1964   *Sense and Non-sense*, Northwestern Chicago Press, Chicago.

MERTON, ROBERT K.
1957   *Social Theory and Social Structure*, Free Press, New York.

MILLER, E.
1950   *An Analysis of the Hindu Caste System in its Interaction with the Total Social Structure in North Kerala*, Unpublished Ph. D. Thesis, University of Cambridge. Cambridge.

MINES, M.
1972   'Muslim Social Stratification in India: The Basis for Variation', *South Western Journal of Anthropology*, 28, 333-49.

MUKHERJEE, KALYAN AND RAJENDRA SINGH YADAV
1980   *Bhojpur: Naxalism in the Plains of Bihar*, Radhakrishna, New Delhi.

O'MALLEY, L.S.S.
1932   *Indian Caste Customs*, Cambridge University Press, Cambridge.

1975   *India's Social Heritage*, Curzon Press, London.

1941   *Modern India and the West: General Survey*, Oxford University Press, London.

PANIKKAR, K. M.
1955   *Hindu Society at the Crossroads*, Asia Publishing House, Bombay.

PARKIN, FRANK
1982　　*Max Weber*, Ellis Harwood and Tavistock, Chichester and London.

PATEL, S.J.
1952　　*Agricultural Labourers in Modern India and Pakistan*, Current Book House, Bombay.

PETTIGREW, JOYCE
1975　　*Robber Nobleman: A Study of the Political System of the Sikh Jats*, Routledge and Kegan Paul, London.

PIKE, KENNETH, L.
1967　　*Language in Relation to a Unified Theory of the Structures of Human Behaviour*, Mouton, The Hague.

POCOCK, D.F.
1972　　*Kanbi and Patidar*, Clarendon Press, Oxford.

———
1973　　*Mind, Body and Wealth*, Blackwell, Oxford.

PRADHAN, M.C.
1966　　*Political System of the Jats of Northern India*, Oxford University Press, London.

RAMASWAMY, E.A.
1977　　*The Worker and his Union: A Study in South India*, Allied, Delhi.

RAO, M.S.A.
1957　　*Social Change in Malabar*, Popular Book Depot, Bombay.

———
1964　　'*Caste and the Indian Army*', The Economic Weekly, 16, 1439-43.

RCL
1929　　*Royal Commission on Indian Labour-Memorandim of Written Evidence of Government Witnesses*, Bombay Presidency (for official use only), Government Central Press, Bombay.

REY, P.P.
1975   'The Lineage Mode of Production', *Critique of Anthropology*, 3, 27-79.

RISLEY, H.H.
1891   *The Tribes and Castes of Bengal*, 2 vols., Bengal Secretariat Press, Calcutta.

ROWE, WILLIAM L.
1960   'The Marriage Network and Structural Change in a North Indian Community', *South-western Journal of Anthropology*, xvi, 299-311.

―――――
1968   'The New Cauhan: A Caste Mobility Movement in North India', in James Silverberg, ed., *Social Mobility in the Caste System in India*, Mouton, The Hague.

RUDOLPH, LLOYD I, AND SUSSANNE H.RUDOLPH
1960   'The Political Role of India's Caste Associations', in *Pacific Affairs*, 33, 5-22.

―――――
1969   *The Modernity of Tradition*, Orient Longmans, Bombay.

SACHCHIDANAND
1979   'Bihar's Experience', *Seminar*, 243, 31-3.

SAHLINS, M.
1966   *Tribesmen*, Prentice Hall, Englewood Cliff.

SCHURMANN, F.
1971   *Ideology and Organization of the Communist Party of China*, University of California Press, Berkeley.

SEAL, A.
1968   *The Emergence of Indian Nationalism*, Cambridge University Press, Cambridge.

SENGUPTA, NIRMAL
1979   'Caste as an Agrarian Phenomenon in Twentieth Century

Bihar', in Arvind N. Das and V. Nilakant, ed., *Agrarian Relations in India*, Manohar, New Delhi.

SHAH, A.M.
1964   'Political System in Eighteenth Century Gujarat', *Enquiry*, 1, 33-95.

————

1988   'Division and Hierarchy: An Overview of Caste in Gujarat', in A.M. Shah and I.P. Desai, eds., *Division and Hierarchy: An Overview of Caste in Gujarat*, Hindustan Publishing Corporation, Delhi.

SHAH., A.M. AND R.G.SHROFF
1959   'The Vahivanca Barots of Gujarat: A Caste of Geneologists and Mythographers', in Milton Singer, ed., *Traditional India: Structure and Change*, American Folklore Society, Philadelphia.

SHAH, GHANSHYAM
1982   'Rural Politics in Gujarat', in Gail Omvedt, ed., *Land, Caste and Politics in Indian State*, Authors Guild Publications, Delhi.

SHAH, M.M.
1941   *Labour Recruitment and Turnover in the Textile Industry of Bombay Presidency*, Unpublished Ph. D. dissertation, Bombay University.

SHARMA, U.
1973   'Therodicy and the Doctrine of Karma', in *Man* n.6, 8, 347-64.
SHERRING, M.A.
1881   *Hindu Tribe and Castes*, Bengal Secretariat Press, Calcutta.

SIDDIQI, MAJID H.
1978   *Agrarian Unrest in North India: The United Provinces, 1919-22*, Vikas, Delhi.

SINGH, K. SURESH
1971   'State Formation in Tribal Society: Some Preliminary Obser-

vations', *Journal of the Indian Anthropological Soceity*, 6,2.

SINGH, YOGENDRA
1977   *Social Stratification and Social Change in India*, Manohar, Delhi.

1985   *Sociology of Social Stratification: Survey of Research in Sociology and Social Anthropology*, ICSSR and Satvahan, New Delhi.

SINHA, ARUN
1977   'Murder of a Peasant Leader', *Economic and Political Weekly*, 12, 1214-15.

SINHA, SURAJIT
1962   'State Formation and Rajput Myth in Tribal Central India', *Man in India*, 42, 35-80.

SOROKIN, PITRIM
1967   'Social Stratification', in T. Parsons, E. Shils, K.D. Naeghele and J.R. Pitts, eds., *Theories of Society: Foundations of Modern Sociology*, vol.1, Free Press, Glencoe.

SRINIVAS, M.N.
1952   *Religion and Society among the Coorgs of South India*, Clarendon Press, Oxford.

1956   'A Note on Sanskritization and Westernization', *Far Eastern Quarterly*, ·15, 481-96.

STEIN BURTON
1968   'Social Mobility and Medieval South Indian Hindu Sects', in J. Silverberg, ed., *Social Mobility in the Caste System in India*, Mouton, The Hague.

TERRAY, EMANUEL
1975   'Classes and Class Consciousness in the Abron, Kingdom of Gyaman', in Maurice Block, ed., *Marxist Analysis and Social Anthropology*, Malaby Press, London.

WEBER, MAX
1948   'Politics as a Vocation', in H.H. Gerth and C.W. Mills, eds.,
            From Max Weber: Essays in Sociology, Routledge, London.

1958   Religon of India, Free Press, New York.

WESOLOWSKI, M.
1969   'The Notions of Status and Class in Capitalist Societies', in
            André Béteille, ed., *Social Inequality*, Penguin, Harmond-
            sworth.

Index